2nd Edition

Consumer Behavior
and CULTURE

2nd Edition

Consumer Behavior
and CULTURE

Consequences for Global Marketing and Advertising

Marieke de Mooij

⑤SAGE

Los Angeles | London | New Delhi
Singapore | Washington DC

For information:

SAGE Publications, Inc.
2455 Teller Road
Thousand Oaks, California 91320
E-mail: order@sagepub.com

SAGE Publications Ltd.
1 Oliver's Yard
55 City Road
London EC1Y 1SP
United Kingdom

SAGE Publications India Pvt. Ltd.
B 1/I 1 Mohan Cooperative Industrial Area
Mathura Road, New Delhi 110 044
India

SAGE Publications Asia-Pacific Pte. Ltd.
33 Pekin Street #02-01
Far East Square
Singapore 048763

Printed in the United States of America

Library of Congress Cataloging-in-Publication Data

Consumer behavior and culture : consequences for global marketing and advertising/editor, Marieke de Mooij. — 2nd ed.
    p. cm.
Rev. ed. of: Consumer behavior and culture / Marieke de Mooij. c2004.
Includes bibliographical references and index.
ISBN 978-1-4129-7990-0 (pbk.)
    1. Consumer behavior—Cross-cultural studies. 2. Consumers—Psychology. 3. Marketing.
I. Mooij, Marieke K. de, 1943- II. Mooij, Marieke K. de, 1943- Consumer behavior and culture.

HF5415.32.M66 2011
658.8'342—dc22   2010019234

This book is printed on acid-free paper.

10   11   12   13   14   10   9   8   7   6   5   4   3   2   1

Acquisitions Editor:	Deya Saoud Jacob
Editorial Assistant:	Megan Krattli
Production Editor:	Astrid Virding
Copy Editor:	Pam Suwinsky
Permissions Editor:	Adele Hutchinson
Typesetter:	C&M Digitals (P) Ltd.
Proofreader:	Ellen Brink
Indexer:	Kathleen Paparchontis
Cover Designer:	Candice Harman
Marketing Manager:	Helen Salmon

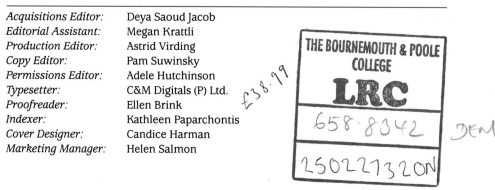

Contents

Chapter 4. The Consumer: Attributes 109

Preface

It has been seven years since the first edition of this book. Since then, increased research results have become available to support the understanding of culture's influence on consumer behavior. In these seven years also the Internet has become integrated in people's lives worldwide, and differences in usage have become manifest. Increasing spending power of consumers worldwide runs parallel to increasing choice. Most consumers, wherever they live, are not rational in their choice behavior. With increased wealth, people's values become manifest in the decision-making process and these values vary across cultures. Western marketing managers are driven by the need for consistency, which is an innate need of their own culture, but they shouldn't project this need to other cultures where it isn't relevant. It is the fundamental error of consistency that makes Western marketing managers develop consistent brand identities and universal advertising campaigns for the rest of the world, where they don't apply or are not understood and thus are less effective.

This book is written for those who have understood that markets are people and that people are not the same everywhere. The focus of this book is consumption and consumer behavior; it is about people—what they buy, why they buy, and how they buy. The basic message is that there are no global consumers, and consumer behavior is not converging across countries. As a result, understanding the differences in behavior across countries is of utmost importance.

To provide evidence of how culture explains variance of consumption, I have collected and analyzed recent and past data on consumption. What I learned from these data is the importance of history. Consumer behavior appears very stable, and habits of the past often can best explain current and future behavior. Behavior that is considered new is often only a new format of old behavior.

In many models of consumer behavior, culture is viewed as an environmental factor, whereas it is in the heads of consumers. This book goes to the roots of culture's influence, the mind of the consumer. I have structured the various elements of consumer behavior in an—to users of U.S. consumer behavior textbooks—unusual way, using a model that integrates culture in all aspects of the human being, in the self, in personality, and in people's relationships with others. I could do this thanks to the increasing evidence of how culture influences the self gained from cross-cultural psychology. Much of this work has not yet been used for explaining consumer behavior across cultures; little has reached the academic world and marketing professionals.

The structure of the book follows this model. After the introductory Chapter 1, which reviews the current myths of global marketing and explains the structure of the book, Chapter 2 explains the concept of culture. This chapter compares several cultural models that are most used in theory and practice and explains my choice of the Hofstede model.

Chapter 3 deals with my findings of convergence and divergence of consumption and consumer behavior. It also reviews national income and sociodemographic variables that tend to be used to analyze cross-country differences.

Chapter 4 deals with the self, personality, and identity—concepts that are central for understanding human behavior and that are also used as metaphors in branding and corporate strategy. In particular, personality theories, developed mostly by Anglo-Saxon psychologists, have been adopted by Western brand managers. These theories are not as universal as generally thought, which has major implications for strategy development. I learned this myself when dealing with Japanese companies, who have very different perceptions than, for example, American companies of what makes a strong brand. Chapter 5 deals with the self in the social environment. In a large part of the world, the context in which the self operates defines the self, which is very different from what Western psychology teaches.

Chapter 6 describes mental processes, such as perception, learning, language, and information processing. There is increased evidence that around the world people process information in different ways. How these processes vary is of great importance for marketing communications.

Chapter 7 is new to this second edition. Part of it extends the communication theories and advertising styles that were covered in Chapter 6 of the previous edition. Part of it is new and covers differences in media usage, both the classic media and the new electronic media.

Chapter 8 includes most statistical evidence of how culture influences product ownership and usage. In addition, it covers consumer behavior domains such as complaining behavior, brand loyalty, shopping and buying behavior, including Internet shopping.

Some of the practical implications in the first edition Chapter 8 were moved to different chapters where applicable.

Many explanations of my findings are based on my own analysis and practical experience, statistical analysis of a growing database, and increased research results as found in literature. I hope this book, like the first edition, will be a challenge for academics and researchers to do further research. Although availability of data from Latin America and Asia is improving, most data are still from the European Union. There is no other area that provides so many data that are also available in the public domain.

For this new edition, SAGE has provided a companion website and will provide instructor-specific materials, such as presentations, illustration material, and student activity at http://www.sagepub.com/demooij2einstr.

ACKNOWLEDGMENTS

I am greatly indebted to Geert Hofstede who again supported me. Also to the reviewers: Georgiana Craciun, Sujata Ramnarayan, Jose Rojas Méndez, Vassilis Dalakas, Ute Jamrozy, Silvia Hodges, Stephen Marshall, and Kenneth Yang. I also thank those who helped explain various cultural phenomena and those who provided literature and data: Carlo Praet at Otaru University in Japan; Vivek Gupta at IMRB International, Bangalore, India; Michael Minkov, Sofia University, Bulgaria; Angel Arrese and Charo Sádaba at the University of Navarra, Spain; Reinier Schaper of Synovate in Amsterdam and Clare Lui of Synovate in Hong-Kong; Jonathan Fletcher at Amsterdam Worldwide, Leo van Deutekom at Sara Lee/DE, and Gerard Foekema who provided photographs. I thank several users of the first edition who gave me feedback, students in the various countries where I have been teaching, who provided their own examples. I also acknowledge the support from SAGE, specifically Lisa Shaw, Deya Saoud Jacob, and Astrid Virding. The most important supporter was again my husband, Anne van't Haaff.

Marieke de Mooij
Burgh-Haamstede
www.mariekedemooij.com

ACKNOWLEDGMENTS

Consumer Behavior
Across Cultures

When the Canadian media philosopher Marshall McLuhan[1] coined the concept of the global village, he was referring to Plato's definition of the proper size for a city—the number of people who could hear the voice of the public speaker. By the global village, McLuhan meant that the new electric media of his time, such as telephone and television, abolished the spatial dimension. By means of electricity, people everywhere could resume person-to-person relations, as if on the smallest village scale. Thus, McLuhan viewed the electronic media as extensions of human beings. They enhance people's activities; they do not make people the same. If you assume people are the same everywhere, global media extend homogeneity. If you realize that people are different, extensions reinforce the differences. McLuhan did not include cultural convergence in the concept of the global village. In fact, he said the opposite: that uniqueness and diversity could be fostered under electronic conditions as never before.

This is exactly what technological development has accomplished. Contrary to expectations, people have embraced the Internet and other new technology mostly to enhance their current activities. In the cold climates, where people used to preserve food in the snow, they have embraced deep-freeze technology most intensely. The colder the climate, the more deep freezers. In Korea, where people used to preserve the national dish *Kimchi* in pots in the ground, they developed a special refrigerator to be able to do this in the home. The mobile phone penetrated fastest in countries that already had advanced fixed telecommunications infrastructures. It was assumed that the Internet would undermine authoritarian regimes, but in fact it is used to strengthen them. The Internet has not changed people. It has reinforced existing habits that, instead of converging, tend to diverge. There is no evidence of converging consumer behavior across countries. This phenomenon is a core topic discussed in this book that provides evidence of consumer behavior differences that are too large and too stable to ignore.

Technology and national wealth have converged in the developed world to the extent that the majority of people can buy enough to eat and have additional income to invest in new technology and other durable goods. As a result, countries will become similar with respect to penetration of many of such goods, but what people do with their possessions does not converge. Much of consumer behavior varies across borders. As national wealth converges across countries, its explanatory power declines, and mainly cultural variables can explain cross-country differences. Cultural values are at the root of consumer behavior, so understanding culture's influence is necessary for those who want to succeed in the global marketplace. Culture is pervasive in all aspects of consumption and consumer behavior and should be integrated into all elements of consumer behavior theory. That is what this book attempts to do. This first chapter reviews the assumptions of homogenization and the underlying causes of these assumptions.

GLOBAL CONSUMERS IN A GLOBAL VILLAGE?

One of the greatest myths of global marketing is of global consumers living in a global village. In a sense, new communication technology has made the world into a global city or village in which we, in theory, can hear and see everything at any time in any place. The question is whether in practice we *do* hear and see everything at any time and in any place. And then, even if we do, the core question is whether this makes us similar to each other. Jeremy Bullmore says, "In many ways, consumers are growing more alike, and we all know why. Mass communications, travel, multinational companies, the whole apparatus of the global village."[2] Because we adopt some consumption symbols, such as jeans and trainers, from people in other parts of the world, the assumption has been that other aspects of our behavior will likewise change. In particular, Western international news journals have made us believe that a homogenization process would work toward universal (American) values. A single youth culture was expected to form across Europe, mimicking a kind of American model because teenagers listen to the same music, surf the net. and talk to each other on their mobile phones.[3]

Also, in academia the belief is that convergence of technology, global media, increased trade, and travel act to bring people together. In textbooks of international marketing and consumer behavior, there are plenty of statements about convergence of lifestyles and values, but these statements are not accompanied by empirical evidence. Assael,[4] author of one of the leading textbooks on consumer behavior, states that world cultures are becoming closer in many respects, that tastes in music, fashion, and technology among the young are becoming more similar across the world. With more consumers craving American goods, consumption values abroad are Americanizing. In particular, teenagers across the world have become similar.

> As teens across the world watch the same television shows and similar commercials, they begin to develop similar consumption patterns. . . . Teens in the United States, Europe, Latin America and the Far East find being with friends and watching TV to be the most enjoyable ways to spend time. . . . Greater travel, better global

communications, and increased access to the web have spurred the development of common norms and values among teens worldwide.[5]

In reality, few people watch international (English language) television programs regularly. The English language cross-border channel CNN has had to introduce national language versions. MTV has localized its content all over the world. The degree of exchange of people is limited, and there is no empirical evidence that global media make consumer behavior converge across countries. How young people spend their leisure time varies. Watching TV and meeting friends are activities of young people everywhere, but the degree to which they do this varies. Whereas 45% of Portuguese youngsters watch TV, only 8% of German youngsters do so. Also in some countries other activities like playing sports are preferred to watching TV or meeting friends. Figure 1.1 illustrates the differences for 13 European countries.

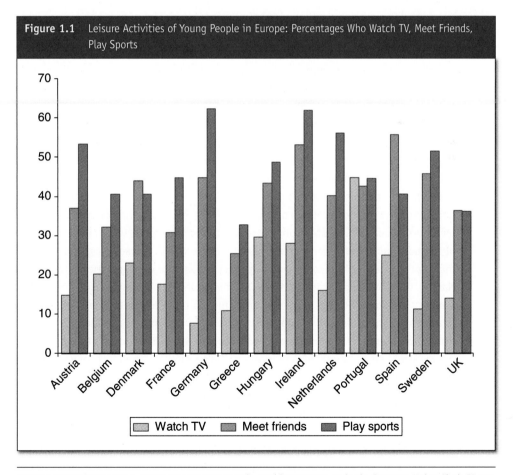

Figure 1.1   Leisure Activities of Young People in Europe: Percentages Who Watch TV, Meet Friends, Play Sports

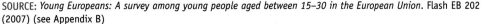

SOURCE: *Young Europeans: A survey among young people aged between 15–30 in the European Union*. Flash EB 202 (2007) (see Appendix B)

GLOBALIZATION AND GLOBAL CONSUMER CULTURE

Globalization is a recurrent theme in the newspapers, with particular focus on its negative effects. People feel dominated by large multinational corporations more than by their local and national governments. Global trade is supposed to result in a global consumer culture. What are *globalization* and *global consumer culture*?

Globalization

According to Robertson,[6] *globalization* became a common term in intellectual, business, media, and other circles with a number of meanings and with varying degrees of precision. In 1990 he related the term *globalization* to modernity and postmodernity. The concept of globalization per se should be applied to a particular series of developments concerning the structuration of the world as a whole. These are the spread of capitalism, Western imperialism, and the development of a global media system. The notion of Western imperialism in particular has linked negative connotations to the term *globalization*. Critics of globalization tend to protest against an emerging global monoculture consisting of McDonald's, Nike, Levi's, Barbie dolls, and American television. Use of the term *cultural imperialism* suggests a passive consumer who has no free will to withstand the attractive propositions of effective marketing techniques applied by a few American brands.

Globalization is largely visualized as a few ubiquitous global brands such as Coca-Cola, McDonald's, and Nike, and such brands are frequently targeted because of their symbolic function. This is partly caused by American marketing executives who would like us to believe that the global village means we drive the same cars, eat the same food, and watch the same television programs. This idea is reinforced by journalists and editors of international (mostly Anglo-American) newspapers who, whenever they discuss globalization, use pictures of Coca-Cola and McDonald's to illustrate the process, which is basically the spread of a small number of American brands across the world. These few global brands are neither representative of the total consumption package nor of transnational trade. The United Nations Conference on Trade and Development (UNCTAD) constructs an "index of transnationality." It works out the ratios of companies' foreign assets to total assets, foreign sales to total sales, and foreign employment to total employment; the index is the average of these three numbers. By this measure, Nestlé, the Swiss food company, is the world's most foreign-oriented company: 87% of its assets, 98% of its sales, and 97% of its workers are outside its homeland. Several of the most transnational companies are from small, advanced economies with small home markets. America's Coca-Cola and McDonald's, makers of the best-known global brands, rank only 31st and 42nd respectively.[7] Yet these brands have become the symbols of globalization and "Western cultural imperialism."

Consumers have varying views on globalization. A majority of inhabitants of the European Union are of the opinion that globalization has a positive effect on scientific and technological progress, employment, health, and cultural exchanges, although the degree of these positive responses varies across countries. Whereas 66% of the Irish view globalization as advantageous to themselves and their families, only 33% of the Greeks do so. Seventy-five percent of Europeans are of the opinion that the United States has too much influence on the globalization process. Whereas 45% trust their national governments, only 31% trust the multinationals and only 28% trust the United States. Although only 42% trust anti-globalist movements, 79% say that these movements raise points that deserve to be debated.[8]

In some non-Western countries, global culture is equated with new, modern, scientific, and results-oriented behavior. The global market is associated with scientific knowledge and technology.[9]

Global Consumer Culture

Global communications are assumed to create a global, homogeneous consumer culture. Views on this homogenization process, however, are stronger in the United States than in other parts of the world. Alden, Steenkamp, and Batra,[10] who analyzed the representation of global consumer culture in advertising, view global consumer culture as shared sets of consumption-related symbols (product categories, brands, and consumption activities) that are meaningful to segment members. Mass media programming, flowing primarily from the United States, has played a major role in the creation, learning, and sharing of such consumption symbols. As a result, the symbols of global consumer culture are basically American symbols that in the United States are viewed as local. In the sample of advertisements that was analyzed, only 5.5% were viewed as including global culture symbols compared with 25.6% in the other countries. The spread of global symbols, however, does not necessarily include homogeneity of people's habits or values.[11]

In practice, notwithstanding the worldwide reach of television and the Internet, in many areas of people's lives, in consumption or entertainment habits, be it music or sports, the people of different nations continue to have different habits, tastes, and loyalties. Instead of causing homogenization, globalization is the reason for the revival of local cultural identities in different parts of the world.[12]

Different nations play different sports: Cricket is the sport of Britain and its old dominions. Rugby is the sport of New Zealand. Cycling is an important sport of the Netherlands, France, and Spain. Badminton is strong in Malaysia. Maybe only football (soccer) can be considered to be a global sport, but it is by no means as popular in the United States as it is in Europe or Latin America. Even within Europe, interest in soccer varies from 49% in the United Kingdom to 65% in Portugal. Whereas 60% of Belgians are interested in tennis, only 15% of Norwegians share this interest. Interest in golf varies from 46% in Ireland to a meager 7% in Belgium. Of the Irish, 58% are interested in rugby, as compared to 2% of the Danes.[13]

Increasingly, music is local. Local music has gained market share throughout most of the world. In many European markets, demand for local films is increasing. In Germany, 26.6% of cinema attendants choose national films.[14] There are a limited number of global products and global brands, and there are no global consumers. This book presents evidence that in the foreseeable future economic development and technology will not lead to homogenization of consumption.

CONVERGING AND DIVERGING CONSUMER BEHAVIOR

In his famous article, "The Globalization of Markets," Harvard professor Ted Levitt[15] argued that new technology would lead to homogenization of consumer wants and needs because consumers would prefer standard products of high quality and low price to more customized high-priced products. Levitt's argument was based on the assumption that consumer behavior is rational and that consumers always want to maximize profit. The assumption of rationality is increasingly regarded as unrealistic and places consumers outside of a cultural context.[16] No empirical evidence has been brought to show homogenization of tastes or the appearance of universal price-minded consumer segments.[17]

Empirical evidence of convergence is usually based on macro-developmental data, such as the numbers of telephones, television sets, or passenger cars per 1,000 population. The U.S. sociologist Alex Inkeles[18] finds that such macro-level data often mask diversity at the micro level. Convergence at macro level (e.g., convergence of GNI [gross national income] per capita) does not necessarily imply convergence of consumer choice. As people around the globe become better educated and more affluent, their tastes diverge. With increased wealth, people increasingly accord greater relevance to their civilizational identity.

There is no support for the argument that increased global mobility for business and vacations will cause people to homogenize. People do not travel to an extent that they are frequently confronted with other cultures. Even if all people were to have enough money to travel abroad, they would not all travel to the same extent. Across European countries, the degree to which people travel varies widely. Whereas in 2008 only 11% of Swedes and 14% of the Irish had not made any short business or private trips, 54% of Hungarians and 47% of Portuguese had not made a business or private trip.[19] Also, young people do not travel to an extent that induces them to adopt different habits and values. In 2001 in Europe, 44% of young people ages 15–24 had not visited another country in the previous 2 years. This was the same percentage as in 1997. Of those who have visited other European countries in the past 2 years, 86% went on vacation.[20] White[21] adds to this that people on vacation are not in a mood that has much to do with their domestic purchasing behavior, so the relevance of any advertising they see is limited. Annually, only 0.4% of Europeans (1.5 million) work in another European Union (EU) state, compared with 2.4% of Americans who work in a state other than where they grew up.[22]

In regions other than Europe, the trend is also toward divergence. Initially, with increased wealth, standards of living appear to converge, but a closer look makes clear that there are large differences. In Latin America, because of the large differences between rich and poor, the rich in each country have more in common with each other than with their poorer compatriots, but middle-income people differ from one country to another. They vary in the use of their discretionary income. All Latin Americans use toothpaste and shampoo each day, but there are varying brand preferences. Although 25% of Latin Americans eat cold cereal for breakfast, the national figures vary from 48% in Central America to 11% in the South.[23] Japan was the country that developed earliest and fastest of all Asian countries, and it was expected that development patterns of other countries in Asia would follow the pattern of Japan. This has not happened. The way other economies, like Malaysia and Indonesia, have developed is different. Even the values gap of American and European elites has widened, according to studies conducted in 2002.[24]

What convergence can be found is at macro level and follows economic development—household penetration of products like refrigerators, washing machines, and color television sets. Only at a certain level of economic development, when people's stomachs are filled, when most people can afford proper housing and durable products such as cars and television sets, do people reach a higher level of unsatisfied needs. That is the moment when cultural values become manifest and are reflected in the different choices of products and brands. The interesting question is what people do with their incremental income, the extra money they have after they have bought the necessary durables to live a comfortable life. At that level, countries tend to diverge. (This phenomenon is further discussed in Chapter 3.)

POST-SCARCITY SOCIETIES AND THE CULTURE PARADIGM

A point of agreement among economists is that people will spend more as they become richer, so it would be surprising if there were no effect of increased national wealth on consumption. But the effect can take many different forms. One reason may be that consumption is a matter of habit. Much of consumer behavior is based on long-time habits.

An assumption by sociologists is that with increased wealth people's values will change. The idea is that with increased wealth, expenditures on education and media increase, resulting in more egalitarian values and democratic systems that in turn would lead to convergence of consumption. However, better education also makes people more aware of their value preferences. The expectations were that with increased openness and capitalism in China, the Chinese would turn to Western values. Instead, the Chinese are rediscovering the teachings of Confucius, which for centuries have been the moral guidance of the Chinese people. The Chinese want to become modern while retaining their core values.[25]

> Instead of homogenizing, continents are becoming more heterogeneous. In 1945, Europe had 31 independent countries. Today there are 51. In Africa, the number of countries grew over the same period from 21 to 53. The European Union has not harmonized people's values or national feelings. Consumers tend to feel most comfortable with their "own" products or brands, the images and emotions they are used to.

The paradigm of economics is that consumers will maximize their own utility and will prefer low-priced, high-quality products to high-priced, added-value brands. This paradigm fits the old scarcity societies where people had to make either/or decisions, for example either a washing machine or holidays. In post-scarcity societies, people have more choices that make them less rational in their buying behavior. When comparing post-scarcity societies that have converged economically, one observes that national wealth is no longer a useful variable for explaining consumption differences. The new paradigm is culture, which becomes an increasingly important variable to explain consumption differences and brand preferences.

Chapter 3 presents data of longer time periods of consumption that demonstrate that people's habits do not converge and that with converging wealth some habits even diverge. For many new commodities, initially national income explains differences in ownership across countries. At some point in time, ownership across countries has reached maximum convergence. When that point is reached, ownership and usage start to diverge. The differences can be explained by culture. In Europe, around 1995, both ownership of television sets and cars per 1,000 inhabitants had converged. At the end of the century, countries had diverged with respect to the numbers of television sets owned per family, ownership of wide-screen TVs, viewing time, and numbers of cars owned per family. The patterns followed by "old" technology can be used to predict the pattern of "new" technology. New technology (e.g., computers) has not reached the point of convergence, so differences between countries are related to national wealth, but future development can be predicted.

Generally speaking, the older the product category, the stronger the influence of culture. This explains why consumption of food products is persistently culture bound. The wealthier countries become, the more manifest the influence of culture on consumption. When people possess more or less enough of everything, they will spend their incremental income on what most fits their value patterns. Americans will buy more cars, the Dutch will buy more luxurious caravans (holiday trailers), and the Spanish will eat out even more than they do now. So greater wealth will not make people spend more on the same products in all countries. With converging wealth, the influence of income on consumption decreases. Cultural values are the main variable to explain differences in consumer behavior. (The convergence-divergence process is a major topic of Chapter 3.)

GLOBAL COMMUNITIES?

One of the preconditions of global advertising is the existence of homogeneous global segments across borders with similar values. Focus on similarities or marketing universals rather than the differences has led international marketers to search for market segments of people with similar lifestyles and values across countries that are called *global communities* or *global tribes*. The assumptions are that 18-year-olds in Paris have more in common with 18-year-olds in New York than with their own parents.[26] Business travelers and teenagers are most often cited as examples of such homogeneous groups. Samuel Huntington speaks of a "Davos culture," referring to people who speak fluent English, hold university degrees, who travel frequently outside their own country and dress alike.[27] These people are only superficially alike; their ways of thinking and behavior in the home country are not necessarily the same.

The European youth market is considered to be homogeneous because these people were reared on the same movies and global brands, like Coca-Cola and Levi's, and watch MTV, all of which have supposedly encouraged the development of a global teenager with common norms and values. However, several value studies show that between countries, young people vary as much as do grown-ups. General evidence is the fact that cross-cultural psychologists who measure value differences across cultures tend to use students as subjects. Youths from Stockholm to Seville may use the same type of mobile phone or computer, but they may have bought it for different reasons and they use it in different ways and places. Young people may buy and use the same technology worldwide, but to a different degree, for different purposes, and in different ways. Everywhere young people may play sports, listen to music, or play video games, but they do this to a different extent. These differences are related to culture.

Young people use computers in different ways. A survey by the advertising agency Euro RSCG in 2001 showed that attitudes toward technology vary enormously among youth in the large European cities. For example, 16% of respondents in Amsterdam said entertainment was their primary reason for using technology, compared with 9% in Helsinki and London, and only 4% in Milan.[28]

Western magazines suggest that Asian teens, in the way they behave and dress and express themselves, increasingly resemble American and European teens and mistake it for Western individualistic behavior, but this behavior is not driven by individualistic values. Moreover, there is not one teenage culture in Asia; there is enormous diversity among Asian teenage lifestyles.[29] Young Asians may be typically Western on the surface, but traditional values like hard work remain next to aspiration toward money and display of success via branded goods.[30] If you take a typical Indian teenager in Mumbai, Delhi, or Kolkata, he'd be wearing a Lacoste shirt or Nike shoes, but he is very much an Indian in his values. He respects his parents, lives together in a family, and removes his Nike shoes before entering a place of religion.[31] Many Westerners make a mistake when they think Japanese are changing because students between 18 and 25 years old act in an extreme and revolutionary way. Westerners have to realize that these years are the only free years a Japanese has in his entire life. As soon as he gets a job, he conforms to typical Japanese behavior.[32] A study by ACNielsen found that, increasingly, Indonesian youth like to use traditional Indonesian products, prefer advertisements that use Indonesian models, and when sick would rather use Indonesian medicine than Western medicine.[33] In India, family and religion remain solid blocks of society, even as teens experiment with Western music, fashion, and brands. Because of the low penetration of global media, teens may copy a look from pictures but have trouble understanding the attitudinal context for that look. In India, pride in Indianness has increased hand in hand with globalization. Increasingly teens in Asia turn to Japan, not to the West, for their music, books, comics, and television programs.[34] Global media have understood the consequences of diversity. The music channel MTV, originally meant to be a global music channel for the young, has localized its content.

Global homogeneous markets exist only in the minds of international marketing managers and advertising people. Even people with similar lifestyles do not behave as a consistent group of purchasers because they do not share the same values. Yes, there are young people and yuppies (young urban professionals), rich people and graying populations who have economic and demographic aspects in common, but marketing communications cannot use similar motives and arguments because their targets do not have the same values. This is demonstrated by ownership of luxury products as measured by the European Media and Marketing Survey. The high-income European target, consisting of people who read international media, is not one homogeneous, cross-border target group for high-touch and high-tech luxury articles. Expenditures on expensive luxury articles by this high-income group in Europe vary strongly. The differences can only be explained by cultural variables. (More about this is discussed in Chapter 8 of this book.)

Within cultures, lifestyle segmentation is useful, as it adds value to economic and demographic segmentation. For cross-national marketing, the concept is less applicable because value differences of national culture are overriding. It may be that only very small groups of people, such as the NYLON,[35] jet setters who live between New York and London, have some common habits with respect to restaurants and theaters visited. This is relevant only for a limited number of products and services. Even if across countries certain groups of people can be defined by common ownership of some products, the motives for buying these products vary so strongly that for developing effective marketing programs across countries these lifestyle distinctions are not useful. (Differences in buying motives and their relationship with culture are discussed in Chapters 5 and 8 of this book.)

Business people are generally considered to be a "culture-free group" because of assumed rational decision making as compared with consumer decision making, but decision making by business people, like many business habits, is also culture bound. Whereas the French and the Belgians will prefer meeting in a restaurant for lunch, the Dutch will prefer meeting in the office with some sandwiches.

NEW MEDIA

The new media have facilitated doing business and intensified existing behavior. Satellites, mobile phones, and the Internet are helping people in developing countries to better their lives. Faster information by satellite (as in Figure 1.2) about prices for buying and selling has helped farmers in India, but it hasn't made them dress as farmers do in the United States.

Expectations of the Internet were that it would homogenize people's values. In the year 2000, Nicholas Negroponte of the Massachusetts Institute of Technology declared that "thanks to the Internet the children of the future are not going to know what nationalism is."[36]

Figure 1.2   Information by Satellite in India. Photograph Gerard Foekema

Bill Clinton was quoted as saying "the Internet, with foreign involvement, would eventually bring democracy to the Middle Kingdom," but as yet, that hasn't happened. Indeed, Internet diffusion has been correlated with democracy, but positive democratic effects of the Internet have primarily been observed in countries that were already developed and at least partially democratic. The Internet amplifies and modifies existing patterns of governmental conflict and cooperation. In many developing and nondemocratic countries, access to the Internet is limited by filtration software, state laws, self-censorship, cost, speed, and other factors.[37]

Whereas in the Western world, the adoption of the Internet is bottom-up, in Asian countries it is pushed and controlled by governments. In 1999 the government of Taiwan wanted 50,000 companies to be online by 2001, and in Thailand a law was passed requiring all export and import documents to go online before 2000.[38] In Korea, the government saw to it that all Korean households have a broadband connection.

The Internet is not a homogenizing factor. Instead, there is growing demand for the ability to adapt language and advertising and to apply local laws based on the geographic locations of individual Internet users. The expectation of convergence has caused many to ignore that the basic principles of effective communication also apply to the new media.[39]

The Internet does not change people's habits or values. It confirms and enhances existing values, habits, and practices. An Asian example of adoption of the Internet for a culture-specific activity was the Bandai i-service in Japan. In Japan, cartoon magazines have always been very popular. One of the first, most popular services to the subscribers of NTT DoCoMo's i-service (Internet by mobile phone) was by Bandai, allowing subscribers to download cartoon characters to their mobile phones.[40]

Online sellers are not changing people's preferences. They are selling things that people already buy. Online selling is mainly a new retail method. Across cultures similar differences in product buying via the Internet are found as via conventional retail channels.[41]

People will use the new media for the interests and habits they acquired in the country where they grew up. These interests and habits have existed for a long time, and the Internet is not going to change them. The new media may even lead to divergence in Europe and probably more so worldwide. Oliver Cleaver, media director at Kimberly Clark Europe, subscribes to this point of view. He states:

> The new media belong to global business and to a minority of consumers who are affluent, smart and wired enough to be able to use its potential to make themselves more affluent, smarter and better wired. . . . The new media are not creating a global village, they are helping to destroy it.[42]

UNIVERSALISM

At the root of many assumptions about convergence is universalistic thinking. By the term *convergence*, people often mean Westernization, whereby "Western" usually is American. Trends spotted in the United States are indiscriminately extended to other areas where different circumstances and habits will prevent their materializing. An example is a statement like, "In Western society 15% of meals eaten outside the home are in the car."[43] Dashboard dining is a typical American habit that is alien to most people of Europe and is unlikely to become a European habit.

Americans, but also northern Europeans, tend to be universalistic in their perception and assumptions. They genuinely think that their values are valid for the whole world and should be shared by all.[44] In contrast, most Asians are particularistic and focus more on the differences than on the similarities. They think their own culture to be so unique that no outsider can understand it. The way the Japanese try to demonstrate their cultural uniqueness in the world is called *nihonjinron,* a body of discourse that demonstrates Japan's cultural identity. A survey by Kazufumi Manabe,[45] a Japanese professor of sociology, shows that 82% of the Japanese are interested in the subject and read about it in the media, and 63% think foreigners are incapable of completely understanding Japanese culture.

From the Western point of view, democracy and human rights should be universal, and these are the regular topics that pop up in many articles by American journalists. This selective focus annoys many Chinese. The reaction by the Chinese is that they are depicted as slaves with no freedom.

In an interview, *Newsweek's* George Wehrfritz asked a journalist for the official Xinhua News Agency which stories upset Chinese young people. The answer was

The Western press is always talking about human rights. To you in the United States, human rights mean the right to be elected president, change your government or establish a political party. But to 1.3 billion Chinese people, human rights means the right to be with family and friends, the opportunity to make money and go to school and have access to good health care.[46]

Many international marketing managers are convinced that their own ideas or practices represent universal wisdom and try to impose them on everybody. Most global advertising agencies and many multinational companies have Anglo-American management. Their universalism makes them focus on the similarities and ignore the differences. These similarities are often pseudo-similarities.

In advertising, American values are viewed as universally valid, whereas the values of other cultures are not acceptable for advertising in the United States. Although Americans easily export their marketing and advertising concepts abroad, they rarely take an ad campaign from abroad into the United States.

Universalism can also be the cause of mistaking habits or values of one European country for all of them, for example, taking the United Kingdom as representative of Europe or categorizing all European countries as hierarchical societies,[47] whereas the differences between European countries with respect to hierarchical thinking and acting are large. Another mistake is grouping Europe into Nordic and Latin, or Mediterranean, groups or grouping the countries of the Benelux. There are important cultural differences between countries in Europe that influence consumer behavior, also between the Mediterranean cultures, for example, Italy and Spain. In Europe no two countries are more different than Belgium and the Netherlands, although they share a language and a border. Yet companies tend to take the countries together, present them as the Benelux, and extend research findings for Belgium to the Netherlands or vice versa.

A problem that reinforces universalistic thinking is lack of knowledge of other countries and cultures. A previous boss of Coca-Cola, Doug Ivester, after a contamination incident in Belgium, was said to have dismissed the problem with the comment: "Where the fuck is Belgium?"[48] CEOs, when traveling, hardly meet the average consumer. It is easy to pretend everybody is the same when you are at the top of a company and business partners are inclined to agree with you to avoid conflicts.

Lack of knowledge of separate countries makes people also see more similarities than there actually are. In international marketing, Americans tend to view all Europeans as similar; Europeans tend to view all Asians as similar; and Asians, when referring to Western culture, usually mean American culture.

Language is a related cause of misunderstanding. Some 380 million people speak English as their first language and perhaps two thirds as many as their second. Yet, understanding of English as a second language tends to be overestimated. In 2001 nearly half of all EU citizens spoke no language other than their own,[49] and 31% of young Europeans ages 15–24 spontaneously claimed not to know any foreign languages.[50] Some expect that the advance of English as a global language will damage or destroy local culture. However, just adding English to one's native language doesn't change one's culture. The problem is actually the native English speakers who think that use of English by others elsewhere makes them also think like native English speakers. Although the English language is widely spoken in many countries, it often is not spoken well enough to understand a native English or American speaker, which can cause misunderstanding in international advertising.

> An example of difficult to interpret use of the English language was a U.K. commercial for Bacardi Breezer in spring 2002 that was also aired in the Netherlands, referring to a "tomcat." The word for tomcat (*kater*) in the Netherlands is used for what is a "hangover" in the English language. This was probably not intended to be the effect of the alcoholic beverage advertised. In addition, the tomcat is asked whether he has been "chasing birds" (which means chasing women in English), the sort of word play that is beyond the understanding of most inhabitants of the Netherlands.

(Language as one of the mental processes related to culture is a topic discussed in Chapter 6 of this book.)

Finally, universalism has led to the application of Anglo-American marketing theories worldwide. This is not due to American imperialism but to the fact that advanced marketing and advertising practice and theory originated in the United States. Not only have these theories been exported to other cultures, practitioners and academics elsewhere have enthusiastically copied practices and theories from the United States without realizing that not all these concepts and theories are equally valid in their own countries. This has happened in all regions of the world, both in Europe and in Asia. In developing countries in particular, because Western concepts are regarded as "proven," Western ideas are readily acceptable to clients of advertising agencies.[51] With increased marketing literacy, people in business have slowly started to understand that not all American concepts and theories can be applied to their own cultures.

SENSE OF HISTORY

Another cause of mistakes is lack of a sense of history. Many recent phenomena are perceived as new, whereas they are often only a new format of the past. Knowledge of history helps to understand phenomena that seem to be new but are not. Those who hadn't known people's behavior in the former European Eastern bloc prior to the Soviet occupation thought new behavior resulted from Western capitalism or globalization after the Communists had left, whereas, in reality, people just resumed their old ways.

> The following is a reader's reaction to an article in *Newsweek* about patterns of Hungarian behavior that were seen to be the result of globalization:
>
> > In your insightful article, you write of the Hungarian executive who "thinks nothing of popping over to Vienna to hear U2 or Whitney Houston." This may not be as much a sign of globalization as a return to the way things were. In their day, our great-grandparents thought nothing of heading to Vienna for a night at the opera. They took the train, not their Alfa Romeo, and listened to Verdi, not Whitney. The difference is that back then not only the elite were able to afford this kind of entertainment.[52]
>
> Mate Hegedus, Budapest, Hungary

Austrians and Hungarians have much in common because Austria and Hungary have belonged to one empire (the Habsburg Empire), which makes it understandable that people easily and frequently travel through each other's countries. Only the Communist occupation prevented that temporarily.

Behavior that is understandable in the context of history is often interpreted as new by the historically ignorant. Many differences between countries can be traced to history. What most people mean by globalization is increasing flows of trade and investment between parts of the world and between countries, but many nations have been global from their origin.

One of the most important themes in the history of world economy is the balance between nationalism and internationalism, not in the ideological sense but in organization.

The historian George Holmes[53] states that the economic relationship of the modern world existed in embryo within late medieval Europe. The city-states of the fourteenth century, such as Venice, Florence, and Genoa, were republics, where state and commercialism were integrated. Venice provided its trading nobility with a state-controlled shipping service. There were Italian trading communities in every city from London to Alexandria. Marco Polo, who at the end of the thirteenth century described China for Westerners, was one of a family of Venetian merchants. At that time journeys by Italian merchants across Asia from the Black Sea to China were commonplace. Venice, a city without much industry, came to control an empire through trading enterprise. The most famous commercial family of the fifteenth century, the Medici, established a network of branches at Rome, Geneva, Bruges, London, Lyons, Naples, and Milan. They were experts in the international exchange business, transferring money by letters of exchange from one part of Europe to another.

Increased worldwide interconnectedness has intensified global trade, money exchange, and flow of information. Individuals like Bill Gates or Richard Branson, or families like the Wallenbergs or Guccis, can span the globe with their trade like the Medici did in their times on a smaller scale. What has changed is that modern branding and media have made the phenomena of globalization more visual. Family names have become brands.

Technological advances have always played a role in altering the economic importance of certain areas. Advanced technology came from the Silicon Valley in the twentieth century, and it came from China in the fifteenth century, where it may come from again in the twenty-first century. The degree to which some nations or areas have embraced new technology has changed their structural role in the world economy. During the Middle Ages, a reasonable trade balance existed between Christian Europe and the Arabian world. Gold and silver flowed eastward, and spices and precious stones went westward. However, a shortage of gold caused problems for Florence and Genoa, which needed gold to produce coins for their trade activities. Gold had to be obtained elsewhere. The Portuguese were the only people interested in traveling further afield than the usual kind of discovery voyages. Due to its geographical position, Portugal could only expand via the sea. Financed by Genoa, the Portuguese set out on their voyages of discovery. Europeans traveled the world in order to obtain exotic commerce and to trade. Looking at China during that same period, it seems that Europe and China had similar population levels between the thirteenth and sixteenth centuries. From the second century to the fifteenth century, China had a technological advantage. It was only around 1450 that Europe began to increase its technological development. One reason was political: Europe could not afford to lag behind in the development of its arms industry because of many wars between the different states. In China, on the other hand, the government decided to restrict the development of the arms industry in order to improve internal peace.

The Portuguese and the Chinese went on their voyages of discovery in the same period. After 18 years, however, the Chinese stopped abruptly with the death of eunuch-admiral Cheng Ho in 1434. The main reason lay in an important cultural difference: the Chinese did not travel to *obtain* something but to *bring* something. By bringing gifts of high quality to faraway countries, they wanted to assure those countries of their superiority. They were not interested in colonizing because they believed that they were already the whole world. When their treasuries were depleted due to the escapades of Cheng Ho, the discovery voyages were stopped and China cut itself off.[54]

Historical, political, and cultural factors explain the economic development of nations that have played an integrated role in global trade. That has not changed. Despite the existence of a World Trade Organization, there still are trade wars between nations. What has changed is that there are no more military wars between commercial communities. The armies of the government do not support the cola wars.

Many current global developments can be better understood by knowing the history of global trade and the varying national contexts in which global trade has developed. Habits of inhabitants of India can be explained by the former British colonial influence. How China in the far past dealt with technological development can explain how that country deals with new developments in the present. The Chinese people are, as in the past, eager to embrace new technology, but a historically strongly centralized government wishes to guide (control in Western eyes) the people in the way they adopt it.

When entering new markets with new products or brands, a sense of history can help. In a country like the Czech Republic, where people have been drinking fruit juice and herbal teas for centuries, it will not be easy to change their habits to drinking cola. Perceptions of brands are often formed by their history in the market place. In 1996 in China, Panasonic was seen as the leading electronics brand in Beijing, Shanghai, Guangzhou, and Chengdu, according to a survey by advertising agency Grey, but ironically, Panasonic was introduced to Chinese consumers when the manufacturer shipped a load of what were actually outdated cassette players to the country in the early 1980s. For many Chinese households, Panasonic was their first foreign brand.[55]

BRANDING AND ADVERTISING: FROM GLOBAL TO MULTI-LOCAL

The discussion about the advantages and disadvantages of standardizing advertising across countries has been a long one. One of the most frequently heard advantages is cost reduction because of economies of scale. Other reasons are quality control and consistency in an era when many media reach various countries at the same time. It is good international business practice to want to control one's communications, but standardization of global branding and marketing communications is wrong in principle and impossible in practice. Global advertising can only be effective if there are global consumers with universal values. As consumers' values and behavior vary across cultures, global standardized advertising is not equally effective in all markets. Much of it is wasted in markets where consumer values are different from the values of the advertising campaign. Because of this, even

Saatchi & Saatchi, the advertising agency that was first to embrace the concept of global advertising, changed their opinion. Kevin Roberts, CEO worldwide of Saatchi & Saatchi, stated in 2002, "Anyone who wants to go global has to understand the local—their own local and the locals of all their customers. People live in the local. I've never met a global consumer. I never expect to. We define ourselves by our differences. It's called identity—self, family, nation."[56] In an interview in *BusinessWeek,* Martin Sorrell, CEO of WPP group, says that the idea that globalization would lead consumers to buy goods and services the same ways everywhere now looks to be flawed. According to Sorrell, truly global products and services such as soft drinks or computers only account for 15% of WPP's revenues. What has been going on may not have been globalization but the Americanization of markets.[57]

The old marketing paradigm says that markets are people. There may be global products, but there are no global people. There may be global brands, but there are no global motives for buying these brands. There may be global markets, but most consumption patterns are local. Douglas Daft, Coca-Cola's CEO, stated in 2000, "People don't buy drinks globally."[58] Coca-Cola is one of the brands that are frequently used as examples of longtime successful global advertising. Probably the most important success factor of Coca-Cola, however, has been its efficient distribution system, not its global advertising. For a long time Coca-Cola's main goal was "to be within an arm's reach of desire,"[59] and its longtime slogan was "Always, everywhere Coca-Cola." In the year 2000 the Coca-Cola Company, which had until then been the prototype of a global advertiser, decided to get closer to local markets because of declining profitability. CEO Douglas Daft was quoted in the *Financial Times,* "We kept standardizing our practices, while local sensitivity had become absolutely essential to success."[60] According to Daft, the general direction is away from global advertising. "We need to make our advertising as relevant as possible to the local market."[61] This approach is a better way to control the marketing process than exporting universal brand values to global publics without knowing what the takeout will be. As the sociologist-anthropologist David Howes says, "The assumption that goods like Coca-Cola, on entering a culture, will retain and communicate the values they are accorded by their culture of origin must be questioned. Often these goods are transformed in accordance with the values of the receiving culture."[62] This results in loss of control instead of control, which is the purpose of global standardized marketing and communications.

Many of the large multinationals that have standardized their operations and brands since the 1990s have seen their profits decline because centralized control lacks local sensitivity. In the mid-1990s, Ford centralized global management. "That move, Ford execs now say, took Ford of Europe's focus off local strategy. As a result it lacks competitive offerings in segments that make up 35 percent of the European market."[63] The continental European clothing retailer C&A standardized buying and advertising in Europe in 1997. In June 2000 the company decided to close all 109 shops in the United Kingdom and Ireland because of substantial losses. The taste of the British and Irish consumers is different from that of continental Europeans.[64] Also, tastes vary across continental Europe. Casual clothing, for example, sells better in the Netherlands than in Germany. At the end of the year 2000, C&A had relocalized both buying and advertising. The British retail chain Marks & Spencer, which until then had made different advertising campaigns for each country where it operated, changed to uniform advertising for the whole of Europe. At the end of 2001, Marks & Spencer withdrew from the European continent. Differences in local tastes not only prevent selling standard products; they also affect the way retailers sell their goods. In 1996 the American retailer Wal-Mart set up efficient, clean supercenters in Indonesia, only to find that Indonesians preferred Matahari, the shabbier shop next door, which reminded shoppers of a street market where they could haggle.[65] Many international companies underestimate the strength of local products in the markets they enter. And they overestimate the value of their reputations.

Perhaps one of the causes of success of McDonald's in foreign markets is the fact that, in addition to maintaining a strong brand image and consistent service standards around the world, its product offer has a local touch and its advertising until 2003 has been local. Examples are the Kiwi burger in New Zealand; the Maharaja Mac in India; the Prosperity burger in Malaysia; the Teriyaki burger in Japan; the McKroket in the Netherlands; McLaks, a grilled salmon burger, in Norway; and the Croque McDo in France that refers to the popular French "Croque Monsieur," a hot ham and cheese sandwich. Advertising by McDonald's tied into local habits, values, and symbols. In 2001, for example, advertising for McDonald's in France tied into "Asterix and Obelisk," the most famous historical cartoon of the nation. Figure 1.3 shows a few pictures from this commercial.

Figure 1.3   McDonald's Advertising in France, 2001

In Asia, McDonald's follows cultural habits and uses celebrities. Figure 1.4 shows pictures from a Japanese commercial that is hardly understandable to outsiders. We see a young woman putting on all sorts of different hats and in the end eating a hamburger. What is special is that her name is Yuri Ebihara. McDonald's Japan annually has a special filet-o-fish with shrimp inside, which is called *ebi filet-o*. *Ebi* means shrimp in Japanese. Since Ebihara is such a famous model, and her name is actually a bit strange, including the word *ebi*, anybody in Japan can easily relate Ebihara to *ebi filet-o*, even without saying anything about the hamburger.

Instead of consistency, flexibility will become increasingly important in global marketing. The strength of many national or multilocal brands is demonstrated by the

Figure 1.4   McDonald's Advertising in Japan, 2009

Reader's Digest surveys, "European Trusted Brands,"[66] conducted annually since 2000 and asking respondents which brands they trusted most for several product categories. There are several national brands that have remained strong in the face of the power of the large multinationals. These are national brands that are either old or include important national values in their advertising, or both. In France, the French car brand Renault is most trusted; in Germany and Austria it is the German brand Volkswagen; and in the Czech Republic, it is Skoda, an originally Czech car brand. The most trusted car brand in India is the Indian brand Maruti.

The trend from global to local is reinforced by localization of media. Many originally global or pan-regional television channels have localized, that is, adapted to local languages and offered local ad windows to advertisers. CNN International programming regionalized in September 1997 and now comprises five separately scheduled international television channels: Asia Pacific; South Asia; Europe/the Middle East/Africa; Latin America; and North America. CNN is available on television in Spanish on CNN+, Spain; in Turkish on CNN Turk, Turkey; and in German on n-tv, Germany. On the Web it is available in Japanese on CNN.co.jp, and Arabic on CNNArabic.com. A CNN headline news service is also available in Korean at CNN.com/Korean. Nearly 90% of programs on CNN International are exclusively produced for the international feeds. Only about 10% are derived from CNN/U.S.[67]

Localization makes it increasingly important for marketing and advertising people to understand the influence of culture. Cultural effects are often less obvious and more difficult to research than economic consequences, but they can be more pervasive and serious in the long run.

CONSUMER BEHAVIOR

Consumer behavior can be defined[68] as the study of the processes involved when people select, purchase, use, or dispose of products, services, ideas, or experiences to satisfy needs and desires. In this definition, consumer behavior is viewed as a process that includes the issues that influence the consumer before, during, and after a purchase. In some models of consumer behavior, the elements of consumer behavior are classified according to the academic disciplines psychology and sociology, from which consumer behavior theory borrows. Whereas psychology studies human behavior at the individual level, sociology studies human behavior at group level. But culture operates at each level. Personality and culture are inextricably bound together. How people learn is studied at the individual level, but what and how human beings learn varies with the society in which they live. Culture is more than a social or environmental influence. Instead of viewing culture as the environment of people's behavior, nowadays anthropologists view culture as "interiorized." People used to be imagined *in* a culture. Now, culture is in their *heads.*[69]

To understand culture's consequences for consumer behavior, culture must be integrated in the various aspects of consumer behavior theory. Ideally, theories of consumer behavior are developed within cultures, studying people's behavior within each nation. For comparing cultures, variables and constructs must be found that allow discovering how these cultures or groups of cultures are different from or similar to each other. Following this "etic" approach (see also Chapter 2) includes the risk of overlooking some unique aspects of unique cultures, but it is the most practical approach and is common to current research in cross-cultural psychology and other comparative social sciences.[70] This book approaches consumer behavior across cultures by reviewing various existing theories and integrating culture in these theories. Instead of categorizing behavior aspects according to the separate disciplines, we need an integrated view of the individual, culture, and society. This approach is reflected in the model that structures the various components of consumer behavior process described in this book.

A MODEL OF CROSS-CULTURAL CONSUMER BEHAVIOR

The components of human behavior can be summarized as *what people are* ("Who am I?"), the *self* and *personality,* defined by people's attributes and traits ("What sort of person am I?"), *how people feel, how people think and learn,* and *what people do.* The terms of the social sciences for feeling, learning, and doing are *affect, cognition,* and *behavior.* These elements are included in the definition of consumer behavior of the American Marketing Association as "the dynamic interaction of affect and cognition, behavior, and the environment by which human beings conduct exchange aspects of their lives."[71]

For understanding the influence of culture on consumer behavior, marketers must integrate culture in the various components of human behavior. U.S. marketing scholars Manrai and Manrai[72] point out that in the definitions, culture is a complex concept. Many items defined as consequences of culture are also included in the definition of culture, either as artifacts (e.g., food, dress) or as abstract elements (e.g., values and norms). These must be separated, so that consumer behavior consequences of culture can be specified beyond other types of behavior that are implicitly included in the definition of culture itself. Cultural values should be included as an integrated part of the consumer and not as an environmental factor. In this book also *national income* is not viewed as an environmental factor as in so many textbooks, so I do not use the term *economic environment.* Income interacts with the consumer's values and culture, in particular in post-scarcity societies. In this I follow Süerdem,[73] who defines economic rationality as a "value system" appropriate for a certain social system.

The model presented in Figure 1.5 structures the cultural components of the *person* in terms of consumer *attributes* and *processes,* and the cultural components of *behavior* in con-*sumer behavior domains.* Wealth is influenced by culture, but in turn it influences culture, so *income* is placed in a separate box, shown as interacting with the culture of the consumer.

ORGANIZATION OF THE BOOK

This book is organized according to the framework shown in Figure 1.5. It discusses topics found in American consumer behavior textbooks, but it is structured in a different way.

Core differences in the approach of this book are with respect to the influence of culture on the self and information processing. In U.S.-based textbooks, the self and information processing are described from the perspective of an individualistic culture only. The group is viewed as an external factor and not as part of the self. Information is described as an instrument that empowers consumers with the ability to make informed decisions.[75] Culture is usually viewed as merely an environmental influence on consumer behavior instead of interiorized in the person. Another major difference is that most textbooks start with the decision-making process, whereas this book views decision making as a mental

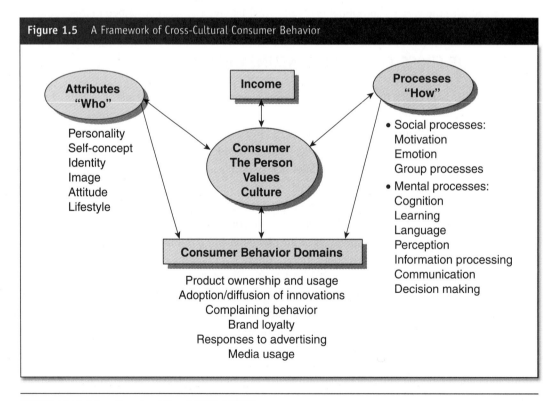

Figure 1.5   A Framework of Cross-Cultural Consumer Behavior

SOURCE: Adapted from Manrai and Manrai (1996, 2001)[74]

process, and influences on decision making are found all through the book. Consumer behavior textbooks of U.S. origin—apart from an introductory chapter that includes varying topics in different textbooks—generally consist of the following major parts: (1) consumer decision making; (2) the consumer as an individual; (3) group and cultural influences. Table 1.1 shows how these topics are covered in this book.

Table 1.1 Comparison of Organization of Topics in U.S. Consumer Behavior Textbooks and in *Consumer Behavior and Culture*

General Consumer Behavior Textbooks	Topics	Consumer Behavior and Culture (Chapter Number)
Consumer decision making	Buying, consumption	(8) Consumer behavior domains
	Brand loyalty	(8) Consumer behavior domains
	Individual decision making	(6) Mental processes
	High-, low-involvement decision making/processing	(6) Mental processes
	Situational influences on decision making	(5) Social processes
	Dissatisfaction	(8) Consumer behavior domains
	Shopping behavior	(8) Consumer behavior domains
Consumer as individuals	Motivations and values	(5) Social processes
	The self, personality, image, lifestyle	(4) The consumer: Attributes
	Attitude	(4) The consumer: Attributes
	Perception, learning, memory	(6) Mental processes
	Categorization	(6) Mental processes
	Information processing	(6) Mental processes
	Demographics	(3) Convergence/divergence in consumer behavior
Group and cultural influences	Cultural values	(2) Values and culture
	Group influence, roles of group members, reference groups	(5) Social processes
	Influentials, opinion leaders	(5) Social processes
	Household decision making	(5) Social processes
	Group communication	(7) Culture and communication
	Link values-behavior	(7) Culture and communication
	Diffusion of innovations	(7) Culture and communication
	Opinion leaders	(7) Culture and communication

CONCLUSION

The topics reviewed in this chapter illustrate assumptions generally found in academic literature and in practice. The assumptions are that there are global consumers or global communities with universal values who can be reached by global advertising. Reality is different, and examples are given of companies that have standardized their products and communications with bad results. Global advertising was conceived from the assumption that consumer behavior across countries would converge with converging media, technology, and national wealth. There is little evidence to support this thesis. Instead, with converging wealth, when people increasingly live in post-scarcity societies, the differences become more pronounced. At the root of misunderstanding are universalism, the spread of the English language, and lack of a sense of history. For comparing post-scarcity societies, income can no longer serve as an explaining variable, and culture becomes the new paradigm.

NOTES

1. McLuhan, M. (1964). *Understanding media: The extensions of man.* New York: McGraw-Hill, 225, 268, 276.
2. Bullmore, J. (2000). Alice in Disneyland: A creative view of international advertising. In J. P. Jones (Ed.), *International advertising realities and myths* (pp. 41–56). Thousand Oaks, CA: Sage, 48.
3. Rossant, J. (2000, November 20). A common identity for Europe? You better believe it. *BusinessWeek,* 72.
4. Assael, H. (2004). *Consumer behavior: A strategic approach.* Boston: Houghton Mifflin, 378.
5. Assael (2004), 386.
6. Robertson, R. (1990). Mapping the global condition: Globalization as the central concept. In M. Featherstone (Ed.), *Global culture* (pp. 15–30). London: Sage.
7. Financial indicators. (1997, September 27). *The Economist,* 123; Worldbeater, Inc. (1997, November 22). *The Economist,* 108.
8. *Globalisation.* (2003, October–November). Flash Eurobarometer report 151b.
9. Fu, J. H. Y., & Shiu, C. Y. (2007). Local culture's responses to globalization. Exemplary persons and their attendant values. *Journal of Cross-Cultural Psychology, 38*(5), 636–653.
10. Alden, D. L., Steenkamp, J. B. E. M., & Batra, R. (1999). Brand positioning through advertising in Asia, North America, and Europe: The role of global consumer culture. *Journal of Marketing, 63,* 75–87.
11. Featherstone, M. (1991). *Consumer culture and postmodernism.* London: Sage.
12. Giddens, A. (2000). *Runaway world.* New York: Routledge.
13. European Media and Marketing Survey. (2007). Synovate.
14. European Audiovisual Observatory. Retrieved April 18, 2009, from http://www.obs.coe.int/about/oea/pr/berlinale2009.html
15. Levitt, T. (1983, May–June). The globalization of markets. *Harvard Business Review,* 2–11.
16. Süerdem, A. (1993). Social de(re)construction of mass culture: Making (non)sense of consumer behavior. *International Journal of Research in Marketing, 11,* 423–443.
17. Usunier, J. C. (1996). Consommation: Quand global rime avec local (Consumption: When global rhymes with local). *Revue Française de gestion, 110,* 100–116.

18. Inkeles, A. (1998). *One world emerging?: Convergence and divergence in industrial societies.* Boulder, CO: Westview.

19. *Survey on the attitudes of Europeans towards tourism.* (2008). Flash Eurobarometer report 258.

20. *Young Europeans in 2001.* (2001). Eurobarometer report 151.

21. White, R. (1998). International advertising. How far can it fly? In J. P. Jones (Ed.), *International advertising* (pp. 29–40). Thousand Oaks, CA: Sage, 34.

22. Theil, S. (2004, November 1). Not made for walking. *Newsweek, 36–37.*

23. Allman, J. (1997, January). Variety is the spice of Latin life. *M&M Europe, 49–50.*

24. Living with a superpower. (2003, January 4). *The Economist,* 18–20.

25. Mooney, P. (2002, May 27). Learning the old ways. *Newsweek,* 29.

26. Assael (2004), 386.

27. Huntington, S. P. (1996). *The Clash of Civilizations and the remaking of world order.* New York: Simon & Schuster, 57.

28. Galloni, A. (2002, February). Marketers face divergent tech targets. *Marketing & Media,* 26.

29. Lau, S. (2001, March). I want my MTV, but in Mandarin, please. *Admap,* 34.

30. Cooper, P. (1994, October 17). Western at the weekends. *Admap,* 18–21.

31. Malkin, E. (1994, October 17). X-ers. *Advertising Age International,* 1–15.

32. Dijkgraaf, M. (1999, December 17). Interview with Amélie Nothomb. *NRC Handelsblad,* 5.

33. *Insights 88.* (1998, November). ACNielsen, 8.

34. Advance of the amazones. (2000, July 22). *The Economist,* 69.

35. High rollers. (2001, June 16). *The Economist,* 43.

36. What the Internet cannot do. (2000, August 19). *The Economist,* 9; Wired China. (2000, July 22). *The Economist,* 24–25.

37. Groshek, D. (2009). The democratic effects of the Internet, 1994–2003: A cross-national inquiry of 152 countries. *The International Communication Gazette, 71*(3), 115–136.

38. Moore, J., & Einhorn, B. (1999, October 25). A biz-to-biz e-boom. *BusinessWeek,* 30–31.

39. Percy, L. (2001, February). Marketing communication in evolution. *Admap,* 31.

40. *Nikkei trendy.* (2000, March).

41. Goodrich, K., & De Mooij, M. K. (2011). New technology mirrors old habits: Online buying mirrors cross-national variance of conventional buying. *Journal of International Consumer Marketing,* forthcoming.

42. Cleaver, O. (2000, January). The digital divide. *M&M Europe,* 38–39.

43. Nuttall, C. (2001, September). Trend-spotters don't have to follow fashion. *M&M Europe,* 18.

44. Adler, N. J. (1991). *International dimensions of organizational behavior* (2nd ed.). Belmont, CA: Wadsworth, 47.

45. Manabe, K. (2004). Cultural nationalism in Japan. In H. Vinken, J. Soeters, & P. Ester (Eds.), *Comparing cultures: Dimensions of culture in a comparative perspective.* Leiden-Boston: Brill.

46. Wehrfritz, G. (1997, February 17). The great stone curtain. Do American journalists obscure the real China? *Newsweek,* 39.

47. Rossant, J. (2001, January 31). Old world, new mandate. *BusinessWeek,* 49.

48. Who's wearing the trousers? (2001, September 8). *The Economist,* 29.

49. English is still on the march. (2001, February 24). *The Economist,* 33; A world empire by other means. (2001, December 22). *The Economist,* 33–35.

50. *Young Europeans in 2001* (2001).

51. Interview with Jimmy Lam, Regional Executive Creative Director and Chairman of D'Arcy Greater China. (2000, November 12). *New Sunday Times* (Malaysia), p. 12.

52. Letters to the editor, re: "Globalization in Eastern Europe," September 25. Special Report on Prague's IMF summit. (2000, October 23). *Newsweek.*

53. Holmes, G. (1975). *Europe: Hierarchy and revolt 1320–1450.* Glasgow: William Collins Sons, 71–72, 119.

54. Wallerstein, I. (1974). *The modern world system* (Vol. I). New York: Academic Press.

55. Liang, E. (1996, July 12). Solving the consumer jigsaw puzzle. *Asian Marketing, 10.*

56. Roberts, K. (2002, January). Running on empty. *M&M Europe, 8.*

57. Capell, K. (2003, July 7). Martin Sorrell on the ad game. *Business Week, 23.*

58. Debunking Coke. (2000, February 12). *The Economist, 74.*

59. New Doug, old tricks. (1999, December 11). *The Economist, 59.*

60. Daft, D. (2000, March 27). Back to classic Coke. Personal view. *Financial Times.* Retrieved March 30, 2000, from http://news.ft.com

61. Crawford, A. M. (2000, March). New Coke chief cans "universal" message. *M&M Europe, 8.*

62. Crawford (2000), 5.

63. Welch, D., & Terney, C. (2000, October 16). Can the Mondeo get Ford back into the race? *Business Week, 29.*

64. C&A heft alle Britse winkels op. (2000, June 15). *NRC Handelsblad.*

65. Shopping all over the world. (1999, June 19). *The Economist, 73–75.*

66. *European trusted brands.* London: Reader's Digest. Retrieved from http//:www.rdtrustedbrands.com

67. Retrieved November 6, 2009, from http://www.cnnasiapacific.com/factsheets/?catID=9

68. Solomon, M., Bamossy, G., & Askegaard, S. (1999). *Consumer behaviour: A European perspective.* London: Pearson Education, 8.

69. Munroe, R. L., & Munroe, R. H. (1997). A comparative anthropological perspective. In J. W. Berry, Y. H. Poortinga, & J. Pandey (Eds.), *Handbook of cross-cultural psychology* (Vol. 1, pp. 171–213). Boston: Allyn & Bacon, 173.

70. Luna, D., & Forquer Gupta, S. (2001). An integrative framework for cross-cultural consumer behavior. *International Marketing Review, 18,* 377–386.

71. Luna & Forquer Gupta (2001).

72. Manrai, L. A., & Manrai, A. K. (1996). Current issues in cross-cultural and cross-national consumer research. In L. A. Manrai & A. K. Manrai (Eds.), *Global perspectives in cross-cultural and cross-national consumer research* (pp. 9–22). New York: International Business Press/Haworth Press, 13.

73. Süerdem (1993).

74. Manrai, L .A., & Manrai, A. K. (2001). Current issues in the cross-cultural and cross-national consumer research in the new millennium. *Journal of East-West Business, 7*(1), 1–10.

75. Assael (2004), xix.

CHAPTER 2

Values and Culture

For some time it has been understood that different value orientations cause variations in preferences for products and brands.[1] Values of both consumers and marketers are defined by their culture, hence the importance of understanding the value concept and culture. To understand how culture operates, we have to vocalize it. Models of culture that enable observing and tabulating cultural differences facilitate this. This chapter deals with such models. It describes the value concept, culture, and the various dimensions of culture that can explain consumer behavior differences.

VALUES

A *value* is defined by Rokeach, one of the early U.S. researchers of values, as

> an enduring belief that one mode of conduct or end-state of existence is preferable to an opposing mode of conduct or end-state of existence. A *value system* is an enduring organization of beliefs concerning preferable modes of conduct or end-states of existence along a continuum of relative importance.[2]

In a value system, values are ordered in priority with respect to other values. This is why some authors use the term *value priority* interchangeably with *values*.

Because values are preferences of one state of being over another, they are often measured on polar scales, for example,

Healthy versus ill

Clean versus dirty

Active versus passive

Optimist versus pessimist

Modern versus traditional

A *value* refers to a single belief of a very specific kind, as opposed to an *attitude* that refers to an organization of several beliefs around a specific object or situation.[3] Values have cognitive, affective, and behavioral components. Although values are expressed in abstract terms, people generally *know* what their preferred "state of being" is (e.g., being healthy, not ill). Values are *affective* in the sense that people can *feel* emotional about them. A value has a *behavioral* exponent in the sense that it is an intervening variable that leads to *action* when activated.

Rokeach distinguishes two levels of values: terminal values and instrumental values. *Terminal* values refer to desirable end-states of existence. *Instrumental* values refer to desirable modes of conduct; they are motivators to reach end-states of existence. Examples are the instrumental values "ambitious" and "capable" that lead to the terminal values "a comfortable life" and "a sense of accomplishment."

The Rokeach Value Survey (RVS) has been used in other cultures, but with different results, in particular with respect to value priorities. Whereas in the United States being honest, ambitious, and responsible have been consistently shown as the most important instrumental values, in China being cheerful, polite, and independent appear to be the most important values. Being cheerful and polite are values of the doctrine of Confucianism.[4]

The Desirable and the Desired

Two aspects of values must be distinguished: (1) values as guiding principles in life and (2) a value as a preference for one mode of behavior over another. The distinction refers to the *desirable* and the *desired,* or what people think ought to be desired and what people actually desire—how people *think the world ought to be* versus *what people want for themselves.*[5] The desirable refers to the general norms of a society and is worded in terms of right or wrong, in absolute terms. The desired is what we want, what we consider important for ourselves.

We speak of *norms* as soon as we deal with a collectivity. In the case of the desired, the norm is statistical: It indicates the values held by the majority. In the case of the desirable, the norm is absolute, pertaining to what is ethically right. The desired relates more to pragmatic issues, the desirable to ideology. The desired relates to choice, to what is important and preferred; it relates to the "me" and the "you." The desirable relates to what is approved or disapproved, to what is good, right, what one ought to do, and what one should agree with; it refers to people in general (see Table 2.1).[6]

Rokeach states that conceptions of the desirable are deliberately excluded from his definition. In his definition of values, he refers to preferable states of being, not to moral principles. When measuring values, asking people for moral guidelines is likely to result in different answers than asking them, directly or indirectly, for their preferred state of being. An example is the question about equality. In some cultures inequality is implicitly accepted

Table 2.1   The Desirable Versus the Desired

The Desirable	The Desired
The norm, what ought	What people want for themselves
Words	Deeds
Approval, disapproval	Choice
What is good, right	Attractive, preferred
For people in general	For me and for you
Ideology	Pragmatism

in relationships with higher-placed persons (e.g., bosses), yet people tend to say Yes when asked if there should be greater equality between people.

Market researchers Grunert and Muller[7] point at an additional type of interference in research. The desirable can signify something that guides one's day-to-day life, as well as something one wishes to have, but cannot attain given present circumstances. In research we have to distinguish between "real" life values and "ideal" life values.

The desired and the desirable do not always overlap, and often are seemingly opposing or paradoxical. Each society has its specific *value paradoxes* as a result of these opposing elements in values.[8] An example is a value found in many lists of values of the United States: "belonging," which seems paradoxical in view of the equally important value "rugged individualism." An example of a paradoxical element in Chinese culture is the combination of modernity and tradition that go together in Chinese advertising, whereas from the Western value perspective, it seems the two are opposing values.[9] Understanding the value paradoxes of cultures is of great importance when analyzing advertising, which tends to focus on the desirable, what should be, what people want, or what they don't have. For example, in cultures where the family is an integrated part of the self, advertising need not focus so much on the importance of the family. In cultures where family values are lacking, advertising focuses more on the role products play in a desirable happy family life.

Values Are Enduring

Values are among the first things children learn, not consciously, but implicitly. Development psychologists believe that by the age of 10, most children have their basic value systems firmly in place.[10] Values are stable through generations. Several studies demonstrate this stability. Yankelovich[11] found that many of Americans' most important traditional values have remained firm and constant over time. Examples are freedom, equality, fairness, achievement, patriotism, democracy, and religion. Since 1934, Gallup polls have

measured the opinions and beliefs of American people that have remained stable over time. The United States, for example, remains much more religious than any other religious country. A Gallup poll of 1995 found that 61% of Americans say that democracy cannot survive without a widespread belief in a god of some kind.[12] Time and again, Japan is expected to converge with the West, but Japanese values have remained relatively stable. Examples of stable values are pragmatism and hard work. In China, throughout the changes brought by the Cultural Revolution, Confucian values have remained important.[13]

Also, value differences across Europe have remained quite stable over time. Data from Eurobarometer surveys between 1973 and 2008 show that across countries the levels of satisfaction with life in general have remained more or less the same, and there are remarkable cross-cultural differences: consistently, the Danish, Dutch, and British publics show a higher level of satisfaction than the Italian, French, and German. These differences have remained stable over time.

Figure 2.1 illustrates the stability of the differences. An important finding is that similar differences are found for young people 15 to 24 years old. Eurobarometer also asked young

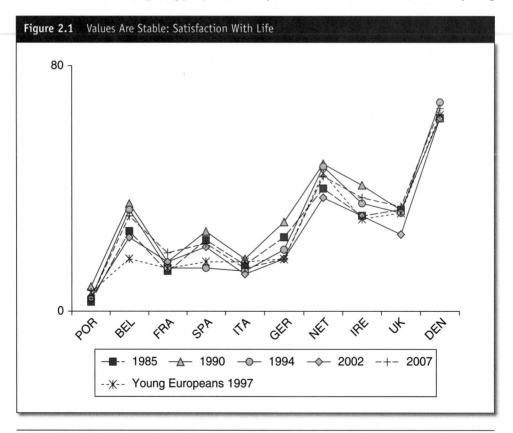

Figure 2.1   Values Are Stable: Satisfaction With Life

SOURCES: Data from Eurobarometer (1985, 1990, 1994, 2002, 2008); Young Europeans, Eurobarometer (1997) (see Appendix B)

people in Europe to what degree they are satisfied with their lives, and, as the chart shows, this line runs parallel to the one of the general public.

Also, Chinese values appear to be resistant to change. Traditional moral values such as filial piety are still the top moral concerns among young people in Beijing and Hong Kong China.[14]

Scholars of advertising also have reported stability of values. Commercial communication has been relatively consistent in its cultural character, both in the Western world and in Asia. Despite the rapid changes in Hong Kong society, for example, people continue to hold many traditional attitudes that influence what they buy and how they respond to advertising messages.[15] Pollay and Gallagher[16] found strong consistency in values in advertising between 1970 and 1980 in the United States. Similar values were found in print advertising and in television advertising. Wiles et al.[17] compared U.S. values found in a comparative study with a similar study conducted 20 years earlier and found the same values. People tend to think that inequality between males and females is decreasing, along with wealth and better education, but there is evidence of persistent or even increasing role patterns in the United States,[18] where between 1975 and 1993 the differences between the sexes with respect to certain duties, obligations, and beliefs in the roles of fathers had increased.[19]

Values in Marketing

The Rokeach Value Survey was one of the first value studies that served as an example for many others. A simpler approach to values, called list of values (LOV), was developed by Kahle and Goff Timmer.[20] LOV consists of nine values: sense of belonging, excitement, fun and enjoyment in life, warm relationship with others, self-fulfillment, being well-respected, a sense of accomplishment, security, self-respect. The nine items of LOV became the basis of the development of a measurement scheme by the United States Marketing Science Institute, called MILOV (Multi-Item List of Values). Clawson and Vinson[21] were among the first scholars who applied the value concept to marketing. They state also that consumer values are derived from and modified through personal, social, and cultural learning. Many lists of U.S. values have been used in value studies in other countries.

In marketing and advertising, the value concept is often used in an ethnocentric way. Value studies developed in one culture are applied to other cultures where they do not fit. An example is the lists of values, applicable to advertising, as defined by Pollay,[22] that contains only American values. This is logical, as they result from analysis of American advertising. The cultural values extracted from an examination of hundreds of ads from more than 60 years reveal that these values are fundamental to American cultural life and have found their way into consumer culture. Yet, Pollay's list of values has been used in cross-cultural advertising studies. Applying sets of values derived from one culture in cross-cultural contexts without regard to the substance of the cultures in question is called *ethnoconsumerism*.[23] One cannot assume that the same set of values will influence two different groups of consumers' responses for the same marketing stimuli, or that causes of behavior in one country are the same as in another.[24] Both values and related behavior vary by culture.

Cultures can overlap with respect to some values and related habits. Some values are found everywhere, but they are more prevalent in some cultures than in others. Figure 2.2 illustrates this overlap. The distribution of values of a culture follows the normal distribution. The averages of one culture are different from the averages of another culture, but they may overlap to a certain extent. For international marketers, such overlaps can be niches. A marketer's choice is to adapt the brand values and advertising to the target culture or stick to the specific values of the home culture. This will result in having only a niche market in the target market for what is a mass market of the home market. An example is the Italian car brand Alfa Romeo. Italians are more aggressive drivers than are the British or the Dutch, and the Alfa Romeo caters to aggressive drivers. In the Netherlands, there will be some people who like to drive aggressively, but this is a minority. Alfa Romeo, which can cater to a mass market in Italy, will, without adapting their positioning strategy, have only a niche market in the Netherlands.

Figure 2.2   Culture Overlap

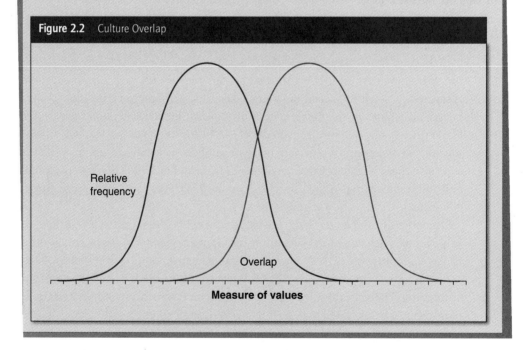

CULTURE DEFINED

Culture is the glue that binds groups together. Without cultural patterns—organized systems of significant symbols—people would have difficulty living together. Culture is what defines a human community, its individuals and social organizations. The anthropologist Clifford Geertz[25] views culture as a set of control mechanisms—plans, recipes, rules, instructions (what computer engineers call "programs")—for the governing of behavior. People are dependent upon the control mechanisms of culture for ordering their behavior. In line with this, Hofstede defines culture as "the collective mental programming of the people in an environment. Culture is not a characteristic of individuals; it encompasses a number of people who were conditioned by the same education and life experience."[26]

Individuals are products of their culture and their social groupings; therefore, they are conditioned by their sociocultural environment to act in certain manners. Culture cannot be separated from the individual; it is not a system of abstract values that exists independently of individuals. Neither can culture be separated from the historical context. Culture is to society what memory is to individuals. It includes the things that have "worked" in the past. It includes shared beliefs, attitudes, norms, roles, and values found among speakers of a particular language who live during the same historical period in a specific geographic region. These shared elements of subjective culture are usually transferred from generation to generation. Language, time, and place help define culture.[27]

The U.S. sociologist Alex Inkeles[28] uses the term "national character" because individuals make up societies, and patterned conditions of life in a particular society give rise to certain distinctive patterns in the personalities of its members. The national character is the set of psychosocial characteristics manifested by a given national population. Some of those characteristics are shared by some other populations. The total profile, however, is likely to be distinctive.

COMPARING CULTURES

Cultural differences manifest themselves in several ways. Hofstede[29] distinguishes symbols, heroes, rituals, and values. Symbols, heroes, and rituals are the practices or expressions of culture that are the visible aspects of culture. The underlying values are invisible. Often when people suggest that cultures converge, they refer to the symbols of culture.

The Emic and the Etic

Two different ways to compare cultures are from the emic or from the etic point of view. The terms *emic* and *etic* are derived from the "phonemic" and "phonetic" classification in linguistics. The phonemic is the specific, the phonetic is the general. In line with this, the emic approach tries to describe behavior of one particular culture, the etic approach uses external criteria to describe and compare behavior of different cultures. The usefulness of culture as an explanatory variable depends upon our ability to "unpackage" the culture concept. To do so, the etic approach must be used, and cultural values must be arrayed along interpretable dimensions.[30] Differences in the locations of cultures along these dimensions can then be used to explain differences between cultures in their distributions of behavior patterns, norms, attitudes, and personality variables.

Measuring Cultural Values

The values that characterize a society cannot be observed directly. They can be inferred from various cultural products (fairy tales, children's books, or advertising) or by asking members of society to score their personal values by stating their preferences among alternatives and then calculating the central tendency of the answers. When value differences are derived from cultural products, or artifacts of culture, we run the risk of circular reasoning.[31] Values should be related to information about cultures derived from the study of individuals. This is not an easy job. Because values are learned unconsciously, people are only partly aware of them. They work as an automatic pilot and people can only describe them in an abstract way.[32] When measuring values at the individual level, culture always plays a role. Many (cultural) value studies use self-reflective reports; that is, they ask respondents to agree or not agree with statements about themselves (e.g., "I tend to do my own thing"). According to the cross-cultural psychologist Kitayama[33] such reports fail to accurately reflect mental responses that are produced spontaneously as people behave in actual social settings. When individuals make certain judgments about themselves, they implicitly draw comparisons with others. These referent others, however, are different for people in different cultures. In a society where on average people are aggressive car drivers, an individual driver may not judge himself to be an aggressive driver, whereas he would notice his driving as being aggressive in a society where most people are more tolerant drivers.

For conducting value surveys following the etic approach, similar questionnaires have to be used and questions have to be translated. Language, however, is also an expression of culture. Questions about values must be translatable and meanings must have conceptual equivalence across all cultures where the questions are used. Some values that are specific for certain cultures alone cannot be measured directly by the etic method but only by interpreting the values included in the various etic scales. For culture-specific values there are often no linguistic or conceptual equivalents. An example is the concept of competitiveness linked with individuals. In the English language, one can say about an individual that he or she is "a competitive person." The Dutch language does not link competitiveness to a person. Language also has an impact on the way people respond to questions relating to cultural values. When using questionnaires with questions about cultural norms and values and other preferences, researchers observe that differences across countries are considerably smaller when the English-language questionnaire is used than when local languages are used.[34]

For making international comparisons, data should have the same meaning across countries—they must be equivalent—because biased information leads to ambiguous or even erroneous conclusions.[35] Three types of equivalence can be distinguished: *sample* equivalence, *linguistic* and *conceptual* equivalence, and *metric* equivalence. Similar people must be compared as to age, gender, profession, and so on. The questions must have the same meaning to all respondents. Translation and back-translation is not always sufficient. A scale that has been developed in one culture will not always have a similar effect in another culture. Response style and tendencies to use extreme points on verbal rating scales (Extreme Response Style, ERS), as well as yea-saying and nay-saying (Acquiescence Response Style, ARS) have been found to differ from country to country.[36]

Individual and Culture Level

Cultural elements are held by individuals and influence both individuals and society. For comparison across nations, the *average* value priorities of individual members of one society are compared with the *average* value priorities of individual members of other societies. The average value priorities of a group are what the members of that group or nation have in common. Individual values are partly a product of shared culture and partly a product of unique individual personality and experience. There is overlap between individual values and cultural values because institutions reflect the societal values shared by the individual members. If they would not do so, individuals would not be able to function adequately. Individual members of a society have internalized values that help them conform to the requirements of societal institutions. Individuals are guided by their cultural priorities and in their behavior reinforce the social system.[37]

Consumer psychologists generally measure individual behavior within social systems (countries, cultures, states). Individuals are sampled from a population in order to reach conclusions on that population.[38] In comparative research, the properties of individuals as observed within a country (e.g., age or literacy) are aggregated and then treated as country-level variables. To find explanations for some phenomena at country level (e.g., differences in ownership of computers across countries) the aggregate data can be correlated to other country-level variables (e.g., gross national income [GNI] per capita). This is called "between-system" or "between-country" comparison, although data are used that were originally collected among individuals of countries. Because the data have been aggregated, we cannot use them anymore to explain within-system differences. Hofstede[39] states that cultures are wholes and their internal logic cannot be understood in the terms used for measuring individuals. Patterns observed at the culture level (also called *ecological level*) can be different from patterns at the individual level. Culture is no king-sized personality; cultures are formed through the interactions of different personalities, both conflicting and complementary, that create a whole that is more than the sum of its parts.[40] Thus, patterns of associations for specific values at the culture level can be different from those at the individual level. For example, Schwartz[41] has shown that patterns of associations with "freedom" are different at the individual and at the cultural (national) level. Within countries, individuals who score high on the importance of "freedom" also tend to score high on the importance of "independence of thought and actions." But if the scores for all individuals in each nation are averaged, the nations where on average "freedom" is scored as more important than in other nations are not those scoring higher on the importance of "independence," but those scoring higher on "protecting the welfare of others." The individual associations are based on psychological logic, the national associations on the cultural logic of societies composed of different, interacting individuals.

Using a culture-level correlation to interpret individual behavior (for this the term *ecological fallacy* is used) can lead to misinterpretations. Within-system correlations can be different from between-system correlations. So, conclusions about individual-level relationships drawn from relationships between culture-level variables may be fallacious. A classic example was a strong correlation between the percentage of blacks and percentage of illiteracy across states in the United States, whereas the relationship between blacks and illiteracy might be nonexistent within each American state.[42] Reverse ecological fallacy is committed in the construction of ecological indexes from variables correlated at the individual level. Cultures cannot be treated and categorized as if they were individuals. An example of a reverse ecological fallacy is the use of a ready-made U.S. scale for comparing cultures, for example, Rokeach's structure of central and instrumental values for comparing countries.

Because of their strong belief in the uniqueness of individuals, generally, individualists are in favor of individual-level studies; they feel reluctant categorizing people on the basis of group characteristics and insist that people should be treated, analyzed, and interpreted as individuals, not as group members. In more collectivistic cultures, the opposite bias can be found. Group differences are exaggerated and viewed as absolute. There is a tendency to treat people on the basis of the group that they belong to rather than as individuals.[43]

Searching for Similarities or for Differences

Studies that search for *similarities* across countries are studies that use culture-level (ecological) variables to determine types or subsets of cultures that are similar among themselves but differ from other types or subsets (e.g., the young, business people, or lifestyle groups). Studies that focus on the *differences* determine dimensions of societies consisting of societal variables. Next to dimensions, *typologies* are used, as in most value and lifestyle studies. A typology describes easy-to-imagine ideal types; hence typologies are popular among marketing and advertising people who develop messages for imaginary consumers. For such research, usually large numbers of questions on activities, interests, and opinions are reduced to two basic and bipolar dimensional structures resulting from factor analysis, and the resulting factors are given labels that cover the factor items, as interpreted by the creators of the studies. As a result, the labels will reflect the culture of the developers of the study. This leads to labels like "strivers," "devouts," or "fun seekers" if the study is directed by Americans, or to labels like "mythical" or "emotional" by French researchers, whereas British researchers tend to include class-based segment labels. Both concepts and dimensions used in value studies reflect the culture of the home country and cannot be extended to other cultures without losing meaning.

The Stanford Research Institute's values and lifestyles (VALS) program was one of the first value and lifestyle studies. VALS, developed by SRI International, Menlo Park, California,[44] is based on the Rokeach value system. It uses a questionnaire asking motivations and demographic characteristics that are seen as predictors of consumer preferences. Later, a parallel system called RISC International (after the International Research Center for Social Change in Paris) emerged in Europe. Such studies were developed in several other countries as well.

The common aspect of these studies is the use of two-dimensional space in which consumption, respondents, and values are placed. The primary dimensions of VALS are motivations and resources. RISC distinguished three dimensions: *expansion-stability* (openness to new ideas versus resistance to change), *enjoyment-responsibility*, and *flexibility-structure*.[45] The VALS segmentation system was developed in the United States, and the values included are typical for the United States. Nevertheless, international research and advertising agencies apply it to other cultures.

CCA, a French system developed in the 1990s, worked with the dimensions "progressive-conservative" and "material-spiritual." The Belgian market research agency Censydiam uses theories by the psychoanalyst Alfred Adler.[46] According to this theory, consumers develop basic strategies for the management of tension.

A commercial segmentation system developed by Gallup in Scandinavia, Kompas works with the dimensions "modern" versus "traditional" and "individual" versus "social" values.[47] A Japanese model developed by Dentsu[48] used the dimensions "achiever" versus "membership dependent" and "group merit" versus "intelligent, nonconformist" that both reflect the individualism-collectivism paradox. An originally German study of social milieus extended its study to other markets in Europe.[49] Social milieus describe the structure of society in terms of social class and value orientations. Within cultures, groups of people are delineated who share a common set of values and beliefs about, for example, work, leisure, and relationships. Groups are labeled in terms of "modern," "conservative," "proactive," or "materialist." These groups are not necessarily similar across cultures.

The previous discussion may have demonstrated that most lifestyle studies have strong local roots. The cross-cultural validity of international lifestyle instruments remains to be demonstrated. The results of such studies are also often presented without saying that the findings are based on a study among respondents of one specific culture and are not applicable to subjects who are of a totally different culture.

NATIONAL CULTURES

A point of discussion is the delineation of cultural groups by national borders. A country is not necessarily equivalent to a culture or society in the anthropological sense. A country (or nation-state) is a politically unified population; it may, and often does, contain more than one culture or society, anthropologically speaking. Conventionally, a culture is the set of customary beliefs and practices characteristic of a society, the latter being the population that occupies a particular territory and speaks a common language not understood by neighboring populations. There may be great variation in the learned behavior that may be found in "the population that occupies a particular territory and speaks a common language."[50]

Hofstede[51] states that indeed nations should not be equated to societies. Societies are, historically, organically developed forms of social organizations and, strictly spoken, the concept of a common culture applies to societies, not to nations. Nevertheless many nations do form historically developed wholes even if they consist of clearly different groups. Within nations that have existed for some time, there have been strong forces toward further integration: (usually) one dominant language, common mass media, a national education system, and national markets for products and services. Nations as political bodies also supply all kinds of statistics about their populations. To assess the potential of international markets, companies generally compare nations with respect to demographics, GNI per capita, and consumer usage and attitudes. National mass media, such as television, newspapers, and magazines, are important means of communication that mostly target national audiences.

Simon Anholt, one of the leading consultants in global advertising, bases his culture mapping on Hofstede's dimensions of national culture. He states:

> For advertising agencies and their clients, culture mapping [i.e., working with the Hofstede dimensions] really comes into its own: it's absolutely *made* for mass marketing, an area where individual personality is of very secondary importance, and what you really want is reliable, true, but *gross generalizations*. You need to know what *most people* in a country are like, and how most of them will behave in response to certain stimuli.[52]

Yet with respect to values, some nations are more homogeneous than others, although differences between nations are substantially larger than differences within nations. One of the most heterogeneous nations is the United States, where the white, Caucasian American population is decreasing and other groups, in particular Americans of Hispanic origin, are increasing. According to the U.S. Census Bureau, in 2006 white Americans made up 76% of the population, but part of the white population is of Hispanic descent. African

Americans made up 12.4% and Americans of Hispanic origin composed 14.8% of the population, of which 64% were Mexican Americans.[53]

As we'll see throughout this book, neither Europe nor Asia are homogeneous regions with respect to national values, and heterogeneity within nations varies. Some nations are clearly more homogeneous than others. Cross-cultural consultant Arne Maas used regional data from the European Social Survey[54] to calculate a measure of cultural cohesion by cluster analysis of 21 value questions that were answered by people from all provinces in a country. The questions measured value preferences, like the importance of having friends, family, equality, the importance of work, or of being rich. These are not representative of the total value system of countries, but variety gives an indication of the degree of coherence of countries. The coherence measure found for 19 countries ranged from 1.4 for Norway to 14.9 for Spain, indicating that of these 19 countries, Norway is most homogeneous and Spain most heterogeneous. The score for the whole region, comprising the 19 countries, was 27.

The northern European countries are evidently culturally coherent. Their measures ranged from 1.4 for Norway to 2.4 for Sweden. Only Denmark appears to be less coherent, with a measure of 5.3. The United Kingdom seems to be somewhere in the middle, with 7.0, but this changes dramatically when Northern Ireland is left out of the analysis, and the measure changes from 7.0 to 1.6. A similar change occurs in Switzerland (coherence = 7.2) when Ticino, the Italian part of Switzerland, is left out. The figure then drops to 2.6. Spain is the least culturally coherent of all countries measured. It has a score of 14.9, the highest of all 19 countries. This is not so strange for a country with at least three regions with different languages and histories (Castilia, Cataluna, and Pais Vasco). Also, Greece is not very coherent (12.2), although the regions within Greece have more in common with other Greek regions than with regions in other countries. This means that Greek culture is quite different from other European cultures.

A third country that is culturally not very cohesive is Germany (8.5). It is interesting to see that the differences are especially large in former Western Germany (13.7) and that the former DDR is quite cohesive (4.3). Some southern German regions cluster with Austria and Switzerland rather than with other German regions. Also, Hamburg is quite different from the rest of Germany. Table 2.2 provides the measures for the 19 countries.

Devinderpal Singh found regional cultures in India that were quite different with respect to cultural values. For example, the state of Gujarat in western India is far more hierarchical and power is distributed unequally as compared to the West Bengal in the east and Punjab in the north. Whereas Tamil Nadu is collectivistic, in West Bengal people are more individualistic.[55]

The consequences of heterogeneity of countries is that companies, when testing products or advertising, have to be careful which region to select as a test market in a country if it is a heterogeneous one. For international research, using a too homogeneous or too heterogeneous country as a test market is risky.

Table 2.2   Measures of Coherence for 19 Countries

1. Norway	1.4	11. Austria	5.7
2. Finland	1.9	12. Netherlands	5.7
3. Sweden	2.4	13. U.K.	7.0
4. Hungary	2.9	14. Switzerland	7.2
5. Slovenia	3.0	15. Israel	7.5
6. Belgium	3.6	16. Portugal	8.3
7. Ireland	3.6	17. Germany	8.5
8. Poland	4.5	18. Greece	12.2
9. Czech Republic	5.0	19. Spain	14.9
10. Denmark	5.3	20. All 19 countries	27.0

DIMENSIONS OF CULTURE

Cultures can be described according to specific *characteristics* or categorized into *value categories* or *dimensions* of national culture. Cultural characteristics distinguishing countries described by international management consultants Harris and Moran[56] are sense of self and space, communication and languages, food and feeding habits, time consciousness, values and norms, beliefs and attitudes, and work habits and practices. These characteristics are based on observations, and many of these are found in dimensional models derived from large surveys.

The advantage of dimensions over descriptions is the empirical base. Dimensions are generally developed from large numbers of variables by statistical data reduction methods (e.g., factor analysis) and provide scales on which countries are scored. Dimensions that order cultures meaningfully must be empirically verifiable and more or less independent.

Reducing culture to dimensions with numbers on scales has been criticized. But we have to understand that dimensions are useful constructs that explain behavior. As Hofstede states:

> We cannot directly observe mental programs. What we can observe is only behavior: Words or deeds. Mental programs are intangibles and the terms we use to describe them are *constructs*. A construct is a product of our imagination, supposed to help our understanding. Constructs do not "exist" in an absolute sense: We define them into existence. In the same way values and dimensions do not exist.

They are constructs, which have to prove their usefulness by their ability to explain and predict behavior. . . . Culture is not the only thing we should pay attention to. In many cases economic, political or institutional factors provide better explanations. But sometimes they don't, and then we need the construct of culture.[57]

The most common dimension used for ordering societies is their degree of economic evolution or modernity, from traditional to modern. One of two dimensions used by U.S. political scientist Ronald Inglehart, who leads the World Values Survey (WVS), follows this order of societies. Inglehart[58] arranges world values in two broad categories. The first is "traditional" versus "secular-rational," and the second looks at "quality of life" attributes ranging from "survival" to "well-being," the latter including so-called post-materialist values.

Increasingly more complex models are developed. Most of them define patterns of basic problems that are common to all societies and that have consequences for the functioning of groups and individuals. Few are true dimensions in the sense of being statistically independent. Such categories are better called *value orientations* or *value categories*.

The idea that basic common problems exist is not new. An early analysis by Alex Inkeles and Daniel Levinson[59] suggested that the following issues qualify as common basic problems worldwide: (1) relation to authority; (2) the conception of self, including ego identity; and (3) primary dilemmas of conflict and dealing with them. These basic problems have been found in many other studies. American anthropologists Kluckhohn and Strodtbeck[60] proposed five value orientations on the basis of their investigations of small communities in the southwestern United States: (1) perception of human nature (good/evil); (2) relationship of man to his environment (subjugation/mastery); (3) time orientation (past/present); (4) orientation toward the environment (being and doing); (5) orientation toward human relationships (hierarchical/individualistic). The five value orientations are recognized in later studies, for example, by Trompenaars[61] who applied these orientations to countries and presented seven categories of work-related values. These are universalism-particularism, achievement-ascription, individualism-collectivism, emotional-neutral, specific-diffuse, time orientation, and orientation to nature, but these categories were not combined into country scores. Trompenaars's database was analyzed by the British psychologist Peter Smith,[62] who only found two independent dimensions in the data that basically measured various intercorrelated flavors of individualism. Trompenaars's dimensions are not statistically independent and he produced no country scores, so his findings are not useful for analysis of consumption data.

Fiske[63] proposed four elementary forms of sociability that occur within and across cultures: (1) communal sharing, (2) authority ranking, (3) equality matching, and (4) market pricing. Fiske's theory was supported by ethnographic field work and experimental studies covering five cultures. Authority ranking and equality matching are similar to forms found in classifications by others, such as by Schwartz and by Hofstede, models that we deal with in more detail later.

The anthropologist Edward Hall[64] distinguished patterns of culture according to context, space, time, and information flow. In particular, the context concept is useful for understanding consumer behavior across cultures. Also, Hall did not develop country scores, but the context orientation is related to individualism-collectivism, one of Hofstede's dimensions that provides country scores. Differences between cultures with respect to the relationship between man and nature still are viewed as unique. The nature and context orientations are described in later sections of the chapter.

Only a few dimensional models provide country scores that can be used as independent variables for the analysis of consumption differences and other aspects of consumer behavior across cultures. These are the models by Geert Hofstede, by Shalom Schwartz, and the more recent GLOBE study. The Dutch scholar Geert Hofstede was the first who, starting in 1973, developed five independent dimensions of national culture that are used in this book to analyze differences in consumer behavior.[65] His five dimensions are labeled: *power distance, individualism/collectivism, masculinity/femininity), uncertainty avoidance,* and *long-/short-term orientation.*

The Israeli psychologist Shalom Schwartz[66] developed seven value types, labeled *embeddedness, intellectual and affective autonomy, hierarchy, mastery, egalitarianism,* and *harmony.*

Both models describe similar basic value orientations of countries and are based on large quantitative surveys. Further similarities are (a) focus on the etic in comparisons, (b) the perspective of values being at the core of culture, and (c) the notion of culture being located within national boundaries. The models are different with respect to the level of analysis (individual versus culture level) and the dimension structure. For marketing purposes, the Schwartz dimensions are not as useful, first because the model covers fewer countries and, second, because they do not show results that are as consistent as the Hofstede dimensions, which may be caused by conceptual and methodological differences between the models. The Schwartz country scores are not easily accessible, and the country scores in the original paper of 1994 are different from a later publication of 2007.[67]

The most recent large-scale dimensional model is GLOBE,[68] developed by Robert House of the Wharton School of Management and his associates, who initiated a cross-national project for the study of leadership and societal culture. They discovered nine cultural dimensions at the level of society, labeled *uncertainty avoidance, power distance,* two types of *collectivism, gender egalitarianism, assertiveness, future orientation, performance orientation,* and *humane orientation.* The GLOBE survey asks respondents to report how things are done or should be done in their societies; like Schwartz, House measures several aspects of the desirable.

Analysis of existing databases can also deliver useful classifications. From factor analysis of country means of items in the World Values Survey, Michael Minkov[69] defined three dimensions: *exclusionism* versus *universalism,* which is similar to Hofstede's dimension individualism-collectivism; *indulgence* versus *restraint,* which is analogous to Schwartz's hedonism, and *monumentalism* versus *flexumility,* which is close to Inglehart's dimension secular vs. traditional and which includes some values that are also part of Hofstede's dimension masculinity-femininity.[70] As the latter dimension is even more comparable to Hofstede's LTO dimension, he has extended his LTO database with Minkov's findings. All country scores for LTO in Appendix A are derived from Minkov's database.

A reason for widespread adoption of Hofstede's classification of culture lies in the simplicity of his dimensions, which are straightforward and appealing to both academic researchers and business people. Increasingly, international companies want to analyze foreign markets with respect to the cultural distance to their home markets. Although Hofstede's work has been thought to be outdated, several reviews and analyses of the validity of different models for the purpose of measuring cultural distance for international marketing strategy show that the more recent cultural frameworks provide only limited advancements compared with Hofstede's original work.[71] Two of these models are described in more detail: Hofstede's five dimensions of national culture and seven motivational domains by Schwartz. First, context, concepts of time and nature are described.

RELATIONSHIP OF MAN WITH NATURE

There are basically three types of relationship between man and nature: *mastery-over-nature* (man is to conquer nature), *harmony-with-nature* (man is to live in harmony with nature), and *subjugation-to-nature* (man is dominated by nature). In the Western world, man is viewed as separate from nature. The North American relationship to nature in particular is that it should be conquered and controlled for human convenience. To most North Americans the expression "to move a mountain" is not a metaphor symbolizing the impossible but rather an optimistic challenge. The view of U.S. culture is that it is the person's responsibility to overcome obstacles that may stand in his or her way. The Japanese experience of nature is one of communion, of exchange, characterized by a subtle intimacy. It is an experience of identification with nature. Westerners tend to explain the Asian reverence of nature as a relationship with God, which involves living in harmony with the world of nature. Takeo Doi,[72] a Japanese psychiatrist, says that in Japan, God as a creator is absent and, therefore, human beings seek comfort by attempting to immerse themselves completely in nature. Other cultures, such as many African cultures, see people as dominated by nature, and supernatural forces play a dominant role in religion. This subjugation-to-nature involves the belief that nothing can be done to control nature.

HIGH-CONTEXT COMMUNICATION CULTURE AND LOW-CONTEXT COMMUNICATION CULTURE

In a high-context communication or message, most of the information is either part of the context or internalized in the person; very little is made explicit as part of the message. The information of a low-context message is carried in the explicit code of the message. In general, high-context communication is economical, fast, and efficient. However, time must be devoted to programming. If this programming does not take place, the communication is incomplete. To the observer, an unknown high-context culture can be completely mystifying because symbols, not known to the observer, play such an important role. Thus, high-context culture communication can also be defined as inaccessible to outsiders. Low-context communication cultures are characterized by explicit verbal messages. Effective verbal communication is expected to be direct and unambiguous. Low-context communication cultures demonstrate high value and positive attitudes toward words. Argumentation and rhetoric in advertising are more found in low-context cultures, whereas advertising of high-context cultures can be characterized by symbolism or indirect verbal expression.

> For the purpose of shaping and maintaining corporate identity, companies develop an "identity standards manual," which is a guide to managing the application of the corporate identity visual system, or how an organization uses logotypes, typography styles, names, and architecture to communicate its corporate philosophy. In high-context cultures, these manuals include more nonverbal features (logo and symbol), traditions and customs (history, values), features defining the context of the communication, accessories or decorative elements and people (uniforms). In low-context cultures, these manuals include more textual features (name and publications) and direct messages (e.g., incorrect applications) manuals are more prescriptive and simpler than in high-context cultures where manuals use more indirect language and are more complex because of use of indirect language and also have more sections.[73]

Hofstede suggested a correlation between collectivism and high-context in cultures. In collectivistic cultures, information flows more easily between members of groups, and there is less need for explicit communication than in individualistic cultures. Another explanation of high context is homogeneity of cultures. Homogeneous cultures have more in common with respect to cultural heritage, and thus their members, more than members of heterogeneous cultures, can rely on shared symbols.

Cultures are on a sliding scale with respect to context. Most Asian cultures are high-context, whereas most Western cultures are low-context, extremes being Japan and China (high-context) on the one end of the scale and Germany, Switzerland, and the United States (low-context cultures) on the other end.

DIMENSIONS OF TIME

Time is more than what the clock reads. Different cultures have different concepts of time. Western advertisers tend to use clocks in their international advertising to symbolize efficiency. Clocks are not recognized as symbols of efficiency in cultures where people have a different sense of time. Time is a core system of cultural, social, and personal life. Each culture has its own unique time frame. Hall's[74] important study of time as an expression of culture provides an explanation of differences in behavior and language. He distinguishes different types of time, among others biological time (light-dark/day-night, hot-cold/summer-winter), personal time (how time is experienced), and sync time (each culture has its own beat). Hall developed his theories during his stay with Native Americans, discovering how differently they dealt with time than did Anglo-Americans. Different concepts of time can explain significant differences in behavior. A few aspects of time that are relevant to consumer behavior—closure; linear versus circular time; and monochronic versus polychronic time—are summarized following.

Closure

Americans are driven to achieve what psychologists call "closure," meaning that a task must be completed or it is perceived as "wasted." What Hall saw as characteristic of Hopi (Native Americans of the Southwest) villages was the proliferation of unfinished houses. The same can be seen in Turkey, in southern Europe, and in other collectivistic cultures where additional rooms will be built only when family needs arise. American novels or films always have a "happy ending," including solutions to problems, which are rare in Japanese novels.

Time Is Linear or Circular

Time can be conceived as a line of sequential events or as cyclical and repetitive, compressing past, present, and future by what these have in common: seasons and rhythms. The latter time orientation is linked with Asian culture; the former is the Western time orientation. The linear time concept causes people to see time as compartmentalized, schedule dominated. Americans have a linear time concept with clear structures, such as beginning, turning point, climax, and end. Time is used as a measuring instrument and a means of controlling human behavior by setting deadlines and objectives. Time is tangible, like an object; it can be saved, spent, found, lost, and wasted. Temporal terms such as *summer* and *winter* are nouns; they are treated as objects. For Native Americans, summer is a condition: hot. The term is used as an adverb, not related to time but to the senses.

In Japan, time is circular and is related to the special meaning of seasons. Japanese time-thinking is not in terms of today, tomorrow, or the day after tomorrow. The seasons form an automatic, upward spiral; everything returns automatically. Saying "back to the old values" in Japan does not imply a step backward but a step forward. It means progressing through an upward spiral, using what was good in the past for progress.

Monochronic and Polychronic Time

Another distinction by Hall[75] of how people handle time is between monochronic (M-time) and polychronic (P-time) cultures. People from monochronic cultures tend to do one thing at a time; they are organized and methodical, and their workdays are structured to allow them to complete one task after another. Polychronic people, on the other hand, tend to do many things simultaneously. Their workday is not a chain of isolated, successive blocks; time is more like a vast, never-ending ocean extending in every direction. The Germans adhere to the more rigid and compartmentalized way of dealing with time. To people who do many things at the same time, however, such as the Spanish, Arabs, Pakistani, or South Americans, punctuality is nice but by no means an absolute necessity in the middle of a hectic day. This polychronic behavior that is so natural to polychronic cultures, has received a special term in monochronic cultures: *multi-tasking*. In monochronic cultures, time spent on the Internet takes time from other activities, such as TV viewing. In polychronic cultures, people do both at the same time.

When two people of different time cultures meet, they may easily offend each other because they have different expectations of time. In particular, the fact that in polychronic cultures people interfere during meetings is very annoying to people of monochronic cultures. Not all M-time cultures are the same, however. In Japan, tight M-time is for business, and P-time is for private life.

HOFSTEDE: FIVE DIMENSIONS OF NATIONAL CULTURE

Geert Hofstede[76] developed a model of five dimensions of national culture that helps to explain basic value differences. This model distinguishes cultures according to five dimensions: power distance (PDI), individualism/collectivism (IDV), masculinity/femininity (MAS), uncertainty avoidance (UAI), and long-/short-term orientation (LTO). The dimensions are measured on a scale from 0 to 100, for 75 countries, and each country has a position on each scale or index. Although the model is most used to explain differences in work-related values, I have applied it to consumption-related values and motives. This was validated in two ways: (1) by content analysis of television commercials and print advertisements and (2) by linking the Hofstede data to secondary data on consumption, attitudes, and behavior. Many product data and data on related behavior appear to correlate with culture. Hofstede's dimensions are increasingly used as independent variables for comparative cross-cultural studies and provide many useful explanations of cross-cultural differences in consumer behavior. A list of country scores is in Appendix A. His country scores allow us to make cultural maps for cross-cultural segmentation. Often a configuration of two dimensions explains differences in product usage or other consumption-related phenomena. It makes more sense to cluster countries based on cultural closeness than on geographical closeness.

Power Distance

Power distance can be defined as "the extent to which less powerful members of a society accept and expect that power is distributed unequally." It is reflected in the values of both the less powerful and more powerful members of society. It influences the way people accept and give authority. In large power distance cultures (those scoring high on the power distance index), everyone has his or her rightful place in a social hierarchy, and as a result acceptance and giving of authority come naturally. To the Japanese, behavior that recognizes hierarchy is as natural as breathing. It means "everything in its place." In cultures scoring low on the power distance index, authority can have a negative connotation; focus is on equality in rights and opportunity. In high power distance cultures, there are strong dependency relationships between parents and children, bosses and subordinates, professors and students. In low power distance cultures, children are raised to be independent at a young age. Americans will avoid becoming dependent on others, and they do not want others, with the possible exception of immediate family members, to be dependent on them. In high power distance cultures, one's social status must be clear so that others can show proper respect. Global brands serve that purpose.

> *Power distance* explains, for example, differences in the way people behave in the public and private domains and the importance of appearance as well as status brands. It explains differences in communication behavior, such as information gathering for making a buying decision and reading newspapers. It explains differences in usage of the Internet and mobile phones as well as credit card usage. It explains differences in complaining behavior of consumers and behavior of personnel in retail. Examples of values reflected in advertising are independence/dependence of children, importance of authority, and social status.

Individualism/Collectivism

"People look after themselves and their immediate family only, or people belong to in-groups who look after them in exchange for loyalty." In individualistic cultures, values are in the person, and people want to differentiate themselves from others. In collectivistic cultures, identity is based in the social network to which one belongs. In individualistic cultures people are "I" conscious and express private opinions; self-actualization is important. Individual decisions are higher valued than group decisions. Individualists attach priority to variety and adventure, whereas collectivists prefer harmony. There is more explicit, verbal communication. In collectivistic cultures people are "we" conscious—their identity is based on the social system. Harmony with in-group members and avoiding loss of face is important. Between 70% and 80% of the world's population is more or less collectivistic. All of Asia, Africa, and Latin America are collectivistic. In Italy, the data were collected in the north, where people appeared to be individualistic. Other studies[77] indicate that the Italians as a whole are collectivistic. Individualistic cultures are universalistic cultures, whereas collectivistic cultures are particularistic.

Individualism/collectivism explains, for example, many differences in communication behavior, both interpersonal and mass communication. It is related to high/low context communication, so it explains differences in direct versus indirect communication, information gathering from the media or word-of-mouth communication. It explains differences in Internet buying, owning insurances and cars. It explains differences in Internet usage such as e-mailing or blogging. It explains differences in the importance of pleasure and adventure for spending leisure time and fun shopping. It explains differences in demonstrating uniqueness versus wanting to conform, which can be recognized in buying behavior of fashion and luxury articles. Examples of values reflected in advertising are self-confidence, self-expression versus conformance, and sharing.

Masculinity/Femininity or the Gender of Nations (Tough Versus Tender)

"The dominant values in a masculine society are achievement and success, the dominant values in a feminine society are caring for others and quality of life." In masculine societies, performance and achievement are important. Status is important to show success. Big and fast are beautiful. Societies that score low on the masculinity index are more service oriented, have a people orientation, and regard small as beautiful. There is a tendency to strive for consensus. Quality of life is more important than competition. Status is not so important to show success. Being a "winner" is positive in masculine cultures and negative in feminine cultures. In masculine cultures, children learn to admire the strong, whereas in feminine cultures children learn sympathy for the underdog. A consequence of this dimension is variation in the degree of role differentiation: small in feminine societies, large in masculine societies. In feminine cultures, a male can take a typical female job without being seen as a "sissy." In masculine cultures, people consume for show; in feminine cultures people consume for use. The masculine/feminine dimension discriminates between cultures particularly with respect to values related to winning, success, and status as used in advertising appeals, so it is an important dimension for marketing and advertising.

Masculinity/femininity explains, for example, differences in household roles like cleaning, child care, cooking, and shopping as well as differences in working part-time, by both males and females. It explains differences in frequency of Internet access and using the Internet for leisure and other personal reasons, to enhance the quality of life. It explains differences in nights staying in hotels for pleasure. It explains differences in buying status brands, luxury goods, jewelry and coffee consumption. In the masculine cultures of Latin America, men must be real men. In a Latin American survey across seven countries, the percentages of answers agreeing with the statement "Real men don't cry" correlated with masculinity.[78] Examples of values reflected in advertising are winning and success as compared versus modesty, as well as role differences.

Uncertainty Avoidance

"The extent to which people feel threatened by uncertainty and ambiguity and try to avoid these situations." Some people do not mind ambiguity, whereas others hate uncertainty or ambiguity and try to cope with it by making rules and prescribing behavior. In cultures of strong uncertainty avoidance (those scoring high on the index), there is a need for rules and formality to structure life and belief in experts. People are more interested in the process of how a product works than in the results. Purity is an important value. There is more formal communication. People in high uncertainty avoidance cultures have a higher level of anxiety and aggressiveness, and showing emotions is accepted. Conflict and competition are threatening. Weak (low-scoring) uncertainty avoidance cultures feel that there should be as few rules as possible. They are more result oriented than process oriented. They believe more in generalists and common sense, and there is less ritual behavior. Conflict and competition are not threatening. The uncertainty avoidance dimension discriminates between cultures where innovations are adopted early and cultures where people lag in the adoption process.

> *Uncertainty avoidance* explains, for example, differences in the adoption of innovations, differences in access to the Internet and ownership of personal computers. It explains differences in the degree to which people read books and newspapers. It explains differences playing sports, in use of medication, numbers of physicians per 1,000 people, and consumption of mineral water. It explains differences in traveling, foreign language speaking, and contacts people have with foreigners. Examples of values reflected in advertising are details and precision versus use of humor.

Long-/Short-Term Orientation

The fifth dimension was originally discovered in cooperation with Michael Bond.[79] Bond, who called it "Confucian Work Dynamism," sampled a domain of values formulated by Chinese scholars. He assembled a group of researchers, named the Chinese Culture Connection (CCC), who presented these values to students from 23 countries. The resulting dimension referred to a long-term versus a short-term orientation in life.

Consequences of long-term orientation are that there is not one truth; there is perseverance, thrift, and pursuit of peace of mind, elements of Confucian philosophy. The opposite is a short-term orientation in which spending now is more important than saving for tomorrow. Most East Asian countries scored high on this fifth dimension, particularly the ones with large Chinese populations. Anglo-Saxon societies scored low. Because measurements started later than for the other dimensions, scores were available for fewer countries. One of Michael Minkov's[80] dimensions, called "monumentalism versus flexhumility," appeared to share common values with the original LTO dimension, but it also included other values that are not linked with Confucian philosophy.[81] Country scores are available for nearly all countries for which scores of the other dimensions are available. Included in short-term orientation are values of national pride, tradition, low thrift, self-enhancement, appeal of folk wisdom and witchcraft, and talent for theoretical, abstract sciences. Included in long-term orientation are thrift, perseverance, pragmatism, and talent for applied, concrete sciences. In short-term-oriented cultures, there is a need for the absolute truth, which is less relevant to members of long-term-oriented cultures. In long-term-oriented cultures, parents are more lenient toward children than in short-term-oriented cultures. The country scores for LTO in Appendix A refer to this new dimension.

> *Long-/short-term orientation* explains, for example, differences in use of cosmetics, deodorants, and convenience products such as soft drinks, all sorts of processed food, microwave ovens, and dishwashing machines. It explains differences in time spent eating and shopping and visits to museums. It explains adoption of all sorts of applications of the Internet as well as relationships between parents and children. Examples of values reflected in advertising are long-term symbols like thick trees or other time-related references versus convenience.

Validation

Hofstede's dimensions are increasingly used as independent variables for comparative cross-cultural studies and have led to many useful explanations of cross-cultural differences in consumer behavior. One of the reasons may be that his dimensions are independent. Only power distance and collectivism are interdependent. Both are correlated with wealth (GNI per capita at PPP [purchasing power parity]), but when that is controlled for, the correlation almost disappears.

An often-posed question is whether his country scores, produced in the late 1960s and early 1970s are valid to use some 30 years later. Also, because Hofstede's dimensions were derived from answers by IBM employees only, often the question is asked whether the same dimensions are found among other matched samples of respondents. Several replications of Hofstede's study on different matched or nonmatched samples have proved that his data are still valid. Søndergaard[82] analyzed applications and replications of Hofstede's work in the 1980s, which showed that the differences predicted by Hofstede's dimensions were largely confirmed. There are remarkably few nonconfirmations. In the second edition of his book *Culture's Consequences*, Hofstede describes more than 200 external comparative studies and replications that have supported his indexes.

For marketing, the most useful replication was conducted in 1996 for 15 countries in Western Europe in the 1996–1997 EMS survey. This resulted in country scores that, taking into account the fact that the samples were not as well matched as they should be, were beyond expectations. Three of the four original dimensions (IDV, MAS, and UAI) correlated significantly with the Hofstede country scores from the IBM sample, and for the first time in Europe, scores for the fifth dimension were found. Due to the heterogeneity of the sample, the power distance dimension could not be measured.

Hofstede's dimensions are increasingly used as a conceptual framework outside their original setting and are used to classify and explain the influence of culture on various research topics.

SCHWARTZ: SEVEN VALUE TYPES OR MOTIVATIONAL DOMAINS

The Israeli psychologist Shalom Schwartz[83] presents an alternative conceptual and operational approach for deriving cultural dimensions of work-related values in a study of value priorities in 87 samples of teachers and students from 41 cultural groups in 38 nations. The analysis was expected either to support Hofstede's dimensions and refine them into finer tuned dimensions or to reveal that a different set of cultural dimensions emerges when a more comprehensive set of values is analyzed. Originally, Schwartz and Bilsky[84] searched for a theory of a universal psychological structure of human values. Individual-level value types were distinguished that were extended to the culture level.

A set of 56 value questions was used. Respondents rated each value for importance as "a guiding principle in their own life." From these 56 values, 10 (individual-level) value types were derived. The technique used was smallest space analysis. A consequence of this technique is that the value types are not independent. The 10 value types were organized on two basic bipolar dimensions. Each pole constitutes a higher-order value type that combines two or more of the 10 types. One dimension opposes openness to change (self-direction and stimulation) to conservation (conformity, tradition, and security). The other opposes self-transcendence (universalism and benevolence) to self-enhancement (achievement and power). Although this structure applied to individual values, it was used as hypothesis for the structure of culture-level values. Analysis across 47 cultures established that of the 56 values, 45 had nearly equivalent meanings across cultures. The following values did *not* have equivalence of meaning across cultures: social recognition, intelligent, self-respect, inner harmony, true friendship, a spiritual life, mature love, meaning in life, detachment, sense of belonging, and healthy. From the 45 questions, seven value types were distinguished for use across cultures, called conservatism (later changed to embeddedness), autonomy, mastery, harmony, hierarchy, and egalitarianism. Schwartz's distinctions refer more to categories than to dimensions, as dimensions should be statistically independent, whereas the Schwartz value types partly overlap. The seven value types (or motivational domains) are basically three dimensions with different polar locations. They are summarized following.[85]

Autonomy (Intellectual or Affective) Versus Embeddedness

Autonomy values are important in societies that view the person as an autonomous entity entitled to pursue his or her individual, independent interests and desires, who relates to others in terms of self-interest and negotiated agreements. A core value is the pursuit of personal interest. Related aspects are emphasis on self-direction, stimulation, and hedonism. This value type is negatively correlated with the value type conservatism. Thus, a polar opposition exists of autonomy versus conservatism. Values included in *intellectual autonomy* are autonomy of individual thought, curiosity, creativity, freedom, and broadmindedness. Values included in *affective autonomy* are varied life, stimulating activity, exciting life.

The value type *embeddedness* includes values that are important in societies based on close-knit harmonious relations, in which the interests of the person are not viewed as distinct from those of the group. Emphasis is on maintenance of the status quo and avoidance of actions of individuals that might disturb the traditional order. The self lacks autonomous significance but has meaning as part of the collectivity. Cultures that emphasize conservatism values are primarily concerned with security, conformity, and tradition. Included are the values devout, obedient, social order, and family security.

Hierarchy Versus Egalitarianism

The *hierarchy* value type emphasizes the legitimacy of hierarchical roles. Values included are social power, authority, influential, humble, and self-enhancement. This value type forms a broad self-enhancement region together with the next type mastery, the type with which it is correlated most positively.

Egalitarianism includes promoting the welfare of other people or transcendence of selfish interests. Social commitment occurs among equals. Values included are social justice, responsible, helpful, loyal, honest, equality.

Mastery Versus Harmony

Mastery values emphasize active mastery of the social environment through self-assertion. Mastery values promote active efforts to modify one's surroundings and get ahead of other people. Values included in this value type are daring, capable, success, ambition, independence, social recognition, self-direction at the individual level, and the pursuit of personal interest.

The *harmony* value type emphasizes harmony with nature. It is found opposite mastery, just as Kluckhohn and Strodtbeck's relationship, man/nature. Social harmony as a value is also included. Other values are world at peace, social justice, helpful, and world of beauty. Harmony values stand in opposition to value types that promote actively changing the world through self-assertion and exploitation of people and resources.

Overlap With the Hofstede Dimensions

There are several relationships between the Schwartz and Hofstede models. Schwartz states that, for example, his dimension autonomy/embeddedness to some degree conceptually overlaps with individualism/collectivism. Both concern relationships between the individual and the collective and both contrast an autonomous with an interdependent view of people. A difference is that autonomy includes openness to change versus maintaining the status quo being part of embeddedness. Individualism/collectivism doesn't include that distinction. National scores on individualism correlate negatively with national scores on embeddedness and positively with autonomy. The hierarchy pole of the hierarchy/egalitarianism dimension is correlated with Hofstede's power distance dimension, but is not fully conceptually equivalent. The mastery pole of mastery/harmony is correlated with Hofstede's masculinity and has some conceptual overlap.[86] All Schwartz categories except harmony correlate significantly with GNI per capita.[87] The model by Schwartz is less used in quantitative cross-cultural studies, but it is attractive to the Western advertising world because it describes value types in terms that are appealing to people in advertising who like to describe imaginary consumers in terms of abstract preferences like pleasure, sensuous gratification, excitement, novelty, challenge, or hedonism. Yet, whereas Hofstede has validated his dimensions by correlating them with a large number of national level data—also on consumption-related issues—Schwartz doesn't seem to have done so.

A problem of the Schwartz model is that country scores are not readily available and different scores have been published in different publications. Country scores published by Schwartz in 1994 are different from those published in 2007.[88] When used to analyze cross-cultural consumer behavior data, the two models lead to additional explanations but also to incomparable results. This may be caused by a few conceptual and methodological differences between the models.

COMPARING DIMENSIONAL MODELS

Cultural dimensions are human constructs. Although they are based on objectively existing phenomena, they are not the phenomena themselves but ways of describing them. One and the same reality can be explained and presented in different ways, through different constructs.[89] The three major large-scale worldwide dimensional models—by Hofstede, Schwartz, and GLOBE—overlap in some ways but vary with respect to sampling and type of questions used. What they have in common is aggregating self-descriptive responses by individuals drawn from a series of different national samples. The predominant emphasis has been upon characterizing cultures in terms of shared values, shared beliefs, or shared sources of guidance.[90]

The samples of the three models are different. Hofstede used matched groups of employees in seven occupational categories within one global company in 66 countries, of which two were managerial. Schwartz also used matched samples: students and teachers in 54 countries. GLOBE surveyed managers in 951 local organizations in food processing, financial services, and telecom services in 62 societies.

The types of questions used are based on different value concepts. Hofstede asks people about individual behavioral preferences, preferred or actual states of being, which is the desired. Examples are questions about time available for family life, variety in the job, or frequency of feeling nervous or tense. Schwartz asks respondents for guiding principles in people's lives with respect to social issues, such as social justice, humility, creativity, social order, pleasure, ambition.[91] The GLOBE study originally was concerned with leadership issues, not with people's work motivations, although later the questions were meant to clarify Hofstede's dimensions. Researchers measure respondents' perceptions of the organizations or societies in which they live or work *as it is* and *as it should be*. As the desired and desirable often are opposed, for 7 of the 9 GLOBE dimensions, cultural values and practices are negatively correlated. [92]

The respondents used by Schwartz are students and teachers, whereas Hofstede has used matched samples of all categories of people who work in organizations. The value instrument employed by Schwartz requires respondents to evaluate the importance of abstract values, which makes the questions easier to answer by educated people than by less educated people. This aspect of the method has implications for the universality of the method. According to Schwartz and Bardi,[93] this abstract task is likely to be inappropriate for some of the world's populations and is likely to elicit unreliable and invalid value ratings. The survey is also based on people's self-reports of the importance they attribute to values. It is therefore critical to establish that self-reports of value priorities relate meaningfully to actual behavior. A problem of Hofstede's questions is that, next to general questions about people's condition (e.g., nervousness), questions are asked about work-related behavior and preferences that can only be answered by people who are in relevant work situations. The results have to be translated to other situations.

Hofstede's scales are bipolar; they include a positive and negative pole for each dimension, which makes results easy to interpret. The Schwartz scales are unipolar that are seemingly opposites; but a negative correlation with one does not imply a positive correlation with the opposite scale, and results are often difficult to interpret.

The three models can be applied for different purposes. Those who want to study both individual-level values and culture-level values may opt for the Schwartz model. The Hofstede model is suggested to be more useful in predicting behavior, and the GLOBE value dimensions could prove more useful in studying aspects of intergroup and international relations.[94] Gouveia and Ros[95] find that the Hofstede model is better explained by macroeconomic variables, while the Schwartz model is better accounted for by macro-social variables, and believe that this is due to conceptual and measurement differences.

Several inventories of cultural classifications applied to international marketing show that of available models the Hofstede model has been used most frequently to understand differences across markets. It has been used for analyzing market entry modes, for innovation, research and development, for personality and for motivation studies, for understanding emotions across cultures as well as for analyzing advertising. Marketing managers have a need to estimate cultural differences between the firm's home and host markets, for which the Hofstede model is used.[96] It is useful to segment the world on a country level so international marketers can adopt similar advertising campaigns in a country segment.[97]

APPLICATION TO CONSUMER BEHAVIOR

Dimensions of national culture provide excellent variables that can be employed to analyze cross-cultural consumer behavior. Together with national wealth, Hofstede's cultural dimensions can explain more than half of the differences in consumption and consumer behavior.[98] In the following chapters many of these findings are presented.

The Schwartz dimensions do not show results that are as consistent as the Hofstede dimensions, although the Schwartz dimensions include values similar to the Hofstede dimensions. Analysis of the same data can result in different, sometimes seemingly opposing explanations, but the Schwartz dimensions in some cases provide additional explanations. A few examples may demonstrate the phenomenon, as summarized in Table 2.3, which for a number of consumer behavior data show the significant correlation coefficients with both Hofstede's and Schwartz's dimensions for 20 countries worldwide and 13 countries in Europe.[99]

Two types of data are used for Table 2.3: data on PC ownership and Internet users of 2005 from the World Development Report 2007, results from a Eurobarometer survey among young people in Europe in 2001 (as in the first edition of this book); and a Eurobarometer consumer survey with data on consumers and use of information.[100]

Country scores on the Schwartz dimensions are from his publication of 2007.[101] For the data on PCs and Internet, 20 common countries for both models were available, and for the Eurobarometer data, 13 countries. For a number of topics, Table 2.3 shows the significant correlations with Hofstede's power distance, individualism, and uncertainty avoidance, and for the Schwartz dimensions embeddedness, hierarchy, intellectual autonomy, egalitarianism, and harmony. The most confusing differences are correlations with power distance and egalitarianism that share values of equality. PC ownership, for example correlates negatively with power distance ($r = -.51**$) and positively with individualism ($r = .59***$), which both include egalitarian values. One would expect a positive relationship with the Schwartz dimension egalitarianism, but the correlation is negative ($r = -.47*$). Internet users per 1,000 correlate negatively with uncertainty avoidance ($r = -.39*$) and positively with individualism ($r = .43*$). The combination of low uncertainty avoidance and individualism seems to be a logical explanation, as independence and willingness to try new things are values found in cultures of small power distance and weak uncertainty avoidance. The Internet is by definition an egalitarian means of communication. Yet, the only significant correlation with the Schwartz dimensions is a *negative* correlation with egalitarian commitment ($r = -.43*$). So egalitarianism may include values that are not the same as equality, or this example points at the difference between the desirable and the desired.

Table 2.3 Comparing Hofstede and Schwartz: Significant correlations with Hofstede & Schwartz dimensions for 20 countries worldwide and 13 countries in Europe

	Hofstede			Schwartz				
	PDI	IDV	UAI	EMB	HRCH	IntAUT	EGAL	HARM
PCs/1,000	− .51**	.59***	− .66***				− .47*	
Internet users/1,000		.43*	− .39*				− .43*	
Young people: Leisure activities								
Watch TV					.58*	.14	− .62*	
Shopping	− .53*	.51*	− .70***	− .52*	.56*		−.63*	− .59*
Use PC, Internet, v-game	− .49*			− .53*	− .73***	.58*	−.54*	
Play instrument	− .54*		.49*			.52*	−.64**	
Do some work for money	− .65**		− .74***				−.57*	− .56*
Do-It-Yourself activities		.52*			.50*		−.63**	
Member of organization								
Sports club	− .51*	.57*	− .70***	− .61*			−.50*	
No club	.62*	−.53*	.68**				.57*	
Visit other country for								
Holidays			− .58*				−.60*	
Youth exchange program						.61*		
Learn language						.84***		.50*
No other country visited	.57*		.50*	.59*			.60*	
% who speak English well enough to take part in a conversation (U.K. and IRE excluded)	− .73**		− .54*				−.75***	

	Hofstede			Schwartz				
	PDI	IDV	UAI	EMB	HRCH	IntAUT	EGAL	HARM
Use once a week								
Laptop	− .68**	.53*	− .72***	− .56*				
E-mail	− .64**		− .68***				− .57*	
Internet	− .57*		− .63**				− .54*	
Information behavior								
Consumers who view themselves as well-informed (%)	− .51*	.73***	− .56*			.49*	− .53*	
% who often get information from the Internet	− .81***		− .71***				− .66**	
% who get information from newspapers	−.73***						−.69***	
% who do not consult any information sources	.75***						.54*	

SOURCES: Hofstede et al. (2010); Schwartz (2007); World Development Report (2007); EBS 151 *Young Europeans in 2001*; Flash EB 117, Consumer Survey (2002) (see Appendix B)

The Eurobarometer study used to compare the models among young Europeans ages 15–24[102] shows similar puzzling results for using a laptop, e-mail, and Internet. Although egalitarianism and hierarchy are presented as two poles of basically one dimension, young people's use of a personal computer, Internet, or video games correlates negatively with both hierarchy and egalitarianism. On the other hand, some interesting relationships are between intellectual autonomy—that includes values of curiosity and broadmindedness—and the percentages of young people who travel to other countries for the purpose of language learning or youth exchange programs. Also, similar values of individualism and low embeddedness can be recognized in the positive correlation between individualism and shopping as leisure activity as well as a negative correlation with embeddedness.

Correlations with several aspects of information behavior are puzzling. Information gathering to make a buying decision is related to low power distance and low uncertainty avoidance, but also to low egalitarianism. The percentages of consumers who view themselves as well informed correlate with individualism, low power distance, and with low uncertainty avoidance. They also correlate with intellectual autonomy, which seems logical, but the correlation with low egalitarianism doesn't seem logical.

Literature shows that most applications of cultural dimensions to marketing and advertising have used the Hofstede model, which covers a larger number of countries, than the Schwartz model does. Hofstede's dimensions have become key variables or explanatory features in a wide variety of research.[103]

CULTURE RELATIONSHIPS

Because the Hofstede model is the most robust, it is used in this book to explain culture's influence on consumer behavior. The model was developed for people's behavior in organizations, so the relationship with behavior of consumers needs some additional analytical skills. It is easy to draw the wrong conclusions of cause and effect of culture. Problems can arise in the formulation of hypotheses and in selecting countries or groups of countries for analysis. A few general points of caution are dealt with in the following sections.

Cause-Effect

A frequently asked question is about the cause-effect relationship between culture and social phenomena. Are the characteristics of a social system (e.g., legal, political, or economic system) produced by the personal qualities of the population, or are the personal qualities of people generated by the nature of the social system in which they live? In many cases, common historical learning that has shaped national culture is the best factor to explain variance. But problems of determining whether what is observed is caused by history or is a functional relationship are frequent. A classical controversy of this nature concerns the meaning of the Weberian hypothesis relating Protestant values to capitalist orientations. Is it a "functional" relationship between Protestant values and entrepreneurship, or is it based on shared contacts or common historical learning?[104] The latter is probably the case. Capitalism thrived in countries of a specific cultural configuration that also harbored Protestantism.[105] Religious affiliation by itself is less culturally relevant than it is often assumed. If we trace the religious history of countries, what religion a population has embraced seems to have been a result of previously existing cultural value patterns more than a cause of cultural differences.[106]

Another example is the relationship (in continental Europe) between low English-speaking skills and low usage of the Internet. Both are related with Hofstede's dimension uncertainty avoidance. In strong uncertainty avoidance cultures, people avoid difficulties of language learning[107] as well as innovative behavior with respect to new technology (see also Chapter 7). So the functional relationship is with uncertainty avoidance.

Another assumed cause-effect relationship is between economic development and culture. Some theorists see culture as a major determinant of socioeconomic success, whereas others see national wealth as a determinant of culture. Schwartz[108] states that socioeconomic and cultural variables powerfully influence each other. Inglehart's findings suggest that economic development is related to culture change away from traditional values and toward self-expression values. However, further analysis of the WVS data by Van de Vliert[109] led to the conclusion that higher levels of economic growth are not related to decreases in traditional values and increases in secular-rational values.

Comparing Groups of Cultures

Evolutionary theory states that only cultures in the same stage of development can be meaningfully compared.[110] Comparisons that include both modern and developing countries produce differences that are very hard to interpret—if they make sense at all. In youth surveys, for example, one observes young people in developing countries such as India reacting with high degrees of optimism that are factually completely inappropriate. By way of contrast, young people in Sweden or in the Netherlands exude gloom in the wake of incomparably greater opportunity.[111] So, the choice of which nations to compare can influence the validity of the findings and reduce the possibility of generalizing findings. It is not easy to get subclasses of cultures for which valid comparison is possible. Correlations of different groups of countries will have different results. Hofstede's dimension power distance can serve as an example of how different groups of countries show different relationships. Worldwide, for a group of 33 countries of mixed levels of development, power distance is correlated with wealth; that is, the higher the GNI per capita, the lower countries score on power distance, so there is a negative correlation between national wealth and power distance. This relationship does not exist among a group of developed countries.

The relationships between dimensions can also vary for different regions. For example, Hofstede's dimension uncertainty avoidance correlates positively with power distance in a wealthy subgroup of countries, but this correlation is nonexistent in a poorer subgroup of countries.[112] This may be related to findings that in richer countries uncertainty avoidance is negatively related to the penetration of new products, but this relationship tends to be positive under poorer economic conditions.[113]

Different selections of countries can result in different significance of correlations. For several communication technology products, our finding is that the wealthier the group of countries, the more significant the correlations with culture. When comparing cultural relationships over time, the same groups of countries have to be selected.

Comparing Groups Within Cultures

In line with the distinction individual-level and culture-level, comparing subgroups (within-country groups) can lead to different results than when countries are compared. Power distance, measured by Hofstede at the culture level, can only be used as a characteristic of social systems, not of individuals or groups within countries. When for the group of 33 countries worldwide, populations are segmented in subgroups of different levels of wealth, these subgroups show different correlations with power distance. The groups that have the 20% highest share of national wealth, for example, correlate positively with power distance, whereas at national level, GNI per capita correlates negatively with power distance. If the 20% highest income groups correlate positively with power distance, and the 20% lowest correlate negatively, such results demonstrate that the subgroups are not functionally equivalent. The findings say that in high power distance cultures, differences in income equality are larger than in low power distance cultures. Similar effects are found when comparing groups of students: Students from some countries belong to the elites in their countries.

Value Shift

Although values are enduring, some values may change in the long term. Value shift can be caused by economic change, modernization, maturation and generation effects, zeitgeist, and seniority effects.

Economic change, like increased wealth, can lead to individualism, and poverty leads to collectivism. With better education, the level of power distance goes down. Yet relative differences remain, and some differences may even become stronger. At face value, people tend to become more individualistic, but individuation follows different patterns.

Modernization, including industrialization and urbanization, is assumed to turn collectivistic societies into individualistic societies. Although urbanization tends to break up the joint household of the extended family in favor of more nuclear households, this does not imply decreasing extended family values.

Maturation effects[114] mean that people's values shift as they grow older. Stress, for example, is highest at middle age. Masculinity decreases with increasing age. Young people who want to make it in life generally adhere more to masculine values than do those who have already made it. Youngest and oldest age categories are less individualistic.

Generation effects occur when values are fixed in the young from a certain period and then stay with that age cohort over its lifetime. Drastic changes in the conditions of life during youth may lead to generations having different fixed values. The value shift of the generation of the 1960s in Europe and the United States is an example of a generation effect.

Zeitgeist effects occur when drastic systemwide changes in conditions cause everyone's values to shift, regardless of age. In times of recession, the degree of power distance may increase because equality is less functional, or it may lead to increased bureaucracy and shift to a stronger level of uncertainty avoidance. *Seniority effects* occur when the values of people who are more senior in an organization are measured. Seniority and age effects cannot be separated easily.

The degree of uncertainty avoidance of countries can change with environmental factors. Natural disasters and war will cause higher levels. When in 1996 we measured the dimensions in the EMS survey, Finland's score on uncertainty avoidance had lowered and the score of the United Kingdom had become higher. The United Kingdom was in an economic crisis at that time, and Finland had been delivered from the pressure of the Soviet Union.

CONCLUSION

People of different countries have different value orientations that cause variation in preferences of products and brands. For effective international marketing and communications, people must understand these differences. Much consumer behavior research is conducted at the individual level. This chapter discussed comparative research at the culture level. Models that distinguish value categories or dimensions of culture can help to analyze differences at culture level. They allow statistical analysis that can discover relationships between country scores on cultural dimensions and data on consumption and consumer behavior. Not all models are equally practical. Several models were reviewed in this chapter. The model that is most applied to marketing and advertising is the model of national culture developed by Geert Hofstede. Analysis of the effect of culture becomes increasingly important, because value differences are stable over time and become manifest with increased wealth. This is the topic that will be further pursued in Chapter 3.

NOTES

1. Vinson, D. E., Scott, J. E., & Lamont, L. M. (1997, April). The role of personal values in marketing and consumer behavior. *Journal of Marketing*, 44–50.
2. Rokeach, M. (1973). *The nature of human values.* New York: Free Press, 5.
3. Rokeach (1973), 18.
4. Wang, Z., Rao, C. P., & D'Auria, A. (1994). A comparison of the Rokeach Value Survey (RVS) in China and the United States. In J. A. Cote & S. M. Leong (Eds.), *Asia Pacific advances in consumer research* (Vol. 1, pp. 185–190). Provo, UT: Association for Consumer Research.
5. Hofstede, G. (1991). *Cultures and organizations: Software of the mind.* London & New York: McGraw-Hill, 9.
6. Hofstede, G. (2001). *Culture's consequences* (2nd ed.). Thousand Oaks, CA: Sage, 6–7.
7. Grunert, S. C., & Muller, T. E. (1996). Measuring values in international settings: Are respondents thinking "real" life or "ideal" life? In L. Manrai & A. Manrai (Eds.), *Global perspectives in cross-cultural and cross-national consumer research* (pp. 169–186). New York and London: International Business Press/Haworth Press.
8. De Mooij, M. (2010) *Global marketing and advertising, Understanding cultural paradoxes* (3rd ed.). Thousand Oaks, CA: Sage.

9. Cheng, H., & Schweitzer, J. C. (1996, May/June). Cultural values reflected in Chinese and U.S. television commercials. *Journal of Advertising Research,* 27–45.

10. Hofstede (1991), 8.

11. Yankelovich, D. (1994). How changes in the economy are reshaping American values. In H. J. Aaron, T. E. Mann, & T. Taylor (Eds.), *Values and public policy* (pp. 23–24). Washington, DC: Brookings Institution.

12. Dr Gallup's finger on America's pulse. (1997, September). *The Economist,* 102.

13. Inkeles, A. (1997). *Continuity and change in popular values on the Pacific Rim.* Stanford, CA: Stanford University, Hoover Institution.

14. Fu, J. H. Y., & Chiu, C.Y. (2007), Local culture's responses to globalization. Exemplary persons and their attendant values. *Journal of Cross-Cultural Psychology, 38*(5), 636–653.

15. Tai, S. H. C., & Tam, J. L. M. (1996). A comparative study of Chinese consumers in Asian markets—a lifestyle analysis. *Journal of International Consumer Marketing, 9,* 25–42.

16. Pollay, R. W., & Gallagher, K. (1990). Advertising and cultural values: Reflections in the distorted mirror. *International Journal of Advertising, 9,* 359–372.

17. Wiles, C. R., Wiles, J., & Tjernlund, A. (1996, May/June). The ideology of advertising: The United States and Sweden. *Journal of Advertising Research,* 57–66.

18. Inkeles, A. (1998). *One world emerging?* Boulder, CO: Westview, 173.

19. Cafferata, P., Horn, M. I., & Wells, W. D. (1997). Gender role changes in the United States. In L. Kahle & L. Chiagouris (Eds.), *Values, lifestyles, and psychographics* (pp. 249–262). Mahwah, NJ: Lawrence Erlbaum, 258.

20. Kahle, L. R., & Goff Timmer, S. (1983). *A theory and method for studying values and social change: Adaptation to Life in America.* New York: Praeger.

21. Clawson, C. J., & Vinson, D. E. (1978). Human values: A historical and interdisciplinary analysis. In H. K. Hunt (Ed.), *Advances in consumer research* (Vol. 5, pp. 396–402). Ann Arbor, MI: Association for Consumer Research.

22. Pollay, R. W. (1984). The identification and distribution of values manifest in print advertising 1900–1980. In R. E. Pitts Jr. & Arch G. Woodside (Eds.), *Personal values and consumer psychology* (pp. 111–135). Lexington, MA: Lexington Books.

23. Venkatesh, A. (1995). Ethnoconsumerism: A new paradigm to study cultural and cross-cultural consumer behavior. In J. A. Costa & G. J. Bamossy (Eds.), *Marketing in a multicultural world* (pp. 26–67). Thousand Oaks, CA: Sage.

24. Lowe, A. C-T., & Corkindale, D. R. (1998). Differences in "cultural values" and their effects on responses to marketing stimuli: A cross-cultural study between Australians and Chinese from the People's Republic of China. *European Journal of Marketing, 32,* 843–867.

25. Geertz, C. (1973). *The interpretation of cultures.* New York: Basic Books, 44.

26. Hofstede (1991), 5.

27. Triandis, H. (1995). *Individualism and collectivism.* Boulder, CO: Westview.

28. Inkeles, A. (1997). *National character.* New Brunswick, NJ: Transaction, 3–17.

29. Hofstede, G. (2001). *Culture's consequences* (2nd ed.). Thousand Oaks, CA: Sage, 11.

30. Schwartz, S. H. (1994). Beyond individualism/collectivism: New cultural dimensions of values. In U. Kim, H. C. Triandis, Ç. Kâgitçibasi, S.-C. Choi, & G. Yoon (Eds.), *Individualism and collectivism* (pp. 85–119). Thousand Oaks, CA: Sage, 85.

31. Inkeles (1997), 103.

32. Hofstede (1991), 8.

33. Kitayama, S. (2002). Culture and basic psychological processes: Toward a system view of culture: Comment on Oyserman et al. *Psychological Bulletin, 128,* 89–96.

34. Harzing, A. W. (2005). Does the USE of English-language questionnaires in cross-national research obscure national differences? *International Journal of Cross Cultural Management, 5*(2), 213–224.

35. Van Herk, H., Poortinga, Y. H., & Verhallen, T. M. M. (2005). Equivalence of survey data: Relevance for international marketing. *European Journal of Marketing, 39*(3/4), 351–364.

36. Douglas, S. P., & Craig, C. S. (1983). *International marketing research.* Englewood Cliffs, NJ: Prentice-Hall International Editions, 192.

37. Hofstede (2001), 15–17; Schwartz (1994), 92–93.

38. Van Raaij, W. F. (1998). Micro and macro economic psychology. In M. Lambkin, G. Foxall, F. van Raaij, & B. Heilbrunn (Eds.), *European perspectives on consumer behaviour* (pp. 335–347). London: Prentice Hall.

39. Hofstede (2001), 16–17.

40. Hofstede (2001), 463.

41. Schwartz (1994), 104.

42. Przeworski, A., & Teune, H. (1970). *The logic of comparative social inquiry.* New York: Wiley-Interscience, 59–60.

43. Minkov, M. (2007). *What makes us different and similar.* Sofia, Bulgaria: Klasika I Stil, 35.

44. Holman, R. H. (1984). A values and lifestyles perspective on human behavior. In R. E. Pitts Jr. & A. G. Woodside (Eds.), *Personal values and consumer psychology* (pp. 35–54). Lexington, MA: Lexington Books, D. C. Heath.

45. RISC International. (1995). *Why people buy* [Brochure]. Paris. http://www.risc-int.com

46. Callebaut, J., Janssens, M., Lorré, D., & Hendrickx, H. (1994). *The naked consumer: The secret of motivational research in global marketing.* Antwerp: Censydiam Institute, 106.

47. Hansen, F. (1998). From lifestyle to value system to simplicity. *Advances in Consumer Research, 25,* 181–195.

48. De Mooij, M. (1994). *Advertising worldwide* (2nd ed.). London: Prentice Hall International, 178–183.

49. Homma, N., & Ueltzhoffer, J. (1990, 18–20 June). *The internationalization of everyday-life research markets and milieus.* ESOMAR Conference on America, Japan and EC '92: The Prospects for Marketing, Advertising and Research. Venice, Italy. See also http://www.motivaction.nl

50. Denton, T. (2007). Unit of observation in cross-cultural research: Implications for sampling and aggregated data analysis. *Cross-Cultural Research, 41*(1), 3–31.

51. Hofstede, G., & Hofstede, G. J. (2004). *Cultures and organizations: Software of the mind* (2nd ed.). New York: McGraw Hill.

52. Anholt, S. (2000). *Another one bites the grass.* New York: Wiley, 66.

53. *American Community Survey.* (2006). U.S. Census Bureau.

54. *The European Social Survey.* See Appendix B. This study provides answers to value questions that can be isolated for the various provinces of the participating countries. In the cultural cohesion analysis, France and Italy could not be included, as the respondents hadn't answered the particular set of questions.

55. Singh, D. (2007). *Cross cultural comparison of buying behavior in India.* Doctoral thesis. Chandigarh: Panjab University, University Business School.

56. Harris, P. R., & Moran, R. T. (1987). *Managing cultural differences.* Houston, TX: Gulf Publishing, 190–195.

57. Hofstede, G. (2002). Dimensions do not exist: A reply to Brendan McSweeney. *Human Relations, 55*(11), 1355-1361

58. Inglehart, R., Basañez, M., and Moreno, A. (1998). *Human values and beliefs.* Ann Arbor: University of Michigan Press.

59. Inkeles (1997), 45–50.

60. Kluckhohn, F., & Strodtbeck, F. (1961). *Variations in value orientations.* Evanston, IL: Row, Peterson.

61. Trompenaars, F. (1993). *Riding the waves of culture: Understanding cultural diversity in business.* London: Nicholas Brealey.

62. Smith, P. B., Dugan, S., & Trompenaars, F. (1996). National culture and the values of organizational employees: A dimensional analysis across 43 nations. *Journal of Cross-Cultural Psychology, 27,* 231–264.

63. Fiske, A. P. (1992). The four elementary forms of sociality: Framework for a unified theory of social relations. *Psychological Review, 99,* 689–723.

64. Hall, E. (1976). *Beyond culture.* New York: Doubleday; Hall, E. (1984). *The dance of life.* New York: Doubleday, 85–128.

65. Analysis is through correlation and regression analysis. Throughout this book for correlation analysis, the Pearson product-moment correlation coefficient is used. Correlation analysis is one-tailed. Significance levels are indicated by $*\ p < .05$, $**\ p < .01$, and $***\ p < .005$. When regression analysis is used, multiple linear regression analysis is done stepwise. The coefficient of determination or R^2 is the indicator of the percentage of variance explained. The examples in the charts are of significant correlations between secondary data and one or more dimensions. Usually, for presentation clarity not all countries are included. If more countries are available than presented in the chart, the original number of countries with the related correlation coefficient are included in an endnote.

66. Schwartz, S. H., & Bilsky, W. (1987). Toward a universal psychological structure of human values. *Journal of Personality and Social Psychology, 53,* 550–562.

67. Schwartz, S. H. (2007, June). Cultural and individual value correlates of capitalism: A comparative analysis. *Psychological Inquiry, 18*(1), 52–57.

68. House, R. J., & associates. (Eds.). (2004). *Culture, leadership, and organizations: The GLOBE study of 62 societies.* Thousand Oaks, CA: Sage.

69. Minkov (2007).

70. Littrel, R. F. (2008). Adding Minkov's dimensions to the panoply. *Journal of Cross-Cultural Psychology, 39*(5), 655–657.

71. Magnusson, P., Wilson, R. T., Zdravkovic, S., Zhou, J. X., & Westjohn, S. A. (2008). Breaking through the cultural clutter: A comparative assessment of multiple cultural and institutional frameworks. *International Marketing Review, 25*(2), 183–201.

72. Doi, T. (1985). *The anatomy of self.* Tokyo: Kodansha International.

73. Jordá-Albiñana, B., Ampuero-Canellas, O., Vila, N., & Rojas-Sola, J. I. (2009). Brand identity documentation: a cross-national examination of identity standards manuals. *International Marketing Review, 26*(2), 172–197.

74. Hall (1984), 16–27, 32–34.

75. Hall (1984), 17–24.

76. The descriptions of the dimensions are summaries of the dimension descriptions from Hofstede, G., Hofstede, G. J., & Minkov, M. (2010). *Cultures and organizations: Software of the mind* (3rd ed.). New York: McGraw-Hill; and Hofstede, G. (2001). *Culture's consequences* (2nd ed.). Thousand Oaks: Sage. With permission.

77. Michael Hoppe, a German American management educator, replicated the IBM study on a population of political and institutional elites and found that Italy is much more collectivistic than the IBM scores lead one to believe. Hoppe's study [(1990). *A comparative study of country elites: International differences in work-related values and learning and their implications for management training and development.* Unpublished doctoral dissertation. Chapel Hill: University of North Carolina] also found differences with respect to Finland, which may be more individualistic than the IBM scores indicate. Contradictory information about the level of individualism or collectivism in Italy is probably due to

the fact that Italy is bicultural: The north is individualistic, but the rest of the country is collectivistic. Hofstede's IBM data were mainly collected in the north, and he found strong individualism. Consumption and media behavior data are based on a country average; where these relate to individualism or collectivism, Italy tends to score similar to Spain, which is much more collectivistic.

78. Soong, R. (2003, December 23). Argentina, Brazil, Chile, Colombia, Ecuador, Mexico and Peru. Message posted to TGI Latina (http://www.zonalatina.com/Zldata332.htm).

79. Hofstede, G., & Bond, M. H. (1988, Spring). The Confucius connection: From cultural roots to economic growth. *Organizational Dynamics, 16,* 4–22.

80. Minkov (2007).

81. Hofstede et al. (2010).

82. Søndergaard, M. (1994). Research note: Hofstede's consequences: A study of reviews, citations and replications. *Organization Studies, 15,* 447–456.

83. Schwartz, S. H. (1994). Beyond individualism/collectivism. In U. Kim, H. C. Triandis, et al. (Eds.), *Individualism and collectivism: Theory, method, and applications: Vol. 18. Cross-cultural research and methodology* (pp. 85–119). Thousand Oaks, CA: Sage.

84. Schwartz, S. H., & Bilsky, W. (1987). Toward a universal psychological structure of human values. *Journal of Personality and Social Psychology, 53,* 550–562; Schwartz, S. H., & Bilsky, W. (1990). Toward a theory of the universal content and structure of values: Extensions and cross-cultural replications. *Journal of Personality and Social Psychology, 58,* 878–891.

85. Schwartz, S. H. (2004). Mapping and interpreting cultural differences around the world. In H. Vinken, J. Soeters, & P. Ester (Eds.), *Comparing cultures: Dimensions of culture in a comparative perspective* (pp. 43–73). Leiden: Brill.

86. Schwartz (2004), 51–52.

87. Hofstede (2001), 265.

88. Schwartz (2007).

89. Minkov (2007), 23.

90. Smith, P. (2006). When elephants fight, the grass gets trampled: The GLOBE and Hofstede projects. *Journal of International Business Studies, 37,* 915–912.

91. Schwartz (2004), 48.

92. Javidan, M., House, R. J., Dorfman, P. W., Hanges, P. J., & Sully de Luque, M. (2006). Conceptualizing and measuring cultures and their consequences: A comparative review of GLOBE's and Hofstede's approaches. *Journal of International Business Studies, 37,* 897–914.

93. Schwartz, S., & Bardi, A. (2001). Value hierarchies across cultures: Taking a similarities perspective. *Journal of Cross-Cultural Psychology, 32,* 268–290.

94. Smith (2006).

95. Gouveia, V. V., & Ros, M. (2000). Hofstede and Schwartz's models for classifying individualism at the cultural level: their relation to macro-social and macro-economic variables. *Psicothema, 12* (Suppl.), 25–33.

96. Magnusson et al. (2008).

97. Vanderstraeten, J., & Matthyssens, P. (2008). Country classification and the cultural dimension: A review and evaluation. *International Marketing Review, 25*(2), 230–251

98. De Mooij, M. (2001). *Convergence and divergence in consumer behavior. Consequences for global marketing and advertising.* Doctoral dissertation. Pamplona, Spain: Universidad de Navarra.

99. The 13 countries in Europe for which country scores by both Hofstede and Schwartz are available are Austria, Belgium, Denmark, Finland, France, Germany, Ireland, Italy, the Netherlands, Spain, Portugal, Sweden, and the United Kingdom.

100. In the *Young Europeans* report, one of the questions used was "From the following list of activities, which, if any, do you do regularly during your leisure time?" Answer categories used were Watch TV, Go shopping, Use a computer/Internet/video game, Play an instrument, Do some work for money, and Do-it-yourself activities. Another question was about membership in organizations. Answer categories used in our analysis were Sports club, and an answer category "No club or organization." In the survey also a number of questions were asked about young people visiting other countries, the purposes and the difficulties. Purposes used are Holidays, Youth Exchange programs, and Language learning. Also the category "Did not visit any other country" was used. Also the answers "English" to the question "Do you speak another language well enough to take part in a conversation?" (United Kingdom and Ireland excluded). Answer categories used were Laptop computer, E-mail, and the Internet used at least once a week. From the Eurobarometer report *Consumer Survey* 2002, the percentages agreeing to the statement "I view myself as well-informed" were used and answers to questions on sources of information consulted to make an informed purchase decision: Internet, newspapers, or none at all.

101. Schwartz (2007).

102. *Young Europeans in 2001*. (2001). Eurobarometer report 151. (See Appendix B.)

103. Milner, L. M., & Collins, J. M. (2000). Sex-role portrayals and the gender of nations. *The Journal of Advertising, 29*, 67–79.

104. Przeworski & Teune (1970), 51–56.

105. Hofstede (2001) 114.

106. Hofstede & Hofstede (2004).

107. Several data on foreign language speaking show a relationship with uncertainty avoidance: the higher countries score on this dimension, the fewer foreign languages people speak. With respect to the English language, the argument can be that the countries with a language structure that is similar to the English language (all Germanic languages) have an advantage in learning English. Quite a few Germanic languages are spoken in cultures of low uncertainty avoidance. However, also within the group of Germanic language countries (United Kingdom and Ireland excluded), a significant correlation is found between English speaking and low uncertainty avoidance.

108. Schwartz (2004), 65.

109. Van de Vliert, E. (2007). Climatoeconomic roots of survival versus self-expression cultures. *Journal of Cross-Cultural Psychology, 38*(2), 156–172.

110. Van Raaij, W. F. (1978). Cross-cultural research methodology as a case of construct validity. In K. Hunt (Ed.), *Advances in consumer research* (Vol. 5, pp. 693–701).

111. Scheuch, E. K. (1996). Theoretical implications of comparative survey research: Why the wheel of cross-cultural methodology keeps on being reinvented. In A. Inkeles & M. Sasaki (Eds.), *Comparing nations and cultures* (pp. 57–73). Englewood Cliffs, NJ: Prentice Hall, 68.

112. Müller, H. P., & Ziltener, P. (2004). The structural roots of values: An anthropological interpretation of Hofstede's value dimensions. In H. Vinken, J. Soeters, & P. Ester (Eds.), *Comparing cultures. Dimensions of culture in a comparative perspective* (pp. 122–140). Leiden/Boston: Brill, 139.

113. Yeniurt, S., & Townsend, J. D. (2003). Does culture explain acceptance of new products in a country? *International Marketing Review, 20*(4), 377–396.

114. Hofstede (2001).

Convergence and Divergence in Consumer Behavior

Chapter 1 reviewed the assumptions of converging consumer behavior and the counter-arguments. The universalism of Western marketing professionals presupposes the emergence of a unique world culture following the maturity of consumer markets in which the United States leads the world. As American advertising professor John Philip Jones states, "Logic points to similar patterns emerging in other countries when their per capita income levels approach that of the United States." [1] Also, consumer behavior theorists follow this idea—that consumers in all parts of the world want American goods as status symbols—and in the process they adopt American consumption values. This chapter reviews the underlying socioeconomic phenomena of assumed convergence of consumer behavior, such as modernization, urbanization, rising education levels, changing demographics, and convergence of national wealth. Convergence theory and forms of convergence and divergence in consumer behavior are discussed.

CONVERGENCE THEORY

Convergence theory proposes that, along with industrialization and modernization, nations are becoming increasingly alike despite different cultural and historical legacies and diverse political and economic systems. [2] Aspects of socioeconomic convergence are patterns of social relationships, increasing dependence on science and technology, popular attitudes, and systems of political and economic control. [3] Almost every society on Earth has at least begun to industrialize, and it seems likely that within the next century most of humanity will live in predominantly urban industrialized societies. This does not mean that all societies will be identical. Industrial societies have a wide variety of cultures and institutions. But their common characteristics are also striking: virtually without exception, they are characterized by high degrees of urbanization, the use of science and technology, and high levels of formal education.[4] However, the assumption that industrialization and modernization will bring a universal civilization, including universal values and consumption patterns, is a distinctive product of Western thinking.[5]

The convergence debate is not new; it resulted from modernization theory of the 1960s. Advocates of convergence argued that all or nearly all societies were, at different speeds, moving toward the same point, mainly as a result of industrial man,[6] whereas adherents to the divergence thesis emphasized the idea of there being different forms of modernity and that in that sense there is no convergence.[7] In order not to mistake the spread of American consumption symbols for cultural convergence, we have to understand the various aspects of modernization that underlie the global convergence hypothesis.

MODERNIZATION

Taken literally, the word *modern* refers to anything that has more or less recently replaced something that in the past was the accepted way of doing things.[8] Being modern is opposed to being traditional, whereby the modern is viewed as positive and the traditional as negative. The terms are used to characterize individuals and nations. When societies or nations are defined as modern, they are characterized by mass education, urbanization, industrialization, bureaucratization, and rapid communication and transportation. Some add to these cultural homogeneity and the secularization of belief.[9] *Economic modernization* includes intense application of scientific technology and inanimate sources of energy, high specialization of labor, interdependence of impersonal markets, large-scale financing combined with concentration of economic decision making, and rising levels of material well-being. The *socio-psychological* approach to modernization treats it mainly as a process of change in ways of perceiving, expressing, and valuing.

American social scientists Alex Inkeles and David Horton Smith[10] developed dimensions of individual modernity, including personal qualities such as openness to new experience, readiness for social change, a disposition to form or hold opinions and acknowledge differences of opinion, information, sense of time, control of the environment, orientation toward planning, calculability versus trust, educational and occupational aspirations, sense of dignity, and respect for others. The dimensions were developed to measure individual modernity in order to find scientific knowledge as to how far the qualities of a nation's people are important in fostering development. With the exception of Japan, all the major nations that can be considered modernized according to these dimensions are part of the European tradition. Although business people and the elites in most of the (from the Western point of view) developing societies have adopted the Western businessman's suit and shoes, the societies to which they belong are considered to be traditional societies. This approach demonstrates that the term *modern* is often equated with *Western,* and the assumption is that with modernity people also will adopt Western values. This also applies to popular thought in marketing and advertising. According to the French marketing professor Jean-Claude Usunier,[11] some researchers, even though they acknowledge national differences, envision multinational marketing activities merely as processes of innovation and change that would bring worldwide convergence, with "traditional" cultures being progressively replaced by "modern" ones.

Although technological modernization is an important force to societal change, it does not wipe out variety. It may even increase differences, as on the basis of preexisting value systems societies cope with technological modernization in different ways.[12] Varying use of the Internet demonstrates this thesis. Associations with modernization vary. Whereas Westerners view modernization as a matter of changing values, Asians view modernization as involving technology, behavior, or material progress, without cultural implications.[13]

From Premodern to Postmodern

The distinction of societal stages of development from premodern to modern to postmodern and the effects on people's behavior and values reflects the development of Western societies. *Premodern times* tend to be characterized by agriculture as the dominant means of sustaining life, households containing three-generation extended families, feudal societies with landowners and nobility, and a cyclical perception of time. Industrialization brought *modern times,* characterized by increased urbanization, the nuclear family of husband, wife, and children, mass production, and a linear time orientation. A third societal development stage is postindustrialization, when most professions deal with obtaining, transforming, and integrating information. A variety of names using the prefix *post-*, meaning "after," are used to describe a new social order after the industrial development phase. Examples are *postmodern* or *post-scarcity society, postindustrial society, information society, service society,* or *knowledge society.* The term *postmodernism* is not a well-defined concept. It is used in many different ways. For example, postmodernity is a condition of Western society after modernity, and postmodernism is a movement that reacts to earlier modernist principles. According to Inglehart,[14] in postmodern society, emphasis on economic achievement is giving way to an increasing emphasis on quality of life.

Modernization is often equated with individualism in the sense of increased autonomy of individuals and decreasing sense of community that could even lead to the disintegration of society. However, modernization should be distinguished from individualism/collectivism. Equating individualism with modernization amounts to psychologizing a sociological phenomenon.[15]

In the economic development process of nations, the change from agriculture to indus-trialization is a universal process, including changing living conditions, although different countries are passing through these phases at different speeds. The assumption that these changes have similar societal implications and consequences for the behavior of individu-als is a product of Western thinking. In the strongly urbanized and modern Japan, planning and the linear time concept have not become mainstream. They are restricted to business practice. Many manifestations of Japanese culture, such as strong focus on the seasons (spring blossoms and autumn leaves), indicate that circular thinking has not disappeared with modernization.

Modernization, frequently mentioned as a cause of convergence, is not synonymous with convergence of values. Perkin refers to modernization as just "one of the neologisms like postmodernism that tend to conceal a preference for the values and practices of an author's own national culture."[16]

CONVERGENCE: MACRO AND MICRO LEVEL

For the analysis of convergence, we have to distinguish between convergence at macro and micro level, although the macro/micro dichotomy is not well defined. The following sections describe definitions of the macro/micro dichotomy.

The Macro/Micro Dichotomy

Various fields of study define the dichotomy macro/micro in different ways. In international marketing textbooks, *macro information* generally includes population data, gross national income (GNI) per capita, and growth rates of production and consumption.[17] Another term used is the *macro environment,* which includes political, legal, economic, social, cultural, and technological dimensions.[18] Descriptions of the macro-economic environment also can include, in addition to purely economic factors, human, technological, and natural resources, skills of a country's population (education), infrastructure (traffic, communica-tion, and technology), and level of technology.

Measurements of economic advancement at macro level can be energy available, GNI per capita, consumption, transportation and communication facilities, urbanization, capital for investment, technology, media, and the structure of consumption. The *micro-economic envi-ronment* generally refers to the environment surrounding a product and/or market of inter-est to a company and essentially concerns competition. Different competitors may satisfy different types of demand (existing, latent, incipient). This description points only partly at the consumer.

Hunt distinguishes between macro and micro at the level of aggregation. "Micro refers to the marketing activities of individual units, normally individual organizations (firms) and consumers or households. Macro suggests a higher level of aggregation, usually marketing systems or groups of consumers."[19]

According to Peterson and Malhotra[20] macro criteria are typically traditional and stereotypical and represent features of the country that can be counted, recorded, and shared as secondary data. The micro criteria are generally measured in consumer surveys. Consumer behavior researchers are typically concerned with micro and "somewhat macro" processes of consumption behavior. At the micro level is the study of how individuals seek information, evaluate alternatives, develop affective responses, plan actions, and then decide, act, and evaluate. At the "somewhat macro" level is the attempt to understand group behavior of households, neighborhoods, or lifestyle segments.[21]

For comparative analysis at the national level, the distinction between macro and micro at the level of aggregation is not useful, as all data are at the aggregate level. What the descriptions of Hunt and Peterson and Malhotra have in common is that they point at micro-level data being more concerned with buying behavior of consumers, as opposed to macro-level data being indicators of the macro-economic environment of countries. This rough distinction is followed in this book. Statistical indicators of a country's development, which often are also composites or summaries of other phenomena, are indicated as macro-level data. Examples are numbers of telephone main lines, cars, personal computers and television sets per 1,000 people. Most other data are at micro level and represent differences in consumption, consumer behavior, attitudes, values, and so on. Examples are product usage, such as time spent watching television, what people do on the Internet or with their computers, liters per capita mineral water consumed.

Convergence and Divergence at Macro Level

The convergence thesis at macro level deals with aspects of national income, infrastructure, health, social welfare, education levels of countries, possession of communication means such as telephone lines, computers, cars, television sets, newspapers, and increased leisure and physical security. The macro variables generally are the characteristics of the industrial but even more of the postindustrial world.

National wealth converges in the rich regions of the world, but not on a worldwide basis. This goes against popular thinking that with increased free trade and international access to information and technology, developing economies will catch up with the developed world. Analysis of longer historical periods questions this simple convergence hypothesis. Hollanders et al.[22] analyzed longer-term trends in economic development both in the developing and the developed world. They found that, whereas the period up to 1973 was characterized by a period of rapid growth and catching up between European and U.S. consumption patterns, in the 1973–1991 period this catching up disappeared.

Between 1991 and 1998, growth diverged among the United States, Europe, and Japan, with the United States leaping forward as compared with Europe and Japan. An explanation is that the U.S. economy has benefited faster from the implementation of new technology. Global inequality is reinforced by what is called the "digital divide." In the year 2000, about 87% of people online lived in postindustrial societies.[23] Worldwide data on ownership of computers and use of the Internet still correlate positively with national wealth.

World income distribution has become much more unequal in the past several decades. The World Bank publishes for each country a so-called Gini coefficient, a commonly used measure of inequality: zero signifies perfect equality; 100 means that one person holds all the income. In the short period between 1988 and 1993, world inequality increased from a Gini coefficient of 62.5 to 66. The implications are that the majority of the populations of poor countries are able to buy fewer and fewer of the goods and services that enter into the consumption patterns of rich-country populations.[24] Generally, in low-income countries, Gini coefficients are high. Worldwide GNI per capita explains 50% of variance. Examples of Gini coefficients of 2005 are 56.7 for Brazil, 59.2 for Bolivia, 28 for France, and 23 for Sweden. In the developed world, it is the degree of power distance that explains variance. High power distance means inequality. In economically homogeneous Europe, however, the differences are small and there is no relationship with income or culture.

> At the end of the 20th century, the north-south divide had increased. Between 1950 and 1992, the gap in the standards of living between the richer countries in the Northern Hemisphere and the poorer countries in the Southern Hemisphere had widened. Countries of the north experienced convergence among themselves. The bottom 16 countries of the north (real GNI/cap < US$5,000) experienced a catching up with the average standard of living of the top nine countries (real GNI/cap > US$5,000).[25]

International market researchers Craig, Douglas, and Grein[26] found that rather than converging in terms of macro-environmental characteristics, countries are becoming more divergent. They examined a set of 15 macro-environmental variables of the years 1960–1988 (e.g., infant mortality, cost of living, passenger motor vehicles, telephones in use, students, book production, daily newspaper circulation) among a set of industrialized nations. The results suggest that despite increased interaction and communication between industrialized nations, they are not becoming more similar in terms of macro-economic characteristics.

Convergence of Markets?

Most of the developments accelerating the trend toward global market unity are macro developments. For example, in some world regions, demographic convergence takes place with respect to age distribution and household size. Often-mentioned converging aspects in marketing are increased buying of services, increased demand for health and convenience products, convergence of distribution systems, and convergence of advertising expenditures.[27] Next to macro-level convergence, there is increasing evidence that at micro level there is not so much convergence. Infrastructural and economic integration usually occur at a higher speed than the cultural and mental integration of consumers. As people around the globe become well educated and more affluent, their tastes diverge. With increased wealth, people increasingly accord greater relevance to their civilizational identity.[28]

Forms of Convergence

Inkeles[29] reviewed various societal convergence effects of industrialization and modernization, such as of educational systems and family patterns. He did not find univocal evidence of convergence, but instead a variety of forms and levels of convergence and divergence. He summarized several patterns.

- Change may stop short of actual convergence, and a critical threshold of stable differences may remain. Moreover, on some dimensions there is a ceiling that most of the advanced countries reached long ago, leaving no room for further convergence. An example is the percentage of primary school enrollment.

- Movement toward a common point does not necessarily mean movement in the same direction. An example is convergence of age of marriage, which may come down in some countries, but move upward in others. Convergence and crossover take place when two converging lines meet, fuse, cross, and start to diverge.

- There may be thresholds that are more important than absolute differences. An example is education. Once a modern school system has been introduced, further expenditures in education seem not to produce any significant improvements.

- Parallel change takes place without convergence. An example is the remaining gap in wealth separating the less developed and more industrialized countries.

- Convergence masks diversity. Macro-level statistical indicators are by definition summaries of many single, discrete subsystems. These statistics are composites of several different indicators. Such summary indicators may become more alike with economic development, but they may mask diversity or actual divergence in the component elements of the summary indicator. An example is convergence of the percentage of GNI devoted to public expenditure on education in the West. Underneath this common convergence there was a marked divergence in how the extra money was apportioned among the three levels of education.

- Change patterns may vary by subsystem and within subsystems. Some types of clothing may diffuse and converge fast (blue jeans), while this is not representative for the clothing category.

- With respect to consumption, some patterns converge significantly, whereas others do not, and the rate of convergence varies between product categories.[30]

Measuring Convergence/Divergence

Convergence or divergence can be measured by computing the coefficients of variation (the ratio of the standard deviation to the mean) and comparing them over time. The coefficient of variation (CV) is explained in Williamson and Fleming, who prefer the coefficient of variation rather than

> the more common alternatives such as the standard deviation or variance because the coefficient of variation is adjusted for shifts in the mean (i.e., a 10-point spread is likely to have a different interpretation around a mean of 150 than around a mean of 15). The greater the decrease in the coefficient of variation over a specified period of time, the greater the convergence.[31]

When data from one source are available for different time periods, the mean convergence per year can be calculated. Williamson and Fleming express the mean convergence per year symbolically as follows:

$$\text{MC/year} = \frac{(CV_{t1} - CV_{t2})}{CV_{t1}} \times 100 \,/\, (t_2 - t_1)$$

where MC/year = mean convergence per year, CV_{t1} = coefficient of variation at the earlier date, CV_{t2} = coefficient of variation at the later date, t_1 = the earlier date, and t_2 = the later date. Implicit in this statistic is the simplifying assumption that any 10-, 20-, or 30-year period is equivalent to another. When comparing convergence trends for different length time spans, one will notice some variation in the rate of convergence from one period to another.

If convergence is calculated for the degree of industrial and economic development of countries, rates of convergence or divergence will vary for different groups of countries. In order to analyze the varying influence of national wealth, several groups should be assembled of economically heterogeneous and homogeneous countries. Examples provided in this book are for three groups of countries: an economically heterogeneous group of 44 countries worldwide,[32] an economically more homogeneous group of 26 countries worldwide (GNI/capita > US$8,000),[33] and an economically homogeneous group of 15 countries in Europe.[34] If no time series are available, differences in convergence can be demonstrated by comparing CVs of heterogeneous and homogeneous economic regions.

CONVERGENCE/DIVERGENCE IN CONSUMER BEHAVIOR

Analysis of time series data on consumption and ownership of various product categories demonstrates that at macro level and at micro level both convergence and divergence take place, but to varying degrees in different regions. If products converge across countries, convergence is weakest in economically heterogeneous regions and strongest in economically homogeneous regions. But even in economically homogeneous regions, such as Europe, only a few cases of true convergence can be demonstrated. In many cases differences are stable over time or countries diverge. If ownership of products converges, it does not imply that usage also converges. People may own modern technology, but they do not use it the same way and for the same purposes across countries. So, even if convergence is found at macro level, substantial differences are likely to exist at micro level.

In Europe, for 20 product categories reviewed[35] in 1997, the coefficients of variation (CVs) varied from 0.66 for sales of real jewelry per capita to 0.11 for television sets per 1,000 people. Only three product categories had a CV below 0.20, which suggests a threshold of convergence across countries. These are television sets per 1,000 people (0.11), fixed telephone lines per 1,000 people (0.17), and automobiles per 1,000 people (0.18).

A few examples illustrate the convergence/divergence process. Between 1960 and 1997, in Europe the CV for television sets owned per 1,000 people decreased from 1.00 in 1960 to 0.30 in 1975 and to 0.11 in 1997, with the mean rate of convergence per year being 2.4%. Between 1996 and 2000 (the last year the World Bank published data on ownership of TV sets per 1,000 people), ownership diverged, with a mean rate of divergence per year being 5.77%. The CV for radios was 0.33 in 1960 and decreased to 0.24 in the next 10 years. After that year it increased to 0.38 in the year 2000, with mean divergence per year being 1.94%. In the 40 years between 1960 and 2000, the average annual rate of divergence of radios per 1,000 people was 0.38%. After the year 2000, no more data on radio ownership were published, because nowadays people listen to radio broadcasts in many different ways. The differences between countries with respect to newspaper circulation have remained more or less stable in the past 50 years and have slightly diverged in Europe. The examples are illustrated in Figures 3.1, 3.2, and 3.3.

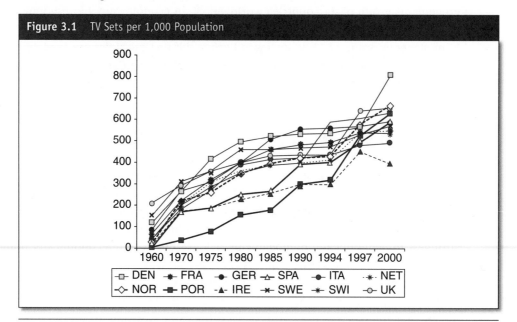

Figure 3.1 TV Sets per 1,000 Population

SOURCES: United Nations Statistical Yearbooks and World Bank Development Indicators (see Appendix B)

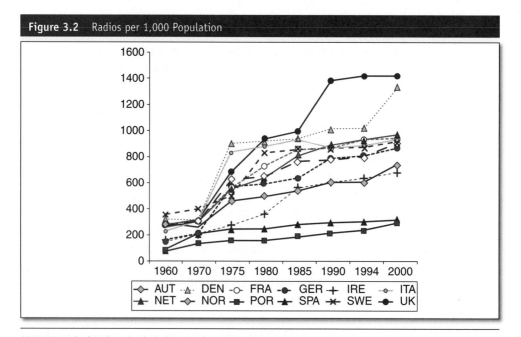

Figure 3.2 Radios per 1,000 Population

SOURCES: United Nations Statistical Yearbooks and World Bank Development Indicators (see Appendix B)

Figure 3.3   Newspaper Circulation per 1,000 Population

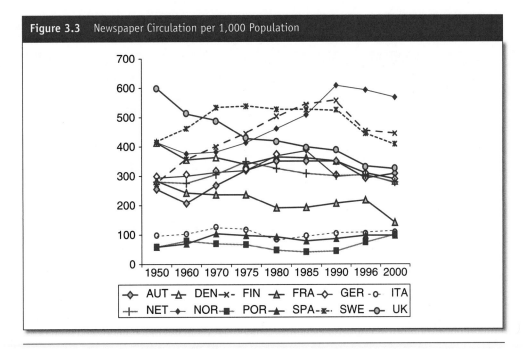

SOURCES: United Nations Statistical Yearbooks and World Bank Development Indicators (see Appendix B)

Table 3.1 presents the means of convergence or divergence per year at macro level for GNI per capita and eight product categories (fixed telephone lines, passenger cars, television sets, radios, newspapers, PCs per 1,000 population, Internet users per 100 people, and mobile phone subscribers per 100 people) for several time periods, for the country groups worldwide 44, developed 26, and for Europe 15. In the long term, in economically homogeneous Europe, at macro level the more expensive products that are linked with economic development converged fastest, whereas older, cheaper products such as radios and newspapers diverged. As a result of replacing fixed telephone lines with mobile phones in Europe, countries diverged after 1996 with respect to fixed telephone lines.[36]

The previous examples are all at macro level. More interesting are micro-level data—what people actually do with the products they own. Data for calculating convergence/divergence at micro level are not readily available worldwide. Some data are available for Europe, but only for shorter time spans. These data provide evidence of both convergence and divergence. There may be 100% or higher penetration of TV sets, but viewing time varies considerably and diverges across Europe. This is illustrated in Figure 3.4.

Countries have converged for the total number of passenger cars per 1,000 people, but the distribution across populations, numbers owned per household, or type of car owned

Table 3.1   Mean Convergence or Divergence per Year (%) at Macro Level

		Worldwide 44	Developed 26	Europe 15
GNI/capita	1994–2006	**−0.57**	0.30	1.39
Fixed telephone lines per 1,000 population	1966–1996	1.34	2.11	2.28
	1996–2007	0.60	1.05	**−0.05**
Passenger cars per 1,000 population	1960–1990	1.52	1.98	1.96
	1990–2003	0.81	1.90	3.68
Television sets per 1,000 population	1960–1996	1.83	2.13	2.42
	1996–2000	0	**−1.79**	**−5.77**
Radios per 1,000 population	1960–2000	0.75	0.79	**−0.38**
Newspapers per 1,000 population	1950–2000	0.18	**−0.11**	**−0.04**
PCs per 1,000 population	1996–2006	0.75	1.25	1.91
Internet users per 100 population	2002–2007	5.32	6.80	9.00
Mobile phone subscribers per 100 population	2000–2007	7.35	2.04	**−16.6**

SOURCES: UN Statistical Yearbooks; World Bank Development Indicators; ITU: ICT Development Index (see Appendix B)

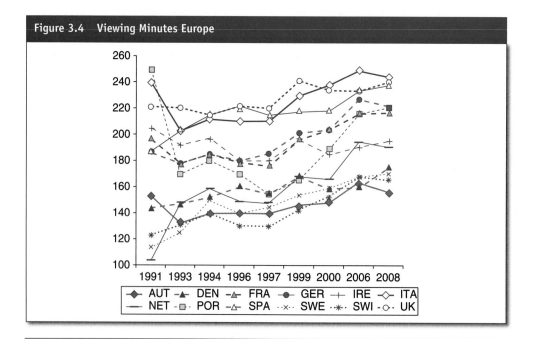

Figure 3.4   Viewing Minutes Europe

SOURCE: IP TV (see Appendix B)

diverge. Table 3.2 presents convergence and divergence at micro level for a few product categories in 15 European countries. Countries diverged with respect to having "only one" car in the family, but converged with respect to having two cars and three cars.[37] For daily viewing minutes, countries converged between 1991 and 1993 and diverged after 1993. Between 1999 and 2008 the differences were stable. Taking the groups of people in a country that were heavy TV viewers from EMS, countries slightly diverged. Countries also diverged with respect to heavy print usage. Whereas countries converged with respect to visits to the theatre, they diverged with respect to visiting the cinema. Countries also diverged with respect to consumption of fresh coffee.

Examples of divergence are noted in many other product categories, for example, consumption of milk and ice cream diverging in the past 20 years. For many food products, the differences have remained more or less the same.

Stability

In addition to convergence or divergence, in many cases differences are stable over time. In Chapter 2 we pointed at the stability of cultural values over time. The percentages of general life satisfaction as presented in Chapter 2 are consistently correlated with low uncertainty avoidance. In some cases cultural relationships are even becoming stronger.

Table 3.2   Convergence/Divergence per Year at Micro Level

Cars: One car in family	1997–2007	−4.70
Cars: Two cars in family	1997–2007	3.30
Cars: Three cars in family	1997–2007	1.14
TV: Daily viewing minutes	1999–2008	0
Heavy TV viewing	1997–2007	−0.60
Heavy print usage	1997–2007	−4.50
Three to five visits to theatre past year	1997–2007	4.30
Three to five visits to cinema past year	1997–2007	−0.50
Consumption of fresh coffee	1997–2008	−2.90

SOURCES: EMS 1997 and 2007, IP TV, Euromonitor (see Appendix B)

An example of how value differences can increasingly be explained by cultural variables can be found in the Reader's Digest (2001) report, "European Trusted Brands." In the survey, a few questions about the degree of trust in institutions such as the police and the legal system were repeated from an earlier survey by Reader's Digest (1991). Differences in trust in the police and the legal system correlate significantly with Hofstede's cultural dimension power distance: in cultures of high power distance there is less trust than in cultures of low power distance. Regression analysis shows that for the 13 countries[38] involved in both surveys, in 1991 the percentage of variance explained by power distance was 52% for trust in the police and 41% for trust in the legal system. In 2001 the figures were 72% and 69%. In 10 years, with increased wealth, the differences between countries increased and the explanation by culture became more pronounced.

With respect to some consumption differences, we also find stable or increasing cultural relationships. The Belgians drink 10 times as much mineral water as the British and 6 times as much as the Dutch, their neighbors in Europe. Although the quality of tap water has improved all over Europe, consumption of mineral water has increased, and differences have remained similar since 1970 or have become larger. These differences are related to Hofstede's dimension uncertainty avoidance, which includes values of purity. The significance of the correlations has become stronger over time. In France, Germany, Italy, and Belgium, all high uncertainty avoidance cultures, people drink increasing volumes of mineral water, as compared to the United Kingdom and Scandinavia, cultures of low uncertainty avoidance. Table 3.3 presents the correlation coefficients and percentages of variance explained in stepwise regression analysis for 15 European countries.

Table 3.3   Mineral Water Consumption, Europe

	Product Moment Correlations					Stepwise Regression
	GNI/cap	PDI	IDV	MAS	UAI	Predictors
1970	.31	.32	−.21	.24	.46*	None
1991	.21	.32	−.05	.53*	.57*	UAI+ ($R^2 = .32$)
1997	.04	.56*	−.10	.57*	.73***	UAI+ ($R^2 = .53$)
2003	−.23	.60*	−.14	.56*	.73***	UAI+ ($R^2 = .53$); MAS ($R^2 = .69$)

SOURCES: Reader's Digest Surveys 1970 and 1991, Euromonitor 1997 and Bottled Water Corporation 2004 (see Appendix B)

NOTE: 1970: Drink taken in the past year: mineral spring water; 1991: Drinking mineral water almost every day; 1997: Mineral water sales, liters per capita; 2003: Sales bottled water in liters per capita

Convergence/Divergence: A Pattern

There is a pattern of convergence/divergence. For durable products—in particular those related to wealth, such as passenger cars, television sets, and computers—initially, with increased wealth, countries converge, but in the developed world, at a certain level of wealth, convergence reaches a ceiling after which there is no further convergence, and differences remain stable or increase. With converging wealth, convergence of consumption turns into divergence. For "old" products such as newspapers and radio, that ceiling was reached long ago; for numbers of TV sets, the ceiling was reached in 1997. New products such as computers have not yet reached a ceiling, and differences between countries are still large. The point of convergence lies in the future. But it can be predicted by understanding the pattern of the old products.

At macro level, products linked with economic development of countries have converged fastest in the economically converging Europe, whereas older, cheaper products such as radios and circulation of newspapers have diverged. However, this convergence at macro level is not accompanied by convergence at micro level, what people do with products they own. New media and technology are converging at macro level, but differences at micro level emerged soon after introduction. Internet penetration converges, but the way the Internet is used varies, as is described in Chapter 7.

NATIONAL WEALTH AS AN EXPLAINING VARIABLE

The assumed strongest influence on consumer behavior is income. The amount of disposable income is expected to determine buying behavior once basic needs are fulfilled. This sounds logical, yet what must be considered to be basic needs are not the same all over the world. In affluent societies, basic needs may include television-watching capability in the home; in others it is just limited to food and shelter. In the developed world, what is viewed as a necessity will not only vary by country but also will change over time.

> In 1999 the standard package of items considered as necessity in the United States consisted of an answering machine, a cordless phone, at least one television, cable TV, a VCR, a stereo cassette player and CD player, a microwave oven, dishwasher, washer and dryer, air conditioning, two cars. Twenty-seven percent of households making more than US$100,000 said they couldn't afford everything they really need.[39]
>
> In 2006, on top of the list of things Americans said they couldn't live without were a car (91%), a clothes washer (90%), a clothes dryer (83%), home air conditioning (70%), a microwave (68%), TV set (64%), car air conditioning (59%), and a home computer (51%).[40]

A commonly used measure to compare national wealth is the *gross domestic product* (GDP) or the similar measure *gross national product* (GNP*)*. In 2001 the terminology was changed to *gross national income* (GNI).[41] There are some problems when comparing countries using GNP data. First, for comparison, the data must be converted into a common currency. The U.S. dollar is commonly used for this purpose. Fluctuations in the exchange rates disturb the picture. A second problem with the conventional GNP calculation is that it includes all efforts in a country. That does not, however, necessarily reflect the exact welfare of the community. In an effort to improve comparability, the United Nations and the World Bank developed a method to calculate a "real" GNP on an internationally comparable scale. Originally this "new" GNP was called ICP, named after the UN International Comparison Program. Later it was called "GNP measured at PPP" (purchasing power parity). The World Bank publishes the data in the annual World Development Reports. The World Bank definition of GNP measured at PPP is "GNP converted to U.S. dollars by the purchasing power parity (PPP) exchange rate." At the PPP rate, one dollar has the same purchasing power over domestic GNP that the U.S. dollar has over U.S. GNP; dollars converted by this method are sometimes called "international dollars."[42] Because differences between countries with respect to purchasing power parity are expected to better explain product consumption than GNP per capita, PPP data of the relevant years should ideally be used. As these data are only available from 1990 onward, they cannot be used for time-series analysis starting at an earlier date. However, income per capita at PPP and GNP per capita are closely related. The correlation coefficients between GNP and PPP vary between .93 and .95 for the group of 44 countries worldwide. For the 15 countries in developed Europe, the correlation coefficients vary between .90 and .95. In this book we use GNI, and in all calculations in this book GNI per capita at PPP is used.

Whereas between 1995 and 2005 worldwide, 62 countries slightly converged with respect to GNI per capita (0.95% per year), convergence was stronger for a group of 28 wealthy countries (2.4% per year). Whereas in Europe and Asia countries converged, in Latin America they diverged. In 2005 worldwide individualism explained 55% of variance and low power distance an additional 6%.

Composite Development Indicators

Much cross-national consumer research uses macro-environmental indicators of economic development. Countries tend to be classified on a single dimension (e.g., GNI per capita) or on composite variables consisting of other developmental variables, for example, resource development, economic and demographic mobilization, and societal development, such as urbanization, literacy, or energy consumption. In such studies,[43] researchers form comparative clusters of countries and compute economic development factors from a large number of phenomena related to economic development. Examples of variables used are electricity production, urbanization, school enrollment per capita, imports and exports per GNI, number of air passengers/km, life expectancy, literacy, percentage of population in agriculture, average work week, percentage employed in service, physicians per capita, manufacturing percentage of GNI, and private spending as a percentage of GNI. Examples of consumption-related macro variables used in comparative studies are per capita ownership of cars, radios, television sets, telephones, energy consumption, hospital beds, foreign visitors per capita, tourist's expenditure per capita, newspaper circulation, and other aspects of media availability.[44] Such composite macro indicators are used for many purposes, for example, to study patterns of media use in Europe,[45] to measure the degree of materialism,[46] or for calculating modernity.[47] Most of such indicators that make up composite variables (e.g., possession of cars, TVs, PCs, video cameras, and the like) are interdependent and are each correlated with per capita GNI. Such factors are basically a function of economic development and an indirect measurement of national wealth. Consumer researcher Alladi Venkatesh points out:

> Many economically oriented consumer studies are conducted without regard to the intrinsic values studied. . . . Poverty is studied abstractly as a condition related to lack of education, infrastructure, or adequate housing. . . . The object . . . [of a] study may be poverty, but it is never poor people. In particular, economists trained in the neoclassical tradition cannot deal with the whys and wherefores of their questions, either in historical or cultural terms, and they avoid, therefore, culture-theoretical explanations.[48]

OVER TIME, CULTURE REPLACES INCOME AS AN EXPLANATORY VARIABLE

Europe is an interesting area for analyzing the effects of converging wealth. The region can serve as an example of how, with convergence of national wealth, cultural variables can better explain differences in consumption. Analysis of time series data reveals that country-level ownership of many products and services is initially best predicted by national wealth. At a certain point in time, culture replaces wealth as a predictor variable for ownership and/or usage. The same effect is found when selecting a group of wealthy countries from a worldwide database. Several examples demonstrate this process.

Radios, TV Sets, and Cars

Consider the adoption of radio, television sets, and automobiles in Europe. Table 3.4 contains CVs for these products for 15 European countries for selected years from 1960 to 2000 as well as the proportion of variance (R^2) respectively explained by national wealth or Hofstede's dimensions individualism and long-term orientation. Time series data for radios per 1,000 population show a breaking point between 1980 and 1990, when culture replaced income as an explanatory variable. In 1990 individualism explained 72% of variance of radio ownership, and radios per 1,000 people were no longer significantly correlated with national wealth.

In 1960, country differences in ownership of television sets per 1,000 people were related to individualism. From 1970 to 1994, country differences in television ownership were related to GNI per capita. After 1990, the differences between countries became so minor that neither national wealth nor individualism was an effective predictor.

A similar pattern was found for passenger cars. Until 1970, differences in the numbers of automobiles per 1,000 people across 15 countries in Europe were

Table 3.4   CV and R^2 Values for Durable Products Over Time

	Radios/1,000			TV Sets/1,000			Passenger Cars/1,000		
	CV	GNI/cap R^2	IDV R^2	CV	GNI/cap R^2	IDV R^2	CV	GNI/cap R^2	IDV/LTO R^2
1960	.33	.81		1.00		.37	.56	.80	
1970	.24	.69		.30	.61		.34	.82	IDV .91
1980	.36	.58		.24	.55		.23	.69	IDV .82
1990	.35		.72	.17	.35		.18	.47	LTO .66
1997	.36		.48	.11	none		.17	none	LTO .61
2000*	.38		.42	.16	none		.12	none	LTO .46

SOURCES: Hofstede et al. (2010) (see Appendix A); United Nations Statistical Yearbooks; World Development Indicators (see Appendix B)

*Data for passenger cars are from 2003

explained by national wealth only. After 1970, individualism became another explaining variable. After 1997 in Europe, only long-term orientation explained differences in ownership.

If we look at a larger scale, worldwide (41 countries,[49] see Table 3.5) from 1960 to 1970 GNI is the main explaining variable for ownership of cars. From 1970 onward, individualism is the second explaining variable, and in 1980 individualism becomes the first

Table 3.5   Passenger Cars per 1,000 People 1960–2003: CVs and Explaining Variables

Worldwide 41 Countries							
Year	CV	Pred.1	R^2	Pred.2	R^2	Pred.3	R^2
1960	1.39	GNI	.81				
1970	1.04	GNI	.88	IDV	.91		
1980	.90	IDV	.79	GNI	.88		
1990	.84	IDV	.76	GNI	.87		
1998	.77	IDV	.70	GNI	.82	UAI	.87
2003	.68	IDV	.57	GNI	.68	UAI	.76

Worldwide 26 Countries GNI/capita at PPP More Than US$17,000 in 2006					
Year	CV	Pred.1	R^2	Pred.2	R^2
1960	1.00	GNI	.81		
1970	.63	GNI	.80		
1980	.50	IDV	.76	GNI	.82
1990	.42	IDV	.74	GNI	.81
1998	.37	IDV	.62	LTO	.69
2003	.31	IDV	.43		

SOURCES: Hofstede et al. (2010) (see Appendix A); World Development Indicators (see Appendix B)

explaining variable, with after 1998 uncertainty avoidance being an additional predictor. The same pattern is found for 26 rich countries worldwide, where in 1998 long-term orientation became an additional explaining variable.

Next to this, many aspects of cars are culture related. Consumers in masculine cultures are more interested in the size and power of the engine than are consumers in feminine cultures. In high power distance cultures, consumers are particularly interested in the design of an automobile (for car motives, see Chapter 5).

Information Technology

Another example is how information technology developed at the end of the 20th century when ownership of new technology was concentrated in developed countries. In 2000, the 29 OECD (Organisation for Economic Cooperation and Development) member states representing the postindustrial economies contained 97% of all Internet hosts, 92% of the market in production and consumption of computer hardware and services, and 86% of all Internet users. The whole of sub-Saharan Africa contained less than 1% of the world's online community.[50] In 2007, Internet use and computer ownership worldwide were still mainly related to GNI per capita, and the convergence process is slow.

In the developed world, low uncertainty avoidance, a measure of innovativeness, tends to explain variance of penetration of new technology products. Countries scoring low to medium on the uncertainty avoidance index (e.g., the United States, New Zealand, Australia, the Netherlands, and the Scandinavian countries) were the first to embrace the Internet and still are leading with respect to usage of it, whereas countries of high uncertainty avoidance (e.g., Italy, France, and Germany) have been lagging. In 2007, across a group of 26 relatively wealthy countries, worldwide GNI per capita was still the main explaining variable, but in addition long-term orientation explained variance as well as low uncertainty avoidance, low masculinity, and low power distance. With increasing penetration of computers and the Internet, differences in usage are also found. Frequent usage is related to low masculinity. In feminine cultures, people use new technology to enhance quality of life more than productivity. Collectivists prefer person-to-person contact and have been late adopting the Internet for personal communication. Individualists use the Internet more for buying products as well as using it for e-mail (see Table 3.6). The data are from different databases, but all for a similar number of mostly wealthy countries.

In sum, when countries have converged with respect to national wealth, cultural variables start to explain more of the differences in country-level consumer behavior.

Table 3.6   Internet Usage Differences in Developed World: Explaining Variables

	Predictors	R^2
Proportion of Households With Internet 2007	GNI/cap	.51
26 countries, worldwide	LTO	.62
	UAI–	.74
	MAS–	.81
	PDI–	.85
Use Internet every day 2007, 24 countries, Europe	MAS–	.43
Almost never access Internet for personal use	IDV–	.20
25 countries, Europe	MAS	.35
Buy on the Internet, 25 countries, Europe	IDV	.38
Use for e-mail, 25 countries, Europe	IDV	.31

SOURCES: Hofstede et al. (2010); ITU report 2009; EBS 278 (2007); Flash EB 241 (2008) (see Appendix B)

WITH INCREASED WEALTH, CULTURAL VALUES BECOME MANIFEST

The previous data have shown that the wealthier countries become, the more manifest is the influence of culture on consumption and consumer behavior. This phenomenon is reflected in many changes of the past decades, such as increased interest in local music and TV programs, which in turn resulted in localization of some of the international media such as MTV and CNN. With increased wealth, cultural relationships are stable or become stronger.

Higher levels of wealth do not change traditional values. Longitudinal comparisons of economy and culture by Van de Vliert show that higher levels of economic growth are not related to decreases in traditional values.[51] More discretionary income gives people more freedom to express themselves, and that expression will be based in part on their national value system. Wealth brings choice. It enables people to choose leisure time or buy status products or devote free time to charitable work or to self-education. Two distinct philosophies on what people are expected to do with their incremental income are (1) that increased wealth leads to greater materialism and overconsumption, or (2) that with increased wealth people turn away from more consumption. Inglehart's[52] study of changing values from materialist to postmaterialist values follows the latter line. According to Inglehart, with prosperity and economic security, further income does not lead to higher levels of subjective well-being. People take their prosperity for granted and transfer their focus to other parts of life, such as politics and the quality of physical and social environment. However, no evidence can be found that people consume less with increased wealth.

New Manifestations of "Old" Values

Whereas in many East Asian countries with economic development and modernity some practices changed dramatically, important cultural values have not changed or have become even stronger. Inkeles[53] measured change and stability in five countries on the Pacific Rim (Japan, Taiwan, Singapore, Korea, and China). Whereas in Chengdu in China in 1933, 68% of marriages still were "arranged" by the parents, in the 1980s it was only 2%. A similar change was found in Taiwan. At the same time there are indications that some Asian populations are reinvigorating traditions. With increased wealth, people also seek outward signs of social respectability, which is expressed by participating in rituals such as ancestor worship and religious practices. An important East Asian value is "filial piety," a son's obligations of duty that affiliate him to his father. In surveys in Japan, the preference for filial piety has been rising year after year. In 1963, the first year this question was asked, filial piety was selected by 61% of the respondents, but by 1983 it had risen in popularity to 73%; it held its rank as the number one value in subsequent surveys through 1993. In the early 1990s, in Baoding, China, approximately 95% of both elders and adult children stressed their commitment to filial piety. Also among young people, both in Beijing and Hong Kong China, Chinese moral values such as filial piety are still heavily emphasized.[54]

When values become manifest, this can be recognized in behavior. An example is the change in women's roles. Everywhere women's roles change, but they change more in some cultures than in others. With economic development, variance in role differentiation becomes manifest. Cultural values influencing role behavior, which are latent in the more traditional societies, become manifest when countries modernize. An example is for shopping behavior. In 1991 the Reader's Digest survey divided main food shoppers into males and females. For 16 countries in Europe, there was a significant correlation between cultural masculinity and the proportion of main food shoppers who are women ($r = .50*$). Because of stronger role differentiation, more females will do the daily food shopping in masculine cultures than in feminine cultures. In feminine cultures, males will be relatively more involved in the daily household chores than in masculine cultures. When the more traditional countries of Spain, Portugal, and Greece are excluded from the calculation, significance becomes much stronger ($r = .77***$).

OTHER MEASUREMENT VARIABLES

Economic development is linked to a syndrome of changes that include urbanization, mass education, and communications development that are interdependent. Such socioeconomic variables are frequently used in cross-cultural studies, but they are indirect measures of economic development. Levels of education are indicators of economic development, and education influences income levels. Education also indoctrinates people to learn specific values.[55] In the following sections, several sociodemographic variables are discussed: urbanization, population density, education, age distribution, household and family, social class, and ethnicity. Also, the function of climate as an explanatory variable is discussed.

URBANIZATION

There is no universally accepted standard for distinguishing *urban* and *rural*. The World Bank's definition for urban population is the midyear population of areas defined as urban in each country and reported to the United Nations.[56] Most countries have adopted an urban classification related to the size or characteristics of settlements, others have based their definition on certain infrastructure, and some are based on administrative characteristics.

The distinction *urban/rural* is mainly important for understanding differences within large developing economies, such as China, where consumer spending still is concentrated in a number of key cities and provinces, and urban household disposable income is much higher than rural income. In 1996 in China, urban residents accounted for about 43% of China's population, according to a World Bank estimate, but this is changing fast. Populations of the world's largest metropolitan conglomerations have been growing. In 2000, the Tokyo metropolitan area consisted of 34.5 million inhabitants; next was Mexico City with 18.1 inhabitants.

The divide, urban/rural, is less pronounced in developed economies, and there is not one pattern. In Luxemburg, Denmark, and the United Kingdom, for example, in 1999, in sparsely populated areas average household expenditure was higher than in densely populated areas. In Portugal, Italy, and Spain, with larger rural areas, it was the other way around.[57] In the developed world, urbanization differences have little explaining power.

Urbanization and Housing

There are relationships between urbanization and type of housing, but this relationship rarely has explanatory power. In the less urbanized countries, people live more in apartment blocks, whereas in the more urbanized countries, people live more in one-family houses and have more private gardens. A better explanation is the relationship with individualism. In individualistic cultures, people live more in one-family houses and have more private gardens, whereas living in apartment blocks generally is correlated with collectivism. The type of housing in Britain and in the United States can be viewed as an expression of the individualistic lifestyle in general.[58]

Increased urbanization is assumed to turn collectivistic societies into individualistic societies because people cannot live anymore in the extended household. As yet, there is no evidence to support this assumption. Although urbanization tends to break up the joint household of the extended family in favor of more nuclear households, this does not imply decreasing extended family values. Despite changing living conditions, the Indian family always remains an extended one. The extended family maintains strong family ties, gets together on holidays, makes mutual decisions on important matters, and sometimes maintains joint ownership.[59] Close emotional bonds between generations may continue even though material interdependence weakens.[60] There is no evidence of convergence of family and kin patterns resulting from increased urbanization. Analysis of social relationships between parents and children, brothers and sisters, and friends has not shown a declining frequency of contact with relatives. The mobile phone has become an important communication means to maintain these social relationships. An important argument for using the mobile phone is to keep contact with family and friends, and in 2008 this correlated negatively with individualism ($r = -.38*$).[61]

Urbanization and Retail Structure

One would expect that the degree of urbanization would influence the retail structure of countries. Low urbanization would be expected to influence remote buying methods such as mail order or cyber-shopping. Data of 2000[62] on the percentage share of mail order in total retail trade sales, however, do not show such a relationship. The only relationship is with GNI per capita. It is not a lack of infrastructure that makes people adopt new distance buying opportunities. Increased wealth offers more choice that people, irrespective of urbanization, want to exercise. Additional facilities mainly attract people to do more of what they were used to do. If people like shopping and buying, they will try all sorts of new types of distribution. Findings from Roper Starch Worldwide[63] confirm this phenomenon. A survey of 1997 found that people who live in countries with well-established infrastructures are most likely to buy things in a remote fashion. Japanese and Britons, for example, ranked high in their propensity to buy things over the phone, followed by Americans and the Dutch. There are few meaningful significant correlations between urbanization and consumption or consumption-related phenomena. If significant correlations are found, other variables usually are better predictors.

POPULATION DENSITY

Another variable that is thought to be useful for measuring country-level differences is population density. *Population density* is defined as "midyear population divided by land area."[64] A more simple definition is the number of people per square kilometer. The degree of population density might influence various habits and product ownership, such as housing, the use of cable versus satellite television, and mobile phones. However, there are few significant correlations between consumer behavior data and population density. Only one meaningful significant correlation was between population density and mobile phone ownership in Europe ($r = -.53*$), but correlations with the cultural variables are much more significant. In the food category, significant correlations exist between population density and volume sales of milk and soft drinks, but correlations with other variables are much more significant. Worldwide and in the group of 26 developed countries, population density correlates significantly with uncertainty avoidance ($r = -.41***$ and $r = -.40*$). This relationship does not—as far as our knowledge goes—explain the differences. Because of the interdependence with other variables, population density is not a useful measurement of consumption differences.

EDUCATION

Education levels of countries are a function of national wealth. With respect to secondary education, worldwide (44 countries), countries converged until 1980, but after that year convergence stopped. There still are differences between countries, and these remain stable. A threshold of convergence has been reached at a CV of 0.35 worldwide and of 0.06 in Europe, which demonstrates that with respect to education levels, Europe is a truly homogeneous area. Convergence also takes place with respect to tertiary education. GNI per capita consistently explains variance of education levels, so wealth is the driver of education. Only in Europe, the relationship disappeared after 1990. Because of the interdependence with economic development, education is not a meaningful explaining variable at the national level.

AGE DISTRIBUTION

The age distribution of populations influences buying patterns of societies. In economically developed countries, senior citizens generally have a sizeable disposable income that is spent on goods that are often of little interest to the younger generation.

Age distribution is related to economic development and to culture. Worldwide,[65] the percentages of people under 15 years old are negatively correlated with GNI per capita, and the percentages of people over 65 years old are positively correlated with GNI per capita. The wealthier nations are, the longer the life expectancy people have. This relationship is much weaker in the developed countries. In particular in Europe, where economies have converged, in all countries people have increasingly longer life expectancy and lower birth rates, although the decline of birthrates varies by culture. Birthrates are lower in long-term orientation cultures, but also in higher uncertainty avoidance cultures. Worldwide (57 countries) GNI per capita explains 36%, long-term orientation an additional 22%, and uncertainty avoidance an additional 4%. In a group of 28 wealthy countries worldwide, long-term orientation is the main explaining variable, with 32% explained. It looks like in the long-term oriented cultures parents have deeper thoughts about the consequences of having children. Michael Minkov offers the following quote about this:

> When my father worked in Algeria (whose birth rate is second only to some equatorial countries in Africa), he asked some poor people why they had so many children and who would feed them. Their answer was "Who feeds the birds in the sky? Allah takes care of everything as he sees fit."[66]

Figure 3.5 illustrates differences and similarities in age distribution for four sets of four countries each. Figure 3.5a shows the age distributions for Mexico, the United States, United Kingdom, and Spain. It shows the large percentage of people over 65 years old in Spain and the United Kingdom as compared to the United States that shows a distinct pattern, probably because of the heterogeneity of the population. Mexico is an example of a developing economy with a large percentage of young people and a small percentage of old people. Differences in economic development can also be recognized when comparing four Latin American countries in Figure 3.5b, with Bolivia showing the

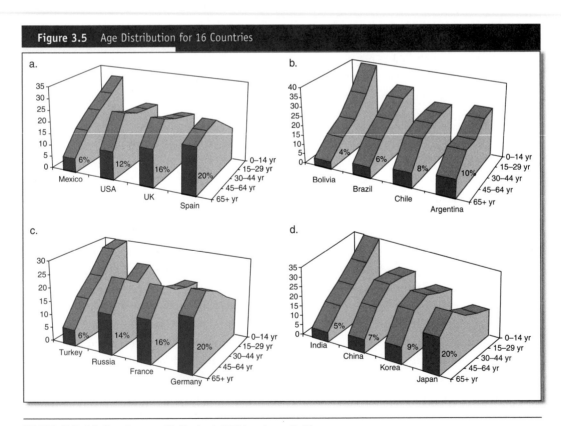

Figure 3.5   Age Distribution for 16 Countries

SOURCE: United Nations Demographic Yearbook 2006 (see Appendix B)

typical age distribution of a developing economy with a small percentage of old people and a large percentage of young people, whereas Argentina has the age distribution of a more developed economy. Figure 3.5c shows three European countries and Turkey. The age distributions of Germany and France represent the typical developed "old" countries, comparable to Spain and Japan. Turkey shows the shape of a developing economy. Russia, however, has a quite specific shape, with a clear dip for the age group 30–44. According to the World Health Organization,[67] this adult mortality is due to alcoholism in Russia. In that age group, alcohol not only affects mortality from cirrhosis of the liver and cardiovascular disease, but also through violence and road accidents caused by alcohol abuse. In countries with similar high alcohol consumption as the Russian federation, the same age distribution pattern is found. Such countries are Ukraine, Moldova, and the Slovak Republic.

Finally, Figure 3.5d illustrates the pattern for four Asian countries that show similar differences between developed and developing economies as in the other regions.

In consumer research, different age distributions are used across countries. One reason can be that attitudes to age vary by culture. In high power distance cultures, for example, middle age starts earlier than in low power distance cultures.[68]

HOUSEHOLD AND FAMILY

Household structures vary worldwide. Household size—the number of people per household—varies from 2.13 in Sweden to 6.71 in Pakistan.[69] Generally in lower-income and collectivistic cultures household sizes are larger. In collectivistic cultures, multigenerational families are common, where children care for their parents in their homes. The age at which people marry varies. In particular in Europe, couples are waiting longer to get married, if they get married at all. Living alone and cohabitation, even if a couple gets children, has become more popular in northern European countries. Table 3.7 shows for 24 countries differences in age of women to get married. There are significant differences between countries with respect to the age women marry. Low GNI explains variance of the group 20–24, and high GNI explains variance of the age group 30–34, so in the wealthy countries women get married later. Variance of the group 25–29 is explained by long-term orientation, so in the long-term-oriented cultures a marriage age between 25 and 29 is viewed as the ideal age. In a few of the countries in the table, the percentages of age group 15–19 also are substantial, for example, in Brazil (18%) and in Mexico (25%).

The different stages of people's lives, from single to married, raising a family, and old age, are lifestyle stages that follow different age levels across countries. The classical—typically individualistic—distinction of lifestyle stages that influence buying behavior is young singles, newly married or cohabitating, full nest (parents with children), empty nest (children have left home). Developments like increased divorce rates add other distinctions,

Table 3.7   Marriage by Age of Bride, 2005

Country	Age of Marriage		
	20–24 %	25–29 %	30–34 %
Korea	15	47	18
Japan	20	41	23
Singapore	23	42	18
Kuwait	39	19	9
Venezuela	29	27	13
Chile	30	30	15
Brazil	32	24	12
Mexico	33	21	9
Czech Republic	23	41	16
Romania	34	28	11
Bulgaria	35	33	13
Poland	44	34	8
Spain	13	42	26
France	15	32	20
Austria	18	27	21
Italy (2003)	18	39	24
Greece	18	39	24
Portugal	26	37	16
Denmark	7	28	23
Sweden	9	24	26
Norway	14	29	23
U.K. (2002)	16	28	21
Australia	18	32	22
Canada	21	31	21

SOURCE: United Nations Demographic Yearbook 2007 (see Appendix B)

such as divorced single parents with children. In collectivistic cultures, there is a greater reliance on extended families for household chores and child care, and many children live with parents after they are married. In some European countries, children also remain living at home longer. In Italy, increasingly, young adults stay home with their mothers, reinforcing the role of the mother in the home.[70] Generally, the countries where young people stay at home longer because they get married later score high on uncertainty avoidance (UAI), which explains 24%, also in a group of rich countries where high UAI explains 30% of variance.[71]

In all societies, women have traditionally performed roles of mother, carer, and home provider more than do men. In the various phases of economic development, some of these roles were more pronounced than others. In the developed world, "housewives" used to be a category to be targeted by companies because of the sole involvement in the household by a majority of women. From the economic point of view, women could afford to stay home and dedicate themselves solely to doing household chores and raising children, whereas in the developing world working was a necessity, which was facilitated by the existence of an extended family that took care of the children.

In developed economies, increased education levels made women look for work outside the home, and the housewife in the old sense does not exist anymore. Increasingly, women have entered the labor force. The percentages of working women[72] of countries have converged between 1970 and 2004, but there still are differences.

Until 1998, variance of female share of the labor force was explained by national wealth. In that year, low masculinity started explaining variance. In order to become wealthy, women have to work. In turn, wealth leads to higher levels of education that lead to a greater drive for women to enter the labor force. However, in some cultures more women will work than in others. Table 3.8 (on page 98) shows how over time cultural variables take over income's explaining function. Gender equality of the low masculine cultures facilitates working by women because men share the caring roles. This is demonstrated by variance of working parttime by men, which is also explained by low masculinity (40%). In 1996, in the Netherlands 17% of working males worked part time; in 2007 this was 16%. In Denmark it was 10.8% in 1996, as compared with 12% in 2007. In Italy it was 3.1% in 1996 and 5% in 2007. In poor countries, part-time work by women is a luxury. In 2007, across 42 countries worldwide, 36% of variance of women's share of part-time employment was explained by GNI per capita and an additional 13% by masculinity. For a group of 25 wealthy countries (GNI per capita > US$17,000), masculinity is the only explaining variable, explaining 23% of variance. In the wealthy masculine cultures, the majority of men work full time and women part time, so the female share of part-time work is higher. In Austria it was 84%, in Germany 81%, and in Denmark 63%. Also in Asia we see these differences reflected: in Japan it was 72% and in Korea 59%.[73]

In 2008, when asked for the most practical ways to combine work and children, GNI per capita explained 21% of variance of the choice for both parents working part time; low

Table 3.8 Women's Share of Labor Force 1970–2004: Income and Cultural Variables

Worldwide 44	GNI/cap	PDI	IDV	MAS	UAI	Predictors	R^2	R^2
1970	.47***	−.32*	.51***	−.00	−.31*	IDV	.26	
1980	.59***	−.37**	.54***	−.17	−.40***	GNI/cap	.35	
1990	.62***	−.47***	.58***	−.17	−.29*	GNI/cap	.34	
1998	.63***	−.45***	.61***	−.24	−.29*	GNI/cap	.40	MAS– .46 IDV .52
2004	.64***	−.51***	.51***	−.03	−.14	GNI/cap	.41	

Developed 26	GNI/cap	PDI	IDV	MAS	UAI	Predictors	R^2	R^2
1970	.54***	−.47**	.42*	.07	−.22	GNI/cap	.29	
1980	.60***	−.38*	.32	−.35*	−.34*	GNI/cap	.36	
1990	.58***	−.47**	.49**	−.47**	−.40*	GNI/cap	.34	MAS– .52
1998	.46**	−.35*	.47**	−.48**	−.33*	MAS–	.23	IDV .42
2004	.48**	−.63***	.57***	−.43*	−.32	PDI–	.40	MAS– .53

Europe 15	GNI/cap	PDI	IDV	MAS	UAI	Predictors	R^2
1970	.55*	−.44*	.27	.09	−.31	GNI/cap	.30
1980	.47*	−.35	−.03	−.37	−.26	none	
1990	.39	−.26	.08	−.56*	−.35	MAS	−.32
1998	.29	−.08	.02	−.63**	−.21	MAS	−.40
2004	.46*	−.30	−.04	−.50*	−.35	none	

SOURCES: Hofstede et al. (2010) (see Appendix A); World Bank Development Reports (see Appendix B)

masculinity explained an additional 16%. For a group of 18 rich countries, low masculinity was the main explaining variable, explaining 27% of variance. In the masculine cultures, females prefer to stay home to look after the children. High masculinity explained 17% of variance of the choice for one parent working full time, and the other looking after children full time. For a group of 18 rich countries, masculinity explained 24%.[74]

In Italy and Germany, women tend to choose between work and children, whereas in the northern European countries women are more able to compromise and combine children and work because partners help more in the house. The percentages who say it is difficult to find the right work-life balance relates to high uncertainty avoidance, which explains 42%. For 28 rich countries, high uncertainty avoidance explains 53%.[75]

SOCIAL CLASS

Definitions of class structure vary from country to country. Next to changeable categorizations, there are more permanent, organized class structures. For marketing purposes, people are categorized in groups that are *not organized*. Classifications can be by gender (male-female), age, education, income, or occupation. Basically for marketing purposes, the Western social class system categorizes people according to wealth, which provides an indication of disposable income. However, with increased wealth, disposable income is decreasingly a factor that can explain variance. Other categorizations are by age group (e.g., teenagers, gray populations) or by life stage, such as yuppies (young urban professionals) or DINKs (double income, no kids). Not only do class systems differ in various parts of the world, the relative sizes of the classes vary with the relative prosperity of countries. Some class systems have a greater explanatory power of buying behavior than others.

An example of *organized* class is the Indian caste system that, although officially nonexistent, determines a person's rank in all areas of life. In developing economies that tend to be collectivistic and of high power distance, income inequality goes together with social inequality. Whereas in individualistic cultures individuals can categorize themselves according to social strata, in collectivistic cultures class does not belong solely to oneself but also to one's group, usually one's family, relatives, and kinship clan.[76]

The social class structure most often used in marketing in developed economies is that of the United States or adaptations of it. American society is usually described as a three-tier society, divided into upper, middle, and lower classes. Another distinction is between blue-collar and white-collar, a simple classification by occupation.

In the developed world, many class distinctions have become irrelevant with increased wealth. In the developing world, growing middle classes with increased spending power are expected to become new markets for multinational companies. However, both within countries and across countries, income inequality, popularly said the gap between the haves and have-nots, is increasing. In Latin America, the proportion of society considered to be middle class has shrunk since the 1990s. Real wages and purchasing power for the middle and lower classes have steadily declined, whereas the top 8–10% of its citizens hold a disproportionate amount of its wealth. In Brazil the median income of the wealthiest 10% of the population is almost 30 times greater than that of the poorest 40%, and their disposable income (after taxes, food, and housing are paid) is 80–100 times greater.[78]

Measuring Class

There are different ways to measure social class, and they produce different results. Consumers can be asked to self-assign themselves to social classes, people can be asked to assign others to class, or social class can be objectively measured. A most used objective measurement is by occupation, referring to the household head. An example is the measurement system of the United Kingdom, distinguishing among (a) upper middle class, consisting of professional, higher-managerial, senior civil servants; (b) middle class, consisting of middle managers or principle officers in local/central government; (c1) lower middle class, consisting of junior managers, routine white-collar or non-manual workers; (c2) skilled working class, consisting of skilled manual workers; (d) semiskilled and unskilled working class, consisting of manual workers, apprentices to skilled workers; (e) residual, consisting of those dependent on long-term state benefits. This sort of classification can be useful for understanding different habits, but not necessarily all consumption, because some working-class people may have more disposable income than higher-class categories. Linking class to profession implies that people may move from one class to another. Whereas in the United Kingdom in 1949, 43% said they were working class, in 1989 67% said they were working class. The percentages for middle class changed from 52% in 1949 to 30% in 1989. When people classify themselves to specific class categories, they may assume a class position that may be different from the position others would ascribe them to. In the United Kingdom in 1993, of 1,004 people questioned, 3 in 10 said they thought of themselves as belonging to a particular class. Nearly 4 in 10 of those in occupational classes (a) or (b), such as judges, professors, stockbrokers, and psychiatrists, described themselves as working class. Conversely, 1 in 7 in classes (d) or (e), including unskilled, manual workers, were convinced they were middle class.[79]

Whereas the need to categorize the self and others is strong in cultures of the configuration individualism/masculinity, it is much weaker in feminine cultures where people are less inclined to consider themselves better than others. Asking people to place themselves in a category that may be higher than others is suspect. Whereas, for example, in the United States (a masculine culture), students know their rank in class, this is not viewed as interesting knowledge in feminine cultures like the Netherlands and Scandinavian countries.

Class is a sensitive subject. So are ethnicity and race, and, to a lesser degree, religion and age. In the United States, people are categorized according to race, and people are asked to define their own race. Asking people to do so in the Netherlands would be unthinkable. This applies to many countries in Europe, where asking people to categorize themselves according to race and religion is illegal. In France, in 2007 an effort to make official records on ethnic, religious, or racial backgrounds of immigrants was overturned as unconstitutional.[80] On the other hand, in the United States one does not ask another's age, whereas this is usually a lesser problem in most of the countries in Europe. Another sensitive area in the United States is the male-female categorization. Usage of the terms *sex, masculine,* or *feminine* is considered not to be politically correct. The term used for the social functions of sex is *gender*. As a result, another term that is used for Hofstede's dimension masculinity/femininity is the "gender of nations," on which scale countries can score high ("tough") or low ("tender").[81]

ETHNICITY

In many countries, ethnic minorities have become interesting marketing target groups. The term *ethnic* is used for minority groups that are culturally or physically different from the dominant cultures of societies. Minorities in the world include a great variety of groups, from original populations overrun by immigrants (Native Americans, Australian Aborigines), to descendants of imported labor (African Americans, Turkish Germans), to natives of former colonies (Indians and Pakistanis in Britain), to international nomads (Roma or "Gypsies"), to ethnic migrants or refugees.[82] Ethnicity can be viewed as a catchall collective term that has replaced several other identifiers—race, religion, language, nationality—as a way to determine the social identity of groups.[83]

In consumer behavior, research interest in ethnicity is increasing because of the changing ethnic landscapes in the United States and in Europe. In the United States, the metaphor describing the American ethnic landscape as a "melting pot" is supplanted by the "tossed salad" metaphor. In some states, minorities have become majorities, which makes them attractive as market segments. In 2000, of the population of Starr County in Texas, 98% was Hispanic, and 86% of the population of Jefferson County in Mississippi was African American. The largest white population (96%) was found in Slope County in North Dakota.[84] The top four ancestry groups in the United States are German (23.3%), Irish (15.6%), English (13.1%), and African American (9.6%).[85]

Newcomers are expected to retain their cultural identities and integrate less in mainstream American than earlier generations did. For understanding their behavior, analysis of the values of their country of origin can be helpful, but it may be questioned if the ethnic minorities within the United States resemble the cultural groups outside of the United States from which they originated. African Americans and Asian Americans are higher in collectivism compared to European Americans,[86] but it is unclear whether African Americans resemble Africans in their cultural orientation. In other respects African Americans are as, or even more, individualistic than European Americans, as they emphasize their own uniqueness and independence.[87] This may be due to the fact that African Americans, more than other ethnic groups, have been the targets of stereotyping and prejudice.[88]

A frequently asked question is about the validity of Hofstede's country scores for the United States because of the expected underrepresentation of minorities. Hofstede states that the IBM populations measured were essentially middle class. Because IBM was a socially advanced company, minorities were part of the research population.[89] This proportion may not be representative for the current situation, although replications of Hofstede's work indicate that with respect to work-related values, the IBM country scores for the United States are still valid. Although the expectations are that large ethnic groups in the United States will not assimilate to the original European values of the early Americans, in the long run, the middle-class values of any society are aspirational values for lower classes and for minorities.

In Europe most ethnic minorities originate from collectivistic cultures, and related values are in contrast with the strong individualism of most receiver cultures. In some European cities, ethnic minorities are large groups. In Amsterdam in 2002, approximately 25% of the population was not born in the Netherlands. Many behavioral differences can be explained by the difference individualism/collectivism.

A question for the future is about the degree to which minorities will adapt to, or acculturate to, the values of the receiver culture. A rule of thumb is that integration takes three generations, but this depends on various factors, for example, the degree to which integration is stimulated by the receiver culture. Assimilation does take place at longer term. In a study of consumption-related values among students of a number of European countries and black and white students in South Africa, I found that the values of white (English and Afrikaans speaking) students were more similar to the values of black students (Nguni and Sotho) than to the originally English or Dutch values.

CLIMATE

Climate has a direct and indirect influence on consumption. *Climate* is typically defined as "average meteorological conditions specific to a geographic region over a period of several years or decades."[90] The Earth's climates originate from solar radiation that varies in relation to one's absolute latitude from the equator. No two countries have identical climates. A large portion of countries, however, has similar climates across broad classifications (e.g., mostly desert or tropical). Geographical latitude is an unambiguous measure of a country's geographical position and a crude measure of climate. At face value, average temperature may be a better indication, but in some countries extreme temperatures may vary widely between low and mountainous countries. Another problem is the "average" character of the data, which makes them not very credible for large countries like the United States, Russia, and China.

Parker[91] sees climate as the primary cause of behavioral differences. His findings are that solar climate (absolute latitude squared, to account for the Earth's curve), explains the largest variances in behavior. Cultural differences can be traced back to ecological differences,[92] and there is a relationship between temperature and wealth.[93] Countries with colder climates are wealthier than countries with warm climates.

A direct effect of climate is on energy consumption. In hotter climates people will use less fuel for heating and eat less, especially of foods that require high energies to digest such as meat. The indirect effect is via the relationship with wealth and cultural variables. Although worldwide, total calories consumed per day are correlated with climate, they are more significantly correlated with GNI per capita and individualism. The relationships with wealth and climate do not exist in economically homogeneous Europe where the only explaining variable is masculinity. The more masculine cultures consume more calories as well as confectionery products. Eurostat[94] data on everyday consumption of chocolate and soft drinks by students show significant correlations with masculinity. Individualism explains variance of calorie intake best. In the developed collectivistic world, people take time for meals and have them at regular times, together with other people. They eat less in between meals, whereas in individualistic cultures people seem to eat all the time, both meals and snacks.

A climate-related process is *homeostasis*,[95] a system of controls in the hypothalamus. The hypothalamus mediates the effects of sunlight and temperature on the production of hormones and neurotransmitters. Changes in levels of hormones and neurotransmitters are theorized to influence consumer behavior. Certain stimulants, such as alcohol, cigarettes, coffee, and tea, are assumed to mediate the effects of climate. In cold climates, with less sunshine, its stimulating effect is stronger than in warm climates, which should explain higher consumption of coffee, tea, alcohol, and cigarettes in colder climates than in warmer climates. According to Parker, the ability to institutionalize climate (heating, air conditioning) can reduce the effects of the physical environment and may decrease psychological differences across cultures in the future.

Against this reasoning goes the working of collective memory. Consistently in the colder climates people drink more milk, eat more ice cream, and own more deep freezers than in the warm climates. In Europe, consistently in the warmer climates, fresh milk is not trusted. The differences in trust in food across the countries in Europe are explained by uncertainty avoidance, a dimension that includes purity needs in several consumption domains. Fresh milk, as well its modern replacement ice cream, is a perishable product; and in the past, without refrigerators, fresh milk perished faster in the warm climates than in cold climates. With a nearly 100% penetration of refrigerators throughout Europe, there is no need whatsoever to have less trust in fresh milk in warm climates than in cold climates. This looks more like an indirect effect of climate than a direct effect. Because milk cannot be kept in warm climates, people have historically not consumed as much fresh milk in the warm climates as in the cold climates, and a fresh milk industry has not developed. And still, in the collective memory of people, there is an attitude toward milk (and related products) that it cannot be trusted, because it is perishable. This distrust in perishable food products has become a cultural factor. The phenomenon also demonstrates the stability of people's habits. Logically one would expect more deep freezers in warm climates than in cold climates, but it is the other way round. The colder the climate, the more people were used to preserve food in the snow, and the more they keep doing that, helped by the latest technology.

CONSUMER BEHAVIOR, NATIONAL WEALTH, AND CULTURE

The previous sections described how at country level, the explanatory role of income decreases and culture becomes an increasingly important variable that can explain cross-country differences in consumption.

When observing the relationship between national income and penetration of some new products at macro level, one may be tempted to conclude that the richer countries become, the more their inhabitants will spend on these products. We have seen that for some investment-type products, income is the initial explaining variable, but over time cultural variables better explain variance. Analysis at micro level often points at relationships with culture. For many products, income differences have no explanatory power at all, and only cultural variables can explain variance. So greater wealth will not make people spend more equally in all countries.

The Concept of the Rational Consumer

Economists have viewed the consumer as a rational human being or *homo economicus* whose decisions are based on the principle of maximizing utility and profit in an environment of perfect knowledge. Individuals are assumed to be able to use reason to make personal choices. Scholars from various disciplines have objected to the overstated influence of income, also at national level. "Differences, which, toward the end of the fifties, seemed to social scientists to be characteristics of countries—such as variations in the value of GNI and living standards—are viewed over time as quite unreliable indicators."[96] In Chapter 6 we will see that information based decision making is not universal.

There are many consumption differences across nations that cannot be explained by income differences. *Homo economicus* is a social construct of the Western world, assuming people spend their income in a rational way, first deciding on primary needs, and only when these are met considering luxury goods. This is not the case. For example, in the poorer countries, income often is an irrelevant criterion for buying luxury goods. Poorer consumers in developing economies may buy symbolic products (of little functional value in the eyes of Western economists) for social status needs that are not viewed as a necessity to Western economists. The importance of the symbolic function of brands is not limited to the wealthy. In 2009, low GNI per capita was the main explaining variable of differences in answers to the question about the importance of brand or brand name for making a buying decision.[97]

Another assumption is about the influence of education on consumer behavior. Information technology is expected to cause better-educated consumers. Better-educated consumers are assumed to be better informed. Better-informed consumers are assumed to make better (i.e., more rational) buying decisions. In Chapter 6 we will see that in collectivistic and high power distance cultures people don't search for information the way they do in individualistic and low power distance cultures. The concept of a rational consumer, consciously searching for information to make an informed buying decision—if it ever was a valid concept—is less valid in other than individualistic and low power distance cultures.

Engel's Law

Another economic theory that needs justifying for cross-cultural use is Engel's law, which has tried to generalize consumers' spending patterns. Engel states that as a family's income increases, the percentage spent on housing will be roughly constant and the amount saved or spent on other purchases will increase. The percentage of private consumption spent on food should decrease with increasing incomes. The theory was developed for single countries. Indeed, in all countries in Europe, the percentage of total household expenditure spent on food is lower in the 20% lowest-income households than in the 20% highest-income households.[98] Between countries, however, at the national level, the differences remain large over time and are culture bound. The percentage of consumption expenditures dedicated to food[99] is correlated with low individualism. In collectivistic cultures in Europe, people allocate a higher percentage of consumption expenditure to food than do people in individualistic cultures. Generally, in collectivistic cultures food has an important social function. Providing food and having food in the

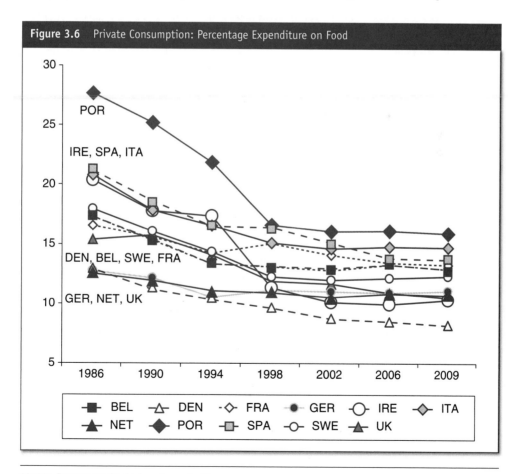

Figure 3.6   Private Consumption: Percentage Expenditure on Food

SOURCE: Eurostat Yearbooks (see Appendix B)

home for any guest who drops by is an important social value. So expenditures on food are likely to remain relatively high in collectivistic cultures as compared with individualistic cultures.

Figure 3.6 illustrates how in each of the 13 European countries over time the percentage of private consumption spent on food has decreased. But after 1998 the percentages do not converge; the differences remain more or less the same. Thus, the universality of Engel's law is in the fact that for each separate country the percentage spent on food decreases with increased wealth. The modification is in the fact that the differences at country level remain the same. In the collectivistic cultures (e.g., Portugal, Spain), people continue to spend a relatively large amount of their income on food. With increased wealth, the percentage is even likely to increase. Whereas in individualistic cultures fast food is an increasingly important phenomenon, in collectivistic cultures increasing time and money is spent on quality and variety of food as well as on eating out. Food carries cultural meaning. It provides emotional and social security. It provides comfort and may also be used to relieve anxiety or cope with stress. It may be used to gain acceptance, friendship, to influence others, to establish communication with others.[100]

How Engel's law operates across countries is demonstrated by the development in Ireland. Ireland was, until the mid-1990s, a relatively poor country but it has developed remarkably fast at the end of the past century. Although Ireland is an individualistic culture, the percentage spent on food in Ireland used to be similar to that of a more collectivistic culture like Spain, because levels of wealth were similar. After 1995, however, with increased wealth, Ireland's percentage spent on food became similar to the percentage of the other individualistic cultures.

CONCLUSION

This chapter discussed convergence, divergence, and stability of consumption. It provided evidence of the stability of values and behavior. Instead of expected convergence, people's behavior is rather stable, and this is reflected in socioeconomic and consumption differences across countries. One of the assumed causes of convergence is modernization. When countries go through development stages from premodern to modern and postmodern, whatever convergence takes place is at macro level and rarely at micro level. It was argued that with converging wealth across countries, value differences become manifest and consumer behavior diverges. With disappearing income differences at country level, cross-country differences in consumption and consumer behavior cannot anymore be explained by GNP per capita. Because other demographic variables such as urbanization are related to national wealth, these variables cannot be used as explaining variables. Cultural variables are the best variables to explain differences.

NOTES

1. Jones, J. P. (2000). Introduction, the vicissitudes of international advertising. In J. P. Jones (Ed.), *International advertising, realities and myths* (pp. 1–10). Thousand Oaks, CA: Sage, 5.
2. Williamson, J. B., & Fleming, J. J. (1996). Convergence theory and the social welfare sector: A cross-national analysis. In A. Inkeles & M. Sasaki (Eds.), *Comparing nations and cultures* (pp. 348–355). Englewood Cliffs, NJ: Prentice Hall.

3. Inkeles, A. (1998). *One world emerging?: Convergence and divergence in industrial societies.* Boulder, CO: Westview, 20–23.

4. Inglehart, R. (1997). *Modernization and postmodernization: Cultural, economic, and political change in 43 societies.* Princeton, NJ: Princeton University Press, 18.

5. Huntington, S. P. (1996). *The clash of civilizations and the remaking of world order.* New York: Simon & Schuster, 58.

6. Kerr, D., Harbison, F. H., & Myers, C. A. (1992). *Industrialism and industrial man.* London: Heinemann, 1960. Quoted in Robertson (1992). *Globalization.* London: Sage, 11.

7. Robertson, R. (1992). *Globalization.* London: Sage.

8. Inkeles, A., & Smith, D. H. (1999). *Becoming modern.* Cambridge, MA: Harvard University Press, 15.

9. Giddens, A. (1991). *Introduction to sociology.* New York: W. W. Norton, 795.

10. Inkeles & Smith (1999) 16–25.

11. Usunier, J.-C. (1996/1997). Atomistic versus organic approaches. *International Studies of Management and Organization, 26,* 90–112.

12. Hofstede, G. (2001). *Culture's consequences* (2nd ed.). Thousand Oaks, CA: Sage, 34

13. Fu, J. H. Y., & Chiu, C. Y. (2007). Local culture's responses to globalization: Exemplary persons and their attendant values. *Journal of Cross-Cultural Psychology, 38*(5), 636–653.

14. Inglehart, R., Basañez, M., & Moreno, A. (2001). *Human values and beliefs.* Ann Arbor: University of Michigan Press.

15. Kagitçibasi, Ç. (1997). Individualism and collectivism. In J. W. Berry, M. H. Segall, & Ç. Kagitçibasi (Eds.), *Handbook of cross-cultural psychology* (Vol. 3, pp. 2–49). Boston: Allyn & Bacon, 31.

16. Perkin, H. (1999). Review: One world emerging? Convergence and divergence in industrial societies. By Alex Inkeles. *Journal of Social History, 33,* 461–462.

17. Jain, S. C. (1989). Standardization of international marketing strategy: Some research hypotheses. *Journal of Marketing, 53,* 70–79.

18. Mühlbacher, H., Dahringer, L., & Leihs, H. (1999). *International marketing: A global perspective* (2nd ed.). London: International Thomson Business Press, 50, 85.

19. Hunt, S. D. (1976). The nature and scope of marketing. *Journal of Marketing, 40,* 17–28.

20. Peterson, M., & Malhotra, N. (2000). Country segmentation based on objective quality-of-life measures. *International Marketing Review, 17,* 56–73.

21. Andreasen, A. R. (1990). Cultural interpenetration: A critical consumer research issue for the 1990s. In M. Goldberg & R. W. Pollay (Eds.), *Advances in consumer research* (Vol. 7, pp. 847–849). Provo, UT: Association for Consumer Research.

22. Hollanders, H., Soete, L., & Ter Weel, B. (1999, March 11–13). *Trends in growth convergence and divergence and changes in technological access and capabilities.* Paper presented at the Lisbon Workshop on Cliometrics, Econometrics and Appreciative History in the Study of Long Waves in Economic Development. Lisbon.

23. Norris, P. (2001). *Digital divide: Civic engagement, information poverty and the Internet in democratic societies.* New York: Cambridge University Press. 2001.

24. Wade, R. (2001, April). Winners and losers. *The Economist,* 79–82.

25. Sarkar, P. (1999, February 20). Theory of convergence and real income divergence 1950–1992. *Economic and Political Weekly.*

26. Craig, C. S., Douglas, S. P., & Grein, A. (1992). Patterns of convergence and divergence among industrialized nations: 1960–1988. *Journal of International Business Studies, 23,* 773–786.

27. Usunier, J.-C. (1996). Consommation: quand global rime avec local (Consumption: when global rhymes with local). *Revue Française de gestion, 110,* 100–116.

28. Huntington, S. P. (1996). The goals of development. In A. Inkeles & M. Sasaki (Eds.), *Comparing nations and cultures* (pp. 469–483). Englewood Cliffs, NJ: Prentice Hall.

29. Inkeles (1998), 30–45.

30. Van Mesdag, M. (2000). Culture-sensitive adaptation of global standardization: The duration-of-usage hypothesis. *International Marketing Review, 17,* 74–84.

31. Williamson, J. B., & Fleming, J. J. (1996). Convergence theory and the social welfare sector: A cross-national analysis. In A. Inkeles & M. Sasaki (Eds.), *Comparing nations and cultures* (pp. 348–355). Englewood Cliffs, NJ: Prentice Hall.

32. The 44 countries of this group are Argentina, Australia, Austria, Belgium, Brazil, Canada, Chile, Colombia, Costa Rica, Denmark, Ecuador, El Salvador, Finland, France, Germany, Great Britain, Greece, Indonesia, India, Ireland, Israel, Italy, Japan, South Korea, Malaysia, Mexico, Netherlands, Norway, New Zealand, Pakistan, Panama, Peru, Philippines, Portugal, South Africa, Singapore, Spain, Sweden, Switzerland, Thailand, Turkey, Uruguay, United States, Venezuela.

33. The 26 countries of this group are Argentina, Australia, Austria, Belgium, Canada, Denmark, Finland, France, Germany, Greece, Ireland, Israel, Italy, Japan, Korea, the Netherlands, New Zealand, Norway, Portugal, Singapore, Spain, Sweden, Switzerland, United Kingdom, United States, Venezuela. In 1998, Venezuela's GNI per capita was below US$8,000, but Venezuela used to be part of the "top 25 income countries" until 1988, when South Korea took its place. For continuity's sake I kept including both Venezuela and South Korea in all time series calculations. The same group of countries in 2006 had a minimum GNI per capita of US$15,000, except Venezuela, which still lagged.

34. When I refer to calculations for Europe, these are generally for 15 countries: Austria, Belgium, Denmark, Finland, France, Germany, Ireland, Italy, Netherlands, Norway, Portugal, Spain, Sweden, Switzerland, United Kingdom. When Eurostat data (available only for EU countries) are used, calculation generally is for 14 countries (Norway and Switzerland excluded) or 13, Greece excluded. (See Appendix B.)

35. The examples of convergence and divergence are computed from data from annual reports of the World Bank, Eurostat, and the United Nations, Euromonitor, and data from surveys like Eurobarometer, Reader's Digest, and the European Media and Marketing Surveys (EMS), as in Appendix B. The 20 product categories are telephony, passenger cars, television, radio, the press (newspapers, books), food, mineral water, soft drinks, alcoholic drinks, cigarettes, jewelry, personal computers, Internet, audio, household appliances, watches, cameras, personal care products, household cleaning products, and financial products.

36. The varying time spans for these calculations are due to the fact that data definitions changed over time. For example, until 2000 data for mobile phones were based on ownership, and after 2000 data are for mobile phone subscribers. For Internet I used data on usage, not on Internet connections, which data were used earlier.

37. Data EMS 1997 and 2007.

38. Belgium, Denmark, Finland, France, Germany, Italy, Netherlands, Norway, Portugal, Spain, Sweden, Switzerland, United Kingdom.

39. Helm, J. (1999, October 1). *Advertising's overdue revolution.* Paper presented to the *Adweek* creative conference. San Francisco.

40. Pew Research Center. Retrieved November 21, 2009, from http://pewresearch.org/assets/social/pdf/Luxury.pdf

41. I use GNI consistently in this book in order not to confuse the reader. Information on this terminology change from the World Bank at http://www.worldbank.org/data/changinterm.html

42. *Technical notes.* World Development Report 1998/99. Washington, DC: World Bank.

43. Sethi, S. P. (1971). Comparative cluster analysis for world markets. *Journal of Marketing Research, 8,* 348–354; Craig, C. S., Douglas, S. P., & Grein, A. (1992). Patterns of convergence and divergence among industrialized nations: 1960–1988. *Journal of International Business Studies, 23,* 773–786.

44. Helsen, K., Jedidi, K., & DeSarbo, W. S. (1993). A new approach to country segmentation utilizing multinational diffusion patterns. *Journal of Marketing, 57,* 60–71.

45. McCain, T. (1986). Patterns of media use in Europe: Identifying country clusters. *European Journal of Communication, 1,* 231–250.

46. Ger, G., & Belk, R. W. (1996) Cross-cultural differences in materialism. *Journal of Economic Psychology, 17,* 55–77.

47. Roth, M. S. (1995). The effects of culture and socioeconomics on the performance of global brand image strategies. *Journal of Marketing Research, 32,* 163–175.

48. Venkatesh, A. (1995). Ethoconsumerism: A new paradigm to study cultural and cross-cultural consumer behavior. In J. A. Costa & G. J. Bamossy (Eds.), *Marketing in a multicultural world* (pp. 26–67). Thousand Oaks, CA: Sage, 41.

49. For three countries of the group of 44 countries no LTO data are available, so these calculations are for only 41 countries.

50. Norris, P. (2000, April 10–13). *The worldwide digital divide: Information poverty, the Internet and development.* Paper presented at the annual meeting of the Political Association of the United Kingdom. London School of Economics and Political Science.

51. Van de Vliert, E. (2007). Climatoeconomic roots of survival versus self-expression cultures. *Journal of Cross-Cultural Psychology, 38*(2), 156–172.

52. Inglehart (1997), 603–604.

53. Inkeles, A. (1997). *Continuity and change in popular values on the Pacific Rim.* Stanford, CA: Hoover Institution, 8–10, 14–15.

54. Fu & Chiu (2007).

55. Abrahamson, P. R., & Inglehart, R. (1995). *Value change in global perspective.* Ann Arbor: University of Michigan Press, 84.

56. *Urbanization Table 3.10.* (2007). World Development Indicators. Washington, DC: World Bank, 165.

57. *Consumers in Europe: Facts and figures: Data 1996–2000.* (2001). Eurostat. Luxembourg: Office for Official Publications of the European Communities, 21.

58. Höllinger, F., & Haller, M. (1996). Kinship and social networks in modern societies: A cross-cultural comparison among seven nations. In A. Inkeles & M. Sasaki (Eds.), *Comparing nations and cultures* (pp. 147–170). Englewood Cliffs, NJ: Prentice Hall.

59. Roland, A. (1988). *In search of self in India and Japan.* Princeton, NJ: Princeton University Press, 302.

60. Kagitçibasi, Ç. (1997). Individualism and collectivism. In J. W. Berry, M. H. Segall, & Ç. Kagitçibasi (Eds.), *Handbook of cross-cultural psychology* (Vol. 3, pp. 1–49). Boston: Allyn & Bacon, 35.

61. *Information society.* (2008). Flash Eurobarometer 241.

62. *Consumers in Europe* (2001), 36.

63. The global marketplace. (1997). *The Public Pulse* (10, 11), 12. Roper Starch Worldwide, 7.

64. *Technical notes World Development report 1998/99.* Washington, DC: World Bank.

65. Data United Nations Demographic Yearbook 1999 and 2005.

66. Personal communication, November 17, 2009.

67. *Dying too young.* (2005). World Bank. Europe and Central Asia Human Development Department. Retrieved April 26, 2009, from http://siteresources.worldbank.org/INTECA/Resources/DTY-Final.pdf

68. Hofstede (2001).

69. Jennings, Y., Lloyd-Smith, B., & Ironmonger, D. (2002*). Three dimensional modeling of household size distributions*. Paper. University of Melbourne, Economics Department. Retrieved November 16, 2009, from http://www.apa.org.au/upload/2002-5C_Jennings.pdf

70. Why Italians don't make babies. (1998, May 9). *The Economist, 39.*

71. *Young Europeans.* (2007). Flash Eurobarometer report 202.

72. Female share of labor force data, World Bank Development reports for 1994 and 2006.

73. *United Nations statistics.* Retrieved November 16, 2009, from http://unstats.un.org/unsd/demographic/products/indwm/tab5b.htm

74. *Satisfaction with family life.* (2008). Flash Eurobarometer report 247.

75. *Satisfaction with family life* (2008).

76. Usunier, J. C. (2000). *Marketing across cultures* (3rd ed.). Harlow, UK: Pearson Education, 60–61.

77. Empires without umpires: Survey of Asian business. (2001, April 17). *The Economist, 6.*

78. Price, J. (2000, July/August). Mining for opportunities in Latin America. *ESOMAR Research World,* no. 7, 5.

79. Hadfield, G., & Skipworth, M. (1994). *Class: Where do you stand?* London: Bloomsbury, 10–18.

80. Dickey, C. (2008, November 24). Reflecting on race barriers. *Newsweek,* 26–30.

81. See also Hofstede (2001), 279–280.

82. Hofstede (2001), 429.

83. Venkatesh (1995), 31–35.

84. U.S. Census 2000 data.

85. Berry, J. (1993, July 19). America's family tree. *Brandweek,* 19.

86. Coon, H. M., & Kemmelmeier, M. (2001). Cultural orientations in the United States. *Journal of Cross-Cultural Psychology, 32,* 348–364.

87. Oyserman, D., Coon, H. M., & Kemmelmeier, M. (2002). Rethinking individualism and collectivism: Evaluation of theoretical assumptions and meta-analyses. *Psychological Bulletin, 128,* 3–72.

88. Coon & Kemmelmeier (2001).

89. Hofstede (2001), 42, and private communication.

90. Parker, P. M. (1997). *National cultures of the world.* Westport, CT: Greenwood, 23–34.

91. Parker (1997).

92. Kim, U., Triandis, H. C., Kâgitçibasi, Ç., Choi, S. C., & Yoon, G. (1994). *Individualism and collectivism.* Thousand Oaks, CA: Sage.

93. Van de Vliert, E., Kluwer, E. S., & Lynn, R. (2000). Citizens of warmer countries are more competitive and poorer: Culture or chance? *Journal of Economic Psychology, 21,* 143–165.

94. *Consumers in Europe* (2001), 73.

95. Parker, P. M., & Tavassoli, N. T. (2000). Homeostasis and consumer behavior across cultures. *International Journal of Research in Marketing, 17,* 33–53.

96. Scheuch, E. K. (1996). Theoretical implications of comparative survey research: Why the wheel of cross-cultural methodology keeps on being reinvented. In A. Inkeles & M. Sasaki (Eds.), *Comparing nations and cultures* (pp. 57–73). Englewood Cliffs, NJ: Prentice Hall.

97. *Europeans' attitudes towards the issue of sustainable consumption and production.* (2009). Flash Eurobarometer report 256.

98. *Consumers in Europe* (2001), 25.

99. Eurostat annual yearbooks (see Appendix B).

100. Magrabi, F. M., Chung, Y. S., Cha, S. S., & Yang, S. J. (1991). *The economics of household consumption.* New York: Praeger. 211.

CHAPTER 4

The Consumer: Attributes

The attributes of the person refer to *what people are*. The central question is, "Who am I?" or the *self*, and in what terms people describe themselves, their personalities, traits, and identities. Related to the *who* are attitudes and lifestyles, because they are a central part of the person.

The concepts of self, personality, identity, and image are central to consumer behavior and are also used as metaphors in branding strategies. They have been derived from psychological studies in the United States and northwest Europe, so these and other psychological models presented in consumer behavior textbooks are derived from an individualistic worldview. Increasingly, other models are being developed for other groups.[1] Both attitude formation and the relationship between attitude and behavior vary across cultures. Whereas in Western models attitude is used to predict behavior, this is much less the case in other parts of the world.

Although ideally the emic approach should be followed for the study of consumer behavior in different countries, at this point in time it is more pragmatic to evaluate the cross-cultural usefulness of existing constructs. In this chapter, findings from cross-cultural psychology are presented to help understand the differences of the various aspects of the person across cultures.

THE CONCEPT OF SELF

Psychologists agree that the self-concept plays a central role in behavior and psychological processes. It consists of whatever individuals consider to be theirs, including their bodies, families, possessions, moods, emotions, conscience, attitudes, values, traits, and social positions.[2] The cross-cultural psychologists Markus and Kitayama state:

> The self or the identity is critical because it is the psychological locus of cultural effects. It functions as a mediating, orienting and interpretative framework that will systematically bias how members of a given socio-cultural group will think, feel and act.[3]

The self is shaped by the cultural context, and in turn it strongly influences social behavior in various ways, including an individual's perceptions, evaluations, and values.[4] This mediating role of the self makes it an intermediary variable for understanding behavior.

The concept of self, as used in consumer psychology, is rooted in individualism. It includes the following ideas about a person: A person is an *autonomous entity* with a distinctive set of attributes, qualities, or processes. The configuration of these internal attributes or processes causes behavior. People's attributes and processes should be expressed consistently in behavior across situations. Behavior that changes with the situation is viewed as hypocritical or pathological.

In the collectivistic model of the self, persons are fundamentally interdependent with one another. The self cannot be separated from others and the surrounding social context. This concept of self is characteristic of Asia, South America, Russia, the Middle East, Africa, and the south of Europe. The interdependent view of human nature includes the following ideas about a person: A person is an *interdependent entity* who is part of an encompassing social relationship. Behavior is a consequence of being responsive to the others with whom one is interdependent, and behavior originates in relationships. Individual behavior is situational; it is sensitive to social context and varies from one situation to another and from one time to another.[5] People follow different norms and values at different places, times and with different people. For example, the behavior norm in public space (e.g., work) is different from the norm in private space (e.g., family).[6]

In individualistic cultures focus is on individual autonomy. A youth has to develop an identity that enables him or her to function independently in a variety of social groups, apart from the family. In collectivistic cultures youth development is based on encouragement of dependency needs in complex familial hierarchical relationships, and the group ideal is being like others as opposed to being different.[7]

> The very first words of children in China are people related, whereas children in the United States start talking about objects.[8] In Japan, feeling good is more associated with interpersonal situations such as feeling friendly, whereas in the United States feeling good is more frequently associated with interpersonal distance, such as feeling superior or proud. In the United Kingdom, feelings of happiness are more related to a sense of independence, whereas in Greece, good feelings are negatively related to a sense of independence.[9]

Kagitçibasi[10] distinguishes between a *relational self,* a *separated self,* and the *family model of emotional interdependence,* which is a combination of the first two. The relational self develops in collectivistic cultures in rural areas, where intergenerational interdependence functions for family livelihood. It is the family model of emotional and material interdependence. The separated self develops in the family model of independence in the urban context of Western, individualistic cultures, where intergenerational interdependence is not required for family livelihood. The third category of self combines a relational orientation with autonomy. It develops the family model of emotional interdependence in the developed urban areas of collectivistic cultures, where material interdependency weakens, but emotional interdependence continues.

> The mobile phone is the ultimate communication means to support emotional interdependence of members of collectivistic cultures in urban environments. Although in 2008 ownership of mobile phones was still related to wealth and individualism, an important motive for using it was to keep contact with family and friends. In a Eurobarometer[11] survey the percentage of people who strongly agreed with the statement "Use of the mobile phone helps to keep contact with family and friends" correlated negatively with individualism ($r = -.38*$).

Although the relational self is characteristic of collectivistic cultures, a different type of relationship orientation exists in individualistic cultures that are also feminine.[12] This relationship orientation is called *horizontal individualism* by the cross-cultural psychologist Harry Triandis,[13] who distinguishes between two types of individualism: vertical (independent and different) and horizontal (interdependent and different) individualism. What he calls horizontal interdependent is the relationship orientation of individualistic and low masculine cultures that are on the one hand characterized by self-reliance but on the other hand by interdependence, which translates to needs for consensus, low social status needs, and not wanting to "stick out." Whereas "family values" are part of the self-concept in collectivistic cultures, comparable social aspects characterize the self-concept in individualistic cultures that are also feminine.[14] Both collectivism and femininity can explain variance in relationship orientation. Across seven countries in Latin America, in the more feminine cultures young people think the Internet is isolating. Low masculinity explains 59% of variance.[15]

> A study by Yankelovich Clancy Shulman[16] in the United States found that Hispanics do not believe they have to blend in with American culture at the expense of losing their own identity, which is based on a "relational self." The study found that for nearly 75% of U.S. Hispanics, personal satisfaction comes mostly from home and family, a significantly higher percentage than in the general population. Even though the percentage of working women among U.S. Hispanics is not much below general market levels, nearly 90% of Hispanic men and women believed that "a housewife's role is interesting and challenging," a view that was more than three times higher than other Americans. Nearly half the adult Hispanics said it is best to fit in rather than be different from others. They were less likely to search for new brands, try new products, or gather information on new products.

Adapting to situation suggests different self-concepts across contexts. Singh[17] writes that Indians tolerate inconsistency more than Westerners, and their thinking is more contextual, which leads to contradictory self-concepts. Zhang[18] suggests young Chinese, next to their local identity, may develop a global identity that allows them to communicate with people from other cultures either face to face or through interactive media. Their local identity is likely to be used most in daily interaction with family and friends and community members.

In the eyes of Westerners, behavior of Chinese or Japanese when in the West may suggest they are like Westerners because they are able to adapt so much to the situation and norms of the hosting country. This doesn't mean they share the same values, but they are much more than Westerners able to adapt to the situation.

Self-Descriptions and Self-Evaluations

In order to develop a distinctive, unique self, in individualistic cultures people learn to describe themselves in terms of psychological characteristics, but reporting one's distinctive characteristics is not a natural task in collectivistic cultures. Individualistic Westerners seem relatively more practiced in describing themselves in abstract and global ways than are members of collectivistic cultures. Individuals with interdependent selves may have difficulty describing themselves in absolute terms without any contextual or situational references. To the Japanese, abstract categorizations of the self seem unnatural or artificial because they reflect a claim of being a separate individual without the constraints of specific roles or situations.[19] So collectivists are more likely to refer to social roles and present themselves as a relational part of a greater whole. Markus and Kitayama[20] describe studies that demonstrate that Korean and Japanese students twice as often as American students use context-specific and social self-descriptions or refer to some features of the situation or social context. People may, for example, describe themselves as "I am in the gymnastic club." This difference has consequences for opinion or attitude research. In collectivistic cultures, opinions are much less individual opinions, and references to group membership or situational aspects should be included in questions.

In particular, American descriptions of the self tend to contain almost only positive self-evaluations. Whereas American adults tend to rate themselves as more attractive and intelligent than average adults, Japanese adults rate about 50% of others as higher on a given trait or ability. In American psychology it is said that Americans display a "false uniqueness bias," whereas Japanese and Chinese tend to show a "modesty bias."[21] Within Japanese culture, self-criticism (*hansei*) serves a functional purpose. It aids individuals in pointing at the areas in which they need to improve themselves. Self-improvement serves to aid Japanese in fulfilling their role obligations. This is in sharp contrast to North American practice, where negative self-features would symbolize lack of the ability to be self-sufficient, autonomous, and to make one's own unique mark in the world.[22] The modesty bias is a reflection of collectivistic culture. A study comparing Congolese with Americans showed that, in general, fewer Congolese evaluate themselves positively than Americans. Enhancing the self is likely to be more common in the United States than in Congo.[23]

IMPLICATIONS FOR MARKETING, BRANDING, AND ADVERTISING

A central aspect of Western marketing is the focus on product attributes that are to distinguish the user's self from others. People will buy products that are compatible with their self-concepts or rather that enhance their "ideal self" images.

Ownership of products or brands transfers the meaning of products to consumers. By owning an item, the item can become part of the "extended self." The product's image should contribute to the consumer's self-concept.[24] This process is likely to vary with the different self-concepts. Whereas product ownership in individualistic cultures can express uniqueness and independence, in collectivistic cultures the extended self is the group, and product ownership may have the function of demonstrating life stage and group identity. In Japan, brands do not enhance a unique personality but confirm social status. The extreme brand-related behavior of Japanese youths is often falsely interpreted as Japanese youths becoming individualistic. It is the context that allows such behavior. When one is a student one can behave in specific autonomous ways; in other roles one cannot.

> Key associations for fashion in France are individuality, symbolism, meaning, interpretation, pleasure, and seduction. In Japan, to be fashionable is to be dynamically integrated in a community that defines the self and proves that it exists by its ability to adapt to all new expressions of fashion.[25] To be fashionable in the United States is to demonstrate your unique individuality.

The Self-Concept and Branding

To many collectivists, abstract self-descriptions seem unnatural; characteristics can only be asked in the context of specific situations and relationships, for example, "Describe yourself at home with your family." An important lesson for branding is that if people are not able to describe *themselves* in abstract terms, they are likely not able to do so for *brands* either. For members of collectivistic cultures, the brand concept is too abstract to be discussed in a comparable manner as in individualistic cultures. The Reader's Digest Trusted Brands survey in 2002 asked people in 18 different countries[26] in Europe about the probability of buying a brand they had heard of but not tried before. In individualistic cultures people are more likely to buy unknown brands than in collectivistic cultures. The responses "Extremely/quite likely to consider buying a brand which I've heard of but haven't tried before" correlate significantly with individualism ($r = .82***$). The relationship is illustrated in Figure 4.1. A brand out of context is less relevant to members of collectivistic cultures than to members of individualistic cultures.

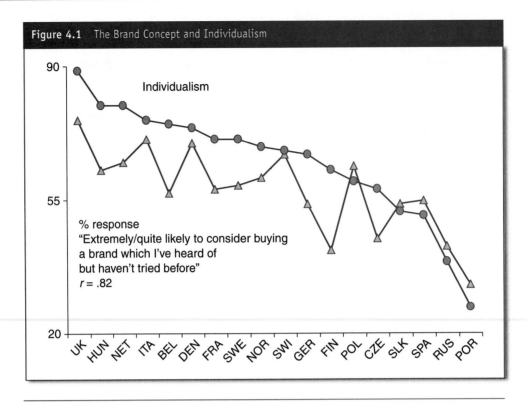

Figure 4.1   The Brand Concept and Individualism

SOURCES: Hofstede et al. (2010) (see Appendix A); Reader's Digest Trusted Brands (2002) (see Appendix B)

The context specificity of the self in collectivistic cultures may imply that, in contrast to individualistic cultures, where a brand is supposed to be consistent with respect to its attributes and values, in collectivistic cultures one brand can have different attributes and/or values in different contexts. The innate need for cross-situational consistency of Western marketing managers induces them to develop consistent brand identities across countries. This is a fundamental error that may limit cross-cultural success.

In Asia, marketing managers are not inclined to develop brands or brand strategies by adding abstract characteristics to brands, the way it is done in the West. Hu[27] analyzed the content of 30 issues of the Chinese professional advertising magazines *Modern Advertising* and *China Advertising,* including 10,000 titles, and found zero articles including *brand* as a keyword.

Another limitation is the Western concept of creativity that is historically based on originality and uniqueness. The practices of Western branding and design are a reflection of the uniqueness concept that is seen as a precondition to differentiation. That is why marketers and designers insist that their brands should be *unique.* In Asian cultures the concept of originality does not exist as it does in the West. Instead, everything comes from somewhere else, because everything and everybody is part of a greater whole, out of which everything can be taken, assimilated, and remade even while it retains its own cultural origins, and code.[28] The wish to be consistent is reflected in the ubiquitous use of standard—often English language—logos and pay-offs. What might, for example, for a Chinese consumer be the meaning of the pay-off "Wella, perfectly you" under a logo for a shampoo brand consisting of stylized waving hair?[29] (See Figure 4.2.)

Figure 4.2   Wella Logo

The Self-Concept and Advertising

The difference between the independent and interdependent self has its impact on advertising. In collectivistic cultures, such as China and Korea, appeals focusing on in-group benefits, harmony, and family are more effective, whereas in individualistic cultures like the United States, advertising that appeals to individual benefits and preferences, personal success, and independence is more effective.[30] A commercial in which a guy breaks out from a group and starts doing something on his own that the group hasn't thought of would be seen as positive in the individualistic cultures of the West but negative in collectivistic Asian cultures.[31] For collectivists, one's identity is in the group. Depicting someone alone may imply he or she has no identity. A pan-European campaign by Vodafone depicted a lone individual, but the Vodafone brand Airtel in Spain depicted the group identity, as illustrated in Figure 4.3.

Members of individualistic and collectivistic societies will respond differently to advertisements emphasizing individualistic or collectivistic appeals. In the United States, people will be more persuaded by ads emphasizing individualistic benefits such as personal success and independence, whereas in Korea people will be more attracted to ads emphasizing collectivistic benefits, such as in-group benefits, harmony, and family.[32]

Advertising appeals that present a brand in a way that matches consumers' self-concepts appear to result in more favorable brand attitudes. This was confirmed in a study by Wang et al.,[33] who use the terms *separated* versus *connected* for appeals that are attractive for people in individualistic cultures or collectivistic cultures. A connected advertising appeal stresses interdependence and togetherness. A separated advertising appeal stresses independence and autonomy.

The importance of both context and the relationship orientation of the self in collectivistic cultures can explain the frequent use of celebrities in Japanese advertising. The use of celebrities in advertising varies across cultures. There are indications that in Western societies these variations are related to the degree of masculinity (need for success), which is likely to explain why in the United States the cult of personality and obsession with celebrity and stardom is pronounced. However, in the collectivistic Japan, the use of celebrities in advertising

Figure 4.3 Vodafone and Airtel Advertisements

is even stronger than in the United States. In his description of the celebrity phenomenon in Japan, Praet[34] provides explanations that refer to two collectivistic aspects: the relational self and context. In Japan, unlike in most countries, celebrity appearances are not limited to famous actors, singers, sports stars, or comedians. Advertising is a stage for established celebrities to capitalize their fame; it also is the steppingstone for models and aspiring actors toward fame. In Japan, the word *talent* (*tarento*) is used to describe most celebrities in the entertainment world, and *star* is reserved for those who are seen to have long-lasting popularity. Many of these talents are selected on the basis of their cute looks. First, in the context of entertainment and advertising, this phenomenon seems not to pose problems of distinctiveness, which it might give in the context of the family or a work-related environment. Second, the function of using such *tarento* is to give the brand "face" in the world of brands with similar product attributes. Instead of adding abstract personal characteristics to the product, it is linked to concrete persons. This is also explained as part of the creative process, in which a creative team in the advertising agency prefers to explain a proposed campaign by showing the client a popular talent around whom the campaign is to be built rather than talking about an abstract creative concept. In a large study comparing 25 countries, Praet found that mainly collectivism explains differences in the use of celebrities in advertising, where the function of a celebrity is to give face to the brand in a world of brands with similar product attributes.[35]

SELF-ENHANCEMENT AND SELF-ESTEEM

European Americans show a general sensitivity to positive self-relevant information, which is named *self-enhancement*.[36] To Americans, self-enhancement leads to *self-esteem*, and self-esteem is a natural and valid barometer of human worth and psychological health, a belief that is unheard of in many other cultures. To Americans, self-esteem is important for a general sense of well-being, whereas in Japan, as well as in many other collectivistic cultures, subjective well-being depends on the appraisal of the self as actively responding to and correcting shortcomings. For collectivists, absence of negative features is more important for their well-being than presence of positive features.[37]

How much self-esteem is integrated into the concept of self in Anglo-American culture is demonstrated by the definition of self-concept by Eysenck:

Self-concept is all the thoughts and feelings about the self; it combines self-esteem and self-image (the knowledge an individual has about himself or herself). Self-esteem is the evaluative aspect of the self-concept; it concerns how worthwhile and confident an individual feels about himself or herself.[38]

Self-enhancement and self-esteem have been thought to be a phenomenon typical of individualistic cultures, because associated with individualism and the independent self is the tendency to maintain and enhance self-esteem through efforts to stand out or be superior to others.[39] Cross-cultural studies have shown that the self-enhancement tendency is indeed weaker in collectivistic cultures. Among Americans, success situations are considered to be more important than failure situations, whereas the opposite is true for Japanese. The independent self-system, typical of Western individualistic societies, stresses the uniqueness and well-being of the individual, whereas the interdependent self stresses the importance of fitting in, restraining oneself, and maintaining social harmony. Having self-attributes that are more positive (the main advantage of self-enhancement) seems to be less central to the interdependent self than to the independent self.[40]

Among individualistic cultures, differences in self-enhancement are also considerable. These differences can be explained by cultural masculinity, but even better by the new long-/short-term orientation dimension. Feelings of pride and self-esteem are strong in short-term-oriented cultures. This explains the self-enhancement phenomenon in the United States, which is short-term oriented and scores high on masculinity.

Self-enhancement practices like ego boosting, performance, and showing off are integrated aspects of the North American self. American sociologist Erving Goffman saw the structure of self in terms of "how we arrange for performances in Anglo-American society." He described the individual as "a harried fabricator of impressions involved in the all-too-human task of staging a performance."[41]

> Making pictures of themselves in celebrations or other self-enhancing situations is what people do more in individualistic and masculine cultures than in collectivistic and/or feminine cultures. In some countries people indeed make more photographs than in others. Usage of films (more than six used in the past 12 months) in 1995 (data EMS) correlated with masculinity, which explained 38% of variance. In 2007, 44% of variance of interest in photography was explained by short-term orientation.

Acceptance of advertisements appealing to personal status and self-enhancement differs as much between the United States and Denmark, both individualistic cultures, as between the United States and Korea. This is because self-enhancement appeals may be judged in poor taste in the self-reliant yet egalitarian societies of Scandinavia, whereas they may be rejected for being too self-focused in Korea.[42]

Differences in how women judge their own bodies, beauty, or appearance, in an enhanced way or more critical, is related to differences in self-enhancement.

> For the Dove campaign for Real Beauty, Unilever sponsored a study[43] on the self and beauty, asking questions to young girls about satisfaction with their own beauty and opinions on beauty in 10 different countries worldwide. Individualism and short-term orientation were the main predictors of variance. The percentage of girls who were satisfied with their beauty correlated with short-term orientation, which explained 58% of variance; short-term orientation also explained 69% of agreement with the statement "Society expects women to enhance their physical attractiveness." Agreement with the statement "It would be better if the media depicted women of different shapes" varied with individualism, explaining 53% of variance and short-term orientation explaining an additional 25%. One statement to a larger group of women (18–64 years old) was, "My mother has positively influenced my feelings about myself and beauty." Sixty-five percent of variance of the percentages who agreed was explained by short-term orientation. Self-enhancement goes from generation to generation.

Across 14 wealthy European countries, short-term orientation explains differences between countries with respect to consumers' relationships with brands, like finding that some brands are worth paying more for (42% explained) and consumers' desire to be among the first to try new brands (40% explained).[44] In short-term-oriented cultures, brands appear to be self-enhancing phenomena.

A need for self-esteem may exist across cultures, but people arrive at self-esteem in various ways. Self-esteem is not necessarily the cause of behavior; behavior can be the cause of self-esteem. Because different cultural behavioral practices lead to self-esteem, the content of self-esteem can vary across cultures. In individualistic and masculine cultures, self-esteem means being competent, talented, able to take care of oneself, and able to compete successfully. The pursuit of self-esteem is facilitated by self-enhancing motivations. In contrast, in collectivistic and high power distance cultures, in particular in East Asia, self-esteem is tied to maintaining face, implying meeting the consensual standards associated with their roles. The pursuit of face is facilitated by self-improving motivations.[45]

In collectivistic cultures, respect from others is more important than self-esteem. This can be recognized in answers to a question in the European Social Survey[46] that asks respondents across western and eastern European countries to mark the importance of getting respect from others. Collectivism explains 47% of variance, and masculinity explains an additional 13% of variance. The relationship between respect from others and collectivism is illustrated in Figure 4.4, which also shows that feminine cultures like Sweden, Norway, and Finland score lower than masculine cultures like Ireland, Switzerland, and Poland.

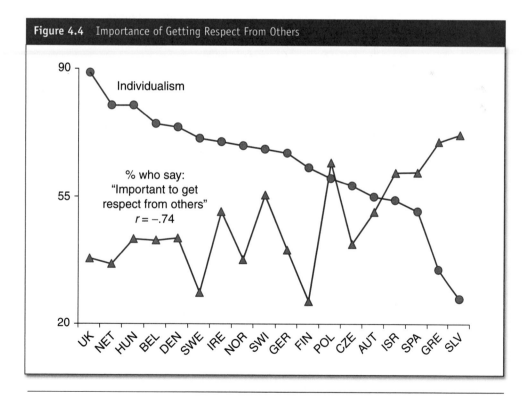

Figure 4.4 Importance of Getting Respect From Others

SOURCES: Hofstede et al. (2010) (see Appendix A); European Social Survey (2002/2003) (see Appendix B)

The differences in self-enhancement are mapped in Figure 4.5. The *X*-axis contains Hofstede's country scores for individualism, and the *Y*-axis for short-/long-term orientation. In the cultures in the lower quadrants, we find need for respect from others, feelings of pride and self-enhancement. In the upper quadrants, maintaining face, self-improvement, and self-criticism are more common. Figure 4.5 shows that, although self-enhancement is often thought to be a universal human characteristic, the countries where it is strongest are the United States, United Kingdom, Ireland, and Australia, a limited number of countries.

Figure 4.5   Self-Enhancement

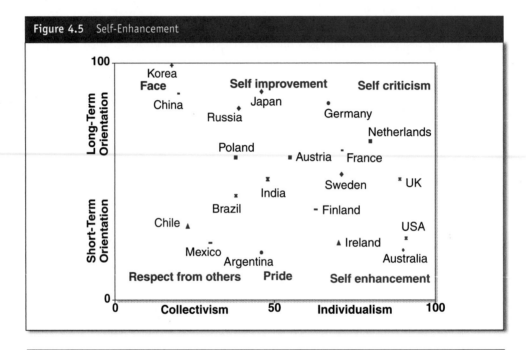

SOURCE: Data Hofstede et al. (2010) (see Appendix A)

PERSONALITY

Broadly defined, *personality* is the sum of the qualities and characteristics of being a person. Generally, the person is defined in the European-American psychological context in which the person is viewed as an "independent self-contained, autonomous entity who comprises a unique configuration of internal attributes (e.g., traits, abilities, motives, and values) and who behaves primarily as consequence of these internal attributes."[47] Definitions of personality in consumer behavior and marketing textbooks reflect this. Persons have distinct personalities that influence their buying behavior.

What is meant by *personality* are the person's distinguishing psychological charac-teristics that lead to relatively consistent and enduring responses to his or her environ-ment. Like the self, the personality is assumed to be cross-situationally consistent. Increasingly, cultural psychologists argue that consistency is greater in individualistic cul-tures than in collectivistic cultures, because in the latter behavior is more strongly influ-enced by contextual factors.[48]

Descriptions of the concept of personality generally include three Western-based ele-ments: (1) People should distinguish themselves from others. (2) Consistency is an integral part of the concept. (3) Personality is described in terms of abstract personal traits.

According to the Western view, the study of personality should lead to understand-ing, predicting, and controlling behavior. In individualistic cultures, because of con-sistency between personal traits and behavior, these traits are used to predict behavior. Collectivists place a higher value on situational cues and upholding "face." Emphasis on behavior that should not bring public shame to one's family and social group sug-gests that individuals behave irrespective of their individual characteristics. As a result the utility of personal traits may not be as strong in collectivistic cultures as it is in indi-vidualistic cultures.[49]

In individualistic cultures, once people have chosen to comply with a request, they will more than will collectivists comply with subsequent, similar requests. Comparison of consistency in compliance among Americans and Asians showed some differences. Differences in compli-ance were measured by (a) compliance with an initial request, (b) willingness to comply with future, related requests, and (c) compliance with a larger subsequent request. Although in both cultures participants were more likely to comply with a request if they had chosen to com-ply with a similar request one month earlier, this tendency was more pronounced among the U.S. participants than among Asian participants. Despite their lower rate of compliance with an initial request, once committed, the U.S. respondents were more likely than the Asian respondents to agree to a larger, related request.[50]

Western individualists view personal traits as fixed; they are part of the person. East Asian collectivists view traits as malleable; traits will vary with the situation. When individualists describe themselves or others, they use elements of the personal self in objective, abstract words, out of context (I am kind, she is nice). People from collectivistic cultures tend to use mostly elements of the collective self or describe actions of people in context (My family thinks I am kind, she brings cake to my family).[51] Easterners believe in the continuous shap-ing of personality traits by situational influences.[52]

People in Eastern cultures often use a "tree" as a metaphor for a person, which emphasizes the endless shaping of internal dispositions by the external environment. For instance, in Korea a person is believed to be like a white root that takes on the color of the soil in which it grows. If a white root is planted in red soil, it becomes red. In China a person is likened to a white silk cloth. If placed in red dye, it becomes red; if placed in green dye, it becomes green. Once the self is likened to a plant, it is evident that the environment is essential for the development, nourishment, and cultivation of the person.[53]

THE BRAND PERSONALITY CONCEPT

The human personality is used as metaphor in branding strategies. The *brand personality* concept is rooted in Anglo-American presumptions. The core of a sophisticated advertising campaign is the brand positioning statement, including a description of the brand personality in terms of human characteristics. In international marketing, the descriptions are usually in Anglo-American terms. A brand personality that can be recognized by or is attractive to the average public of one culture will not necessarily be recognized or found attractive to the average public of another culture. As a result, advertising campaigns that are effective in one culture because they are based on a strong brand personality are not necessarily as effective in another culture. Brands acquire their personalities over time, and these are largely derived from the market context in which they develop. This context consists of a series of peculiarities that might not repeat itself in the same ways in other intended markets.[54]

Whereas in individualistic cultures brands have to be unique, distinct, and contain consistent characteristics, in collectivistic cultures the brand personality should be viewed as being part of a larger whole, being a person in the world of other brands. In Asia a brand is probably better defined as being part of a *brand world* rather than being a *unique personality.*

Because of the nonexistence of the Western personality concept in Asia, Asian languages such as Japanese and Chinese do not have linguistic equivalents for the term *personality* as a person separate from the social environment. As a result the Western brand personality metaphor is not well understood in Asia, and brand personalities are more corporate personalities. This is recognized in branding practice of Asian companies. Whereas American companies have concentrated on promoting product brands, Japanese companies have generally emphasized company brands. In essence this means inspiring trust among consumers in a company and so persuading them to buy its products. Western companies that tend to insist on consistency in their uniqueness, using one logo worldwide, run the risk of being perceived as arrogant or even insulting. In line with the idea of a brand world, another option may be to use the concept of *face of the brand,* a visual representation of the company's attributes that is more like a mosaic than a logo. It consists of a unified set of visual symbols that is tailored to depict the brand. "A global 'face of the brand' can have the same graphic roots but appear somewhat different depending on the local markets targeted. The idea is to depict unity, without forcing sameness."[55]

> A study by Linda Derksen at the advertising agency PPGH/JWT Amsterdam surveyed the practice of brand personality in four countries in Europe. The JWT agencies in Germany, United Kingdom, France, and Spain were asked to what extent they worked with the brand personality concept when developing advertising campaigns. One of the questions was to select a definition of brand personality from a choice of three possible definitions: (1) the unique characteristics of a brand that distinguish it from other (competitive) brands; (2) the brand as a "human being" with human characteristics that are associated with a brand; (3) the reflection of a brand in its environment, just like people who are part of their environment, their family, and work. The British and Germans viewed the brand as a person who is characterized by unique qualities that differentiate it from other brands. The French saw the brand as a human being with human characteristics associated with the brand. The Spanish opted for the definition of brand personality as a reflection of how a brand fits in its environment, family, and work.[56]

PERSONAL TRAITS

The Western habit of describing people in terms of abstract characteristics has led to the development of characterization systems of personal traits. *Traits* can be defined as "dimensions of individual differences in tendencies to show consistent patterns of thoughts, feelings, and actions."[57] Examples of traits are *altruism* (helpfulness and generosity to others), *modesty* (self-effacing attitudes and behaviors), and *trust* (beliefs about others' actions and intentions).[58] In the Western world it has been argued that there are only a relatively small number of universal trait dimensions.[59]

Personality traits can be found in the natural language used when people describe themselves. Such natural language adjectives are used in questionnaire scales for developing trait dimensions. Factor analysis is used to develop trait structures. The five-factor model (FFM or "Big Five") is one of the most used models to organize personality traits. It was developed in the United States and based on analyses of the colloquial usage of the English language, on people's descriptions of themselves and others.

There are various problems when developing trait structures across cultures. Whereas American descriptions include psychological trait characteristics, self-descriptions in collectivistic cultures tend to refer to social roles. A difficulty when using scales across cultures is finding linguistic equivalents for the trait descriptions. Nevertheless, with the cooperation of psychologists of many different cultures, the FFM has developed into a universal model for measuring personality trait structure across cultures, using a scale called the NEO-PI-R facet scale. The universal five-trait factors have been named *neuroticism, extraversion, openness to experience, agreeableness,* and *conscientiousness.* These five basic trait factors are supposed to capture the many meanings of personality characteristics. Table 4.1 shows the factors and components of each factor.[60]

Table 4.1   Five-Factor Model of Personality Traits

Neuroticism	Extraversion	Openness to Experience	Agreeableness	Conscientiousness
Anxiety	Warmth	Fantasy	Trust	Competence
Angry hostility	Gregariousness	Aesthetics	Straightforwardness	Order
Depression	Assertiveness	Feelings	Altruism	Dutifulness
Self-consciousness	Activity	Actions	Compliance	Achievement striving
Impulsiveness	Excitement seeking	Ideas	Modesty	Self-discipline
Vulnerability	Positive emotions	Values	Tender-mindedness	Deliberation

SOURCE: McCrae (2002)

Across cultures, several variations were found. There were, for example, more within-culture differences in European than in Asian cultures. A cause of this may be that in collectivistic cultures, individual differences are muted because individuals avoid emphasizing their distinctive personal attributes. Another reason can be more homogeneity of personality among Asians than among European groups.[61]

In particular, Asian psychologists have been eager to find whether the model applies to collectivistic cultures. Chinese psychologists Cheung et al.[62] developed an indigenous scale for China (Chinese Personality Assessment Inventory) and merged it with the five-factor model. They found similar five factors, but the components varied across the factors. A cause can be that the trait adjectives, when translated, get different meanings. The Chinese researchers also found a sixth dimension, which they called *interpersonal relatedness,* that included the components optimism versus pessimism, *Ren Qing* (relationship orientation), flexibility, *Ah-Q* mentality (defensiveness), harmony, face, and logical versus affective orientation. The interpersonal relatedness factor addresses the interdependent aspects of personality that are important to the Chinese as well as to other collectivistic cultures. If Chinese researchers had dominated personality research, the leading theory would have excluded the openness factor, which is a decidedly non-Asian factor.[63] For measuring an open person in collectivistic cultures, interpersonal tolerance and social sensitivity are more relevant than the items included in the Western scales.[64] Generally, in collectivistic cultures openness may take on a different form or function. Differences may be caused by translating concepts for which there are no linguistic equivalents. Openness also is difficult to translate in African languages, such as Shona and Xhosa, in which there is a shortage of openness-related terms. The Korean language version of the NEO-PI-R scale submitted to Korean respondents also produced differences between Korean and American respondents.[65]

From longitudinal studies psychologists find increasing evidence that our personality traits are partly biologically inherited and partly shaped by the interaction of the individual with the environment, at the broadest level. One of these environments is the culture of the country where we were raised.[66] The relationship with culture was found by correlating Hofstede's cultural variables with culture-level means of individual-level scores on the NEO-PI-R factors for 36 cultures.[67] Neuroticism scores are higher in cultures of strong uncertainty avoidance and high masculinity. This fits with other findings that anxiety, stress, and expression of emotion are more found in high uncertainty avoidance cultures than in low uncertainty avoidance cultures. Masculinity stands for focus on ego and money orientation, whereas femininity stands for focus on relationships and people orientation. The latter orientation probably relates to lower neuroticism. Impulsiveness, one of the elements of this dimension, does not necessarily include impulse buying. Data by TGI[68] among consumers in seven Latin American countries show a relationship with low, not high, uncertainty avoidance, with buying on impulse ($r = -.70*$). Extraversion score levels are higher in individualistic cultures, where autonomy, variety, and pleasure are valued over expertise, duty, and security. Furthermore, they correlate with low power distance. Openness to experience was correlated with high masculinity and low power distance. In cultures of high masculinity, people tend to overrate their own performance, and low power distance stimulates independent exploration. Agreeableness correlated with low uncertainty avoidance, so in cultures with higher tolerance, people score themselves as more agreeable. Conscientiousness correlated with high power distance, but it is even stronger related to gross national income (GNI) per capita. Hofstede concludes that "prosperity allows people to behave less conscientiously or more wasteful."[69]

How consumer experiences reflect elements of personality is demonstrated by findings of a pan-European (13 countries) study of ecological awareness among drivers by the tire company Goodyear.[70] A typology of European drivers was developed from questions about attitudes toward driving and driving behavior. Respondents could categorize themselves in terms of personal driving characteristics. Considerable culture-related differences were found between countries. The percentages of respondents who considered themselves to be *responsible drivers* (= conscientiousness) correlated positively with power distance. The percentages of respondents who considered driving their car as an *adventure* (= extraversion) correlated with individualism. The percentages of respondents who considered themselves to be *social drivers*, who considered their car as a means of supporting their social life (= agreeableness), correlated with low uncertainty avoidance and low power distance. The percentages of respondents who considered their car to be a means to *show off*, a status symbol, saying something about themselves (= openness to experience), correlated with masculinity.

The problem with trait studies is that instead of factors emerging from native conceptions of personhood across cultures, findings mainly confirm that when the same set of English items that form five factors are translated into other languages, they result in similar five-factor structures across cultures. This doesn't imply that these are the only existing conceptions of personhood. It merely shows that a set of English language questions, when translated, result in similar five-dimensional structures.[71]

As in value studies, in addition to translation problems when measuring personal traits, there are other measurement problems. When individuals make judgments about themselves, they implicitly draw comparisons with others. These referent others, however, are different for people in different cultures. This is particularly relevant for measuring personality traits. In a large study of the geographic distribution of the "Big Five" personality traits, the researchers were surprised to find Chinese, Korean, and Japanese people in the very bottom on the conscientiousness scale. It seems unlikely that most people would think of individuals of these cultures as extremely undisciplined and weak willed—a profile indicative of low conscientiousness. However, where the standards for being punctual, strong willed, and reliable are very high, a respondent may report that he or she is less disciplined than is generally the case in the particular culture.[72] A similar phenomenon can be recognized when measuring Spanish *simpatía* (agreeableness), which is associated with striving to promote harmony in relationships by showing respect toward others, avoiding conflict, emphasizing positive behaviors, and deemphasizing negative behaviors. However, self-report data show that Hispanics rate themselves lower on agreeableness than do European Americans. When *simpatía* is the norm, people will not score themselves high on this trait.[73]

BRAND PERSONALITY TRAITS

Marketing people tend to develop trait dimensions for brands as if brands are human beings. Thus, brand personality is defined as a set of humanlike attributes associated with a particular brand. An example is a study by Aaker et al.[74] that developed personality dimensions in several countries by asking individuals to rate a representative set of commercial brands on a battery of personality attributes. In the United States, five dimensions were found and labeled *sincerity* (down-to-earth, real, sincere, honest); *excitement* (daring, exciting, imaginative, contemporary); *competence* (intelligent, reliable, secure, confident); *sophistication* (glamorous, upper class, good looking, charming); and *ruggedness* (tough, outdoorsy, masculine, and Western). The authors noted that three of the dimensions—sincerity, excitement, and competence—resemble personality dimensions that are also present in human personality models such as the Big Five model, relating respectively to agreeableness, extraversion, and conscientiousness. Sophistication captures aspirational images associated with wealth and status, and the ruggedness dimension represents typical American values such as strength, masculinity, and ruggedness. Similar studies were conducted in Japan and Spain, which resulted in two more sets of five dimensions. The five Japanese dimensions overlapped with the American ones with respect to excitement, competence, sincerity, and sophistication. One dimension, named *peacefulness,* was defined by a unique blend of attributes (e.g., shy, peaceful, naïve, dependent), which was assumed to be indigenous for Japan. Of the five dimensions found in Spain, three overlapped with the American dimensions sincerity, excitement, and sophistication. The latter included some of the competence associations. One dimension was similar to the Japanese dimension peacefulness, and one dimension seemed to be an indigenous Spanish one. It was named *passion* and included components like fervent, passionate, spiritual, and bohemian. The dimension peacefulness that Spain and Japan have in common is likely related to the collectivistic aspects they share. A Korean study of brand personalities[75] of well-known global brands like Nike, Sony, Levi's, Adidas, Volkswagen, and BMW found two specific Korean brand personalities. The first, labeled *passive likeableness,* included traits like easy, smooth, family oriented, playful, and sentimental. The second was labeled *ascendancy* and included traits like strict, heavy, intelligent, and daring. These findings suggest that, even if companies wish to be consistent, having connected one specific personality trait to a global brand, across cultures consumers attach different personalities to these brands. These are the traits that are viewed as fitting by consumers, but they can be very different from what the company wanted.

Comparison of the image of Red Bull in the United Kingdom, Singapore, Austria, Germany, the Netherlands, and the United States show differences in perceptions of the Red Bull brand personality. Although the global advertising campaign pushed competence and excitement as brand characteristics, these seem mostly to appeal to the U.K. public.[76]

Similar brand personality dimensions may exist across cultures, but the similarities are often based only on partial equivalents, meaning that superficially similar dimensions consist of different associations. Constructs tend to shift in meaning when examined in different cultural contexts. Excitement, for example, is associated with being young, contemporary, spirited, and daring, but in the United States and Spain it also conveys imaginativeness, uniqueness, and independence, whereas in Japan it includes talkative, funny, and optimistic. Sophistication takes on a different meaning in Spain than it does in Japan.

The previous discussion may demonstrate the difficulty in using personality descriptors for brand positioning across cultures. First, there are culture-specific personality dimensions, such as ruggedness in the United States and peacefulness in Japan. Brand personalities fitting in such indigenous dimensions are not likely to be as successful in

A cross-cultural brand value study[77] showed that a brand characteristic like friendly is most attributed to strong global brands in high uncertainty avoidance and low power distance cultures. This fits with findings from a Eurobarometer study asking for the importance of friends. The percentages of answers saying that friends are very important correlate with low power distance ($r = -.59***$).[78] Prestigious is a characteristic attributed to global brands in high power distance, and trustworthy is most attributed to strong brands in high uncertainty avoidance cultures. In the low power distance and low uncertainty avoidance cultures, people attributed innovative and different to these brands. Figure 4.6 presents a map of different brand personalities attributed to strong global brands.

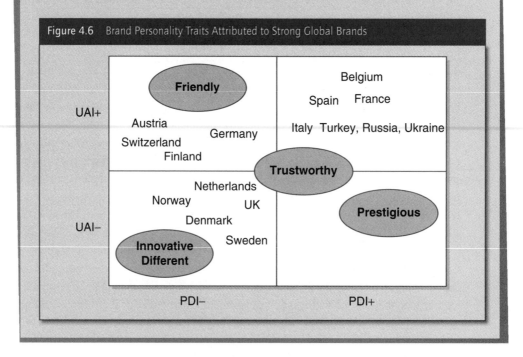

Figure 4.6   Brand Personality Traits Attributed to Strong Global Brands

other countries as they are in the home country. Second, although some studies suggest that there are similar personality dimensions across countries, similar labels can have different associations, so the meaning of seemingly similar trait descriptions can be very different.

One reason for developing consistent brand personalities may be the need for *control.* If consumers elsewhere perceive these global brands as having different personality traits than the company intended, the process is *out of control,* and to keep control, it may be better to define specific brand personality traits for the various cultures in which the company operates.

IDENTITY AND IMAGE

Identity is the idea one has about oneself, one's characteristic properties, one's own body, and the values one considers important. *Image* is how others see and judge a person.[79] The importance of a unique identity for individualists emerges from a Eurobarometer[80] survey asking respondents to what degree people believe in a shared cultural identity. The percentages of respondents who agreed correlated negatively with individualism, whereas the percentages disagreeing correlated positively with individualism. Figure 4.7 illustrates this relationship for 12 countries in Europe.

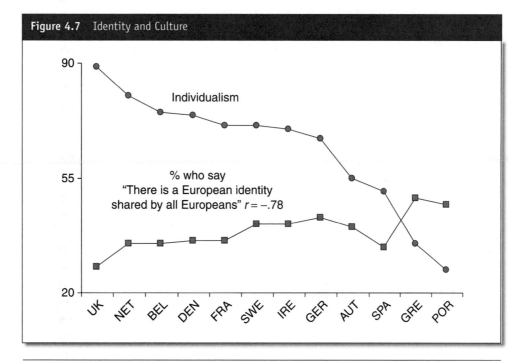

Figure 4.7   Identity and Culture

SOURCES: Data from Hofstede et al. (2010) (see Appendix A); Eurobarometer Report *How Europeans See Themselves* (2001) (see Appendix B)

Identity among collectivists is defined by relationships and group memberships, whereas individualists base identity on what they own and their experiences. Identity also is one's capacity to fulfill expectations. When a person is asked what her identity is, she can categorize herself in terms of desirable values ("I believe that . . ."), as a member of social groups (e.g., a mother, a student), or by personality traits (e.g., ambitious, cheerful.)[81] In most Western cultures, people tend to assess the identity of self and others based on personality traits, on other individual characteristics such as age and occupation, and on material symbols.[82]

A distinction can be made between achieved identity and ascribed identity. *Achieved identity* means one is judged by what one does, one's being: one is a "good father," a "good student." *Ascribed identity* involves fixed expectations based on non-chosen traits such as gender, age, and inherited position. The perception of people having fixed, ascribed identities is stronger in high power distance cultures, where people have more clearly defined positions in society than in cultures of low power distance. In Western societies, the possession of tangible goods provides achieved identity. Housing, transportation, and other visible consumption are assumed to reflect one's values, career success, and personality. In the United States social standing is fluid—one *buys* one's status—whereas "the French still believe that it is noble to inherit a fortune and dirty to earn one."[83]

Individuals can be pleased with personality traits that form a part of their *real identity*, or they may want to change them, as a function of an image they would like to have. This produces an identity that reflects what psychoanalysts have termed the "ideal self." These two dimensions of identity can be close or far apart from each other. If they are far apart, efforts are usually made to reduce the gap.[84] In individualistic cultures, material possessions can serve this purpose.

The Body and Identity

In Western psychology the body is viewed as part of the identity. Body esteem is related to several constructs of the self, such as self-esteem, body consciousness, and social anxiety. One of the central terms in the field is *body image,* which is the picture of our own body that we form in our mind.[85] In Western societies, people attribute more desirable characteristics to physically attractive persons. This is called the "physical attractiveness stereotype."[86]

What is considered attractive varies. The Japanese, for example, rate large eyes and small mouths and chins as attractive, whereas Koreans prefer large eyes, small and high noses, and thin and small faces.[87] The vast majority of research on what constitutes physical attractiveness has been conducted in Western societies, but mostly in the United States, where physical attractiveness of women is judged according to strict criteria, which leads to dissatisfaction. The typical American woman begins to voice dissatisfaction with her body early in life and continues to do so into the adult years. The general idea is that a desirable appearance leads to greater self-esteem. In Japan, where people attribute success more to external than to internal sources, there is less emphasis on the body as a source of esteem.[88] Confucian belief suggests that external physical appearance is less important than success in social role performance in the development of self-esteem and happiness.[89]

Attractiveness does not result in similar conclusions about people's characteristics across cultures. In Korea, for example, attractiveness is seen as being associated with lineage: high-status families are expected to produce better-looking children because their greater financial and social resources would permit considerable selection in mating.[90]

Each cultural group has its own unique definition of physical attractiveness (human beauty), and its own set of bodily ideals, that shape its collective body image.

> Chinese women view Caucasian men as wealthy, and this presumed wealth makes Caucasian men attractive. Chinese women's views on what makes attractive men differ completely from the South Korean perspective that overwhelmingly prefers images of immature young men who have a "pretty face with big eyes and fair skin and a moderately masculine body." It is a criterion also shared by young Japanese women. In contrast, Chinese women are adamant in their rejection of immature males. Chinese women prefer a more serious pose associated with an integrated or well-balanced character.[91]

Body image concerns, weight concerns, and eating disorders are more prevalent among Western women than among non-Western women.[92] Within the United States, disordered eating and dieting behaviors are more frequent among European Americans than among Asian and African Americans.[93] A study in 1995 found that 90% of white schoolgirls were dissatisfied with their weight, whereas 70% of African American teens were satisfied with their bodies.[94] Body images as displayed in the media are assumed to influence ideal body images. The continual exposure of good-looking, thin models creates pressure to have an attractive body. This thought is most pronounced in Western individualistic culture, although a relationship between TV viewing and body image dissatisfaction was also found in Hong Kong.[95] In particular in the United States, the ideal is to be thin, and advertising shows thin people. Yet, the United States also is the country with the highest percentage of obese people. Obesity is—as yet—a problem of individualistic cultures. In 1999, in 18 countries of the developed world, the differences between countries with respect to the percentage of population with a body mass index (BMI) over 30[96] correlated significantly with individualism ($r = .59$***). So, in the individualistic cultures the discrepancy between the real and ideal body image is largest.

Although both Japanese and American young adults are concerned with physical attractiveness, female body images in the Japanese media are different from those in American media. Poses of American (thin) models are rebellious or defiant, offering a sultry facial expression, to represent the individual self, independent from and equal to others, whereas poses of Japanese (also thin) models emphasize youthful "girlishness" reflecting dependence needs. The faces show happy, broad smiles reflecting nonchallenging innocence.[97] Figure 4.8 illustrates the differences. These are covers of a British magazine (*Harpers*) for adult women, an American magazine (*Cosmopolitan*) for young women, a Japanese magazine (*Madam*) for adult women, and a Chinese language magazine from Malaysia (*Nuyou*) for young women.

Figure 4.8   Magazine Covers

CORPORATE IDENTITY, BRAND IDENTITY, AND BRAND IMAGE

Like the self, identity in individualistic cultures is supposed to be unique and consistent, as opposed to a collectivist's identity, which can change according to varying social positions and situations. This is reflected in the definitions of *corporate identity* that are based on the Western identity concept. The British communication consultant Nicholas Ind defined *corporate identity* as "an organization's identity in its *sense of self,* much like our own individual sense of identity. Consequently, it is unique."[98] Corporate identity is concerned with the impressions, the image, and the personality projected by an organization.

The individualistic identity metaphor is probably not well understood in collectivistic cultures. Like the personality concept, identity doesn't have a linguistic equivalent in many Asian languages like Japanese and Chinese.

Usually the task of creating a corporate identity begins with the selection of an appropriate corporate name. Other factors that contribute to corporate identity include the logo of the organization and marketing communications. All this, including language, lettering, and associations, is logically a reflection of the home country of the organization. Western organizations in particular prefer worldwide consistency of all these elements, without realizing that this is not an equally effective approach to business in all countries.

Ideally brands have clearly defined images created by advertising, packaging, and other positioning elements, and theory says that these brand images should be congruent with consumers' self-images. The question is whether people buy brands because they are similar to the self, or whether people assume that these brands are similar to the self because they bought them. There is general agreement in (American) marketing literature that consumers tend to favor brands they perceive as similar to themselves, so self-image should match brand image, and similarity of the self-image and brand image should lead to attraction. The Dutchman Bosman,[99] however, found evidence that it works the other way around. In his study the causal flow is not from liking brands because they are similar to the self, but liking a brand for other reasons leads to perceiving it as similar to the self. The subjects in the study were probably Dutch,[100] so his findings may apply to Dutch respondents, whereas the findings presented in American marketing literature may apply to American respondents. Within the Western world, the relationship between brand image and self-image may vary, and even more so between individualistic and collectivistic cultures, where the self-image is likely to be more situational.

Culture does influence how consumers organize the brand image in their minds, in particular the associations consumers have when perceiving a brand. The brand image is a set of perceptions about a brand as reflected by the brand associations held in the consumers' memories. Three main types of brand associations can be distinguished: (1) the product attributes; (2) the benefits; and (3) the brand attitude, including values. Benefits and attitudes are at a higher level of abstraction than the attributes and are assumed to have a closer relationship with the consumer self than do product attributes. Culture influences how consumers perceive and organize these abstract associations. For some, "latest technology" may be associated with "prestige," for others it may be negatively related with "fuel economy."[101]

ATTITUDE

Western consumer behaviorists view *attitudes* as learned predispositions to respond to an object or class of objects in a consistently favorable or unfavorable way.[102] This reflects an individualistic worldview, including the assumption that attitudes lead people to behave in a fairly consistent way. Attitudes drive behavior, but behavior also drives attitudes. In collectivistic cultures, attitudes may vary along with the context in which they operate. A more neutral definition of *attitude* is the individual predisposition to evaluate an object or an aspect of the world in a favorable or unfavorable manner. Attitudes have affective and cognitive components. The affective component includes the sensations, feelings, and emotions one experiences in response to an attitude object. The cognitive component includes various attributes and functions of the object.[103]

In the Western definitions, attitudes serve as knowledge function, helping to organize and structure one's environment and to provide consistency in one's frame of reference. Individualists want consistency across their attitudes, feelings, and behaviors.[104] In collectivistic cultures, people are supposed to form attitudes that fulfill their social identity functions.

Western theory distinguishes three components of attitudes: cognitive, affective, and behavioral, which for attitudes toward brands translate as brand belief, brand evaluations, and intention to buy. The relationship among these three components is known as a *hierarchy of effects*, as if consumers consistently step from one component to another. The sequence varies with the degree of involvement with the product. Brand belief and brand evaluations are knowledge and information based. The role of information in this process will vary with culture as well. (This is discussed further in Chapter 6.)

In Western theory, many attitudes are supposed to serve a utilitarian function, helping to maximize the rewards and minimize the punishments obtained from objects in the environment. An example is one's attitude toward ice cream, which serves a utilitarian function because it can be based on the rewards (enjoyment) and punishment (weight gain). The cross-cultural relevance of this functional theory has not been tested.[105] The reward-punishment effects are a reflection of the typical Western value of guilt.

ATTITUDE AND BEHAVIOR

Consistency between attitude and behavior in individualistic cultures implies that under certain conditions, the behavior of consumers can be predicted from their attitudes toward products, services, and brands, and a purchase prediction is derived from a positive attitude. In collectivistic cultures, however, people form attitudes that fulfill their social identity functions, and there is not a consistent relationship between attitude and future behavior. It may be a reverse relationship: usage comes first and defines attitude. In collectivistic cultures, shared experiences influence brand attitude positively, more than in individualistic cultures.[106]

For measuring advertising effectiveness, the attitude to the advertisement (A_{ad}) tends to be measured, which in turn is used as an indication of buying intention. This practice is logical in individualistic cultures where individuals want consistency between their personal attitudes and behaviors. In collectivistic cultures, where situational factors can influence the various elements of attitude and behavior, the practice may not work the same way.

> Behavior of Japanese youngsters is not consistent with their attitudes to life in general.
>
> Japanese kids like to shop, they curl their hair, they wear this really outrageous clothing that's really influenced by the West, but if you talk to these girls with piercing everywhere, they say that what they really want to do is get married, have a nice house and have kids.[107]

The most widely known model that measures the relationship between attitude and behavior is the Fishbein behavioral intentions model, also referred to as the theory of *reasoned action*. Fishbein hypothesizes that a person's behavioral intentions are determined by an *attitudinal* or *personal component* and a *normative* or *social component*. The personal attitude component, or *attitude toward the act,* refers to personal judgment of behavior, whereas the normative or social component refers to social pressures on behavior such as expectations of others. Cross-cultural findings are that attitude toward the act is the primary determinant in the United States, whereas social norm is more important in Korea. What in Western terms is called *social pressure,* put on Korean consumers, has relatively weak influence on Americans, who refer to their own personal attitudes as having influenced their buying decisions.[108] What is called *social norm* in American theory has a different loading in collectivistic cultures. The social component in the theory does not capture "face." Face motivates collectivists to act in accordance with one's social position. If one acts contrary to expectations of one's social position, a shadow is cast over one's moral integrity.[109] Thus, in collectivistic cultures face pressure is more like a personal norm, capturing personal perceptions of living up to the standards of one's position, whereas the social norm component included in the Fishbein model mainly measures perceptions of opinions of other persons.

Attitudes and intentions are what we feel and know and are derived from what we say. Intentions are often poor predictors of behavior, with large variance across cultures. Intentions must be measured, and differences in response styles are a cause of varying relationships between buying intention and actual buying. For example, if 55% of the people who try a new product in Italy say they will definitely buy it, the product will probably fail. If in Japan 5% say they will definitely buy it, the product is likely to succeed. If people are used to external, uncontrollable factors, such as fate or power holders interfering at any time in the realization of an expressed intention, people will more readily express positive intentions that will not transform into behavior. This difference is reflected in the way people answer in semantic scales in survey research.

Italians like extremes and mark toward the end of any semantic scale, whereas the Germans are more restrained and mark toward the middle. The effect is that a "Completely agree" answer in Italy is not worth the same as a "Completely agree" answer in Germany. This tendency to use extreme points in verbal rating scales is called Extreme Response Style (ERS). One cause of ERS is the type of Likert scale. If high-ERS participants are given a survey using a 7-point Likert-type scale, their responses tend to be either 1 (Strongly agree) or 7 (Strongly disagree). If low-ERS participants are given the same survey, their responses will tend to cluster around 4 (Neither agree nor disagree).[110] Another difference occurs when one group systematically gives higher or lower responses than another group, resulting in a scale displacement. This is called Acquiescence Response Style (ARS). To American respondents a response of 3 on a 5-point Likert scale may mean "No opinion," whereas it may mean "Mild agreement" to Korean respondents. As a result of this scale displacement, Korean 3s are equivalent to American 4s, and Korean 4s are equivalent to American 5s. Overall, ERS and ARS will influence most traditional quantitative marketing techniques, and a strong bias can make market researchers draw wrong conclusions. Market researchers may be erroneously reporting differences in product preferences, consumer attitudes, or perceptions across countries that are wholly or partially attributable to ERS.

When attitudes are measured and compared at national level, there are examples of congruence and incongruence of attitudes and behavior. An example of congruence of national-level attitudes, knowledge, and self-reported behavior is attitude toward the environment among drivers. The tire company Goodyear[111] measured general ecological attitude and knowledge across 13 countries in Europe by asking a number of questions about what is good or bad for the environment (e.g., burning coal, the effects of nuclear waste, human-made chemicals, and the greenhouse effect). The percentages of respondents who answered all questions correctly correlated positively ($r = .61*$) with questions about attitudes to environmental developments (e.g., worry about the destruction of the rain forest, global warming, and environmental pollution). So knowledge and attitudes matched. There was also a significant positive correlation between attitudes and self-reported behavior ($r = .53*$) from questions about how people handle their cars (e.g., rapid acceleration, proper maintenance of their cars, or avoiding use of their cars for short distances).

An example of incongruence of attitudes and behavior is with respect to the euro, the European currency. Whereas the collectivistic and high uncertainty avoidance cultures have shown positive attitudes toward the euro[112] during the years before its introduction in January 2002, after introduction these were the cultures where people still calculated more in their own currencies than in the euro. In some restaurants in Spain, in 2003, the bills were still written in pesetas.

Analysis of differences in attitudes can help explain differences in consumer behavior across cultures. Different attitudes toward the press explain differences in press readership. Attitudes toward technology and information explain differences in acceptance of computers and related technology. In the mid-1990s in Germany, consumers had lots of reservations against the computer. In contrast, U.S. consumers saw the computer mainly as a means to success and prestige.[113] These differences reflected actual penetration differences of computers. Differences in confidence in specific food categories parallel consumption differences. In the following sections of the chapter, several examples of specific culture-bound attitudes are discussed. These are attitudes toward food, health, the media, materialism, national pride, environmentalism, country of origin, and love-related attitudes.

Attitudes Toward Food

Attitudes toward food vary across cultures. There are important differences in the degree to which food is considered to be safe. In 1998 Eurobarometer asked the inhabitants of the European Union (EU) member countries to which degree they had confidence in food. The question asked was, "For each of the following food products, please tell me if you think it is safe or not safe." Products were bread and bakery products, fresh fruit, fresh vegetables, fresh fish, fresh meat, fresh milk, cheese, eggs, canned foods, frozen foods, precooked meals and other prepacked food. Variance among the 13 countries of the European Union was considerable. A number of responses to confidence in food products correlate with actual consumption. Confidence in fresh milk is significantly, positively, correlated with actual consumption of fresh milk, so in countries where people drink more fresh milk, they also have more confidence in fresh milk. There is also a positive relationship between confidence in frozen food and consumption of frozen food. The common explaining factor is uncertainty avoidance. Whereas low confidence in several processed food categories correlates with high uncertainty avoidance, consumption of processed food products correlates with low uncertainty avoidance. Table 4.2 shows the relationships with three cultural variables for the answers "Not safe" for five food products and for consumption data of related products.

Low trust in processed food explains the aversion to genetically modified food (GMF) that is stronger in high than in low uncertainty avoidance cultures. The strong protests against genetically modified food in Europe originated in France, a culture of high uncertainty avoidance.

Table 4.2   Confidence in Food and Consumption of Processed Food

	PDI	IDV	UAI	Predictor	R^2
Not Safe (13 countries)					
Fresh milk	.72***	−.31	.71***	PDI	.51
Cheese	.58*	−.34	.64**	UAI	.42
Frozen foods	.54*	−.60*	.75***	UAI	.56
Precooked meals	.43	−.50*	.67**	UAI	.45
Other prepacked	.49*	−.45	.64**	UAI	.40
Consumption, Liters or Kilograms per Capita (15 countries)					
Milk	−.65*	.11	−.79***	UAI (−)	.63
Ice-cream	−.57*	.45*	−.76***	UAI (−)	.57
Frozen food	−.33	.45*	−.69***	UAI (−)	.48
Frozen ready meals	−.31	.41	−.62**	UAI (−)	.57

SOURCES: Hofstede et al. (2010) (see Appendix A); EBS 120 (1998); Euromonitor (1997) (see Appendix B)

Attitudes Toward Health

People's attitudes toward their health are related to behavior. People's concern for health can be recognized in consumption patterns, in expenditures on health, and in the variations of fitness practice across countries. In Chapter 3 (section on stability), we mentioned the consistent relationship between mineral water consumption and uncertainty avoidance. Whereas in Europe people of high uncertainty avoidance cultures search for health in the purity and quality of their food, in low uncertainty avoidance cultures people's attitudes toward health make them pursue fitness activities. People's positive perception of their health is related to being actively involved in sports. The 1990 World Values Survey asked people to describe their health and also asked questions about membership in sports organizations. There is a significant correlation between the percentages of respondents who describe their health as good or very good and membership in a sports organization. The common explaining variable is uncertainty avoidance. All sorts of data measuring an active attitude toward health, such as involvement in sports, correlate negatively with uncertainty avoidance, whereas all sorts of data relating to a passive orientation, such as use of antibiotics[114] and numbers of physicians per 100,000 people, correlate positively with uncertainty avoidance. An inventory of the results is provided in Table 4.3.

Table 4.3   Attitudes Toward Health: Active and Passive

	Uncertainty Avoidance (r)
1990: Health very good (worldwide, 26 countries)	−.74***
1990: Member sports organization (worldwide, 26 countries)	−.68***
2000: Member sports organization (Europe, 18 countries)	−.56**
1999: Expenditures on recreational & sports services (Europe, 12 countries)	−.71***
2001: Play sports as leisure activity (Europe, 13 countries)	−.47*
2001: Member sports organization (Europe, 13 countries)	−.71***
2007: % active in sports club (Europe, 24 countries)	−.63***
1990: % who neither sport nor exercise (Europe, 15 countries)	+.69***
2004: % who never play sports (Europe, 21 countries)	+.68***
2008: % who say health most important in connection with idea of happiness (Europe, 26 countries)	+.48**
2008: % of household consumption spent on health (Europe, 25 countries)	+.48**
2006: Number of physicians per 10,000 people (worldwide 18 countries GNI/cap US$17,000+)	+.38*

SOURCES: 1990 data: Inglehart et al. (1998); 1999 data: Eurostat (2001); 2000 data: EB 151 *Young Europeans* (2001); 2007 data: EBS 273 (2007); 1990 data: Reader's Digest Eurodata (1991); 2004 data: EBS 213 (2004); 2008 data: Standard EB 69 (2008); 2008 data: Eurostat (2008); 2006 data: World Health Organization (2002/2009) (see Appendix B)

Attitudes Toward Consumption: Materialism

Materialism is described as an attitude toward consumption, an enduring belief in the desirability of acquiring and possessing things. Materialism can also be viewed as a function of one's personality, reflecting traits of possessiveness, envy, nongenerosity, and preservation. Another approach is to view materialism as a value, as a desirable goal in life. It can also be viewed as part of a self-concept, when people use material possessions to construct personal identities. More often than not materialists tend to judge their own and others success by the number and quality of possessions accumulated. The value of possessions stems not only from their ability to confer status but from their ability to project a desired self-image and identify one as a participant in an imagined perfect life.[115]

As a consumption orientation,[116] materialism is the importance a consumer attaches to worldly possessions. Materialism is also a competitive striving to have more than others. Possessions make people happy and things are more valued than people. Materialistic people display an excessive desire to acquire and keep possessions, including objects, people, and memories (photographs). Materialism consists of three belief domains.

1. Acquisition centrality: Materialism brings meaning to life and provides an aim for daily endeavors.

2. Acquisition as the pursuit of happiness: Materialists view their possessions and their acquisitions as essential to their satisfaction and well-being in life.

3. Possession-defined success: The number and quality of possessions accumulated form a basis for judgment of the materialist's own and others' success. [117]

Attitudes toward materialism vary across cultures. A study among American, British, German, and Austrian students showed that *success* played a vital role in attitudes toward materialism, but also differences in associations with materialism were found, related to job matters, personal development, health, and happiness. For the Germans and Austrians, for example, happiness was more related to stability and social security than to materialism. Because all four groups score high on cultural masculinity, the similar associations with success are understandable. The differences are likely related to the differences in uncertainty avoidance.

Chiagouris and Mitchell describe how much materialism is ingrained in American society:

Materialism is the foundation of an inherently competitive humanity. A philosophy ingrained in the history of the United States of America and the capitalist society we hold so dear. We strive to accumulate goods, products, things that carry with them the external status symbolism that fosters perceived power and influence. It is the core of consumer behavior that has, throughout time, evolved through numerous phases of development.[118]

With increased wealth, materialism should increase. Inglehart,[119] however, assumes that after a certain level of affluence is reached, materialism declines as consumers turn to higher-order needs, and so-called postmaterialist values become more important. He defines *materialist* values as emphasizing economic and physical security above all, whereas *postmaterialist* priorities include emphasis on the quality of life. If this assumption were true, there would be evidence of ownership of expensive luxury articles becoming less important with increased wealth. This cannot be demonstrated at the national level. Inglehart's country scores for postmaterialist values do not show any significant correlations with data on ownership of luxury articles, such as watches, PCs, cars (three or four owned), expensive clothes, shoes, and handbags, and spending on cosmetics, skin care, and perfume.[120] In Europe, Inglehart's postmaterialist country scores are correlated with individualism ($r = .47^*$). In sum, at the culture level there is no relationship between Inglehart's postmaterialist values and ownership of luxury articles. Instead, the relationship between individualism and postmaterialist values leads us to conclude that Inglehart's definitions of postmaterialism and materialism are mainly reflections of values of individualistic cultures.

Analysis of other data supports this conclusion. Ger and Belk[121] developed scales to measure various aspects of materialism across nations, which were labeled *nongenerosity*, *possessiveness*, *envy*, and *preservation* (the conservation of events, experiences, and memories in material form). The four together were thought to be the underlying views of materialism. When the country scores of the four scales (factors) were correlated with the cultural variables,[122] nongenerosity correlated with individualism ($r = .60^*$), and envy correlated with power distance ($r = .53^*$). Preservation correlated with GNI per capita ($r = .69^{**}$), small power distance ($r = -.72^{***}$), and individualism ($r = .67^{**}$), a configuration of dimensions that fits the Western world. From the various studies, it looks like materialism is a specific Western concept, although the various separate elements of materialism are related to different cultural dimensions.

Findings from another study, comparing Australia, France, Mexico, and the United States, suggest that materialism is indeed less strong in collectivistic than in individualistic cultures. Across cultures, the values associated with materialism also vary. For example, security is a value more related to materialism in individualistic cultures than in collectivistic cultures.[123]

National Pride and Consumer Ethnocentrism

Countries vary with respect to the importance people attribute to their own national identities, their attitudes toward their nations. National identity is the extent to which a given culture recognizes and identifies with its unique characteristics. "National pride designates the positive affective bond to specific national achievements and symbols."[124] According to the World Values Survey data from the years 1995–2004, Venezuelans are the most patriotic people in the world: 92% say they are very proud of their country. Americans and Australians also score high, with respectively 72% and 73%. In Asia, the Philippines score high with 87%. In Europe, feelings of national pride are strong in Portugal and Ireland. In Portugal, 80% said that they were very proud to be Portuguese, and in Ireland 73% of respondents said they were proud to be Irish. National pride is weakest in Germany, where only 14% said they were proud to be German, and in Belgium, where 23% said they were proud to be Belgians. Feelings of national pride are not strong in Japan (23%) and Korea (17%) but are high in Thailand (85%). There is a strong relationship between national pride and short-term orientation, which explains 82% of variance. In short-term-oriented cultures, self-enhancement is strong, and so are feelings of pride that obviously are associated with the country one belongs to.

When consumers prefer products or brands from their own country to products or brands from other countries, this is called consumer *ethnocentrism*. Generally, in developed countries preferences for domestic products are stronger than in developing countries.[125] The inclination to favor in-groups over out-groups in collectivistic cultures would suggest a relationship with collectivism,[126] but among consumers in developing countries that are usually also collectivistic—for reasons that go beyond quality assessments—nondomestic brands are attitudinally preferred to brands viewed as local. Brands from other countries, especially from the West, are seen as endowing prestige and cosmopolitanism and thus enhancing the buyer's social identity.[127] Status seeking by buying international brands is also a phenomenon of collectivistic cultures.

Consumer ethnocentrism is related to the degree of national pride. Across Latin America, where feelings of national pride generally are strong, 67% agree with the statement "I prefer to buy products manufactured in my own country."[128] Thai consumers have an overall preference for national brands, and they are willing to pay a premium for brands with strong reputations.[129]

Feelings of national pride can be reinforced after political turbulence. In 1995, a study of consumer patriotism and attitudes toward purchasing in Eastern Europe found that Czech, Slovakian, and Polish consumers considered their goods to be better value for money than those of Western countries. Hungarian consumers had the best opinion of their own food production, closely followed by consumers in the Czech Republic and Poland. Domestic brands had more loyal buyers than foreign brands.[130] Over time, preferences for domestic products had become stronger. By 1998, local brands had gained significant share from international brands. In Poland, when asked, "If you have two similar products at the same price which one do you prefer: a local one or a foreign one?" the majority (77%) of adults said they would prefer the local product.[131]

In the year 2000, in the European car market, national brands dominated. The top three brands in the United Kingdom were Ford, Vauxhall, and Rover, all three British made. In Germany the top five car brands were Volkswagen, Ford (German made), Opel, BMW, and Audi. In France, the top three brands were Renault, Peugeot, and Citroën, all three of French heritage. In Spain, the third brand was Seat, the Spanish-made Volkswagen brand.[132] The extreme patriotism that motivates Americans to support national business and to continue buying in difficult economic or political times does not exist in Europe.

Attitudes Toward Country of Origin

Consumers are sensitive to the country of origin of products and brands. Country of origin of products or brands or foreign-sounding brand names influence consumer perceptions.[133] Consumers use country of origin as stereotypical information in making evaluations of products.[134] Consumers who have positive or negative attitudes toward a particular country will show favorable or unfavorable responses to country-related advertisements.[135]

Attitudes toward foreign products vary by country of origin of the product. Whereas Japan is judged best for technologically advanced and attractively priced products, Germany is the home of reliable, solid products. France and Italy share the preeminence for style, design, and refinement.[136]

Attitudes are related to the combination of the product category and country of origin. "Fashionable" for clothes will relate to French origin, whereas "quality" for cars will relate to Germany. A positive product-country match exists when a country is perceived as very strong in an area (e.g., design or technology), which is also an important feature for a product category (e.g., furniture, cars). Such product-country match is called *prototypicality.* Views of what product categories are prototypical for which countries vary. The role of the country image acts differently in different target countries.[137] Whereas, for example, in Korea refrigerators are viewed as prototypical for the United States,[138] this is not the case in Europe.

Country of origin can reflect on specific product categories or on a variety of products when a country represents a *way of life.* Both effects can change over time. In the past, Japan stood for shoddy, cheap products, but that image has changed into one of quality and technology. For Asian youth, "American" has long represented an aspirational lifestyle. It used to offer freedom, independence, and opportunity, but in 2000, this attitude was changing, and European goods became more popular. Europe represents a more understated style, compared with the brashness of America.[139]

Attitudes toward developed countries are more favorable than attitudes toward developing countries, although in some cultures people tend to prefer anything from outside to domestic products. In the eyes of Nigerian consumers, for example, mere foreignness is a reason for product preferences. Even products from Ghana, which is economically and technologically not superior to Nigeria, are preferred to Nigerian products.[140]

Attitudes Toward the Environment

Across countries, people vary with respect to their attitudes toward the environment. Only in the past decades have environmental problems become widespread matters of concern among the general publics. But attitudes to the environment vary. In the less wealthy countries, economic development has higher priority than the environment. In 2008, the percentage of inhabitants of European Union countries who said that "economic growth must be a priority for our country, even if it affects the environment" correlated with low GNI per capita and high power distance.[141]

The associations people have with the concept of the environment vary. The word *environment* is associated with a wide variety of thoughts that, in equal measure, suggest negative images (pollution, disasters) and positive ideas (pleasant landscapes, protecting the natural world). German consumers tend to adopt a holistic perspective (i.e., humans are seen very much as a part of the ecological system). In Britain, environmentalism is very much about the destruction of the inner cities, the preservation of the fabled English countryside, and the war on waste. In France, environmentalism is mostly about the depletion of the rain forests or problems stemming from the use of harmful products like aerosols.[142] Differences in associations are culture bound.[143] Whereas in high power distance cultures people think first of pollution in towns and cities, in low power distance cultures a first association is with climate change. Loss in biodiversity, depletion of natural resources, and consumption habits are worries of rich countries. Air pollution and noise pollution are worries of the poorer countries that also score high on power distance. Variance of air pollution worries is explained by high power distance (31%). Variance of natural disasters worries is explained by low individualism (36%) and masculinity (additional 26%).

In high uncertainty avoidance cultures, larger percentages of people agree with the statement that environmental problems have a direct effect on their daily life, but in the countries that score low people do more about it. In low power distance and low uncertainty avoidance cultures, more people say they intend to buy and also actually buy environmentally friendly products. In all countries the differences between intention to buy environmentally friendly products and actual buying are large. In Greece, for example the percentage difference between intention and buying was 75%, in Portugal 68%, in Sweden 46%, and in Denmark 45%. The higher countries score on uncertainty avoidance, the larger the gap between intention and actual behavior. In the individualistic countries of Europe people feel well informed about the environment ($r = .70***$), which fits the general pattern of variance of information behavior (discussed in Chapter 6).

Whether people take responsibility for the environment themselves or expect their governments to take responsibility varies by culture. The World Values Survey of 1990 asked questions to find whether people refer to the government as the responsible institution for caring for the environment or whether they want to pay for the environment themselves and accept higher taxes for this purpose. Viewing the environment as a government responsibility was significantly correlated with high uncertainty avoidance, both for 25 countries worldwide ($r = .61***$) and for Europe ($r = .75***$). In the low masculine cultures, people think they should pay for the environment themselves (worldwide $r = -.61***$, in Europe $r = -.71***$).

Sex- and Love-Related Attitudes

Although love often is mentioned as a universal value, attitudes toward romantic love vary widely across cultures. Generally, romantic love is valued highly in individualistic cultures and is less valued in collectivistic cultures where strong family ties reinforce the relationship between marriage partners. Asians are more friendship oriented in their love relationships than are Americans.[144] Japanese value romantic love less than do Germans. Comparative research on intimacy shows that Americans conceptualize intimacy more concretely than do Japanese, especially in ways that are associated with direct behavioral manifestations. Americans also prefer to express intimacy through a greater variety of means and channels than do Japanese, who prefer high-contextual interaction in intimate relationships.[145] Compared with Swedish young adults, American young adults differentiate love and sex more strongly.[146] In feminine cultures the distinction between love and sex is less rigid than in masculine cultures. In spite of the sexual revolution of the 1950s, culturally masculine countries continue to manifest a stronger taboo on addressing sexual issues openly than do culturally feminine ones.[147]

In some cultures nudity is related to sex, whereas in others nudity symbolizes purity or beauty. Whereas nudism is popular in Germany, it is unthinkable in the United States, where people are extremely sensitive to nudity, which tends to be confused with sex. In Sweden and Finland, on the other hand, people do not confuse nakedness with sexiness. That is why schoolchildren can see a naked boy or say "penis" without collapsing into giggles. The fact that the Swedes tend to be matter-of-fact about both nudity and sex does not mean they are sexually more promiscuous than people elsewhere in Europe or America.[148] In Scandinavia and in the Netherlands, in the sauna one is nude. In Britain, a bathing costume is obligatory. While "streaking" was trendy in several countries in Europe in the 1970s, it still is done in the United Kingdom because it shocks. In countries where nudity is not viewed as shocking, there is no fun in streaking. In Europe, toddlers commonly run around naked on the beach and nobody pays attention, whereas in the United States, people are easily shocked, and parents are told to cover the kids up. Americans tend to categorize nudity in advertising as sex appeal and may hypothesize a relationship with cultural masculinity, but such a relationship is not found.[149]

Likewise, the use of nudity in advertising varies across countries. Germans don't perceive female nudity in advertising as an affront or as sexist exploitation. They might see it as nothing more than a cheap advertising trick. In France naked women are more or less acceptable icons of the advertising language. The female body is used as a metaphor for beauty. The British, on the other hand, think it is sexist and exploitative first, and bad advertising second. Italy is probably the closest to Britain. Although on TV images of scantily clad women are commonplace, full nudity is rare.[150]

LIFESTYLE

Lifestyle is described in terms of shared values or tastes as reflected in consumption patterns. Personal characteristics are viewed as the "raw" ingredients to develop a unique lifestyle. In an economic sense, one's lifestyle represents the way one allocates income, but lifestyle is more viewed as a mental construct that explains but is not identical with behavior.[151]

A comprehensive definition by Dutch consumer psychologists Antonides and Van Raaij shows how the lifestyle concept is embedded in culture: "Lifestyle is the entire set of values, interests, opinions and behavior of consumers."[152] Lifestyle descriptions tend to include attitudes, values, and behavioral elements that often are a reflection of culture. Lifestyles transcend individual brands or products but can be specific to a product class. Thus, it makes sense to talk about a food-related lifestyle, or a housing-related lifestyle.

> An example of an American lifestyle description is one of the "new materialists" from a study by Backer Spielvogel Bates as described by Chiagouris and Mitchell.
>
> The youthful materialists referred to as "New Materialists" are financially independent, have acquired "spending ability" and have compulsion toward its exercise. As the children of the decade of greed, they have grown accustomed to immediate gratification. They are not conscious of the ethics of saving. They want to consume as much as they can, even if it is sometimes beyond their means. Possession is the central concern of proving one's independence and success. . . . They view themselves as opinion leaders and trendsetters. It is ingrained in their quest to make an impression in society. They have an unbridled desire to be the first to discover, purchase, and possess the newest in material goods. Material goods comprise a central and defining part of their identity.[153]

In the professional world, lifestyle research originated from what is called *psychographic* research, as a response to the decreased usefulness of *sociodemographic* and *economic* variables to explain differences in behavior. Classical psychographic segment descriptions could be in terms of behavior and attitudes or could relate to a particular consumer activity. An early example of five motorist segments in terms of attitudes and behavior by Esso was (1) the uninvolved, (2) the enthusiast, (3) the professional or business driver, (4) the tinkerer, and (5) the collector.[154] Generally lifestyle studies search for attitudes, interests, and opinions (AIOs) that do not relate directly to specific product characteristics. Examples of such AIOs are "sense of fashion," attitude toward money, or opinions on roles of males and females.[155] Working with AIO variables, segments were identified such as "the happy housewife," "the affluent consumer," or "the price-conscious consumer."[156]

Today many lifestyle studies and systems exist across countries. (A few examples were given in Chapter 2.) In academia, the lifestyle research instruments developed and used by most of the larger market research firms are criticized on several grounds; we mention five.

1. There is no agreement on what lifestyle actually means.

2. The methods used are purely inductive and not guided by theory. Lifestyle types come about based on dimensions derived by exploratory data analysis techniques like factor analysis or correspondence analysis.

3. The derivation of the underlying dimensions is unclear and unsatisfactory. Because commercially marketed instruments are proprietary, the information necessary to evaluate statistical soundness of the derived dimensional solutions is often missing.

4. The explanatory value of lifestyle types or dimensions with regard to consumer choice behavior is low and not well documented.

5. The cross-cultural validity of the international lifestyle instruments remains to be demonstrated.[157]

Lifestyles Across Cultures

Lifestyle may be a useful within-country criterion; it is less useful for defining segments across cultures because lifestyles are country specific. No one has ever produced an empirical base to support the argument that lifestyle similarities are stronger than cultural differences. In contrast, increasingly evidence is found that culture overrides lifestyle.

An early example of a cross-cultural lifestyle study is by Douglas and Urban,[158] who compared lifestyles of women in the United States, the United Kingdom, and France. They found similarities in the degree to which women accepted or rejected their traditional homemaking job. They also found large differences in underlying values of lifestyle elements. French women identified their own self-concepts relative to those around them, suggesting less self-reliance than found among U.S. and U.K. women. Whereas in the United Kingdom and United States innovativeness primarily took the form of willingness to experiment and try new things, in France innovativeness and interest in buying new products was strongly associated with interest in fashion and in being well dressed.

In a comparative study in France, Brazil, Japan, and the United States, Eshgi and Sheth,[159] using the modern/traditional dichotomy as a lifestyle variable, demonstrated that more than lifestyle, national, and cultural influences determine consumption patterns of stereo equipment, soft drinks, fruit juices, alcoholic beverages, automobiles, and deodorants.

Studies among consumers in different countries in Asia also demonstrate the continuing impact of culture on lifestyle. When comparing, for example, Singapore and Hong Kong lifestyles that are superficially similar, Singaporeans are more home oriented and place a higher value on family relationships and education, whereas Hong Kong consumers are more fashion conscious and concerned about their personal appearance, but they also adhere strongly to specific traditional cultural values.[160]

Although lifestyle studies are popular among advertising agencies, they are very general, which is their major weakness. To understand consumer behavior across cultures it is necessary to go beyond lifestyle and distinguish value variations by product category. Even if across cultures certain groups of people can be identified with respect to ownership of specific products, the motives for buying these products vary so strongly that, for developing advertising, these lifestyle groups are not useful.

Global Communities?

Pan-European or global lifestyle studies aim at identifying similar lifestyle segments across borders, assuming that national and cultural influences on consumption patterns are less significant than modern lifestyle patterns. Certain lifestyle groups are assumed to be so similar between countries that their behavior is more similar to the same group across borders than to other groups within borders. Ownership of similar products or brands across countries would create consumption communities that, like neighborhoods, provide a sense of community with other people who own the same products. Even though there is some evidence for psychological feelings of community in relation to people engaging in common consumption behaviors, the individuals sharing these feelings do not constitute a community.[161] Usually groups that are given one label across countries are very different as to content. The British TGI (Target Group Index),[162] for example, categorizes age categories of women and labels the 15- to 24-year-old group as the "@ generation." What members of this group have in common is that they are mostly single women. However, young Italian and Spanish women mostly live at home with their parents, whereas young Germans start to live as a couple early on. All spend money on pleasure articles: CDs, makeup, sportswear, or snack products. However, Italians and Spaniards—probably because they live at home and have more spending power—spend more on personal and luxury goods and going out. They live in larger households and share products and brands, so brands must address the collective, not individual. Italian and British women are more involved in appearance. Snack consumption is high among this age group, but snacks are consumed in different situations. In Britain potato chips are an around-the-clock, individual snack product, but in Spain they are used as *tapas,* when people are socializing.

The difference between Western and Asian lifestyles of young people is even more pronounced. The image of a fun-loving, brand-conscious, and free spending Western-type teenager is a myth in many countries in Asia, including Singapore. Whereas in Europe most youth live for the moment and are hedonistic, youth in Singapore are more idealistic in their expectations than hedonistic. Next to being happy and healthy, doing well in school is an important goal. Teenagers of different countries live in different social and cultural environments with shared historical events that shape their lives. The promotion of products based on the typical youth themes of rebellion, individuality, freedom, confidence, sexiness, and even Americanness, as typified by brands such as Levi's, may communicate very little to teenagers in Asia.[163]

Studies among parents and students in the United States, Japan, New Zealand, France, Germany, and Denmark demonstrate the strong influence of culture on the values of both parents and students. The values of parents and students within a culture are relatively similar, with the greatest similarity between Japanese students and parents.[164] Jones[165] presents major differences in attitudes and behavior of young people across four European countries.

Asked for what was really important in life, young people show unanimity only in placing friendship, health, and love as the top three items. There are considerable differences with respect to the other 23 items.

CONCLUSION

This chapter discussed the relationship among values, culture, and personal attributes: personality, the self, attitude, and lifestyle. Personality and trait structure are Western concepts. For marketing and branding, understanding these cultural variations is necessary because the concepts are used as metaphors for brand personality. Similarly, the concepts of self and identity vary across cultures. The most pronounced difference is between individualistic and collectivistic cultures, where the self is independent or interdependent. The Western approach is that the self and personality are consistent and unchangeable. Because the self is a relational self in collectivistic cultures, it varies along with the context and situation. Similarly, attitudes vary across cultures. Several examples of culture-related attitudes were given in this chapter. Finally, the concept of lifestyle was discussed as a not-so-well-defined concept that is used worldwide to find and describe similar segments. These are pseudo-similarities. There is little evidence that there are culture-free lifestyle groups that can be targeted in similar ways. On the contrary, there is evidence that cultural differences override lifestyle similarities.

NOTES

1. Oyserman, D. (2006). High power, low power, and equality: Culture beyond individualism and collectivism. *Journal of Consumer Psychology, 16*(4), 352–356.
2. Díaz-Loving, R. (1998). Contributions of Mexican ethnopsychology to the resolution of the etic-emic dilemma in personality. *Journal of Cross-Cultural Psychology, 29,* 104–118.
3. Markus, H. R., & Kitayama, S. (1991). Culture and the self: Implications for cognition, emotion and motivation. *Psychological Review, 98,* 224–253.
4. Singelis, T. M. (2000). Some thoughts on the future of cross-cultural social psychology. *Journal of Cross-Cultural Psychology, 31,* 76–91.
5. Markus & Kitayama (1991).
6. Singh, D. (2007). *Cross cultural comparison of buying behavior in India.* Doctoral thesis. Chandigarh: Panjab University, University Business School.
7. Roland, A. (1988). *In search of self in India and Japan.* Princeton, NJ: Princeton University Press; Triandis, H. C. (1995). *Individualism and collectivism.* Boulder, CO: Westview.
8. Tardif, T., Fletcher, P., Liang, W., Zhang, Z., Kaciroti, N., & Marchman, V. A. (2008). Baby's first ten words. *Development Psychology, 44*(4), 929–938.
9. Nezlek, J. B., Kafetsios, K., & Smith, V. (2008). Emotions in everyday social encounters. *Journal of Cross-Cultural Psychology, 39*(4), 366–372.

10. Kagitçibasi, Ç. (1997). Individualism and collectivism. In J. W. Berry, M. H. Segall, & Çi. Kagitçibasi (Eds.), *Handbook of cross-cultural psychology* (Vol. 3, pp. 2–49). Boston: Allyn & Bacon, 19.

11. *Information society.* (2008). Flash Eurobarometer report 241.

12. Kashima, Y., Yamaguchi, S., Kim, U., Choi, S. C., Gelfand, M. J., & Yuki, M. (2001). Culture, gender, and self: A perspective from individualism-collectivism research. *Journal of Personality and Social Psychology, 69,* 925–937; Hofstede, G. (2001). *Culture's consequences* (2nd ed.). Thousand Oaks, CA: Sage, 294.

13. Triandis (1995).

14. Watkins, D., Akande, A., Fleming, J., Ismail, M., Lefner, K., Regmi, M., et al. (1998). Cultural dimensions, gender, and the nature of self-concept: A fourteen-country study. *International Journal of Psychology, 33,* 17–31.

15. *Ibero-America interactive generation.* (2008). See Appendix B.

16. Stelly, P. Jr. (1992, May 11). Tuning in to the next big thing. *Adweek,* 42–46.

17. Singh (2007).

18. Zhang, J. (2009). The effect of advertising appeals in activating self-construals: A case of bicultural generation X consumers. *Journal of Advertising, 38*(1), 63–81.

19. Harb, C., & Smith, P. B. (2008). Self-construals across cultures: Beyond independence-interdependence. *Journal of Cross-Cultural Psychology, 39*(2), 178–197.

20. Markus, H. R., & Kitayama, S. (1998). The cultural psychology of personality. *Journal of Cross-Cultural Psychology, 29,* 63–87.

21. Singelis, T. M., Bond, M. H., Sharkey, W. F., & Lai, C. S. Y. (1999). Unpackaging culture's influence on self-esteem and embarrassability. *Journal of Cross-Cultural Psychology, 30,* 315–341.

22. Heine, S., Kitayama, S., & Lehman, D. R. (2001). Cultural differences in self-evaluation. *Journal of Cross-Cultural Psychology, 32,* 434–443.

23. Westerhof, G. J., Dittmann-Kohli, F., & Katzko, M. W. (2000). Individualism and collectivism in the personal meaning system of elderly adults. *Journal of Cross-Cultural Psychology, 31,* 649–676.

24. Barone, M., Shimp, T. A., & Sprott, D. E. (1999). Product ownership as a moderator of self-congruity effects. *Marketing Letters, 10,* 75–85.

25. Becker, C. (1997). Hair and cosmetic products in the Japanese market. *Marketing and Research Today,* 31–36.

26. Belgium, Czech Republic, Denmark, Finland, France, Germany, Hungary, Italy, Netherlands, Norway, Poland, Portugal, Russia, Slovakia, Spain, Sweden, Switzerland, United Kingdom.

27. Hu, X. (2009). Mainstream and trends: Brand research in China. In H. Li, S. Huang, & D. Jin (Eds.), *Proceedings of the 2009 American Academy of Advertising Asia-Pacific conference* (p. 44). American Academy of Advertising in conjunction with China Association of Advertising of Commerce, and Communication University of China.

28. Gagliardi, M. (2001, Fall). Alchemy of cultures: From adaptation to transcendence in design and branding. *Design Management Journal,* 32–39.

29. Personal observation by the author when traveling through Henan Province, China.

30. Han, S-P., & Shavitt, S. (1994). Persuasion and culture: Advertising appeals in individualistic and collectivistic societies. *Journal of Experimental Social Psychology, 30,* 326–350; Zhang, Y., & Gelb, B. D. (1996). Matching advertising appeals to culture: The influence of products' use condition. *Journal of Advertising, 25,* 29–46.

31. Bowman, J. (2002). Commercials rise in the East. *Media and Marketing Europe Pocket Guide on Asian TV.* London: Emap Media, 8.

32. Han & Shavitt (1994).

33. Wang, C. L., Bristol, T., Mowen, J. C., & Chakraborty, G. (2000). Alternative modes of self-construal: Dimensions of connectedness-separateness and advertising appeals to the cultural and gender-specific self. *Journal of Consumer Psychology, 9,* 107–115.

34. Praet, C. L. C. (2001). Japanese advertising, the world's number one celebrity showcase? A cross-cultural comparison of the frequency of celebrity appearances in TV advertising. In M. Roberts & R.L. King (Eds.), *Proceedings of the 2001 special Asia-Pacific conference of the American Academy of Advertising* (pp. 6–13).

35. Praet, C. L.C. (2008). The influence of national culture on the use of celebrity endorsement in television advertising: A multi-country study. In *Proceedings of the 7th international conference on research in advertising (ICORIA).* Antwerp, Belgium, s.1., CD-ROM.

36. Kitayama, S., Markus, H. R., Matsumoto, H., & Noraskunkit, V. (1997). Individual and collective processes in the construction of the self: Self-enhancement in the United States and self-criticism in Japan. *Journal of Personality and Social Psychology, 72,* 1245–1267.

37. Kitayama, S. (2002). Culture and basic psychological processes—toward a system view of culture: Comment on Oyserman et al. *Psychological Bulletin, 128,* 89–96.

38. Eysenck, M. W. (2000). *Psychology: A student's handbook.* Hove, East Sussex, UK: Psychology Press, 458.

39. Twenge, J. M., & Crocker, J. (2000). Race and self-esteem: Meta-analyses comparing whites, blacks, Hispanics, Asians and American Indians and comment on Gray-Little and Hafdahl. *Psychological Bulletin, 128,* 371–408.

40. Kurman, J. (2002). Measured cross-cultural differences in self-enhancement and the sensitivity of the self-enhancement measure to the modesty response. *Cross-Cultural Research, 36*(1), 73–95.

41. Goffman, E. (1959). *The presentation of self in everyday life.* Harmondsworth, Middlesex, UK: Penguin, 244.

42. Maheswaran, D., & Shavitt, S. (2000). Issues and new directions in global consumer psychology. *Journal of Consumer Psychology, 9,* 59–66.

43. Etcoff, N., Orbach, S., Scott, J., & Agostino, H. (2006, February). *Beyond stereotypes: Rebuilding the foundation of beauty beliefs.* Retrieved November 4, 2008, from http://www.campaignforrealbeauty .com/DovebeyondStereotypesWhitePaper.pdf

44. Reader's Digest trusted brands, 2005 and 2007.

45. Heine, S., & Hamamura, T. (2007). In search of East Asian self-enhancement. *Personality and Social Psychology Review, 11*(1), 4–27.

46. Jowell, R., et al. (2003). *European social survey 2002/2003* (technical report). London: City University, Centre for Comparative Social Surveys.

47. Markus & Kitayama (1998).

48. Church, A. T., et al. (2006). Implicit theories and self-perceptions of traitedness across cultures. *Journal of Cross-Cultural Psychology, 37*(6), 694–716.

49. Eap, S., DeGarmo, D. S., Kawakami, A., Hara, S. N., Hall, G. C. N., & Teten, A. L. (2008). Culture and personality among European American and Asian American men, *Journal of Cross-Cultural Psychology, 39*(5), 630–643.

50. Petrova, P. K., Cialdini, R. B., & Sills, S. (2006). Consistency-based compliance across cultures. *Journal of Experimental Social Psychology, 43,* 104–111.

51. Triandis, H. C. (2004) Dimensions of culture beyond Hofstede. In H. Vinken, J. Soeters, & P. Ester (Eds.), *Comparing cultures: Dimensions of culture in a comparative perspective.* Leiden and Boston: Brill, 37; Kashima, Y., Kashima, E. S., Kim, U., & Gelfand, M. (2005). Describing the social world: How is a person, a group, and a relationship described in the East and the West? *Journal of Experimental Social Psychology, 42,* 388–396.

52. Norenzayan, A., Choi, I., & Nisbett, R. E. (2002). Cultural similarities and differences in social influence: Evidence from behavioral predictions and lay theories of behavior. *Personality and Social Psychology Bulletin, 28,* 109–120.

53. Choi, I., Nisbett, R. E., & Norenzayan, A. (1999). Causal attribution across cultures: Variation and universality. *Psychological Bulletin, 125,* 47–63.

54. Campana Carramenha, P. R. (1999, November). Evaluating the value of global brands in Latin America. *Marketing and Research Today,* 159–167.

55. Blumenthal, D. (2001, Fall). "Face of the Brand": A design methodology with global potential. *Design Management Journal,* 65–71.

56. Derksen, L. (2002). *Brand personality study.* Unpublished report, PPGH/JWT. Amsterdam.

57. McCrae, R. R., & Costa, P. T. Jr. (1990). *Personality in adulthood.* New York: Guildford, 23.

58. McCrae, R. R., Costa, P. T. Jr., Del Pilar, G. H., Rolland, J. P., & Parker, W. D. (1998). Cross-cultural assessment of the five-factor model. *Journal of Cross-Cultural Psychology, 29,* 171–188.

59. Church, A. T., & Lonner, W. J. (1998). The cross-cultural perspective in the study of personality. *Journal of Cross-Cultural Psychology, 29,* 32–62.

60. McCrae, R. R. (2002). NEO-PI-R data from 36 cultures. In A. J. Marsella & R. R. McCrae (Eds.), *The five-factor model of personality across cultures* (pp. 105–125). Dordrecht, The Netherlands: Kluwer.

61. McCrae (2002).

62. Cheung, F. M., Leung, K., Zhang, J. X., Sun, H. F., Gan, Y. Q., Song, W. Z., et al. (2001). Indigenous Chinese personality constructs: Is the five-factor model complete? *Journal of Cross-Cultural Psychology, 32,* 407–433.

63. Yoon, K., Schmidt, F., & Ilies, R. (2002). Cross-cultural construct validity of the five-factor model of personality among Korean employees. *Journal of Cross-Cultural Psychology, 33,* 217–235.

64. Cheung, F. M., Cheung, S. F., Zhang, J., Leung, K., Leong, F., & Yeh, K. H. (2008). Relevance for openness as a personality dimension in Chinese culture. *Journal of Cross-Cultural Psychology, 39*(1), 81–108.

65. Yoon, Schmidt, & Ilies (2002).

66. Hofstede, G., & McCrae, R. R. (2004). Personality and culture revisited: Linking traits and dimensions of culture. *Cross-Cultural Research, 38*(1), 52–88.

67. McCrae (2002).

68. Data provided by TGI, United Kingdom. http://www.tgisurveys.com. © TGI—All Rights Reserved. Countries: Argentina, Brazil, Chile, Colombia, Mexico, Peru, and Venezuela.

69. Hofstede. Personal communication.

70. *Pan-European market research into ecological awareness amongst drivers.* (2001, September). Received from Goodyear Dunlop Tires Nederland BV. Merwedeweg 4c, 3621 LR Breukelen.

71. Schmitt, D. P., Allik, J., McCrae, R. R., & Benet-Martínez, V. (2007). The geographic distribution of big five personality traits. *Journal of Cross-Cultural Psychology, 38*(2), 173–212.

72. Schmitt et al. (2007).

73. Ramírez-Esparza, N., Gosling, S. D., & Pennebaker, J. W. (2008). Paradox lost: Unraveling the puzzle of simpatía. *Journal of Cross-Cultural Psychology, 39*(6), 703–715.

74. Aaker, J. L., Benet-Martínez, V., & Garolera, J. (2001). Consumption symbols as carriers of culture: A study of Japanese and Spanish brand personality constructs. *Journal of Personality and Social Psychology, 81,* 492–508.

75. Sung, Y., & Tinkham, S. F. (2005). Brand personality structures in the United States and Korea: Common and culture-specific factors. *Journal of Consumer Psychology, 15*(4), 334–350.

76. Foscht, T., Maloles III, C., Swoboda, B., Morschett, D., & Sinha, I. (2008). The impact of culture on brand perception: A six-nation study. *Journal of Product and Brand Management, 17*(3), 131–142.

77. Crocus (Cross-Cultural Solutions) was a cross-cultural study that measured brand value (called "brand pull") and provided a cultural explanation of strong or weak brand value in different countries. Conducted by the research agency chain Euronet, in cooperation with the advertising agency chain Interpartners.

78. *European social reality.* (2007). Special Eurobarometer report 225.

79. Antonides, G., & Van Raaij, W. F. (1998). *Consumer behaviour: A European perspective.* Chichester, UK: Wiley, 162–163.

80. *How Europeans see themselves.* (2001). Eurobarometer.

81. Camilleri, C., & Malewska-Peyre, H. (1997). Socialization and identity strategies. In J. W. Berry, P. R. Dasen, & T. S. Saraswathi (Eds.), *Handbook of cross-cultural psychology* (Vol. 2, pp. 41–67). Boston: Allyn & Bacon, 48.

82. Belk, R. W. (1984). Cultural and historical differences in concepts of self and their effects on attitudes toward having and giving. In T. C. Kinnear (Ed.), *Advances in consumer research* (pp. 753–760). Provo, UT: Association for Consumer Research.

83. Edmondson, G. (1999, August 9). France: A CEO's pay shouldn't be a secret. *BusinessWeek,* 24.

84. Camelleri & Malewska-Peyre (1997), 48.

85. Kowner, R. (2002). Japanese body image: Structure and esteem scores in a cross-cultural perspective. *International Journal of Psychology, 37,* 149–159.

86. Shafer, D. R., Crepaz, N., & Sun, C. Ru. (2000). Physical attractiveness stereotyping in cross-cultural perspective. *Journal of Cross-Cultural Psychology, 31,* 557–582.

87. Matsumoto, D. (2000). *Culture and psychology: People around the world* (2nd ed.). Delmar, CA: Wadsworth Thomson Learning, 411.

88. Kowner (2002).

89. Prendergast, G., Leung Kwok, Y., & West, D. C. (2002). Role portrayal in advertising and editorial content, and eating disorders: An Asian perspective. *International Journal of Advertising, 21,* 237–258.

90. Wheeler, L., & Kim, Y. (1997). What is beautiful is culturally good: The physical attractiveness stereotype has different content in collectivistic cultures. *Personality and Social Psychology Bulletin, 23,* 795–800.

91. Jankowiak, W., Gray, P. B., & Hattman, K. (2008). Globalizing evolution: Female choice, nationality, and perception of sexual beauty in China. *Cross-Cultural Research, 42*(3), 248–269.

92. Wan, F., Faber, R. J., & Fung, A. (2001, December 12–15). Perceived impact of thin female models in advertising: A cross-cultural examination of third person perception and its impact on behaviors. In *Proceedings of the 8th cross-cultural research conference, Association for Consumer Research and American Psychological Association* (pp. 13–16). Hawaii.

93. Matsumoto (2000).

94. Ingrassia, M. (1995, April 24). The body of the beholder. *Newsweek,* 50.

95. Prendergast et al. (2002).

96. Data OECD. (2001, December 15). *The Economist,* 88.

97. Maynard, M. L., & Taylor, C. R. (1999). Girlish images across cultures: Analyzing Japanese versus U.S. *Seventeen* magazine ads. *Journal of Advertising, 28,* 39–48.

98. Ind, N. (1992). *The corporate image: Strategies for effective identity programmes.* London: Kogan Page, 19.

99. Bosman, J. (1996). The relation between self image and brand image: An alternative perspective. *Communications, 21,* 27–47.

100. Unfortunately the author—like more authors of such studies do—assumes his findings to be universal because he does not mention the culture of the participants, which may have explained the outcome.

101. Hsieh, M. H., & Lindridge, A. (2005). Universal appeals with local specifications. *Journal of Product and Brand Management, 14*(1), 14–28.

102. This is the definition by Gordon Allport, in Assael, H. (2004). *Consumer behavior: A strategic approach.* Boston and New York: Houghton Mifflin, 216.

103. Cervellon, M. C., & Dubé, L. (2002). Assessing the cross-cultural applicability of affective and cognitive components of attitude. *Journal of Cross-Cultural Psychology, 33,* 346–357.

104. Gudykunst, W. B., Matsumoto, Y., Ting-Toomey, S., Nishida, T., Kim, K., & Heyman, S. (1996). The influence of cultural individualism-collectivism, self construals, and individual values in communication styles across cultures. *Human Communication Research, 22,* 10–543.

105. Shavitt, S., & Nelson, M. R. (2002). The role of attitude functions and social judgment. In J. P. Dillard & M. Pau (Eds.), *The persuasion handbook: Theory and practice* (pp. 137–154). Thousand Oaks, CA: Sage, 137.

106. Chang, P. L., & Chieng, M. H. (2006). Building consumer-brand relationship: A cross-cultural experiential view. *Psychology and Marketing, 23*(11), 927–959.

107. Bowman, J. (2002). Commercials rise in the East. *Media and Marketing Europe pocket guide on Asian TV.* London: Emap Media, 11.

108. Lee, C., & Green, R. L. (1991). Cross-cultural examination of the Fishbein behavioral intentions model. *Journal of International Business Studies, 22,* 289–305.

109. Malhotra, N. K., & McCort, J. D. (2001). A cross-cultural comparison of behavioral intention models. *International Marketing Review, 18,* 235–269.

110. Cheung, G. W., & Rensvold, R. B. (2000). Assessing extreme and acquiescence response sets in cross-cultural research using structural equations modeling. *Journal of Cross-Cultural Psychology, 31,* 187–212.

111. Goodyear Dunlop Tires (2001).

112. Data Eurobarometer and EMS of various years. (See Appendix B.)

113. Mundorf, N., Dholakia, R. R., Dholakia, N., & Westin, S. (1996). German and American consumer orientations to information technologies: Implications for marketing and public policies. In L. A. Manrai & A. K. Manrai (Eds.), *Global perspectives in cross-cultural and cross-national consumer research* (pp. 125–144). New York, London: International Business Press/Haworth Press.

114. American Medical Association (AMA), in De Rijck, K. (2002, April 2). Vlaming grijpt naar antibiotica, Nederlander "ziekt uit" (Belgian people take antibiotics while the Dutch just wait till they recover without antibiotics). *De Standaard.*

115. Kamineni, R., & O'Cass, A. (2000). The effect of materialism, gender and nationality on consumer perception of a high priced brand. *ANZMAC 2000 visionary marketing for the 21st century: Facing the challenge,* 614–618.

116. Ger, G., & Belk, R. W. (1996). Cross-cultural differences in materialism. *Journal of Economic Psychology, 17,* 55–77.

117. Sinkovics, R. R., & Holzmüller, H. H. (2001). National differences in materialism: Using alternative research strategies to explore the construct. *Journal of International Consumer Marketing, 13,* 103–134.

118. Chiagouris, L., & Mitchell, L. E. (1997). The new materialists. In L. R. Kahle & L. Chiagouris (Eds.), *Values, lifestyles and psychographics* (pp. 263–282). Mahwah, NJ: Lawrence Erlbaum, 263.

119. Inglehart, R. (1997). *Modernization and postmodernization: Cultural, economic, and political change in 43 societies.* Princeton, NJ: Princeton University Press, 4.

120. Data EMS (1997).

121. Ger & Belk (1996). The twelve countries were Romania, United States, New Zealand, Ukraine, Germany, Turkey, Israel, Thailand, India, United Kingdom, France, and Sweden.

122. Ukraine excluded.

123. Clarke III, I., & Micken, K. S. (2002). An exploratory cross-cultural analysis of the values of materialism. *Journal of International Consumer Marketing, 14*(4), 65–89.

124. Müller-Peters, A. (1998). The significance of national pride and national identity to the attitude toward the single European currency: A Europe-wide comparison. *Journal of Economic Psychology, 19,* 702–719.

125. Usunier, J. C. (1999). *Marketing across cultures* (3rd ed.). Harlow, UK: Pearson Education, 158.

126. Balabanis, G., Mueller, R., & Melewar, T. C. (2002). The relationship between consumer ethnocentrism and human values. *Journal of Global Marketing, 15,* 7–37.

127. Batra, R., Ramaswamy, V., Alden, D., Steenkamp, J. B., & Ramachander, S. (2000). Effects of brand local and nonlocal origin on consumer attitudes in developing countries. *Journal of Consumer Psychology, 9,* 83–95.

128. *Patriot games: Consumer preferences for national products.* (2004, May). Retrieved May 2004 from http://www.zonalatina.com/Zldata19.htm

129. Mandhachitara, R., Shannon, R. M., & Hadjicharalambous, C. (2007). Why private label grocery brands have not succeeded in Asia. *Journal of Global Marketing, 20*(2/3), 71–87.

130. Home-grown appeal. (1995, June). Special report. *M&M Europe,* 6.

131. Bartonova, M. (1998). Consumer attitudes to brands. *ESOMAR Newsbrief, 10,* 7.

132. Mareck, M. (2000, March). The European car market: National brands dominate. *M&M Europe,* 49.

133. Diamantopoulos, A., Schlegelmilch, B. B., & Du Preez, J. P. (1995). Lessons for pan-European marketing? The role of consumer preferences in fine-tuning the product-market fit. *International Marketing Review, 12,* 38–52; Keillor, B. D., & Hult, G. T. (1999). A five-country study of national identity: Implications for international research and practice. *International Marketing Review, 16,* 65–82.

134. Maheswaran, D. (1994). Country of origin as a stereotype: Effects of consumer expertise and attribute strength on product evaluations. *Journal of Consumer Research, 21,* 354–365.

135. Moon, B. J., & Jain, S. C. (2002). Consumer processing of foreign advertisements: Roles of country-of-origin perceptions, consumer ethnocentrism, and country attitude. *International Business Review, 11,* 117–138.

136. Dubois, B., & Paternault, C. (1997, May). Does luxury have a home country? An investigation of country images in Europe. *Marketing and Research Today,* 79–85.

137. Lee, C. W., Suh, Y. G., & Moon, B. J. (2001). Product-country images: The roles of country-of-origin and country-of-target in consumers' prototype product evaluations. *Journal of International Consumer Marketing, 13,* 47–62.

138. Moon & Jain (2002).

139. Murphy, G. (2000, August). From geisha to Gucci. *M&M Europe,* 24–25.

140. Agbonifoh, B. A., & Elimimian, J. U. (1999). Attitudes of developing countries towards country-of-origin products in an era of multiple brands. *Journal of International Consumer Marketing, 11,* 97–116.

141. *Europeans' state of mind.* (2008). Standard Eurobarometer 69.3.

142. Homma, N. (1991). The continued relevance of cultural diversity. *Marketing and Research Today,* 251–259.

143. *Attitudes of European citizens towards the environment.* (2008). Special Eurobarometer report 295.

144. Matsumoto (2000), 416.

145. Seki, K., Matsumoto, D., & Imahori, T. T. (2002). The conceptualization and expression of intimacy in Japan and the United States. *Journal of Cross-Cultural Psychology, 33,* 303–319.

146. Best, D., & Williams, J. E. (1997). Sex, gender, and culture. In J. W. Berry, M. H. Segall, & Ç. Kagitçibasi (Eds.), *Handbook of cross-cultural psychology* (Vol. 3, pp. 163–212). Boston: Allyn & Bacon, 174.

147. Hofstede, G. (1998). Comparative studies of sexual behavior: Sex as achievement or as relationship? In G. Hofstede (Ed.), *Masculinity and femininity: The taboo dimension of national cultures* (pp. 106–116). Thousand Oaks, CA: Sage, 157.

148. Naked truths for Swedes. (1998, February 28). *The Economist,* 31.

149. Nelson, M. R., & Paek, H. J. (2008). Nudity of female and male models in primetime TV advertising across seven countries. *International Journal of Advertising, 27*(5), 715–744.

150. Archer, B. (2000, September). Sex in advertising. *M&M Europe,* 44–45.

151. Grunert, K. G., Brunsø, K., & Bisp, S. (1997). Food-related lifestyle: Development of a cross-culturally valid instrument for market surveillance. In L. R. Kahle & L. Chiagouris (Eds.), *Values, lifestyles and psychographics* (pp. 337–354). Mahwah, NJ: Lawrence Erlbaum, 343.

152. Antonides & Van Raaij (1998), 377.

153. Chiagouris & Mitchell (1997), 272–273.

154. Sampson, P. (1992, November). People are people the world over: The case for psychological market segmentation. *Marketing and Research Today,* 236–244.

155. Vyncke, P. (1992). *Imago-management: Handboek voor reclamestrategen* (Image management: Handbook for advertising strategists). Gent, Belgium: Mys & Breesch, Uitgevers & College Uitgevers.

156. Hansen, F. (1998). From life style to value systems to simplicity. *Advances in Consumer Research, 25,* 181–195.

157. Grunert et al. (1997), 337–338.

158. Douglas, S. P., & Urban, C. D. (1977, July). Lifestyle analysis to profile women in international markets. Can the same segmentation strategies be used? *Journal of Marketing,* 46–54.

159. Eshgi, A., & Sheth, J. N. (1985). The globalization of consumption patterns: An empirical investigation. In E. Kaynak (Ed.), *Global perspectives in marketing* (pp. 133–148). New York: Praeger.

160. Tai, S. H. C., & Tam, J. L. M. (1996). A comparative study of Chinese consumers in Asian markets: A lifestyle analysis. *Journal of International Consumer Marketing, 9,* 25–42; Wei, R. (1997). Emerging lifestyles in China and consequences for perception of advertising, buying behavior and consumption preferences. *International Journal of Advertising, 16,* 261–275.

161. Friedman, M., Vanden Abeele, P., & De Vos, K. (1993). Boorstin's consumption community concept: A tale of two countries. *Journal of Consumer Policy, 16,* 35–60.

162. TGI, European women report. http://www.bmrb.co.uk. womensreportch2.htm

163. Wee, T. T. T. (1999). An exploration of a global teenage lifestyle in Asian societies. *Journal of Consumer Marketing, 16,* 365–375.

164. Rose, G. M. (1997). Cross-cultural values research: Implications for international advertising. In L. R. Kahle & L. Chiagouris (Eds.), *Values, lifestyles and psychographics* (pp. 389–400). Mahwah, NJ: Lawrence Erlbaum, 395.

165. Jones, J. P. (2000). Media may be global, but is youth? In J. P. Jones (Ed.), *International advertising, realities and myths* (pp. 117–140). Thousand Oaks, CA: Sage, 121.

CHAPTER 5

Social Processes

A human is human because of other people, as they say in the South African languages Xhosa and Zulu (*umuntu ngumuntu ngabanty*). In short, the term *ubuntu* means, "I can only be me through your eyes."[1] The self is not an isolated unity; it is always part of a social environment, but in some cultures the self is less integrated into the social environment than in others. The self in the social environment is the topic of this chapter, which deals with the processes, or the *how*'s of consumer behavior, that mostly are derived from social and cognitive psychology. Social psychology examines how we relate to other people, and cognitive psychology is concerned with internal processes, or what goes on in the mind. This chapter covers the social processes that include motivation, needs and drives, emotion, and group processes. All are processes that steer behavior. Although some emotions are internal, many relate to interaction with the social environment. Motivation theories such as those developed by Abraham Maslow, or Sigmund Freud's theories of structure and functioning of the mind, implicitly carry the culture of the country of origin because they were formed in the social environment of the theorists.

MOTIVATION, NEEDS, AND DRIVES

The study of motivation, the mixture of wants, needs, and drives within the individual, is of prime importance to understanding behavior. Motivation research seeks to find the underlying *why* of our behavior; it seeks to identify the attitudes, beliefs, motives, and other pressures that influence our purchase decisions. Understanding the variation of what motivates people is important for explaining product behavior, brand preference, and for developing effective advertising.

Motivation can be defined as the internal state of an organism that drives it to behave in a certain way.[2] *Drives* are the motivational forces that cause individuals to be active and to strive for certain goals. There are three main types of explanations of motivation.

1. Physiological explanations that emphasize the importance of *internal* drives or needs, also called *primary* drives, because of their importance to the organism. Hunger and thirst are the primary drives for food or drink. Internal physiological drives are based on the process of *homeostasis* by which we maintain a reasonable constant internal (biological/physical) environment.

2. Behavioral explanations that rely on acquired drives through learning are called *external* drives. We have learned to adapt to external circumstances, for example, avoiding extreme temperatures.

3. Psychological explanations tend to apply to complex human behaviors. "Motivation in the psychological sense is generally conceived in terms of process, or a series of processes, which somehow start, steer, sustain and finally stop a goal-directed sequence of behavior."[3]

In Chapter 3 the relationship between climate and homeostasis was discussed. Both external drives, because they are based on learning, and psychological drives, because they concern the self, are culture bound.

Freud

Many motivation theories are based on Freud's idea of anxiety. In consumer behavior theory, Freud's theory is applied to motivation and needs.[4] Freud assumed that the mind is divided into three parts. First, there is the *Id* that contains sexual and aggressive instincts and is located in the unconscious mind. The sexual instinct is known as libido. The Id works in accord with the pleasure principle. Second, there is the *Ego,* or the conscious rational mind. It works on the reality principle. Third, there is the *Superego* that is partly conscious and partly unconscious. It consists of the conscience and ego ideal. Conscience makes people feel guilt. The ego ideal is formed through the use of reward. The Id contains basic motivational forces.

In developing his concepts of the Id, Ego, and Superego, Freud was a true product of Austrian-Hungarian culture. Austria and Hungary score extremely low on power distance and high on uncertainty avoidance. Strong uncertainty avoidance implies that parents raise their children with the message that life is threatening and dangerous, so the children have to create structures to cope with threat. If combined with large power distance, this attitude does not pose a problem for children, as parents will create the structures for them. Parents guard and guide their children. Low power distance, however, implies that children become independent at an early age and have to structure reality themselves. This leads to frustration. Freud's Superego is meant to control the Id, thus take the role of the parent. It serves as an inner uncertainty-absorbing device.[5] One conclusion is that if Freud's theory is true or useful, it will be most useful for Austrians and Hungarians and other cultures of a similar configuration of dimensions. It will be less useful for cultures of weak uncertainty avoidance, such as the U.K. and Scandinavia, or for cultures of large power distance, such as France and most Asian cultures.

Maslow

Maslow[6] arranged human needs in a hierarchy of importance: physiological needs, safety needs, social needs, esteem needs, and self-actualization. His *hierarchy of needs* concept is based on the assumption that a person's behavior is directed at satisfying needs and that some needs take precedence over others when the individual is faced with choices as to which needs to satisfy. *Physiological* needs will take precedence over *security* or *safety,* the need for *group membership* or *esteem* needs. The ultimate need then is *self-actualization.* Figure 5.1 depicts Maslow's hierarchy of needs.

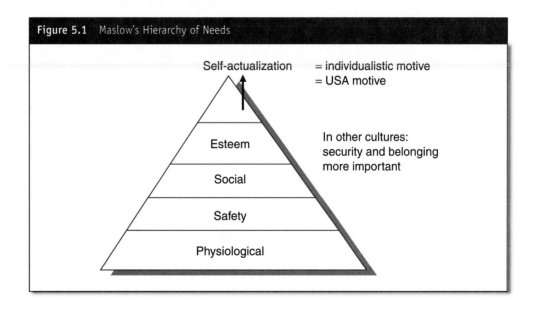

Figure 5.1 Maslow's Hierarchy of Needs

This order is generally presented as universal for mankind, but several authors have argued that it is defined by culture. A universal human pattern may be that physiological needs take precedence over higher-order needs, but the nonphysiological needs as such and their ranking varies across cultures. Self-actualization is a highly individualistic motive. In collectivistic cultures, what will be actualized is the interest and honor of the in-group rather than its individual members. In collectivistic cultures, belonging and safety will converge: it is very unsafe to distinguish oneself from the group.[7]

> How much *self-actualization* is defined from the individualistic, Anglo-American perspective can be understood from the description of self-actualized individuals by the British psychologist Eysenck: "Self-actualized individuals are characterized by an acceptance of themselves, spontaneity, the need for privacy, resistance to cultural influences, empathy, profound interpersonal relationships, a democratic character structure, creativeness and a philosophical sense of humor."[8]

McClelland

According to David McClelland, there is a theory of motivation to go with every field of human endeavor. "People do various things frequently and infer that therefore they must want to do them. People eat, so they must want to eat. Some people do well in school, so we infer they have a need for academic success."[9] McClelland distinguished three specific needs: achievement, power, and affiliation. He defined the need for *achievement* as a desire to do things better or to surpass standards of excellence. If food is the reward or incentive for the hunger drive, "doing something better" is the natural incentive for the achievement motive. A high need for achievement is assumed to affect performance. The goal of the *power* motive is exerting influence. One way individuals can appear powerful in a socially acceptable way is to collect symbols of power or *prestige* possessions. At the time of measurement (1975) in the United States, such prestige objects included a color television set, a rifle or pistol, and a convertible car for adults. Prestige possessions for students were cars, wine glasses, college banners, a tape recorder, wall hangings, and an electric typewriter. *Affiliation* was linked with harmonious relations, fear of rejection, and intimacy.

Like Maslow's theory, McClelland's theory of achievement motive is directly related to two cultural dimensions of U.S. culture: high masculinity and low uncertainty avoidance. People of this cultural configuration are motivated by the expectancy of some kind of results from their acts, and by extrinsic reasons and rewards.[10] In collectivistic cultures the motivation to achieve includes the self and others. When one's group succeeds, the success accrues to the self, and, similarly, when the self succeeds, so does the group. In a study that compared Turkish and Belgian participants, the Turkish motivation for achievement included a component of loyalty (to their families and the larger society) as well as a component of self-realization, which was the sole motivating factor among the Belgian participants.[11] Group achievement need in collectivistic cultures of high masculinity explains the problems that arise when Japanese companies merge, where groups of workers of the original companies remain hostile for a long time. Workers of one company have historically competed with workers of the other company's collectivities. Nelson and Shavitt[12] relate achievement needs to vertical individualism, rather than to horizontal individualism (see Chapter 4, section on the concept of self).

CULTURE-RELATED CONSUMER NEEDS AND MOTIVES

Consumption can be driven by functional or social needs. Clothes satisfy a functional need; fashion satisfies a social need. A house serves a functional need; a home serves a social need. A car may satisfy a functional need, but the type of car can satisfy a social need. Products can be distinguished between those that are products bought mainly for utilitarian reasons and those that are bought for more symbolic reasons, but often there is no clear-cut distinction between the two types. In some countries, high quality has a symbolic function, and in others a utilitarian function. For a car, latest technology may be viewed as a universal motive, but the associations linked to technology may be different across individuals and across cultures. *Latest technology* may be associated with *sporty* in one culture, with *fuel economy* in another culture, and with *prestige* in again another culture.[13]

People's behavior is not only determined by their needs and motivations but also by their surroundings and the context in which they make decisions. These contextual variables vary considerably from one country to another. "People across cultures can do the same thing for different reasons or motives, and people in different countries may do different things for the same reasons."[14] Buying motives are strongly related to the social environment. Many global standard products, assumed to be culture free, are bought for different reasons across cultures.

> Already in 1975 differences were found in product attribute appeals of soft drinks and toothpaste in the United States, France, India, and Brazil. Even though the basic products essentially served the same need in each country, several cultural and environmental factors influenced the characteristics of the product that people emphasized in its purchase. For soft drinks, people from Brazil, France, and India rated the attribute "contains no artificial ingredients" higher than did the U.S. sample. Americans placed high importance on "taste" and "convenience." For toothpaste the French rated high "kills germs in the mouth." Americans placed greater emphasis than the French on attributes not directly associated with the primary function of the product, such as "well-known brand," "freshens the mouth," and "brightens teeth." For the Brazilians other nonfunctional attributes were important, such as "color of toothpaste" and "tube squeezes easily." In addition, the Brazilians rated the family-oriented attribute "children like it" higher than the U.S. sample did.[15]

Differences in sensitivity to certain product attributes and varying buying motives can be explained by the underlying cultural values that vary by product category. In some cultures certain motives may be considered "prototypical" for a specific product category. For example, for mineral water, in the high uncertainty avoidance cultures a generic motive is purity; for luxury alcoholic beverages it may be social status in high power distance cultures and self-enhancement in short-term-oriented cultures. For cars, motives vary among safety, status, design, and prestige, all based on different cultural values.

Buying motives can be recognized in the appeals used in advertising. Several scholars have developed lists of consumption motives by analyzing advertising. Pollay's[16] list of values in advertising is one of the early inventories. Some motives may exist across cultures, but the degree of importance will vary. One product attribute that seems appealing across different markets cannot be generalized, as it may differ as to level of importance.[17] Examples of motives that vary by culture are the status motive, environmentalism, purity, and convenience.

The Status Motive

There are substantial differences in status needs across countries, and income differences have no explanatory power. In India, for example there is demand for high-status consumption goods among the low-income groups.[18] Status motives vary with power distance, individualism/collectivism, and masculinity, for different reasons.

Because luxury articles can be used as manifestations of one's material success, they are more attractive to members of masculine cultures than to members of feminine cultures. They can serve as symbols to express success and achievement. In the United States, a masculine culture, the need for success and the search for status symbols is strong. Table 5.1 gives an overview of the correlations among masculinity, GNI per capita, and a few luxury

Table 5.1 Status Needs and Masculinity: Correlation Coefficients for Selected Products

	GNI/cap	MAS/FEM
Watches Owned		
1997 Value main watch under $150	−.70***	−.50*
1997 Value main watch over $1,600	.38	.56*
2007 Value main watch over €750	−.001	.62**
1997 More than four watches in use	−.01	.53*
1997 Own suit or dress over $800	.01	.68***
2007 In past year bought suit or dress over €750	−.38	.58*
2007 In past year bought jewelry over €1,500	−.30	.77***
Sales Real Jewelry (in value)		
Worldwide 44 countries	.34	.44*
26 developed countries worldwide (GNP/cap > $8,000)	.25	.61***
Europe 15 countries	.18	.51*

SOURCES: Hofstede et al. (2010) (see Appendix A); EMS 1997 and 2007; Euromonitor, 1997 (see Appendix B)

articles. EMS provides data on ownership of various luxury articles and the value of watches owned across Europe. Euromonitor provides sales data for real jewelry. For this category, data are used for various areas to demonstrate that national wealth has no explaining power for variance of real jewelry in any part of the world.

Although ownership of cheap watches is related to low national income, there also is a relationship with low masculinity that includes low status needs. Ownership of really expensive watches (1997: > US\$1,600; 2007: > €750) is not related to income; it is only correlated with high masculinity. Having more than four watches in use also is a matter of status, in view of the correlation with high masculinity. Other items that serve as status symbols are expensive clothes. Also the wish to wear the latest fashion is a matter of status. As early as 1970,[19] the percentage of answers "wholly true" to the statement "I dress as far as possible according to the latest fashion" correlated with high masculinity ($r = .53*$). Generally brands are more important in masculine cultures than in feminine cultures, where fewer people say that the brand name is an important factor that influences food choice.[20]

Whereas in masculine cultures cars have high status value for young men, this is less so in feminine cultures. In Japan, young men need a car to attract girlfriends. In Malaysia, attitudes to cars are different. In 1995, a commercial for a new sports car, the Bufori, showed four women going to a marriage bureau in search of an ideal husband, and ended with the line by a model who said, "I don't care who you are, or what you look like, if you drive a Bufori, I am yours." Two women's organizations objected and the campaign had to stop. The advertising agency reacted saying the commercial was intended to be funny and cheeky and entertaining.[21] Playing with important cultural values can cause resistance.

Differences in status needs are also explained by power distance, but the type of status need is different. In high power distance cultures, positions and social status are not fluid, and people want to demonstrate their position in society.

Many Western brands have served the purpose of social status in high power distance and collectivistic cultures. Indians, for example, tend to drink Coca-Cola for the image, not for the taste. The choice is dependent on the context. Whereas in a simple restaurant one might just choose an orange- or lemon-flavored drink, in a more expensive hotel or restaurant one would order a cola.

In collectivistic cultures a high price delivers status. A high price is associated with quality, and high quality contains social meaning for consumers in collectivistic cultures more than in individualistic cultures. This also explains the success of pricey luxury brands in Asian markets, in which price not only signals high quality but also social status, prestige, and belonging. Some perfume companies have reported that in Asia they sell more perfumes by increasing prices than by lowering prices.[22] Also in Russia, which scores very high on power distance, luxury brands have become very popular.

A retail study in 2007 showed that for East Europeans, in particular Russian women, the most important criteria to select a retail store were style and quality of clothing/merchandise. Estimates from the European Fashion and Textile Export Council indicated that Russian women were one of the biggest evolving consumer markets for high-end fashion and accessories. These customers were also found to be very label conscious. Highly visible items are chosen to be "status symbols" of wealth, sophistication, or success. More "value for the dollar" variables were not ranked among the top attributes in the shopping criteria for the retail stores in Eastern European countries.[23]

An example of a luxury product that fulfills the desire for the latter type of status in Europe is Scotch whisky. For 13 countries in continental Europe,[24] there is a significant correlation between regular consumption of Scotch whisky and power distance ($r = .74$***). Also, drinking aperitifs and champagne are social status-reinforcing habits. Figure 5.2 shows how cultures can be mapped according to the two different status motives.

Figure 5.2   Status Needs and Motives

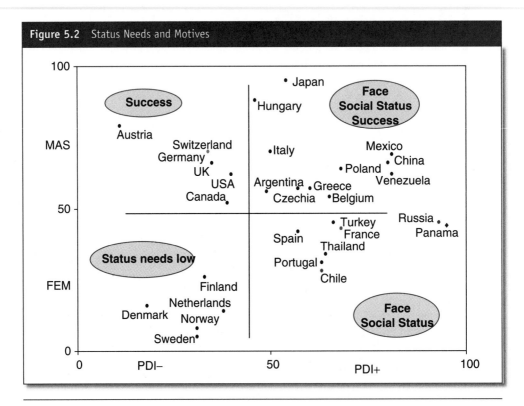

SOURCE: Data Hofstede et al. (2010) (see Appendix A)

Face

An expression related to social status that entered the English language from the Chinese is *face*, a characteristic of collectivistic cultures. In general, *face* describes the proper relationship with one's social environment, which is as essential to a person (and that person's family) as the front part of his or her head. Other collectivistic cultures have linguistic equivalents, for example, the Greek *philotimos*. Face is lost when an individual, either through his action or that of people close to him, fails to meet essential requirements placed upon him by his social position.[25]

Avoiding loss of face is of overriding concern. Losing face is a damaging social event in which one's action is publicly and negatively judged by others, resulting in a loss of moral or social standing. Failure to maintain or protect one's face has adverse implications for social functioning. Consumption of luxury goods is regarded as a behavior to maintain and enhance one's face.[26] In 2004, 29% of the total turnover of LMVH and 58% of turnover of Cognac producer Rémy Martin was concentrated in Asia.[27] In China, status appeals are heavily used in advertising.[28]

Upholding face goes with avoiding social embarrassment. Social embarrassment occurs when seen by others when buying, for example, intimate products. Avoidance of social embarrassment has been used in India as advertising appeals for several product categories such as deodorants or detergents, for example, being punished by your teacher for not wearing clean clothes.[29]

Green Motives, the Environment

Awareness of the environmental impact of consumption is increasing, but more in some areas than in others. (Some of the attitudes toward the environment were discussed in Chapter 4.) Overall awareness of environmental issues is relatively high, but it varies by country. Across 25 European countries, the percentages of people who say they are *fully aware* of the impact vary between 4.4% in Finland and 32.4% in France. In most countries the majority of people agree with the importance of taking into account a product's impact on the environment for making a buying decision, which is more than the percentage of people who attribute the same importance to the product's brand or brand name for making a buying decision; the environment is viewed of greater importance in collectivistic cultures of high uncertainty avoidance, which explains 32% of variance.[30] However, various data show that in the low power distance and low uncertainty avoidance cultures, people's behavior is more active with respect to environmental behavior. In cultures where people think the environment of high importance, they don't necessarily act accordingly.

The degree to which countries recycle and compost their municipal waste correlates with low power distance ($r = -.72**$),[31] and so does the recycling rate of container glass ($r = -.50*$)[32] and the degree to which people reduce consumption of disposable items ($r = -.48**$), which also correlates with low uncertainty avoidance ($r = -.54***$).[33] Across Europe, willingness to buy environmentally friendly products, even if they cost a little bit more, is stronger in the low power distance cultures; actually having bought environmentally friendly products relates to low power distance and low uncertainty avoidance. However, the percentages are low and vary from 7% in Bulgaria to 42% in Sweden. Across Latin America, overall 75% of people are willing to pay more for a product made by a company that respects and improves the environment; the higher percentages are found in the countries with lower scores on uncertainty avoidance, which explains 66% of variance.[34] Overall, the environment as a motive to prefer some products to others is not strong.

Purity

The need for purity is manifested in different ways and related to the product categories food, drink, and cleaning products. Cross-cultural variations in purity needs are explained by uncertainty avoidance. In Japan, high on uncertainty avoidance, cleanliness has historically been an important need. European visitors already reported it around the turn of the 16th century. The Japanese have a horror of filth. Most people have at least one bath a day.[35] Modern technology, providing all sorts of antibacterial products, has reinforced this need for purity. Shops sell germ-free pens, bicycle handles, telephones, tea towels, toothpaste, and underwear, all impregnated with antiseptic chemicals. Such products are called *kokin guzzu,* or antibacterial goods designed to get rid of germs on things with which people come into contact.

Varying purity needs are reflected in the differences in consumption of mineral water and all sorts of processed foods, as well as in the varying volume of soap powder used. In Europe, in high uncertainty avoidance cultures, people drink more mineral water and use more soap powder and household cleaning products. The need for purity in food is related to perceived food safety. In 1998 Eurobarometer measured the elements that determine food safety. The response "absence of preservatives" correlated with high uncertainty avoidance ($r =. 67***$).[36] The purity motive is recognized in advertising for many beverages, but also for soap powder. Figure 5.3 gives examples from various countries.

Freshness in food is another culture-bound motive but is more related to individualism/collectivism. What is considered fresh in food merchandise varies. In the south of Europe, what is considered fresh is what people prepare themselves, so the whole salad or fish, not fresh fish cut into pieces and presented in a Styrofoam dish covered with plastic. In the north of Europe, anything that is not tinned or frozen is considered fresh.

Convenience

The convenience motive refers to the value placed on, and the active search for, products and services that provide personal comfort and/or save time in performing various activities. Convenience-driven demand is assumed to exist for products and services like frozen food, food processors, microwave ovens, and drive-in restaurants. The need for convenience is related to individualism, low uncertainty avoidance, and short-term orientation, but the relationships vary

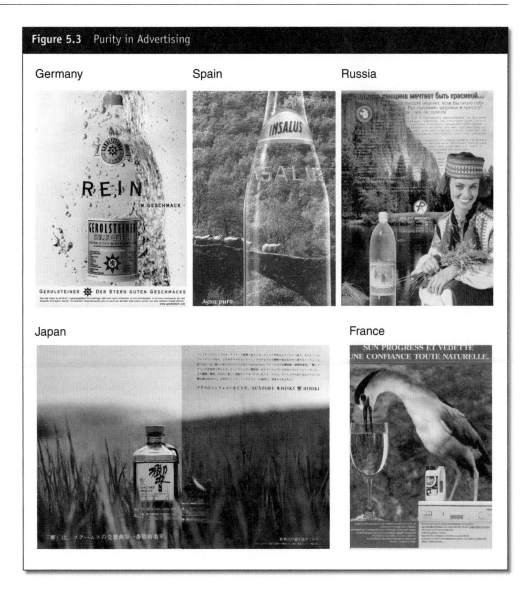

Figure 5.3   Purity in Advertising

by product type. Low long-term orientation (LTO) explains variance of usage of ready-made food products such as breakfast cereals (60%), potato crisps (22%), fizzy soft/energy drinks (30%), and ready-to-drink fruit and vegetable juices (19%). It also explains differences in usage of electric dishwashers (36%).[37] In 2001, 41% of variance of convenience as a motive for food choice was explained by low uncertainty avoidance, and an additional 25% by low masculinity.[38] Low uncertainty avoidance explains 36% of variance of convenience that influences food choice.[39] Thirty percent of variance of minutes spent on eating is explained by long-term orientation.[40] Figure 5.4 illustrates the latter relationship for 14 countries.

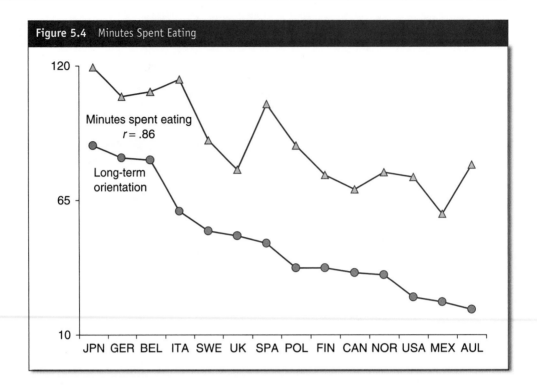

Figure 5.4   Minutes Spent Eating

SOURCE: Hofstede et al. (2010) (see Appendix A); Society at a Glance (2009) OECD Social Indicators (see Appendix B)

The configuration of dimensions explaining convenience orientation is the opposite of the cultural configuration of Italy, the country that harbors the propagators of "slow food." In 1986 in Rome, the Slow Food International Movement was founded. It claims 60,000 members, holds conferences, and protests fast food through education and information.[41]

One function of convenience is saving time, but this is not a universal motive for buying microwave ovens. Whereas in the United States, a nation of snack food and dashboard dining, the buying motive for microwave ovens may be the timesaving feature, in other cultures the motive is different. Similar to food processors, in cultures where food consumption is considered to be a social event, the microwave oven is a device that enables people to prepare more refined dishes, so people can spend even more time on cooking. Whereas in the United States people tend to think of food as something to pop into the microwave oven, in Spain much attention is given to cooking two meals a day or at least the main meal or *comida*. Microwave ovens are used to make meals even more perfect. Even on vacation, people cook meals. At some Spanish camping sites, every section has a special tent for placing your oven.

Car-Buying Motives

Several surveys have asked consumers questions about car-buying motives. EMS, for example, asks respondents, "Which of the following factors are the most important in choosing your main car?" Four of the response choices in 1997 were "safety," "fuel economy," "enjoyment to drive," and "distinctive design." Another four in 1999 were "car interior," "environmentally friendly," "importance of an international image," and "I would always choose a European make of car." In 2007 these motives were repeated, adding a few others like "engine performance," "price," and "technology." All motives vary by culture and are related to different dimensions. Table 5.2 shows the correlation coefficients of the cultural variables with the different factors of car choice.

Table 5.2   Factors of Importance for the Choice of Car, Europe

	GNI/cap	PDI	IDV	MAS	UAI	LTO
Factor to Choose Car (1997/1999)						
Safety	.02	−.29	−.59*	−.39	.03	−.21
Design	−.50*	.51*	.24	.15	.10	−.17
Joy to drive	.36	−.22	.48*	.16	−.18	.33
Car interior	.38	.15	.12	.49*	.36	.77***
Env't friendly	.37	−.55*	−.17	.03	−.20	.23
Fuel economy	−.47*	−.08	−.57*	.06	.14	−.61**
European make	.27	.24	−.11	.51*	.53*	.60**
Intl image	−.56*	.49*	−.84***	.11	.70***	−.29
Factor to Choose Car (2007)						
Safety (airbags etc.)	−.31	−.06	−.45*	−.29	.15	−.19
Design	.14	.12	.46*	−.02	−.32	−.19
Joy to drive	.55*	−.44*	.54*	−.25	−.47*	.12
Car interior	−.22	.19	−.20	.41	.48*	.70***
Env't friendly	.17	−.25	.07	.27	−.17	.22
Engine performance	−.19	.05	−.20	−.14	−.10	−.66***
Price	−.26	.04	−.14	−.14	−.02	−.58*
Technology	−.10	.18	−.36	−.02	.46*	.23

SOURCES: Hofstede et al. (2010) (see Appendix A); EMS 1997, 1999 and 2007 (see Appendix B)

International image is a status motive, related to high power distance and collectivism. Fuel economy is related to short-term orientation. Enjoyment to drive is related to high individualism, reflecting pleasure seeking, a typical individualistic motive. Safety generally is viewed to be a universal attribute, because everybody wants a safe car, but nowadays basically all cars are safe. As a motive, however, it is culture bound. In other surveys we have found a negative correlation with masculinity. Here we find a correlation with low individualism. The function of safety is likely to be more to protect the family and other loved ones than to protect oneself. Preference of cars of European make is related to long-term orientation. Design can be associated with status feelings but also be an expression of individuality. Environmental friendliness is a motive for small power distance cultures. This fits the general environmental sensitivity as discussed in the earlier section on environmentalism. Engine performance and price are specifically important in short-term-oriented cultures, and technology is an issue of most importance in high uncertainty avoidance cultures.

Figure 5.5 shows motives for buying automobiles by cultural clusters according to two of Hofstede's dimensions, masculinity and uncertainty avoidance. These motives are recognized in the design of cars and in the appeals used by advertisers of successful car brands.

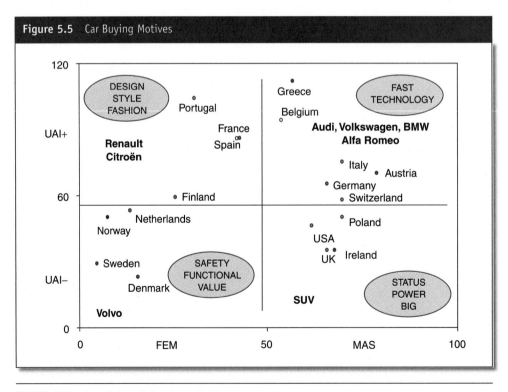

Figure 5.5   Car Buying Motives

SOURCE: Hofstede et al. (2010) (see Appendix A)

The lower left quadrant shows the configuration of low masculinity and weak uncertainty avoidance. In this culture cluster, people have a preference for safety to protect the family and value for money. Safety (to protect the weak) and the functional aspects of a car are more important than technology or design. The Swedish Volvo car brand is well known for the safety claim. In feminine cultures, people have little interest in the motor of their car. Data from several surveys show that they don't even know the size of their car engines, as compared with masculine cultures. The lower right quadrant shows a cluster of cultures with the configuration masculinity and weak uncertainty avoidance. People in these cultures have status needs to show their success and prefer cars with big, powerful motors. This is the culture cluster where people will be most attracted to the sturdy SUV (sport utility vehicle). The upper right quadrant shows the cluster of cultures with the configuration of masculinity and strong uncertainty avoidance. People in these cultures are aggressive drivers, and they prefer cars with rapid acceleration. Speed of a car is an important motive. This seems paradoxical, as one would expect to see risk aversion translated into a safety motive. Not so: the explanation is that people of strong uncertainty avoidance cultures build up stress, which they also want to release. Fast and aggressive driving serves as an emotional safety valve. It demonstrates that uncertainty avoidance is not the same as risk avoidance. But cars must also be technologically advanced, well designed, and well tested. These are the cultures where people prefer the German brands like Audi and BMW and the Italian Alfa Romeo. Volkswagen's claim, *Vorsprung durch Technik* ("Headstart through technology"), reflects the technology motive. In the upper left quadrant, in the combination of low masculine and strong uncertainty avoidance, one sees the need for "sporty" driving, fast acceleration but not so aggressive. This is combined with a preference for design (but more in the art/fashion sphere), pleasure, and enjoyment. This is the area where the stylish brands like Renault and Citroën originate. Most of the countries in the upper quadrants are also high power distance, so social status is a motive in both quadrants.

EMOTION

Emotion is not a well-defined concept, neither in psychology nor in advertising. In psychology, emotion is generally described as a process that involves interaction between cognition and physiology, meaning the mind influences the body and vice versa. Emotion involves bodily (physiological) changes and, on the mental side, a state of excitement or disturbance marked by a strong feeling.[42] The basic emotions concept includes the notion that emotions form independent and integral wholes in which various components (e.g., experience, facial expression, and physiological response) are closely linked together.

In Anglo-Saxon literature, emotions and thinking are classified as different kinds of phenomena. Emotions appear to be natural phenomena governed by biological mechanisms that are beyond control. In contrast, thinking appears to be voluntary, learned, controlled, and dependent upon cultural symbols and concepts. Emotions are associated with art, beauty, poetry, and music. Thinking is associated with logic, science, calculation. Clear thinking supposedly requires eliminating emotions. Other cultures have different concepts of emotions.

Numerous peoples have no word or concept for emotions, per se. They regard emotions as integrated with thinking, attitudes, motives, behavior, and fate/fortune rather than being something distinct. Western parents indulge children's emotions and encourage them to pay a great deal of attention to their emotions, while non-Western parents usually do not. American mothers tend to encourage their children to introspect about, analyze, and discuss their feelings, which Chinese mothers don't do.[43]

Emotions are affective responses that are learned. This aspect of emotion makes it culture bound. It is unlikely that people in all cultures have learned to express their own feelings and to recognize feelings of others in the same way. Yet, emotion psychologists have argued that many emotions are universal, although the components of emotion are embedded in the sociocultural environment.[44] Whereas in European-American culture, emotions, such as joy and anger, are constructed primarily as internal experiences, they are inherently more social and relational in non-Western cultures.[45] The psychologists Mesquita and Frijda[46] reviewed various elements of emotions across cultures and concluded that global statements about cross-cultural universality of emotion, or about their cultural determination, are inappropriate. Several elements of emotion, but not all, are related to culture. For example, among individualistic independent selves, "ego-focused" emotions (e.g., anger, frustration, and pride) are more marked than among collectivistic, interdependent selves where "other-focused" emotions (such as sympathy, shame, and feelings of interpersonal communion) are more marked. Whereas in the United Kingdom happiness is positively related to feelings of independence, in collectivistic Greece happiness is negatively related to independence.[47] The very concepts, definitions, understandings, and meanings of emotion can differ across cultures.

American prize-winning TV commercials tend to display the quintessential American type of feelings and emotions as described by the Japanese American psychologist David Matsumoto.

In the United States, we place a premium on feelings. We all recognize that each of us is unique and that we have our own individual feelings about the things, events, situations and people around us. We consciously try to be aware of our feelings, to be "in touch" with them, as we say. To be in touch with our feelings and to understand the world around us emotionally is to be a mature adult in society.... Much psychotherapeutic work is focused on helping individuals freely express the feelings and emotions they may have bottled up inside.[48]

Happiness is one of the strongest American emotions. "Life, liberty and the pursuit of happiness" is one of the most famous phrases in the U.S. Declaration of Independence, and Americans are obsessed by the pursuit of happiness. In 2008, 4,000 books were published on happiness, up from 50 in the year 2000.[49]

Universal, Basic Emotions?

Much research on emotions has been designed to test the hypothesis of the universality of basic emotions. Basic emotions were supposed to be a part of the human potential and therefore universal. One argument in favor of universal basic emotions is that most languages possess limited sets of central *emotion-labeling* words, referring to a small number of commonly occurring emotions. Examples of such words in the English language are *anger*, *fear*, *sadness*, and *joy*. Another argument is based on research on *recognition of facial expressions*. People from different cultures can recognize facial expressions in similar ways. From this it was concluded that there is also similarity in showing facial expressions, but there is no evidence that these facial expressions actually occur across cultures.[50] The question is whether it is justified to take facial expression as an index of the presence of emotions, because it is possible that in some societies emotions occur without facial expressions whereas in others facial expressions occur without emotions.[51] Seeing a facial expression allows an observer to draw a conclusion about a situation, but one specific facial expression is not necessarily connected to one specific emotion. For example, a smile is generally viewed as an expression of happiness. However, seeing a friend can make a person smile, but this does not imply that the person is happy. He or she can, in fact, be sad or lonely.

Facial expressions are only a crude measurement of emotions, and labeling a facial expression is not the same as conceptualizing emotion. Yet, many people in Western cultures implicitly believe that certain categories of emotion are natural kinds and that specific facial actions express these emotions.

Emotion and Language

English words are the core of psychologists' theories of emotion, but words for emotions vary from one culture to another. English words often assumed to denote natural basic categories of emotion have no equivalents in some other languages, and other languages provide commonly used emotion words that have no equivalent in English.[52]

Lists of English language emotion words do not cover the important emotions that exist worldwide. Examples are emotions like shame and guilt, important East Asian emotions that are generally lacking in lists of emotion words. The concept of emotion per se is not universal either. In a culture that lacks the concept of emotion, it is difficult to find out whether words refer to emotions. For many emotion words, there are no linguistic equivalents, or seemingly linguistic equivalents cover different concepts. Anger, for example, appears to be natural in Western cultures, but even across Western cultures the content varies. The American experience and organization of anger is American specific, stressing the expression of one's rights, goals, and needs. Anger occurs when these are blocked, and the person has a sense of "I was treated unfairly." By contrast, in collectivistic cultures anger would be a different experience because it produces separation and disconnection where connection and interdependence are so important.[53] The fact that anger is related to the concept of fairness makes it all the more culture bound because concrete notions of what is considered fair in a specific situation also vary among cultures.[54] Americans usually interpret behavior as motivated by personal traits that are consistent and persistent. Consequently, when someone hurts them they assume that this person is "an injurious person" who warrants continued anger to defend against likely new attacks.[55]

Whereas the dominant American associations with anger identify the *causes* of anger, the Korean associations center on the *consequences* of anger,[56] which obviously implies disturbing harmony. In many English-language emotion words, the cause and situation are incorporated. *Fear* implies that a danger has appeared. *Anxiety* implies that the cause is vague or unknown. *Guilt* implies that you yourself are the causal agent of a bad outcome. *Anger* implies that another has caused some harm. In collectivistic cultures emotion words are often seen as statements about the relationship between a person and an event, rather than as statement about introspection on one's internal states.

There are important cross-language differences in the meaning of *disgust*, in particular in conceptions of disgust toward the body and its products. For the Germans, the word for disgust, *Ekel,* means "what leads to vomiting," which also is included in the Swedish word for disgust, but not in the Dutch word. To Americans the common understanding of the word *disgust* reflects both disgust and anger. Causes of disgust are also shaped by culture. Whereas spiders are a source of disgust in many Western countries, this is not the case in China, where they are eaten as a delicacy.[57]

Some emotion terms can superficially include similar emotions, but that can be misleading. A desire typical of Japanese culture is *amae,* the desire to be dependent upon another's love and kindness, which is accepted in the context of family and other group members, in interactions between children and parents, spouses, siblings, friends and lovers, and even to a certain extent in a Japanese organizational context, but tends to be inappropriate outside a non-*amae* interaction when it is viewed as manipulative. Although in a Midland English dialect the term *mardy* suggests similar emotional elements of dependency, it comprises mainly unacceptable components, like spoilt, sulky, whining, and moody.[58]

Face and shame are typical East Asian emotions. The idea of face is Chinese in origin. In Chinese as well as Japanese, the idea of losing face is found in numerous expressions. Linguistic representation of shame and embarrassment is far richer in Chinese than in English. Chinese people are better equipped to make refined discriminations between nuances of these emotions. Avoiding shame is of overriding concern—as is the avoidance of losing face.[59]

In some cultures emotion words include multiple emotions or feelings. An example is from Japan, where *jodo* includes several emotional states, such as angry, happy, sad, and ashamed. However, *jodo* also includes what might not be called emotions: considerate, motivated, lucky, and calculating. In African languages one word covers both anger and sadness. There is no word for depression among many non-Western cultural groups. Anger is missing in some cultures. Guilt is missing in many Asian and Pacific languages. About 20% of the world's languages make no distinction between envy and jealousy, which in the United States are two different concepts.[60]

The commonly given examples of culture-specific emotion words are the German words *Schadenfreude* and *Angst*. *Schadenfreude* means malicious delight, enjoying other people's suffering or bad luck. In Dutch we have a similar word: *leedvermaak*. The German *Angst* is more related to anxiety than the English word *fear*. Korean words that have no linguistic equivalents in German are *uulhada* and *dapdaphada,* which can be interpreted as subcomponents of sadness. *Dapdaphada* is a feeling of loneliness resulting from the inability to express oneself in a foreign environment. *Uulhada* expresses a sort of depressive feeling, not wanting to laugh, but not wanting to cry either because there is no reason for it.[61]

Expression of Emotions

Much research in the field of human emotions is on facial expressions. For more than 100 years the argument has been whether facial expressions are innate and thus universal or socially learned and culturally controlled. The *neuro-cultural* position[62] states that there are distinctive movements of the facial muscle for each of a number of primary affect states, and these are universal for mankind. However, the emotion-eliciting stimuli, the linked feelings, the display rules, and the behavioral consequences all can vary from one culture to another. The *universalists* argue that the face reveals emotion in a way that is universally understood because a number of universal emotions, such as happiness, surprise, fear, anger, contempt, disgust, and sadness, are universally recognized from facial expressions. They base their ideas on studies of recognition of facial expressions against lists of basic emotions, based on a standard set of English terms. In the major studies, respondents have been asked to categorize the basic emotions against still photographs of facial expressions of Caucasian actors, who posed according to instructions by Anglo-American researchers (e.g., a smile for happiness, crying face for grief, wide open mouth and eyes for surprise, frown for anger, and wrinkled nose or tongue protrusion for disgust). Usually the choice respondents have to make is forced, meaning that they have to select basic emotions from a fixed list and options are mutually exclusive. This sort of study has led to high levels of recognition rates for several basic emotion categories across countries. Accuracy rates have been reported ranging from 86% for Americans down to 53% for tribal people in New Guinea (judging American facial expressions).[63] Cultural differences have been found in the level of recognition and ratings of intensity.

An alternative approach is free choice, when respondents can freely use their own descriptions of an emotion related to each facial expression. In free choice studies, facial expressions are rarely interpreted in terms of one specific category, more often in a broad range of overlapping categories that are not always emotions but are often situations. In particular, free responses by members of collectivistic cultures tend to include non-emotions, more situations.

In the process of measuring emotion by facial expression, several aspects can go wrong: the correct *recognition* of facial expressions, the *judgment of intensity,* and the *labeling* of the related emotion. Another aspect of the measurement of facial expression is the *absence of context or situation,* as such studies tend to be conducted in a laboratory setting, with no other communication or contextual cues.[64] People may judge expressions differently according to the context or event surrounding the emotion. The problem is that operationalizing context is a difficult task. Edward Hall states, "Context never has a specific meaning. Yet the meaning of a communication is always dependent on context."[65]

Several researchers have contributed to the understanding of the role of emotions in advertising across cultures. Many such studies try to measure the difference in persuasiveness of emotional appeals in individualistic and collectivistic cultures. An experimental approach is to use alternative (mock) advertisements with different emotions that are hypothesized to be more appealing to members of one culture than to members of another culture. An example is the measurement of the effectiveness of ego- versus other-focused emotions, using varying appeals, featuring, for example, *pride* (ego-focused emotion) or *empathy* (other-focused emotion) or *happiness*-related emotions (e.g., happy, cheerful, delighted) versus *peacefulness*-related emotions (calm, peaceful, serene). The logical approach to such studies is to keep other variables constant in order to be able to isolate the effect of the different appeals. So ads are made as similar as possible, varying only in the target emotion.[66] However, the constant variables provide the context of the emotion. Unlike individualists, collectivists have difficulties understanding the emotion properly outside the context. It is nearly impossible to find a culture-free context. Variation of copy only leaves out the role of context, which is so important in advertising. An example of background used in such studies is a beach, which is not culture free. Whereas a beach to Westerners is a place to relax, to play active sport, or have fun and adventure, in Asian countries it has different connotations. It is associated with many different activities and events, varying from special celebrations or funerals, to taking wedding pictures, to even use as public toilet. So a beach is likely to be associated with different emotional events.

Recognition and Judgment of Expressions of Emotions

Both recognition of expressions of emotion and judgment vary across cultures. How people express their emotions, but also how people judge the expressions of emotion, are learned behavior. People of different countries and cultures learn culture-specific rules of decoding the meaning of emotion expressions. This can be due to the difference in meanings and associations of the emotion terms used as response alternatives. It can also be related to differences in *intensity* in the expression of emotions. When the Japanese express emotions, they express them less intensely than do Americans, which leads to lower intensity ratings when judging expressions.

Across cultures, people weigh facial cues differently. When interpreting emotions of others, the Japanese focus more on the eyes, whereas Americans focus on the mouth. This difference may explain why stylized facial icons seem to differ between Japan and the United States. In Internet text mails, Americans use emoticons that vary the direction of the mouth, e.g., :) and :(. Japanese emoticons vary the direction of the eyes and may not vary the direction of the mouth, e.g., ^_^ and ;_; .[67]

In China people do not generally correlate facial expressions with a discrete emotion category. Many Chinese phrases that describe facial expressions refer to more than one part of the face, for example, "eyes wide open (with strength), mouth dumbstruck," suggests that speaker's mind goes blank and they are unable to say anything ("I can't say anything"); sticking out one's tongue may indicate that someone wants to say something now, but does not know what to say as if still being in a state of disbelief. [68]

Matsumoto[69] correlated the Hofstede dimensions with recognition accuracy levels and found that in individualistic cultures people are better at recognizing negative emotions than in collectivistic cultures. Hofstede[70] explains differences in emotion recognition by the level of uncertainty avoidance. In low uncertainty avoidance cultures, where emotions are less expressed, people have learned to take cues from faces, as compared with high uncertainty avoidance cultures, where emotions are expressed in more powerful ways. There also is a relationship with the personality trait dimensions of the five-factor model.[71] (See Chapter 4, section on personal traits.)

The Canadian psychologist James Russell[72] reviewed a number of studies and summarized many discrepancies in recognition of emotions. The hypothesis that happiness, surprise, fear, anger, disgust, and sadness would be universally recognizable from facial expressions fit the data only for *happiness*. There are many examples of confusion of the other basic emotions. In particular, non-Western subjects tend to categorize expressions incorrectly. Examples are "disgust" being confused with *contempt,* "sadness" with *contempt* and *fear,* "anger" with *contempt, frustration,* and *disgust,* and "fear" being confused with *surprise*. In a study using a set of photographs of facial expressions of emotion posed by Chinese people living in Beijing, "anger" expressions were also rated as *disgust* (and vice versa), "surprise" as *fear,* and "sadness" as *disgust* and *fear.*[73]

Researchers from Waseda University in Japan teamed up with Kyushi-based robot manufacturer tmsuk to develop a humanoid robot, called Kobian, that uses its entire body to express a variety of emotions. Kobian expresses seven different feelings, including delight, surprise, and disgust, as depicted in Figure 5.6. Kobian expressing delight, surprise and disgust.[74] The journalists who reported on this expressed difficulties in recognizing these expressions.

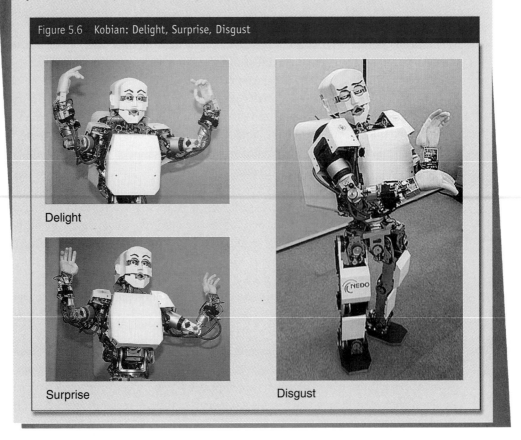

Figure 5.6   Kobian: Delight, Surprise, Disgust

Delight

Surprise

Disgust

Other studies have demonstrated that the match between the cultural background of expresser and judge is important. When members of a cultural group judge emotions expressed by members of that same cultural group, cross-cultural significance is higher. This suggests that emotions may be more accurately understood when members of the same national, ethnic, or regional group that express the emotion judge them. In heterogeneous societies, minority groups are better able to judge the emotions of majority group members than majority group members are able to judge the emotions of minority group members.[75] Emotional experience and linguistic expression are culture specific; they are learned either by growing up in a culture or by later exposure to the culture. The match between the emotional expressor and perceiver has implications for communication effectiveness. For effective advertising, the facial expression should be interpretable by the target group. This implies that for a culturally correct interpretation for each cultural group, the correct expression must be found. An example was described in Chapter 4 in the section on the body and identity. A sultry facial expression of American models is meant to express independence, whereas Japanese models present happy broad smiles to express dependence needs.

If emotions are better understood from faces of the same national or ethnic group, it should be important for advertisers to select not only the right expressions but also the right faces. In international advertising, for efficiency reasons companies tend to select faces that they think are recognizable to people of various countries in a region. An example is the Egyptian advertisement for Nivea (Figure 5.7), showing a Lebanese face. The differences may not be easily recognizable for Europeans or Americans, but I have been told by Egyptians that they recognize this face instantly as being not Egyptian.

Figure 5.7 Nivea Ad

Emotions are also expressed vocally. Comparative analysis of expression of emotions from voices shows that happiness is least recognizable from vocal portrayals. In a study in Germany, Switzerland, Great Britain, the Netherlands, United States, Italy, France, Spain, and Indonesia, the accuracy of recognition of emotions was related to the similarity of languages. The best recognitions of German speakers were by the Dutch and English speakers, also Germanic languages. This was followed by Romance languages (Italian, French, and Spanish). The lowest recognition was obtained for Indonesia.[76] People are not just faces. Other senses are likely to play an additional and complementary role in recognizing emotions. Whereas happiness is the most accurately understood emotion in the face, it is the least accurately understood emotion in the voice. Anger is the most accurately understood in the voice, whereas it is relatively less understood in the face.[77]

Recognition of facial expressions may be a human capacity, but it does not imply universality of emotions. In some cultures people hide their emotional states according to the social norms of their culture, called *display rules*. Cultural display rules also cause people of different cultures to attribute different meanings to emotional expressions. Americans, for example, rate smiling faces as more intelligent than neutral faces, whereas Japanese do not.[78]

Display Rules

The degree to which people display their emotions (and how) is culturally defined. *Meaning* and *intensity* of emotions vary. Emotions are, for example, more subdued in hierarchical, high power distance and collectivistic cultures.[79] In individualistic cultures personal feelings and their free expression are more important than in collectivistic cultures. A comparison of emotion expression across 32 countries showed a significant correlation with individualism for overall emotion expressivity, and in particular expressing happiness and surprise.[80] East Asian collectivists try to display only positive emotions and tend to control negative emotions. Probably this is the reason why in emotion recognition studies Chinese people are less able to identify expressions of fear and disgust.[81] To the Chinese the eyes and the eyebrows can convey rich emotions. However, such expressions of emotion are discouraged. Thus, when one speaks, one generally should not move one's eyebrows or one's eyes, otherwise the risk is being considered frivolous. As in other East Asian cultures, Chinese people are discouraged from having very dramatic facial expressions.[82]

Within Europe, members of cultures of weak uncertainty avoidance are less inclined to show emotions than cultures of strong uncertainty avoidance. The British "stiff upper lip" can serve as an example. Also the vocal expression of emotion by Chinese young adults is more restrained than by Italian young adults.[83]

The same expressions may have different meanings in different cultures. Children in Western societies who protrude their tongue show *contempt;* among Chinese it means *surprise*. A smile may be an expression of pleasure or friendliness everywhere, but showing friendliness may be arrogant in one culture, a reason for distrust in another, and a requirement in social interaction in a third.[84] East Asian collectivists, instead of suppressing expression of displeasure, may display an expression of polite intercourse, what Westerners may perceive as a smile.[85] Matsumoto[86] mentions that in collectivistic cultures the expression of shame is more often accompanied by laughter and smiles than in individualistic cultures. In personal encounters, the author of this book has often seen Chinese or Indonesians smile or even laugh to hide their embarrassment. This sort of smile is certainly not a reflection of happiness. Not knowing this phenomenon can lead to misunderstanding.

Members of individualistic cultures display a wider variety of emotional behaviors than do members of collectivistic cultures, who will also emphasize emotional displays that facilitate group cooperation, harmony, and cohesion. For collectivists, the specific emotions displayed depend on the context and target of the emotion. In a public context in a collectivistic culture, it would be inappropriate to display a negative emotion because it would reflect negatively on the in-group. If the emotion is a reaction to an out-group member, it would be acceptable to express it because this would foster cohesion in the in-group.[87] So the group and the context influence the display of emotions.

> Mesquita and Frijda[88] reported an experiment by Friesen,[89] who compared display of emotions between Americans and Japanese. When watching disgusting films, both Americans and Japanese displayed disgust when filmed outside the presence of the scientist, whereas the Japanese no longer indicated disgust but were found to smile more instead when the scientist was present.

Hofstede[90] reports studies that show significant correlations between uncertainty avoidance and the expression of embarrassment. In low uncertainty avoidance cultures, people control their emotions, claim not to express embarrassment and guilt, whereas in high uncertainty avoidance cultures, display of emotions is normal and people claim the expression of embarrassment and guilt. Individualistic cultures tolerate the expression of individual anger more easily than do collectivistic cultures.

Display of emotion is also influenced by social motivation. Evidence comes from observation of Olympic gold medal winners. Experiencing some of the happiest moments in their lives, the winners smiled much during specific social presentations, but little before or after.[91]

Emotion-Eliciting Events

Emotions are usually the results of specific events, and the events that cause similar emotions vary across cultures. Happiness may be a universal emotion, but what makes us happy can be very different across cultures. Whereas Americans, for example, relate achievement goals to happiness, what makes Danes most happy is time spent with friends and family.[92]

In 2008, Eurobarometer[93] asked the question, "Which is the most important in connection with your idea of happiness?" Respondents had to make a choice of various options. Respondents in low power distance cultures most selected friendship ($r = .51$***) and love ($r = -.43$*). In high individualistic cultures they selected tolerance ($r = .33$*) and pleasure ($r = .42$*). In low individualistic cultures the choice was money ($r = -.49$**). In high masculine cultures it was tradition ($r = .43$*) and self-fulfillment ($r = .38$*). In low uncertainty avoidance cultures they selected love ($r = -.54$***), friendship ($r = -.63$***), and freedom ($r = -.51$***), and in high uncertainty avoidance cultures they chose solidarity ($r = .44$*). In short-term-oriented cultures, the choice was equality ($r = -.61$***).

Mesquita et al.[94] point at three variations in the effects of emotion-eliciting events: (1) the same situations are interpreted differently across cultures, and therefore lead to different emotions; (2) living conditions vary across cultures, resulting in different events; or (3) events derive their significance from certain culture-specific events. For example, various cultures interpret the condition "being alone" differently. In collectivistic cultures being alone can mean not being among kin and not showing or being shown affection, implying unhappiness. Sitting alone can mean that the relationships between the individual and those considered as kin are not running smoothly. In contrast, in individualistic cultures being alone can serve the need for privacy, leading to happiness, or it can mean relaxation from stress.

Events that have an impact on the family or in-group will have greater importance in collectivistic cultures than in individualistic cultures. To reach an emotional state of happiness, Americans are more likely than Japanese to seek "fun" situations, and Japanese are more likely than Americans to seek situations that produce harmonious interpersonal atmospheres.

The same type of situation or event will not necessarily trigger the same emotion in people across cultures. *Sadness* is more produced by problems in relationships for the Japanese than for Americans or Europeans. Strangers and achievement-related situations elicit more *fear* for Americans, whereas novel situations, traffic, and relationships are more frequent elicitors of fear for the Japanese. Situations involving strangers are more frequent elicitors of *anger* for the Japanese than for Americans or Europeans.[95]

Mesquita et al.[96] state that cross-cultural similarities in emotional phenomena are more likely to be found when these phenomena are described at a high level of abstraction. The differences are found when the more concrete features of emotions are taken into account. This is exactly what happens in global advertising. The argument for standard global advertising—that there are universal emotions such as love, pride, and motherhood—only holds for emotions described at a highly abstract level. When expressed in advertising, emotions must be made concrete; they must be displayed and placed in the cultural context. Universality of emotions exists only in theory, not in practice.

Emotions and expressions of emotion elicited by romantic love vary. In China romantic love is more "embedded" than in the United States, where love is based on personal preferences and intense desire. *Embedded* means it is incorporated in a larger context, namely the natural world and long-term aspects of the relationship, including devotion, commitment, loyalty, and enduring friendship. This is in contrast to the Euro-American style of love characterized by physical attraction, intense feelings of desire, and dependency in the relationship. Whereas Chinese dependency needs are diffused into a web of multiple close relationships, including their relationship with nature, Americans' dependency needs are focused on their sexual partners. This can be recognized by the characteristics of love songs. Many American songs reflect sexual dependency by using the term *baby*. In Chinese love songs, contextual forces play a role, including harmony with both society and nature, expressed by flowers, rivers, and stars. This is recognized in expressions in songs, for example, "having you, me, feelings, heaven, sea, and earth." Chinese songs also include aspects of suffering and more negative expectations about the future of the relationship.[97]

In sum, cultural variations in emotion are relative to the cultural orientations from which they derive. The culture-specific American patriotism, with the American flag as a symbolic device, may serve as an example. The ubiquitous emotional reaction of individuals after the terrible events of September 11, 2001, was carrying the national flag, in whatever sort of form: big, small, or lapel pins. Emotional reactions to ETA killings in Spain are always collective marches. In 2002 the Dutch football coach Guus Hiddink helped the Korean football team win several matches in the World Cup finals, played in Korea and Japan. The Koreans were extremely emotional about this, and thankful, because he had given them "face" to the world. Soon, groups of Koreans even went to visit his birthplace, Varsseveld, an until-then insignificant village in the Netherlands.

EMOTIONS IN ADVERTISING

For a long time international advertising strategists have thought that emotional or "feeling" appeals would travel better than "thinking" ones because of the assumption that certain emotions are shared around the world.[98] Thus, international advertising has been dominated by emotional appeals such as love and happiness.[99] This is caused by the assumed universality of emotions, in particular happiness. A global brand like Coca-Cola uses happiness in global advertising worldwide showing happy people and using the payoff "open happiness" next to the bottle. Figure 5.8 shows a few pictures from a Coca-Cola commercial.

The thought of universality of emotions in advertising has been stimulated by consumer behavior theorists like Morris Holbrook,[100] who used a number of basic emotions

Figure 5.8   Pictures from a Coca-Cola Commercial

to categorize emotional responses in advertising in the United States. "Disgust" would be an appropriate basic emotion related to cleaning products, "anger" and "frustration" would be recognized in a commercial for a bank, and "joy" would be recognized in a commercial for a telephone company. The use of Anglo-American basic emotions in advertising may have been effective for advertising in the United States; the use of the typical American emotions, and in particular the way these emotions are expressed, is not likely to be equally effective in many other cultures.

An example of the use of disgust is a commercial for Johnson Flushable wipes. The commercial shows a woman throwing away a nonflushable wipe and after that she walks past the dustbin, acting in a disgusted way, viewed from inside the dustbin. The solution is Johnson Flushable wipes. This problem-solution approach may be less effective in collectivistic cultures where people avoid negative emotions and also don't want to be confronted with problems. Figure 5.9 shows a few pictures from the commercial.

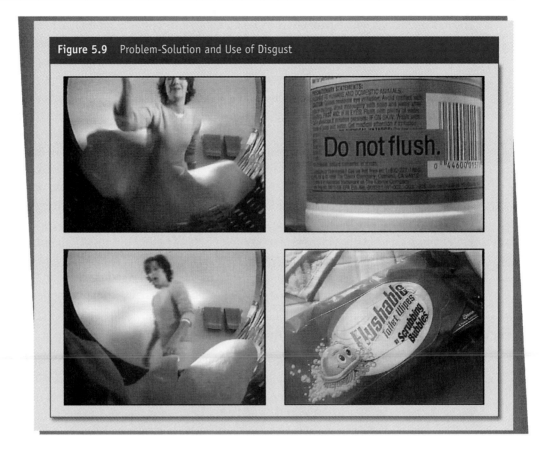

Figure 5.9   Problem-Solution and Use of Disgust

Emotional Versus Rational Advertising

In (American) advertising theory, the concept of emotion is used in the rough classification of advertising in "rational" and "emotional," where "emotional" means *feeling, pleasure,* or *mood,* whereas "rational" advertising includes mainly information about the product. The simple distinction is between "thinking" ads and "feeling" ads. Basically, any claim or appeal that is not rational is considered to be emotional. Examples of emotional appeals are sex appeals, humorous appeals, and fear appeals. The distinction represents the two schools of thought about advertising strategy in the United States: the "head" and the "heart." *Head* stands for rational argumentation, whereas *heart* stands for emotional or image advertising, "which doesn't barrage the consumer with words, facts, or claims."[101] The distinction is typical of American advertising. The strong focus on feelings and emotions in the United States is related to the values of American culture, where emotions are highly personalized and individual, and being in touch with one's feelings is a condition for mental health. This helps to understand the impact of emotional appeals in American advertising, like "Reach out and touch someone" as in the classic campaign for Bell Telephone long distance and use of phrases like "The heartbeat of America." In other parts of the world such emotional statements may be viewed as exaggeration or pure sentimentality.

The distinction "rational/emotional" is also used to distinguish simply between the direct and the indirect approach in advertising or even between verbally and visually oriented advertising. Because much of advertising in Asia is more visual and indirect than American advertising, advertising in Asia tends to be characterized as emotional as opposed to more rational Western advertising. However, what is labeled as emotional in Japanese or French advertising is merely high-context, indirect style (see Chapter 7). Jean-Marie Dru, cofounder of the international advertising agency BDDP, observes, "Japanese advertising is not simply emotional. It taps into the richness of imagination."[102] Using the concept of emotion to classify advertising across cultures is often more confusing than clarifying, leading to obscure statements like "Even when Japanese commercials use an informational strategy, such as hyperbole or a unique selling proposition, their executions are emotional in appeal."[103]

Facial Expressions: Application to Advertising

In order to understand the emotional responses to advertising, researchers of advertising agencies apply the facial expression recognition method, a system based on the assumption that emotion can be recognized from facial expressions. An example is the emotional measurement system developed by BBDO in the United States that followed the method of still photographs of posed facial expressions. For developing such instruments, enormous investments have to be made as a pool of facial expressions ("photo decks") must be developed. At BBDO, 26 categories of emotion were selected and six professional actors, representing 20-, 30-, and 40-year-old age groups, were hired to pose for all the emotional categories. This resulted in the production of 1,872 facial expressions. Samples of consumers rated these in order to arrive at the best selection. This provided a standard for discussing the facial expressions in terms of the emotional meaning ascribed to them by consumers. Such emotional photo decks are useful instruments for nonverbally assessing the emotional impact of advertising. Consumer respondents who view television ads can select photographs from the deck that represent how the commercial makes them feel. The advantage of the method is that respondents do not have to verbalize the emotions elicited by advertising. The disadvantage is that it is only useful for international advertising if for each country different photo decks are made. Experience at BBDO in Europe has taught that photographs of facial expressions produced in the United States could not be transplanted to Europe. European respondents could not recognize the way American actors expressed specific moods. The same is true within Europe: no useful single "photo deck" could be developed for the whole of Europe.[104]

Similar experiences are reported from New Zealand, where photographs of people's faces or stylized faces (smiley faces) are frequently used in projective techniques. Several groups other than the New Zealand Europeans, for example Tongans and Koreans, cannot associate easily with pictures of European faces. New Zealand Europeans can better associate brands with photographs that are similar to themselves. Also Koreans identify more closely with Korean photographs if they have the appropriate expressions. Cues in smiley faces developed for Koreans and Tongans tend to be viewed as offensive because the characteristics, such as eye shapes, are seen as offensive caricatures. Both Koreans and Tongans view representing the mouth as a straight horizontal line—meant to be a neutral cue—as indicating a negative reaction. Peripheral cues, such as distinctive hairstyles, tend to distract attention away from the expression of the face, which demonstrates the importance of context.[105]

GROUP PROCESSES

According to Western consumer behavior theory, the behavior of individuals is based partly on their personal characteristics and partly on their group memberships. The group influences individual consumer behavior. Norms concerning perceptions, opinions, attitudes, and behaviors frequently develop within a group. A distinction is made between *formal* (associations) and *informal* groups (family and friends) that may influence behavior and decision making. Other groups that are distinguished as influencing consumer behavior are *reference group* and *aspirational group*.

Western examples of reasons why people are part of or join a group are (1) to achieve a task that cannot be completed alone; (2) to obtain friendship, companionship, and support; (3) to get a source of warmth and psychological security; (4) because we have no choice—we are born male or female and we are born in a particular family. The first three are Western-centric reasons. The basic assumption is that people can choose group membership, which is true for individualistic cultures, whereas in collectivistic cultures group membership is a central aspect of identity.

The degree to which group members depend on others in consumer decision making varies. In collectivistic and high power distance cultures, dependence on others is stronger than in individualistic and low power distance cultures. Comparative content analysis of Chinese and American advertising demonstrates that group consensus and conformity to family preference rather than individual choice is more found in Chinese than in American advertising.[106] Differences in family relationships and interdependence, however, are quite complex. Studies within the United States found that European Americans equated obligation to family with relationship quality and closeness to family members, and therefore viewed obligation to family as personal choice; whereas for Mexican Americans, obligation related to the social role of being family or group. As compared with Chinese American students, European American undergraduate students saw their parents as more respectful of their independence, felt supported in their independence, and rated their relationship with their parents as emotionally supportive and mutual and felt more comfortable asking their parents for support.[107] For understanding group influences on consumer behavior the in-group versus out-group distinction is important.

In-Group and Out-Group

Triandis defines in-groups as "groups of individuals about whose welfare a person is concerned, with whom that person is willing to cooperate without demanding equitable returns, and separation from which leads to anxiety."[108] Members of collectivistic cultures are born as part of a group, which defines their identity. In-group behavior can be different from out-group behavior. The Japanese divide their lives into inner and outer sectors, each with its own different standards of behavior. In the inner circle the individual is automatically accepted, there is interdependence and automatic warmth, love, or *amae,* the best translation of which is "passive love" or dependency. Members of the inner circle experience this *amae* between each other, but it does not exist in the outer circle. You lose *amae* when you enter the outer circle. You don't expect *amae* in the outer circle.[109] In-group relationships in collectivistic cultures are more intimate than in individualistic cultures. Members of individualistic cultures belong to many specific in-groups, which they join willingly. Because of this, these in-groups have less influence than in-groups do in collectivistic cultures.[110]

In collectivistic cultures there is a sharp distinction between in-group and out-group. People in collectivistic cultures interact more frequently, more widely, more deeply, and more positively with in-group members than members of individualistic cultures do in their in-groups. Processes of mutual influence, harmony enhancement, and in-group favoritism are stronger in collectivistic cultures than in individualistic cultures.

Studies among students have shown that Japanese and Hong Kong students spend more time with in-groups than with out-groups. A within-U.S. study showed that European Americans spend equal time with in- and out-groups and have more freedom to decide which groups to belong to than Indian or Asian Americans. Americans also belong to more groups than do Indian students.[111] The difference between in-group and out-group is particularly visible in Chinese restaurants that generally have round tables for eight persons and where families or other in-groups can have their own sections in restaurants. Family birthday parties are characterized by a lot of noise, which is why restaurants have several special rooms to host celebrating groups. In-group noise is part of the celebration, but out-group noise can have a negative influence on the goals of the in-group. Figure 5.10 shows a restaurant in Shanghai.

Several elements of the McDonald's brand play a role in the evaluation of McDonald's in China. These are the way the food is ordered and delivered, the price, the decor, the noise, and the way the tables are set up. What makes McDonald's unique is the standardized menu and low price, cleanliness, and tables for two. These are exactly the reasons why McDonald's is not the place to go for a typical event celebrated in a restaurant, such as birthday parties with several generations of family. The tables are not right. There is too little choice of food and the price is too low to give proper face to the honoree. There is too much noise from out-groups. At Chinese birthday parties people order special food that sets them apart from other restaurant guests.

They also get a special section where they are not disturbed by the noise of outsiders. The standardized approach of McDonald's does not allow for that sort of service. However, because of the two-person tables, McDonald's is a place that enables a couple on a date to find privacy. It offers social space outside of the home in which two people can be "alone" and sit for a long time. This is in contrast to Chinese restaurants where people typically eat and leave immediately afterward. So in China, McDonald's offers the opposite of fast food.[112]

Figure 5.10   Large Round Tables in Chinese Restaurants. Photograph Gerard Foekema

Interaction with strangers (out-groups) varies with uncertainty avoidance. In high uncertainty avoidance cultures people tend to think what is strange or unknown can be threatening. Behavior toward strangers may be ritualized and/or very polite, or strangers can be ignored, treated as if they don't exist. In low uncertainty avoidance cultures there is more interaction with foreigners. A Eurobarometer survey asked for the degree to which respondents interacted with foreigners, such as e-mailing with foreigners or having job contacts with foreigners. Variance of answers to both questions was explained by low uncertainty avoidance (respectively, 37% and 45%).[113]

Collectivistic cultures vary with respect to the type and rank-order of importance of in-groups. In-groups vary from the extended family (whether they live in joint or unitary households is not relevant) with neighborhood and school friends absorbed in the extended family, to the larger community such as the Indian *jati* or Spanish *barrio*, or the occupational unit.[114] Some put kinship organizations (family) ahead of all other in-groups, whereas others put their companies ahead of other in-groups. In-group relationships in collectivistic cultures are usually limited to three groups: brother/sister (family group), coworker and colleague (company in-group), and classmate (university in-group). In Japan, modernization has made the occupational unit more important than kinship links. Even in the medium collectivistic cultures in Europe, one's city or region is an important part of one's identity, more than in individualistic cultures. This is demonstrated by correlation between individualism and the attachment to one's town ($r = -.66***$) or region ($r = -.79***$).[115]

Members of the collectivistic in-group are implicitly what in individualistic cultures are called your "friends." Members of individualistic cultures have to invest time in friendship, and they belong to many specific in-groups that may change over time. Across Europe, the percentages who state that friendship is very important correlate with individualism, low power distance, and low uncertainty avoidance.[116] Friendship is important because people have to make an effort to get and preserve friendship, other than in collectivistic cultures where people automatically belong to a group. Seven out of ten Americans belong at least to one club or association,[117] whereas membership in associations is not very popular in Japan. Also, Spaniards do not tend to subscribe in great numbers to clubs and associations, political or otherwise. Although many Americans have close friends to whom they feel special attachments and strong obligations, such friendships are small in number. Many other people are labeled "friends" without the element of mutual obligations that comes so natural in the collectivistic in-group. In collectivistic cultures there is more communication and interaction between friends than in collectivistic cultures; they meet each other much more frequently. Across 25 European countries, the percentages who say they meet their friends every day correlate negatively with individualism ($r = -.41*$) but also with short-term orientation ($r = -.53***$).[118] In short-term-oriented cultures people spend more money on enjoying themselves with others. This is included in an aspect of short-term orientation called "service to others" by Minkov, who developed this long- short-term orientation and labeled it *flexhumility* versus *monumentalism*.[119] This same dimension was adopted by Hofstede (see Chapter 2).

> Giving gifts is much more important for in-group members than for out-group members. When the self is group based rather than individual based, gift giving within the group or family takes on a unique meaning. Giving to others can be seen as giving to self.[120] Gift buying for members of the in-group is a special art in Japan, and even pets are part of that group. In 2001, "Posh dog products and accessories have become hot items, and Hermes, Louis Vuitton, Gucci, Prada and others sold 175,000 yen bags, 200,000 yen beds, and 50,000 yen collars for their canine clients." Buyers say, "He's family, so I don't mind spending up to 15,000 yen on things for him."[121]

The advantage of branded pet articles is that customers can match their own fashions with those of their pets, be in harmony. Also in Europe there is a relationship between gift giving and collectivism. Annual spending on cosmetics and skin care, as measured by EMS, correlates with low individualism. Of the respondents of EMS, 68% are males. So, the answers are likely to refer to buying perfume, cosmetics, and skin care as gifts when traveling.

FAMILY AND RELATIONSHIPS: PARENTS-CHILDREN

The traditional definition of a *family* is two or more people living together who are related by blood or marriage. What is called the *nuclear family* is one couple with children. If more generations are living together, it is called the *extended family*. In the individualistic Western world there are many varieties to the traditional family, and increasing numbers of babies are born with parents who are not married. In the Netherlands in 2007, 4 out of 19 babies born were from no-married parents.[122] Increasing divorce rates in the Western world also lead to more single parents. In collectivistic cultures, economic development has led to the decrease of the extended family with a weakening of material interdependence, but that has not led to decreasing psychological interdependence.

Whereas in individualistic cultures, children are reared to develop an autonomous, independent identity, in collectivistic cultures parents tend to foster a high level of dependence in their children, to socialize them to successfully adapt to an interdependent society; children to some extent are allowed autonomy, without desiring separateness in the child. This influences the way parents and children relate to each other. Indian parents are found to be more authoritarian, whereas Japanese parents are more permissive.[123] Korean parents grant autonomy to their children but they must accept in-group obligations. From the Western point of view in collectivistic cultures, the way young children are raised looks like permissiveness, with little interference by parents. But in collectivistic cultures small children get more freedom to learn to conform and preserve harmony with their siblings. Parental control also is more "order setting" than "dominating."[124] This is confirmed by a study among young people 10–18 years old across seven Latin American countries that showed that in the more individualistic cultures, fathers and mothers more decide which programs children watch on TV than in the more collectivistic cultures. Also the percentages who say they use the Internet with their mothers correlate with individualism.[125]

Another dimension that explains differences in parental control is long- /short-term orientation. In short-term-oriented cultures there are more strict rules to which people adhere in raising children. Long-term-orientation cultures are more pragmatic and lenient. Parents place few restrictions on their children's media exposure. In short-term-oriented, cultures parents check what their children do on the Internet; they stay near the child and sit with them when they are on the Internet. In long-term-oriented cultures there are fewer restrictions, and more parents say they never sit with their child; they allow them to use e-mail and chat rooms.[126] In long-term-oriented cultures children also have more say in important family decisions.[127]

In high power distance cultures, adults and children tend to live in different worlds, the world for children and the world for grown-ups. This has implications for the type of toys that are popular. LEGO, for example, developed in Denmark, is meant for parents and children to play together. Parents teach their children how to construct LEGO buildings. In France, a high power distance, dependency culture, LEGO never became as popular as in Denmark. In communications, children are also addressed in the context of their own world. This is a likely explanation of the fact that Chinese children's commercials are less likely to use an adult spokesperson or voice-over than are those in the United States.[128]

Worldwide, parents have to find solutions to combining work and child care. As we have seen in Chapter 3, the degree to which women work varies with the masculinity/femininity of their cultures. This is also the case for their view on how they ideally organize child care. In the masculine cultures, the general norm is that a woman's first priority is the family $(r = .67***)$[129] and women are responsible for running the household. The Japanese house-wife manages household budget, decides on the choice of school of the children, the house, holidays, and often also the car to buy. In the Indian family hierarchy, age and gender are the main ordering principles, and men have more decisive authority and property rights. The elders and both parents enjoy more respect and woman as a mother is more respected.[130]

CONFORMITY

In collectivistic cultures, people conform more to others, both of in-groups and of out-groups, than they do in individualistic cultures. A famous experiment by Asch[131] measured the degree of conformity in the United States by showing participants a stimulus line and a set of three lines, in which one line was the same length as the stimulus line. The partic-ipants had to say which of the three lines was similar to the stimulus line. All but one par-ticipant were told to give the same wrong answer. Individuals who had to judge in a group where the other participants all gave the same wrong answer also gave the wrong answer, while this was not the case in groups where no such pressure took place. Hofstede[132] reports cross-analysis of Asch-like studies in the United States and 36 studies in 16 other countries that point at greater conformity in collectivistic cultures than in individualistic cultures. Young people conform more to their peers. For young girls in collectivistic and high power distance cultures, the most powerful influences on beauty and body image are their girl-friends.[133] Singh reports that young people in India are more influenced by their peers than by family members. Conformance to peers may be more important than family influence.[134]

Branded luxury products like Vuitton purses fulfill the need to conform. In Japan, 1 in 3 women and 1 in 6 men own a Vuitton product. Teenaged girls want Vuitton because "Everyone has it."[135] Vuitton's sales have risen by double digits every year since 1990. Japanese sociologists state that by owning a Vuitton purse, anonymous young women can feel kinship with other Vuitton owners and not feel the stigma of being excluded.[136] The Japanese term is *wa,* meaning to be similar to others, look the same as others.

In China, friendship circles or people living in the same area (e.g., apartment building) often consume similar product categories, select the same brands within a category, and purchase them in the same department store.

The need for conformity is also related to low masculinity. Feminine cultures can be characterized by a need for leveling; they are also said to be "jealous" societies. Envy can be a motive to buy or not buy products or brands. In 2001, in Korea, a feminine culture, 70% said buying imported cars would lead to greater "social disparity," and nearly half avoided imports for fear of "dirty looks" from fellow Koreans.[137]

> The typical individualistic definition of conformity is "yielding to group pressure," but in collectivistic cultures conformity is not a matter of "yielding" to pressure. Group conformity is an automatic process caused by the need for social harmony. Whereas conformity, obedience, and compliance are viewed negatively in American culture, they generally are positively valued behavior in collectivistic cultures. The American bias can be recognized when conformity-related values are discussed, like using the phrase "yielding to group pressure" or "sacrificing the self for the common goal" as done by Oyserman et al.[138] and Lee.[139]

Unilever found that the Chinese bought ice cream mainly when they saw other people eat ice cream. As a result Unilever marketers intensified the distribution of ice cream in order to make it more visible in the streets.[140] In China/Taiwan people may line up when they see a line, even when they don't know what it is for. When so many people spend time standing in line, it must be good.[141]

The Heineken beer distributor in Hong Kong tapped into this key value by asking on-premise staff to leave Heineken bottles on the table. The key to marketing in Asia is perceived popularity. The bottles on the table, the restaurant with the queues. The "Be like others" appeal works.[142]

> In 2000, in Japan, cheaper "chic" was challenging the Western luxury labels the Japanese had come to embrace as symbols of prosperity. People were increasingly wearing casual clothes. In an interview by *Newsweek*'s Kay Ito in Tokyo with Tadashi Yanai, president of the Fast Retailing Company, the parent of the successful casual brand Uniqlo, Ito referred to *Newsweek* stories that the Japanese are becoming more diverse and asked whether Yanai believed this. Yanai was quoted saying:
>
> > Japanese people are extremely interested in how different they are from each other. They want to be a little different, but they hate to be very different. Most people receive
>
> *(Continued)*

(Continued)

the same education, read the same magazines and watch the same television programs. They couldn't be different even if they wanted to. In the U.S. and Europe, there is more diversity in incomes people earn and how much information they receive.[143]

Whereas in individualistic cultures women are more fashion conscious, in collectivistic cultures there is more dress conformity. Fashion consciousness deals with an individual's interest in and attention to the latest fashion trends. It is about being up to date with respect to dressing. Dress conformity refers to dressing in line with the associative group, wearing the "right" clothes.[144]

Inner-, Outer-Directedness

In the VALS (values and lifestyles) typology, people are described as outer directed who look more to the expectations of others and societal norms to fulfill their psychological needs, and inner directed when their personal needs and priorities take precedence over the expectations of others.[145] Collectivists can be characterized as more outer directed whereas individualists are more inner directed. Outer-directedness applies to the concept of *self-monitoring*—the degree to which a person takes his or her behavioral cues from the behavior of others. The self-monitoring individual is particularly sensitive to the self-presentations of others in social situations that are used as guidelines for monitoring his or her own self-presentation.[146] In individualistic cultures, prototypic individuals are used as examples, whereas in collectivistic cultures context and status relationships are more taken into consideration when deciding how to behave in a particular situation.

Public and Private Self-Consciousness

A concept related to the inner/outer distinction is *self-consciousness*. A distinction is made between *public* and *private* self-consciousness. Private self-consciousness is concerned with attending to inner thoughts and feelings, and involves introspection about the self. Public self-consciousness involves a general awareness of the self in relation to others, as a social object.[147] Hofstede views public self-consciousness (measured by answers to the question "I am concerned about what other people think of me") as presenting oneself as an individual, which is related to individualism.[148] In individualistic cultures self-consciousness implies concern for the self as viewed by unknown others, a concept that is not very well developed in collectivistic cultures where the self exists only in relation to known others, involving the concept of face. Introspection about the self is most relevant in masculine cultures that value performance and ambition, both of which require introspection about individual abilities. Research by cross-cultural communication researchers Gudykunst and

Ting-Toomey[149] revealed that people in Japan are higher on private self-consciousness than those in Korea, whereas the United States fell in between. Both private and public self-consciousness are involved in the need for status luxury articles and may serve as an explanation of the extreme dependence on foreign, status-enhancing brands by the Japanese.

> The market research agency Salles D'Arcy in São Paulo[150] conducted a survey among 14- to 24-year-old girls and women in Latin America. There were several answer categories to the question "What are the three things that Latin girls can't be without when going out?" Fifty-nine percent of Mexican respondents and 60% of Venezuelan respondents said, "Trendy clothes," as compared with 27% of respondents from Chile and 36% from Brazil. The responses correlated significantly with masculinity ($r = -.98***$). To the question what sort of women they related to, the percentages answering "Liberated" correlated significantly with low masculinity ($r = -.99***$).

PUBLIC AND PRIVATE SPACE

Some products are used more privately (toothpaste, deodorants), others more in public (drinks, luxury articles). Next to culture, public or private use affects advertising appeals across countries. In general, advertising in individualistic cultures appeals more to individualistic values such as self-reliance and personal rewards, whereas advertising in collectivistic cultures tends to appeal more to values like family well-being, in-group goals, and interdependence. This difference, however, is not uniform across products. The differences are larger for products that are shared and used in public than for personal products that are more used in private. So the type of product advertised moderates the cultural differences. For example, Han and Shavitt[151] found that individualistic appeals were more effective in the United States and collectivistic appeals were more effective in Korea, but for personal products that are used privately, individualistic appeals were generally favored in both countries.

> Zhang and Gelb[152] compared the acceptance of culture-bound appeals in the United States and China for two different products: toothbrushes and cameras. The cultural dimension used was individualism/collectivism. They found that for cameras, a product used for self-expression, in China the collectivistic appeal worked better, whereas the individualistic appeal worked better in the United States. For the toothbrush it did not make a difference. The product use condition made the difference: a toothbrush is a product used for personal purposes and not meant to show in public, so in the collectivistic China the individualistic appeal worked equally well as the collectivistic appeal. The collectivistic appeal did not work in the individualistic United States, but the individualistic appeal did work in China.

Behavior in private space can be different from behavior in public space. Members of individualistic cultures have a greater need for privacy than have members of collectivistic cultures, which has implications for usage of various products. Whereas mobile phones are used ubiquitously in public space in the collectivistic cultures in the south of Europe, this is not tolerated in the north. In 2001, some 56% of those over age 50 in the United Kingdom thought that mobile phones should be banned in public places.[153]

Culture influences the type of houses people live in and the activities in and around people's homes. In individualistic cultures people prefer one-family houses with private gardens. Every home should have its own garden, however small. Members of collectivistic cultures prefer to live in apartment buildings and own relatively few private gardens. Data on possession of private gardens correlate significantly with individualism (1970: $r = .74***$; 1991: $r = .72***$).[154] The two correlations are illustrated in Figure 5.11. As a result, mean consumption expenditures on garden plants and flowers is also significantly correlated with individualism (2001: $r = .65**$; 2005: $r = .53***$), as is the

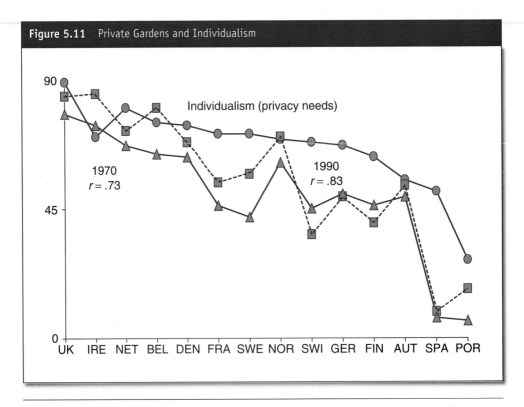

Figure 5.11   Private Gardens and Individualism

SOURCE: Hofstede et al. (2010) (see Appendix A); Reader's Digest Reports 1970 and 1991 (see Appendix B)

proportion of European inhabitants who do gardening during a typical week ($r = .49*$), but there also is a relationship with low power distance ($r = -. 78***$).[155] In high power distance and collectivistic cultures a private garden is more viewed as public space, and not tended the way the house is tended inside, whereas in individualistic cultures the garden is viewed as an extension of the house.

Whereas in Europe, in individualistic cultures people get together with friends and family in the home or garden, in collectivistic and/or high power distance cultures people get more together in public places such as parks and bars and keep the home mainly for the family. Preferences for spending nearly all of one's free time out of home correlate high power distance ($r = .67**$) and low individualism ($r = -.56*$), whereas preferences for spending free time mostly in the home are correlated with low power distance ($r = -.77***$).[156] Comparative data on numbers of cafés per million population[157] are significantly correlated with low individualism ($r = -.55*$). The percentages of people who have a meal in a restaurant or visit a bar every day correlate with low individualism ($r = -.76***$), which explains 58% of variance.[158] Expenditures in restaurants and cafés correlate with low individualism ($r = -.38*$), but also with short-term orientation ($r = -.40*$).[159]

If collectivists are used to socializing more in the public than in the private domain, they can also be expected to do other things in the public domain that individualists might be reluctant to do outside the privacy of the home. In Europe, in the countries where people more frequently visit cafés and bars, they also access the Internet more in cyber cafés. In 2000,[160] individualism explained 47% of variance of the percentages of Internet users who did not access the Internet outside the home and 53% of variance of the percentages of respondents who said they accessed the Internet in the cyber café. In 2009 the percentages of individuals who accessed the Internet at home in the past three months correlated with low uncertainty avoidance ($r = -.71***$), individualism ($r = .67***$), and low power distance ($r = -.60***$).[161] Also children in individualistic cultures access the Internet mostly inside the home, whereas in collectivistic cultures they also do so in Internet cafés.[162] Figure 5.12 is a graphic illustration of the correlations across individualism, numbers of cafés per 10,000, percentage of people who have a meal in a restaurant or visit a bar every day, access to the Internet in a cyber café and not outside the home, for nine countries in Europe.

Mixing home and work life is also related to individualism. Whereas in individualistic cultures people may want to take work into their homes, this is not the usual behavior in collectivistic cultures. Another dimension that explains differences is cultural masculinity. The task orientation of high masculine cultures versus needs for quality of life of low masculine cultures explains the division between public work life and private home life. The cultural configuration explains differences in penetration of computers and use of the Internet (further discussed in Chapter 7).

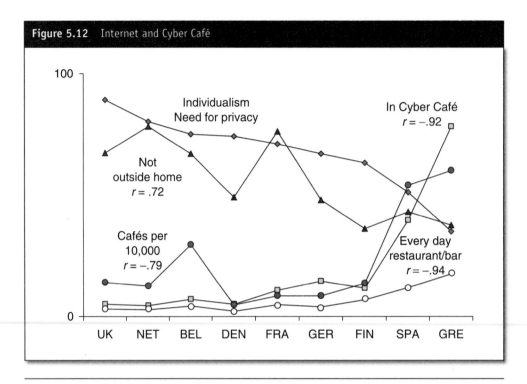

Figure 5.12 Internet and Cyber Café

SOURCE: Hofstede et al. (2010) (see Appendix A); Eurostat (2001); Flash EB 241 (2008) (see Appendix B); Hotrec data on numbers of cafés per 10,000 people (1997) (http://www.hotrec.com)

In an interview by Bill Powell of *Newsweek* with Seijiro Yokoyama, NEC executive vice president, the latter expressed his doubts about the emergence of virtual offices in Japan resulting from the information superhighway.

Far more so than in the West, business in Japan is a powerful social phenomenon. For 100 years Japanese businessmen have been coming to offices to work. Technology isn't going to change that any time soon. In Japan—and indeed, throughout much of East Asia—personal contact is still critically important, digital revolution or no digital revolution. Personal relationships matter more than contracts, and personal relationships are established within groups. No matter how good the latest technology, you can't go out and get drunk with your customers or your suppliers on the Infobahn. . . . In Japan, many men have two families. Their families at home and their families at the office. Both are very important. In Japan, this is the bottom line that doesn't appear on any balance sheet. For a lot of men, business and social life are simply one and the same. Many salary men have no interest in "telecommuting." They would be at a loss if they didn't have an office to go to—no matter what they actually do while they are there.[163]

Appearance

How people deal with their appearance is very much related to variations of the self in the social environment as discussed in the previous sections of the chapter. Three cultural dimensions can explain variance of people's needs for appearance: uncertainty avoidance, power distance, and individualism/collectivism. Strong uncertainty avoidance makes people want to be well groomed when they go out into the streets. It helps to structure an ambiguous world. This is confirmed by the relationship between uncertainty avoidance and the percentage of private consumption spent on clothing and footwear. In collectivistic cultures people dress well in order to preserve harmony, and in high power distance cultures dependence on others makes people more other-directed in their self-presentation. In collectivistic cultures being properly dressed when going out into the streets, facing out-groups, is important for not causing loss of face to the in-group. The psychoanalyst Alan Roland[164] notes that urban Indian women spend much more time and effort on personal grooming and dress when they go out in public in India than they would do when going out in public in New York.

> In India, your position in society is defined by the clothes you wear, your shoes, your posture, your facial expression, and the volume of your voice. The combination provides you with your rightful place in the endless hierarchy of class and power. It defines the type of seat, the number of pillows, or the height of seat you are offered when shopping.[165] In the United States the workplace is the only place left that asks for role-consistent and situation-specific public clothing: the suit—which stands for tradition, hierarchy, conformity, and money.[166] In all other places there are few situation-specific ways of dressing. People wear in public whatever they wear in private. Presidents go jogging in shorts and baseball caps, film stars walk in the streets in jeans and T-shirts, and people go to church barefoot in shorts. Shanghai is known for, among other things, its middle-aged women who saunter onto the street in their sleepwear. Some even venture as far as the subway or the shopping mall. They view their pajamas as casual wear.[167]

Particularly for social occasions—and there are many in collectivistic and high power distance cultures—people buy new clothes. It is not a necessity to be dressed according to the latest fashion, which is more related to individualistic self-enhancement.

Several surveys have measured interest in fashion by asking positive or negative confirmation to the statement, "I like to dress according to the latest fashion," or "I like to be well-dressed," or "I try to look stylish all the time." Table 5.3 shows the correlations with three dimensions and percentages of variance explained in regression analysis. The relationship between individualism and fashion consciousness was confirmed by Manrai et al.,[168] who compared fashion consciousness of consumers in Hungary, Romania, and Bulgaria. Hungarian (individualist) consumers scored higher in fashion consciousness than (collectivist) Bulgarian and Romanian consumers.

Group processes as discussed in the previous sections play a role in explaining variance of the importance of appearance. Countries can be clustered according to these variations, using the dimensions individualism-collectivism and uncertainty avoidance (see Figure 5.13).

Table 5.3 Appearance

	PDI	IDV	UAI	Predictor	R^2
No to latest fashion 1970 (15 countries)	.57*	−.56*	.59**	UAI	.35
No to latest fashion 1997 (15 countries)	.22	−.51*	.22	IDV−	.26
				MAS−	.48
Well-dressed 1997 (15 countries)	.39	−.60**	.48*	IDV−	.36
Physical attractive women are more valued by men (10 countries)	.87***	−.60*	.71**	PDI	.75
Try to look stylish all the time (20 countries)	.63***	−.60***	.69***	UAI	.47
				PDI	.70

SOURCES: Hofstede et al. (2010) (see Appendix A); Reader's Digest Surveys 1970 and 1991; EMS 1997; Dove Report *Beyond Stereotypes* 2006; Nielsen 2007 (see Appendix B)

Figure 5.13 Appearance

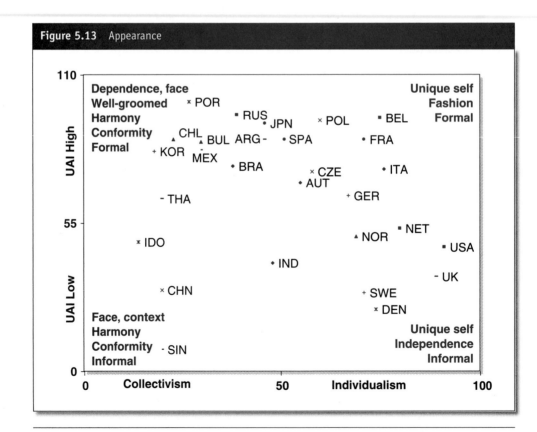

SOURCE: Data Hofstede et al. (2010) (see Appendix A)

Dependence needs are found in the two left-hand quadrants that are collectivistic. Face and context are important, as well as conformity. The differences between the two left-hand quadrants are in the degree of uncertainty avoidance. In the upper left-hand quadrant, of high uncertainty avoidance, people need structure—they ritualize life by the way they dress. This is where people want to match colors of shoes and handbags or the designer brand of their own clothes and even the attributes of their pets. The Spanish ad for Honda (Figure 5.14) refers to this need for matching colors. In the lower left-hand quadrant anything goes, but social context must be taken into account.

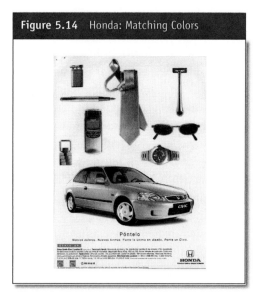

Figure 5.14   Honda: Matching Colors

In the two right-hand quadrants of Figure 5.13 the unique self operates. In the upper right-hand quadrant it is combined with structure and ritualization. In this corner is a small group of countries that combine individualism with high power distance and high uncertainty avoidance. The self must be presented in a unique, but ritualized way, and social context is important. This leads to high importance of fashion, design, and art-orientation. In the lower right-hand quadrant are the countries where the unique self is combined with low ritualization needs. Anything goes—people don't dress up in the public domain; they don't care what they look like. The Norwegian ad for Prior (Figure 5.15) illustrates this.

Figure 5.15   Prior, Norway: No Special Attention to Appearance

REFERENCE GROUPS

A *reference group* is a group that serves as a reference point in forming people's attitudes and behavior. In Western consumer behavior theory, three reference group influences are distinguished: informational, utilitarian, and value-expressive. *Informational* influence comes from groups or associations of professionals or experts (formal groups), from friends, or neighbors. *Utilitarian* influence comes from preferences of family members or other people with whom one has social interaction. *Value-expressive* influence is on the image, when the individual feels that the purchase or use of a particular product or brand will enhance the image others have of him or her.

The strongest cultural determinant of reference groups is individualism/collectivism. All aspects discussed in the previous sections of this chapter, such as dependency, harmony, or self-consciousness, will influence the role of reference individuals or groups. In collectivistic cultures, people do not belong to associations to the degree they do in individualistic cultures, so the influence of information from associations is less relevant. The influence of professionals and associations is strongest in individualistic and high uncertainty avoidance cultures. Consumer organizations may also be viewed as authorities, which is appealing to members of high power distance cultures. Whereas companies are mentioned as favorite source of information in the low power distance cultures, consumer organizations are more mentioned in high power distance cultures. Colleagues and relatives are consulted more in individualistic cultures than in collectivistic cultures.[169] Expert groups will have a stronger reference function in high uncertainty avoidance cultures.

> An indication of the influence of different types of reference groups across cultures is provided by a Eurobarometer survey on risk issues that asked who would be most trusted to inform people if a serious food risk would occur. The answer "public authorities" correlated with low power distance ($r = -.54***$) and short-term orientation ($r = -.56***$); "food manufacturer" correlated with low uncertainty avoidance ($r = -.37*$); "the media" correlated with short-term orientation ($r = -.45*$); "consumer groups" correlated with individualism ($r = .49**$); "physician/doctor" correlated with high uncertainty avoidance ($r = .59***$).[170]

Because members of high uncertainty avoidance cultures have respect for expertise and professionalism, formal or professional reference groups are likely to have greater influence in high than in low uncertainty avoidance cultures. The degree of dependency on elders and other family members will be stronger and different in collectivistic cultures than in individualistic cultures. In high power distance cultures experts are viewed as authorities.

The importance of others influencing a buying decision will vary with the type of product. If a product is consumed privately (e.g., necessities), the opinions of others are viewed to be less important than if a product is used publicly (e.g., luxury goods). In China friends and colleagues have a particularly strong influence on buying cosmetics. Friends (particularly girlfriend/boyfriend) and sisters are viewed as being appealing in cosmetics advertisements. The mother and daughter relationship, like the husband and wife relationship, has less relative influence.[171]

OPINION LEADERS

In Western decision-making theory, specific individuals are assumed to influence the decision-making process through word-of-mouth communication, generally within a certain product category. Rogers,[172] in his theory of diffusion of innovations, called these people *opinion leaders*. Opinion leaders are strong, informal sources of product information. Opinion leaders get their status because of technical competence and social accessibility. They serve as role models and play an important role in the process of diffusion of innovations (to be discussed in Chapter 8). Rogers's concept of opinion leadership is basically an American concept. The concept as marketers know it today was derived from the diffusion of innovation theory, which resulted from investigation of the speed and pattern of the spread of new farming techniques across the United States. Herein lies a trap for non-U.S. practitioners of marketing, for the assumption typically made is that the U.S.-developed theory has universal applicability. This is doubly dangerous in that foreigners may assume that (at least) the basic theoretical constructs of opinion leadership can be applied without adjustment in other countries.

The roles of opinion leaders, like reference groups, vary across cultures. For example, people with technical competence or competent people in general, are likely to be favored in strong uncertainty avoidance cultures.

An important difference is in the way opinion leaders get their information. Whereas they get their information from the media in individualistic culture, they obtain their information from the social network in collectivistic cultures. However, some doubts arise if in collectivistic cultures the opinion leader phenomenon is as relevant in collectivistic cultures as it is in individualistic cultures. In collectivistic cultures, information gathering is an unconscious process. There is a strong flow of information between people with so much informal communication that people are not aware of the fact they are getting information or from whom they got the information. So when asked which sources of information they consult, collectivists tend to say "none" much more than do individualists. Information is like air; it is there and you don't know where you got it. (This is further discussed in Chapter 6, information processing.)

In a comparative study in eight countries worldwide that tested the roles of opinion leaders, some characteristics of opinion leaders appeared to vary across cultures. In 3 of 8 countries, marketers tended to select opinion leaders from an older age group. All three countries were Asian.[173] Green and Langeard[174] found differences in opinion leadership between U.S. and French consumers. The U.S. sample indicated a significantly higher level of group membership than the French sample. Thirty-two percent of the members of the U.S. sample belonged to more than three formal organizations, as compared with only 3% of the members of the French sample. Conversely, only 22% of the U.S. respondents said they did not belong to any formal organizations, as compared with 56% of the French respondents.

CONCLUSION

In this chapter a number of aspects related to the self in the social environment were discussed. Most motivations are not innate, but formed by culture. Motivation theories are culture bound, and they tend to reflect the culture of the theorist who developed the theory. That doesn't mean these theories are useless, but the user must be aware of the cultural bias. Buying motives are not only culture bound, they are also product-category related. Different cultural dimensions explain specific motives for specific product categories. For example, status motives are relevant for luxury goods. Purity is a motive that is most relevant for food and household cleaning products. Needs for dependence and harmony relate to how people dress in public space.

Emotions are not universal, although many students of psychology have learned they are. The emotions referred to as universal are of Anglo-Saxon origin. Although many can be found in other cultures, the connotations with these emotions vary across cultures. In particular, display rules vary. This is important for advertising. Even if there would be universal emotions, advertising that would display such emotions would not be very relevant or effective in countries where people are not supposed to display them.

Group processes include the functions of in-groups and out-groups and the need to conform to others. With respect to conformity the big difference is between the West and the East, but also between the countries in the south and north-west of Europe and between the east and the west of Europe. Such differences are important for the marketing of many products.

NOTES

1. Ubuntu, and other management tips. (1995, March 18). *The Economist, 72.*
2. Cardwell, M. (2000). *The complete A-Z psychology handbook* (2nd ed.). London: Hodder & Stoughton, 160.
3. Eysenck, M. (2000). *Psychology: A student's handbook*. Hove, East Sussex, UK: Psychology Press, 127–134.
4. Antonides, G., & Van Raaij, W. F. (1998). *Consumer behaviour: A European perspective*. Chichester, UK: Wiley, 165.
5. Hofstede, G. (2001). *Culture's consequences*. Thousand Oaks, CA: Sage.
6. Maslow, A. H. (1954). *Motivation and personality*. New York: Harper & Row.
7. Adler, N. J. (1991). *International dimensions of organizational behavior*. Belmont, CA: Wadsworth, 30–31.
8. Eysenck (2000), 28.
9. McClelland, D. C. (1988). *Human motivation*. Cambridge, UK: Cambridge University Press, 32.
10. Usunier, J.-C. (1999). *Marketing across cultures* (3rd ed.). Harlow, UK: Pearson Education, 67.

11. Singelis, T. M. (2000). Some thoughts on the future of cross-cultural social psychology. *Journal of Cross-Cultural Psychology, 31*, 76–91.

12. Nelson, M. R., & Shavitt, S. (2002). Horizontal and vertical individualism and achievement values. *Journal of Cross-Cultural Psychology, 33*, 439–458.

13. Hsieh, M. H., & Lindridge, A. (2005). Universal appeals with local specifications. *Journal of Product and Brand Management, 14*(1), 14–28.

14. Williams, J. (1991, August). Constant questions or constant meanings? Assessing intercultural motivations in alcoholic drinks. *Marketing and Research Today*, 169–176.

15. Green, R. T., Cunningham, W. H., & Cunningham, I. C. M. (1975). The effectiveness of standardized global advertising. *Journal of Advertising, 4*, 25–30.

16. Pollay, R. W. (1984). The identification and distribution of values manifest in print advertising 1900–1980. In R. E. Pitts Jr. & A. G. Woodside. *Personal values and consumer psychology* (pp. 111–135). Lexington, MA: Lexington Books, D. C. Heath.

17. Papavassiliou, N., & Stathakopoulos, V. (1997). Standardization versus adaptation of international advertising strategies: Towards a framework. *European Journal of Marketing, 31*, 504–527.

18. Singh, D. (2007). *Cross cultural comparison of buying behavior in India.* Doctoral thesis. Chandigarh: Panjab University, University Business School.

19. *A survey of Europe today.* (1970). Reader's Digest.

20. *Risk issues.* (2005). Special Eurobarometer 238, 16 wealthy countries.

21. Malaysian feminists drive car ad off air. (1995, February 24). *Asian Marketing and Advertising*, 6.

22. Jo, M. S., & Sarigollu, E. (2007). Cross-cultural differences of price-perceived quality relationships. *Journal of International Consumer Marketing, 19*(4), 59–74.

23. White, D. W., & Absher, K. (2007). Positioning of retail stores in Central and Eastern European accession states: Standardization versus adaptation. *European Journal of Marketing, 41*(3/4), 292–306.

24. EMS (1997).

25. Hofstede (2001), 230.

26. Jiang, Y., & Li, N. (2009). An exploratory study on Chinese only-child-generation motives of conspicuous consumption. In H. Li, S. Huang, & D. Jin (Eds.), *Proceedings of the 2009 American Academy of Advertising Asia-Pacific conference.* (pp. 121–129). American Academy of Advertising in conjunction with China Association of Advertising of Commerce and Communication University of China.

27. Roll, M. (2006). *Asian brand strategy.* London: Palgrave McMillan, 50–51.

28. Zheng, L., Phelps, J., & Hoy, M. (2009). Cultural values reflected in Chinese Olympics advertising. In H. Li, S. Huang, & D. Jin (2009), 26-27.

29. Information from Vivek Gupta, Senior Vice President IMRB BrandScience at Kantar Group, Bangalore, India.

30. *Europeans' attitudes towards the issue of sustainable consumption and production.* (2009, April). Flash Eurobarometer report 256.

31. Data, House of Commons, UK In: More rubbish. (2002, August 24). *The Economist,* 29–30.

32. *Consumers in Europe: Facts and figures: Data 1996–2000.* (2001). Eurostat, 10 countries.

33. *Attitudes of European citizens towards the environment.* (2008). Special Eurobarometer 295. 25 countries.

34. Soong, R. (2004, May). *Environmentalism in Latin America.* Retrieved May 2004, from http://www.zonalatina.com/zldata59.htm

35. Very clean people, the Japanese. (1997, August 2). *The Economist,* 70–71.

36. *Consumers in Europe* (2001), 63.

37. *TGI product book 2009*. Data used for 22 wealthy countries worldwide, GNI/capita > US$17,000.

38. *Consumers in Europe* (2001), 733.

39. *Risk issues* (2005).

40. *Society at a glance.* (2009). OECD Social Indicators.

41. Power, C. (2000, July 10). McParadox. *Newsweek,* 15.

42. Eysenck (2000), 137.

43. Ratner, C. (2000). A cultural-psychological analysis of emotions. *Culture and Psychology, 6*(1), 5–39

44. Markus, H., Kitayama, S., & VandenBos, G. R. (1996). The mutual interactions of culture and emotion. Psychology Update. *Psychiatric Services, 47,* 225–226.

45. Kitayama, S., Markus, H. R., Matsumoto, H., & Norasakunkit, V. (1997). Individual and collective processes in the construction of the self: Self-enhancement in the United States and self-criticism in Japan. *Journal of Personality and Social Psychology, 72,* 1245–1266.

46. Mesquita, B., & Frijda, N. H. (1992). Cultural variations in emotions: A review. *Psychological Bulletin, 112,* 179–204.

47. Nezlek, J. B., Kafetsios, K., & Smith, C. V. (2008). Emotions in everyday social encounters: Correspondence between culture and self-construal. *Journal of Cross-Cultural Psychology, 39*(4), 366–372.

48. Matsumoto, D. (2000). *Culture and psychology: People around the world* (2nd ed.). Belmont, CA: Wadsworth, 305–310.

49. Flora, C. (2008, December 15). The pursuit of happiness. *Psychology Today.* Retrieved January 1, 2009, from http://www.psychologytoday.com/articles/200812/the-pursuit-happiness

50. Mesquita, B., Frijda, N. H., & Scherer, K. R. (1997). Culture and emotion. In J. W. Berry, P. R. Dasen, & T. S. Saraswathi (Eds.), *Handbook of cross-cultural psychology* (Vol. 2, pp. 258–260). Boston: Allyn & Bacon.

51. Russell, J. A. (1995). Facial expressions of emotion: What lies beyond minimal universality? *Psychological Bulletin, 118,* 379–391.

52. Russell, J. A. (1991). Culture and the categorization of emotions. *Psychological Bulletin, 110,* 426–450.

53. Markus et al. (1996).

54. Scherer, K. R. (1997). The role of culture in emotion-antecedent appraisal. *Journal of Personality and Social Psychology, 73,* 902–922.

55. Ratner (2000).

56. Kim, H-J J., & Hupka, R. B. (2002). Comparison of associative meaning of the concepts of anger, envy, fear, romantic jealousy, and sadness between English and Korean. *Cross-Cultural Research, 36*(3), 229–255.

57. Olatunji, B., and 11 co-authors. (2009). Confirming the three-factor structure of the disgust scale-revised in eight countries. *Journal of Cross-Cultural Psychology, 40*(2), 234–255.

58. Lewis, J. R., & Ozaki, R. (2009). *Amae* and *Mardy:* A comparison of two emotion terms. *Journal of Cross-Cultural Psychology, 40*(6), 917–934.

59. Ho, D. Y. F., Fu, W., and Ng, S.M. (2004). Guilt, shame and embarrassment: Revelations of face and self. *Culture and Psychology, 10*(1), 64–84.

60. Kim & Hupka (2002).

61. Schmidt-Atzert, L., & Park, H. S. (1999). The Korean concepts *dapdaphada* and *uulhada:* A cross-cultural study of the meaning of emotions. *Journal of Cross-Cultural Psychology, 30,* 646–654.

62. Ekman, P. (1994). Strong evidence for universals in facial expressions: A reply to Russell's mistaken critique. *Psychological Bulletin, 115,* 268–287.

63. Elfenbein, H. A., & Ambady, N. (2003). Cultural similarity consequences: A distance perspective on cross-cultural differences in emotion recognition. *Journal of Cross-Cultural Psychology, 34*, 92–110.

64. Biehl, M., Matsumoto, D., Ekman, P., Hearn, V., Heider, K., Kudoh, T., & Ton, V. (1997). Matsumoto and Ekman's Japanese and Caucasian facial expressions of emotion (JACFEE): Reliability data and cross-national differences. *Journal of Nonverbal Behavior, 21*, 3–21.

65. Hall, E. T. (1976). *Beyond culture.* New York: Doubleday, 81–82.

66. Aaker, J. L., & Williams, P. (1998). Empathy versus pride: The influence of emotional appeals across cultures. *Journal of Consumer Research, 25*.

67. Yuki, M., Maddux, W. W., & Masuda, T. (2007). Are the windows to the soul the same in the East and West? Cultural differences in using the eyes and mouth as cues to recognize emotions in Japan and the United States. *Journal of Experimental Social Psychology, 43*, 303–311.

68. Ye, Z. (2004). The Chinese folk model of facial expressions: A linguistic perspective. *Culture and Psychology, 10*(2), 195–222.

69. Matsumoto (2000), 286.

70. Hofstede (2001), 157.

71. Matsumoto, D., LeRoux, J., Wilson-Cohn, C., Raroque, J., Kooken, K., Ekman, P., et al. (2000). A new test to measure emotion recognition ability: Matsumoto and Ekman's Japanese and Caucasian brief affect recognition test (JACBART). *Journal of Nonverbal Behavior, 24*, 179–209.

72. Russell, J. A. (1994). Is there universal recognition from facial expression? A review of the cross-cultural studies. *Psychological Bulletin, 115*, 102–141.

73. Wang, L., & Markham, R. (1999). The development of a series of photographs of Chinese facial expressions of emotion. *Journal of Cross-Cultural Psychology, 30*, 397–410.

74. Retrieved November 30, 2009, from http://pinktentacle.com/2009/05/emotional-robot-kobian-pics-video/

75. Elfenbein, H. A., & Ambady, N. (2002). On the universality and cultural specificity of emotion recognition: A meta-analysis. *Psychological Bulletin, 128*, 203–235.

76. Scherer, K. R., Banse, R., & Wallbot, H. G. (2001). Emotion inferences from vocal expression correlate across languages and cultures. *Journal of Cross-Cultural Psychology, 32*, 76–92.

77. Elfenbein et al. (2002).

78. Matsumoto (2000), 287.

79. Kagitçibasi, C. (1997). Individualism and collectivism. In J. W. Berry, Ma. H. Segall, & C. Kagitçibasi (Eds.), *Handbook of cross-cultural psychology* (Vol. 3., pp. 2–49). Boston: Allyn & Bacon, 23.

80. Matsumoto, D., with 19 coauthors. (2008). Mapping expressive differences around the world: The relationship between emotional display rules and individualism versus collectivism. *Journal of Cross-Cultural Psychology, 39*(1), 55–74.

81. Wang, K., Hoosain, R., Lee, T. M. C, Meng, Y., Fu, J., & Yang, R. (2006). Perception of six basic emotional facial expressions by the Chinese. *Journal of Cross-Cultural Psychology, 37*(6), 623–629.

82. Ye, Z. (2004). The Chinese folk model of facial expressions: A linguistic perspective. *Culture and Psychology, 10*(2), 195–222.

83. Anolli, L., Wang, L., Mantovani, F., & De Toni, A. (2008). The voice of emotion in Chinese and Italian young adults. *Journal of Cross-Cultural Psychology, 39*(5), 565–598.

84. Mesquita, B., Frijda, N., & Scherer, K. R. (1997). Theoretical and methodological issues. In J. W. Berry, P. R. Dasen, & T. S. Saraswathi (Eds.), *Handbook of cross-cultural psychology* (Vol. 2, pp. 255–297). Boston: Allyn & Bacon, 285.

85. Triandis, H. C. (1995). *Individualism and collectivism.* Boulder, CO: Westview.

86. Matsumoto (2000), 295.

87. Gudykunst, W. B., & Bond, M. H. (1997). Intergroup relations across cultures. In J. W. Berry, M. H. Segall, & C. Kagitçibasi (Eds.), *Handbook of cross-cultural psychology* (Vol. 3, pp. 119–161). Boston: Allyn & Bacon, 145.

88. Mesquita, B., & Frijda, N. H. (1992). Cultural variations in emotions: A review. *Psychological Bulletin, 112*, 179–204.

89. Friesen, W. (1972). *Cultural differences in facial expression in a social situation.* Unpublished doctoral dissertation. San Francisco: University of California, Department of Psychology.

90. Hofstede (2001), 156, 157, 160.

91. Russell (1995).

92. Nelson & Shavitt (2002).

93. *Values of Europeans.* (2008, November). Standard Eurobarometer 69.1.

94. Mesquita et al. (1997), 270.

95. Matsumoto (2000), 300.

96. Mesquita et al. (1997), 287.

97. Rothbaum, F., & Tsang, B. Y. P. (1998). Lovesongs in the United States and China. *Journal of Cross-Cultural Psychology, 29*, 306–319.

98. Domzal, T. J., & Kernan, J. B. (1994). Creative features of globally-understood advertisements. *Journal of Current Issues and Research in Advertising, 16*, 29–47.

99. Huang, M. H. (1998). Exploring a new typology of advertising appeals: Basic versus social, emotional advertising in a global setting. *International Journal of Advertising, 17*, 145–168.

100. Holbrook, M. B., & Westwood, R. A. (1998). The role of emotion in advertising revisited: Testing a typology of emotional responses. In P. Cafferata & A. M. Tybout (Eds.), *Advertising and consumer psychology* (pp. 353–371). Lexington, MA: D.C. Heath, 356.

101. Moriarty, S. E. (1991). *Creative advertising, theory and practice.* Englewood Cliffs, NJ: Prentice-Hall, 79.

102. Dru, J.-M. (1996). *Disruption.* New York: Wiley, 9.

103. Ramaprasad, J., & Hasegawa, K. (1992). Creative strategies in American and Japanese TV commercials: A comparison. *Journal of Advertising Research, 32*, 59–67.

104. Majorie Dijkstal, advertising researcher at FHV/BBDO, the Netherlands (personal communication, 1995).

105. Cooper, H. R., Holway, A., & Arsan, M. (1998, February). Cross-cultural research—should stimuli be psychologically pure or culturally relevant? *Marketing and Research Today*, 67–72.

106. Lin, C. (2001). Cultural values reflected in Chinese and American television advertising. *Journal of Advertising, 30*, 83–94.

107. Oyserman, D., Coon, H., & Kemmelmeier, M. (2002). Rethinking individualism and collectivism: Evaluation of theoretical assumptions and meta-analyses. *Psychological Bulletin, 128*, 3–72.

108. Triandis (1995), 9.

109. Doi, T. (1973). *The anatomy of dependence.* Tokyo: Kodansha International.

110. Gudykunst, W. B., & Ting-Toomey, S. (1988). *Culture and interpersonal communication.* Newbury Park, CA: Sage, 42–43.

111. Oyserman et al. (2002).

112. Eckhardt, G. M., & Houston, M. J. (2002). Cultural paradoxes reflected in brand meaning: McDonald's in Shanghai, China. *Journal of International Marketing, 10*, 68–82.

113. *European cultural values.* (2007). Special Eurobarometer 278.

114. Roland, A. (1988). *In search of self in India and Japan.* Princeton, NJ: Princeton University Press, 134 and 149.

115. Standard Eurobarometer 55, 2001.

116. *European social reality.* (2007). Special Eurobarometer Survey 273.

117. America's strange clubs: Brotherhoods of oddballs. (1995, December 23). *The Economist*, 63.

118. *Information society.* (2008). Flash Eurobarometer 241.

119. Minkov, M. (2007). *What makes us different and similar.* Sofia, Bulgaria: Infopartners, 175.

120. Belk, R. W. (1984). Cultural and historical differences in concepts of self and their effects on attitudes toward having and giving. In T. C. Kinnear (Ed.), *Advances in consumer research* (pp. 753–760). Provo, UT: Association for Consumer Research.

121. Dog accessories go through the "woof." *The Asahi Shimbun.* Retrieved September 16, 2002, from http://www.asahi.com

122. Centraal Bureau voor de Statistiek, July 28, 2008.

123. Rose, G. M., Dalakas, V., & Kropp, F. (2003). Consumer socialization and parental style across cultures: Findings from Australia, Greece, and India. *Journal of Consumer Psychology, 13*(4), 366–376.

124. Kagitçibasi, C. (2005). Autonomy and relatedness in cultural context. Implications for self and family. *Journal of Cross-Cultural Psychology, 36*(4), 403–422.

125. Bringué Sala, X., & Sádaba Chalezquer, C. (2008). *The interactive generation in Ibero-America: Children and adolescents faced with the screens.* Colección Fundacion Telefónica.

126. *Towards a safer use of the Internet for children in the EU: A parents' perspective.* (2008, December). Flash Eurobarometer report 248.

127. *Family life and decision making.* (2009). Future Foundation, 12 countries in Europe.

128. Mindy, F. J., & McNeal, J. U. (2001). How Chinese children's commercials differ from those in the United States: A content analysis. *Journal of Advertising, 30*, 79–92.

129. EMS (2007).

130. Singh (2007).

131. Asch, S. (2000). Studies of independence and conformity: A minority of one against a unanimous majority. *Psychological Monographs, 70* (Whole no. 416). Quoted in Eysenck. (2000), 556.

132. Hofstede (2001), 232.

133. Etcoff, N., Orbach, S., Scott, J., & D'Agostino, H. (2006, February). *Beyond stereotypes: Rebuilding the foundation of beauty beliefs.* Findings of the 2005 Dove Global Study.

134. Singh (2007).

135. Thomas, D. (2002, October 14). Addicted to Japan. *Newsweek, 48.*

136. Zielenziger, M. (2002). Young Japanese gobble up luxury items. *Free Press.* Retrieved September 6, 2002, from http://www.free com/news/nw/japan

137. Lee, B. J. (2001, June 25). Invisible barriers. *Newsweek, 38–39.*

138. Oyserman et al. (2002).

139. Lee, J. A. (2000). Adapting Triandis's model of subjective culture and social behavior relations to consumer behavior. *Journal of Consumer Psychology, 9*, 117–126.

140. De Bruyne, M. (1997, September 25). Het verschil zit in de smaakpapillen (The difference is in the taste). *Nieuwstribune*, 25.

141. Warden, C. A., Huang, S. C. T., Liu, T. C., & Wu, W.Y. (2008). Global media, local metaphor: Television shopping and marketing-as-relationship in America, Japan, and Taiwan. *Journal of Retailing, 84*(1), 119–129.

142. Robinson, C. (1996). Asian culture: The marketing consequences. *Journal of the Market Research Society, 38*, 55–62.

143. Itoi, K. (2000, November 13). Dress down for success. *Newsweek, 40–44.*

144. Manrai, L. A., Lascu, D. N., Manrai, A. K., & Babb, H. W. (2001). A cross-cultural comparison of style in Eastern European emerging markets. *International Marketing Review, 18*(3), 270–285.

145. Holman, R. H. (1984). A values and lifestyles perspective on human behavior. In R. G. Pitts & A. G. Woodside (Eds.), *Personal values and consumer psychology* (pp. 35–54). Lexington, MA: D.C. Heath, Lexington Books, 38.

146. Gudykunst & Ting-Toomey (1988), 138–141.

147. Gudykunst & Ting-Toomey (1988), 143.

148. Hofstede (2001), 231.

149. Gudykunst & Ting-Toomey (1988), 143.

150. Rocha, G. (2001, December). What women want. *M&M Europe, Latin America,* xii-xiii. Countries surveyed were Argentina, Brazil, Chile, Mexico, and Venezuela.

151. Han, S. P., & Shavitt, S. (1994). Persuasion and culture: Advertising appeals in individualistic and collectivistic societies. *Journal of Experimental Social Psychology, 30,* 326–350.

152. Zhang, Y., & Gelb, B. D. (1996). Matching advertising appeals to culture: The influence of products' use conditions. *Journal of Advertising, 25,* 29–46.

153. Research Watch. (2001, May). *M&M Europe,* 41.

154. Reader's Digest Surveys 1970 and 1991.

155. *Consumers in Europe* (2001), 251.

156. *Family life and decision making in the household.* (2009). Future Foundation.

157. Data Hotrec 1997. In Sociaal Cultureel Planbureau, 2000. Sociaal en Cultureel Rapport 2000.

158. *Information society.* (2008). Flash Eurobarometer 241.

159. *Structure of consumption.* (2005). Eurostat.

160. *Consumers in Europe* (2001), 203. (See Appendix B.)

161. *Euro indicators.* (2009). Eurostat statistics database.

162. Flash Eurobarometer 248.

163. Powell, B. (1994, June 6). But we like it at the office. *Newsweek,* 25.

164. Roland (1988).

165. Ramdas, A. (2000, October 2). Onbegrijpelijke democratie (Incomprehensible democracy). *NRC Handelsblad.*

166. Adler, J. (1995, February 20). Is America a nation of slobs? *Newsweek,* 42–49.

167. Zhou, R. (2009, November 11). In defense of pajamas. *China Daily.* Retrieved November 27, 2009, from: http://www.chinadaily.com.cn/opinion/200911/06/content_8923160.htm

168. Manrai, L. A., Lascu, D. N., Manrai, A. K., & Babb, H. (2001). A cross-cultural comparison of style in Eastern European emerging markets. *International Marketing Review, 18,* 270–285.

169. *Consumer survey.* (2002). Flash EB 117.

170. *Risk issues.* (2005).

171. Bradley, R., Barnes, B. R., Kitchen, P. J., Spickett-Jones, G., & Yu, Q. (2004). Investigating the impact of international cosmetics advertising in China. *International Journal of Advertising, 23,* 361–387.

172. Rogers, E. M. (1962). *Diffusion of innovations.* New York: Free Press.

173. Marshall, R., & Gitosudarmo, I. (1995). Variation in the characteristics of opinion leaders across cultural borders. *Journal of International Consumer Marketing, 8,* 5–22.

174. Green, R. T., & Langeard, E. (1975). A cross-national comparison of consumer habits and innovator characteristics: What makes French and U.S. consumers different? *Journal of Marketing, 39,* 34–41.

CHAPTER 6

Mental Processes

How people see, what they see and do not see, how they think, how language structures their thinking, how they learn, and how they communicate are mental processes that apply to consumer behavior. These processes—in psychology called *cognitive processes*—deal with understanding of several *how*'s of behavior. Consumer behavior is learned in the context of a specific social system. Consumer learning theories generally focus on repetition and the creation of simple associations between elements (e.g., a brand name becomes associated over time with a picture or a slogan), whereas more sophisticated approaches to learning are concerned with how advertising messages are stored in memory. These processes of storage and retrieval are the major focus of the dominant perspective in cognitive approaches to advertising, that of information processing.[1] With the acceptance of the person as a carrier of culture, cognitive processes are also considered as being shaped by culture. They will systematically vary as a function of the manner in which the self is culturally constituted.[2]

COGNITION AND COGNITIVE STYLES

Cognition covers the main internal psychological processes that are involved in making sense of the environment and deciding what action might be appropriate. These processes include thinking and reasoning, understanding and interpreting stimuli and events, attention, perception, learning, memory, language, and problem solving. *Cognitive styles* are defined as "characteristic, self-consistent modes of functioning that individuals show in their perceptual and intellectual activities."[3] This definition reflects the Western, individualistic approach that views cognitive styles typically as part of relatively stable personality traits. But variations of the self influence how people think and process information, either as an independent self, isolated from the context, or context dependent.[4]

Chinese, for example are situation centered; they are obliged to be sensitive to their environment. Americans are individual centered; they expect their environment to be sensitive to them. Whereas the West is object focused, the East is context focused. This difference underlies different thinking styles, namely abstract versus concrete and analytic versus holistic. In collectivistic cultures, more concrete styles of thought are found, because thought is more contextual and concrete as compared with individualistic cultures in which thought can be more abstract because it is not necessarily linked to the social environment. The implication for marketing communications is that the Chinese place relatively greater emphasis on the more concrete product attributes when evaluating products than on abstract affective (emotion) aspects.[5]

In the West, context dependent thinking is viewed as opposite to logic. The way collectivists, and in particular Asians, think and communicate in symbols and metaphors is viewed as illogic. Most theories of consumer behavior, their spending and decision making, are based on Western, logical thinking. From the early 1900s onward, economists have assumed that consumers have a stable and consistent set of preferences that they try to satisfy, and their decision making is based on rational evaluation of alternatives. Consumers are supposed to make self-interested choices, but they are limited by lack of information. As a result, much attention is paid to trying to understand information behavior.

Culture also influences how people categorize objects. Whereas Americans are likely to group objects on the basis of category membership or on the basis of shared features, Chinese are more likely to group objects or people on the basis of relational contextual criteria. For example, when shown a picture of a man, a woman, and a child, Chinese are likely to group the woman and the child together, because the woman takes care of the child. Americans would group the man and the woman because they are both adults. The American orientation may inhibit the perception of objects in terms of relationships or interdependence. Americans see the behavior of an individual fish moving in various ways in relation to a group of fish as due to internal properties of the individual fish; Chinese are more likely to see the behavior of the individual fish as a reaction to the behavior of the group.[6]

> Inhabitants of European countries have distinctly different information wants for car purchases. Germans look out for detailed product specification data for car purchase research (categorization), whereas Italians are more interested in car images and subjective editorial (i.e., the context in which the car is used).[7]

Categorization differences can explain differences in company structure and marketing strategy. Many Asian companies produce a variety of product categories, all under the same company brand name. Companies and marketing departments in Western societies are split into divisions by product category. In the West, specific advertising styles have been developed for specific product categories. Whereas much Western advertising is structured analytically, following rules for the placement of headline, brand name, and pay-off, the total picture is more important for the holistically thinking Asians.

LEARNING AND MEMORY

Most human behavior is learned. When people act, they learn. *Learning* describes changes in an individual's behavior arising from experience. Consumers learn from past experience. A person's learning is produced through the interplay of needs, stimuli, and reinforcement. Reinforcement results from product usage and satisfaction with the product, and this continuous reinforcement leads to habitual buying.

Culture is learned behavior. It is learned unconsciously. That unconscious process is called *socialization*. Socialization is the process whereby the young of a society learn the values, ideas, practices, and roles of that society. The socialization process is a semiconscious one, in that the major participants in socialization of young people, the family, would not see themselves consciously in this role, whereas others, such as educators, function deliberately for this purpose.

Education systems as well as the concepts behind education vary by culture. In the West, intelligence assumes a key role in human learning, and intelligence involves mostly logical-mathematical and verbal skills. African conceptions of intelligence focus on wisdom, trustworthiness, social attentiveness, and responsibility. Japanese conceptions include different kinds of social competence, such as individuals' sociability and ability to sympathize with others. The Western theoretical framework focuses on the outcome of learning (achievement) rather than on learning itself. This is different from the Chinese people's orientation to lifelong learning, which does not have achievement as an objective, although at long term it will result in higher levels of achievement.[8]

Memory involves acquiring information and storing it for later retrieval. Learning and memory have great practical significance for many activities in life. Culture also affects memory. There is evidence for better recall of stories consistent with people's own cultural knowledge.[9]

A Chanel No.5 television commercial with fairy tale moral based on the Little Red Riding Hood fairy tale, well understood by Europeans, had limited meaning for Asian immigrant populations. The narrative advertisement referred to the European fairy tale of Little Red Riding Hood and the Wolf. There are multiple close-ups of a young woman wearing a short red dress and hooded cape. Rich colors (red and gold) are repeatedly used throughout the advertisement, which is set in Paris. It deploys a strong linear narrative technique and the story is essentially a multilayered allegory where, paradoxically, a wolf is under the control of a young woman who is wearing Chanel No.5 perfume.[10]

The information a person has acquired must be *organized* in order for it to be placed in one's memory. The human memory is arranged according to *schemata,* structures of knowledge a person possesses about objects, events, people, or phenomena. To place the acquired information in memory, it must be *encoded* according to the existing schemata. A schema relating to activity is called a *script*. One's generic schema for a product would include what to do with the product, the consequences of using it, and the environment in which it is used.[11] The independent self of individualistic cultures forms context-independent schemata, whereas the interdependent self of collectivistic cultures forms context-dependent schemata.[12]

The information we gather about products or brands consciously and unconsciously form networks of associations in our memories related to usage, people, places, occasions, and so on. The associations in the consumer's mind will relate to a number of aspects of the brand (see Figure 6.1):

- The brand name and the brand's visual images: the package, logo, brand properties, and other recognizable aspects
- The product or products linked with the name
- Product attributes: what the product is or has (characteristics, formula)
- Benefits or consequences: rewards for the buyer or user, what the product does for the buyer
- Places, occasions, people, moments, moods when using the product
- Users: users themselves or referent persons or groups
- Values

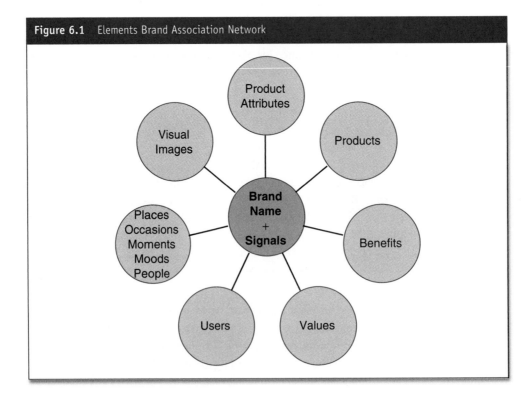

Figure 6.1   Elements Brand Association Network

Associations are structured in the human mind: attributes and benefits will be linked with users and may be specific for the product category or for the brand. An example is an association network for the beer brand Corona Extra, a Mexican beer exported to many countries in the world. It distinguishes itself by its transparent white bottle with a long neck and the ritual of drinking from the bottle with a slice of lime pushed into the neck. A mixed group of Spanish and German students developed the association network presented in Figure 6.2. This association network includes attributes and benefits as well as values. Two clusters of values can be distinguished. Those of the Germans are success, self-esteem, independence, and freedom; those of the Spanish are belonging, happiness, and sophistication.

Many of the elements of an association network will vary across countries, depending on the people one associates with, places and occasions, and the product's benefits and values. One problem is that values are abstract properties, which people in individualistic cultures can formulate better than can people in collectivistic cultures. As associations with brands are part of the method for measuring brand equity, the results of these measurements will vary with individualism/collectivism. Hsieh[13] demonstrated that the brand value calculated based on brand associations for 19 car brands in 16 countries varied significantly. In

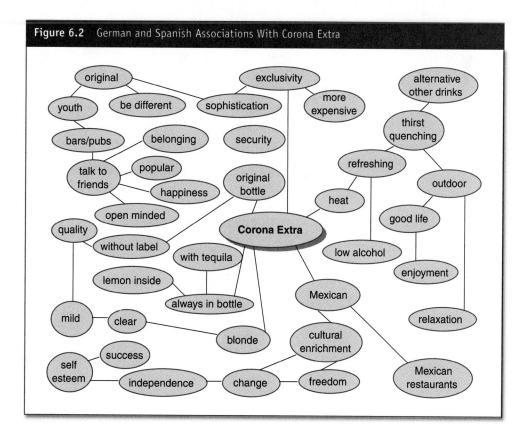

Figure 6.2   German and Spanish Associations With Corona Extra

Europe, the average brand value of the 19 brands was higher than in the Asian countries. These differences appear to correlate with individualism ($r = .68***$). Different cultural conditions lead consumers to different brand evaluations.[14] The associations conveyed in advertising may be different from the associations consumers derive from their own cultural environments.

Diesel, the Italian clothing manufacturer, developed an advertising campaign called "Global warming ready." Sophisticated models are posing in Diesel clothing in a world affected by raised water levels and temperatures. The models were shown in several world cities, such as New York, Paris, Rio, London, and Venice. We see the Chinese wall covered by desert sand and Antarctica in the sun with models in swim suits. Figure 6.3 shows New York in high water and Paris as a tropical jungle[15] as well as a picture of a young boy wearing a Diesel T-shirt in Tobolsk, Siberia. Associations with the Diesel brand will be quite different in New York, Paris, and Tobolsk.

Figure 6.3   Diesel Advertising: New York and Paris; Diesel T-shirt Tobolsk. Photograph Gerard Foekema

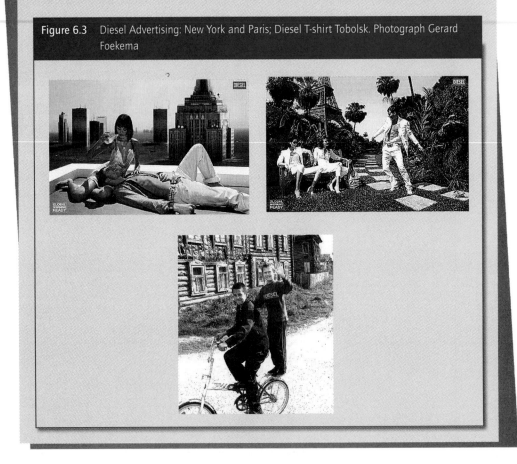

Different learning conditions also lead to differences in the way people communicate with each other—to different communication styles. Consumption behavior is part of the society in which people live; it is learned behavior. As consumers gain experience in purchasing and consuming products, they learn not only what brands they like and do not like but also the features they like most in particular brands. Communication and advertising draw on a shared visual vocabulary and a learned system of pictorial conventions.[16] These are based on letters, words, pictures, maps, and models that are all part of what people have learned in a particular culture and what has become part of the collective memory of a culture.

COGNITION AND AFFECT

Emotions, feelings, and moods are viewed as affective responses to stimuli, whereas knowledge, meanings, and beliefs are cognitive responses to stimuli. Usually the combination of affective and cognitive components contributes to one's general disposition or attitude toward objects, goods, events, persons, or brands.

Western consumer psychology states that the cognitive and affective systems interact, and affective responses (e.g., emotions, feelings) are interpreted by the cognitive system (e.g., "I wonder why I am so happy"). Examples of cognitive interpretation of a *physical stimulus* are "This toilet paper is soft," "There are no artificial ingredients in this food product," or "Ice cream is fattening." An example of cognitive interpretation of a *social stimulus* is "The salesperson was helpful." An example of cognitive interpretation of an *affective response* is "I love this ice cream."[17] Research on the cognitive and affective components of attitudes has mainly been done in the Western world. Cross-cultural psychologists have found that the idea that people interpret feelings, emotions, and mood—and even attribute these to phenomena, personal behavior, or personal characteristics—is not a universal phenomenon. The cognition-affect interaction varies across cultures and product categories.

In Western branding strategy, creating a favorable brand attitude, increasing the already favorable brand attitude, or modifying a brand attitude are viewed as basic objectives of advertising. Brand attitude consists of cognitive and affective components. Buying intention models include affective and cognitive components of attitudes to predict buying behavior. Understanding how the two components function across cultures is important for developing measurement tools to assess consumers' attitudes and buying intentions.

Cognitive and Affective Components of Attitudes Toward Food

An example of a product category that in the West involves a different interaction of cognition and affect than in the East is food. In the food domain, examples of affective components are hedonism, pleasure, and sharing food with family and friends. Examples of cognitive components are nutrition, health consequences, and convenience. Cervellon and Dubé[18] use food as an object of study of how affective and cognitive components vary among France, China, and Chinese immigrants in French-speaking Canada. They present a model (Figure 6.4) of attitude, including at the higher level affect and cognition, and at the lower level the object-specific attributes and consequences.

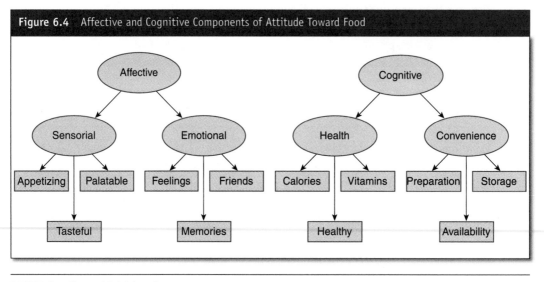

Figure 6.4 Affective and Cognitive Components of Attitude Toward Food

SOURCE: Cervellon and Dubé (2002)

Food attitudes in Western cultures reflect ambivalence between affective and cognitive components. The French value the pleasure of food but also are conscious of possible negative effects on their health. The English and American focus is on health consequences, but this includes paradoxical aspects. Lots of unhealthy fast food is consumed—together with diet drugs and vitamins to compensate for bad eating. So in each cultural group people are convinced that hedonism and health are incompatible, but across Western cultures this phenomenon varies. Whereas Americans combine bad eating with a fitness culture and/or drugs, the French look for purity in their food. So the affective and cognitive components of attitudes toward food seem to be inconsistent and conflicting. When taste or other affective beliefs attached to food are positive, health and other cognitive beliefs tend to be negative. For the Chinese, however, food attitudes do not reflect ambivalence between affective and cognitive components. Health value and sensory pleasure are viewed as necessary to a person's equilibrium. Food intake reflects a balance in filling and nutritional properties to satisfy physiological and taste properties. For the Chinese, the affective and cognitive components are positively linked. The difference is likely related to individualism/collectivism because of the difference between guilt and shame cultures. In individualistic cultures, people can develop guilt feelings after doing something incompatible, like enjoying unhealthy food. People of collectivistic cultures lack this sense of guilt.[19]

Cognitive Dissonance

In individualistic cultures, the choice between two desirable alternatives can lead to *cognitive dissonance*. The theory of cognitive dissonance is based on the premise that people have a need for order and consistency in their lives and that tension is created when beliefs or behaviors conflict with one another.[20] A state of dissonance occurs when there is a psychological inconsistency between two or more beliefs or behaviors, and people tend to reduce this dissonance by finding arguments to convince themselves their behavior was right. A frequently used example is cigarette smoking. People know that smoking cigarettes causes cancer, so cigarette smoking will cause dissonance. This dissonance is reduced by referring to examples of people who have grown old while smoking 25 cigarettes per day all of their lives. An effect of cognitive dissonance is that people will collect more information after they have bought a product than before because they want to confirm that they made a good decision. People may also like the product even more after than before buying it because of the need to prevent dissonance.

The cognitive dissonance effect is typical for individualistic cultures where people are driven by a need to classify their emotions, to evaluate them as positive or negative, and do not tolerate conflicting emotions. Seeking internal causes and consistency need generates the dissonance effect. Collectivists realize that people behave differently under different circumstances and may be aware that their behavior often is caused by situational constraints.[21] They can cope with the two types of emotions simultaneously without needing to resolve the incongruity between them. Individualists tend to react to incongruity by discounting one piece of information in favor of another, whereas collectivists tend to give weight to both pieces of information.[22]

LANGUAGE

Language is an abstract system of rules and a medium of communication. Abstract rules are translated into a channel (spoken, written, sign language) in order to create messages. When the channel is the spoken word, speech is involved.[23] One of the most powerful generalizations discovered about language is that all known writing systems encode spoken language. Writing is speech put into visible form.[24]

Language is a manifestation of culture. At different language acquisition stages, children do not learn language per se; rather they learn the various patterns and styles of language interaction that enable them to function as competent communicators in different situational contexts. They develop a culture-specific communication style that is, for example, direct and explicit in individualistic cultures or indirect and implicit in collectivistic cultures. Examples of words linked with the direct style are categorical words like *absolutely*, *certainly*, or *positively*. By contrast, the cultural assumptions of interdependence and harmony require that collectivists limit themselves to implicit and even ambiguous use of words, using terms like *maybe*, *perhaps*, or *probably*.[25] The English language is the only language in the world that spells *I* with a capital letter. This phenomenon may reflect the fact that the roots of individualism are in England.[26] There is no Japanese equivalent for the English *I*. Different words are used to refer to the self, depending on the social situation, the speaker's gender, age, and the other social attributes relative to the listener. The terms reflect status differences, and the speaker usually attempts to elevate the status of the other, while reducing his or her own status, by choosing the correct wording. Similarly, *you* changes wording, depending on the social context.[27]

Language reflects values, and the expression of values varies by the language used. Several studies have shown that "forcing" bilinguals to complete a test in their second language can often mean that they will express the values stereotypically associated with that language. In a projective test in both languages, the narratives of French American bilinguals were more romantic and emotional in French than in English. The reverse can operate with respondents who strongly identify with their cultural group. When students in Hong Kong were asked to complete a values test in either English or Cantonese, they expressed more traditional Chinese values in English than in Chinese.[28]

How the structure of language is a reflection of culture was demonstrated by Kashima and Kashima,[29] who studied the relationship between pronoun drop and culture. In some languages—including English—the use of subject pronouns is obligatory: *I* or *you* must be mentioned. By contrast, other languages do not require the utterance of subject pronouns, and these words can be dropped by the speaker's choice. In some Indo-European languages (e.g., Spanish), personal pronouns are not obligatory, partly because the referents can be recovered from the verb inflections. This phenomenon is called *pronoun drop*. Explicit use of *I* signals highlights the person. Its absence reduces the prominence of the speaker's person. Pronoun-drop languages are more associated with a contextualization of the person than languages that do not allow pronoun drops. Drop of the subject pronoun (*I*, *we*, or *you*) was found to correlate significantly with low individualism. Thus, languages licensing pronoun drop are associated with lower levels of individualism than those that require the obligatory use of personal pronouns such as *I* or *you*.

Language reflects culture. Expressions of culture are particularly recognizable in the use of metaphors. Examples are expressions like "He is a team player," "He drives me up the wall," a "ballpark estimate," "the sweet spot," all derived from American baseball in the American language, whereas British English has a number of expressions relating to cricket. The elements used in metaphors will vary. In Egypt, for example, the sun is perceived as cruel, so a girl will not be described as "my sunshine," but may be compared with moonlight.[30] *Moonlighting* in English means having a second job in the evening.

Some languages have more words for a phenomenon than other languages have, for example, for the different substances of ice or rain in Nordic countries. The Norwegian language reflects a historic seafaring nation, having one strong word for "wind in your favor": *bør*. Some languages have words that do not exist in others. The English *pith,* the archaic word for "marrow," refers to the white under the skin of oranges and other citrus fruit. This seems to be directly linked with the British "marmalade culture." There is no equivalent in the Dutch language for the English *to fudge* (empty talk, refusing to commit oneself). The Dutch are not inclined to fudge, which may explain their image of being blunt.

Some culture-specific words migrate to other languages if they express something unique. Examples of such words are *management, computer, apartheid, machismo, perestroika, geisha, sauna, Mafia,* and *kamikaze.* Often, these words reflect the specific values of a culture. They cannot easily be translated into words of other cultures, or they have been borrowed from another culture from the start. The English language does not have its own words for *cousin* and *nephew.* These were borrowed from French (*cousin* and *neveu*). The way a person describes kin is closely connected with the way he or she thinks about them. In extended families, a father and a father's brother may both be termed "father." The Hungarians differentiate between a younger sister (*húg*) and an older sister (*növér*). The Russian language has different names for the four different brothers-in-law. In Indonesian, *besan* is the word for "parents of the children who are married to each other."[31] Even terms of abuse vary: whereas the most used term of the Germans, Spanish, Italians, and Greek is related to lack of mental capabilities, the French, Brits, Americans, and Dutch use sexually loaded terms. Norwegians use the devil.[32]

The Dutch language shows frequent use of diminutives; so does the Spanish language. In both languages, use of the diminutive suffix reflects something positive, whereas using the enlargement suffix turns it into something negative.

The English language reflects the way Anglo-Saxons deal with action and time. They have a rich vocabulary expressing this, such as "down to earth," "feedback," "deadline." The English word *upset* expresses the way the English handle their emotions, with self-constraint. *Upset* is not translatable into most other languages. The Dutch and the Scandinavians have words for "togetherness" that express much more than "being together" and that do not exist in the Anglo-Saxon world. The words are *gezellig* (Dutch), *hyggelig* (Danish), *mysigt* (Swedish), and *kodikas* (Finnish). The Danes use it even in combinations like *hyggetime* ("together time") and *hyggemad* ("together food"). It means sharing your feelings and philosophies in a very personal way while being together in a small group. To an Englishman, this sort of behavior is too intrusive. The concept means preferring a dinner party for four people to a larger group, whereas a small group is not considered to be a dinner party by the British or the Americans. For the Dutch and the Scandinavians, the concept can be used very effectively in advertising for the type of product used during such meetings, such as coffee, sweets, and drinks. The concept will not be understood by members of other cultures. Swedes even have a word for the combination of this feeling together with drinking coffee: *kafferep*.

German examples include the word *Reinheit,* which has a wider meaning than the word *purity.* The word *ergiebig* is another example, meaning delivering quality and efficiency, or more for the same money. The Spanish word *placer* means much more than the translation *pleasure*. It includes pleasure while eating, enjoyment, sharing a social event, softness, warmth, the good life, contentment, and satisfaction. Some words represent interpersonal relations of one culture that do not exist in others. The French notions of *savoir faire* and *savoir vivre* include a vast array of values specific to French culture and cannot be properly translated. The Japanese expression for "computer graphics" carries the meaning of a picture, a drawing, and illustration or sketch, but not of a graph. Another example is the Japanese word for "animation," which in translation carries the meaning of "comics" or "cartoons."[33] In Japan, the word for "heart" associates with "warmth," not necessarily with "love," as love is not expressed the same as in the Western world. There are no proper equivalents to the words *identity* and *personality* in the Japanese language, as the concept of personality separate from the social environment is alien to the Japanese people.

Untranslatable concepts often are so meaningful to members of a specific culture that they are effective elements of advertising copy. They refer to collective memory. This implies that words that are labels of culturally meaningful concepts are too ambiguous to use in international campaigns.

A European campaign for the KitKat candy bar was based on the concept of the "break": "Take a break, take a KitKat." The break was an English institution: the 11 o'clock morning tea break, when working people had their morning tea, and brought a KitKat as a snack. Because of this, KitKat in the United Kingdom was called "Elevenses." This type of break did not exist in any other country in Europe, so the break concept had to be "translated" in a different way for the other countries. Continental Europeans do not have the same "break" memory as do the British.

Language is much more important than many international advertisers realize. It is common knowledge among those who are bi- or trilingual that copy carrying cultural values is difficult to translate. Monolingual people generally do not understand this. If translations are needed, particularly for research purposes, the best system is translating and back-translating the questions to be sure that at least the questions have the same meaning. Yet the values included in the words cannot be translated, and often conceptual equivalence cannot be attained.

The view that language reflects culture is opposed to the Sapir-Whorf hypothesis, which states that the structure of language influences culture via perception and categorization. This would imply that the worldview and social behavior of people depend on the structure and characteristics of the language they speak.[34] The assumption is that certain thought processes are more likely to occur in one language than in another because of the structure of the language. A frequently found assumption is that there are systematic differences between Western and non-Western language and thinking.[35] This idea originated from the work by Bloom,[36] who suggested that in some cultures people use a more abstract form of reasoning, whereas in others forms of reasoning are more concrete, and that this phenomenon would be due to differences in language structure. He investigated reasoning in Hong Kong and concluded that English has a particular constellation of linguistic patterns encouraging a mode of abstract thinking among speakers of English that cannot be found in the Chinese language. Other studies have not supported this finding. It is unlikely that the Chinese are less capable of abstract thinking than Americans.

Language, Perception, and Memory

The structure of a language (e.g., its grammar and type of writing system) has consequences for basic consumer processes such as perception and memory. Structural differences, such as in scripts of Indo-European and Asian languages, seem to affect mental representations, which in turn influence memory. Chinese native speakers rely more on visual representations, whereas English speakers rely primarily on phonological representations (verbal sounds). Written Chinese contrasts with the Latin system because it is ideographic instead of alphabetic. Consumers who use ideographic languages evaluate brand names more in terms of visual features, while speakers of alphabetic languages view brand names with respect to their phonological codes.[37] In the English language, verbal sounds are most used to encode the brand name and facilitate memory. Explicit repetition of words enables consumers to encode and recall the brand name. An example is, "If anyone can, Canon can," used as pay-off in ads for Canon in the United Kingdom. Chinese and Japanese languages make it relatively easy for consumers to visually encode and remember the topic and theme (e.g., the brand's function).

Because of their own focus on sound and pronunciation, Western companies are inclined to adapt their brand names to other cultures more vocally than visually.

A first try to "translate" the brand name Coca-Cola in China was *Ke-kou-ke-la* because when pronounced it sounded roughly like Coca-Cola. It wasn't until after thousands of signs had been printed that the Coca-Cola company discovered that the phrase could mean "bite the wax tadpole" or "female horse stuffed with wax," depending on the dialect. Second time around things worked out better. After researching 40,000 Chinese characters, Coke came up with *ko-kou-ko-le* which translates roughly to the much more appropriate "happiness in the mouth."[38]

Chinese consumers are more likely to recall information when the visual memory rather than phonological memory trace is accessed. This information draws from a study by Schmitt et al.,[39] who found that Chinese native speakers were more likely to recall brands when they could write them down than when they generated a spoken response. The authors suggest that marketers, instead of translating Western brand names into Chinese via sound, should enhance the natural tendency of Chinese consumers to rely on visual representations. Visually distinct brand name writings or calligraphy and logo designs that enforce the writing should be more effective in China, whereas for English native speakers the sound qualities of brand names should be exploited by the use of jingles and onomatopoeic names (resembling the sound made by the object). One reason the written language is so important in Chinese is that there are more variations in writing than in sound. One sound can have different meanings that often can only be specified in the written words. This explains why Chinese people during a conversation sometimes write the words in their hands.[40]

> In China a name is like a work of art, and the art of writing—*shu-fa* (calligraphy)—has a long tradition. A name should therefore "look good" and be rendered in appealing writing. Associations with the brand depend on the way brand names are written. In Japan, specifically, brands that use the oldest writing system, *kanji*, are perceived to be "traditional"; as a result, *kanji* may be appropriate for tea products but not for high-tech products. For high-tech products, the most "modern" language system, *katakana*, is the best. *Hiragana*, written in the eleventh century by a courtesan, has a somewhat feminine image. It is used for beauty products, hair salons, and kimono stores.[41]

Most companies end up with suboptimal solutions. Some Western firms have kept the Western name and Western spelling. This approach may be appropriate in Japan, where consumers are familiar with the Roman alphabet, but it is less appropriate in a fast-growing market such as China, where only a minority of consumers know the Roman alphabet.

Language in Advertising and Value Studies

The availability of specific linguistic devices or tools in a particular language can diminish the load on working memory. Western advertising tends to use efficient value-expressive language to help recognition and memory. But some trait terms that efficiently refer to specific behavior in one language do not exist in other languages. For example, in English, it is possible to combine a number of diverse behaviors under the adjectives *artistic* or *liberal*. These devices do not exist in Chinese. The separate behaviors referred to do exist in China, but there is no encompassing term for them.[42] Whenever in translations it is difficult to find a linguistically or conceptually equivalent word, it likely concerns a concept that represents culturally significant values that cannot be translated into copy for an ad in another culture without losing the value-expressive meaning. Differences between languages can go far beyond mere translation problems. In different cultures, people have different "schemata." These schemata are often linked with both a typical language concept and a specific product category.[43] This explains why copy for meaningful advertising concepts of one culture cannot easily be translated into other languages. One language represents only one cultural framework. Speakers of different languages not only say things differently, they experience things differently; the fact that there are rarely direct translations (especially for abstract words) is a reflection of this.[44] The ultimate consequence is that the more meaningful advertising is, the less it is translatable.

> The international advertising consultant Simon Anholt says:
>
> Translating advertising copy is like painting the tip of an iceberg and hoping the whole thing will turn red. What makes copy work is not the words themselves, but subtle combinations of those words, and most of all the echoes and repercussions of those words within the mind of the reader. These are precisely the subtleties which translation fails to convey. Advertising is not made of words, but made of culture.[45]

Translations can cause bias in value studies. The phenomenon that bilingual people express different values when using different languages is likely to influence translations of questions. The translation and back-translation system may not be able to correct for value-expression variations. Sometimes questions are simply untranslatable, such as the following two statements that appeared in the original VALS (values and lifestyles) questionnaire in the United States that cannot even be translated into U.K. English: "I am a born-again Christian" and "I like to think I am a bit of a swinger."[46]

Foreign Language Speaking and Understanding

Although English is the most spoken second language in the world, fluency varies widely. Whereas in 2001, 79% of the Danish and 75% of the Dutch said they spoke English well enough to take part in a conversation, only 18% of the Spanish, 22% of the Portuguese, 32% of the French, and 44% of the Germans said they did. Of the British, only 11% speak French and 6% speak German.[47] Foreign language speaking correlates with low uncertainty avoidance. Both for the general public and young people, 58% of variance was explained by low uncertainty avoidance. In 2005 the percentages of people who said they could speak at least one language other than their mother language varied from 93% in Latvia and 91% in the Netherlands to 29% in Hungary and 30% in the United Kingdom.[48] In the high uncertainty avoidance cultures, if people do speak a little of a foreign language, they are reluctant to try because they are afraid to make mistakes.

In countries where large percentages of people say they understand English, this doesn't mean they really understand the meaning of everything said. This has consequences for international advertising. In countries like the Netherlands and Denmark, international advertisers assume understanding of English, in particular among young people, is enough to allow them to leave copy and speech untranslated, which is a dangerous thing to do. A study by Gerritsen and Jansen[49] among young people in the Netherlands showed that lack of English knowledge makes the use of English more popular, but also that Dutch young people (14–17 years old) do not know the meaning of many English language words that are regularly used in the Dutch language. Examples are words like *blazer, entertainment, image, research, sophisticated,* and *strapless.* The word *blazer* was thought to mean remote control or laser pistol; *entertainment*: working with a computer; *image*: energy, brains, health, appearance; *research*: rubbish; *sophisticated*: ugly, hysterical, aggressive; and *strapless* was thought to mean whorish. A former payoff by the electronics company Philips, "Philips invents for you" was understood as *Philips invites you.* The watch brand Swatch used the term *boreproof,* which was understood as "drill-proof." In another study,[50] respondents had a high opinion of their understanding of the English language, but more than half could not write down what was said in the ads and only one third understood the meaning of English fragments in TV commercials. The claim by Fa "The spirit of freshness" was understood as *the spirit of fitness.* Copy for L'Oreal's Studioline "style and love for my hair, invisi'gel FX" was understood as *style grow of my hair* and *invisual terrifics.* A claim by Seiko "lifetime precision without a battery" was understood as *goes slow.* Few Germans understand English language slogans like "Be Inspired" (Siemens) or "Impossible Is Nothing" (Adidas).[51]

Some advice about translating television commercials: whereas in large markets such as Germany, France, and Spain, people are used to dubbed television programs, in smaller markets such as the Netherlands, most foreign language programming is subtitled, so people are used to hearing and seeing the lip movements of the original language spoken. Even the best lip-sync looks fabricated to them. Hearing a well-known American soap star speak Dutch with another person's voice doesn't add to credibility. Whether subtitled or dubbed, viewers will note that the commercial is not made for them.

CATEGORIZATION

How people categorize other people and objects varies with individualism/collectivism and with power distance. Collectivists tend to pay attention to relationships between objects, whereas individualists categorize objects according to rules and properties. Chinese children will group items together that share a relationship, whereas Canadian children will group items together that share a category.[52] Ask an African to sort a few objects, say some tools, food items, and clothes, and he will put a knife in a potato, as a knife is needed to slice a potato.[53]

Categorization differences have implications for brand strategy. American consumers view a brand extension of a different product category not as fitting with the parent brand. A brand extension must fit, and this fit is judged on the basis of product class similarity. Collectivists view the parent brand in terms of the overall reputation of or trust in the company. So they perceive a higher degree of brand extension fit also for extensions in product categories far from those associated with the parent brand than individualists would.[54]

Whereas companies of individualistic cultures carefully select line or brand extensions that "fit" the product category, companies from collectivistic cultures stretch their brands in wider directions. The American cola brands wouldn't think of stretching their brands beyond the soft drink and related food category products such as snacks, and if they would do so they would give them different brand names. The European brand Nivea has been careful to limit line extensions to related products and linked them all consistently to the core brand values "purity" and "value for money." Japanese Shiseido, a cosmetics company, has extended its brand into the food category. The overall category they cover is "beauty," and both cosmetics and beauty food appear to fit this category. Examples of beauty food are sweets for shiny eyes, lollipops for full hair, and self-tanning chewing gum.[55] The Spanish brand Chupa Chups, characterized by the yellow-red logo designed by Salvador Dali, includes many different products, from lollipops to sunglasses, clothes, shoes, and stationery.

Categorization differences can explain variance of advertising formats and differences in presentation of goods in shops, by sort or by relationship, or by classifier. An example of categorizing by relationship is presenting food products together that are combined when cooking and/or eating, such as pasta with pasta sauce, herbs, or other ingredients and wine, versus presenting it according to the way they are packaged, for example, pasta sauces in pots together with other sauces in pots, pasta together with rice, and wine with wine.

Chinese department stores, unlike their U.S. counterparts, typically offer products that share a classifier. For example, *tai* products (used for electric and mechanical equipment such as blow dryers, TVs, radios, washing machines, computers, and electric knives) are located on one floor.

Unlike Indo-European languages, Asian languages like Chinese, Japanese, and Korean are *classifier* languages. A classifier is a measure that is used in conjunction with numerals (one, two, three, etc.) or determiners (*a, the, that, this*) and that refer to common physical features of objects, such as shape, size, thickness, or length, as well as other perceptual or conceptual properties associated with objects, such as "bendability" or "graspability." Classifiers categorize a given object into a larger set of objects and describe classes of objects. As such they are different from adjectives that describe specific instances within a class. Adjectives answer the question, "What kind of object is it?" whereas classifiers answer the question, "What kind of object is this a member of?" The use of classifiers is found in Chinese, Japanese, Korean, and Thai languages as well as Navajo and Yucatan-Mayan languages. Some languages (e.g., Japanese) have classifiers that are generally of broader scope than classifiers of other languages (e.g., Chinese). Compared to English native speakers, Chinese speakers perceive objects that share a classifier as more similar than objects that do not share a classifier.[56] Chinese-speaking people have schematic organizations based on classifiers, so the Chinese are more likely to recall classifier-sharing objects in clusters than are English-speaking people.

In advertising in classifier languages, objects are more positively evaluated when they are combined with a visual cue related to the classifier. An example is the difference in judgment of pictures of "graspable" objects (brush, cane, umbrella, broom) using the classifier *ba* in Chinese. A picture showing only the object is judged less positive than one showing the object with a hand. [57]

The classifier system has to be exploited carefully, as it can have positive and negative effects. For example, a classifier for pipe-like thick objects will lead to positive expectations for lipstick, but a classifier for long, thin objects can lead to negative expectations that it will provide less quantity and will not last long. When existing products are modified and change shape, inconsistency can occur. Classifiers used for telephones (objects standing on a frame) cannot be used for cellular phones.[58]

PERCEPTION

Perception gives us knowledge of the surrounding world. Perception of what a picture depicts, and that it means something, depends on both the picture and the perceiver. Failures to recognize a picture and its meaning are related to unfamiliarity with the picture itself and with the context.

Nearly all research on perception has been carried out in Western societies. If the development of visual perception depends on certain kinds of learning experiences, then it might be expected that there would be some important cross-cultural differences in perception. Evidence of a basic cross-cultural difference in perception was reported by Turnbull,[59] who studied a pygmy who lived in dense forests and so had limited experience looking at distant objects. This pygmy was taken to an open plain and shown a herd of buffalo a long way off. He argued that the buffalo were insects and refused to believe that they really were buffalo. When he was driven toward the buffalo, he thought that witchcraft was responsible for the insects "growing" into buffalo. Presumably he had never learned to use depth cues effectively. Because only one person was studied, this study is limited. Moreover, the global spread of images of diverse societies would make such an experiment unrepeatable. However, an important question for international advertising is, When using ads of one culture in another, will people who never ever have been confronted with a phenomenon before be able to recognize the meaning intended by the advertiser? People learn the "rules of seeing," and these are not universal principles but are formed by the natural and social environments that teach us both what to look at and how to look.

Some studies suggest that the integration of pictorial elements varies cross-culturally. The correct naming of elements of a picture does not predict ability to correctly perceive their mutual relationships.[60]

In perception studies the traditional concern is about *what* is perceived. Do people see or recognize pictures or colors? Next to this are the affective consequences of perception—do people like or dislike what they see?

Selective Perception

Perception can be a selective observation of reality. We actually see what we want to see and expect to see, even if it is not there. We do not see what we do not expect to see. The implication of *selective perception* is that people observe some aspects of reality and do not see other aspects. Selective perception is a universal phenomenon, but it is reinforced by culture. People who are used to behavior and phenomena in their own cultures tend to expect similar phenomena and behavior in other cultures, which may not exist or exist in limited ways. This selective perception process is stronger in individualistic cultures, where people are universalistic and tend to expect that everybody elsewhere has similar values. People tend to ignore the differences and only perceive the similarities. In individualistic cultures, reality is a subjective observation. In collectivistic cultures, more phenomena influence perception. In particular, the context influences what people see and hear. This can easily lead to miscommunication between members of individualistic and collectivistic cultures. When communicating in the different languages of individualistic and collectivistic cultures, the words can be the same, but the context in which the words are interpreted can be different and thus influence understanding.[61] What people hear can also depend on what the speaking person looks like.

Aesthetic Experience

Aesthetic experience refers to the experience of pleasure or displeasure caused by stimuli that are perceived as being beautiful or not beautiful, attractive or unattractive, and rewarding or unrewarding.[62] Many historical and geographical differences in styles and conventions in works of art point to cultural influences. The art of a culture is a symbolic representation of its social structure and social practices. In art and design, visual structures realize meanings as linguistic structures do. Visual language is culturally specific. Western visual communication, for example, is deeply affected by the convention of writing from left to right. Other cultures write from right to left or from top to bottom and as a result will attach different meanings to these dimensions of visual space. Whereas the composition of pages in Anglo-Western print media adheres to a basic left-right structure, others place the main stories and photographs in the top section or in the center. In Western visualization, central composition is relatively uncommon, but central composition plays an important role in the imagination of Asian designers. Centering is a fundamental principle in visual art in many Asian cultures. Although differences in composition and design are largest between East and West, differences are also found among Western countries. Composition of pages and images in the British media are characterized by the contrasting use of the left and right, whereas this is less usual in the Greek or the Spanish media.[63]

Also, photography is recognized as the product of cultural forces and is therefore particular to the culture that creates the imagery. There are two basic types of photojournalism:

a descriptive approach and an interpretative approach. For American photojournalists, self-expression is important and creativity is a basic requirement. Subjectivity and objectivity are viewed as mutually supportive values. For Koreans, however, objectivity appears to be the most important value, and subjective values are to be avoided. Artistic creativity is seen as a potential threat. Americans are more comfortable with a mix of descriptive and interpretive approaches. Whereas Korean newspapers use photographs with a more descriptive visual reporting approach, American photographs use a more interpretative approach.[64]

East Asians value decoration and the use of nature symbols such as waterfalls, mountains, spring blossoms, and autumn.[65] In East Asian advertising, nature symbols are ubiquitous. The Japanese psychiatrist Doi[66] explains that the Japanese turn to nature because there is something unsatisfying in the way they deal with human relations. Nature is neutral. Dealing with the complications of in- and out-group behavior in collectivistic cultures is much more complicated than human relations in individualistic cultures.

Variables found to influence aesthetic responses are complexity, novelty, uncertainty, and incongruity, but there is little empirical research on whether and how these variables vary across cultures.

Schmitt and Pan have summarized East Asian aesthetic expression as follows:

A general concern for aesthetics—i.e., for an attractive look, touch and feel, and attention to detail—is widespread in the Asia-Pacific Region; and despite regional variations, the region as a whole seems to share a common aesthetic style. Specifically, aesthetic expressions—whether in the arts or in the form of corporate aesthetic output (e.g. packaging, brochures, advertisements, store designs)—are guided by three aesthetic principles. First, Asians value complexity and decoration: they love the display of multiple forms, shapes and colors. This feature is most pronounced in Chinese, Thai, Malay, and Indonesian aesthetics. Second, beauty means balancing various aesthetic elements; harmony in aesthetic expression is seen as one of the highest goals. Third, Asian aesthetic expression values naturalism. In China, symbols and displays of natural objects—of mountains, rivers, and phoenixes—prevail and are frequently found in packaging and advertising. . . . Finally, colors seem to have different meanings and aesthetic appeal in the Asia-Pacific Region than in the West.[67]

Color Perception

Colors represent different meanings and aesthetic appeals in different cultures. There are two major schools of thought relating color and human behavior that reflect the nature/nurture discussion. Color reactions could be innate or learned. The first school argues that color signals the brain to trigger an affective reaction directly, whereas others suggest that color preferences are learned over time as shared meanings or as result of past experiences or as conscious associations in language.[68]

Color categories are greatly determined by a culture's color language.[69] How people describe colors is related to the linguistic terms of their language and these terms vary by culture. Adult speakers of different languages show different patterns of discrimination and memory for the same set of colors. There are no cognitive color categories that are independent of the terms used to describe them.[70]

Cross-cultural studies of *color preferences* have found similarities and differences.[71] Red is the most preferred color by Americans, green by the Lebanese, and blue-green by Iranians and Kuwaitis. Red is found to be most strongly related to China, purple to France, green to both France and Italy.

Also, color associations vary across countries. In the United States, blue is associated with wealth, trust, and security; gray is associated with strength, exclusivity, and success; and orange denotes cheapness. Yellow, orange, and blue are connected with happiness, whereas red, black, and brown are sad colors. Dutch people designate red as the first color that comes to mind, whereas Americans nominate blue. Cross-cultural surveys of color meanings and associations have found that blue is the most highly evaluated color across cultures, followed by green and white. The most potent colors are black and red. In Japan, China, and Korea, purple is associated with expensive, whereas in the United States purple is associated with inexpensive. In India, Hindus consider orange the most sacred color, whereas the Ndembo in Zambia do not even consider orange a separate color. The pairing of colors shows more variation than separate colors. This is important knowledge when creating brand images and packaging across cultures, as often combinations of colors are used. A few examples are of pairing colors with green and red. The color best paired with green is yellow in Canada, Hong Kong, China, and Taiwan, blue in Colombia, and white in Austria. Only the Chinese and Taiwanese pair green with red. In Brazil and the United States people pair red with black, whereas in Colombia, Hong Kong, China, and Taiwan, red is paired with white. In Austria, Canada, and China, the preferred combination with red is yellow. The most selected color to pair with blue is white.[72]

Table 6.1 provides a summary of different color perceptions in 12 countries, based on an inventory by Aslam.[73]

According to the situation, color associations can vary. Although in China, white traditionally has been associated with mourning, young Chinese are pragmatic and have adopted the white wedding dress as a status symbol.

In marketing and branding, colors can have powerful effects. Colors can alter the meanings of the objects or situations with which they are associated and color preferences can predict consumers' behavior. Color is an integral element of corporate and

Table 6.1   Color Associations for 12 Countries

Associations With Color	White	Black	Red	Yellow	Green	Blue	Purple
Germany		Sorrow Fear Anger	Lucky	Envy Jealousy			
U.K.		Sorrow					
Sweden		Sorrow				Warmth	
Denmark		Sorrow	Lucky				
Belgium		Sorrow			Envy		
France		Sorrow		Infidelity			
Russia		Anger Fear		Envy Jealousy			
USA	Happiness Purity	Sorrow Fear Anger Expensive	Love	Warmth	Good taste Adventure	Wealth Trustworthy Security High quality	Inexpensive Love
China	Mourning	Expensive High quality	Love Lucky	Pleasant Happy Good taste	Trustworthy		Expensive Love
Japan	Mourning	Fear Expensive	Love		Love Happiness	Trustworthy	Expensive Fear, sin
India		Dullness Stupidity	Ambition Desire			Purity	
Korea	Mourning	Expensive	Love			Trustworthy	Expensive Love

SOURCE: Aslam (2006)

marketing communications. It influences consumers' perceptions and behavior and helps companies position or differentiate from the competition. Color evokes strong product associations and category imageries. In the United States blue is associated with toys, health foods, dairy foods, desserts, and financial services; red is related to toys, piz-zas, and some meat products.

The right choice of colors is important for package design. Van den Berg-Weitzel and Van de Laar[74] found that packages for deodorants for women used greater contrast and brighter colors in feminine cultures, whereas they used soft harmonious colors and low contrast in masculine societies to endorse female softness in societies with strong role differentiation.

Color communicates corporate position. In the United States, blue stands for solid, responsible, financial services; green for innovative, caring organizations; and yellow for young, bright, and exciting firms. Whereas blue is the corporate color in the United States, red is the winning business color in East Asia.

Aesthetic Preferences: Paintings and Music

Generally speaking, the little empirical evidence available suggests that with respect to aesthetics, people like most what they are used to. People prefer pictorial images that correspond to the aesthetic traditions of their culture. According to art historian Rudi Fuchs,[75] there is little globalization in art. Art remains linked with a geographic area with its own history.

Preferences for *landscapes* are influenced by the similarity of the landscapes to the living environments of the respondent. Chinese undergraduate students prefer Chinese land-scape paintings to Western landscape paintings, whereas Western undergraduate students prefer Western landscape paintings.[76]

Several studies have suggested that people from East Asian cultures (e.g., China, Korea, and Japan) tend to pay greater attention to contextual information in art products than their counterparts in Western cultures. East Asian landscape paintings place the horizon higher than the horizons appearing in Western paintings. The high horizon broadens the space for context, which allows the painter to include more information about mountains, rivers, and other objects, including people.

With respect to *music* preferences, some studies suggest cultural differences in the perception of consonance and dissonance, but little is known about the nature and extent of such differences. Western tonal music relies on a formal geometric structure that determines distance relationships within a harmonic or tonal space. It follows tonal stability, a consistent set of key notes. This consistency is lacking in African or Indonesian music, where focus is on changing tones, and fixed tone scales like the Western 12-tone scale are not found. A global comparison between the intervals found in Western and in African scales shows that African music does not conform to a fixed chromatic scale nor does it have another fixed scale.[77] Also rhythm in music follows the rhythm of the language of the composer.[78]

When designing products, some shapes can have undesirable associations. IKEA has standardized most of their product offerings. Chinese furniture stores have a broad range of tables with table tops made of glass, and these are also available in IKEA in China. Figure 6.5 shows a table available at IKEA Shanghai, where you can see a circle surrounded by a square through the glass tabletop. To a Western consumer it looks like a normal small table, but for a traditional Chinese consumer it is not right. In China a circle represents the sky, while a square represents the earth. Putting the sky in the earth makes no sense.[79]

Figure 6.5   IKEA China. Courtesy Live Grønlien

Field Dependency

Research from various areas suggests that members of individualistic and collectivistic cultures differ with respect to the degree to which they perceive objects either as single and independent entities (field independent) or as being related to the context in which they appear (field dependent). *Field dependent* people are influenced in their perception by characteristics of their physical and social environment. *Field independent* people will perceive an object separately from its environment.

The amount of field information is restricted in classic Western art—painters include field information only to the extent that it can realistically be observed given the perspective within a given scene. East Asians, in contrast, have employed various ways of emphasizing field information. The Chinese developed the scroll form to depict a panoramic view of landscape that could include a whole succession of mountain ranges, near and far. The bird's-eye view used in Japanese landscape depiction is another mode of representing field information. The artist's standpoint is higher than the objects depicted.

In Western portraits the intention is to distinguish the figure from the ground. For this reason, the model occupies a major fraction of the space. East Asian portraiture is unlikely to emphasize the individual at the expense of the context. For this reason, the size of the model is relatively small, as if the model is embedded in an important background scene. Analyses of paintings of groups of people show similar results: East Asian paintings of people place the horizon higher and present models smaller than do Western paintings of people. When making photographs, East Asians are more likely than Westerners to set the zoom function in order to make the model small and the context large.[80]

If advertising is developed in collectivistic cultures, it is likely designed to be perceived field dependently. Information that can be perceived by the field-dependent target group cannot as easily be perceived by those who are field independent. Field dependents are likely to see more in a message than intended by the sender. This is further discussed in the section on processing visual images later in this chapter.

THE CREATIVE PROCESS

Artistic creativity refers to the creativity expressed in any aspect of the arts, including visual art, music, literature, dance, theatre, film, and mixed media. Several resources contribute to creativity: intelligence, knowledge, thinking style, personality, motivation, and the social environment. The extent to which a person or a product is judged as creative may be influenced by where the person or the product originates. The social environment can have a profound impact on judgments of the level of creativity of persons or products.[81] It is assumed that the Western conception of creativity is primarily concerned with innovation, whereas the Eastern conception of creativity is more dynamic, involving the reuse and reinterpretation of tradition rather than breaks in tradition.[82]

Two aspects of creativity are *creative expression* (i.e., production of creative products) and *judgment of creative products*. Several studies have measured judgment, but the number of cross-cultural studies measuring differences in production of creativity is limited. A general finding is that judges evaluate in-group creations more positively than out-group creations.[83]

A Western assumption is that the creative process is based on divergent thinking. If that were the core of creativity, the need for conformity in collectivistic cultures would inhibit the creative process. Several creativity tests that were developed in the West have been used to measure differences in creativity across Asian and Western cultures, some based on figurative expression (drawing tests), others based on verbal expression. The results of these studies, generally conducted with children or students, are mixed. Some have demonstrated that people of Western societies are more creative; others found that the Chinese are more creative.

There is some variation in the ways creativity can be fostered in different cultures. Countries high on uncertainty avoidance prefer creative individuals to work through organizational norms, rules, and procedures, and countries high on power distance prefer creative individuals to gain support from those in authority before action is taken. In individualistic cultures that are also low on uncertainty avoidance and power distance, creativity can best survive outside organizational constraints. High power distance means individuals are restricted in challenging others, and deviant ideas tend to be suppressed. In the Western sense, deviant ideas are viewed as a precondition of originality and creativity. Another difference is the Chinese inclination to perceive and to cognitively organize things holistically, suggesting that Chinese people see and interpret things in terms of wholes and context, which contrasts with an Anglo-American tendency to fragment, decompose, and decontextualize.[84]

Cultures are creative and innovative within the context of their own systems. No one culture is best for innovation, and no one culture can claim a superiority of ideas. Conceptions and definitions of creativity in one culture should not be applied unthinkingly and uncritically to evaluate and judge creativity in another. The Western view of creativity as a break with tradition and movement beyond what exists contrasts with the Eastern notion of reinterpreting tradition. Classic Chinese visual art has pursued common stylistic and even topical forms for hundreds of years. The aim is not to create a new image or form but to reveal, or better still uncover, an essence through an exploration of or meditation on a long-standing theme.

Differences with respect to photojournalism are related to cultural and educational differences. As individualists, American photojournalists rely on their own individual interpretations, observe and document their subjects as individuals, and focus on distinctive individual personalities. In contrast, Korean photojournalists adhere more strictly to their societal responsibilities. They are part of a larger group, either the journalistic community as a whole or their particular news organization. They act according to the group's interest rather than according to their own interpretations. In terms of subject matter, Korean photojournalists tend to document people as part of larger groups. Education reflects or reinforces these culturally determined roles. American photojournalists are far more likely to have majored in journalism, where storytelling is taught, whereas Koreans are more likely to study history and politics. Another consideration concerns the workplace structure journalists inhabit. American photojournalists tend to work in collaboration with editors, writers, and others in the newsroom. Newsrooms in Korea, however, are strictly hierarchical and rigid. Editors demand particular types of photos following a specific assignment. Photographers are expected to return from assignments with the same shots their colleagues at other papers will have delivered to their editors. If a photographer doesn't have a "required" shot, the photographer has failed, even if he produced a far more creative, innovative shot instead.[85]

Creativity in advertising is an applied form of art. A creative director at an advertising agency has to select properties from what the Canadian anthropologist Grant McCracken calls a culturally constituted world.[86] The selection process proceeds at unconscious and conscious levels. Directors are not always fully aware of how and why a selection is made, even when this selection presents itself as compelling and necessary. The director must decide how the culturally constituted world is to be portrayed in the advertisement. For the creative director, this process works as an automatic pilot. His or her own value system will automatically apply when developing concepts or appeals and when selecting or producing visuals. Generally good creative directors are very much ingrained in their own culture.[87]

Advertising serves as a lexicon of cultural meaning, and the viewer or reader who shares the culturally constituted world with the creator will be able to successfully decode the meaning transferred. The viewer or reader who does not do so may not be able to decode the meaning as meant by the designer of the ad.

Advertising is a reflection of the culture of the designer and his or her design training. In the West, design training generally gives the aspiring designer some insights into art and design history. The learning process, however, stops after school, when the Western designer-artist is required to be an instant genius. In contrast, as in most Asian cultures that favor a lifelong learning process, Japanese designers continue actively seeking out other influences.[88]

ATTRIBUTION

Attribution theory is a theory about searching for causes of human behavior or phenomena. Causal attribution involves predicting and explaining the behavior of other people or finding causal explanations of events in order to predict similar ones in the future. Events can be explained as being due to either internal or external causes. Internal causes are those causes attributed to characteristics of individuals or groups, such as dispositions (efforts, ability of people) or personality traits. External causes are those causes attributed to situational constraints or to contextual factors. In individualistic cultures one's behavior or the result of one's behavior (e.g. success) is explained more by internal attributes than by situational factors, whereas the reverse is true in collectivistic cultures that focus on external, relational attributes such as social support or situational factors.[89]

There are particular differences with respect to attributing failure or success. In individualistic cultures, both attributions to success and failure are internal. In collectivistic cultures, the explanations of failure, but not of success, are more external, referring more to situation and context than to the ability of people. North Americans tend to give internal, dispositional explanations for behavior even when behavior is obviously caused by situational factors. For this phenomenon North American psychology uses the term *fundamental attribution error.*[90]

Another dimension involved in explaining internal versus external attribution is cultural masculinity.[91] In masculine cultures, people tend to take both their problems and their competencies more seriously, as compared with ego-effacing norms in feminine cultures.

When service providers fail to deliver, they want to respond positively to recover. The types and results of service recovery efforts vary across cultures. If service providers offer explanations for failing service, they may shift the American consumer's focus from blaming the service provider's personal characteristics (lazy, incompetent) to paying more attention to the situation as a cause of failure. East Asians are more apt to be aware of situational constraints and seek to maintain social harmony. So offering explanations is not the way to service recovery. Whereas North Americans want to be compensated for service failure, East Asians gain face in the eyes of family and friends by a genuine apology by top management, not just by front-line personnel.[92]

LOCUS OF CONTROL

A phenomenon related to attribution is *locus of control*, introduced by Julian Rotter.[93] Many attribution findings that indicate differences between the West and the East revolve around this locus dimension.[94] *Internal* or *external* locus of control refers to the degree to which persons expect that an outcome of their behavior depends on their own behavior or personal characteristics versus the degree to which persons expect that the outcome is a function of chance, luck, or fate, under the control of powerful others, or simply unpredictable.[95] At the culture level, the difference suggests that in some cultures people are more inclined to take social action to better their life conditions (also called *civic competence*), whereas in other cultures people are more dependent on institutions such as authorities and governments. Understanding the difference is important, because internal locus of control is part of the fundamental assumptions in consumer behavior, for example, in behavior intention models. North Americans tend to experience that they personally control events in their daily experience. They hold an exaggerated sense of control or mastery.[96] Roper Starch found that 84% of adult Americans believe that if you have an unhappy life, you can change it if you try.[97]

The dimensions involved in explaining internal and external locus of control are individualism, power distance, and uncertainty avoidance. Smith et al.[98] found a significant correlation between internal locus of control and individualism across 43 countries. Members of collectivistic cultures are controlled more externally than are members of individualistic cultures. High power distance and high uncertainty avoidance are also explaining variables.

In 2005, Eurobarometer[99] asked the degree of influence people felt they had over things that happen to them. For 27 countries, the percentages agreeing with having little influence correlated with high power distance ($r = .55$***), low individualism ($r = -.54$***), and high uncertainty avoidance ($r = .54$***). Figure 6.6 illustrates the correlation with power distance for 13 countries. The peaks in the chart are countries that score high on uncertainty avoidance.

Triandis[100] reported a 1985 study among American and Soviet students who were asked their opinions on two opposing statements: "Human beings are unable to rule themselves and their government should rule them" versus "Human beings should rule themselves, best government is least government." The Soviet students, high on power distance and uncertainty avoidance, chose the first statement, whereas the American students, of low power distance and uncertainty avoidance, chose the second statement.

Locus of control is about expectations of authority versus the ability and wish of people to rule themselves. Thus, we find that reliance on the government for welfare[101] is related to high uncertainty avoidance, which explains 32% of variance. Reliance and dependence upon authorities also make people feel at the mercy of the authorities, which leads to lack of confidence in government institutions, such as the justice system, the police, and the civil service. Several data support these cultural relationships, for example, data on "confidence

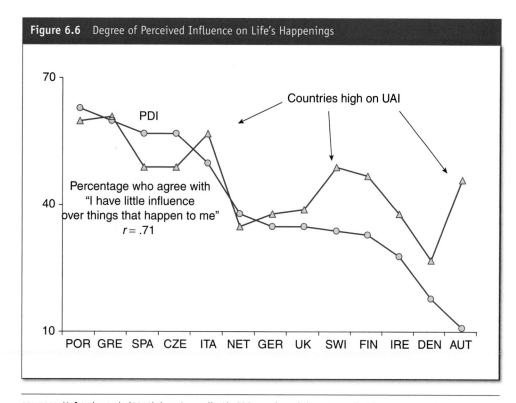

Figure 6.6   Degree of Perceived Influence on Life's Happenings

SOURCES: Hofstede et al. (2010) (see Appendix A); EBS 225 (2005) (see Appendix B)

in institutions" of the European Values Study. The question is, "For each item listed, how much confidence do you have in them, is it a great deal, quite a lot, not very much, or none at all?" The answer categories "a great deal of confidence" and "none at all" are used for confidence in the church, justice system, and police. They are strongly related to power distance and uncertainty avoidance, but also to individualism/collectivism. Data from Eurobarometer show the relationship between trust in the police and low power distance for 19 wealthy countries. Table 6.2 shows the correlation coefficients with the three relevant cultural variables and the percentages of variance explained in regression analysis.

In cultures where external locus of control operates, the church—the moral authority—is trusted, but there is no confidence in the justice system, the civil service, or the police. In particular, low trust in the justice system is remarkable. In the wealthy, western part of Europe (15 countries), the relationship between no confidence in the justice system and power distance is even stronger. Power distance explains 80% of variance.

In cultures where external locus of control prevails, people expect more from their governments than in cultures with internal locus-of-control, and governments can more easily influence people's attitudes. An example is how, across 12 countries in Europe, people

	PDI	IDV	UAI	Predictor	R^2
Table 6.2 Confidence in Institutions					
A great deal of confidence in the church	.54***	−.41*	.52***	PDI	.29
No confidence at all in the justice system	.78***	−.46*	.68***	PDI	.61
				UAI	.69
No confidence at all in the civil service	.63***	−.58***	.70***	UAI	.49
No confidence at all in the police	.70***	−.48**	.57***	PDI	.48
Tend to trust the police	−.71***	.41*		PDI−	.50

SOURCES: Hofstede et al. (2010) (see Appendix A); European Value Study (2000); EB 69 (2008) (see Appendix B)

NOTE: Confidence in institutions and police, 2000; Confidence in police, 2008

answer the question when asked how globalization should be controlled.[102] The higher the countries score on power distance, the higher the percentage of people who say there should be more regulation by their governments to control globalization.

An example of differences in locus of control was acceptance of the European single currency (euro) before and after the introduction. Over time various surveys measured the acceptance of a single European currency. The relationships with culture demonstrate that being for a single currency has been a matter of external locus of control. In 1970, when the idea of a single currency was still an abstract concept, individualism explained variance. After 1990, it was related to large power distance and/or strong uncertainty avoidance. Large power distance means that people are used to others (e.g., government) making decisions for them. The idea that the single currency would be introduced over the heads of the people is something that was more difficult to accept in low power distance cultures than in high power distance cultures. This explains the strong and lasting opposition against the euro in Denmark, a country that scores very low both on power distance and on uncertainty avoidance. It is noticed that neither the young Europeans nor the wealthy target of EMS were very different from the mainstream in Europe in their attitudes to the single currency. Even after the actual introduction on January 1, 2002, in countries like Spain and Belgium many more people were for the euro than in the Netherlands and Finland. Being for the euro, however, didn't fit actual behavior. In the high uncertainty avoidance cultures, higher percentages of people said that they kept converting prices in their national currencies than in low uncertainty avoidance cultures. For example, 78.1% of the French said they converted prices versus 39.7% of the Irish.

With respect to Internet safety, locus of control differences operate. In individualistic cultures that are also low on power distance and uncertainty avoidance, more people feel personally responsible for ensuring security on the Internet. In the high power distance and collectivistic cultures, people are more inclined to not protect because antivirus products are too expensive or because security is too difficult to implement and use.[103]

Also related to locus of control are people's views about the degree to which they can influence their own health. In 1997, Eurobarometer asked questions about people's opinions about the possibility of cancer prevention. The differences between the European countries with respect to belief in prevention are large and culture bound. The questions were "Do you personally think that cancer can be prevented, or not?" If Yes, "How can it be prevented?" Answer possibilities were "By a better balanced diet and a healthy lifestyle" or "By regular medical check-ups." Externals, who are dependent upon and trust experts and authorities, think that cancer can be prevented. They believe in regular check-ups (by experts). Internals believe they are able to influence their health themselves, for example, by a better diet. With respect to the environment, externals associate with natural disasters—beyond their control—and internals view environmental problems related to their own consumption habits.[104] They also think their own actions can make a difference. Table 6.3 shows the correlation coefficients with the three relevant cultural variables and the percentages of variance explained for the examples described.

Table 6.3   Examples of Internal and External Locus of Control

	PDI	IDV	UAI	Predictor	R^2
Belief in Cancer Prevention					
Medical check-ups	.68***	−.45	−.75***	UAI	.57
Better diet	−.59*		−.50*	PDI−	.34
Internet Security					
Personal responsibility	−.57***	.35*	−.48**	PDI−	.33
No protection: too expensive	.46*	−.43*		PDI	.21
No protection: too difficult	.38*	−.36*			
Environmental Impacts					
Our consumption habits	−.44*	.44*	−.62***	UAI−	.38
Natural disasters	.51**	−.60***	.39*	IDV−	.36
My action can make a difference	−.55*			PDI−	.30

SOURCES: Hofstede et al. (2010) (see Appendix A); EB 47 (1997); Flash EB 250 (2009); EBS 295 (2008) (see Appendix B)

Internal versus external locus of control can also be an instrument to explain differences in social and political attitudes or financial systems. External locus of control is likely to make people prefer government or company pension funds, whereas internal locus of control is likely to make people prefer individual pension insurance. In Great Britain, 75% of men of working age have some private pension provision, far more than in continental Europe.[105]

Figure 6.7 shows how countries can be clustered according to internal/external locus of control. This is a two-dimensional map of power distance and uncertainty avoidance. The countries in the left two quadrants are also mostly individualistic, and the countries in the right-hand quadrants are also mostly collectivistic, except France and Belgium that are individualistic.

Understanding the difference is important because internal locus of control is part of the fundamental assumptions in behavior intention models and in decision-making theories. When testing new product concepts, buying intent is regarded as one of the key performance indicators. In external locus of control cultures, people will be more inclined to express buying intention than internally driven consumers would. If one is used to fate or power holders interfering at any time in the realization of an expressed intention, it is easy to express a positive intention even when knowing reality may be different. This is reflected in the way buying intention is expressed. It will predict behavior less than it does in internally driven cultures. So it affects survey results.

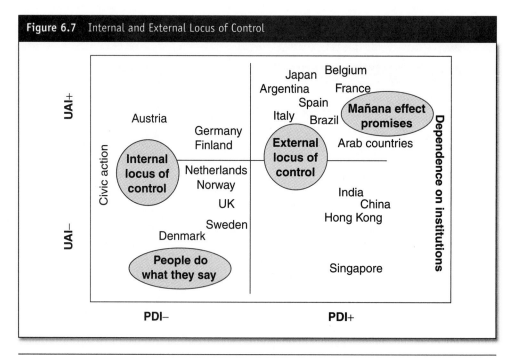

Figure 6.7   Internal and External Locus of Control

SOURCE: Data Hofstede et al. (2010) (see Appendix A)

INFORMATION PROCESSING

Information processing theory is a psychological approach that analyzes how people acquire, organize, and use information to assist choice behavior. The underlying assumption is that people want to solve problems and choose rationally. Theories of consumer decision making, communication behavior and how advertising works are based on a universal assumption that in order to make a buying decision consumers want to inform themselves, but this is not a universal process.

How people acquire information, if they do this consciously, and the importance of information varies with individualism/collectivism and power distance. In individualistic cultures, information is an all-encompassing need. No decision is made without information. Information is the dominant factor that defines attitudes toward Internet advertising in the United States, as compared with trustworthiness as the dominant factor in Korea.[106] In collectivistic cultures, people base their buying decisions on feelings and trust in the company and acquire information mostly via interpersonal communication, whereas in individualistic cultures people will actively acquire information via the media, friends, or organizations to prepare for purchases.

Eurobarometer[107] asked people to what degree they viewed themselves as well-informed consumers. Across 14 western European countries, the answers "well-informed" correlate with low power distance, low uncertainty avoidance, and individualism, which explains 61% of variance. Another question was which information sources (e.g., newspapers, TV, Internet, magazines, friends and relatives, consumer organizations) people consult to prepare for purchases. The percentages of answers "Normally I don't consult any information source" correlate with high power distance, which explains 58% of variance. Figure 6.8 illustrates the relationship for 12 countries.

The explanation is that in collectivistic and high power distance cultures people do not search for information because they don't feel the need. There is much human interaction, people meet their friends daily, they meet people in bars and restaurants, in the streets, they use the mobile phone more and blog more, so there is a constant flow of communication between people, also called *word of mouth*. There are many findings that support this continuous communication process. The percentages of people who say they meet friends every day correlate with low individualism, and so do the percentages who visit a bar or restaurant every day. In collectivistic cultures, people use the mobile phone more to be connected to family and friends. With respect to environmental issues, in the high power distance cultures, although people confirm the importance of eco labels in purchasing decisions, the percentages of people who say they never read any labels correlate with high power distance.[108] In China, the major influence on purchase decisions is word of mouth.[109] Chinese youngsters rely on social networking sites as a source of electronic word of mouth (eWOM) in their decision-making process.[110]

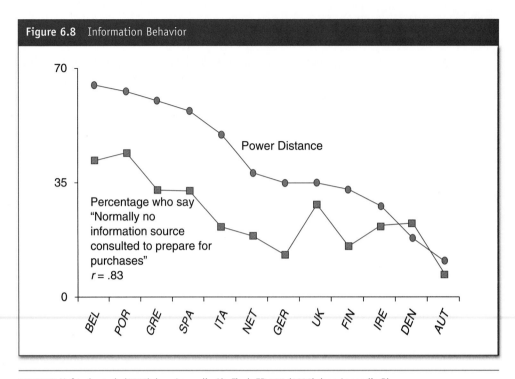

Figure 6.8 Information Behavior

SOURCES: Hofstede et al. (2010) (see Appendix A); Flash EB 117 (2002) (see Appendix B)

If there are such strong flows of information between people, information is like air; it just is there, everywhere, and people cannot easily recall where they got the information from and whether they use it for making a buying decision. Theorists from individualistic cultures tend to call this *intuitive decision making*, suggesting it is not information based without understanding that the information is there, but the process is different.

Individualists of low power distance and low uncertainty avoidance actively search for information to make a buying decision. Across 10 European countries the effect of online research on the brand chosen correlates with low power distance and low uncertainty avoidance.[111] The percentages of respondents that feel well informed about environmental issues across 23 countries in Europe correlate with low power distance, individualism, and low uncertainty avoidance.[112] Also across a group of seven Asian countries searching for information on products or services correlates with low power distance.[113] A number of such cultural relationships are presented in Table 6.4.

Culture influences the way people process positive or negative information. In line with not displaying negative emotions (see Chapter 5), collectivists do not like negative communication and don't want to be confronted with problems. The problem-solving format of advertising that is so popular in the United States will be less effective in collectivistic

Table 6.4   Information Behavior

	PDI	IDV	UAI	Predictor	R²
Europe					
2002: Feel well informed as consumer	−.57*	.78***	−.64**	IDV	.61
2002: No information source consulted for buying decision	.76***			PDI	.58
2008: Feel well informed about environmental issues	−.60***	.70***	−.55***	IDV	.49
2008: Effect of online research on brand chosen	−.65*	.79***	−.75*	IDV PDI−	.63 .78
2008: Internet related activities: search for information	.49**	−.49**		IDV	.24
2008: Mobile phone helps keep contact with family and friends		−.38*			
2008: Mobile phone helps share ideas and material with others		−.42*			
2007: I often recommend brands to others		−.51*			
2007: People often ask my opinion about brands		−.48*			
2009: Never read any labels when making a purchase decision	.35*				
2008: Visit bar every day		−.76***	.52***	IDV−	.58
2008: Meet friends every day		−.41*			
Asia					
2008: Use Internet for personal reasons		−.89***		IDV− UAI−	.79 .93
2008: Read blogs		−.89***		IDV−	.80
2008: Chat		−.95***		IDV−	.91
2008: Activities via PC: search for information on products, services	−.74*				

SOURCES: Hofstede et al. (2010) (see Appendix A); Europe: 2002: Flash EB 117; 2008: EBS 295; 2008: Mediascope Europe; 2007: Reader's Digest Trusted Brands; 2008: Flash EB 241; 2009: Flash EB 256; 2008: Asia: Synovate PAX Asia (see Appendix B)

cultures. Indians would be averse to buying a product category (e.g., deodorants) by which you implicitly admit you have a problem. Even being seen in a shop picking such a product from the shelf is a social risk. A positive approach like freshness or attraction, ignoring the problem, will be more effective.[114] Collectivists are more focused on ignoring negative information than attending to positive information. Because of the importance of face, which is easier lost than gained, avoidance of negative input is important for East Asians. North Americans, however, because of the importance of high self-esteem, are used to focusing on positive self-characteristics to positively distinguish themselves from others.[115]

Processing Advertising

When consumers process advertising, either the information presented in an advertisement will fit existing schema or a new schema will be established. Most acquired information is organized in schemata that already exist in the memory. Often only the information relevant and important to the activated schema is selected; the rest is lost. Next, the meaning (semantic content) is interpreted so as to be consistent with the schema, to make it fit. Finally, schematically stored information can be used to make judgments, evaluations, and choices. However, the information must be retrievable before it can be used; it must be remembered.

Western information-processing theory generally states that distinctive (unusual) information is easier to remember than ordinary information. *Salient* (highly important) information is easier to remember than unimportant information. Many things can go wrong in this process. First, one's own cultural roots may inhibit the perception of stimuli coming from another cultural perspective. Second, interpretation of the meaning may not be as intended. Third, the evaluations and decision-making process may vary.

An example of advertising that did not fit the schemata of the target audience was an ad aimed at housewives in Finland that used quick cuts and short scenes that were associated exclusively with the youth ads the Finns saw on music channels such as MTV. Such styles were uncommon on Finnish terrestrial channels, where the housewives expected to see ads aimed at them. So an ad that used that style was dismissed as a commercial for young people. It might be thought that the ad's distinctiveness would make it stand out for the Finnish target, whereas in fact its execution cut it off from its audience by appearing to target others.[116]

The eternal dilemma of advertising is whether to follow the conventions of advertising for a particular product category in a particular culture or to be distinctive in order to raise awareness and find a place in people's memories. Within countries the danger of using distinctive, unusual information in advertising to attract attention is that it will not fit in consumers' schemata and will be discarded. This risk is even greater across cultures than within cultures because people's schemata vary. How people process information is related to the type of information people are used to processing. People of high-context cultures, used to symbols, signs, and indirect communication, will process information in a different way than will people of low-context cultures who are used to explanations, persuasive copy, and rhetoric. Aaker and Lee[117] show that greater attention is associated with the processing of culture-compatible versus culture-incompatible messages. Briley and Aaker[118] suggest that this is modified by context. Compatibility effects may mostly arise when automatic, effortless processes guide judgments. Culture-based differences in processing arise when a person processes information in a cursory, spontaneous manner, but these differences decrease when a person's intuitions are supplemented by more deliberative processing.

Western Bias in Cross-Cultural Analysis of Advertising

The influence of Western information processing theory has resulted in a biased approach to the way advertising is analyzed across countries. Information-processing research does not emphasize the meanings audiences might ascribe to advertising stimuli; it deals with the processing of details in advertisements, not with the holistically perceived meaning. It assesses, for example, the drawing power of proposed headlines or copy, it can indicate whether a celebrity spokesperson is perceived as credible, and it analyzes the copy points of an advertisement.[119]

Many cross-cultural advertising studies compare the information content of advertising. In order to operationalize the distinction between informative and noninformative content, a typology by Resnik and Stern[120] is often used. If at least one of 14 informational cues is present, an advertisement is considered to be informative. These 14 informational cues are price-value, quality, performance, components, availability, special offers, taste, nutrition, packaging or shape, guarantees and warranties, safety, independent research, company research, and new ideas. An informational cue generally is defined as "a cue that is relevant enough to assist a typical buyer in making an intelligent choice among alternatives." That doesn't make the procedure a proper one for cross-cultural research. What is informational for consumers in one culture may not be informational or relevant for consumers in another culture. In high-context cultures, relevance in advertising isn't even an issue. The type of information cues defined by Resnik and Stern also do not allow for measuring the influence of context. They cannot properly cover other types of information, such as indirect visual cues, which may be interpreted as informative by people of high-context cultures. It is the typical Western analytical system, which is not appropriate for measuring holistically developed Asian advertising. By the use of such Western scales, information of Eastern societies may be missed by forcing these communications to fit into the prescribed Western categories.[121]

Processing Visual Images

There are significant cross-cultural differences in pictorial perception and recognition. Visual language predominantly varies from one culture to another, much in the same way that textual language varies. When processing visual images, field (in)dependency plays a role. East Asians allocate their attention more broadly than Americans, and they are also slower at detecting changes in the center of a picture.[122]

Face recognition is facilitated if people are of the same ethnicity (discussed in Chapter 5). Complex visual images, relying on implicit meaning, can be better processed by members of collectivistic cultures, who are more used to deriving meaning from context, than by members of individualistic cultures, who are more used to simple visual images that carry explicit meaning. In low-context (individualistic) cultures, meaning often relies on explicit information; pictures speak for themselves. In high-context (collectivistic) cultures, much of the information derived from a message is present in the context. People have learned to decode implicit metaphorical messages and contextual language. This difference already exists at early age. Some indirect visual messages—in the English language called *mood metaphors*—are better understood by Chinese children than by British children.[123] When consumers have to quickly process complex information, such as visual information in advertising, familiarity will be a critical factor influencing the resulting brand preferences.[124] In Spain, advertisements including pictures (either alone or with text) are associated with higher levels of attitude toward the ad than those including only text.[125]

A picture that is very meaningful for members of one culture because it expresses important values of that culture can be completely meaningless to members of another culture. An example is the LG advertisement shown in Figure 6.9. East Asians recognize this picture as *continuity*. What the old man cannot finish in his life, the young one can. Most Westerners will not be able to recognize the meaning of this picture. Yet, the ad was placed in a Western business journal. Likewise, Asians may not be able to grasp the meaning of the frog-prince, a European fairy tale written by the German brothers Grimm.

Imagery is an important element of advertising, yet in research it is undervalued because of the historical focus on verbal communication in the United States. This bias is reflected in the use of the phrase "copy theory" instead of "advertising theory." Also the terms "copy research" and "copy testing," used for testing effectiveness of advertising, point at a bias toward thinking in verbal stimuli. As a result little is known about how consumers from different cultures process visual images in print advertisements. Visuals have been used for standardizing print advertisements worldwide with the underlying assumption that consumers from all around the world can "read" a picture, whereas the copy of the advertisement often needs to be translated. However, these highly standardized visual campaigns do not always convey a uniform meaning among audiences. For example, Benetton's ad with a black woman nursing a white baby won awards for its message of unity and equality in Europe. At the same time, the ad stirred up controversy in the United States, since many believed it depicted a black nanny in the subordinate role as a slave.[126] It is a misconception that visuals are understood across cultures. Pictures fit in schemata people have, and schemata vary by culture. A picture, meant in one culture to be associated with freedom (e.g., a lion), may be known in another culture to represent strength.

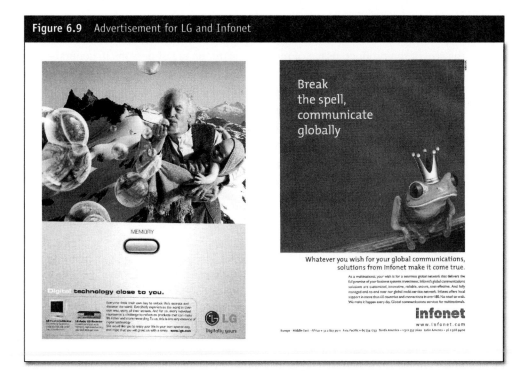

Figure 6.9   Advertisement for LG and Infonet

What may be thought to be a universal picture is likely to be interpreted in different ways. People can derive different meanings from the same message because contextual people will "see" more in the message than was intended by the producer of the message. Because in high-context cultures people are used to contextual messages, they will read more into pictures and derive "hidden" meaning from a visual image. Even for simple visual images with highly explicit information, the high-context audience may try to construct more abstract metaphorical meaning. This effect was demonstrated by Callow and Schiffman,[127] who tested image processing between the United States and the Philippines, countries that contrast strongly with respect to individualism and collectivism. Based on existing ads for perfume, variations were made with single persons or groups of people. The ability to derive implicit meaning from the visuals was measured by two associations, affiliation (collectivistic value) and achievement (individualistic value). The results showed that the higher-context Filipino respondents read higher levels of affiliation into the meaning of a man standing by himself and higher levels of personal achievement into the meaning of a group of women standing together as compared with their American counterparts.

Differences in perception and visual processing result in a range of differences in the use of pictures in advertising. A multi-country comparison in the United States, United Kingdom,

France, Korea, and India[128] of visual components of print advertising found variations with respect to the size of the visual, frequency of usage of photographs and product portrayals, the size of the product, usage of metaphors, frequency of persons in general—and specifically women and children—depicted in advertising. When measuring the effects of visuals in advertising, visuals and words tend to be analyzed as separate items, with the role of visuals as a separate cue, suggesting that the use of an unexpected visual will grab the viewer's attention and get him or her to engage in more effortful and elaborative processing. However, visuals may have a direct and unconscious effect and, consequently, many studies of advertising visuals have not taken into account the context of the visuals or the likelihood of viewers treating the entire advertisement, no matter how incongruous, as information of some sort.[129]

Processing Foreign Words

The use of foreign words in advertising has two purposes. One purpose is to get *attention*. The assumption is that foreign words in advertising make the advertisement distinctive and raise curiosity. The other purpose is *efficiency* in international advertising. Using only one advertisement—usually in the English language—without translation is cheaper because no translation costs are involved. Foreign words in ads are supposed to raise attention and to be remembered as long as these expressions are perceived as unusual, unexpected, yet relevant information. However, the meaning of a foreign expression should be sufficiently apparent to the audience and the expression should add to, not detract from, the existing associations in consumers' schema for the advertised brand. Using French words in a wine advertisement aimed at an English-speaking audience is fine as long as such consumers regard "Frenchness" as an important attribute of wines. If such foreign words are used in ads directed at monolingual audiences, only a limited number of words can be used, and only with the purpose of associating country of origin, for example, phrases like *pasta Italiano*. There is some evidence that to an English language audience product perceptions and evaluations change when the brand name is pronounced in French or English. French names produce a more hedonic perception than English names.[130] However, studies in the Netherlands showed that English language terms used in shop names, although liked, did not lead to more positive associations with the shops or more positive shop images.[131] Neither did the use of English lead to positive attitudes toward brands.

The purpose of English language in international advertising is to appeal to international segments. To young people, English language ads would be more appealing because they would represent the youthfulness and progressivity of the United States and thus add prestige to the brand. To Koreans, the fact that English is the language of international business may give brands expressed in English a cosmopolitan appeal. Among young Japanese, foreign symbols are considered to be exotic.[132]

INVOLVEMENT THEORY

Classic consumer behavior theory poses that people process information, in particular advertising, in what is called a *learning hierarchy*. People would be motivated to seek a lot of information, carefully weigh alternatives, and come to a thoughtful decision. Later theories include variations in a consumer's level of involvement in activating different cognitive processes when a message is received. One of the early sequences in how people were thought to process information and react to advertising was that people first should learn something about a product or brand, then form an attitude or feeling, and consequently take action, meaning purchase the product or at least go to the shop with the intention to buy. This sequence is called *learn-feel-do*. It was later seen as mainly applicable to processing information for products of "high involvement," such as cars, for which the decision-making process was assumed to be highly rational. This so-called *high-involvement* model assumes that consumers are active participants in the process of gathering information and making a decision. In contrast, there are low-involvement products, such as detergents or other fast-moving consumer goods, with related low-involvement behavior when there is little interest in the product. The concept of *low involvement* is based on Herbert Krugman's[133] theory that television is a low-involvement medium that can generate brand awareness but has little impact on peoples' attitudes. The low-involvement sequence was assumed to be *learn-do-feel*. Again, knowledge comes first, after that purchase, and only after having used the product would one form an attitude.

International advertising scholar Gordon Miracle[134] argued that for the Japanese consumer another sequence is valid: *feel-do-learn*. The purpose of Japanese advertising is not to sell or change attitude, like Western advertising. It is based on building a relationship between the company and the consumer. The purpose of Japanese advertising is to please the consumer and to build "dependency" (*amae,* see Chapter 5), and this is done by the indirect approach. As a result, "feel" is the initial response of the Japanese consumer, after which action is taken: a visit to the shop to purchase the product. Only after this comes knowledge. Miracle suggests that this sequence also applies to Korean and Chinese consumer responses. It may well apply to all collectivistic cultures.

According to Petty and Cacioppo's elaboration likelihood model (ELM),[135] information processing follows a central and/or peripheral route depending on the degree of involvement in the message. Within the central route, a person engages in thoughtful consideration (elaboration) of the issue-relevant information (= arguments) within a message. If the person lacks the motivation or ability to undertake issue-relevant thinking, processing follows a peripheral route. Actively thinking about the arguments in the message is the central route. When the person is not motivated to think about the arguments, the peripheral route is followed. In the theory, the peripheral route generally includes visual cues like the package, pictures, or the context in which the message is presented. The theory is embedded in Western advertising practice that uses pictures as illustrations of words. In many Western studies, visual cues are not viewed as informational but as emotional, in contrast to the rational aspects of advertising copy. However, because visuals are convention based, all pictures are interpreted according to learned patterns, just like reading words or recognizing numbers, and thus must be processed cognitively. Using pictures as peripheral stimuli becomes questionable under this theory. In collectivistic cultures, where people process information holistically instead of analytically, the theory may not apply at all. For properly processing an advertisement, the context is likely to be as important or even more important than the verbal message. If the information in the different cues of an advertisement (e.g., picture and words) is incongruent, North Americans tend to increase elaboration to resolve incongruity by discarding one of the incongruent pieces of information, whereas the more holistic East Asians are more likely to tolerate incongruity.[136]

DECISION MAKING

The fundamental assumption in Western decision-making theory is that decisions do not "happen"; someone "makes them." This is a Western view. Japanese are more likely to prefer events to shape whatever actions are required, to stand back from an event rather than attempt to control it by decision making.[137] American-based decision-making theory is based on internal locus of control. People are in control of their own destinies and are fully in charge of their own performance. In many cultures with a more fatalistic approach to life, various uncontrollable higher-order forces are assumed to shape people's acts and future. In cultures where external locus of control operates, people tend to postpone decisions more ("*mañana* syndrome") than in cultures where internal locus of control operates—cultures of the configuration of individualism and weak uncertainty avoidance.[138]

In marketing literature it is generally suggested that the decision-making process of consumers follows several stages, although not in all cases do all consumers pass through all stages. These stages are problem recognition, information search, evaluation of alternatives, purchase decision, and post-purchase behavior. Such models are based on the information-processing approach to consumer decision-making theory that suggests a rational consumer who thinks and evaluates consciously and rationally. The evaluation process is not universal. When presented with contradictory arguments, Americans tend to weigh them and choose the better one. The presence of a weaker argument only strengthens their conviction that they have made the right choice. Chinese often do the opposite. They may accept both options even if they seem mutually exclusive to Americans.[139] Also, the majority of consumer decisions are not based on a large degree of conscious thinking. A lot of information processing is unconscious—in particular in collectivistic cultures—and so is retrieval from memory. Many of these unconscious processes are "automatic" cognitive processes.[140] There also is evidence that in Japan and more generally in Asia, different information is sought than in the West, and that it is used in different decision-making processes.[141] Asians, because of fear of losing face, are careful in ensuring that they know precisely what is on offer before deciding to commit. Due to their nonconfrontational nature, it is not easy for Asians to question certain aspects once they have made up their minds, so they are doubly careful that any decisions are based on close scrutiny and long deliberation.[142] In collectivistic cultures, it often is not information that drives choice behavior. Choices may be driven by loyalty or obligation, which is perfectly rational, although in Western views it may not be so.[143] There are several related influences on choice behavior that vary across cultures, such as price and quality. Chinese are very price conscious for personal use products, but for public use products a high price will enhance face. High quality may reduce the risk of losing face.[144]

Differences also exist with respect to the way people describe their own decision-making styles. Whereas Americans talk more often about the emotional nature of their buyer behavior, Japanese consumers provide more rational descriptions of their decision making.[145] This is likely due to the fact that Americans tend to attribute their behavior to their personal traits and related personal emotions, whereas Japanese are likely to refer to situational facts that in the eyes of the researchers are less "emotional."

The influence of group members on buying behavior will vary with various dimensions, as described in Chapter 5. In China, when it comes to the final decision about what to buy, friends and colleagues have more influence than advertisements or sales people. In cultures of high power distance with related dependency needs elders and superiors will have a more dominant role in decision making. In collectivistic cultures, children are taught to avoid social conflict and utilize parental standards in consumption, whereas in individualistic cultures, where children are encouraged to have opinions and evaluate all sides of an argument, there is a tendency toward lower consumption dependence at a relatively young age (3–8 years). Japanese children make fewer purchase requests and exhibit lower levels of communication about consumption with their parents than American children do.[146] In the United States, household money decisions are often joint decisions, but in China and Japan usually the woman handles the household budget.[147]

In collectivistic cultures, decisions will be made in consensus with the group, so decisions are not individual decisions. Also, people will behave according to the expectations of group members. Consensus seeking is also important in feminine cultures. The degree of role differentiation influences the involvement of partners in decision making. An example is for buying cars. The EMS surveys asked who is involved in choosing the make and model in the purchase of one's main and second car. The answer categories were *you, your partner, another household member, your employer/business partner, someone else.* In 1995, 50% of variance of the answers "your partner" was explained by low masculinity. In the feminine cultures, partners decide on this sort of purchase together, whereas in the masculine cultures selection of the make and model of car is likely to be the task of the male in the relationship. This influence is likely to be noticeable in the decision-making process for many durable household goods.

Consumer Decision-Making Styles

Consumer decision-making style can be defined as "a mental orientation characterizing a consumer's approach to making choices."[148] The underlying thought of most Western consumer decision-making models is that consumers engage in shopping with certain fundamental decision-making modes or styles, including conscious evaluations regarding brand, price, and quality. The search for a universal instrument that can describe consumers' decision-making styles across cultures seems to be problematic.

An approach that focuses on consumers' orientations in making decisions is the consumer characteristics approach of Sproles and Kendall,[149] who developed an instrument, analogous to the personality traits concept, to measure consumer decision-making styles, called the *consumer style inventory* (CSI). The CSI identifies eight mental characteristics of consumer decision making: (1) perfectionism or high-quality consciousness; (2) brand consciousness; (3) novelty-fashion consciousness; (4) recreational, hedonistic shopping consciousness; (5) price and "value-for-money" shopping consciousness; (6) impulsiveness; (7) confusion over choice of brands, stores, and consumer information; (8) habitual, brand-loyal orientation toward consumption. Hafstrom et al.[150] applied the CSI to young Koreans and found similar decision-making styles. The brand conscious and perfectionist styles were among the top three decision-making styles. Lysonski et al.[151] tested the CSI among young people in Greece, India, New Zealand, and the United States and found that 6 of the 40 items that were used by Sproles and Kendall (e.g., price conscious and value-for-money) did not apply to the Greek and Indian samples. So, some of the original items had to be deleted. In the end, 34 items were used, which resulted in seven factors: perfectionist, brand-conscious, novelty-fashion conscious, recreational, impulsive, confusion over choice, and habitual, brand-loyal. Commercial research agencies use similar consumer characteristics to distinguish consumer decision-making styles. For example, in the lower-income countries, people were more brand loyal.

Business Decision Making

Businesspeople are generally considered to be a culture-free group because their decision-making process is assumed to be rational, as compared with more emotional consumer decision making. There is evidence that decision making by businesspeople is also culture bound. Because businesspeople are also part of their culture, they will exhibit similar differences as consumers. In addition to that, the culture of the company will influence cross-cultural differences.

In major purchases in all cultures, a number of people are involved. This is generally called the *decision-making unit* (DMU). In Europe, this DMU contains an average of nine people, varying by country between 3 and 20. The groups are largest in France and Sweden for making purchases within their own countries. Between-country buying involves different DMU sizes (e.g., the French, buying from a German supplier, need only 7 people in the DMU, whereas buying from a French supplier they use 20).[152]

In business in Japan, intermediaries are used, such as bankers, accountants, or trade associations representatives, whereas American businesspeople tend to find their own way. Japanese firms tend to consult more personal sources than do American firms. Whereas American firms get their information about suppliers from the Yellow Pages or industry trade shows, Japanese find suppliers from information from good friends or municipal agencies and prefer to do business with "someone the founder's family knows very well."[153]

Finding the influence of others in decision making is not easy, as culture influences the degree to which people think they are involved in decision making (which may be different from actual decision-making power). Because of egalitarian values in low power distance cultures, more people think they are involved in decision making on corporate buying aspects than in high power distance cultures. Whereas in Denmark a secretary who assists the boss in gathering information on products to buy may view this as involvement in decision making, a secretary in France giving the same assistance probably will not view this as being involved in making the decision, because the boss implicitly makes all decisions. This can be concluded from EMS, which asks the question, "When decisions are made for business purchases several people may have responsibility for different aspects of the decision. Please indicate for each of the product or service areas below whether you have (a) responsibility (this could be for determining needs, choosing brands and suppliers, or authorizing purchase or finance); (b) some involvement (assisting in these decisions) or (c) no involvement."

The questions referred to 26 product categories. Analysis of the mean answer scores shows that for 16 of 26 categories, the answers suggesting that people are involved in the decision-making process are related to low power distance.

Because of centralized decision making in high power distance cultures, the boss in a company more frequently has the final say in buying decisions than in low power distance cultures. This is a likely explanation of differences in the time it takes to pay invoices in Europe. In 1996 the differences between countries in Europe with respect to average agreed payment days and average actual payment days were significantly correlated with power distance ($r = .69***$ and $r = .73***$). In the high power distance cultures there is less delegation, lower-level employees do not have much decision making power, and payment decisions are likely to be carried to the boss through the layers of the organization, which takes more time.

In the sales process, what are considered to be positive influences on decision making vary. In high power distance cultures, seniority is preferred to skills and procedural discipline is preferred to trust. Personal relationships between seller and buyer are fine in individualistic and low power distance cultures, but personal favors are not.[154]

CONCLUSION

The mental processes relevant for understanding consumer behavior discussed in this chapter are cognition, learning, perception, creativity, attribution, information processing, communication, and decision making. All are processes that vary with culture. The basis of understanding is that culture is learned behavior. People who grow up in one culture have learned to see things in certain contexts that people in other countries have learned to see in different contexts. Our thinking and the way we process information defines what and how we communicate. Knowledge of the differences is of utmost importance to international marketers and advertisers. Communication is only effective if the receiver of the message understands the message as the sender intends it. Only recently cross-cultural psychologists and marketing researchers have found evidence of how culture influences these processes. The accumulated knowledge described in this chapter is only the beginning of a knowledge base that should further develop in the next decades.

NOTES

1. Percy, L., Rossiter, J. R., & Elliott, R. (2001). *Strategic advertising management.* Oxford, UK: Oxford University Press, 22.
2. Semin, G. R.. & Zwier, S. (1997). Social cognition. In J. W. Berry, M. H. Segall, & Ç. Kagitçibasi (Eds.), *Handbook of cross-cultural psychology* (Vol. 3, pp. 51–75). Boston: Allyn & Bacon, 61.
3. Eysenck, M. W. (2001). *Principles of cognitive psychology* (2nd ed.). Hove, East Sussex, UK: Psychology Press, 1–2.
4. Kühnen, U. (2001). The semantic-procedural interface model of the self: The role of self-knowledge for context-dependent versus context-independent modes of thinking. *Journal of Personality and Social Psychology, 80,* 397–409.
5. Malhotra, N. K., & McCort, J. D. (2001). A cross-cultural comparison of behavioral intention models. *International Marketing Review, 18,* 235–269.
6. Choi, I., Nisbett, R. E., & Smith, E. E. (1997). Culture, category salience, and inductive reasoning. *Cognition, 65,* 15–32.
7. Hicks, R. (2002, March). Back to the drawing board. *M&M Europe,* 18–21.
8. Li, J. (2002). A cultural model of learning: Chinese "heart and mind for wanting to learn." *Journal of Cross-Cultural Psychology, 33,* 248–269.
9. Mishra, R. C. (1997). Cognition and cognitive development. In J. W. Berry, P. R. Dasen, & T. S. Saraswathi (Eds.), *Handbook of cross-cultural psychology* (Vol. 2, pp. 143–175). Boston: Allyn & Bacon, 160.
10. Bulmer, S., & Buchanan-Oliver, M. (2006). Advertising across cultures: Interpretations of visually complex advertising. *Journal of Current Issues and Research of Advertising, 28*(1), 57–71.
11. Domzal, T. J., Hunt, J. M., & Kernan, J. B. (1995). Achtung! The information processing of foreign words in advertising. *International Journal of Advertising, 14,* 95–114.
12. Kühnen, U. (2001). The semantic-procedural interface model of the self: The role of self-knowledge for context-dependent versus context-independent modes of thinking. *Journal of Personality and Social Psychology, 80,* 397–409.
13. Hsieh, M. H. (2004). Measuring global brand equity using cross-national survey data. *Journal of International Marketing, 12*(2), 28–57.
14. Koçak, A., Abimbola, T., & Özer, A. (2007). Consumer brand equity in a cross-cultural replication: An evaluation of a scale. *Journal of Marketing Management, 23*(1–2), 157–173; Yoo, B., & Donthu, N. (2002). Testing cross-cultural invariance of the brand equity creation process. *Journal of Product and Brand Management, 11*(6), 380–398.
15. Retrieved January 23, 2010, from http://theinspirationroom.com/daily/2007/diesel-global-warming-ready/
16. Scott, L. (1994). Images in advertising: The need for a theory of visual rhetoric. *Journal of Consumer Research, 21,* 252–273.

17. Peter, J. P., Olson, J. C., Grunert, K. G. (1999). *Consumer behaviour and marketing strategy* (European ed.). London: McGraw-Hill, 39.

18. Cervellon, M. C., & Dubé, L. (2002). Assessing the cross-cultural applicability of affective and cognitive components of attitude. *Journal of Cross-Cultural Psychology, 33*, 346–357.

19. Hofstede (2001), 229.

20. Solomon, M., Bamossy, G., & Askegaard, S. (1999). *Consumer behaviour: A European perspective.* London: Pearson Education, 96.

21. Choi, I., Nisbett, R. E., & Norenzayan, A. (1999). Causal attribution across cultures: Variation and universality. *Psychological Bulletin, 125*, 47–63.

22. Aaker, J. L., & Sengupta, J. (2000). Additivity versus attenuation: The role of culture in resolution of information incongruity. *Journal of Consumer Psychology, 2*, 67–82.

23. Gudykunst, W. B., Ting-Toomey, S., Hall, B. J., & Schmidt, K. L. (1989). Language and intergroup communication. In M. K. Asante & W. B. Gudykunst (Eds.), *Handbook of international and intercultural communication* (pp. 145–162). Newbury Park, CA: Sage, 145.

24. Munroe, R. L., & Munroe, R. H. (1997). A comparative anthropological perspective. In J. W. Berry, Y. H. Poortinga, & J. Pandey (Eds.), *Handbook of cross-cultural psychology* (Vol. 1, pp. 171– 213). Boston: Allyn & Bacon, 183.

25. Gudykunst, W. B., & Ting-Toomey, S. (1988). *Culture and interpersonal communication.* Thousand Oaks, CA: Sage.

26. Macfarlane, A. (1978). *The origins of English individualism.* Oxford, UK: Blackwell.

27. Triandis, H. C. (1995). *Individualism and collectivism.* Boulder, CO: Westview, 69.

28. Giles, H., & Franklyn-Stokes, A. (1989). Communicator characteristics. In M. K. Asante & W. B. Gudykunst (Eds.), *Handbook of international and intercultural communication* (pp. 117–144). Newbury Park, CA: Sage, 127.

29. Kashima, E. S., & Kashima, Y. (1998). Culture and language: The case of cultural dimensions and personal pronoun use. *Journal of Cross-Cultural Psychology, 29*, 461–486.

30. Hofstede, G. (personal communication, 1996).

31. Burger, P. (1996, June). Gaten in de taal. *Onze Taal, 293.*

32. Van Oudenhoven, J. P., & De Raad, B. (2008). Eikels en trutten over de grens. (Abusive behavior across eleven countries). *Onze Taal, 77*(9), 228–231.

33. Miracle, G. E., Bang, H. K., & Chang, K. Y. (1992, March 20). *Achieving reliable and valid cross-cultural research results.* Working paper panel of Cross-Cultural Research Design, National Conference of the American Academy of Advertising. San Antonio, TX.

34. Usunier, J. C. (1996). *International marketing: A cultural approach.* Harlow, UK: Pearson Education, 7.

35. Semin, & Zwier (1997), 51–75.

36. Bloom, A. H. (1981). *The linguistic shaping of thought: A study of the impact of language on thinking in China and the West.* Hillsdale, NJ: Lawrence Erlbaum. In Semin & Zwier (1997), 66.

37. Li, F., & Cheng, H. (2009). Brand naming in China's globalized economy: Summarizing and elaborating power of key symbols. In H. Li, S. Huang, & D. Jin (Eds.), *Proceedings of the 2009 American Academy of Advertising Asia-Pacific conference* (p. 256). American Academy of Advertising, in conjunction with China Association of Advertising of Commerce, and Communication University of China.

38. Retrieved September 1, 2002, from http://www.essentialaction.org/tobacco/funny.html and http://www.us-expatriate-handbook.com/chpt3.htm

39. Schmitt, B. H., Pan, Y., & Tavassoli, N. T. (1994). Language and consumer memory: The impact of linguistic differences between Chinese and English. *Journal of Consumer Research, 21*, 419–431.

40. Hofstede, G. (personal communication, August 2002).

41. Schmitt, B. H., & Pan, Y. (1994). Managing corporate and brand identities in the Asia-Pacific region. *California Management Review, 36,* 32–48.

42. Semin & Zwier (1997), 65.

43. Müller, W. (1998). Verlust von Werbewirkung durch Standardisierung. (Loss of advertising effectiveness through standardization). *Absatzwirtschaft, 9,* 80–88.

44. García, S. (1998, October). When is a cat not a cat? *Admap,* 40–42.

45. Anholt, S. (2000). *Another one bites the grass: Making sense of international advertising.* New York: Wiley, 5.

46. Williams, J. (1991, August). Constant questions or constant meanings? Assessing intercultural motivations in alcoholic drinks. *Marketing and Research Today,* 169–177.

47. Standard Eurobarometer 55, 2001; *The Young Europeans,* Special Eurobarometer 151, 2001.

48. *Europeans and their languages,* (2006, February). Special Eurobarometer report 243.

49. Gerritsen, M., & Jansen, F. (2001). Teloorgang of survival? (Loss or survival?). *Onze Taal, 2/3,* 40–42.

50. Gerritsen, M., Gijsbers, I., Korzilius, H., & Van Meurs, F. (1999). Engels in Nederlandse TV reclame (English in Dutch TV advertising). *Onze Taal, 1,* 17–19.

51. Paulick, J. (2007, November 16). *Impossible is nothing, except understanding ads in English.* Deutsche Welle. Retrieved November 20, 2007, from http://www.dw-world.de/dw/article

52. Unsworth, S. J., Sears, C. R., & Pexman, P. M. (2005). Cultural influences on categorization processes. *Journal of Cross-Cultural Psychology, 36*(6), 662–688.

53. Ramdas, A. (2008, March 10). Geef mij maar onzin kennis. *NRC/Handelsblad, 7.*

54. Monga, A. B., & Roedder John, D. (2007). Cultural differences in brand extension evaluation: The influence of analytic versus holistic thinking. *Journal of Consumer Research, 33,* 529–536.

55. Gemmen, P. (2002, September 12). Eet u smakelijk (Enjoy the food). *Adformatie,* 24–26.

56. Schmitt, B. H., & Zhang, S. (1998). Language structure and categorization: A study of classifiers in consumer cognition, judgment, and choice. *Journal of Consumer Research, 25,* 108–122.

57. Zhang, S., & Schmitt, B. (1998). Language-dependent classification: The mental representation of classifiers in cognition, memory and evaluations. *Journal of Experimental Psychology: Applied, 4,* 375–385.

58. Schmitt & Zhang (1998).

59. Turnbull, C. M. (1961). *The forest people.* New York: Simon & Schuster. In Eysenck (2001), 105.

60. Russell, P. A., Deregowski, J. B., & Kinnear, P. R. (1997). Perception and aesthetics. In J. W. Berry, P. R. Dasen, & T. S. Saraswathi (Eds.), *Handbook of cross-cultural psychology* (Vol. 2, pp. 107 – 142). Boston: Allyn & Bacon.

61. Giles, H., & Franklyn-Stokes, A. (1989). Communicator characteristics. In M. K. Asante & W. B. Gudykunst (Eds.), *Handbook of international and intercultural communication* (pp. 117–144). Newbury Park, CA: Sage, 133.

62. Russell et al. (1997), 125.

63. Kress, G., & Van Leeuwen, T. (1996). *Reading images: The grammar of visual design.* London: Routledge, 4, 206.

64. Kim, Y. S., & Kelly, J. D. (2008). A matter of culture: A comparative study of photojournalism in American and Korean Newspapers. *The International Communication Gazette, 70*(2), 155–173.

65. Schmitt, B. H. (1995). Language and visual imagery: Issues of corporate identity in East Asia. *Columbia Journal of World Business, 3,* 28–37.

66. Doi, T. (1985). *The anatomy of self: The individual versus society.* Tokyo: Kodansha International, 151.

67. Schmitt & Pan (1994).

68. Aslam, M. M. (2006). Are you selling the right colour? A cross-cultural review of colour as a marketing cue. *Journal of Marketing Communications, 12*(1), 15–30.

69. Jameson, K. A. (2005). On the role of culture in color naming: Remarks on the articles of Paramei, Kay, Roberson, and Hardin on the topic of cognition, culture, and color experience. *Cross-Cultural Research, 39*(1), 88–106.

70. Roberson, D. (2005). Color categories are culturally diverse in cognition as well as in language. *Cross-Cultural Research, 39*(1), 56–71.

71. Madden, T. J., Hewett, K., & Roth, M. (2000). Managing images in different cultures: A cross-national study of color meanings and preferences. *Journal of International Marketing, 8,* 90–107.

72. Madden et al. (2000).

73. Aslam (2006).

74. Van den Berg-Weitzel, L., & Van de Laar, G. (2001). Relation between culture and communication in packaging design. *Brand Management, 8,* 171–184.

75. Berkhout, K. (2007, March 2). Chinese storm. De hausse van de hedendaagse kunst uit China. *NRC Handelsblad,* 17.

76. Niu, W., & Sternberg, R. J. (2001). Cultural influences on artistic creativity and its evaluation. *International Journal of Psychology, 36,* 225–241.

77. Janata, P., Birk, J. L., Van Horn, J. D., Leman, M., Tillmann, B., & Bharucha, J. J. (2002). The cortical topography of tonal structures underlying Western music. *Science, 298,* 2167–2170; Moelants, D., Cornelis, O., & Leman, M. (2009). *Exploring African tone scales.* 10th International Society for Music Information Retrieval conference.

78. Van Maris, B. (2006, December 10). Lettergreepritme. *NRC handelsblad/Wetenschap,* 51.

79. Grønlien, L. (2005). *Understanding the challenges of entering the Chinese market.* Trondheim: Norwegian University of Science and Technology, Department of Product Design.

80. Masuda, T., Gonzalez, R., Kwan, L., & Nisbett, R. E. (2008). Culture and aesthetic preference: Comparing the attention to context of East Asians and Americans. *Personality and Social Psychology Bulletin, 34*(9), 1260–1275.

81. Niu & Sternberg (2001).

82. Paletz, S. B. F., & Peng, K. (2008). Implicit theories of creativity across cultures. *Journal of Cross-Cultural Psychology, 39*(3), 286–302.

83. Chen, C., Kasof, J., Himsel, A. J., Greenberger, E., Dong, Q., & Xue, G. (2002). Creativity in drawings of geometric shapes: A cross-cultural examination with the consensual assessment technique. *Journal of Cross-Cultural Psychology, 33,* 171–187.

84. Westwood, R., & Low, D. R. (2003). The multicultural muse: Culture, creativity and innovation. *International Journal of Cross-Cultural Management, 3*(2), 235–259.

85. Kim, Y. S., & Kelly, J. D. (2008). A matter of culture: A comparative study of photojournalism in American and Korean Newspapers. *The International Communication Gazette, 70*(2), 155–173.

86. McCracken, G. (1988). *Culture and consumption: New approaches to the symbolic character of consumer goods and activities.* Bloomington: Indiana University Press, 78–79.

87. To find out whether creative directors at advertising agencies deviate from their own culture, I asked several to complete the Hofstede questionnaire. The resulting country scores usually mirrored Hofstede's scores for their country.

88. Gagliardi, M. (2001, Fall). Alchemy of cultures: From adaptation to transcendence in design and branding. *Design Management Journal,* 32–39.

89. Gelfand, M. J., Spurlock, D., Sniezek, J. A., & Shao, L. (2000). Culture and social prediction: The role of information in enhancing confidence in social predictions in the United States and China. *Journal of Cross-Cultural Psychology, 31,* 498–516.

90. Carpenter, S. (2000, February). Effects of cultural tightness and collectivism on self-concept and causal attributions. *Cross-Cultural Research, 34*(1), 38–56.

91. Hofstede (2001), 304.

92. Mattila, A. S., & Patterson, P. G. (2004). The impact of culture on consumers' perceptions of service recovery efforts. *Journal of Retailing, 80*, 196–106.

93. Rotter, J. B. (1966). Generalized expectancies for internal versus external control of reinforcement. *Psychological Monographs, 80*, Whole No. 609.

94. Lieber, E., Yang, K. S., & Lin, Y. C. (2000). An external orientation to the study of causal beliefs. *Journal of Cross-Cultural Psychology, 2*, 160–186.

95. Rotter, J. B. (1990). Internal versus external control of reinforcement. *American Psychologist, 45*, 489–493.

96. Yamaguchi, S., Gelfand, M., Ohashi, M. M., & Zemba, Y. (2005). The cultural psychology of control: Illusions of personal versus collective control in the United States and Japan. *Journal of Cross-Cultural Psychology, 36*(6), 705–761.

97. Roper Starch Worldwide Conference. (1993, November 1). Has America changed as much as you think it has? *Brandweek*, 24–25.

98. Smith, P. B., Trompenaars, F., & Dugan, S. (1995). The Rotter locus of control scale in 43 countries: A test of cultural relativity. *International Journal of Psychology, 30*, 377–400.

99. *Social values, science and technology.* (2005, June). Special Eurobarometer 225, 27 countries.

100. Triandis (1995).

101. Data Reader's Digest, 1991.

102. *Globalisation.* (2003, October). Flash Eurobarometer 151b.

103. *Confidence in the information society.* (2009). Flash Eurobarometer 250.

104. *Attitudes of European citizens towards the environment.* (2008, March). Special Eurobarometer report 295.

105. *The Economist.* (1999, September 4), 37.

106. An, D., & Kim, S. H. (2007). Advertising visuals in global brands' websites: a six country comparison. *International Journal of Advertising, 26*(3), 303–332.

107. *Consumer survey.* (2002, January). Flash Eurobarometer Report 117.

108. *European's attitudes towards the issue of sustainable consumption and production.* (2009). Flash Eurobarometer 256.

109. Schultz, D. E., & Block, M. P. (2009). Understanding Chinese media audiences: An exploratory study of Chinese consumers' media consumption and a comparison with the U.S.A. In Li, Huang, & Jin (2009), 1–12.

110. Chu, S. C., & Choi, S. M. (2009). Use of social networking sites among Chinese young generations. In Li, Huang, & Jin (2009), 50–57.

111. *Online shoppers.* (2008). Mediascope Europe, EIAA. Europe, 10 countries.

112. *Attitudes of European citizens toward the environment.* (2008, March). Special Eurobarometer Report 295.

113. *PAX digital life.* (2008). Synovate.

114. Information from Vivek Gupta, Senior Vice President IMRB BrandScience at Kantar Group, Bangalore, India.

115. Hamamura, T., Meijer, Z., Heine, S. J., Kamaya, K., & Hori, I. (2009). Approach–avoidance motivation and information processing: A cross-cultural analysis. *Personality and Social Psychology Bulletin, 35*(4), 454–462.

116. Banister, L. (1997, October). Global brands, local contexts. *Admap,* 28.

117. Aaker, J. L., & Lee, A. Y. (2001, June). "I" seek pleasures and "We" avoid pains: The role of self-regulatory goals in information processing and persuasion. *Journal of Consumer Research, 28*, 33–49.

118. Briley, D., & Aaker, J. L. (2006, August). When does culture matter? Effects of personal knowledge on the correction of culture-based judgments. *Journal of Marketing Research, XLIII*, 395–408.

119. Domzal, T. J., Hunt, J. M., & Kernan, J. B. (1995). Achtung! The information processing of foreign words in advertising. *International Journal of Advertising, 14*, 95–114.

120. Resnik, A., & Stern, B. L. (1977). An analysis of information content in television advertising. *Journal of Marketing, 41*, 50–53.

121. Mindy J. F., & McNeal, J. U. (2001). How Chinese children's commercials differ from those of the United States: A content analysis. *Journal of Advertising, 30*, 79–92.

122. Boduroglu, A., Shah, P., & Nisbett, R. E. (2009). Cultural differences in allocation of attention in visual information processing. *Journal of Cross-Cultural Psychology, 40*(3), 349–360.

123. Jolley, R. P., Zhi, Z., & Thomas, G. V. (1998). The development of understanding moods metaphorically expressed in pictures. *Journal of Cross-Cultural Psychology, 29*, 358–376.

124. Bu, K., Kim, D., & Lee, S. (2009). Determinants of visual forms used in print advertising: A cross-cultural comparison. *International Journal of Advertising, 28*(1), 13–48.

125. Salvador Ruiz, S.., & Sicilia, M. (2002). The impact of cognitive and/or affective processing styles on consumer response to advertising appeals. *Journal of Business Research, 5717*, 1–8.

126. Callow, M., & Schiffman, L. (2002). Implicit meaning in visual print advertisements: A cross-cultural examination of the contextual communication effect. *International Journal of Advertising, 21*, 259–277.

127. Callow & Schiffman (2002).

128. Cutler, B. D., Javalgi, R. G., & Erramilli, M. K. (1992). The visual components of print advertising: A five-country cross-cultural analysis. *European Journal of Marketing, 26*, 7–20.

129. Bulmer, S., & Buchanan-Oliver, M. (2006). Visual rhetoric and global advertising imagery. *Journal of Marketing Communications, 12*(1), 49–61.

130. Leclerc, F., Schmitt, B. H., & Dubé, L. (1994). Foreign branding and its effects on product perceptions and attitudes. *Journal of Marketing Research, 31*, 263–270.

131. Renkema, J., Hallen, E., & Hoeken, H. (2001). *Tuinapparatuur* [garden equipment] or garden equipment? *Onze Taal, 10*, 257–259.

132. Taylor, C. R., & Miracle, G. E. (1996). Foreign elements in Korean and U.S. television advertising. *Advances in International Marketing, 7*, 175–195.

133. Krugman, H. E. (1965). The impact of television advertising: Learning without involvement. *Public Opinion Quarterly, 29*, 349–56.

134. Miracle, G. E. (1987). Feel-do-learn: An alternative sequence underlying Japanese consumer response to television commercials. In F. G. Feasley (Ed.), *Proceedings of the 1987 conference of the American Academy of Advertising,* R73 – R78.

135. Petty, R. E., & Cacioppo, J. T. (1986). The elaboration likelihood model of persuasion. In L. Berkowitz (Ed.), *Advances in experimental social psychology* (pp. 123 – 192). New York: Academic Press, 1986; and in L. Berkowitz (Ed.), *Communication and persuasion: Central and peripheral routes to attitude change* (Vol. 19, pp 123–205). New York: Springer-Verlag.

136. Aaker, J. L., & Sengupta, J. (2000). Additivity versus attenuation: The role of culture in the resolution of information incongruity. *Journal of Consumer Psychology, 2*, 67–82.

137. Stewart, E. C. (1985). Culture and decision making. In W. B. Gudykunst, L. P. Stewart, & S. T. Ting-Toomey (Eds.), *Communication, culture, and organizational processes* (pp. 177-211). Beverly Hills, CA: Sage.

138. Abe, S., Bagozzi, R. P., & Sadarangani, P. (1996). An investigation of construct validity of the self-concept: Self-consciousness in Japan and the United States. In L. A. Manrai & A. K. Manrai (Eds.), *Global perspectives in cross-cultural and cross-national consumer research* (pp. 97–124). London: International Business Press/Haworth Press.

139. Minkov, M. (2007). *What makes us different and similar.* Sofia, Bulgaria: Klasika I Stil Publishing House, 181.

140. Grunert, K. (1988, August). Research in consumer behaviour: Beyond attitudes and decision-making. *European Research,* 172–183.

141. Usunier, J. C. (1996/1997). Atomistic versus organic approaches. *International Studies of Management and Organization, 26,* 90–112.

142. Simpson, L., & Fam, K. S. (2000). Are Asian students' values similar across Asia? An empirical investigation. ANZMAC 2000 *Visionary marketing for the 21st century: Facing the challenge,* 1180–1184.

143. Katzner, D. (2000). Culture and the explanation of choice behavior. *Theory and Decision, 48,* 241–262.

144. Cai, Y. (2007, September 4–6). Investigating the relationship between personal values and mall shopping behavior: A generation cohort study on the new generation of Chinese and their previous generation. *Proceedings of the Fourth Asia Pacific Retail Conference* (pp. 62–87). Bangkok: Manidol University, College of Management.

145. McDonald, W. J. (1995). American versus Japanese consumer decision making: An exploratory cross-cultural content analysis. *Journal of International Consumer Marketing, 7,* 81–93.

146. Rose, G. M., Boush, D., & Shoham, A. (2002). Family communication and children's purchasing influence: A cross-national examination. *Journal of Business Research, 55,* 867–873.

147. Ackerman, D., & Tellis, G. (2001). Can culture affect prices? A cross-cultural study of shopping and retail prices. *Journal of Retailing, 77,* 57–82.

148. Lysonski, S., Durvasula, S., & Zotos, Y. (1996). Consumer decision-making styles: A multi-country investigation. *European Journal of Marketing, 30,* 10–21.

149. Sproles, G. B., & Kendall, E. L. (1986). A methodology for profiling consumer decision making styles. *The Journal of Consumer Affairs, 20,* 267–279. In Lysonski et al. (1996).

150. Hafstrom, J. L., Jung S. C., & Young S. C. (1992). Consumer decision-making styles: Comparison between United States and Korean young consumers. *The Journal of Consumer Affairs, 26,* 146–158.

151. Lysonski et al. (1996).

152. Wolfe, A. R. (1993, February). The "Eurobuyer": How European businesses buy. *Marketing and Research Today,* 45–49.

153. Money, R. B., Gilly, M. C., & Graham, J. L. (1998). Explorations of national culture and word-of-mouth referral behavior in the purchase of industrial services in the United States and Japan. *Journal of Marketing, 62,* 76–87.

154. Calin Niculescu, G. W. (2006). Cultural differences in decision-making processes and their implications for companies operating in south Eastern Europe countries. Masters thesis. European University Viadrina. Countries covered were Austria, Bosnia, Bulgaria, Germany, Greece, Hungary, Romania, Serbia, and the Slovak Republic.

Culture, Communication, and Media Behavior

Many cross-cultural clashes result from the failure to recognize differences in communication. There is no such thing as a universal form of communication. Differences in cultural background, values, and self-concepts may act as impediments to effective communication across cultures. We have learned that ways of expressing emotions, perceptions of self, others, and of phenomena differ, which also gives rise to miscommunication. Communication between people of different cultures is fraught with difficulties.[1]

Each culture has its own rules of communication. However, there are some patterns. One of the clearest distinctions is between high-context and low-context communication. Related to this distinction is how people process information and their expectations of the role, purpose, and effect of communication. Is advertising persuasive by nature, or can it have another role in the sales process? Understanding how advertising works across cultures is of great importance for international companies. People use different media across cultures and use them in different ways. With advanced information technology, new forms of communication have emerged. The way people use these and how the content is designed, such as websites, are also influenced by culture.

COMMUNICATION AND CULTURE

In classic communication theory, communication in a broad sense includes all the procedures by which one mind may affect another. All communication is viewed as persuasive.[2] The traditional model of communication, as depicted in Figure 7.1, includes the source or sender of a message (person, organization, company, brand), the message itself (story, picture, advertisement), the medium (any carrier of the message: a storyteller, newspaper, television, website) and the receiver of the message (person, consumer).

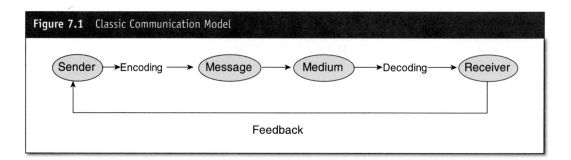

Figure 7.1   Classic Communication Model

In this communication process, the message is selected and encoded in order to transfer meaning. The receiver of the message must be able to receive the message via the medium and decode it. Generally, the sender of the message wants to get feedback to find out if the message has been received and understood. Communication is effective if the message is received as intended by the sender. It is easy to understand that in this process many things can go wrong, even more in mass communications than in interpersonal communication, because the process is difficult to control, and the coding and decoding process may go wrong if the values of sender and receiver do not match.

Advertising, in particular, is a symbolic artifact constructed from the conventions of a particular culture. The sender crafts the message in anticipation of the audience's probable response, using shared knowledge of various conventions. Receivers of the message use the same body of cultural knowledge to read the message, infer the sender's intention, evaluate the argument, and formulate a response. Cultural knowledge provides the basis for interaction. If advertising crosses cultures, it lacks the shared conventions. The purpose of communication may also be different across cultures. Not in all cultures is communication by definition persuasive.

Several cultural dimensions explain variance in communication across cultures, of which individualism/collectivism is the most important. Personal communication styles vary across cultures, along with the self-concept. The independent self, when thinking about others, will consider the other's individual characteristics and attributes rather than relational or contextual factors. An interdependent self emphasizes status, roles, relationships, belonging and fitting-in, and occupying one's proper place.[3] The two types of communication distinguished by Hall—high- and low-context communication (as described in Chapter 2)—fit the differences in communication behavior of interdependent selves of collectivistic cultures and independent selves of individualistic cultures.

High-context communication occurs when most of the information in a message is either in the physical context or internalized in the person; very little is in the coded, explicit part of the message. Meaning may be found purely in the context, for example, when silence is interpreted as disagreement in Japan. Context can also serve to modify the spoken message. Contextual nonverbal factors are facial expressions, body postures, roles, and relationships of communicators. Because in high-context communication the meaning of the message is difficult to assess by outsiders, such communication is viewed to be inaccessible.

Low-context communication occurs when the greatest amount of information is vested in the explicit communication code. In interpersonal communication, individualists emphasize content, whereas collectivists are expected to be able to read the other's mind. Communication in individualistic cultures places the emphasis on speaking skills and speaker strategies for effective communication, whereas collectivistic cultures emphasize listening and interpretation.

Various other factors and cultural dimensions explain differences in communication style. Rapid speech rate, for example, suggests to Americans that the speaker makes true and uncensored statements, whereas for Koreans, slow speech implies careful consideration of others and context.[4]

In low-context communication, information is in the words; in high-context communication information it is in the visuals, the symbols, and the associations attached to them. In individualistic cultures, people are more verbal and textual oriented. They prefer e-mail to the telephone. In collectivistic cultures, people are more visual and oral oriented. They prefer face-to-face conversation or the telephone to e-mail. However, with respect to textual orientation, low uncertainty avoidance is the main explaining variable. In low uncertainty avoidance cultures people read more, write more, and use more textual means of communication.

Textual orientation is reflected in the degree to which people read books and newspapers and use e-mail and other textual devices. Over time, several data on book and newspaper readership show relationships with individualism, power distance, and uncertainty avoidance. Also across Asian countries that are collectivistic to varying degrees, low uncertainty avoidance explains differences in textual orientation. Table 7.1 sums up significant correlations between all sorts of textual behavior and individualism, power distance, and uncertainty avoidance. In particular, low uncertainty avoidance explains various textual behaviors, like reading books, newspapers, use of teletext, e-mail, and the need for written information to protect consumers.

There are important differences between Germans and Russians with respect to the use of e-mail. When Russians use e-mail they tend to make it more personal, for example, by including photographs or graphics. They also like to make within-company e-mail more personal because of their relationship orientation and like to use all sorts of nice greetings. In German individualistic and task-oriented companies, this is not tolerated. The e-mail format must be consistent, and personal salutations are viewed as superfluous, not important for effective communication.

Table 7.1 Textual Orientation: Uncertainty Avoidance, Individualism, and Power Distance

Written Communication Preferences	PDI	IDV	UAI	Predictor	R^2
Europe					
1970: More than 8 books read in past year	−.23	.58*	−.63**	UAI−	.40
1991: More than 12 books read in past year	−.31	.72***	−.68***	IDV	.52
1998: Read a book at least once a month	−.89***	.62*	−.84***	PDI−	.79
2005: Average time spent reading newspapers	−.59***	.44*	−.75***	UAI−	.56
2007: Read 5 books in past year	−.43*	.57***	−.79***	UAI−	.63
2007: Teletext first source or information for news and current affairs	−.55*		−.63**	UAI−	.39
2008: Newspapers first source of information on environmental issues			−.74***	UAI−	.55
2008: Internet activities: e-mail or IM		.56***	−.36*	IDV	.31
2008: Clear written information best way to protect consumers		.34*	−.63***	UAI−	.40
Asia				UAI−	
2008: Mean hours per week reading newspapers	−.71*		−.86***	UAI−	.73
2008: Use e-mail			−.80*		.64

SOURCES: Hofstede et al. (2010) (see Appendix A); 1970 and 1991: Reader's Digest; (1998); *Consumers in Europe* (2001), Eurostat; 2005: European Social Survey; 2007: EBS 278, EMS (2007); 2008: EBS 295, Flash EB 241, EBS 298; Asia: Synovate PAX Asia (2008) (see Appendix B)

The differences between cultures with respect to verbal and visual orientation are reflected in all aspects of marketing communications, such as corporate identity, brand name, package design, and advertising styles. Marketing communications styles are related to personal communication styles. Chinese-speaking consumers tend to judge a brand name based on its visual appeal, whereas English speakers judge a brand name based on whether the name sounds appealing. In Asia, visual symbolism is a key aspect of a firm's corporate identity.[5] A comparative study of package design across seven countries found that packages differ both in three-dimensional design and in the way they communicate through graphical design and vary in the use of textual information; use of color, shape, and symbolism; and degree of structure and detail in the package design. Culture appears to be of great influence on the noted differences.[6]

Whereas U.S. advertising utilizes more copy, Japanese advertising uses more visual elements, and this applies to more Asian countries. Comparative analysis of 642 magazine advertisements of the United States and Korea showed that the proportion of indirect visual forms in Korean ads was significantly higher than in U.S. ads.[7]

COMMUNICATION STYLES

Communication style is made up of verbal and nonverbal styles. Gudykunst and Ting-Toomey have best described the influence of the various dimensions of culture on verbal and nonverbal communication style.[8]

Verbal Styles

Verbal styles can be *verbal personal* or *verbal contextual* according to the degree of context. Another distinction is among elaborate, exacting, and succinct verbal style. *Verbal personal style* is individual-centered language, whereas *verbal contextual style* is role-centered language. Verbal personal style enhances the "I" identity, is person oriented (e.g., English), whereas verbal contextual emphasizes the sense of a context-related role identity (e.g., Japanese, Chinese). The two styles focus on personhood versus situation or status. Verbal personal style is linked with low power distance (equal status) and individualism (low context), whereas verbal contextual style is linked with high power distance (hierarchical human relationships) and collectivism (high context). Verbal contextual style includes different ways of addressing different persons, related to their status. For example, the Japanese language adapts to situations where higher- or lower-placed people are addressed. *Elaborate* verbal style refers to the use of rich, expressive language. *Exacting* or *precise* style is a style where no more or no less information than required is given. *Succinct* or *understated* style includes the use of understatements, pauses, and silences. Silences between words carry meaning. High-context cultures of moderate to strong uncertainty avoidance tend to use the elaborate style. Arab cultures show this elaborate style of verbal communication, using metaphors, long arrays of adjectives, flowery expressions, and proverbs. Low-context cultures of weak uncertainty avoidance (e.g., United States, United Kingdom) tend to use the exacting style. The succinct style is found in high-context cultures of strong uncertainty avoidance (e.g., Japan).

Nonverbal Styles

There are four nonverbal style possibilities: *unique-explicit* and *unique-implicit* style, *group-explicit* and *group-implicit* style. Unique-explicit nonverbal behavior uses expressive nonverbal gestures to express one's unique identity as well as openness and accessibility. It is found in the configuration individualism, low power distance, and low uncertainty avoidance.

Fashion models pose in a defiant way (see Chapter 5). Unique-implicit nonverbal behavior is meant to protect individual privacy while simultaneously using subdued nonverbal gestures to display relational liking, status positions, and power distance. Symbols are used to show position in society; there are behavioral norms that are recognized by the insider, implicit rules of how one should dress, eat, and so on, like French *etiquette*. Group-explicit nonverbal behavior must ensure group norms and regulate public face by the use of expressive nonverbal gestures. This is the style of cultures that combine collectivism with low uncertainty avoidance. Communication is more open. In collectivistic cultures of high uncertainty avoidance, group-implicit nonverbal style upholds group norms and public face, and subdued nonverbal behavior is to display relational liking and power distance. The latter behavior may be related to the extreme use of symbols that support group feelings, like status-enhancing fashion brands and cute characters like Hello Kitty.

The two basic dimensions used are *identity-communality,* which echoes the self-orientation of individualism versus the group orientation of collectivism, and *accessibility-inaccessibility,* which reflects the power distance and uncertainty avoidance dimensions. Accessibility-inaccessibility refers to the degree to which the home environment emphasizes the openness or closedness of occupants to outsiders. Strong uncertainty avoidance people perceive outsiders as more threatening than weak uncertainty avoidance cultures do, and power distance reinforces that. Together, verbal and nonverbal styles are reflected in advertising styles across cultures.

For individuals attempting to function effectively in a foreign cultural setting, nonverbal gestures are a critical facet of interpersonal communication that must be mastered to effectively navigate social situations. The skill to recognize nonverbal language is related to the number of years immigrants have lived in a country.[9]

Interpersonal Communication Styles

Together, verbal and nonverbal communication styles can explain how we communicate. Figure 7.2 clusters countries according to these styles and summarizes the different interpersonal communication styles.

Communication in the cultures in the two left quadrants of Figure 7.2 is direct, explicit, verbal, and personal. People like written communication. In business, they prefer using e-mail to using the phone. They use the exacting style and like data. The sender is responsible for effective communication. Communication in the mostly collectivistic cultures in the two right quadrants is more implicit and indirect. France and Belgium, which are individualistic, are exceptions, and communication can be both explicit and implicit. Communication is role centered. Particularly in Asia communication implies "understanding without words."[10] Children learn to "read the other's mind," to read subtle cues in the communication from others. They are expected to feel the mood or air of each interpersonal situation and improvise appropriate social behavior and communication

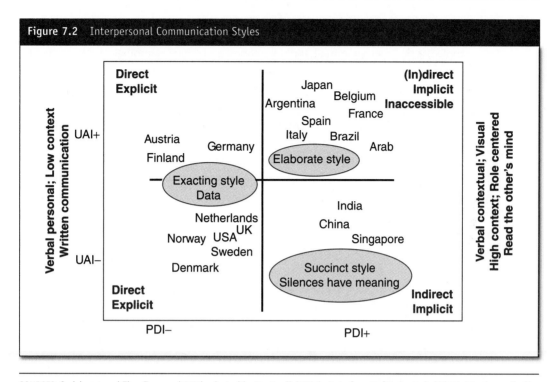

Figure 7.2   Interpersonal Communication Styles

SOURCES: Gudykunst and Ting-Toomey (1988) adapted by De Mooij (2004); Data from Hofstede et al. (2010) (see Appendix A)

depending on the reading of the contextual features.[11] So here the receiver is responsible for effective communication. In cultures in the top right quadrant, the elaborate style is used and communication can be inaccessible. In the lower right quadrant, the succinct style is found. The difference between high and low uncertainty avoidance in Asia does have some implications for differences in explicitness and textual orientation.

In particular, the difference between the indirect style of the East and the direct style of the West can cause grave misunderstandings in international business.[12] In the direct style, wants, needs, and desires are expressed explicitly. Honesty and openness are the norm, and these are achieved through the use of precise, straightforward language behavior. The indirect verbal style refers to verbal messages that conceal the speaker's true intentions. In collectivistic cultures like Japan and Korea, where group harmony and conformity are so important, these are accomplished through the use of imprecise, ambiguous verbal communication behaviors. Wordings such as *absolutely* and *definitely* to express buying intentions are an example of the direct style, whereas *probably* or *somewhat* are examples of the indirect style. In indirect communication cultures, a direct mode of communication can be perceived as highly threatening, whereas in direct style communication cultures the indirect mode can be viewed as too ambiguous.

Communication and the Electronic Media

How people use the Internet, e-mail, mobile phones, and other technological means of communications reflects their interpersonal communication styles. One example is how people deal with the answering machine or voicemail. Japanese—because of stronger emphasis on the relational aspects of communication—find it more difficult than Americans to leave a message on an answering machine. They use their answering machines less often and are more likely to hang up when they reach one than are American callers.[13]

In Asia, usage of technology is related to relationship and context. The mobile phone is used as a medium to communicate with people with strong ties, whereas instant messaging is used as a group-talking tool.[14] People in collectivistic cultures are the leaders in social networking on the Internet, but the number of contacts (what in Western terms are called "friends") can vary. When analyzing the networks people have, it appears that Japanese teenagers have only 7 online "friends" they haven't met, as compared with a global average of 20. Brazilians claim to have most: 46.[15] The key digital device for Japanese youth is the mobile phone, as they generally don't have personal computers until they go to college. The Chinese prefer real-time communications such as instant messaging.[16] Chatting does not necessarily make global communities. It often is a group of existing relations that intensify their communication. Young people of the same city or even in the same street form closed groups that block out strangers with the argument that it is easier to talk to people one knows than to strangers.[17]

In individualistic cultures, social networks are viewed more as providing a path to resources, such as access to people who may have the right information to help deal with a health or medical issue.[18] In collectivistic cultures, Internet networks reinforce the sharing of feelings and ideas. They are a stronger media influence than the traditional media ever were. Of all media, the Chinese say blogs have the strongest influence on purchase decisions.[19] Chinese young generations rely on social networking sites as a source of electronic Word of Mouth (eWOM) in their decision-making process. For social networking sites users, people they communicate with every day, their friends and peers are significant and influential sources of opinions and information on products and services.[20]

Blogging has become a global phenomenon, but the degree to which people blog, their motives and topics vary by country. In 2006 there were more blogs in the Japanese language than in the English language, and the French spent five times as much time blogging as the Americans. For the French, the blog is like the café where they discuss everyday life and politics, fitting in with French argumentative culture.[21] Japanese tend to care less whether their blog influences others, and they are reluctant to reveal their identity, even with the use of aliases.

Whereas in the West the Internet provides an ideal context for self-disclosure, and people tend to release verbal emotions that they wouldn't do in a person-to-person context, self-disclosure has a negative connotation for East Asians. If one partner reveals too much about himself or herself, the other may take it as inappropriate or as an indicator of incompetence.[22] However, also for collectivists the Internet appears to be a context that allows for more self-disclosure than face-to-face relationships do. Yet, North Americans do not perceive East Asians as self-disclosing as much as East Asians perceive themselves to be.[23] Even when East Asians feel they cross their typical cultural constraints and engage in greater self-disclosure than they would do in face-to-face communication, North Americans still view their East Asian partners as indirect, without sufficient self-disclosure. At the same time East Asians feel that their North American partners are overexplicit and rude.[24]

When people of different communication styles interact with each other online, they may encounter unexpected communication behaviors and barriers due to cultural differences. Across cultures, people construct culturally specific norms and patterns of online interactions and relationships and will continue to do so as the role of the Internet evolves and expands.

MASS COMMUNICATION STYLES

Three aspects determine mass communication styles: content, form, and style. Differences in form and style of mass communications reflect interpersonal communication styles. The influence of culture on these three elements can be recognized in literature, mass media programs, advertising, and public relations.

American television, for example, is more action oriented than is Finnish television. Domestically produced Finnish video dramas are much more static. They sacrifice action and setting for dialogue and extreme close-ups.[25] Both the Russians and the Japanese depict boredom in their novels, whereas American novels do not do much with the theme. "Fun is not a Russian concept," says Moscow sociologist Maria Zolotukhina on the difficulties faced by the creators of a Russian version of the popular American children's television program *Sesame Street*.[26] The "happy ending" is rare in Japanese novels and plays, whereas American popular audiences crave solutions. This is reflected in American TV dramas and commercials. The essence of much drama in Western, individualistic literature is an eternal struggle of the hero ("To be or not to be"). Chinese essayist Bin Xin has noted that real tragedy has never existed in Chinese literature because the Chinese have hardly any struggles in their minds.[27] Western readers of Chinese novels find lack of psychological depth and a plot, as most Chinese novels describe what happens without analyzing why it happens.[28] Also, how people behave in literature and what motivates them reflect cultural values. An example from literature is the Italian Carlo Collodi's *Pinocchio,* who is an obedient and dependent child, as compared with the nephews of Disney's Donald Duck, who are much more independent and less obedient. Strong uncertainty avoidance is reflected in the novel *Das Schloss (The Castle),* by Franz Kafka, in how the main character K. is affected by bureaucracy. *Alice in Wonderland,* where the most unreal things happen, is a typical work to originate in a culture of weak uncertainty avoidance: England. No surprise that in the same culture the Harry Potter books originated. U.S. films have been found to be more successful in English-speaking countries,

countries with values similar to the United States.[29] Press releases from American public relations agencies reflect U.S. culture. They are short and to the point.

ADVERTISING STYLES

McCracken states:

> Advertising works as a potential method of meaning transfer by bringing the consumer good and a representation of the culturally constituted world together within the frame of a particular advertisement. The creative director of an agency seeks to conjoin these two elements in such a way that the viewer/reader glimpses an essential similarity between them. When this symbolic equivalence is successfully established, the viewer/reader attributes certain properties he or she knows to exist in the culturally constituted world to the consumer good.[30]

Advertising has developed its own particular systems of meaning. These are by no means universal across borders but rather are often culturally defined and frequently vary from country to country. This suggests a difference in the way advertising is composed and read: that is, a difference in advertising codes. It also suggests that where a different language is spoken, there is likely to be a different set of symbolic references, including myths, history, humor, and the arts. Any ad execution that does not tap into such references is likely to be a blander proposition than one that does.[31]

Although some concepts might be somewhat universal, visual communication of them is not. How the individual reads an advertisement depends on the uses the person has for the interpreted meaning and on his or her unique life experiences and plans. Viewers produce unique interpretations of meaning, often interpreting advertisements in substantially different ways than intended.[32]

Next to viewing advertising as transfer of meaning, in Western advertising theory it is viewed as persuasive communication of which rhetoric is an integral part. *Persuasion* means to "cause someone to do something, especially by reasoning, urging or inducing." It is synonymous for "to win over." The persuasive communication function of advertising is biased toward rational claims, direct address of the public, or "hard sell." All elements of advertising, words and pictures, tend to be evaluated on their persuasive role in the sales process. This is the typical approach of the individualistic-masculine cultural configuration of the culture of origin of advertising theory. Although in other cultures sales will also be the ultimate goal of advertising, advertising's role in the sales process is different. In collectivistic cultures the use of hard sell, or direct address of consumers, turns people off instead of persuading them. Although U.S. studies[33] have shown that persuasion tests (preference shifting) are also adequate for measuring the effectiveness of emotional or image/mood advertising in the United States, it seems inappropriate to use persuasion tests that are based on rational, linear processing to test advertisements meant for people who have a different information-processing system. The effects of advertising in collectivistic cultures in Asia, Latin America, the Arab world, as well as Russia cannot be understood without a thorough knowledge of local beliefs and assumptions.[34]

Jean-Marie Dru, cofounder and Chairman of BDDP Group, writes, "Ads are the mirror of societies, they reflect their respective cultures. . . . Globalization changes nothing. On the contrary, the more sophisticated advertising gets, the more it takes on local colors." Dru characterizes a few advertising styles as follows: "while the British aim for cuteness and are sometimes funny, Americans have gone on to explore a lot of emotions like hunger, sex, fatherhood, etc." In advertising, the Japanese share the French attraction to allegories, showing the brand in context. Half-words are second nature in Great Britain, the country of understatement. Spain makes a specialty of unexpected demonstrations and visual unforgettables. German advertising assumes responsibility for being advertising. German ads seek to sell, they strive to convince. Norwegian advertising is characterized by crazy, random humor. In Asia, there is humility and a humanity that gives messages a very particular sensibility.[35]

Both differences in information-processing and communication styles have resulted in specific advertising styles across cultures. Next to varying appeals and motives, communication styles, including aesthetic preferences, define advertising styles. The strongest distinction is between direct and indirect communication.

Direct Versus Indirect Communication in Mass Communication and Advertising

High-context communication involves transmitting implicit, indirect messages minimizing the content of the verbal message, whereas low-context communication involves being direct, precise, and open. Statements must be to the point and relevant, and people should avoid obscure expressions.

On July 16, 2002, front-page news in India was the high price of the mango. Superficially, one would consider this to be non-news, but for the people in northern India it meant disaster. An expensive mango implied impending drought for 200 million people. Several years without a monsoon had aggravated the lack of water. The mango tree gets water from deep in the soil. If that last bit of water is gone before the fruit ripens, there are few mangos, and the price goes up. Indian journalists are not supposed to predict disaster; they just say that the price of the mango is high.[36]

In advertising the direct style uses the personal pronouns *you* or *we*, whereas the indirect style doesn't address people but uses indirect methods such as metaphors. There are, however, variations in indirectness among collectivistic cultures. Singapore Chinese are, for example, more direct than are people from Taiwan.[37] This is confirmed by a study by Cutler et al.,[38] who examined advertisements from eight different countries (United States, United Kingdom, France, India, Japan, Turkey, Taiwan/Hong Kong, and Korea), measuring the use of a direct, personalized headline, addressing the public by *you* or *your*. The researchers viewed the singular form *you* as an expression of the direct approach, whereas the use of *we* was assumed to be an expression of collectivism. However, both the use of *you* and *we* are in fact reflections of the direct approach. A significant correlation was found between individualism and the measure "personalized headline" used in the content analysis of magazine ads ($r = .62*$). Our own additional analysis of the data published in the article resulted in a more significant correlation with low uncertainty avoidance ($r = -.75***$). Among collectivistic cultures, the degree of uncertainty avoidance explains variation in directness in communications.

A distinction related to direct-indirect is *informational-transformational,* where *informational advertising* refers to advertising that focuses on providing meaningful facts to the consumer, whereas *transformational advertising* is the term used for advertising that uses emotions to move the consumer. Examples of transformational approaches are association, metaphor, storytelling, and aesthetics. Examples of informational approaches are description, comparison, or demonstration. Generally, cross-cultural comparisons of advertising find more informational approaches in individualistic cultures than in collectivistic cultures, where more transformational approaches are used.[39] Figures 7.3–7.6 show examples of direct and indirect advertising style. The direct ones use *you* or *we*. Figure 7.3 shows two examples of the direct approach, an ad for Centrum (UK) and an international

Figure 7.3 Direct Style (United Kingdom, Germany/International)

Figure 7.4   Indirect Style: Metaphor (Belgium, Spain)

Figure 7.5   Direct Style Ads in Indirect Style Culture (France)

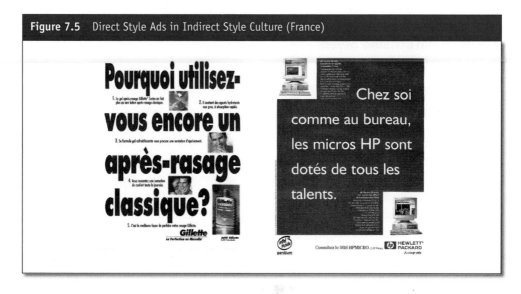

ad for German Bayer. Figure 7.4 shows two examples of Belgian (Audi) and Spanish (Peugeot) car advertising that use the indirect metaphorical approach. The ad for Audi uses the skin care metaphor, saying "We care," and the Spanish ad for Peugeot uses the bull's horns as a metaphor for safety. Figure 7.5 shows two examples of what happens when you only translate the copy without changing the advertising style. The translation may be all right, but this is a direct style message for an indirect style culture. Two Asian examples in Figure 7.6 are ads for Thai Airways International and the Japanese company NSK, selling ball bearings.

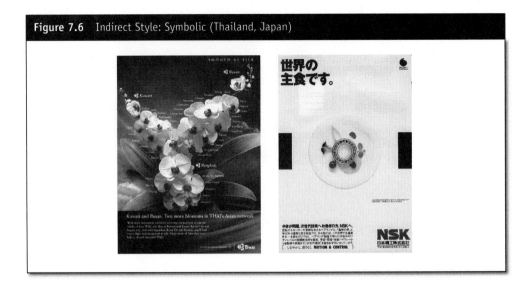

Figure 7.6   Indirect Style: Symbolic (Thailand, Japan)

Mapping Advertising Styles

Countries can be mapped, as in Figure 7.7, according to the different elements of verbal and nonverbal communication style as well as other cultural communication characteristics described previously.

The advertising styles in the lower and upper left-hand quadrant are of individualistic cultures of small power distance. Advertising style is *direct-explicit* and *personal*. The uniqueness of the person or the brand, the importance of identity and personality are reflected in this style. These are the advertising styles of the United States and the countries of northwest Europe. These countries show high use of direct and explicit forms of communication, such as the personalized "lecture" style in advertising. This is the type of advertising in which an identified presenter endorses the product. Many centrally developed television commercials for Anglo-American brands in the category of household products and personal products use this testimonial format. They are carefully directed to focus on the personality of the endorser and not to include any implicit nonverbal behavior. Laskey et al.[40] investigated the effectiveness of different advertising styles for the U.S. market and found that typical person endorser and spokesperson had a positive impact on recall. The person endorser style was used far more frequently than most other styles.

In cultures of strong uncertainty avoidance, positioned in the upper left-hand quadrant of Figure 7.7, advertising is more *serious* and *structured*. The execution of the visuals will be detailed, often including demonstration of how the product works. That is the style of the Germanic cultures, where visuals are more exact and relevant than in weak uncertainty avoidance cultures and verbal information is more detailed. In the weak uncertainty avoidance

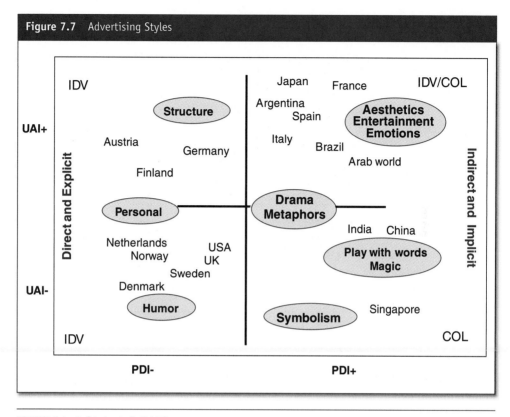

Figure 7.7   Advertising Styles

SOURCE: Data Hofstede et al. (2010)

cultures shown in the lower left-hand quadrant, where ambiguity is tolerated, more humor is used in advertising. In the masculine cultures (United States, United Kingdom), presenters are personalities or celebrities, whereas in the feminine cultures (Scandinavia, Netherlands), the personality of the presenter will be downplayed and the style tends to be softer. Presenters tend to endorse the product and use argumentation.

The two quadrants at the right of the figure include styles that are comparable to the unique-implicit, group-implicit, and group-explicit styles. The upper right-hand quadrant covers several styles. It includes cultures that combine high to medium individualism with high power distance and high uncertainty avoidance (Belgium, France, Poland), showing a unique-implicit communication style that expresses both uniqueness and inaccessibility. *Inaccessibility* is recognized in the frequent references in advertising to other forms of communication such as films, art, or even advertising by others. The upper right-hand quadrant also includes cultures that combine collectivism with high power distance and high uncertainty avoidance, showing an implicit communication style. Countries like Spain, Brazil, and Japan have a more group-implicit and indirect style. Communication is *indirect,* is less likely to offend, and thus upholds public face. Meaning is in the context. Communication is subdued and works on likeability. The preference for *entertainment* as an advertising form is a reflection of this communication style. People like to associate with celebrities more than with abstract values or personal traits. Celebrities are not likely to address the audience directly; they play a more symbolic role and associate more with the product than endorse in a direct way. *Visual metaphors* and *symbols* are used to create context and to position the product or brand in its "proper place," as fits large power distance and collectivistic cultures. Aesthetics are important, and techniques that result in beautiful images are embraced. *Drama* is an advertising form in which actors play actual life or imaginary situations involving a product. The interaction provides the message. It is an indirect style, used in countries like Spain and Italy as well as Latin American cultures. Variations are found between masculine and feminine cultures. In Italy, high on masculinity, a more emotional exaggerated style is favored, and the drama form tends to be theatrical and often not based on real life. In Spain drama style is softer, and metaphorical stories serve to place the product in a context that provides meaning. Although in the United States, the drama style is also used, it is more popular in the countries in the upper right-hand quadrant. Drama in the United States is more slice-of-life, whereas drama in the right-hand quadrants should primarily serve the purpose of entertainment.

The advertising style of collectivistic cultures of medium to large power distance and weak to moderate uncertainty avoidance (displayed in the lower right-hand quadrant of Figure 7.7), is comparable to the group-explicit communication style. Advertising styles must ensure group norms and help maintain face. The use of *visuals,* play with *words* (visually), *songs, magic* and *symbolism* are important in advertising in these cultures, but the audience can be more directly addressed. Advertising in China, Singapore, and India fits this style. These cultures are more direct and textual in their communication, which can be explained by low uncertainty avoidance. A study among business undergraduates from Singapore showed that brands using metaphors were generally perceived to be more sophisticated and exciting, but also less sincere and competent, than brands using literal words and pictures.[41] For India the direct communication style is confirmed by Roland, who states, "Indian modes of communication operate more overtly on more levels simultaneously than do the Japanese."[42]

The Purpose of Advertising

The role and purpose of marketing communications and the way advertising works vary across cultures, in particular between individualistic and collectivistic cultures. In collectivistic cultures, the purpose of advertising is to build relationships and trust between seller and buyer, so positive feelings are included in communication and advertising is entertaining.

Whereas the purpose of advertising in the United States is to sell, persuade, or change attitudes at short term, in collectivistic cultures the purpose of advertising is to build trust and relationships between company and consumer. The desire of Japanese consumers to establish trusting, in-group-like relationships with suppliers and their products is reflected in the tendency of Japanese advertising to focus on inducing positive feelings rather than to provide information.

Miracle[43] summarized the logic of advertising in two distinct ways. The logic of advertising in Western societies is basically to:

1. Tell the audience how you or your product is different.

2. Tell why your product is best, using clearly stated information and benefits.

3. Consumers then will want to buy, because they have a clear reason or justification for the purchase.

4. If they are satisfied, consumers will like and trust the brand, and make repeat purchases.

The logic of advertising in Japan, which is probably valid for most Asian collectivistic cultures, is essentially the reverse:

1. Make friends with the target audience.

2. Prove that you understand their feelings.

3. Show that you are nice.

4. Consumers will then want to buy, because they trust you and feel familiar with you, that is, the company.

5. After the purchase, consumers find out if the product is good or what the benefits are.

This difference is also recognized in Internet advertising. The dominant factor that defines attitudes toward Internet advertising in the United States is information, whereas in Korea the dominant factors are trustworthy and enjoyable.[44] The different purposes explain differences in advertising styles and related models of how advertising works. Persuasion is the model of the Anglo-Saxon world. Likeability is the model of collectivistic cultures, but also of feminine cultures. Likeability can be softness or pure entertainment. The latter is the model of Asia. Figure 5.9 (Chapter 5) showed a U.S. commercial, an example of the persuasion model—problem solving, argumentation, and comparison. Figure 7.8 shows a Spanish example of likeability and softness, and

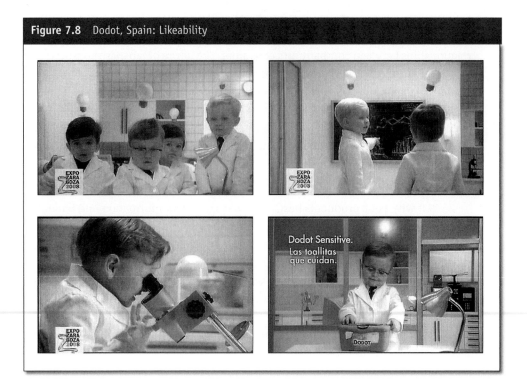

Figure 7.8 Dodot, Spain: Likeability

Figure 7.9 shows a Japanese example of pure entertainment. In the Spanish commercial, the children are the researchers to develop the driest nappy. When they have found it, they shout "Eureka," and they look very satisfied. The Nissin commercial is pure entertainment.

Along with different purposes of advertising, its effectiveness measurement methods should be different. Western measurements of advertising effectiveness use criteria like persuasiveness, attitude change, recall, recognition, brand linkage, message relevance, or likeability.[45] Because of varying mental processes of consumers and those who create advertising, none of these measures can be universal. Persuasiveness is a purpose of advertising mainly applicable to the Western world. The Western proposition is that likeability mediates brand attitude that in turn influences purchase intention. In Chapter 4 (section on attitude and behavior) we discussed the varying relationship among attitude-intention-behavior across individualistic and collectivistic cultures. Because of the importance of situational variables, the relationship is even weaker in collectivistic than it is in individualistic cultures. Relevance is not a condition for effective advertising in collectivistic cultures. In the section on responses to advertising later in the chapter this is further discussed.

Figure 7.9   Nissin Cup Noodle, Japan: Entertainment

In a comparative study among young people in the Netherlands and Japan, Praet[46] found significant differences in advertising likeability of international ads for the global brands Nike, Adidas, Levi's, and Diesel. However, the relationships between likeability and purchase intentions were different. Four measures were used to measure the effect of the ad on purchase intention: ad likeability, brand likeability, personal relevance, and appropriateness. Whereas ad likeability was the strongest predictor of purchase intention in Japan, it did not play a significant role in the Netherlands, where the personal appeal was much stronger. In Japan, ad likeability's main function is to create a favorable feeling toward the advertised brand, which will lead to purchase intention, whereas in the Netherlands the function of ad likeability should be primarily that of gatekeeper for further processing of an ad, which then has to present the viewer with personally relevant information to induce purchase intention. The importance of brand likeability in Japan reflects the strong brand consciousness of the Japanese, as compared with Dutch consumers who are less influenced by brand names and may use a brand's prestige less as a guiding principle for making purchase decisions. The two cultural dimensions at work for explaining the differences are individualism/collectivism and masculinity/femininity.

In sum, the advertising mechanisms that work best are subject to too many specific factors, reflecting market conditions, cultural differences, and brand history, to allow for only one method to measure the effectiveness of advertising across cultures.

WEB COMMUNICATION STYLES

When the Internet became operational for the world, it looked as though its users were part of a global community with similar needs and communication styles, but people soon started to use it for different purposes and in different ways. Subjects from low-context cultures possess a higher degree of information and convenience motivation, and there is more human-message interaction (click into deeper links, using search engine, stay longer for details), while subjects from high-context cultures demonstrate a higher degree of social interaction motivation and human-human interaction (= interacting with other people: participate in customer discussions, provide feedback). High-context communication consumers may trust the information they obtain from their online interpersonal communication, such as chat rooms or online forums, more than do low-context communication consumers who more rely on facts.[47] U.S. citizens are more likely to be motivated to shop online and look for information online than Korean consumers. In contrast, Korean consumers are more motivated than U.S. consumers to head online to fulfill social goals such as making friends, meeting people, and participating in newsgroups. With respect to communication style preferences, U.S. citizens are found to have stronger preferences for verbal styles in comparison to Koreans.[48]

For website design, the same laws operate as for other mass communications. There exists a creative process for generating messages that is independent of the medium and type of message. That is, website and banner designers are not that different from creative directors in the traditional advertising world.[49] Across cultures, people vary in the ways they want to be addressed. Values and motives vary as well as communication styles.

For example, university websites in feminine cultures have a softer approach and are more people oriented than are websites of universities of masculine cultures that are more focused on achievement.[50] Belgian commercial websites reflect hierarchy and more frequent use of proper titles than do Dutch commercial websites.[51] Local websites of India, China, Japan, and the United States are very different and reflect their own cultural values. A striking feature of Chinese websites is the recurrent image of the family theme. Japanese websites exhibit clear gender roles and are rich in colors, aesthetics with pictures of butterflies, cherry blossoms, or other nature scenes. Indian websites prominently depict the titles of the employees to demonstrate hierarchy. U.S. websites are low-context, direct, informative, logical, and success-oriented, with prominent independence themes.[52] Also, local websites for global brands distinguish between low- and high-context communication with more literal visuals in countries like the United States, United Kingdom, and Germany and more symbolic visuals in countries like Japan, Korea, and China.[53]

In 2009 McDonald's used all sorts of culturally relevant approaches in their websites for different countries: people alone or together, images of individuals separate or together with the product, more text or more pictures. In Germany they translate the "I'm loving it" slogan into German *"Ich liebe es,"* and they focus on the origin of the ingredients. The audience is addressed directly. Visuals are more literal than symbolic. Also in the United States and United Kingdom the websites address the public directly, saying "McCafé Your Day" or "Take a look." The websites for Italy, Spain, and France use a more metaphoric style and are more dynamic and animated than the U.K. and German websites. They seem more interested in entertaining than informing about nutritional facts. The Western McDonald's websites use fewer colors than the Asian websites, where symbolism is also stronger. On the main Korean website, the customer is positioned in a McDonald's restaurant; the options are different situations the customer may be in in the restaurant. Young people are seen talking and interacting. Also the Japanese website shows groups. There is little written information. In Japan, products are local, for example, "Nippon All Stars" with the "Chicken Tatsuta."

Generally high-context cultures use more animation and images of moving people in their websites than low-context cultures do, and the images promote values characteristic of collectivistic cultures.[54] The United Kingdom leads both in text-heavy layout and shorter pages, whereas South Korea leads both in visual layout and in longer pages. South Korea utilizes much more multimedia presentation than the United States and the United Kingdom, where presentation more often is based on text only.[55]

There are significant differences between East and West in terms of interactive communication styles used by corporate websites. High-context Eastern websites employ less consumer-message and consumer-marketer interactivity than do low-context Western websites. High power distance explains less consumer-marketer interactivity, as communication between seller-consumer is more hierarchical versus more equal in low power distance cultures where the consumer is treated as a friend. Collectivism explains more group activities among consumers.[56] So in high-context cultures, where people are more motivated by social interaction, online marketers should generate more consumer interaction, such as discussion forums and chat rooms, whereas in low-context cultures, where people search more information, online marketers should emphasize information features such as keyword search and virtual product display.[57] The same applies to government applications of the Internet. In individualistic cultures of low uncertainty avoidance and low power distance, more people use the Internet for obtaining information from public authorities' websites.[58]

In sum, along with culture, there is variation in the way information is presented, the amount of data used, the use of extreme claims, rhetorical style, the use of visuals or animation, the degree to which information is explicit, precise, and direct, and the option to contact people.[59] Companies reaching their local customers through the traditional media do not have international customers to worry about, but the Internet is available for the world to see. Therefore it is critical for companies to develop culturally designed international websites.[60] The more the design of a website conforms to culturally familiar communication styles and cultural habits, the more trust is established and people appear to perform information-seeking tasks faster when using Web content created by designers from their own culture.[61] Cultural adaptation not only enhances ease of use on the website but also leads to more favorable attitudes toward the website, which in turn affects the intention to buy.[62]

MEDIA BEHAVIOR

In Chapter 3, media data were used as examples of the convergence-divergence process. Although at macro level, some media converge, differences at micro level, or what people do with the media, are substantial. This section describes these differences for some of the traditional media, television and newspapers, as well as for the Internet. Generally it was expected that the Internet would be used at the cost of the traditional media, but it has become a medium that is used in addition to the existing media. People now use many media at the same time, which in the Western world is viewed as a negative development. Several words have been developed for this media behavior: *multitasking, parallel processing* or *perpetual partial attention*—watching television, working on the computer and using the mobile phone at the same time. In polychronic cultures like in Asia and Latin America, people have no problems with this and use all sorts of media at the same time with the TV set and computer next to each other. In particular, young people are using a wide variety of media and spending a good part of their time doing so. The biggest media junkies can be found in Malaysia (12.9 hrs a day), Thailand (12.8), and Hong Kong China (12.2).[63]

Television

In Chapter 3 we saw that initially penetration of television sets converged across countries, but since 1997 it has been diverging. Differences in viewing time between countries are more or less stable over time. Of all countries, the Japanese and Americans spend most time watching television. For a mix of poor and wealthy countries, TV viewing is negatively correlated with wealth, that is, in the poorer countries people watch more TV than in the richer countries.[64] Also, more young people mention viewing television as a leisure activity in the lower-income countries in Europe than in the higher-income countries.[65] In the wealthy countries of the developed world, high power distance and masculinity explain variance. In 1998, heavy viewing across 19 countries worldwide[66] was related to high masculinity and large power distance. In 2001 similar relationships were found for 24 countries in western and eastern Europe.[67] High masculinity explained 37% of variance and high power distance explained an additional 14%. In 2006, across 11 wealthy European countries, Japan, and the

United States, 56% of variance of viewing time was explained by masculinity.[68] In 2007, across 18 wealthy European countries, high power distance explained 38% of variance and masculinity an additional 16%.[69] In the Western world television has increasingly become show and violence, to which people in masculine cultures obviously are more attracted than people in feminine cultures.

In collectivistic, polychronic cultures, the TV set tends to be on the whole day, even more so in the masculine cultures. Across Latin American countries, the percentages of people who say they like having the TV set on while doing other things in the house correlate with masculinity.[70]

Across Europe, people hardly watch the programs of other countries, mainly because they do not understand the language. In 1997, 30% of the EMS respondents said they did not understand any foreign language well enough to watch TV news in another language; 54% of Europeans rarely or never watched the news in a foreign language; and 75% rarely or never watched soaps in a foreign language. Even within countries, different language groups will watch different programs. Analysis of People-Meter data from Germany and the three cultural regions of Switzerland showed substantial differences in television viewing.[71] In most countries people prefer watching local programs. The Los Medios y Mercados de Latinoamérica study of 1998 showed that in most Latin American countries, people are more interested in programs from their own countries than from the United States.[72] As a result of these local preferences, many international TV channels have localized language and content. CNN International and MTV started as global channels but have localized content and language.

How people watch TV—alone, with friends or family—is also related to culture. Although in many countries children increasingly have television sets in their bedrooms, French children watch it there less often than do young Swedish children. In France, watching television seems to be a family activity, highly likely to take place in the living room. Also, the degree to which parents give freedom to their children with respect to what they watch varies.[73] Chapter Five discussed relationships between parents and children and differences in the levels of freedom parents allow to children for watching television. Generally in collectivistic cultures, also in Latin American countries, children have greater freedom, whereas in the more individualistic cultures both fathers and mothers decide which programs children may watch.[74]

The more visual orientation of collectivistic and high power distance cultures makes TV more attractive than print media, and within the print media magazines are more attractive than newspapers. High-quality print media are particularly popular among the Japanese, who are avid magazine readers. Magazines are important media for imported luxury brands. The main product categories that dominate the magazine industry in Japan are cosmetics, toiletries, fashion, accessories, automobiles, leisure, and beverage/tobacco.[75]

In addition to watching television programs on the TV set, people can watch them on their computer monitors or on their mobile phone via IPTV (Internet Protocol Television). In Europe, in the feminine cultures where people use the Internet more intensely, they also listen more to Web radio and watch more Web TV.[76]

In the past, TV was something to be enjoyed within the home. As more mobile devices have become available and integrated with IPTV, it has brought more interactivity and flexibility. In countries with limited TV channels, the Internet offers a great deal more. In China in 2006, 70% of adults with broadband at home had watched or downloaded clips from TV programs or whole programs via their PCs; 60% of the Japanese and British had done so, and 39% of the French.[77]

Radio

Radio sets are available in most homes. Ownership of radios per 1,000 persons has been correlated with individualism for the last decades.[78] In individualistic cultures, everybody has his or her own radio or even more than one, whereas in collectivistic cultures one per family may be enough. Even across Latin cultures (Spain, Portugal, and nine Latin American countries)—all scoring more or less collectivistic—the numbers of radio receivers per 1,000 people correlated with individualism ($r = .64*$).[79] Also the time spent on radio listening is related to individualism. For seven countries worldwide, weekly listening hours correlate with individualism ($r = .83***$).[80]

Press Media

As we saw in the section on communication and culture earlier in the chapter, low uncertainty avoidance is the main explaining variable for differences in reading in general, which also explains differences in time spent reading newspapers. National wealth and low power distance explain differences in newspaper readership worldwide, whereas in Europe the configuration of power distance and uncertainty avoidance explains variance. In 1996, for the measurement "Read a newspaper yesterday" for 31 countries worldwide, published by the advertising agency McCann Erickson,[81] .26% of variance was explained by low power distance, and an additional 15% by low uncertainty avoidance. In cultures of high power distance and high uncertainty avoidance, people read fewer newspapers than in cultures scoring low on these dimensions. The latter countries are more participative democracies where people want to be informed about politics and current affairs. The percentages agreeing with the statement "I feel well informed about what is going on in politics and current affairs" are also correlated with low power distance ($r = -.57***$) and low uncertainty avoidance ($r = -.51***$).[82] In the low power distance cultures, young people also are more politically involved, as found in a Eurobarometer survey that asked which political action people viewed as most important. Answers "Join a political party" or "Participate in debates with policymakers" correlated negatively with power distance.[83]

Figure 7.10 illustrates the correlation between newspaper readership and power distance and the stability of the relationship over time for 14 countries in Europe.

The data of 1991 are from Reader's Digest Eurodata and are the percentages of answers to "Read any newspaper yesterday," a more general question than the Eurobarometer

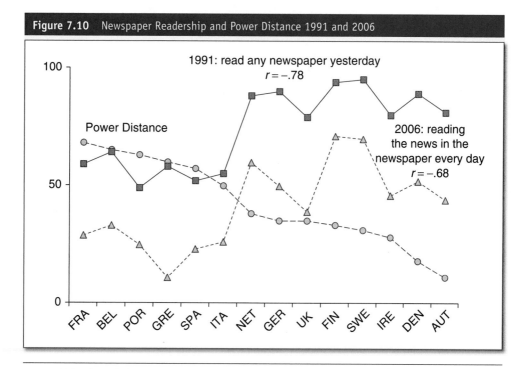

Figure 7.10 Newspaper Readership and Power Distance 1991 and 2006

SOURCE: Hofstede et al. (2010) (see Appendix A); Reader's Digest 1991 and EB 65 (2007) (see Appendix B)

question that asks whether people read the *news* in the newspaper *every day.* So the percentages are lower. But the lines run parallel. A logical result of newspaper reading differences is differences in newspaper ad spending. In 2004, for nine European countries, Japan, and the United States, 72% of variance of newspaper advertising expenditures were explained by low power distance.[84]

In Latin America, press circulation also varies, and variance is partly explained by power distance. In 2007, for 15 Latin countries (Latin America plus Spain and Portugal), 69% of variance of press circulation was explained by gross national income (GNI) per capita and an additional 9% by power distance.[85]

Because the differences in newspaper readership across countries in Europe have existed for more than half a century, they are not likely to disappear. Television will remain a more important medium in the high power distance and masculine cultures than will newspapers.

Magazines have a different function. Differences in readership of news magazines or general interest magazines will be similar to newspaper and book reading. Glossy magazines that have an entertainment function might be compared to television. Across Asian countries, collectivism explains 73% of variance of the percentages of people who say they regularly read fashion or women's magazines.[86] In the 1990s, the magazine share of total advertising expenditures correlated with strong uncertainty avoidance and high power distance.

THE INTERNET

The Internet by its very nature is a global communications channel with the potential to reach consumers anywhere in the world. However, access to the Internet is still concentrated in the developed world. Wealth and individualism are the primary determinants of the structure of international hyperlink flows.[87] Within the developed world, from the start, in the low uncertainty avoidance cultures people have adopted the Internet fastest, and there still are significant relationships between Internet penetration and usage and uncertainty avoidance. In 2004, whereas GNI per capita explained variance of the numbers of Internet users per 1,000 people for 55 countries worldwide, low uncertainty avoidance explained 32% of variance in 26 wealthy countries.[88] In 2002, in Europe the percentages of people without access to Internet, neither at home nor at work were related to high uncertainty avoidance, which across 20 countries explained 46% of variance.[89] The relationship is illustrated in Figure 7.11 for 12 countries ($r = .91***$). The same chart illustrates data of 2007, the percentages of people who never use the Internet apart from professional activity.[90] For 24 European countries, uncertainty avoidance explains 59% of variance ($r = .77***$). For the 12 countries in Figure 7.11, $r = .94***$.

Next to uncertainty avoidance, masculinity explains variance of Internet usage and some of its applications. Low masculinity often is a second or third predictor after GNI per capita and low

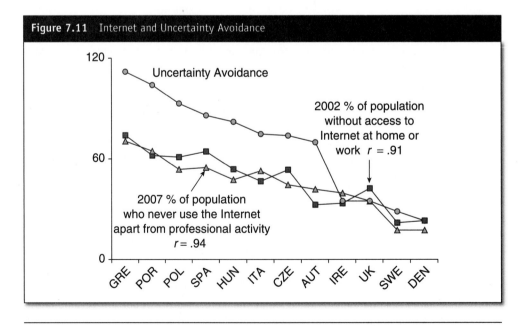

Figure 7.11   Internet and Uncertainty Avoidance

SOURCE: Hofstede et al. (2010) (see Appendix A); European Social Survey (2002); EBS 278 (2007) (see Appendix B)

uncertainty avoidance. For example, in 2007, for 23 countries in Europe and Asia, GNI per capita explained 47% of variance of Internet penetration and low masculinity an additional 14%.[91]

In the masculine cultures people use the Internet more for business, to be more productive or competitive, and in the feminine cultures people will use it more for personal reasons, to enhance the quality of life. Time spent on the Internet is related to femininity. In 2007 in Europe, the percentages of people who said they used the Internet every day correlated negatively with masculinity.[92] In 2007, for 23 countries in Europe and Asia, the average monthly Internet hours per user correlated with low masculinity.[93]

Whereas Internet usage rises with income in the United States, the relationship is not so clear in Japan, where people access the Internet mostly at work.[94] In Japan, the Internet has become more representative with the introduction of new carriers, such as Internet services by mobile phone. Ownership of personal computers in Japan has been relatively low for several reasons. The configuration of high power distance, collectivism, and high uncertainty avoidance explains relatively low penetration of home computers in Japan. In this configuration there is a stronger separation between home and work life; people don't take work home, so for that purpose they don't need home computers. Also, parents don't help children as much with homework, so for that purpose also there is no need for a home computer. Also across countries in Latin America, mostly of high power distance, the Internet is more used for education purposes in the relatively low power distance cultures. This is also relevant for Asia. A study by Roper Starch Worldwide[95] confirms this difference in computer usage. Whereas Americans use their computers for many things related to children and education, in developed Asian countries people are less likely to use computers for teaching or entertaining children or for school or college work. Also Italians rarely use computers on children's behalf. In Chapter 5, we discussed that in high power distance cultures parents participate less in the education of their children, and computer use for educational purposes will be in the schools. In individualistic cultures, children mostly access the Internet in the home or at a friend's home. As discussed in Chapter 5, accessing the Internet in an Internet café happens more in collectivistic cultures, and this also applies to children. Table 7.2 summarizes a number of Internet activities and the significant correlations with the dimensions.

The basic roles of the Internet are *information* (search for, compare, and buy products), *entertainment* (games, online video) and *social* (e-mail, social networks, and chat rooms). The information role is more important in individualistic cultures, whereas the entertainment and social roles are more important in collectivistic cultures. Playing and downloading games, downloading free music, chatting, and blogging are Internet activities that correlate with high power distance and collectivism, whereas in individualistic cultures people use the Internet more for searching information.[96]

Quite a few Internet activities are positively correlated with long-term orientation, which indicates pragmatism. It looks like in long-term orientation cultures people adopt new technology to enhance a large number of existing activities and do these in a more intensive way than in the short-term-oriented cultures that are more traditional.

Table 7.2 Use of Internet for Various Purposes

	PDI	IDV	MAS	UAI	LTO
Internet connection at home[1]	−.55***	.77***		−.81***	
Internet use, % of total population[2]	−.61***	.34*		−.36*	
Use Internet several times a day[3]		.36*	−.45*	−.38*	
E-mail or IM[3]		.56***		−.36*	
E-mail, communicate with foreigners[7]	−.50*		−.53***	−.61***	
Search for information[5]	−.74*				
Buying products or services[3]	−.46*	.61***		−.58***	
Banking[3]	−.45*	.55***	−.41*	−.53***	
Electronic forms for public administration[3]	−.57***	.60***		−.50**	
Digital downloads per head of population[4]			.67*		
Play, download games[3]	.51***	−.47**		.41*	
Download free music[3]	.43*	−.41*		.56***	
Transfer content to other devices[3]	.53***	−.55***		.41*	
Chat, IM[5]		−.89***			
Read blogs[5]		−.89***			
Contribute content[5]		−.79*			
Watch films[5]		−.69*			.83*
Download music[5]		−.78*			
Share files[5]		−.77*			.70*
Video sharing[5]		−.73*			
Young People					
Use Internet[9]			−.34*	−.52***	
Own Internet[6]		.79*			
Use Internet for educational purposes[6]	−.75*				
Use for SMS[6]	−.71*	.72*			
Use for social networks[6]					.77*
Use for watching TV programs[6]					.90***
Use for leisure: Internet, video games[8]	.57***			.36*	
Child allowed to spend a lot of time online[9]				−.54***	
Child accesses Internet from family computer[9]	−.53***	.59***		−.54***	
Child accesses Internet at school[9]	−.35*	.53***		−.53***	
Child accesses Internet at friend's home[9]	−.34*			−.63***	
Child accesses Internet in Internet café[9]		−.39*		.34*	

SOURCES: Hofstede et al. (2010) (see Appendix A); [1]2009 Flash EB 243, 18 countries GNI/cap > $20,000, Europe; [2]2009 TGI product book, 31 countries GNI/cap > $12,000, worldwide; [3]2008 Flash EB 241, 25 countries Europe; [4]2006 Ofcom International Communications Market, 9 countries Europe, United States, Japan; [5]2008 Synovate, Asia PAX digital life, 7 countries, Asia; [6]2008 Ibero-America Interactive generation, 10–18 years, 7 countries Latin America; [7]2007 EBS 278, 24 countries Europe; [8]2007 Flash EB 202, 25 countries Europe; [9]2008 Flash EB 248, 24 countries Europe (see Appendix B)

The Internet takes time from the old media or other activities. In 2000, people across cultures had different views on what activities would be replaced by the Internet.[97] In the various countries, these were the activities on which people already spent relatively little time. An example is Internet usage replacing book reading in collectivistic cultures, where people read fewer books anyway. In masculine and collectivistic cultures, where people generally conduct less active sports, people expected that the Internet would reduce time spent on sport or physical activity. In the United States and in the United Kingdom, where people traditionally have read newspapers and magazines, there are indications that time spent on the Internet will come primarily from time spent watching television rather than from reading newspapers or magazines.[98] In Latin American, mostly collectivistic and polychronic cultures, where people are used to doing more things at the same time, Internet usage and TV viewing are not mutually exclusive activities. In the home, the TV is placed next to the computer monitor so that people can watch the two things at the same time.[99]

The Internet has become part of everyday life. People routinely integrate it into the ways in which they communicate with each other, moving among phone, computer, and in-person encounters. Instead of social relationships disappearing, people's communities are transforming; however, people's networks continue to have substantial numbers of relatives and neighbors—the traditional bases of community—as well as friends and workmates. E-mail and social network services are indeed used for contacting distant friends and relatives, but even more frequently they are used to contact those who live nearby.

The effects of the Internet confirm the theory of McLuhan[100] who said that technological innovations are merely enhancements or extensions of ourselves. They are generally used by people to enhance current activities; they do not fundamentally change people's values or habits.

RESPONSES TO MARKETING COMMUNICATIONS

Responses to marketing communications are an important consumer behavior domain because expenditures on marketing communications tend to be high. Most research has been done on cross-cultural responses to advertising. This section of the chapter first touches on another marketing communication instrument, sales promotion.

Responses to Sales Promotions

Sales promotions vary across countries, and consumers generally respond positively to the type of sales promotions that they are used to. For example, attitudes toward coupons are influenced by familiarity with coupons. Other attitudes that play a role are attitudes of family and friends toward using coupons, fear of embarrassment or losing face when using coupons, as well as consumers' price consciousness. In the United States, where coupons are a frequently used promotional instrument, Hispanic Americans have negative attitudes toward coupons, partly because they view coupons as a sign of low class or inability to pay full price. Also Japanese and Korean consumers are embarrassed to redeem coupons, although coupons have been used in Japan for quite some time. Thai consumers appear to have the highest relative regard for coupons as compared with sweepstakes. To a lesser extent also consumers in Taiwan prefer coupons to sweepstakes. Malaysians respond least favorably to coupons.[101] What appeals to long-term orientation cultures are promotional activities that offer discounts or long-term saving opportunities, such as saving stamps that build longer-term relationships between consumers and brands. Responses to sweepstakes are likely to vary with the degree to which people like to or are allowed to gamble. Sweepstakes, like gambling, are submitted to varying legal constraints across cultures.

Responses to Advertising

Responses to advertising are related to various aspects: the purpose of advertising, general acceptance of advertising, consumers' relationships with the media, the specific advertising appeal, and executional styles.

Whereas the purpose of advertising in individualistic cultures is to persuade, in collectivistic cultures it is to build trust between buyer and seller, which results in different advertising styles, for example, direct address versus entertainment. Responses to direct style persuasion will be different than responses to entertainment, and thus, measurement of responses should not be the same. An example of a measurement item is "relevance," which in individualistic cultures is used to measure a viewer's affective reaction to a television commercial. The response item used is "As I watched I thought of reasons why I would use the product." For measuring the relevance of a TV commercial, thinking about the product is part of this process. For Asian recipients, no such relationship can be found. Generally, relevance may work in individualistic cultures, but the use for measuring affective response in collectivistic cultures is questionable.[102] In collectivistic cultures, contextual cues are more relevant for predicting attitudes than product-related claims. Whereas, for example, U.S. consumers will list more thoughts related to the product, Taiwanese consumers list more thoughts related to the aesthetic qualities of an advertisement.[103] In collectivistic, high-context cultures there is no direct link between a commercial and product usage in the minds of consumers because advertising works in a different way. Also, within individualistic cultures persuasion is likely to work differently. Psychological research indicates that external locus of control makes people more susceptible to being persuaded, socially influenced, and conform more than internal locus of control does.[104]

Responses to advertising that are typically measured are attitude toward the ad and attitude toward the brand, assuming that consumers' reactions to products and brands are influenced by their evaluations of advertising. The attitude toward the advertisement (A_{ad}) is defined as a predisposition to respond in a favorable or unfavorable manner to a particular advertisement during a particular exposure occasion. A_{ad} is influenced by not only the particular ad but also by the viewer's attitude toward the advertiser and advertising as an institution. The latter is based on a general predisposition to respond in a consistently favorable or unfavorable manner toward advertising in general. The former is related to the credibility of the ad, attitude to the sponsor, and likeability of the ad. These measurement parameters are mostly valid for individualistic cultures. In collectivistic cultures, people's attitudes and behavior are not consistent, so the relationship between the parameters may be different.

Acceptance of Advertising in General

Several factors influence perceptions of advertising in general: the political climate, culture, and the advertising landscape of a country. In small markets, where international advertisers dominate with messages that do not fit the culture of the consumer, people tend to dislike advertising more than in large markets with much homegrown advertising. U.S. students, for example have been found to have a significantly greater number of affective responses to advertising in general than do Danish and Greek students.[105]

The degree to which advertising is praised varies across countries. A universal finding is that advertising in general is praised for its economic effects, and it is criticized for its social effects.[106] In developing economies, because of lesser knowledge of how advertising works, expectations of the economic effects may be higher than in developed economies. A study of 1994 found that Russians at that time viewed advertising very positively. They saw it as an "engine of trade."[107]

Several surveys have asked people general questions about acceptance of advertising, its informative role, and liking of advertising. There are major differences in perception and acceptance of advertising across Europe. In 1992, 71% of the British, 66% of the French, and 56% of the Germans regarded advertising as a positive component of everyday life. In most countries the most-cited benefit of advertising was the informational content of advertising. Advertising as entertainment was acknowledged as a benefit only by the French.[108] La Ferle et al.[109] found that in collectivistic cultures, consumers are less skeptical of advertising. This may be due to the fact that advertising is more entertaining in collectivistic cultures.

Attitudes toward Internet advertising have become increasingly negative. Uncontrollable formats of Internet advertising tend to interrupt and irritate Internet users, thus negatively affecting their attitudes toward Internet advertising.[110]

Consumers' Relationships With the Media

In 2001, liking advertising on TV and radio in Europe was correlated with low individualism and high uncertainty avoidance.[111] In Spain 24% of respondents and in Germany only 6% liked TV advertising more than TV programs. If people prefer specific media, they also like advertising in these media or attribute an informative role to advertising. Across countries, reading the news in newspapers every day goes together with viewing advertising in newspapers as a source of new product information. Also EMS data show a positive correlation between heavy to medium press readership and viewing advertising in newspapers as a useful source of product information. For television we see similar relationships. Heavy TV viewing is related to a positive attitude toward advertising on TV. The percentages of heavy viewers correlate positively with the percentages of respondents saying that advertising on TV is a useful source of product information ($r = .66***$).

The overall explaining variables are cultural. Both a positive attitude to advertising in newspapers and newspaper readership are correlated with low uncertainty avoidance. Viewing advertising on television as a useful source of information correlates with low individualism, so for the more visually oriented collectivistic cultures, television has an informative role. This role is extended to advertising. A conclusion is that if people use specific media, they also like or attribute an informative role to advertising in these media.

Advertising Appeals

Advertising appeals that are effective in one culture may result in different responses when used in another culture. Many American marketers assume Europe to be a homogeneous market with similar responses to their advertising. Also marketers targeting eastern European countries tend to select a region-centric approach without differentiating for the various countries in the area, but as in the West, across Eastern Europe countries are very different. Whereas the Polish like to show off, responses by the Romanians to status advertising tend to be negative.[112] Advertising produced in one culture often is not understood in another one. An example of how responses to specific advertisements across cultures vary is the Benetton campaign. In four different national cultures (British, Norwegian, French, and German), the intended messages that Benetton hoped to convey with the images used in their advertisements have not been interpreted as they had wished.[113]

Advertising appeals generally reflect buying motives that are related to the product category, and for each category these motives are culture specific. Chapter 5 provided several examples of category- and culture-specific motives. In cultures where advertising has a long history, the product-specific appeals are ingrained in the culture. Historically in the United Kingdom, beer advertising uses humorous appeals, and historically German car advertising uses technological appeals. But also such differences have been found in newly emerging markets. In China specific appeals exist for specific product categories. "Modernity," for example, is frequently found in service and automobile advertising. "Family values" occur frequently in household appliance advertising, and "tradition" is mostly found in food and drink commercials. In Hong Kong China, "modernity" is found in service and automobile advertising, but "enjoyment" is found more in food and drink advertising.[114] Important Chinese appeals are harmony between people, harmony between people and society and between people and nature. Also modesty and face are important values found in advertising.[115]

A word about sexual appeals in advertising. Studies searching for explanations of usage and acceptance of sexual appeals in advertising tend to assume cultural masculinity to be an explaining variable, but this is not the case. One study found that sexual appeals are more rejected in high than in low uncertainty avoidance cultures.[116] A major problem when measuring sexual appeals is the definition. Whereas in some countries a nude or scarcely dressed person in advertising is considered to have a sexual appeal, in other countries there is no such association.

Executional Styles

The previous sections of the chapter described how advertising styles follow interpersonal communication styles and different perceptual processes. The way an Asian perceives and evaluates writing differs significantly from the way an American views writing. Aesthetic expression is different, and so is the use of colors. This is reflected in advertising responses.[117] In particular, differences in high- and low-context communication will influence responses to advertising. Responses of members of high-context cultures to low-context communication are likely to be different from what is intended by the creator of a low-context communication advertisement. Like direct verbal address, the use of simple pictures is likely to be viewed as offensive by consumers who have learned to process more complex images. A high-context audience may over-read the meaning of a too simple visual image and develop a negative affective evaluation due to the message's apparent lack of metaphorical complexity. This type of audience is trained to read the metaphorical meaning of messages and will be uninspired by the lack of visual imagery in simple visuals that merely show the product.[118] Or people will take out information the creator of the advertisement has never meant to include.

If people are used to a specific advertising style, that is what they will expect from advertising. TGI[119] found that among Internet users 51.4% of Spanish respondents expected advertising to be entertaining, as compared with only 32.2% of Germans.

Part of advertising style is the basic form companies choose, for example, "lesson," "drama," "entertainment," the use of presenters, or comparative advertising. The culture of producers of advertising makes them prefer some basic forms to others. International advertisers sometimes use executional styles or basic forms of their own culture for other cultures than their own where they do not fit. Responses to advertising that uses basic forms that do not fit may not be as positive as responses to culture-fit executional styles. The result may be loss of effectiveness. The best example is the use of comparative advertising, which is basically a form that fits competitive (individualistic-masculine) cultures. Comparative advertising is not appreciated in most cultures that score low on individualism, low on masculinity, and high on uncertainty avoidance. In collectivistic cultures comparison with the competitor disturbs harmony. Thus, the use of superlative and comparative claims, or terms like "King of the beers," is not acceptable in China.[120] In low masculine cultures, modesty is a value that prevents you from saying that you are better than the other.[121]

In collectivistic cultures, more celebrities are used in advertising because advertisers like to link their brands to concrete personalities. But the roles of celebrities are different from those in individualistic cultures where generally celebrities endorse brands with argumentation. In collectivistic cultures, celebrities convey implicit rather than explicit messages and appeal to conformity rather than uniqueness.[122]

Some basic forms have become the property of specific advertisers. Examples are the testimonial format used by the household good producers Procter & Gamble and Unilever. Some brands (e.g., Ariel, Dove) seem to be exclusively linked to that format. Likewise, the use of humor is likely to be more related to the culture of advertising managers than to the degree to which people in some cultures have a greater sense of humor than in others. Humor doesn't travel because it plays with the conventions of societies that usually are historically defined. When people laugh at humorous advertising of other cultures, it often is for the wrong reasons.

Execution of Advertising

Differences that are generally pointed at as "merely" executional aspects are also related to culture. Preferences for older people in advertising in China, for example, relate to high power distance. The consistent wish of advertisers in the United Kingdom to have a strong headline and pay-off in advertising is related to the direct communication style of that culture. The type of music, the pace of speaking and music, the frequency a brand name is mentioned in an ad, all are reflections of the culture of the country where the ad originates. Because the purpose of much Japanese advertising is to entertain the audience, it takes a long time before any mention is made of the brand or the advertiser. Often in commercials there is no benefit, no "reason why," because the Japanese tend to buy on the basis of their feelings of familiarity with the seller. Whereas in the United States elicited emotions are related to brand or seller from the start of the commercial, in Japan this relationship is absent, and identification with the company or brand comes only at the end of the commercial. Because of the importance of trust in the company as an advertising goal, the company name is more frequently shown in Korean and Japanese advertising than in U.S. advertising. Whereas U.S. advertisements often focus primarily on the brand, not including the company name in countries like Korea or China would be ill advised.[123] In most Asian countries television commercials end with a shot of the company's logo. Procter & Gamble in Japan learned that their commercials worked much better when they incorporated a P&G "talking cow" that conveyed the message that the products were made by a good, solid, credible, and trustworthy company.[124]

It is often said that a central idea or concept can be universal, but execution or executional details must be varied with culture. However, all details of an advertisement work together and, consequently, changing only some executional details will not have the desired result. Advertisements are wholes, not sets of headlines, pictures, and text. For some product attributes that are meaningful for different cultures, the central message may be similar, but for greater effectiveness, style and execution should be different. Examples of how the U.S. brand Kellogg's ties into the various styles and execution of different cultures are presented in Figures 7.12 to 7.17. The U.S. commercial displayed in Figure 7.12 is explicit about values that are typical of the United States. It starts with a field where wheat

Figure 7.12   Kellogg's Frosted Flakes, United States

starts to grow and ends with a sports field. The voice over says, "On the right field it is amazing what can grow. Things like self-confidence, friendship and values that last a lifetime. All it takes is someone to plant a seed. Kellogg's Frosted Flakes is building fields for your kids to play, to grow, to be their very best."

Figure 7.13 shows pictures from a German Kellogg's Day Vita commercial. It shows a tough, independent woman who is repairing something in her kitchen. She is fit because she eats Kellogg's. The commercial shows pictures of how the product works and ends with a picture saying that the effect is proven.

Figure 7.13   Kellogg's Day Vita, Germany

Figure 7.14 shows pictures from a French commercial for Kellogg's Special K. This is soft drama. We see two women friends discussing the product and much more, and they keep talking while the husband of one of them is really getting annoyed. The product attribute here is slimming.

Figure 7.15 shows pictures from an Italian commercial for Kellogg's All-Bran. This commercial is like a thriller. Detectives barge into a house where a couple is sitting eating Kellogg's. There is some argumentation about the product, there are some pictures with details of how it works and in the end they all sit down eating Kellogg's.

Figure 7.16 shows pictures from a Japanese commercial for Kellogg's Special K, with Japanese fashion model Miyuki Koizumi. In an interview, Kellogg's marketing manager in

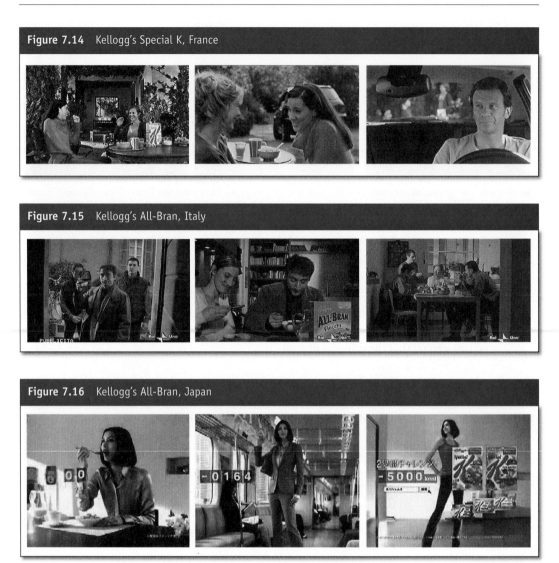

Figure 7.14 Kellogg's Special K, France

Figure 7.15 Kellogg's All-Bran, Italy

Figure 7.16 Kellogg's All-Bran, Japan

Japan[125] states that Kellogg's adapts their products and marketing in each country, so not only advertising, but also the product, ingredients, and taste. In Japan, for example, the product is less sweet. For Japan a special product was developed based on unpolished brown rice (*genmai*), and in India more iron is added as Indians tend to lack iron. In Japan mostly younger women eat cereals.

Figure 7.17 shows pictures from an Indian commercial for Kellogg's Special K. The product attribute is slimming, as in the French commercial. The woman picks out a dress for a party to be given in two weeks time by the boss of her husband. She brings the dress to the tailor to make it smaller. He doesn't believe it will fit her in two weeks time, but it does. We

Figure 7.17   Kellogg's Special K, India

see her in the dress at the party, and all men admire her. In India the wish to be slim seems to catch on as a trend for young women, but more in the north than in the south of India. Slimming is mostly done by fasting, so this is a new way of slimming. The target group clearly is upper class, indicated by showing an occasion like a boss's party and showing the woman eating at a table. A large part of India still sits and eats on the floor, cross-legged, and not on a dining table.

BRAND COMMUNICATIONS ACROSS CULTURES

Chapter 6 discussed brands as association networks in the mind of the consumer. Cultural values are part of such association networks as a result of brand communications that reflect these values in the appeal, in the advertising style, and in execution. Western brand managers select values consciously when formulating their brand strategies, whereas Asian marketers don't do this explicitly, but values are attached to brands by associating them with specific persons. Whether explicit or implicit, all marketing communication carries values. Values offer an opportunity to differentiate brands by going beyond attributes and benefits. Adding values creates association networks that distinguish the brand vis-à-vis the competitive brands in the category and thus can help build strong positions for brands. The attributes, benefits, and values of association networks can be used to develop value structure maps, including similarities and differences across cultures that can help develop a cross-cultural strategy.

Value Structure Maps

A tool for strategy is the *value structure map* (VSM), which describes how a particular group of subjects tends to perceive or think about a specific product or brand.[126] A value structure map links the product's attributes and benefits to values.

Attributes can be concrete or abstract, with variations. For example, in India objects have meanings at three levels, aesthetic, functional, and spiritual, whereas in Western cultures

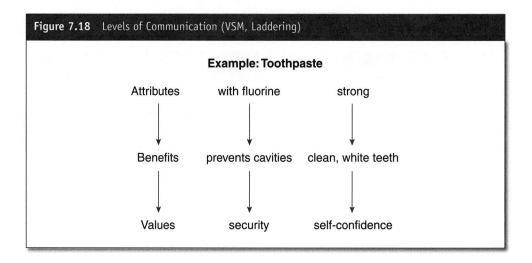

Figure 7.18   Levels of Communication (VSM, Laddering)

meanings are usually restricted to functional and symbolic.[127] Benefits can be functional or psychosocial consequences of the product's attributes. Values, as preferred states of being, can be the consequence of benefits. Value structure maps provide a structure of people's associations with a brand at the three levels: attributes, benefits, and values. They show the connections among the types of associations of people and a specific attribute of a product and its subsequent benefits and values. This connection, developed by Gutman,[128] was presented as the means-end chain model. Gutman formulated the essence as follows: Means are objects (products) or activities in which people engage; ends are valued states of being such as happiness, security, accomplishment. A *means-end chain* is a model that seeks to explain how the choice of a product or service facilitates the achievement of desired end-states. Such a model consists of elements that represent consumer processes that link values to behavior.

The technique used to develop means-end chains is called *laddering,* an in-depth, one-on-one interviewing technique used to develop an understanding of how consumers translate the attributes of products into meaningful associations with respect to the self.[129] By using this laddering technique, sets of linkages can be determined among perceptual elements, which are then represented at different levels of abstraction. Figure 7.18 shows three levels of associations for toothpaste, and Figure 7.19 shows six levels of (hypothetical) associations for Coca-Cola. An example of a value structure map is one for automobiles in Figure 7.20, including values that appeal to different cultures.

Advertisers who want to differentiate a brand can follow different routes via attributes and benefits to reach end values, as shown in Figure 7.20. In this system, the product attributes may be the same worldwide, yet different values may be connected to the attributes (to be found through research), reflecting different cultures. An example of a route in the VSM for automobiles is selecting, for example, one attribute, a Strong motor, and one end

Figure 7.19   Levels of Communication: Coca-Cola

Concrete attributes ⟶ Brown, fizzy, red can

Abstract attributes ⟶ American, modern

Functional benefits ⟶ Everywhere, always

Psychosocial benefits ⟶ My friends drink it, socialize

Instrumental values ⟶ Provides correct user image

Terminal values ⟶ Belonging, security

Figure 7.20   Value Structure Map: Automobiles

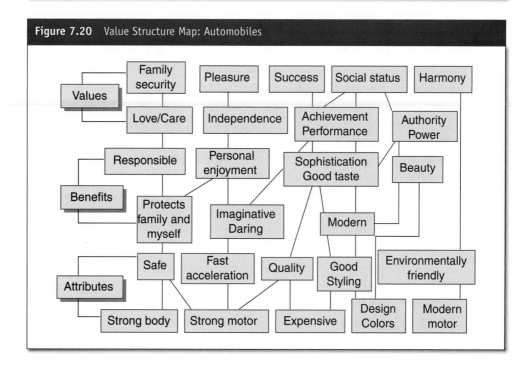

value, Pleasure, and following the route Fast acceleration → Imaginative, Daring → Personal enjoyment → Independence → Pleasure. Another route takes the same attribute as a starting point but continues via Safe → Protects the family and myself → Responsible → Love/Care → Family security. This could be an example of a route for a feminine culture. Volvo has used this route from the attribute Strong body. A route for cultures of the configuration collectivist-high power distance-high uncertainty avoidance would be

Design/Colors → Good styling → Sophistication/Good taste → Authority/Power or achievement → Social status. Different routes can be followed, depending on the target group, the culture, and the competition. Even when similar abstract associations exist in such maps, they can have different links. Value for money, for example, was found to be positively associated with good acceleration and speed in China, but with good styling in Korea and France.[130] In a multinational campaign targeted at countries that are similar with respect to one or more dimensions, it may be possible to select one route with values that the different countries have in common. Yet, depending on the specific cultures, the communication style may have to be different.

THE FUTURE OF GLOBAL ADVERTISING

This book has presented information that can help readers to assess global advertising formats. Decisions on global uniform advertising are based on wrong assumptions and made for the wrong reasons. Short-term pressures on budgets make it tempting to reuse or modify material that has proved to be successful in one country for rollout in others, or a timing issue is involved, when an ad is used until a better one is developed. Supporting ineffective ads may result in waste of media expenditures or even damage the brand in the long term.[131]

Most assumptions underlying the choice of standard global advertising are based on the existence of global communities with similar motives and fundamental universal emotions. In the 21st century the idea is outdated, although in some business schools or advertising agencies the concept is still central. In 2000, Sally Ford-Hutchinson, global director of planning of D'Arcy, a global advertising agency operating in 75 countries around the world, said, "We have to look for similarities across the cultures and we come down to fundamental universal emotions like motherhood, teenage/parental relationships—these are the same in Cairo or Cologne. . . . I believe that a good strategic idea will travel."[132] In such statements "a good creative idea" generally is a creative idea conceptualized in the home country of the person who makes the statement, which is made in abstract terms. Everybody agrees on abstract ideas like love or happiness, but made concrete they don't travel. Those who have read the previous chapters in this book know that the idea of universal emotions is based on ethnocentric research and on personal consistency needs of Western marketing managers that they extend to the strategies they develop. Mental and social processes and consumer behavior vary so fundamentally across cultures that global advertising is a true myth of the past century.

Both market differences and consumer differences make global advertising wasteful. Markets are different because the competitive environment is different and products and brands often are in different stages of the product or brand life cycle. Consumers are different because of historical differences in habits, needs, and motives and the way they process information. Interpersonal and mass communication styles vary, and thus a proposition or appeal that works in one culture will not work in a similar way in another culture.

Companies vary in their strategic thinking. Whereas Western international companies tend to focus on similarities, uniqueness, and universal values and insist on consistency, East Asian companies tend to be flexible because of particularistic thinking and the need for conformance to local values. International companies select international agency chains for efficiency reasons, but they do not sufficiently use the experience and cultural sensitivity of the local agencies that are part of the chain. Western international companies would develop more effective international advertising if they would take the advice of local personnel seriously. Too often such advice is discarded as the "not-invented-here syndrome." For truly effective global branding and advertising, the direction of the future will be toward flexibility and effectiveness instead of uniqueness and consistency. Increasingly, research finds that people better process information that fits their processing styles.

Also, design can be a tool to emphasize uniqueness, or it can be a tool for getting closer to local market conditions and user needs. Whereas Western companies tend to focus on design to strengthen a unique identity that also must be consistent worldwide, collectivistic Asian companies do not focus on a strongly identifiable outward style. They have found that design is the best way to forge connections with the values of their customers. Japanese and Korean companies, eager to connect with the values and tastes of Europeans and U.S. customers, work with local designers in the host countries.[133]

The future of global advertising is multilocal advertising. In 2002, a study comparing advertising in the United States and Hong Kong China found that consumers prefer localized to foreign-sourced, standardized advertisements. When home and host cultures are different, localized advertisements are more favorably viewed, even when consumers are subjected to ongoing exposure to Western cultures, as is the case in Hong Kong China. Although most U.S. brands have a well-established image in Hong Kong, consumers still prefer locally produced advertisements. Local commercials naturally embody cultural traits that local consumers understand and to which they relate.[134]

CONCLUSION

How people communicate varies with culture, and the different communication styles are reflected in advertising and the Internet. Different verbal and nonverbal communication styles can be recognized in both interpersonal and mass communication, and culture clusters can be defined where one or the other style prevails. People process information in different ways. For some, pictures contain more information than words; for others, the only way to convey meaning is verbal. These differences are also relevant for e-communications. Advertising styles follow interpersonal communication styles.

Knowledge of the differences is of utmost importance to international marketers and advertisers. Communication is only effective if the receiver of the message understands the message as the sender intends it. How advertising works, roles and function of advertising, all vary with culture. In one culture, advertising is persuasive by nature; in another, it must be liked in order to build trust between companies and consumers. Thus, models of one culture cannot be projected to other cultures. Marketers have had high expectations of the Internet as a new, interactive medium, unifying consumers worldwide. However it looks like the same principles of culture's influence apply to the new electronic media.

NOTES

1. Craig, C. S., & Douglas, S. P. (2006). Beyond national culture: Implications of cultural dynamics for consumer research. *International Marketing Review, 23*(3), 322–342.
2. Schramm, W., & Roberts, D. F. (1974). *The process and effects of mass communication.* Urbana: University of Illinois Press, 12.
3. Singelis, T. M., & Brown, W. J. (1995). Culture, self, and collectivist communication. *Human Communication Research, 21*, 354–389.
4. Oyserman, D., Coon, H., & Kemmelmeier, M. (2002). Rethinking individualism and collectivism: Evaluation of theoretical assumptions and meta-analyses. *Psychological Bulletin, 128*, 3–72.
5. Schmitt, B. H. (1995). Language and visual imagery: Issues of corporate identity in East Asia. *Columbia Journal of World Business, 3*, 28–37.
6. Van den Berg-Weitzel, L., & Van de Laar, G. (2001). Relation between culture and communication in packaging design. *Brand Management, 8*, 171–184.
7. Bu, K., Kim, D., & Lee, S. (2009). Determinants of visual forms used in print advertising: a cross-cultural comparison. *International Journal of Advertising, 28*(1), 13–48
8. Gudykunst, W., & Ting-Toomey, S. (1988). *Culture and interpersonal communication.* Newbury Park, CA: Sage, 99–133.
9. Molinsky, A. L., Krabbenhoft, M. A., Ambady, N., & Choi, Y. S. (2005). Cracking the nonverbal code: Intercultural competence and gesture recognition across cultures. *Journal of Cross-Cultural Psychology, 36*(3), 380–395.
10. Kobayashi, Y., & Noguchi, Y. (2001). Consumer insight, brand insight, and implicit communication: successful communication planning cases in Japan. In M. S. Roberts & R. L. King (Eds.), *The proceedings of the 2001 special Asia-Pacific conference of the American Academy of Advertising,* 29–40.
11. Miyahara, A. (2004). Toward theorizing Japanese interpersonal communication competence from a non-western perspective. In F. E. Jandt (Ed.), *Intercultural communication* (pp. 279–291). Thousand Oaks, CA: Sage, 286.
12. Sanchez-Burks, J., Lee, F., Choi, I., Nisbett, R., Zhao, S., & Koo, J. (2003). Conversing across cultures: East-West communication styles in work and non-work contexts. *Journal of Personality and Social Psychology, 85*(2), 363–372.
13. Miyamoto, Y., & Schwarz, N. (2006). When conveying a message may hurt the relationship: Cultural differences in the difficulty of using an answering machine. *Journal of Experimental Social Psychology, 42*, 540–547.
14. Kim, H., Kim, G. J., Park, H. W., & Rice, R. E. (2007). Configurations of relationships in different media: FtF, E-mail, Instant Messenger, Mobile Phone, and SMS. *Journal of Computer-Mediated Communication, 12*(4), art. 3.

15. CDTV.net. *New global study from MTV, Nickelodeon and Microsoft challenges assumptions about relationship between kids, youth and digital technology.* Retrieved July 25, 2007, from http://www.cdtv.net/users/node/14372

16. Liu, M., & Zoninsein, M. (2007, December 24). New data suggest China isn't lagging on Internet social networking. It's just innovating differently. *Newsweek,* 48–49.

17. Veilbrief, A. (2007, January). Chattend de puberteit door (Chatting through adolescence). *NRC Handelsblad Maandblad,* 20–25.

18. Boase, J., Horrigan, J. B., Wellman, B., & Rainie, L. (2006, January 25). *The strength of Internet ties.* Washington, DC: Pew Internet and American Life Project. Retrieved from www.pewinternet.org

19. Schultz, D. E., & Block, M. P. (2009). Understanding Chinese media audiences: An exploratory study of Chinese consumers media consumption and a comparison with the U.S.A. In H. Li, S. Huang, & D. Jin (Eds.), *Proceedings of the 2009 American Academy of Advertising Asia-Pacific conference,* 1–12. American Academy of Advertising, in conjunction with China Association of Advertising of Commerce, and Communication University of China.

20. Chu, S. C., & Choi, S. M. (2009). Use of social networking sites among Chinese young generations. In Li, Huang, & Jin (2009), 50–57.

21. Moerland, R. (2006, August 30). Frans weblog is een café (French weblog is a café). *NRC Handelsblad,* 18.

22. Chen, G. M. (1995). Differences in self-disclosure patterns among Americans versus Chinese. *Journal of Cross-Cultural Psychology, 26,* 84–91.

23. Ma, R. (1996). Computer-mediated conversations as a new dimension of intercultural communication between East Asian and North American college students. In S. C. Herring (Ed.), *Computer-mediated communication: Linguistic, social, and cross-cultural perspectives* (pp. 173–185). Amsterdam and New York: John Benjamins.

24. Yum, Y.O., & Hara, K. (2005). Computer-mediated relationship development: A cross-cultural comparison. *Journal of Computer-Mediated Communication, 11*(1), art. 7. Retrieved March 3, 2008, from http://jcmc.indiana.edu/v0111/issue1/yum.html

25. Levo-Henriksson, R. (1994, January). *Eyes upon wings: Culture in Finnish and US television news.* Doctoral dissertation. Oy. Yleisradio Ab., Helsinki, 84.

26. Perspectives. (1996, September 9). *Newsweek,* 11.

27. Li, Z. (2001). *Cultural impact on international branding: A case of marketing Finnish mobile phones in China.* Dissertation. Jyväskylä, Finland: University of Jyväskylä.

28. Marijnissen, S. (2008, June 20). Onbegrepen diepgang. *NRC Handelsblad Boeken,* 1–2.

29. Craig, C. S., Greene, W. H., & Douglas, S. P. (2005). Culture matters: Consumer acceptance of US films in foreign markets. *Journal of International Marketing, 13*(4), 80–103.

30. McCracken, G. (1988). *Culture and consumption: New approaches to the symbolic character of consumer goods and activities.* Bloomington: Indiana University Press, 77.

31. Becatelli, I., & Swindells, A. (1998, March). Developing better pan-European campaigns. *Admap,* 12–14.

32. Bulmer, S., & Buchanan-Oliver, M. (2006). Visual rhetoric and global advertising imagery. *Journal of Marketing Communications, 12*(1), 49–61.

33. Rosenberg, K. E., & Blair, M. H. (1994, July/August). Observations: The long and short of persuasive advertising. *Journal of Advertising Research,* 63–69.

34. Zinkhan, G. M. (1994). International advertising: A research agenda. *Journal of Advertising, 23,* 11–15.

35. Dru, J. M. (1996). *Disruption*. New York: Wiley, 1–19.

36. Ramdas, A. (2002, July 16). Dure mango voorbode van paniek in Noord-India (Expensive mango predictor of panic in North-India). *NRC Handelsblad, 4*.

37. Bresnahan, M. J., Ohashi, R., Liu, W. Y., Nebashi, R., & Liao, C. C. (1999). A comparison of response styles in Singapore and Taiwan. *Journal of Cross-Cultural Psychology, 30*, 342–358.

38. Cutler, B. D., Erdem, S. A., & Javalgi, R. G. (1997). Advertiser's relative reliance on collectivism-individualism appeals: A cross-cultural study. *Journal of International Consumer Marketing, 9*, 43–55.

39. Cutler, B. D., Thomas, E. G., & Rao, S. R. (2000). Informational/transformational advertising: Differences in usage across media types, product categories, and national cultures. *Journal of International Consumer Marketing, 12*, 69–83.

40. Laskey, H. A., Fox, R. J., & Crask, M. R. (1994, November/December). Investigating the impact of executional style on television commercial effectiveness. *Journal of Advertising Research*, 9–16.

41. Ang, S. H., & Lim, E. A. C. (2006). The influence of metaphors and product type on brand personality perceptions and attitudes. *Journal of Advertising, 35*(2), 39–53.

42. Roland, A. (1988). *In search of self in India and Japan*. Princeton, NJ: Princeton University Press.

43. Miracle, G. E. (1987). Feel-do-learn: An alternative sequence underlying Japanese consumer response to television commercials. In F. Feasly (Ed.), *Proceedings of the 1987 conference of the American Academy of Advertising* , R73–R78.

44. An, D., & Kim, S. H. (2007). A first investigation into the cross-cultural perceptions of Internet advertising: A comparison of Korean and American attitudes. *Journal of International Consumer Marketing, 20*(2), 49–65.

45. Wilkins, J. (2002, February). Why is global advertising still the exception, not the rule? *Admap*, 18–20.

46. Praet, C. L. C. (2000, May). *The role of advertising likability: A cross-cultural study of young adults' perception of TV advertising*. Working paper. Sapporo: Otaru University.

47. Ko, H., Roberts, M. S., & Cho, C. H. (2006). Cross-cultural differences in motivations and perceived interactivity: A comparative study of American and Korean Internet users. *Journal of Current Issues and Research in Advertising, 28*(2), 93–104.

48. La Ferle, C., & Kim, H. J. (2006). Cultural influences on internet motivations and communication styles: A comparison of Korean and US consumers. *International Journal of Internet Marketing and Advertising, 3*(2), 142–157.

49. Fourquet-Courbet, M. P., Courbet, D., & Vanheule, M. (2007, June). How Web banner designers work: The role of internal dialogues, self-evaluations, and implicit communication theories. *Journal of Advertising Research*, 183–192.

50. Dormann, C., & Chisalita, C. (2002, September 8–11). *Cultural values in web site design*. Paper presented at the 11th European Conference on Cognitive Ergonomics, ECCEII. Catania, Italy.

51. Brengman, M. (2007, October 10). Cultural differences reflected on the internet: a comparison between Belgian and Dutch e-commerce websites. ECREA Symposium, *The myth of the global Internet*. Brussels.

52. Singh, N. (2005). Analyzing the cultural content of web sites: A cross-national comparison of China, India, Japan, and US. *International Marketing Review, 22*(2), 129–146.

53. An, D. (2007). Advertising visuals in global brands' local websites: A six-country comparison. *International Journal of Advertising, 26*(3), 303–332.

54. Würtz, E. (2005). A cross-cultural analysis of websites from high-context cultures and low-context cultures. *Journal of Computer-Mediated Communication, 11*(1), art. 13.

55. Hermeking, M. (2005). Culture and Internet consumption: Contributions from cross-cultural marketing and advertising research. *Journal of Computer-Mediated Communication, 11*(1), art. 10.

56. Cho, C. H., & Cheon, H. J. (2005). Cross-cultural comparisons of interactivity on corporate websites. *Journal of Advertising, 34*(2), 99–115.

57. Ko et al. (2006).

58. Eurostat Statistics Database (2009).

59. Husmann, Y. (2001). Localization of website interfaces: Cross-cultural differences in home page design. *Wissenschaftliche Arbeit zure Erlangung des Diplomgrades im Studiengang Sprachen-, Wirtschafts- und Kulturraumstudien* (Diplom-Kulturwirt). Universität Passau, Germany.

60. Singh, N., Kumar, V., & Baack, D. (2005). Adaptation of cultural content: evidence from B2C e-commerce firms. *European Journal of Marketing, 39*(1/2), 71–86.

61. Faiola, A., & Matei, S.A. (2005). Cultural cognitive style and web design: beyond a behavioral inquiry into computer-mediated communication. *Journal of Computer-Mediated Communication, 11*(1), art. 18.

62. Singh, N., Fassott, G., Chao, M. C. H., & Hoffmann, J. A. (2006). Understanding international web site usage: A cross-national study of German, Brazilian, and Taiwanese online consumers. *International Marketing Review, 23*(1), 83–97.

63. *Young Asians Survey.* (2008, March 12). Synovate.

64. In 2005 for daily viewing minutes measured by IP for 26 European countries varying between GNI per capita at PPP of $3.450 for Bulgaria and $59.950 for Norway, low income explained 39% of variance.

65. *Young Europeans.* (2007). Flash Eurobarometer 202.

66. Austria, Belgium, Denmark, Finland, France, Germany, Greece, Ireland, Italy, Japan, Netherlands, Norway, Portugal, Spain, Sweden, Switzerland, Turkey, United Kingdom, United States. Source: Initiative Media. [February 24, 2008 http://initiativemedia.com/static/html_home2.htm

67. *Cinema, TV and Radio in the EU.* (2003). Eurostat Statistics on audiovisual services. Data 1980–2002.

68. Ofcom International Communications Market. (2006). *Minutes per day TV viewing per head of the population, 9 countries.*

69. IP Television. (2008). *TV viewing minutes.* Retrieved February 24, 2008, from http://www .ip-network.com/tvkeyfacts

70. http://www.zonalatina.com. Posted by Ronald Soong. December 31, 1998.

71. Krotz, F., & Hasebrink, U. (1998). The analysis of people-meter data: Individual patterns of viewing behavior and viewers' cultural backgrounds. *European Journal of Communication Research, 23*, 151–174.

72. http://www.zonalatina.com. Posted by Ronald Soong on May 11, 2000.

73. Pasquier, D., Buzzi, C., d'Haenens, L., & Sjöberg, U. (1998). Family lifestyles and media use patterns: An analysis of domestic media among Flemish, French, Italian and Swedish children and teenagers. *European Journal of Communication, 13*, 503–519.

74. Bringué Sala, X., & Sádaba Chalezquer, C. (2008). *The interactive generation in Ibero-America: Children and adolescents faced with the screens.* Madrid: Colección Fundacion Telefónica.

75. Voyiadzakis, A. (2001, November). Why magazines and newspapers are so important in the Japanese media mix. *M&M Europe,* 41–45.

76. *Community survey on ICT usage in households and by individuals.* (2006). Eurostat, 21 countries.

77. Ofcom International Communications Market 2006.

78. From 1980 onward, for 44 countries worldwide and for 15 developed countries in Europe, individualism explained between 40% and 72% of variance. Data UN statistical yearbooks.

79. Medios de Comunicacion Annuario de Medios. El escenario Iberoamericano [The Ibero-American media scene]. (2007). Madrid: Fundacion Telefonica.

80. Data Ofcom International Communications Market 2006. United Kingdom, France, Germany, Italy, United States, Japan, China.

81. Coen, R. J. (1997). *The insider's report.* New York: McCann-Erickson.

82. *Social values, science and technology.* (2005, June). Special Eurobarometer 225.

83. *Young Europeans.* (2007). Flash Eurobarometer 202

84. World Advertising Trends 2006. In Ofcom. (2008). The International Communications Market.

85. Medios de Comunicacion Annuario de Medios (2007).

86. *PAX Asia.* (2008). Synovate Asia.

87. Barnett, G. A., & Sung, E. (2005). Culture and the structure of the international hyperlink network. *Journal of Computer-Mediated Communication, 11*(1), art. 11. Retrieved March 3, 2008, from http://jcmc.indiana.edu/v0111/issue1/barnett.html

88. World Development Indicators 2006, Worldbank.

89. European social survey, 2003

90. *European Cultural Values.* (2007). EBS 278.

91. Comscore (2007). (See Appendix B.)

92. *European cultural values.* (2007). Twenty-four countries Europe. 43% of variance explained by low masculinity.

93. Comscore (2007).

94. La Ferle, C., Edwards, S. M., & Mizuno, Y. (2002, April). Internet diffusion in Japan: Cultural considerations. *Journal of Advertising Research,* 65–79.

95. *The Public Pulse.* (1997, October/November). *Roper Starch Worldwide 12*(10, 11), 5.

96. *Information society.* (2008). Flash EB 241; *European cultural values* (2007). EBS 278; Synovate PAX digital life (2008).

97. *Measuring information society.* (2000). EB 53.

98. Mareck, M. (1999, December). Research watch. *M&M Europe,* 47.

99. Los Medios y Mercados de Latinoamérica. (1998). At http//.www.zonalatina.com, posted by Roland Soong, September 4, 1999.

100. McLuhan, M. (1964). *Understanding media: The extensions of man.* New York: McGraw Hill.

101. Huff, L. C., & Alden, D. L. (1998, May–June). An investigation of consumer response to sales promotions in developing markets: A three country analysis. *Journal of Advertising Research,* 47–56.

102. Ewing, M., Salzberger, T., & Sinkovics, R. R. (2001). Assessing responses to standardized TV commercials: Using the Lastovicka "Relevance, Confusion and Entertainment-Scale": A cross-cultural perspective. *Proceedings of the Australian and New Zealand Marketing Academy Conference,* Auckland, NZ.

103. Shavitt, S., Nelson, M. R., & Yuan, R. M. L. (1997). Exploring cross-cultural differences in cognitive responding to ads. *Advances in Consumer Research, 24,* 245–250.

104. Avtgis, T. A. (1998). Locus of control and persuasion, social influence, and conformity: A meta-analytic review. *Psychological Reports, 83,* 899–903.

105. Andrews, J. C., Lysonski, S., & Durvusala, S. (1991). Understanding cross-cultural student perceptions of advertising in general: Implications for advertising educators and practitioners. *Journal of Advertising, 20,* 15–28.

106. Ramaprasad, J. (2001). South Asian students' beliefs about and attitude toward advertising. *Journal of Current Issues and Research in Advertising, 23,* 55–70.

107. Andrews, J. C., Durvasula, S., & Netemeyer, R. G. (1994). Testing the cross-national applicability of U.S. and Russian advertising belief and attitude measures. *Journal of Advertising, 23,* 71–82.

108. Heyder, H., Musiol, K. G., & Peters, K. (1992, March). Advertising in Europe: Attitudes towards advertising in certain key East and West European countries. *Marketing and Research Today*, 58–68.

109. La Ferle, C., Edwards, S. M., & Lee, W. N. (2008). Culture, attitudes, and media patterns in China, Taiwan, and the U.S.: Balancing standardization and localization decisions. *Journal of Global Marketing, 3*(21), 191–205.

110. An, D., & Kim, S. H. (2007). A first investigation into the cross-cultural perceptions of Internet advertising: A comparison of Korean and American attitudes. *Journal of International Consumer Marketing, 20*(2), 49–65.

111. Hielkema, R. (2001). Europa over reclame (Europe about advertising). Results of the study Euro Life & Living by NFO Trendbox. *Adformatie, 24,* 54–56.

112. Lascu, D. N., Manrai, L. A., & Manrai, A. K. (1996). Value differences between Polish and Romanian consumers: A caution against using a regiocentric marketing orientation in Eastern Europe. In L. A. Manrai & A. K. Manrai (Eds.), *Global perspectives in cross-cultural and cross-national consumer research* (pp. 145–168). New York: International Business Press/Haworth Press.

113. Evans, I. G., & Riyait, S. (1993). Is the message being received? Benetton analysed. *International Journal of Advertising, 12,* 291–301.

114. Chan, K., & Cheng, H. (2002). One country, two systems: Cultural values reflected in Chinese and Hong Kong television commercials. *Gazette: The International Journal for Communication Studies, 64,* 385–400.

115. Zhou, D. (2009). Harmony: Advertising situations in China. In Li, Huang, & Jin (2009), 246–253.

116. Garcia, E., & Yang, K. C. C. (2006). Consumer responses to sexual appeals in cross-cultural advertisements. *Journal of International Consumer Marketing, 19*(2), 29–51.

117. Schmitt, B. H., & Pan, Y. (1994). Managing corporate and brand identities in the Asia-Pacific region. *California Management Review, 36,* 32–48.

118. Callow, M., & Schiffman, L. (2002). Implicit meaning in visual print advertisements: A cross-cultural examination of the contextual communication effect. *International Journal of Advertising, 21,* 259–277.

119. TGI Europa Internet Report. (2001, December). Retrieved from http://www.tgisurveys.com

120. Moshavi, S. (1995, October 23). Winding up for the big pitch. *BusinessWeek,* 22–26.

121. This is described more comprehensively in De Mooij, M. (2010). *Global marketing and advertising, Understanding cultural paradoxes* (3rd ed.). Thousand Oaks, CA: Sage.

122. Um, N. H., Kwon, M. W., & Kim, S. (2009). A cross-cultural comparison of creative characteristics of celebrity endorsement in Korea and U.S. magazine advertisment. In Li, Huang, & Jin (2009), 178.

123. Taylor, C. R., & Miracle, G. E. (1996). Foreign elements in Korean and U.S. television advertising. *Advances in International Marketing, 7,* 175–195.

124. Taylor, T. (1997). Cracking Japan. *M&M Europe,* 41.

125. From the Kellogg's Japan website. Translated by Carlo Praet, January 29, 2010.

126. Olson, J. C., & Reynolds, T. J. (1983). Understanding consumers' cognitive structures: Implications for advertising strategy. In L. Perry & A. G. Woodside (Eds.), *Advertising and consumer psychology* (pp. 77–90). Lexington, MA: Lexington Books.

127. Singh, D. (2007). *Cross cultural comparison of buying behavior in India.* Doctoral thesis. Chandigarh: Panjab University, University Business School.

128. Gutman, J. A. (1982). Means-end chain model based on consumer categorization processes. *Journal of Marketing, 46,* 60–72.

129. Reynolds, T. J., & Gutman, J. (1988, February–March). Laddering theory, method, analysis, and interpretation. *Journal of Advertising Research,* 29–37.

130. Hsieh, M. H., & Lindridge, A. (2005). Universal appeals with local specifications. *Journal of Product and Brand Management, 14*(1), 14–28.

131. Wilkins, J. (2002, February). Why is global advertising still the exception, not the rule? *Admap,* 18–20.

132. Vangelder, P. (2000, July/August). Market research for global advertising. *ESOMAR Research World,* 16–17.

133. Grinyer, C. (2001, Fall). Design differentiation for global companies: Value exporters and value collectors *Design Management Journal,* 10–14.

134. Pae, J. H., Samiee, S., & Tai, S. (2002). Global advertising strategy: The moderating role of brand familiarity and execution style. *International Marketing Review, 19,* 176–189.

Consumer Behavior Domains

The previous chapters described how the mental and social processes that drive behavior vary across cultures. This chapter deals with various consumer behavior domains. The consumer behavior domains related to communication, such as responses to communication and the media, were discussed in Chapter 7. *Behavior* refers to the physical actions of consumers that can be directly observed and measured by others. It is also called *overt behavior* to distinguish it from mental activities.[1] A trip to a shop, usage and ownership of products involve behavior. All aspects discussed in the previous chapters, such as motivation, emotion, cognition, and affect, are involved in behavior, but they operate differently across the various consumer behavior domains, such as product acquisition, ownership and usage, shopping and buying behavior, complaining behavior, brand loyalty, and adoption and diffusion of innovations. These topics are discussed in this chapter.

PRODUCT ACQUISITION, USAGE, AND OWNERSHIP

There are substantial differences between countries with respect to product ownership and usage, and an estimated 70% can be explained by culture. People's values have a direct and an indirect effect on product ownership. A product has physical characteristics (attributes) that have functional or psychosocial consequences or benefits. A product can also express the (desired) values of the consumer. A car is not only a means of transportation; it also says something about its owner.

Many cross-country differences in product usage and ownership can be understood by the link between the product category and culture. Category-specific relationships can be found by correlating product category data to cultural dimensions and gross national income (GNI) per capita, thus finding the influence of income and product-specific cultural values. Such findings are presented in the following sections. For food and beverages, climate is also included as an explaining variable. The following categories are reviewed: food and beverages, cigarettes, household cleaning products, cosmetics and personal care products, household appliances, consumer electronics, luxury articles, telecommunications, cars, leisure, and financial behavior.

FOOD AND BEVERAGES

Food consumption varies with climate, historical, economic, and cultural factors. Food carries cultural meaning. Evidence is the variation of the percentages of household expenditures on food and beverages, even within the economically homogeneous Europe. Also with respect to consumption of specific food categories, there are fundamental differences in the patterns of consumption in the different European Union (EU) countries.[2] In Chapter 3 (section on Engel's law), the symbolic function of food was mentioned, which is stronger in collectivistic cultures than in individualistic cultures.

Different attitudes toward food can also be recognized in the presentation of food in shops. In most individualistic cultures, people shop for food in sterile supermarkets where meat is wrapped tightly in layers of plastics or processed into unrecognizable sandwich meat. In most collectivistic cultures, both in small shops and in large supermarkets, there are many counters with fresh food where people can touch, see, and recognize the texture of the food. This is related to differences in convenience needs with respect to food that are related to individualism and short-term orientation.

Countries in Europe differ with respect to associations people have with food. Whereas in collectivistic cultures people associate food with pleasure, in feminine cultures they associate food with conviviality and in masculine cultures more with taste.[3] The Germanic countries are health conscious. The Belgians, French, and Italians have sophisticated food cultures, and sensory enjoyment is important, whereas the Spanish prefer natural products. For the Portuguese, the meal is a social event and consists of small relatively light dishes, as it is in Greece. The British are fond of sweets and pastries as well as instant products. Convenience is important, as in Denmark and Norway, where people don't particularly enjoy cooking. The Swedes prefer heavy meals and have a weak preference for natural products.[4] In India, although young Indian consumers are passionate about visiting fast food outlets for fun and change, home food remains their first choice; they regard home food as better than fast food.[5]

In Chapter 3 (section on climate) the link between *calorie intake* and climate was discussed. Logic says that calorie intake is higher in cold than in warm climates, but national wealth and culture are better explaining variables. Worldwide GNI per capita is the explaining variable, but in the rich world individualism and masculinity explain variance. Americans are the champions of calorie intake, and this has increased over time. In 1960, the average American ate 4 pounds of frozen French fries a year; in 2001 it was more than 30 pounds.[6]

Worldwide climate explains between 20% and 52% of variance of consumption of 7 of 18 food product categories examined: meat, liquid milk, yogurt, cheese, canned foods, chocolate, and sugar confectionery.[7]

In Europe, most fresh fruit is consumed in Italy, Austria, and Spain. In the United Kingdom, people eat the least fruit. Also fish consumption varies enormously: in Spain, which has a long coast line, it is 10 times greater than in landlocked Austria. Modern distribution systems may have caused some convergence, but there still are considerable differences. These consumption habits have been established during the past centuries and are not likely to change in the foreseeable future.

Processed Food

Worldwide GNI per capita and the cultural variables explain most of the differences with respect to processed foods. GNI per capita explains, for example, variance of the volume of consumption of chilled desserts and of soup, and individualism explains variance of frozen foods, biscuits (cookies and crackers), and savory snacks. Data on usage (not volume) of soup show a correlation with individualism that explains 21% of variance for 41 countries worldwide.[8] The colder the climate, the more ice cream consumed. The strong explaining power of climate for the volume of ice cream consumption shows that ice cream is an energy provider in cold climates instead of a cooling mechanism in hot climates. It is basically sweet milk. Ice cream also is related to low uncertainty avoidance, a cultural dimension that is linked with the need for purity in food. How climate explains variance of food consumption in an indirect way and how it is related to trust in food products was discussed in Chapter 3 (in the section on climate). Processed food products are not trusted in cultures of high uncertainty avoidance, which explains variance of most processed foods. The new data for the LTO (long-/short-term orientation) dimension explain several differences in usage of some processed food products, such as breakfast cereals, potato crisps, colas, fizzy soft/energy drinks, ice cream, and ready-to-drink fruit and vegetable juices.[9] These are all ready-to-eat or drink products that fit the convenience orientation of short-term orientation cultures.

Europe is an area where economic convergence has been paralleled by divergence of food habits. In 1997 the Norwegians, with 141 liters per capita, drank twice as much milk as the Belgians, who consumed 70.5 liters per capita. Milk consumption converged in the period 1970–1977[10] and diverged in later years. Also, ice cream consumption has diverged. In 1997[11] in Denmark, the sales volume of frozen food was 40.4 kilograms per capita; in the United Kingdom it was 30.6, and it was 10.3 in Spain. Low uncertainty avoidance explained 60% of variance. Originally, consumption of frozen food was related to penetration of deep freezers, but this relationship has disappeared. This may imply that much frozen food is not bought to keep for later use but to consume right after buying.

Individualism explains variance of biscuits (cookies and crackers) that represents a type of processed food that is rooted in history. Whereas in the individualistic cultures biscuits are consumed as between-meal snacks, they are consumed as breakfast items in countries like Spain.

Soft Drinks

In 1997 Americans consumed twice as many liters of soft drinks as the Dutch. Germans drank 164 liters per capita, nearly twice as much as the Norwegians, who consumed 86.1 liters per capita. The difference is explained by culture. In Europe,[12] in 1997, cultural masculinity explained 60% of variance of soft drink consumption (liters per capita). One of the likely causes of this relationship was global advertising. The soft drinks market has for a long time been dominated by Anglo-American global brands (e.g., Coca-Cola, Pepsi-Cola, Fanta, Seven-Up, Sprite, Schweppes). These early global brands were the first to apply advanced marketing techniques. With growing global competition, the owners of these brands have standardized their marketing and advertising for increased efficiency. Because many global advertising campaigns are developed in London or New York, for decades the global campaigns for soft drinks have reflected Anglo-American values like masculinity, adventure, status, and success, which are not as appealing to all other cultures. Thus, the result of global advertising has been different than intended. Global advertising, instead of causing convergence, may have caused divergence. In countries with values that differ from Anglo-American values, standardized advertising campaigns have resulted in suboptimalization of sales. Consumption of soft drinks by young people varied in a similar way. The percentage of students age 15 years old who in 1998 said they drank soft drinks every day also correlated with masculinity.[13]

Looking not at volumes consumed but at the percentages of people who use colas and soft drinks, there still are large differences. Whereas in the United States 78% of the people drink colas, in France it is 61%, in the Czech Republic it is 55%, in Canada 50%, and in Taiwan 11%. Usage of the whole soft drink category is as different, with 71% in the United States, 79% in Brazil, 48% in Singapore, 29% in Japan, and 13% in Taiwan. Worldwide short-term orientation explains 14% of variance of use of cola drinks, 24% of fizzy soft/energy drinks, and 12% of ready-to-drink fruit and vegetable juices.[14]

Mineral Water

Mineral water consumption varies considerably across countries. The most important explaining variable is uncertainty avoidance, and this relationship has been consistent over time. In Chapter 3 (Table 3.3), mineral water consumption differences over time were used as an example of stability. Although in the past 30 years the quality of tap water has improved everywhere in Europe, the differences between countries have remained similar since 1970 or have become even larger. Since 1970, high uncertainty avoidance has explained between 44% and 53% of variance. In France, Germany, Italy, and Belgium, cultures of high uncertainty avoidance, people drink increasing volumes of mineral water, as compared to the United Kingdom and Scandinavia, cultures of low uncertainty avoidance, where people have different ideas about what is necessary for their health. Figure 8.1 illustrates the relationship between uncertainty avoidance and bottled water consumption for 15 countries.

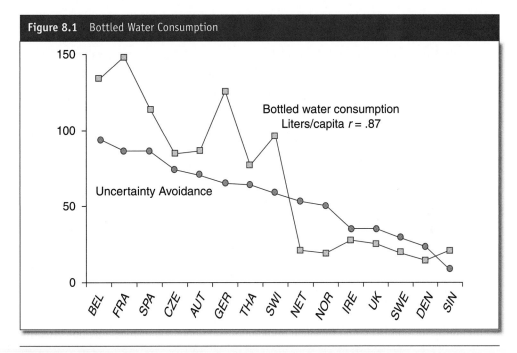

Figure 8.1   Bottled Water Consumption

SOURCES: Hofstede et al. (2010) (see Appendix A); Beverage Marketing Corporation (http://www.beveragemarketing.com) (2003)

Coffee and Tea

The variable that best explains differences in volume of coffee consumption is climate. Consistently, about 35% of variance is explained by latitude.[15] In the colder countries people drink larger volumes of coffee. In Chapter 3 (section on climate), the theory of homeostasis explained the relationship between climate and stimulants such as coffee. Low masculinity also explains variance. In the feminine cultures in Europe that also have colder climates, coffee consumption is connected with the concept of *gezellig* (Dutch), *mysigt* (Swedish), or *hyggelig* (Danish), in particular in the Scandinavian countries. Although tea also is a stimulant, no such relationship with climate exists for tea consumption. There was however, a significant correlation between the volumes of tea consumed and individualism and low uncertainty avoidance, both worldwide and in Europe, but these relationships have disappeared. Differences in use of tea bags are explained by individualism only (19%).[16]

Tea consumption varies from the typical British strong black tea with milk that is consumed during the morning break as well as in the afternoon to all sorts of herbal teas in Germany, to green tea in China, which is consumed with hot meals. Nowadays there are many types of tea, and tea is processed in many different ways. Next to black teas there are green teas, herbal teas, and a variety of chilled, ready-to-drink teas in cans or tetra packs. In Asian countries there are country-specific teas like oolong tea, as, for example, the Taiwanese Tao Ti brand that is very popular. The dominance of tea-based refreshments explains the low consumption of carbonated soft drinks in Taiwan. In Europe, the British and Irish have been drinking the most black tea (1,148 and 1,417 cups per person per year), while the Italians drink least (39.6 cups). Originally tea came from China. The Dutch introduced it to Europe in the 17th century. But the tea rituals of the Chinese or Japanese are far from what they are now in Britain.

Coffee and tea rituals are historically defined. Types of coffee consumed vary from various versions of black coffee to larger cups with milk, called *espresso* and *cappuccino* in Italy—names that have been adopted by other countries in Europe—and *solo* and *cortado* in Spain. The name *latte*, used in the United States, may suggest something continental European, but it is a typical American type of coffee mix. The Italian cappuccino is a drink for the morning in Italy, but the Danes have embraced it for use throughout the day. For them it is "a coffee." Whereas in the north of Europe most coffee is consumed in the home, in the south most is consumed in bars, where contact with people is as important as drinking coffee.

A large coffee café chain like Starbucks reflects American coffee culture. The type of coffee served is different from what people are used to in most other countries. Italian Illy café's owner Andrea Illy says, "In the United States coffee is merely a hot beverage, not an elixir."[17] Illy's aim is to create an exclusive destination with emphasis on quality and aesthetics, whereas Starbucks is more a place to communicate with other people.

Whereas to Americans, Starbuck's offers better coffee than they were used to, Europeans were used to a better coffee already. Also, the idea of a café as a meeting place is not new. In Vienna, as in many European cities, the café has been an important institution in the city's cultural and political life. It is the place to meet friends, to study for an exam, or to listen to Strauss music while reading the newspaper.[18]

In the section "Readers Report" in *Newsweek* of October 7, 2002, an Italian reader reacts to an earlier *Newsweek* story about Starbucks ("Planet Starbucks," the cover story on September 9, 2002).

I was very amused by Starbucks Corp.'s claim that they will come to Italy one day. Automatic espresso machines? Most Italians go to the bar to chat with the cashier or the guy at the coffee machine about the latest actress or football match—hard to do with a machine, even with a Java-enabled one. And what about allowing customers to order their coffee via the Web? What if the customer meets somebody on the way to the bar? "Happy to see you, but my coffee is ready, I'll send you an e-mail!" Come on. Prepaid cards? They've been around for ages here. What we want in Italy (and we have it already) is good coffee at a reasonable price, some nice food just in case, all served quickly but also with a human touch. Not one of these things is Starbucks able to deliver now. And they call themselves a "coffee bar"? Brrr...

Alberto Canesi, Rome

Alcoholic Beverages

Variance of pure alcohol consumption is explained by GNI per capita, high uncertainty avoidance and individualism that explain altogether 46%, but there are differences with respect to consumption of beer, wine, and spirits. Whereas the Czechs and Irish drink most beer, the inhabitants of Luxembourg and France drink most wine, and in the Republic of Moldova, Reunion, and the Russian Federation they drink most spirits.[19] The data on pure alcohol consumption are based on recorded data and don't include home production or so-called cottage-produced alcoholic beverages such as a country liquor called *arrack* in India, corn liquor in Venezuela, rice wine called *tuak* or *tapai* in Malaysia, or home-brewed beers like *talla* in Ethiopia.

In Europe, countries converge with respect to alcohol consumption. This is due to decreased consumption of wine in the wine-growing countries. In the warmer countries people drink more wine, while in the colder climates people drink more beer. This is related to where the two types of alcoholic beverages are produced. A few specific alcoholic drinks are related to cultural variables. Data from EMS show that champagne, port wine, and vermouth are consumed more in high than in low power distance cultures. These drinks are obviously social status drinks. In continental Europe, Scotch whiskey is also correlated with high power distance. Figure 8.2 illustrates that relationship for 13 countries.

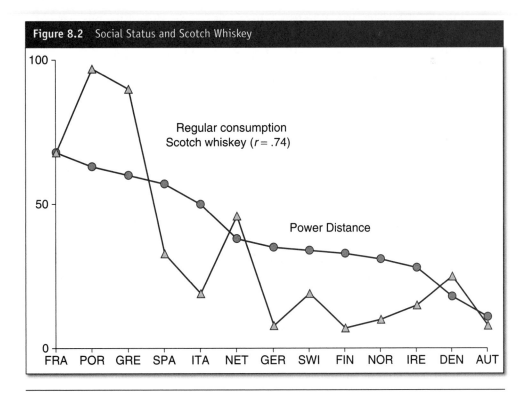

Figure 8.2   Social Status and Scotch Whiskey

SOURCES: Hofstede et al. (2010) (see Appendix A); European Media and Marketing Survey (EMS) (1999) (see Appendix B)

Cigarettes

Whereas in the 20th century variance of cigarette smoking was explained by wealth, this has changed. In 1997 GNI per capita explained 34% of variance of cigarette consumption worldwide, and high uncertainty avoidance explained an additional 13%. Masculinity explained 28% of variance in the developed world and 45% in Europe. In Europe in 2005 the relationship with masculinity had continued.[20] The relationship with uncertainty avoidance confirms that smoking is a stress-reducing mechanism, and the relationship with masculinity that smoking has status value. The relationship with masculinity may also be due to the fact that a few Anglo-American cigarette brands have dominated advertising. In particular, brands like Marlboro and Camel for a long time have reflected rugged masculinity, which obviously has been more appealing to the masculine cultures than to the feminine cultures.

It looks like in high uncertainty avoidance cultures the stress-reducing mechanism of smoking is so strong that protecting others is less relevant. Across Europe the percentages of people who say they smoke in a car in the company of nonsmokers or children correlate with high uncertainty avoidance.[21] Twenty-four percent of the Spanish do so and 21% of the Greeks.

Nowadays the level of economic development in a country appears to be a key determinant of tobacco use. Whereas tobacco use in developed nations has been on the decline, developing nations have in fact experienced an increase in tobacco use. For example, the developing countries' share of world tobacco consumption stood at 49% in 1974–1976. By 2010, the United Nations expected this to reach to 71%. A more educated population tends to be more aware of the health risks posed by smoking. Most developed economies have restricted cigarette sales, cigarette advertising, and smoking in public areas. Restrictions on tobacco advertising are now pervasive for all but low-income countries.[22]

NONDURABLE HOUSEHOLD PRODUCTS

Countries are becoming similar with respect to usage of washing powder and household cleaning products, and whatever differences there are are related to wealth. Volume differences, however, are related to uncertainty avoidance, and this relationship can best be explained by the need for purity that also operates as a value for food preferences (see also Chapter 5). Just to be sure their clothing will be really clean, in high uncertainty avoidance cultures people are likely to throw more washing powder into their washing machines than will people in low uncertainty avoidance cultures. A strong argument found in advertising in high uncertainty avoidance cultures tends to be antibacterial effectiveness and whiteness as a result of washing.

PERSONAL CARE AND COSMETICS

Usage of personal care products like creams and cleansers is mainly related to wealth. For cosmetics in Europe, there are clear cultural patterns for explaining differences in product usage, but this is not the case worldwide. In Europe, for example, in the past 30 years differences in use of lipstick, eye cosmetics, and deodorants have been correlated with low uncertainty avoidance and individualism, of which the relationships with uncertainty avoidance have been strongest. In 1999 the expenditures per inhabitant for the total cosmetics category[23] were significantly correlated with individualism ($r = .71***$). Worldwide these relationships are different. When analyzing the differences, measuring usage, volume, or value sales lead to different results. Data on usage cannot be compared with value or volume data, because for this product category price has a symbolic function. Whereas in some countries fewer people may use makeup, lipstick, or perfume, those who do use these products may prefer more expensive, branded products. Some products are used only in some areas: for example, skin lightening products are popular in Asia because, traditionally, darker skins have been associated with people who work outdoors, and lighter skins are considered more sophisticated. Across Asia, 30% of Chinese use skin lightening products either daily or weekly, followed by 20% of Taiwanese, and 18% of Japanese and Hong Kong Chinese.[24]

Worldwide differences between countries with respect to personal care and cosmetics use are substantial. Whereas 91% of Japanese women use cleansing creams, only 14% of Venezuelans do so. In the United States, 79% of women use lipstick, as compared to 42% in Hungary. Whereas 92% of Americans and 91% of the Germans use deodorant, only 15% of the Japanese do so. Data from 2001 and 2004 show a relationship between short-term orientation and use of perfume, lipstick, and foundation makeup. The need for self-enhancement must be a motive for these products. In Chapter 4 the relationship between short-term orientation and self-enhancement was discussed, with the example of the Dove report, from which statements like "Society expects women to enhance their physical attractiveness" correlated with short-term orientation.

Figure 8.3 illustrates the relationship between short-term orientation and lipstick and makeup for 16 countries.

Different cultural relationships also point at differences in motives for using personal care products and cosmetics. The individualistic cultures are the ones where people want to distinguish themselves from others. Color cosmetics and perfume are a means to do so. In low power distance cultures, cosmetics are used to look young, but in high power distance cultures cosmetics are a social status means to uphold face. Going out into the streets without makeup implies not being properly dressed. In particular, in cultures of short-term orientation, high power distance, and high uncertainty avoidance, people want to look stylish at all times.

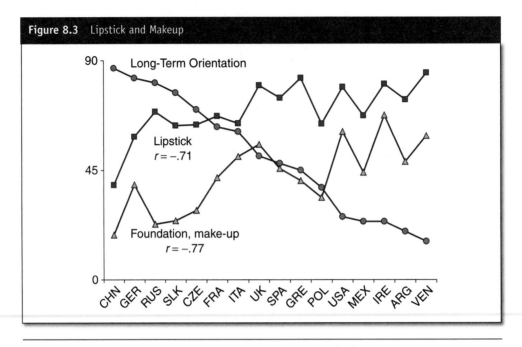

Figure 8.3   Lipstick and Makeup

SOURCES: Hofstede et al. (2010) (see Appendix A); TGI (2001) (see Appendix B)

Color cosmetics can satisfy the need for female self-enhancement, to attract men, to look young, or to differentiate oneself from others, which is an individualistic motive. Cosmetics also are not natural; they are artificial. This explains why usage of all sorts of cosmetics correlates with low uncertainty avoidance. This expresses the need for purity and distrust of the artificial in high uncertainty avoidance cultures. To accept the artificial, in high uncertainty avoidance cultures, scientific claims are used, found in particular in advertising for hair care, toothpaste, and personal care products, and the existence of "scientific" brands such as Laboratoire Garnier in France. Scientific data and arguments are likely to be more effective in strong uncertainty avoidance cultures than in weak uncertainty avoidance cultures, where the results are more important than the process. The preoccupation with purity[25] related to cosmetics has also been recognized in Japanese society, which scores high on uncertainty avoidance. This also explains the high use of cleansing cream.

Figure 8.4 depicts four culture clusters for color cosmetics involving power distance and uncertainty avoidance that together best explain usage motives. As most low power distance cultures (expect France, Belgium, and Poland) are also individualistic, the map includes this dimension too.

In the lower right quadrant of Figure 8.4, people like variety; they will buy any new color, easily change brands, or buy unbranded products at the supermarket. The product or brand

Figure 8.4   Map Color Cosmetics

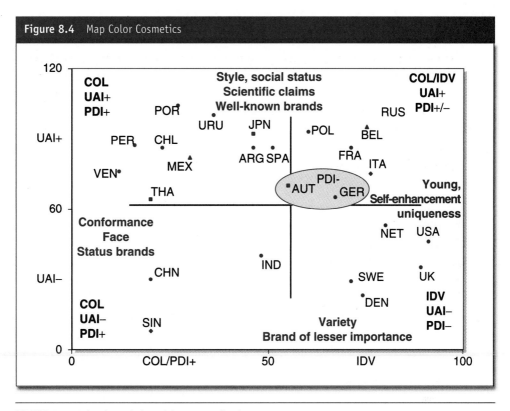

SOURCE: Data Hofstede et al. (2010) (see Appendix A)

sells itself if it offers enough choice. In these cultures there is relatively little advertising by the expensive cosmetics brands. The top right quadrant includes different clusters of cultures that are all high on uncertainty avoidance, but some are low on power distance and some high. High uncertainty avoidance asks for scientific control in both clusters. Low power distance means people will use cosmetics to look young; high power distance means people use them for social status. Products or brands focusing on the natural and purity will sell best in the combination with low power distance and high quality, status brands will sell best in the combination with high power distance. Big cosmetics brands like L'Oréal originated in this culture cluster.

In the culture cluster of the configuration collectivism, high power distance, and high uncertainty avoidance in the upper left-hand corner of Figure 8.4, people want to be stylish and are well groomed for social status reasons and for upholding face. They want to conform. Both the scientific approach and status brands are expected to sell best. Both quality and social recognition are important values. In the lower left-hand quadrant are collectivistic cultures of low uncertainty avoidance. Here conformance and status brands to uphold face are important, but scientific claims may be less relevant. China, Singapore, and India are in this quadrant.

An interesting relationship is between individualism and short-term orientation and deodorant use. Across 39 countries, use of deodorants is explained by short-term orientation, high uncertainty avoidance, and individualism, which together explain 48% of variance. Whereas the need for privacy makes people in individualistic cultures aware of the smell of other people, in collectivistic cultures they don't seem to care so much. In the hotter European countries, perspiration is viewed as the body's natural cooling mechanism; in the United Kingdom they see it as an embarrassment. The relationship with short-term orientation may point at the fact that deodorants help to enhance the self, provide self-confidence.

> Over time several Western companies have tried to sell deodorants to Asians, trying to induce social embarrassment or shame about wetness, sweat stains, and body odor. This negative approach inducing shame has not worked well in Asia, where people avoid negative information. People don't want to admit they have a problem. Indians, for example, would be reluctant to be seen buying a product that demonstrates they have a problem.[26] The positive approach, communicating freshness and attraction, making women more attractive to men or the other way around, is a better approach, which is also effective in other collectivistic cultures. In Russia, Unilever focused on the fact that Russian women spend heavily on cosmetics but not on deodorant. The message was that if you don't use a deodorant you won't look beautiful and will not be attractive to men.[27]

CLOTHING AND FOOTWEAR

In lower-income countries, the percentage of household expenditures spent on clothing and footwear is higher than in the rich countries. In high power distance and collectivistic cultures, people have to be well groomed when going out into the streets, and they may spend more on clothing than in individualistic and low uncertainty avoidance cultures. Generally, people in high uncertainty avoidance cultures are also well groomed. It is one way of facing a threatening world. Spending money on clothing and footwear also serves needs for self-esteem and self-enhancement. In individualistic cultures, variety is important and the percentage of women who say they at least once a month buy new clothes correlates with individualism.[28] Status needs to show one's success can be another explaining variable; for example, in 1999 masculinity explained 46% of the mean household consumption expenditures on clothing and footwear. It also explained the separate expenditures on clothing (42%), garments (43%), and footwear (39%).[29] In Chapter 5 (section on appearance), the social processes were described that explain the varying needs for appearance.

HOUSEHOLD APPLIANCES

Generally, national wealth explains variance of ownership of large electrical household appliances. However, climate explains variance of ownership of deep freezers. In 1970 GNI per capita explained 48% of variance of ownership of deep freezers; in 1991 it explained 57% of variance and in 1997 42%. As explained in Chapter 3 (section on climate), in countries where people used to keep food in the snow, they have embraced electric freezing technology most intensely.

Because of differences in food customs, housing, and cleaning, people will prefer different appliances. An example is the special Kimchi refrigerator developed in South Korea.

Korean *Kimchi* is a cabbage-based dish following century-old recipes. Koreans traditionally make a lot of Kimchi in winter and eat it the whole year, so they need special storage facilities. Koreans used to put Kimchi in a big jar and dig it in the ground, so the temperature was stable and the ground made a perfect ripening temperature for Kimchi. A special breathing brown jar kept the Kimchi fresh. People eat even two-year-old Kimchi. Because urbanization made it difficult to preserve Kimchi in a jar in the ground, a special Kimchi refrigerator was invented, which copies the conditions of the glazed pottery in the ground. If you put Kimchi in a regular refrigerator, it will go bad in one week because of varying temperatures when opening and closing it. By its construction, the Kimchi refrigerator is able to keep a constant temperature. At the beginning it was invented just for Kimchi, but nowadays some Kimchi refrigerators have various functions to keep fresh meat, vegetables, fruits, and so on.[30] Figure 8.5 illustrates the Kimchi jars and refrigerator.

Figure 8.5   Kimchi Pots and Refrigerator. Courtesy Eun Jee Hyun

In 1997 low individualism explained 39% of variance of unit sales of food processors, and low masculinity explained an additional 19%. The link with collectivism explains preferences for slow food instead of fast food. Fast food and convenience are typical needs of individualistic and short-term-oriented cultures, as discussed in Chapter 5 (section on convenience). In 2009, worldwide ownership of electric dishwashers and microwave ovens correlated with wealth, individualism, and low power distance.[31] Across 20 wealthy countries, however, where the influence of GNI per capita is weaker, dishwasher ownership is related to short-term orientation, which explains 36% of variance. No such relationship is found for microwave ovens. Electric dishwashers are convenience products, but the microwave is not. Whereas convenience oriented cultures may use a microwave for warming up precooked dishes, in the cultures where people like cooking, they use it to make more refined dishes.

In 1999, 60% of expenditures on tools and equipment for the house and garden were explained by individualism.[32] This is understandable in view of the relationship between individualism and living in one-family houses as well as ownership of private gardens.

CONSUMER ELECTRONICS AND PERSONAL COMPUTERS

Many consumer electronics serve the individualistic need for variety and stimulation. Ownership of most audio and video consumer electronics correlates with GNI per capita and individualism. Worldwide music sales have been related to national income, and the richer countries have traditionally spent more on CDs, cassettes, and records than the poorer countries. From 1999 onward there have been relationships with individualism and low uncertainty avoidance. Table 8.1 shows correlation coefficients for various video and audio electronics as well as personal computers.

The explaining variables for most audio and video electronics are individualism, low uncertainty avoidance, and low power distance. Ownership and sales of personal stereos, in 1991 first represented by the Sony Walkman, is related to the configuration of individualism, weak uncertainty avoidance, and small power distance. Listening to music all by yourself is an individualistic habit, and individualism explains variance of the whole personal stereo category. The more recent products tend to be related to low uncertainty avoidance. In these cultures people adopt innovations faster than in cultures of high uncertainty avoidance. With the advent of the Internet and the possibilities of downloading music cultural relationships have changed. In collectivistic cultures more music is downloaded from the Internet, both free and paid music (see also Chapter 7, Table 7.2). Ownership of DVD players is still related to wealth.

Ownership of television sets first converged and is now diverging. Radio ownership has diverged, as discussed in Chapter 3. Homogeneity of TV penetration masks heterogeneity at the micro level: numbers of television sets per household, types of

Table 8.1   Video and Audio Electronics and Personal Computers

	GNI/cap	PDI	IDV	MAS	UAI	LTO
Music sales per person 2001[1]	.79***	−.62***	.61***		−.59***	
Recording media 1999, mean consumer expenditures[1]	.66***		.80***		−.65**	
CD players 1999, % owned[2]	.61**			−.65***	−.51*	
Personal stereos 1991, % owned[2]	.54*	−.44*	.56*	−.38	−.65***	
Personal stereos 1997, sales/person[3]		−.48*			−.63***	
VCR 1998, household penetration[4]	.65**	−.47*	.68***		−.73***	
VCR 2005, % households[9]	.78***	−.64***	.68***	−.46*		
DVD player 2000, household penetration[4]			.54*	−.47*	−.55*	
DVD player 2009 % of total population[5]	.48***	−.38**	.28*			−.35*
DVD player 2008, TV households with DVD player[9]	.74***	−.50**	.57**		−.41*	
Expenditures audiovisual equipment, 2005[10]	.65***	−.73***	.61***	−.36*	−.66***	
Game console 2000, % owned[4]			.59*			
Digital audio downloads per head, 2006[8]				.67*		
PC at home, % of total population, 2008[5]	.78***	−.58***	.38*			
PC at home, % of total population, 2008, rich countries[6]	.41*			−.47*	−.46	
PCs per 1,000 people 2004[7]	.62***	−.44*	.38*		−.71***	

SOURCES: Data Hofstede et al. (2010) (see Appendix A); (1) International Federation of the Phonographic Industry, worldwide 22 countries; (2) Reader's Digest Eurodata 1991, Europe 15 countries; (3) Euromonitor 1997, 15 countries; (4) Eurostat, 14 countries; (5) TGI product book 2009, worldwide 38 countries; (6) TGI product book 2009, worldwide 22 countries, GNI/capita > US$17,000; (7) World Development Indicators, 26 countries worldwide, GNI/capita > US$20,000; (8) Ofcom International Communications Market 2006, 9 countries Europe, USA, Japan; (9) IP Television, 25 countries Europe, USA and Japan; (10) Eurostat structure of consumption, 2005, 26 countries (see Appendix B)

television sets, and viewing time vary. Television has become an integral part of life everywhere, but that doesn't mean people watch similar programs or use it in the same way. In Chapter 7 cultural differences with respect to TV viewing and radio listening were discussed. The role of television in social life varies. In modern China the television has emerged as perhaps the most symbolic purchase people make. For many Chinese, owning an automobile is not yet possible, and consumer electronics, particularly the television, play an important role in establishing one's financial image as well as projecting an aura of success. The television one owns must project the right image to others.[33] In countries like China a television set also serves a social need, as an important application is using it for karaoke.

In individualistic cultures everybody has his or her own radio or even more than one, whereas in collectivistic cultures one radio per household used to be enough. In individualistic cultures people have radios in their bedrooms, their kitchens, and in their cars. At the end of the 20th century there were 1,432 radios per 1,000 people in the United Kingdom and 333 in Spain. There were nearly twice as many TV sets as radios in Spain and Portugal, whereas there were twice as many radios as TV sets in the United Kingdom. The best explanation is the difference between individualistic and collectivistic cultures with respect to verbal and visual orientation. Television is more visual and radio is verbal. Figure 8.6 illustrates the significant correlations between the number of radios per 50 people and individualism for 18 countries worldwide. The figure illustrates how these differences have become stronger over time and how they are related to individualism.

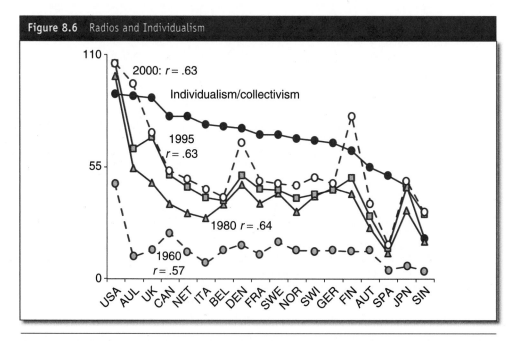

Figure 8.6 Radios and Individualism

SOURCES: Hofstede et al. (2010) (see Appendix A); United Nations Statistical Yearbooks and World Development Indicators (see Appendix B)

In the year 2000, measurement of ownership of radio receivers stopped, because nowadays people listen to radio messages in many different ways, such as via their personal computers or mobile phones.

Worldwide PC ownership is a matter of wealth, but across wealthy countries an important explanation of differences in ownership is uncertainty avoidance, which explains variance of adoption of innovations. Worldwide data correlate with GNI per capita, but across wealthy countries uncertainty avoidance explains 50% of variance.[34] The relationship is illustrated in Figure 8.7 for 20 countries worldwide.

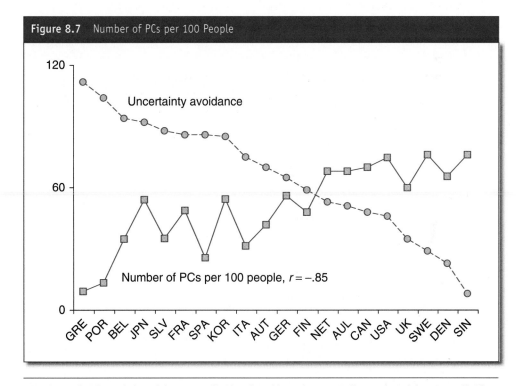

Figure 8.7   Number of PCs per 100 People

SOURCES: Hofstede et al. (2010) (see Appendix A) and World Development Indicators (2006) (see Appendix B)

People do all sorts of different things with their computers: read newspapers, play games, chat, e-mail, shop or buy via Internet, listen to radio, watch television or films, or work at home. These different activities have been discussed in Chapter 7.

TELECOMMUNICATIONS

The quality of a country's infrastructure for transport, technology, and communication[35] depends on the country's wealth. In regions with increased homogenization of national wealth, the differences have decreased but not disappeared. Whereas in 2000 communication expenditures as a percentage of household expenditures still correlated with low GNI per capita, this relationship had disappeared in 2009. Between 1966 and 1998, GNI per capita explained between 95% and 70% of variance of telephone main lines per 1,000 people worldwide. In 1980 culture emerged as an explaining variable next to GNI per capita. After that year, worldwide individualism, and in Europe weak uncertainty avoidance, became additional explaining variables, but after 2006 the main explaining variables were GNI per capita, power distance, individualism, and the new LTO dimension (see Table 8.2). This change is due to the advent of the mobile phone. Table 8.2 presents data on usage of various applications and motives in different sets of countries.

Table 8.2 Telecommunications

	GNI/cap	PDI	IDV	LTO
Fixed telephone lines per 100 inhabitants, 2007[1]	.94***	−.67***	.74***	.40**
Mobile cellular subscriptions per 100 inhabitants, 2007[1]	.52***	−.26*	.38**	
Use mobile phone, 2008 in 33 countries worldwide[2]	.67***	−.61***	.40***	
Use mobile phone, 2008 in 22 wealthy countries[3]			−.40*	
Personal ownership mobile phone, 2009, Asia[4]			−.90***	
Asia: Use mobile phone for[5] taking pictures			−.86**	.72*
playing games			−.96***	.73*
participating in SMS contest, voting				.90***
Europe: Wealthy countries[6]				
% who use mobile phone only occasionally			.46*	.58**
% who use mobile phone at least once a week	.54*		.65***	.64***
% who use mobile phone several times a day			−.53*	−.67***
Using mobile helps in your work			−.54*	−.69***
Not using mobile phone: Miss opportunity to contact family and friends				−.76***
Main benefit of mobile phone: Possibility to be contacted at any place any time[7]	−.58*		−.51*	−.49*

SOURCES: Hofstede et al. (2010) (see Appendix A); (1) ITU measuring the Information Society 2009, 44 countries worldwide; (2) TGI product book, % of total population that use mobile phone, 41 countries worldwide; (3) TGI product book, % of total population that use mobile phone, 22 countries GNI/cap > US$17,000; (4) Synovate Asia PAX Digital life, 7 countries; (5) Synovate Asia PAX 2009, 7 countries; (6) Flash EB 241, 2008, 16 wealthy countries; (7) EBS 249, 2006, 14 wealthy countries (see Appendix B)

At the start of mobile telephony, the general expectation was that mobile phones would penetrate faster in countries where communications infrastructure was weak, but this was not the case. Until 2002 there was a significant correlation between the numbers of fixed telephone lines per 100 inhabitants and mobile cellular subscriptions per 100 inhabitants ($r = .44*$), but this relationship disappeared. Worldwide GNI per capita and individualism explain most of variance of usage of the mobile phone, but across a group of wealthy countries a correlation with low individualism is found. The mobile phone is the typical product that appeals to collectivists to intensify and enhance interpersonal contacts. In the collectivistic cultures, people use the mobile phone more intensively than in the individualistic cultures. Intensive usage is also related to short-term orientation, demonstrating its convenience function. In the long-term-oriented cultures, where pragmatism is valued, all sorts of applications of the mobile phone have been embraced fastest.

In particular, in collectivistic cultures people want to communicate continuously with the members of their in-groups, and all means of communication are used for that. For Japanese youth, the mobile phone is a means to feel connected (*tsunagatte iru*) with other members of their in-group all the time. So people use the new communications technology to satisfy existing needs more intensely.

> In 2002 a Japanese TV station conducted an experiment involving three secondary school girls who were close friends. All three had mobile phones that were used to stay in constant contact by SMS messaging. In the experiment, one of the three girls had to hand over her phone while the other two were allowed to keep theirs. The three girls were continuously followed by the TV station's camera team. At the end of the first day, the viewer could see the three friends singing together in a karaoke box. The two friends with the phones were receiving a continuous stream of SMS messages. Suddenly the girl without the phone started crying because she felt so lonely, although she was with her friends.[36]

So, in contrast to expectations that new technology would fundamentally change people's communication behavior, new technology has made people do more of what they used to do. Although in Europe, initially countries have converged rapidly with respect to penetration of mobile phones, there are differences in usage. In the individualistic North, people use the mobile phone more to inform each other, so conversations are shorter and SMS messaging is preferred in public space in order not to disturb others. In the more collectivistic and high power distance cultures in the South, people use the mobile phone for networking and talk more on the phone. In particular, Italy's ubiquitous mobile phones can be explained by the weblike nature of the family, where everybody wants to talk to everybody else. In Italy, the relationship between young people and their mothers is very strong. Of those who do not live with their mothers, more than two thirds call her every day.[37]

In cultures where interdependence is strong, parents use the mobile phone to stay in touch with their children. In Italy, children as young as 8 years old receive a mobile phone to take to school so that the parents can reach them. As a result, in Italy the mobile phone is called a "communicative feeding bottle."[38]

Many applications to the mobile phone were introduced much faster in Asia than in Europe or the United States. This was caused by the fact that PC and Internet penetration were much lower in Asia, and countries lagged with respect to digital leisure applications. Already in 2000, Japanese NTT DoCoMo introduced its i-mode service with subscriptions to Bandai—known for the Tamagotchi—services that allowed users to download popular cartoon characters and games. As early as 2000, 700,000 people subscribed to these services. In Asia, much faster than in Europe and the United States, a variety of fashionable models entered the market. The Japanese view their phones more as companions and personalize them with ring tones and distinctive images. This process was different from that in the United States, where the mobile phone was more viewed as an instrument for greater productivity.[39] Whereas collectivists use the mobile phone only to intensify what they already were doing—frequently being in touch with family, playing games, and viewing cartoons—in individualistic cultures people view it as an instrument for information. The original mobile phone producers were from individualistic cultures and didn't foresee these differences from the start.

> In Europe mobile phone producers kept standardizing their products and advertising for quite a long time, assuming similarity in behavior. Only in large developing markets like China did Nokia market its cellular phones with features that appealed to local tastes, such as greeting cards with popular Chinese astrological symbols.[40] However, Nokia did not develop specific handset designs for specific markets. Via a subsidiary, Nokia did offer an expensive luxury subbrand (Vertu) in gold or platinum that would appeal to the rich and famous of this world, and Siemens offered so-called fashion accessory phones under the name Xelibri.[41] In China a taste for faux diamond-studded handsets developed that was considered kitschy and thus bad taste in the West. As a result, in China handset brands such as TCL, Ningbo Bird, and Amoisonic quickly gained market share, and Nokia and Motorola were losing. Too late, Motorola started copying the diamond-studded phone designs so popular in China.[42]

LUXURY ARTICLES

Many luxury articles serve status needs. Variance of buying or owning luxury articles is generally explained by masculinity or high power distance that explain the need to demonstrate one's success or social status. Ownership of real jewelry is correlated with cultural masculinity, worldwide ($r = .44*$), in a group of developed countries worldwide

($r = .61***$), and in Europe ($r = .51*$). There is no significant correlation with national wealth. The wealthy, global target groups of travelers and business people are assumed to be homogeneous in their buying behavior, ownership, and preference for luxury products and brands, but data from EMS, covering the 20% highest-income groups of Europe, show a different picture. In 1999 EMS asked questions about the amount of money spent on a range of luxury products and the value of luxury articles owned. Examples are ownership of a suit or dress costing more than US$800 and a briefcase or handbag more than US$300. For expensive clothing, masculinity explained 46% of variance and 27% for expensive handbags or briefcases. The answers "Don't know" to questions about the value of people's possessions likely represent people who don't care if they own expensive products or brands because of low status needs. The answers correlate with low masculinity ($r = -.49*$). In 2007 similar results were found. Variance of buying expensive fragrances was explained by high power distance (40%), and an additional 26% was explained by masculinity. Having bought an expensive briefcase or handbag in the past year correlated with high power distance ($r = .47*$) and having bought an expensive suit or dress correlated with masculinity ($r = .58*$). Masculinity explained 59% of variance of jewelry costing more than €1,500 bought in the past year.

In the modern world everybody can afford to own a wristwatch, but differences in ownership of expensive watches are large. In 1999 low GNI per capita explained 50% of variance of ownership of relatively cheap watches, and low masculinity explained an additional 25%. The relationship between ownership of affordable watches and low income is a logical one. Low status needs explain high ownership of cheaper watches in the feminine cultures, whereas masculinity explains 29% of variance of sales of expensive watches. Of the Italian respondents of EMS, 11.9% reported that the value of their main watch was more than US$1,600, as compared with only 2.1% of the Swedes. In 2007, masculinity explained 38% of variance of ownership of a watch that was more expensive than €750.

In 1999 EMS also asked questions about ownership of specific watch brands. For four brands (Rolex, Seiko, Swatch, and Omega), meaningful relationships with culture were found. These are also the brands with a global positioning based on global advertising. There was no relationship with GNI per capita for any of these expensive watch brands. Judging from the relationship between individualism and ownership of a Rolex, this brand is likely a watch for those who want to distinguish themselves from others. The message of the advertising campaign for Rolex is that it is a brand for unique personalities, singers, musicians, scientists, sports people who have distinguished themselves in their profession. The values included in advertising for Rolex are not just material success, but unique achievement. The advertising campaign shows how the brand distinguishes the dedicated professional from ordinary people. Four examples of ads of the

Figure 8.8 International Advertising for Rolex, with Opera Singer Kiri te Kanawa, Singers Tony Bennett and Diana Kroll, and With Tennis Player Roger Federer

international Rolex campaign are shown in Figure 8.8. Seiko appears to be a no-nonsense brand for those who don't need material status. Ownership of a Seiko as a main watch correlated with low uncertainty avoidance ($r = -.66***$) and with low masculinity ($r = -.61**$).

In Europe ownership of (still) cameras has converged. Whereas in 1970 GNI per capita explained 70% of variance, in later years only ownership of expensive compact cameras (more than US$160) was related to national wealth. Now that digital cameras have become ubiquitous and people also make pictures with their mobile phones, analyzing cameras as a category doesn't lead to further explanations. It may be expected that in the high uncertainty avoidance cultures people will prefer the more specialized cameras with more functions. How people use their cameras varies. Heavy usage is in the masculine cultures. In the no-nonsense feminine cultures, people may own cameras, but they use them less frequently. The measurement "number of films used in the past year" correlated with national income in 1991 and 1999,[43] but heavy usage is also related to masculinity. In 1999 GNI per capita explained 42% of variance, and masculinity explained an additional 36%.

CARS

Worldwide GNI per capita explains differences in car ownership in households, but differences across wealthy countries are explained by individualism.[44] Across countries with GNI per capita more than US$12,000, individualism is the explaining variable. For 18 countries the relationship is illustrated in Figure 8.9.

Also in India, where the different states vary with respect to individualism, in the more individualistic states, car ownership is higher.[45]

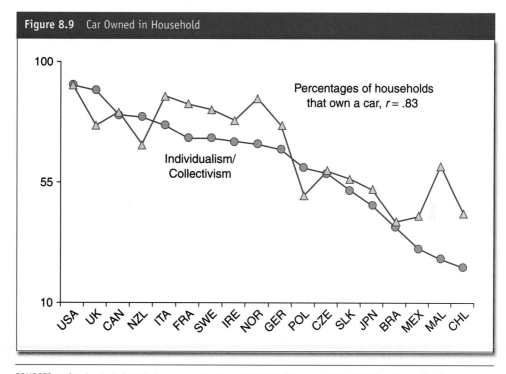

Figure 8.9 Car Owned in Household

SOURCES: Hofstede et al. (2010) (see Appendix A) and TGI Global Surveys 2003–2004 (see Appendix B)

High mobility in the individualistic cultures makes people use their cars more. Individualism explains 50% of variance of the number of passenger kilometers per person per car.[46] Masculinity explains the differences in numbers of cars owned per family. In Italy, Germany, and the United Kingdom, there are more families with two cars than there are in feminine cultures such as the Netherlands and the Scandinavian countries. In these cultures, more people think one car is enough (although they may be able to afford two), and larger percentages of people than in the masculine cultures say they do not want a car. In the United States there are more cars per household than there are licensed drivers per household.[47] Across Europe, among business people differences in having more than three cars in the household are explained by GNI per capita (50%) and masculinity (explaining an additional 17%).[48] Ownership of more than one car is a matter of status.

In the feminine cultures people are less interested in technology than in the masculine cultures. Both the Reader's Digest Surveys and EMS ask questions about the engine size of the car owned by respondents. The answers "Don't know" can be viewed as a measurement of low interest in the engine size. The differences between countries in this respect are large. Of the respondents of EMS in 1999, 30.6% of the Swedes didn't know the engine size of their car, as compared with only 2.6% of the British.

LEISURE

When examples of convergence in Europe are mentioned, a frequent example is convergence of expenditures on services such as leisure activities.[49] Leisure expenditures, however, do not converge. Although worldwide national wealth explains much of variance of leisure expenditures, in the developed world cultural variables are important explaining factors. In Europe, leisure expenditures are highest in individualistic cultures of low power distance and low uncertainty avoidance. The heavy spenders are Sweden and the United Kingdom; the low spenders are Spain and Portugal. An explanation is that free time is spent with family and relatives in the cultures of this cultural configuration, whereas in individualistic cultures of low power distance and low uncertainty avoidance, people spend more time on paid leisure activities. Elements of low uncertainty avoidance that explain expenditures on leisure products and services are low anxiety, innovativeness, and a culture of fitness. Relevant individualistic values are pleasure, stimulation, variety, and adventure. In 1990 the World Values Survey[50] asked respondents how important leisure time was for them. Individualism explained 33% of variance of the answers. The European Value Study of 2000 asked the same question in 25 countries in western and eastern European countries. For that economically heterogeneous group of countries, GNI per capita explained 63% of variance, but for the 15 wealthiest countries[51] low uncertainty avoidance explained 54% of variance. In 2007, in 16 wealthy countries in Europe,[52] low uncertainty avoidance explained 29% of variance of the percentages of people saying that leisure time is very important.[53] Also low uncertainty avoidance explained variance of the percentage of household income spent on recreation and culture in 1999 in Europe,[54] both in the greater European Union (22 countries, 52% explained) and in the 14 member countries of 1999 (64%).

Leisure Activities

The different leisure activities are related to varying cultural dimensions. Low power distance explains variance of visits to amusement facilities such as theme parks or the zoo. Individualism and low uncertainty avoidance explain variance of active participation in sports activities and mean expenditures on sports and recreational services. Collectivism, high power distance, and high uncertainty avoidance tend to explain more passive leisure activities like watching TV, going to the cinema, visiting museums, or regularly dining out in restaurants. Gardening is the typical activity of individualistic cultures, but it is also related to long-term orientation. A few data on playing video games suggest that in masculine cultures people play more video games. However, the type of game may be related to culture. Some Japanese games have conquered the world, but some have not. Pachinko, for example, a gambling game played in nearly every street in Tokyo, has never become popular outside Japan.

For young people, both in Asia and Europe, shopping as a leisure activity is related to individualism.

In the cultures of low power distance and low uncertainty avoidance, sports and fitness activities are a more important leisure activity than they are in the cultures of high power distance and high uncertainty avoidance, where people show relatively more interest in the arts. All sorts of activities are related to this "art orientation," varying from interest in interior design and painting and buying books about it to regular visits to the cinema and doing a cultural tour as holiday activity.

> In Europe, art orientation is most pronounced in Italy. The need for art and show can be traced back far into history. Luigi Barzini writes:
>
> > Italians have always excelled in all activities in which the appearance is predominant: architecture, decoration, landscape gardening, the figurative arts, pageantry, fireworks, ceremonies, opera, and now industrial design, stage jewelry, fashions and the cinema. Italian medieval armor was the most beautiful in Europe: it was highly decorated, elegantly shaped, well designed, but too light and thin to be used in combat.[55]

Several examples of leisure activities and relationships with culture are presented in Table 8.3.

In 1999, 45.8% of Europeans did not go on vacation at all.[56] In 2008, 58% took a vacation, defined by a stay somewhere away from home for at least four consecutive nights for private reasons.[57] In 1999, cultural masculinity and low uncertainty avoidance explained variance of the level of expenditures per vacation trip. In Ireland people spent most on their holidays. Expenditures on packaged holidays were relatively high in the masculine cultures. In the United Kingdom and Austria people spent most.[58] In the feminine cultures people spend more on travel and less on accommodation. People have a greater connectedness to the home than in masculine cultures. This is reflected in the ownership of caravans (*trailers* in American English). Members of feminine cultures want to take a sort of home with them when they go on vacation. Across Europe in 1991, ownership of caravans[59] correlated with low masculinity ($r = -.57**$). Members of feminine cultures like staying in hotels for pleasure less than do members of masculine cultures. In 1997 masculinity explained 56% of variance of 21–30 nights spent in a hotel for personal reasons in the past year. In 2007 masculinity explained 66% of variance of more than 31 nights spent in a hotel for pleasure.[60]

Table 8.3 Leisure Activities and Motives in Europe and Asia

	GNI/cap	PDI	IDV	MAS	UAI	LTO
Worldwide per capita expenditure on tourism[1]	.71***	−.55***	.44***		−.50***	
Europe						
Recreation, culture % of total household expenditures[2]	.79***	−.66***	.59***		−.57***	
% who do active sports at least once a week[3]	.59*	−.54*		−.61*	−.74***	
% who do sports every day and % at least once a week [4]	.80***	−.61***			−.46**	−.42*
6+ visits to cinema in past 12 months[5]	−.55*	.68***			.56*	−.50*
3+ visits to museum or gallery past 12 months[5]			−.47*	.53*	.54*	−.64**
At least once a week[6]						
Watch TV cultural channels					.46**	
Watch TV music channels	−.71***	.60***	−.49**		.53*	
Watch TV movie channels	−.59***	.50***				
Major holiday motive/major attraction[7]						
Wellness, health	−.49**		−.50**		.34*	
Rest, recreation	−.55***	.42*			.60***	
Sports related	.50**	−.44*			−.51**	
% of population visiting amusement facilities[8]		−.85***			−.81***	
Expenditures on recreational/sports services[8]	.53*	−.56*	.75***		−.71**	
Expenditures on gardens, plants and flowers[8]	.74***		.65**			.69**
Expenditures in restaurants, hotels[12]			−.40*		.48*	
Expenditures in restaurants, cafés[12]			−.38*		.43*	−.40*
Europe Leisure Activities Young People						
Watch TV[9]	−.50**	.38*	−.35*			

	GNI/cap	PDI	IDV	MAS	UAI	LTO
Use the Internet, play video games[9]	−.52***	.57***		.36*		
Shopping[10]			.63**		−.77***	
Play instrument[10]	.48*	−.58*		−.53*	−.56*	
Asia Leisure Activities Young People[11]						
Listen to radio		.59*				−.89***
Play any sports			.62*			
Watch video						−.73***
Play hand-held games	.54*			.67**		
Shop	.69**		.55*	.68*		
Camping	.51*				−.62*	
Play TV console games offline by myself			.53*	.83***		

SOURCES: Hofstede et al. (2010) (see Appendix A); (1) United Nations World Tourism Organization, 2004, worldwide 36 countries; (2) Eurostat, Structure of Consumption 2005; (3) EBS 197, 2003, 14 countries; (4) Flash EB 241, 2008; (5) EMS 2007; (6) Flash EB 199, 2007, Europe, Turkey and USA, 27 countries; (7) Flash EB 258, 2009, 25 countries; (8) Eurostat Consumers in Europe, 2001, 13 countries; (9) Flash EB 202 2007, Europe, 25 countries; (10) EBS 151, 2001, Europe 14 countries; (11) Synovate Young Asians 2009, 12 countries; (12) Eurostat Structure of Consumption 2005, 21 countries GNI > US$18,000 (see Appendix B)

What people want for their holidays varies. Whereas people of high uncertainty avoidance cultures search for rest, recreation, wellness, and health, in the low uncertainty avoidance cultures people search more for active sports or sports-related activities. Short-term-orientation cultures, where preservation of the status quo is important, like to visit museums.[61] The numbers of museums per million people[62] are correlated with short-term orientation. An important value of short-term orientation is tradition, and what museums generally do is preserve the past.

People have very different ideas about requirements of facilities for their holidays, and these ideas are related to what they are used to at home. Americans and Asians want air-conditioned hotel rooms, whereas many Europeans think air conditioning is unhealthy. Northern Europeans like dining in the open air in the warm climates of southern Europe, whereas the Spanish will refuse to eat outside; it may spoil the food, or a fly may drop in your wine. Whereas in Asia, Westerners want a mix of sun, sea, and ethnic culture, and in the evening a beer at the poolside, the Japanese, Koreans, and Chinese will want their karaoke bars.

Pets

People mostly enjoy their pets in leisure time. Roles of dogs and cats vary across cultures. In particular the role of dogs in people's lives varies across cultures. In low power distance cultures dogs are companions, equals, and they join in fitness activities of humans. In high power distance cultures, what is appealing to people is that dogs can be trained to obey unconditionally. In high power distance cultures both dogs and cats can serve as status symbols. In individualistic and low power distance cultures, cats are companions and the fact that cats show individual minds fits individualistic cultures. Differences in cat ownership correlate with individualism, and differences in dog ownership correlate with high power distance.[63] Prepared pet food is correlated with wealth. In the lower-income countries, pets tend to be more fed with leftovers of human food.

In pet food advertising, the relationship between humans and pets reflect cultural differences that are similar to relationships between humans. In collectivistic cultures pets live with the family or are shown to be part of a pet family, whereas in individualistic cultures usually a pet is shown as a companion of a single individual. The two pictures in Figure 8.10 are from a German commercial for Sheba cat food, showing a woman alone with a cat, and the Japanese cat food brand Maruha, showing the extended cat family.

Figure 8.10 Cat Food Advertising in Germany and Japan

FINANCE

How people deal with their money is culture bound. Examples are insurance, banking, and private investments. Table 8.4 shows cultural relationships for several financial products and habits.

Insuring oneself and one's property is a habit of the wealthy, individualistic part of the world. Comparison of ownership of all sorts of insurance products over time shows convergence, but differences between countries have remained considerable. Worldwide, in Asia, in Latin America, and in greater Europe, income explains most of variance, although individualism tends to be a second predictor (except in Asia). In Europe, in 1970 and 1991, low uncertainty avoidance explained variance of ownership of insurance products. At face value, one would expect that individuals in strong uncertainty avoidance cultures would own more insurance products than members of weak uncertainty avoidance cultures, but the relationship appears to be the opposite. This demonstrates that uncertainty avoidance is not the same as risk avoidance. Insurance products do eliminate risk, but in low uncertainty avoidance cultures where internal locus of control prevails, people take their future in their own hands by insuring themselves. In high uncertainty avoidance cultures where external locus of control operates, people are more inclined to wait until others take control. External locus of control also explains the relationship between public pension spending and high uncertainty avoidance, whereas private pension funds are related to low uncertainty avoidance, cultures where people save for their pension themselves instead of expecting the government to take care of their pensions. Several OECD data on public pension spending as a percentage of GNI correlate with high uncertainty avoidance.

Life insurances are more sold in individualistic cultures than in collectivistic cultures. In the former, should one die early, one cannot count on family to support one's dependants. Other relationships are with low power distance and low masculinity. In the feminine cultures people are emotionally more sensitive to the needs of their dependants. In high power distance, people rely on their superiors to take care of them.[64]

In some Asian countries, where originally children supported their elderly parents, legislation has been introduced that spells out the children's duties in supporting their parents; increasingly children are not willing to do so because of money and time constraints. In India the so-called Maintenance of Parents Act provides to parents above 60 years old who cannot support themselves the legal means to claim maintenance from their children.

Personal loans are more frequent in individualistic cultures than in collectivistic cultures where people save more for buying expensive products or loan from family and friends. Long-/short-term orientation is a dimension that explains differences in saving or borrowing money. In 2001, the percentage of respondents who tended to agree with the statement "Buying on credit is more useful than dangerous," correlated with short-term orientation.[65]

Table 8.4 Finance and Culture: Insurance, Banking, and Private Investments

	GNI/cap	PDI	IDV	MAS	UAI	LTO
Insurance						
Life 1970[1]	.55*		.61*		−.73***	
Life 1991[1]			.64***		−.67***	
Building 1991[1]			.61**		−.34	
Home insurance[2]	.81***	−.47**	.52***	−.46**		
Pension funds as % of GNI 2001[3]			.53*	−.57*	−.74***	
Banking						
Personal loan (% of pop.) 2000[6]	.65**	−.78***			−.70***	
Household with credit card 1970[1]	.49*	−.45*			−.67***	
Credit card (% of pop.) 2001[6]			.48*			
Use credit card (% of pop.) 2008[2]	.65***	−.68***	.43***			
Online banking (%) 2001[6]	.65*			−.82***		
Use Internet for banking, 2008[5]	.44*	−.45*	.55***	−.41*		
Use computer for searching financial or business information, 2008[8]						.95***
Watch financial websites, 2008[8]						.89*
Private Investments						
Own stocks and shares 1970[1]	.69***		.47*	−.58*	−.63**	
Own stocks and shares 1991[1]	.66***			−.56*	−.56*	
Bought stocks and shares 1999[4]					−.54*	
Personally own stocks and shares on national exchange 2008[7]		−.47*			−.60**	
Traded stocks in past 12 months, 2008[7]						.47*

SOURCES: Hofstede et al. (2010) (see Appendix A); (1) Reader's Digest Surveys 1970 and 1991; (2) TGI product book 2009, 41 countries worldwide; (3) William Mercer, http://www.merceric.com; (4) EMS 1999; (5) Flash EB 241, 2008, 25 countries; (6) EB 56, 2001, 10 countries; (7) EMS 2007; (8) Synovate PAX Digital life, 2008 (see Appendix B)

The Chinese historically have saved much more than people in other countries, and they still do so. In 2009 China's households were saving 25% of their discretionary income, which is about six times the savings rate in the United States and three times the rate in Japan.[66] Credit card ownership and usage are more frequent in individualistic cultures. Online banking started in the feminine cultures, but Internet banking has spread across the world.

Considerable differences exist between countries with respect to private investments. In 1970 and 1991, owning stocks and shares was a characteristic of wealthy societies. This relationship had disappeared by 1999, when low uncertainty avoidance explained variance. In 2007 the percentages of people who said they had traded stocks in the past 12 months correlated with long-term orientation.

SHOPPING AND BUYING BEHAVIOR

Shopping and buying behavior concerns shopping activities, shopping purposes, who does the shopping and with whom, shopping frequency, buyer-seller relationships, and retail preferences. In addition to the conventional retail options there is the Internet, which has introduced a new dimension to buyer-seller relationships.

Shopping activities and purposes in addition to buying can be *searching, learning* about product supply, *bargain hunting, price bargaining, spending money, recreation,* avoiding *boredom,* and *self-gratification* to overcome a depressive mood. Shopping to overcome a depressive mood is not a likely phenomenon in collectivistic cultures where people are not aware of any depressive moods (see Chapter 5). Searching and price bargaining are activities common in collectivistic cultures. Widespread haggling is an important aspect of Chinese shopping behavior. Searching includes comparing shops, prices, and thoroughly inspecting the products, including touching and smelling. In individualistic and short-term-oriented cultures, saving time and convenience are more important, because extensive search takes time away from more important activities.[67] Convenience needs of short-term-oriented cultures make shoppers want to buy groceries as quickly as possible.[68]

Chinese traditional values—related to long-term orientation—emphasize thrift, diligence, and value consciousness, so it is socially desirable to save money and be a meticulous shopper in China.[69] Across 23 countries in Europe, differences in price consciousness with respect to food choice are related to low GNI per capita and high power distance, but in a group of 16 wealthy countries the relationship with low individualism is strongest.[70]

In collectivistic cultures an important shopping distinction is between public and private consumption goods. People are more price conscious for personal goods than for public goods. For members of collectivistic and high power distance cultures where people are status conscious, for public consumption goods, and particularly for gifts, social norms are more important than price. Spending money as such can be a social value, demonstrating allegiance to friends and family. As individualists are more likely than collectivists to seek "fun" situations, fun shopping is typical individualistic behavior. Individualistic Americans, for example, are more recreational and informational shoppers than Chileans, who score a low 23 on the individualism index. Whereas Americans will go to the mall more to look and browse, Chileans will go for a specific purchase, with a plan to buy.[71] Shopping for recreational purposes is related to individualism, among both young Europeans and young Asians (see Tables 8.3 and 8.5).

The term *recreational* covers shopping as leisure activity, but in collectivistic cultures some shopping activities also are a social activity, both for grownups and young people, which is not exactly the same as recreation in the individualistic sense. Donquixote, a Japanese discount retail chain, decided to extend shopping hours in 2002 because young people out on dates were visiting the store late at night.[72] So recreational shopping may have different purposes in the United States and in Japan. In India shopping has become a leisure activity for urban nuclear family women. They love visiting various retail formats and comparing prices and bargaining.[73] In Malaysia, shopping malls offer all sorts of entertainment, like cinemas, bowling, ice skating, and other indoor entertainment, which makes visiting shopping malls a leisure activity.[74]

Both in the search and buying process social relationships between buyers and sellers vary among individualistic and collectivistic cultures. In collectivistic cultures buyers want a relationship with the seller and involve in-group members more than in individualistic cultures.

The importance of in-group members doesn't imply that people always go shopping with their in-group members. Although teenagers may shop in groups when shopping as a leisure activity, for some purposes Chinese prefer to shop anonymously, attracting little community and extended family attention to avoid any resulting gossip and the risk of losing face. They prefer crowded places. The Chinese concept of *renao*—meaning lively, bustling with noise and excitement, opposite to a negative state of being alone—explains preference for crowded and noisy shopping places like markets.[76]

Triandis describes a high-involvement purchase in a collectivistic culture as follows:

> Consider the situation of buying a carpet for the house. Most individualists will shop around, will find one or two carpets that are within the price range they are willing to pay, and will consult one or two members of their family and buy the carpet. Most collectivists are likely to proceed in a more elaborate way. First, they are likely to establish a personal relationship with a storekeeper. Ideally, they will find a member of their kin group who sells carpets, or a friend of a member of the kinship group who does that. They will tell this person about their needs and give details of their income and family life. Having established trust with this merchant, they will examine the stock and find a number of carpets that may be suitable. They will then invite a large portion of their in-group to view the carpets and express their opinions. Finally, after extensive consultations, they will purchase the carpet. Whereas the individualist primarily has an exchange relationship with the merchant—I pay my money and receive the carpet—the collectivist fosters a personal relationship, allowing the merchant to learn a great deal in order to arrive at the best decision.[75]

	GNI/cap	PDI	IDV	MAS	UAI	LTO
Table 8.5 Shopping Behavior						
Shopping						
Women's share of total time spent on shopping[1]			.83***	.72*		
Men's share of total time spent on shopping[1]			−.83***	−.72*		
Proportion of men who spend any time on shopping activities[1]	.62*			−.72*		
Buying groceries as quickly as possible[6]						−.53*
Young people in Asia who enjoy the fun of shopping[7]			.70**			
Mail Order/Internet Shopping						
Purchased goods by post, mail order[4]	.35*	−.39*	.43*		−.44*	.47**
Bought products and services on the Internet[2]	.57***	−.46*	.61***		−.58***	
Bought goods via Internet in past 12 months[4]	.71***	−.57***	.64***		−.67***	
Bought on Internet in the past month[5]	.39*	−.44**	.43*			.33*
Grocery			−.33*	.39*		.64***
Event tickets	.51***	−.48***	.38*			−.43*
Video games, DVDs	.40***	−.56***	.61***			−.33*
Compared on Internet, did not buy[4]	.50**	−.45*	.54***	−.42*	−.71***	
Compared on Internet, bought in shop[4]	.65***	−.47*	.47**	−.45*	−.59***	
Online shopping 10–18 years old, Latin America[3]					−.87**	

SOURCES: Hofstede et al. (2010) (see Appendix A); (1) Eurostat 2002, How Europeans spend their time, 9 countries; (2) Flash EB 241, 2008, 25 countries; (3) Ibero-America Interactive Generation, 2008, 7 countries; (4) EBS 298, 2008, 25 countries; (5) Data Nielsen, 2007, 28 countries worldwide. In Goodrich and De Mooij, 2010; (6) Future Foundation, Trends in clothes shopping and fashion, 2009, Europe, 12 countries; (7) Synovate Young Asians, 2009, 12 countries (see Appendix B)

Living conditions influence shopping habits. Whereas in the United States or the United Kingdom, or even in France, people go to a mega-store once a week to do bulk buying, Japanese housewives make it their routine to visit a familiar nearby supermarket where their friends gather. One reason is the social influence; another is that refrigerators and storage space at Japanese homes are limited.[77] In Europe, in the individualistic and low uncertainty avoidance cultures, important influencing factors for food choice are convenience and availability.[78] People who work full-time will have fewer shopping time opportunities than people who work part-time, so it will influence the number of visits they make to the shop. In low power distance cultures, more women work part-time ($r = -.61***$) than in high power distance cultures.[79] Data for working women were presented in Chapter 3. Table 8.5 shows data that demonstrate how in masculine cultures women do more of the shopping and in the feminine cultures men also go shopping.

Other differences in buying behavior are between *planned buying* and *impulsive buying*. Impulsive buying is involved when a person has no intention to buy a product, yet buys it. A consumer can also intend to buy a product and decide only in the shop which brand to buy. A completely planned purchase occurs if both the product and the brand purchase were planned. If impulsive buying were related to the personality trait "impulsiveness," it should be correlated with strong uncertainty avoidance, but there is little evidence that impulsive buying is related to the overall personality trait impulsiveness. Impulsive buying is likely more related to thrill, variety, and sensation seeking as well as stimulation, traits that are related to individualism and low uncertainty avoidance. A comparison of impulsive buying behavior across five Western and Asian countries[80] showed that the individualistic emphasis on the self, individual needs, and desires encourage impulsive buying behavior.

Collectivistic notions of the self that emphasize interdependence, emotional control, and moderation tend to discourage impulse buying behavior. For a group of seven countries in Latin America[81] there is a relationship between low uncertainty avoidance and the percentages of answers "Agree" to the question "I often buy products on impulse" ($r = -.70*$). Chileans tend to make more planned purchases than Americans, who rely more on spur-of-the-moment decisions.[82]

Out-of-Home Shopping and Buying

Next to the physical retail environment—also called *brick-and-mortar retailing*—there are various means for out-of-home shopping and buying: mail order, television shopping, and Internet shopping.

Mail order buying by catalogue has existed for a long time, and the Internet is partly a replacement of the printed catalogue. Internet shopping has not replaced brick-and-mortar shopping. Between 51% (Poland) and 81% (Hungary) of Europeans prefer shopping personally. These differences are not related to either income or culture. Variance of the percentages of people who purchased goods by post is explained by long-term orientation and low power distance. Across Europe there is a significant correlation between buying by mail and by Internet ($r = .57***$),[83] so basically the Internet is a new medium for out-of-home shopping. Internet buying is, as yet, more commonplace in individualistic cultures of low uncertainty avoidance and low power distance (see Table 8.5).

What people buy online across cultures reflects differences of products or services people buy in regular stores. For example, more event tickets or video games are bought online in the individualistic cultures. The relationship between grocery buying via the Internet and long-term orientation and collectivism reflects historical habits of having grocery products delivered to the home in Asian countries.[84] The Internet offers the opportunity to compare products. Across Europe, in the individualistic, low uncertainty avoidance, and low power distance cultures where decision making is more information based, more people tend to search for information and compare products on the Internet even when they do not buy online or buy in the shop.

Although online sales have been most pervasive in the United States, Chinese consumers, although relatively new to the Internet, are very active online shoppers and buyers. They are willing to make high-risk purchases (e.g., medical, health) and buy high-involvement products such as cosmetics, beauty aids, and travel online.[85] In particular social networking helps them to make better comparisons,[86] and Chinese websites show collectivistic community activities like group buying that you wouldn't find on U.S. websites.[87]

To many, Internet buying is still considered to be risky, so trust in the seller is important. Across Europe, however, the identity of the supplier is of lesser importance than other influences, such as safety, the country of origin where the product was made, and the brand.[88] Several problems like insecurity and privacy are associated with online buying. A study among respondents from the United States, Canada, Germany, and Japan showed differences between countries with respect to concerns about payment security, company legitimacy, and assurance. The Japanese in particular note telephone follow-up as desirable because it is more personal than e-mail. In general people prefer local website design features.[89]

Retail Design

Because of shopping differences, retail design varies across countries with respect to the products offered, variety, shop design, product presentation, shopper behavior, personnel, and service. Consumer preferences for supermarkets or shopping centers vary, and these differences change only slowly over time.[90]

In collectivistic and high power distance cultures, freshness of food is very important. What is considered fresh varies. For the Dutch, prepacked cut lettuce is considered to be fresh, but not so for the Belgians, to whom fresh means you have to cut it yourself. A whole fish is fresh, not so some prepacked bits and pieces. In high uncertainty avoidance cultures, more product information is provided on the shelves. Personnel are better dressed and cleanliness is demonstrated, for example, by white floors and thongs or plastic gloves to pick fresh food products that you don't see so frequently in low uncertainty avoidance cultures. To symbolize freshness of food products or the offer of the day, handwritten information

Figure 8.11 Delhaize, Belgium, and Albert Heijn, the Netherlands

may be provided instead of well-designed, consistent printed information that cannot be produced instantaneously.

Figure 8.11 shows two in-store sales messages. The one on the left, which reads "Suggestion from the Chef," is from the Belgian supermarket Delhaize; the second one is from the Dutch supermarket Albert Heijn, and it says in a much more egalitarian way, "What do we eat today?" The pictures also show how the Belgian supermarket communicates freshness by handwritten text, whereas consistency needs of the Dutch will always have everything printed with the right logo, colors, and type font.

A difference related to individualism and power distance is how products are categorized: by sort or by relationships or even by color, as discussed in Chapter 6. Belgian supermarkets tend to present more products by relationship, whereas in the Netherlands products are categorized by sort. Other differences are visual routing signs versus verbal routing signs.[91] In Belgium, personnel are presented by specialization and hierarchy, whereas in the Netherlands they wear the same uniform to suggest they are all equal. For shoppers in Belgium, it is clear by name and picture who is the manager. In the Netherlands, the manager doesn't make him- or herself known. In supermarkets in feminine cultures more men do food shopping, even with children. This influences the type of shopping carts offered to the public. In low power distance cultures where independence of children is important, small shopping carts are available for children so they can learn to shop independently.

The IKEA formula is based on self-assembly, which is not attractive to high power distance cultures where people want service from human beings. However, IKEA offers total concepts—living rooms, bedrooms—which is attractive to collectivistic and high power distance cultures where people think more holistically. Although Russia scores high on power distance, IKEA is very successful in that country.

Whereas service personnel in retail in the United States learn to be friendly and personal and present themselves at equal level with the customer by conducting some small talk, this is different in Asia. Consumers in Japan look to salespeople to explain a product's attributes without any direct messages. Communication is not personal and small talk can be perceived as artificial or even intrusive. Americans can find the Japanese emphasis on formality and hierarchy (with the retailer on a lower footing) cold.[92] Taiwanese consumers expect service personnel to perform tasks because they genuinely wish to gratify consumer preferences. Service personnel should be willing, enthusiastic, and respectful in fulfilling their service tasks, and Taiwanese consumers expect a genuine attitudinal regard for the "master-servant relationship." Giving and /or preserving a consumer's face is of great importance.[93] Figure 8.12 shows an example of courtesy to the customer in China.

Figure 8.12   *China: Courtesy to the Customer. Photograph Gerard Foekema*

TV sales channels follow cultural preferences and are analogous to department store shopping. In the United States discussions are personalized, and hosts address guests as friends. In Japan little emphasis is placed on any personal details, and each product is shown in detail with extreme close-ups. Conversations stay close to the product.[94]

> Because of differences in shopping behavior retail mergers and acquisitions often fail. There are little advantages of economies of scale because both the product offer and retail design have to be local. Dutch Ahold failed in Spain, British Boots failed in Japan, French Carrefour failed in Japan, British Marks & Spencer failed in continental Europe, German C & A failed in the United Kingdom, and British Tesco failed in Taiwan. One of the reasons of failure of the latter was unclear communication about Tesco's own brands. In Asia retail brands are viewed as cheap and poor quality.[95]

Not all countries have the large shopping malls that exist in the United States or some Asian countries. In many Western countries a shopping center tends to have a variety of stores selling different product categories to a variety of consumers. In collectivistic cultures shops selling the same category are often located in one area to facilitate comparison and price negotiating. Motives for shopping in supermarkets also vary. Whereas in Western societies supermarkets are characterized by a large variety of packaged goods, in Thailand shoppers say they are attracted to supermarkets because of the quality of fresh food and the cleanliness. Because of the importance of fresh food, wet markets continue to dominate shopping behavior in Thailand.[96] Also in the south of Europe, fresh food markets are popular. In Spain only 40% of food is bought in the supermarket, as compared with 59% in the rest of Europe. Across Europe other retailing types vary with consumer preferences. In Germany "hard discounters" like Aldi and Lidl have a far bigger market share than in other European countries. They account for around 30% of food sales, as compared with only the 10% that such firms have in Britain and 8% in France.[97] The degree to which supermarkets offer products under private label varies with individualism. In collectivistic cultures private label products are less popular because they don't contribute to upholding face (see also Chapter 5).

COMPLAINING BEHAVIOR

Consumer complaining behavior can be classified into three categories: (1) voice response to the party directly involved in the complaint; (2) negative word of mouth or brand switching; (3) legal action.[98] With varying concepts of self, perceptions of others, and levels of social activity, consumers across cultures are likely to vary with respect to these three types of responses. Because of harmony needs, collectivistic consumers, compared with individualists, are relatively loyal and are less likely to voice complaints when they experience post-purchase problems. They are more likely than individualists to engage in negative word of mouth to in-group members. Moreover, when collectivists do exit, it is particularly difficult for the offending supplier to regain them as customers.[99] There is evidence that compared with Australians the Chinese are less likely to lodge a formal complaint for a faulty product.[100] Across Europe the percentages of people who say they have made any kind of formal complaint by writing, by telephone or in person, to a seller or provider in the past 12 months vary from 4% in Bulgaria to 25% in the Netherlands. The differences are correlated with GNI per capita, individualism, and low uncertainty avoidance. The percentages of people who took no further action when the complaint was not dealt with in a satisfactory manner varied from 38% in Denmark to 84% in Romania. These differences are related to high power distance and collectivism.[101]

A phenomenon that may only work in collectivistic cultures is a boycott of products. Chinese consumers nowadays are increasingly using boycotts to express their discontent with foreign brands. In 2005 there was a nationwide boycott of Japanese brands after the Japanese prime minister refused to cancel his worship of Yasukini Juja, the burial place of the most notorious Japanese war criminals of the Second World War.[102]

An aspect of American culture is the frequent use of legal action. It may be related to the configuration individualism and masculinity, which makes people want to get the most out of life. This explains the high use of litigation in the United States. Also consumers will take more legal action. For years the cigarette industry has been sued for damaging smokers' health. In 2002 in the United States, obese people even started suing fast food chains, holding them responsible for their gaining weight.

> Fear of legal action has made many companies in the United States and the United Kingdom include all sorts of warnings on label instructions on consumer goods. On a bar of Dial soap: "Directions: Use like regular soap." On a Sears hair dryer: "Do not use while sleeping." On packaging for a Rowenta iron: "Do not iron clothes on body." On Nytol sleep aid: "Warning: May cause drowsiness." On a child's Superman costume: "Wearing of this garment does not enable you to fly." On Sainsbury's peanuts: "Warning: Contains nuts." On Marks & Spencer bread pudding: "Product will be hot after heating." On Boot's child's cough medicine: "Do not drive a car or operate machinery after taking this medication." On a toner cartridge of a photocopying machine: "Do not eat."

BRAND LOYALTY

People in collectivistic cultures of high uncertainty avoidance are expected to be more brand loyal than people of individualistic cultures that are also of low uncertainty avoidance. Trying a new product or brand involves some amount of risk taking, and it may also satisfy a variety-seeking motive.[103] Variety seeking and stimulation are aspects of individualistic cultures. Conformity needs make collectivists more brand loyal. Purchasing products that are well known to the in-group may help to decrease uncertainty about in-group approval of the purchase.[104]

There is little fundamental cross-cultural research on brand loyalty. The 1991 Frontiers[105] study by the Henley Center, conducted in Germany, the Netherlands, Italy, United Kingdom, France, and Spain, asked people of several age categories whether they would replace their car with one of the same brand. For the age group 45–59 years, this study shows a significant relationship between brand loyalty for cars and cultural masculinity ($r = .90***$). Data for seven countries worldwide by the market research agency TGI[106] show a relationship between the wish to stick to a brand and long-term orientation. These findings must be viewed as indicative only, as the number of countries surveyed is limited. Data from Reader's Digest surveys seem to confirm the relationship with long-term orientation in view of the relation-ships between short-term orientation and the percentages of people who say they are among the first to try new brands. In 2005, short-term orientation explained 40% of variance.[107]

Analysis of mean switching rates for service providers of all sorts of services (banking, insur-ance, telecom, energy, etc.) shows for the average of all services across 25 European countries correlations with high GNI per capita, low power distance, and low uncertainty avoidance. Also across 18 of the richest countries wealth explains variance. Maybe as yet mainly the rich countries have better switching facilities for services like energy, banking, and Internet.[108]

Generally the concept of brand loyalty may vary with different brand types, like prod-uct brands or company brands. It makes a difference if one is loyal to a product brand, to a store, or to a company.

Large power distance implies respect for the status quo, the "proper place" of the power brand, the brand with the highest market share. In Asia, big market share brands are the kings of their "brand world," and consumers in Asia believe in them implicitly.[109] This is the reason brands like Coca-Cola, Nescafé, and San Miguel have such high and sustained market shares in a number of Asian countries. Being big automatically promotes trust. This trust, combined with harmony and conformance needs of collectivistic cultures, leads to high brand loyalty. Consequently, it will be difficult for new entrants in these markets to gain market share.

Brand credibility is an important motive for brand loyalty in collectivistic and high uncer-tainty avoidance cultures.[110] For consumers in East Asian cultures, the reputation of the firm contributes to customer loyalty more than in individualistic and low uncertainty avoidance cultures.[111] This is particularly important for e-commerce, when customers don't have per-sonal contacts as they do in shops.

ADOPTION AND DIFFUSION OF INNOVATIONS

Understanding why and how fast people adopt new products and the differences across countries is important for marketers because new product success is linked to profitability.

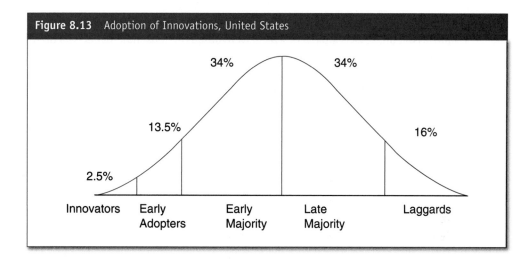

Figure 8.13   Adoption of Innovations, United States

34%   34%

13.5%   16%

2.5%

Innovators   Early   Early   Late   Laggards
              Adopters   Majority   Majority

Consumer innovativeness can be defined as the predisposition to buy new and different products and brands rather than remain with previous choices and consumption patterns.[112] As innovativeness is related to tolerance for ambiguity and deviant ideas, members of weak uncertainty avoidance cultures are more innovative than are members of strong uncertainty avoidance cultures, and new products take off faster. Several studies have demonstrated the relationship between uncertainty avoidance and consumer innovativeness[113] and new product take-off across wealthy countries.[114] High power distance and high uncertainty avoidance are found to hinder the acceptance of new products, so in these cultures it takes longer for new products to penetrate. Individualism has a positive effect because initiating new behavior independently from others is a characteristic of innovativeness.

Lynn and Gelb[115] developed an index of national innovativeness based on ownership of a number of consumer electronics, which was found to be significantly correlated with individualism, low uncertainty avoidance, and purchasing power. However, innovativeness was found to be domain specific; that is, consumers who are likely to adopt the latest new product in one field may be laggards in another. Adoption of one new product reinforces adoption of others in the same category. New product innovators will be drawn from the heavy users of other products within the product category.[116] This also applies to the culture level.

Rogers[117] identified five categories of (American) consumers according to the degree of acceptance of new products. They are called innovators, early adopters, early majority, late majority, and laggards. The *innovators* represent 2.5% of (American) society; they are described as venturesome individuals who are willing to take risks. *Early adopters* (13.5%) are the ones to take up new ideas that are taken up by the innovators who serve as role models. *Early majority* (34%) are risk avoiders; *late majority* (34%) are skeptical and cautious of new ideas; and *laggards* (16%) are very traditional. A two-category distinction is between *innovators* and *imitators*. Figure 8.13 illustrates the curve.

Steenkamp[118] calculated percentages of adoption categories for packaged goods in five countries in Europe (see Table 8.6). These were based on household panel data on the occurrence and timing of first purchases for 239 new consumer packaged goods over a 52-week period after introduction for a large sample of consumers. Correlations with the cultural variables confirm the relationships with uncertainty avoidance and individualism. The category innovators for the five European countries plus the United States is correlated with low uncertainty avoidance and individualism, whereas the category late majority is correlated with high uncertainty avoidance and collectivism.

Table 8.6 Adopter Categories Across Countries

	Innovators (%)	Early Majority (%)	Late Majority (%)	Laggards (%)
United States	16.0	34.0	34.0	16.0
United Kingdom	23.8	43.4	26.4	6.4
France	15.1	25.5	35.6	23.8
Germany	16.8	26.1	34.2	22.9
Spain	8.9	34.1	43.9	13.1
Italy	13.4	30.8	41.0	14.8
Correlation Coefficients				
IDV	−.75*		−.74*	
UAI	−.83*		.83*	

SOURCES: Rogers (1962) and Steenkamp (2002)

Also, in Latin America, where all countries are high on uncertainty avoidance, the percentages of early adopters tends to be lower than in the United States. A Target Group Index (TGI) study in Chile found that 7.5% of the average population could be viewed as early adopters of technological innovations.[119]

Diffusion is the process by which an innovation is communicated through certain channels over time among the members of a social system. The channels are the mass media and word-of-mouth communication. The *adoption rate* is the relative speed with which members of a social system adopt an innovation. New products diffuse at significantly different rates in different countries. For example, in the United States new products diffuse more slowly than in Asia or Europe, but also across Europe there are differences.[120] In Japan, a collectivistic culture of high uncertainty avoidance, adoption of new ideas and products takes long, but the need for conformity leads to fast diffusion as soon as opinion leaders have taken the lead. Cultures of low uncertainty avoidance in Asia adopt innovations faster. Analysis of adoption rates of Japanese, Chinese, Korean, and American consumers showed that the Japanese (high uncertainty avoidance) are cautious until the facts about a novel product are known, whereas the Chinese (low uncertainty avoidance) are the least cautious.[121] A study across 13 European countries found a relationship between diffusion rates of technological innovations with high power distance, collectivism, and masculinity. The explanation was that in these cultures more interpersonal communication causes faster diffusion, and power holders serve as opinion leaders.[122] The measurement and comparison of diffusion across cultures is difficult, because diffusion rates must be compared over longer time periods. The most difficult problem of time-series research across countries is the availability and accuracy of data. If available at all, early data may not be accurate and/or not comparable with later data.

Several studies have used the *coefficients of innovation* (*p*) and *imitation* (*q*) developed by Bass[123] to measure the effects of the media on diffusion of innovations.

The Bass model predicts the spread of innovation, the number of adopters of a new product, and at which time they will adopt it. It assumes that there are two groups in the diffusion process: the innovators and imitators, and two ways a new product diffuses: via the mass media and word-of-mouth. The model is based on Western practice where the innovators are the first ones to buy a product and are mainly affected by the media or advertising. The effects of these influences are captured by the coefficient of innovation, *p*. The imitators are influenced by their peers and are mainly influenced by word-of-mouth, whose effect is captured by the coefficient of imitation, *q*. Diffusion occurs within a system and therefore is a culture-specific phenomenon. The coefficient of innovation is high in countries that are high on individualism, low on uncertainty avoidance, and low on power distance. The coefficient of imitation is high in countries that are low on individualism (word-of-mouth communication is strong) and high on uncertainty avoidance.[124]

Takada and Jain,[125] who have conducted several studies on diffusion of innovations, believed that the coefficient of imitation would represent cross-country differences more clearly and distinctly than the coefficient of innovation, because the latter represents small parts of populations of any country. The innovators are a relatively small segment in the market, and they play a rather limited role in diffusing the innovation to other segments. The imitators, in contrast, play the major role in diffusion of innovations in the marketplace and are a substantially larger segment.

An important conclusion is that culturally similar countries have similar diffusion patterns. Some countries, for some products, will be leaders while others lag. As a result of global media, there is a learning effect between leading and lagging countries. Consumers in a lag country can potentially learn about the benefits of a product from the experience of adopters in the lead country, and this learning can result in a faster diffusion rate in the lag markets.[126] For industrial new products, the learning effect is substantial. It took 17 years for the adoption of scanners (in retail) to peak in the United States, whereas it peaked much faster in the lag markets. Within Europe, the adoption peaked in 9 years in Germany and Belgium, where it was introduced in 1980, whereas in Denmark and Spain it peaked within 4 years, where it was introduced in 1986.[127]

Culture also influences the development of new products. In the new product development process, two stages are important: initiation and implementation. Cultures whose strengths center on initiation are high in individualism but low in power distance, masculinity, and uncertainty avoidance. Cultures whose strengths center on implementation are low in individualism but high in power distance, masculinity, and uncertainty avoidance.[128]

PREDICTING MARKET DEVELOPMENT ACROSS CULTURES

Understanding the role of culture can lead to better predictions of how markets will develop and new products and services diffuse and thus help develop marketing strategy. Although in some cultures people adopt a new innovation or habit quickly, people of other cultures may not. Let's take the Internet as an example. At the end of the 20th century, expectations were that the Internet would cause greater productivity everywhere and make all societies more egalitarian. Instead, people have adopted it for their specific culturally defined purposes.

For better predictions, countries can be mapped according to cultural similarity. An example is a culture map for the development and effects of the Internet. The Internet first penetrated the economically developed markets of low to medium uncertainty avoidance where people adopt innovations faster than in markets of high uncertainty avoidance. These markets are in the lower two quadrants in Figure 8.14.

In the upper two quadrants of Figure 8.14 are the lagging markets, the high uncertainty avoidance cultures. When the Internet became more common in all developed markets, purposes of usage varied. Whereas in the low masculine markets people have adopted the Internet to enhance the quality of life, using it more frequently, and more for leisure and educational purposes, in the high masculine markets the Internet was initially and most important expected to enhance productivity for greater competitiveness.

A third dimension that explains variance of adoption rates is power distance. In the high power distance cultures, governments can exert greater power to influence new developments. In France the government had an early influence on information technology by backing the Minitel system. In Spain the government pushed Internet usage by sponsoring its use in schools. In South Korea the government has pushed broadband communications. As a result, already in 2001 South Koreans spent more time online than the people of any other nation in the world, which also had a beneficial effect on the Korean economy.[129] South Korea is one of the countries with the highest broadband penetration in the world.

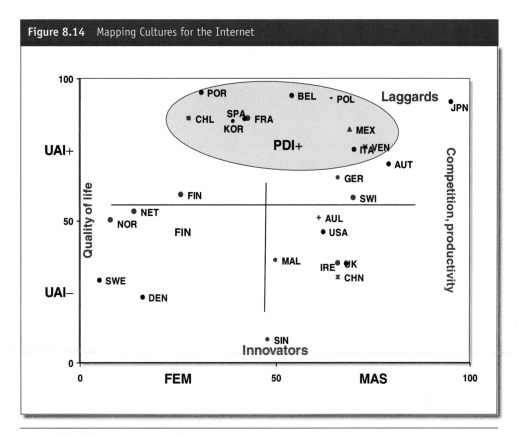

Figure 8.14   Mapping Cultures for the Internet

SOURCE: Data Hofstede et al. (2010) (see Appendix A)

CONCLUSION

This chapter showed that differences exist between countries with respect to ownership and usage of many products. Many data on product consumption, ownership, and usage are available in the public domain and can be submitted to correlation and regression analysis to understand the differences. This chapter provided many examples of how culture explains variance. Many differences are stable over time, and with increased wealth the relationships between GNI per capita and the various cultural dimensions change. In particular, new technology shows different patterns over time. Whereas generally national income combined with low uncertainty avoidance explains variance of new products first, after some time, when new products have penetrated, other dimensions explain variance of usage.

Several aspects of buying and shopping behavior are related to culture. The different concepts of self are reflected in shopping activities and motives. Whether people complain and how they complain is mainly related to individualism and collectivism. The diffusion-of-innovations process and the adopter categories defined by Rogers are based on American culture. Although similar adopter categories do exist across cultures, the distribution across populations varies by culture, and so do the rates of diffusion.

NOTES

1. Peter, J. P., Olson, J. C., & Grunert, K. G. (1999). *Consumer behaviour and marketing strategy* (European ed.). London: McGraw-Hill, 19.
2. Magrabi, F. M., Chung, Y. S., Cha, S. S., & Yang, S. J. (1991). *The economics of household consumption*. New York: Praeger, 210–234, 245–248.
3. *Risk issues*. (2005). Special Eurobarometer report 238.
4. Askegaard, S., & Madsen, T. K. (1995, September). *European food cultures: An exploratory analysis of food consumption in European regions*. MAPP working paper no. 26. Retrieved December 18, 2009, from http://130.226.203.239/pub/mapp/wp/wp26.pdf
5. Singh, D. (2007). *Cross cultural comparison of buying behavior in India*. Doctoral thesis. Panjab University, Chandigarh. University Business School.
6. Nagorski, A. (2001, February 26). Hold the French fries. *Newsweek*, 50–51.
7. Data Euromonitor (1997).
8. TGI product book. (2009).
9. TGI product book. (2009). 41 countries worldwide.
10. *Social indicators*. (1980). Eurostat.
11. Euromonitor (1997).
12. Euromonitor (1997).
13. *Consumers in Europe*. (2001). Eurostat, 73.
14. TGI product book (2009).
15. Data on fresh coffee consumption 1998–2008 from Sara Lee/Douwe Egberts, courtesy Leo van Deutekom.
16. TGI Global Surveys 2003–2004, 36 countries worldwide.
17. Edmondson, G. (2006, August 7). Basta with the venti frappuccinos. *BusinessWeek*, 42–43.
18. Rettenbacher, G. O. (2007, January 8). Vienna's café culture. *Newsweek*, Letters, 8.
19. *Status report on alcohol*. (2004). World Health Organization. Retrieved December 18, 2009, from http://www.who.int/sunstance_abuse/publications/global_status_report_2004_overview.pdf
20. *Attitudes of Europeans towards tobacco*. (2005). Special Eurobarometer report 239. For 16 wealthy European countries low individualism explains 27% of variance and masculinity an additional 34%.
21. EBS 239, 23 countries, $r = .43^*$ for smoking in a car in the company of nonsmokers and $r = .47^*$ for smoking in a car in the company of children.
22. Goel, R. K., & Nelson, M. A. (2004). International patterns of cigarette smoking and global antismoking policies. *Journal of Economics and Finance, 28*(3), 382–394.
23. *Consumers in Europe* (2001), 93.
24. Health, beauty and personal grooming. (2007, March). *A global Nielsen report*. Retrieved December 30, 2007, from http://www.acnielsen.com

25. Becker, C. (1997, February). Hair and cosmetic products in the Japanese market. *Marketing and Research Today, 31*–36.

26. Information from Vivek Gupta, Sr. Vice President Brand Science, IMRB International, Bangalore, India.

27. Mortished, C. (2008, May 26). Sorry, Asia, you smell: The not-so-subtle sales ploy as Unilever scents profits. *Timesonline.* Retrieved December 30, 2009.

28. *Trends in clothes-shopping and fashion-following.* (2009). London: Future Foundation.

29. *Consumers in Europe* (2001), 96.

30. Story and illustration courtesy Eun Jee Hyun, student Master of Retail Design at the Willem de Kooning Academy, Rotterdam, the Netherlands. Autumn 2009.

31. TGI product book (2009).

32. *Consumers in Europe* (2001), 135.

33. Brewer Doran, K. (1997). Symbolic consumption in China: The color television as a life statement. *Advances in Consumer Research, 24,* 128–131.

34. *World Development Indicators.* (2006). PCs per 1,000 people. For 55 countries worldwide, GNI/capita explains 71% of variance and low UAI an additional 4%. For 26 countries worldwide with GNI/capita over US$20,000, low uncertainty avoidance is the only explaining variable and explains 50% of variance.

35. *Structure of consumption.* (2009). Eurostat.

36. Praet, C. (personal communication, January 2003).

37. Mamma mia! (2000, April 1). *The Economist, 24.*

38. Graziella, G., as quoted from the *Corriere della Sera.* Translated in *NRC Handelsblad* (2003, January 18) , 4.

39. Levy, S. (2001, December 17). The next new thing. *Newsweek,* 60–63.

40. Cai, Y. (2001, Fall). Design strategies for global products. *Design Management Journal,* 59–64.

41. The origins of Vertu. (2003, February 22). *The Economist,* 66–67.

42. The local touch. (2003, March 8). *The Economist,* 62.

43. Data 1991 Reader's Digest; data 1999 EMS.

44. *World Development Indicators.* (2006). Number of passenger cars per 1,000 population. For 48 countries worldwide, GNI/capita explains 72% of variance, but for 25 countries with GNI/capita over US$20,000, individualism explains 37% of variance. Data from TGI 2004—car owned in household—show similar results: For 38 countries worldwide, GNI/capita explains 73% of variance. For 16 countries with GNI/capita over US$19,000, individualism explains 43% of variance. TGI data for 2009 (TGI product book) measuring car use show similar results. For 41 countries worldwide, GNI/capita explains 40% and individualism an additional 12%. For 31 countries with GNI/capita over US$12,000, individualism explains 28%.

45. Singh (2007).

46. *Consumers in Europe* (2001).

47. Naughton, K. (2003, December 15). Three for the road. *Newsweek,* 40.

48. *European media and marketing survey.* (2007). Synovate. 15 countries. One car in the household correlates with low uncertainty avoidance, low power distance, and low masculinity. Low uncertainty avoidance explains 46% of variance with low masculinity explaining another 19%. High power distance explains variance of having two cars in the household. Variance of more than three cars in the household is explained by GNI/capita (50%), and an additional 17% is explained by masculinity.

49. Leeflang, P. S. H., & Van Raaij, W. F. (1995). The changing consumer in the European Union: A "meta-analysis." *International Journal of Research in Marketing, 12,* 373–387.

50. Inglehart, R., Basañez, M., & Moreno, A. (1998). *Human values and beliefs.* Ann Arbor: University of Michigan Press.

51. European Value Study, 2000. Countries included in the calculation are France, United Kingdom, Germany, Austria, Italy, Spain, Portugal, Greece, Belgium, Netherlands, Denmark, Sweden, Finland, Ireland, and Slovenia.

52. *European social reality.* (2007). Special Eurobarometer report 273. 26 countries GNI/capita > US$20,000.

53. Hofstede, G., Hofstede, G. J., & Minkov, M. (2010). *Cultures and organizations: Software of the mind.* New York: McGraw Hill. Authors present a sixth dimension called Indulgence versus Restraint, which mainly explains variance of satisfaction with life and importance of leisure time. In particular data that cover the intensity of leisure time activities, such as the frequency of playing sports, correlate with this dimension, but uncertainty avoidance also explains much of variance and correlates with a larger variety of leisure activities.

54. *Consumers in Europe* (2001). Countries are Austria, Belgium, Bulgaria, Czech Republic, Denmark, Estonia, Finland, France, Germany, Greece, Hungary, Ireland, Italy, Netherlands, Poland, Portugal, Romania, Slovenia, Slovak Republic, Spain, Sweden, and the United Kingdom.

55. Barzini, L. (1964). *The Italians.* London: Penguin Books, 111.

56. *Consumers in Europe* (2001), 243.

57. *Survey on the attitudes of Europeans towards tourism.* (2009). Flash Eurobarometer report 258, 25 countries.

58. *Consumers in Europe* (2001), 243.

59. Reader's Digest (1991).

60. EMS (1999, 2007).

61. Flash Eurobarometer 258 (2009).

62. Data UNESCO (1992), Europe, 12 countries.

63. Data courtesy Pets International, Netherlands. For 23 countries worldwide with GNI/capita > US$15,000, 2005. Cats per 1,000 people IDV: $r = .59$***; dogs per 1,000 people PDI: $r = .42$*.

64. Chui, A. C. W., & Kwok, C. C. Y. (2008). National culture and life insurance consumption. *Journal of International Business Studies, 39,* 88–101.

65. *Views on financial services.* (2001, December). Eurobarometer Report 56.

66. Dobbs, R., Grant, A., & Woetzel, J. (2009, September 14). Unleashing the Chinese consumer. *Newsweek,* 42–44.

67. Ackerman, D., & Tellis, G. (2001). Can culture affect prices? A cross-cultural study of shopping and retail prices. *Journal of Retailing, 77,* 57–82.

68. Trends in clothes-shopping and fashion-following. (2009). 12 countries. LTO: $r = -.53$*.

69. Cai, Y. (2007, September 4–6). Investigating the relationship between personal values and mall shopping behavior: A generation cohort study on the new generation of Chinese and their previous generation. In E. Howard (Ed.), *Proceedings of the Fourth Asia Pacific Retail Conference* (pp. 62–87). Bangkok: Manidol University and Oxford: Said Business School.

70. *Risk issues* (2005).

71. Nicholls, J. A. F., Mandakovic, T., Li, F., Roslow, S., & Kranendonk, C. J. (1999). Are U.S. shoppers different from Chilean? A comparative study of shopping behaviors across countries. In *Proceedings of the Seventh Cross-Cultural Consumer and Business Studies Research Conference.* Retrieved July 9, 2010, from http://marketing.byu.edu/htmlpages/ccrs/proceedings99/nicholls.htm

72. Botting, G. (2002, May 23). Buyers be wares—shopping consumes Japan. *The Japan Times.* Retrieved September 16, 2002, from http://www.japantimes.co

73. Mishra, A., & Vishas, R. (2009, August 25–27). Classification and store affiliation of Indian retail consumers: a case study with Bangalore women. In *Proceedings of the Fifth Conference on Retailing in Asia Pacific* (pp. 248–274). Oxford Institute of Retail Management and The Hong Kong Polytechnic University, Institute for Enterprise.

74. Kamarulzaman, Y., & Madun, A. (2009, August 25–27). Attracting patrons to shopping malls: A case of Malaysia. In *Proceedings of the Fifth Conference on Retailing in Asia Pacific* (pp. 174–185).

75. Triandis, H. (1995). *Individualism and collectivism.* Boulder, CO: Westview, 8.

76. Warden, C. A., Huang, S. C. T., Liu, T. C., & Wu, W. Y. (2008). Global media, local metaphor: Television shopping and marketing-as-relationship in America, Japan, and Taiwan. *Journal of Retailing, 84*(1), 119–129.

77. Tanikawa, M. (2001, October 5). French supermarket struggles to fit in. *International Herald Tribune.* http://www.iht.com

78. *Risk issues* (2005).

79. OECD data (2001).

80. Kacen, J., & Lee, J. A. (2002). The influence of culture on consumer impulsive buying behavior. *Journal of Consumer Psychology, 2*, 163–176.

81. Argentina, Brazil, Chile, Colombia, Mexico, Peru, Venezuela. Source TGI, 2001.

82. Nicholls et al. (1999).

83. *Consumer protection in the internal market.* (2008). Special Eurobarometer report 298, 25 countries.

84. Goodrich, K., & De Mooij, M. (2011). New technology mirrors old habits: Online buying mirrors cross-national variance of conventional buying. *Journal of International Consumer Marketing.* In print.

85. Kwak, H., Zinkhan, G. M., Pan, Y., & Andras, T. L. (2008). Consumer communications, media use, and purchases via the Internet: A comparative, exploratory study. *Journal of International Consumer Marketing, 20*(3–4), 55–68

86. Maddox, L. M., & Gong, W. (2009). Online buying decisions in China. In H. Li, S. Huang, & D. Jin (Eds.), *Proceedings of the 2009 American Academy of Advertising Asia-Pacific Conference* (p. 261). American Academy of Advertising, in conjunction with China Association of Advertising of Commerce, and Communication University of China.

87. Ahn, H., Kwon, M. W., & Yuan, L. (2009). When talking about global brands in cyberspace, cultural-free or cultural-bound? A cross-cultural study of the U.S. and Chinese brand community web sites. In Li, Huang, & Jin (2009), 117.

88. *Consumer protection in the Internet market.* (2008). Special Eurobarometer report 298.

89. Cyr, D., Bonanni, C., Ilsever, J., & Bowes, J. (2003). *Trust and design: A cross-cultural comparison.* ACM Conference on Universal Usability. Vancouver, BC.

90. Severin, V., Louviere, J. J., & Finn, A. (2001). The stability of retail shopping choices over time and across countries. *Journal of Retailing, 77*, 185–202.

91. These are examples of findings by students of the Master of Retail Design at the Willem de Kooning Academy at Rotterdam, 2006, 2007, 2008, and 2009. They compared the Dutch supermarket Albert Heijn and the Belgian supermarket Delhaize, of the same size in similar neighborhoods.

92. Warden et al. (2008).

93. Imrie, B. B., Cadogan, J. W., & Durden, G. (2000). The Confucian relational ethic: Respecifying the role of relational norms within service quality evaluation. *Visionary marketing for the 21st century: Facing the challenge* (pp. 574–579). Melbourne: ANZMAC.

94. Warden et al. (2008).

95. Ho, C. W., & Temperley, J. (2009, August 25–27). Consumers' reactions to Tesco's market entry in Taiwan. A comparison with the UK experience. Attracting patrons to shopping malls: A case of Malaysia. In *Proceedings of the Fifth Conference on Retailing in Asia Pacific,* pp. 24–50.

96. Shopping habits die hard in Thailand. (2000, April). *Insights Asia Pacific, 92,* 11.

97. German retailing: Cheap and cheerless. (2000, September 2). *The Economist,* 65–66.

98. Chelminski, P. (2001). The effects of individualism and collectivism on consumer complaining behavior. *Proceedings of the Eighth Cross-Cultural Research Conference.* Kahuku, Hawaii.

99. Watkins, H. S., & Liu, R. (1996). Collectivism, individualism and in-group membership: Implications for consumer complaining behaviors in multicultural contexts. In L. A. Manrai & A. K. Manrai (Eds.), *Global perspectives in cross-cultural and cross-national consumer research* (pp. 69–76). New York/London: International Business Press/Haworth Press.

100. Lowe, A. C. T., & Corkindale, D. R. (1998). Differences in "cultural values" and their effects on responses to marketing stimuli: A cross-cultural study between Australians and Chinese from the People's Republic of China. *European Journal of Marketing, 32,* 843–867.

101. *Consumer protection in the internal market.* (2008).

102. Liu, F., Kanso, A., Wang, W. W., & Li, X. (2009). Negative emotions, attribution, and attitudes towards boycotting a foreign brand in China. In Li, Huang, & Jin (2009), 48.

103. Baumgartner, H., & Steenkamp, J. B. E. M. (1996). Exploratory consumer buying behavior: Conceptualization and measurement. *International Journal of Research in Marketing, 13,* 121–137.

104. Lee, J. A. (2000). Adapting Triandis' model of subjective culture and social behavior relations to consumer behavior. *Journal of Consumer Psychology, 2,* 117–126. Countries studied were Australia, United States, Hong Kong, Singapore, and Malaysia.

105. Stockmann, L. (1991, November 7). Frontiers geeft Euromarketeers grip op de toekomst. (Frontiers offers grip on future to Euromarketers). *NieuwsTribune.*

106. Data TGI (2001). Copyright TGI, all rights reserved.

107. Reader's Digest Trusted Brands reports 2005 and 2007, 14 countries. See Appendix B.

108. *Consumers' view on switching service providers.* (2009). Flash Eurobarometer 243, 25 countries.

109. Robinson, C. (1996). Asian culture: The marketing consequences. *Journal of the Market Research Society, 38,* 55–66.

110. Erdem, T., Swait, J., & Valenzuela, A. (2006). Brands as signals: A cross-country validation study. *Journal of Marketing, 70,* 34–49.

111. Jin, B., Park, J. Y., & Kim, J. (2008). Cross-cultural examination of the relationships among firm reputation, e-satisfaction, e-trust, and e-loyalty. *International Marketing Review, 25*(3), 324–337.

112. Steenkamp, J. B., Ter Hofstede, F., & Wedel, M. (1999). A cross-national investigation into the individual and national cultural antecedents of consumer innovativeness. *Journal of Marketing, 63,* 55–69.

113. Yeniurt, S., & Townsend, J. D. (2003). Does culture explain acceptance of new products in a country? *International Marketing Review, 20*(4), 377–396.

114. Tellis, G. J., Stremersch, S., & Yin, E. (2003). The international take-off of new products: The role of economics, culture and country innovativeness. *Marketing Science, 22*(2), 188–208; Singh, S. (2006). Cultural differences and influences on consumers' propensity to adopt innovations. *International Marketing Review, 23*(2), 173–191.

115. Lynn, M., & Gelb, B. D. (1996). Identifying innovative national markets for technical consumer goods. *International Marketing Review, 13,* 43–57.

116. Gatignon, H., & Robertson, T. S. (1985). A propositional inventory for new diffusion research. *Journal of Consumer Research, 11*, 849–861.

117. Rogers, E. M. (1992). *Diffusion of innovations.* New York: Free Press.

118. Steenkamp, J. B. (2002). *Global consumers.* Presentation at Tilburg University, November 17. Based on *Consumer and market drivers of the trial probability of new consumer packaged goods.* Working paper.

119. *Early adopters of technological innovations.* (2003). TGI Chile. Retrieved November 5, 2004, from http://www.zonalatina.com/Zldata99.htm

120. Tellefsen, T., & Takada, H. (1999). The relationship between mass media availability and the multicountry diffusion of consumer products. *Journal of International Marketing, 7*, 77–96.

121. Samli, A. C. (1995). *International consumer behavior.* Westport, CT, and London: Quorum, 106.

122. Dwyer, S., Mesak, H., & Hsu, M. (2005). An exploratory examination of the influence of national culture on cross-national product diffusion. *Journal of International Marketing, 13*(2), 1–28.

123. Bass, F. M. (1995). Empirical generalizations and marketing science: A personal view. *Marketing Science, 14*, G6–G19.

124. Yaveroglu, I. S., & Donthu, N. (2002). Cultural influences on the diffusion of new products. *Journal of International Consumer Marketing, 14*(4), 49–63.

125. Takada, H., & Jain, D. (1991). Cross-national analysis of diffusion of consumer durable goods in Pacific Rim countries. *Journal of Marketing, 55*, 48–54.

126. Ganesh, J., Kumar, V., & Subramaniam, V. (1997). Learning effect in multinational diffusion of consumer durables: An exploratory investigation. *Journal of the Academy of Marketing Science, 25*, 214–228.

127. Ganesh, J., & Kumar, V. (1996). Capturing the cross-national learning effect: An analysis of an industrial technology diffusion. *Journal of the Academy of Marketing Science, 24*, 328–337.

128. Nakata, C., & Sivakumar, K. (1996). National culture and new product development: An integrative review. *Journal of Marketing, 60*, 61–72.

129. Drewitt, N. (2001, June). Korea opportunities. *M&M Europe,* 15–22.

GNI per Capita at Purchasing Power Parity 2008 (US$) and Hofstede Country Scores for 68 Countries

Country	Abbreviation	GNI/cap	PDI	IDV	MAS	UAI	LTO
Argentina	ARG	14.020	49	46	56	86	20
Australia	AUL	34.040	36	90	61	51	21
Austria	AUT	37.680	11	55	79	70	60
Bangladesh	BAN	1.440	80	20	55	60	47
Belgium	BEL	34.760	65	75	54	94	82
Brazil	BRA	10.070	69	38	49	76	44
Bulgaria	BUL	11.950	70	30	40	85	69
Canada	CAN	36.220	39	80	52	48	36
Chile	CHL	13.270	63	23	28	86	31
China	CHN	6.020	80	20	66	30	87
Croatia	CRO	18.420	73	33	40	80	58
Czech Republic	CZE	22.790	57	58	57	74	70
Colombia	COL	8.510	67	13	64	80	13
Costa Rica	COS	10.950	35	15	21	86	
Denmark	DEN	37.280	18	74	16	23	35
Ecuador	ECA	7.760	78	8	63	67	
Estonia	EST	19.280	40	60	30	60	82
Finland	FIN	35.660	33	63	26	59	38
France	FRA	34.400	68	71	43	86	63
Germany	GER	35.940	35	67	66	65	83
Greece	GRE	28.470	60	35	57	112	45
Guatemala	GUA	4.690	95	6	37	101	
Hong Kong, China	HOK	43.960	68	25	57	29	61
Hungary	HUN	17.790	46	80	88	82	58
India	IND	2.960	77	48	56	40	51
Indonesia	IDO	3.830	78	14	46	48	62
Iran	IRA	10.840	58	41	43	59	14
Ireland	IRE	37.350	28	70	68	35	24
Israel	ISR	27.450	13	54	47	81	38
Italy	ITA	30.250	50	76	70	75	61
Jamaica	JAM	7.360	45	39	68	13	
Japan	JPN	35.220	54	46	95	92	88
Korea, Rep.	KOR	28.120	60	18	39	85	100

(Continued)

Appendix A (Continued)

Country	Abbreviation	GNI/cap	PDI	IDV	MAS	UAI	LTO
Latvia	LTV	16.740	44	70	9	70	69
Lithuania	LIT	18.210	42	60	19	65	82
Malaysia	MAL	13.740	104	26	50	36	41
Malta	MLT	22.460	56	59	47	96	47
Mexico	MEX	14.270	81	30	69	82	24
Morocco	MOR	4.330	70	46	53	68	14
Netherlands	NET	41.670	38	80	14	53	67
New Zealand	NZL	25.090	22	79	58	49	33
Norway	NOR	58.500	31	69	8	50	35
Pakistan	PAK	2.700	55	14	50	70	50
Panama	PAN	11.650	95	11	44	86	
Peru	PER	7.980	64	16	42	87	25
Philippines	PHI	3.900	94	32	64	44	27
Poland	POL	17.310	68	60	64	93	38
Portugal	POR	22.080	63	27	31	104	28
Romania	ROM	13.500	90	30	42	90	52
Russia	RUS	15.630	93	39	36	95	81
Salvador	SAL	6.670	66	19	40	94	20
Serbia	SER	11.150	86	25	43	92	52
Singapore	SIN	47.940	74	20	48	8	72
Slovak Republic	SLK	21.300	104	52	110	51	77
Slovenia	SLV	26.910	71	27	19	88	49
South Africa	SAF	9.780	49	65	63	49	
Spain	SPA	31.130	57	51	42	86	48
Sweden	SWE	38.180	31	71	5	29	53
Switzerland	SWI	46.460	34	68	70	58	74
Taiwan [1]	TAI	29.800	58	17	45	69	93
Thailand	THA	5.990	64	20	34	64	32
Trinidad	TRI	23.950	47	15	58	55	13
Turkey	TUR	13.770	66	37	45	85	46
United Kingdom	UK	36.130	35	89	66	35	51
United States	USA	46.970	40	91	62	46	26
Uruguay	URU	12.540	61	36	38	100	26
Venezuela	VEN	12.830	81	12	73	76	16
Vietnam	VTN	2.700	70	20	40	30	57

SOURCES: Hofstede et al. (2010); Latvia and Lithuania: Huettinger, M. (2006). Cultural Dimensions in Business Life: Hofstede's Indices for Latvia and Lithuania. *Journal of Baltic Management*. GNI/capita 2008 (at Purchasing Power Parity): World Development Indicators database, World Bank, October 7, 2009

[1]GNI/capita Taiwan from CIA World Factbook

Data Sources

Many secondary data sources were used for the cultural analysis in this book. Databases are of several types.

1. Economic statistics published by governmental or nongovernmental organizations: World Bank, United Nations, OECD, and Eurostat.

2. Surveys of opinions and habits of citizens of countries published by governmental organizations. The major studies used are the Eurobarometer reports published by the European Commission Directorate.

3. Academically driven value studies. Examples are the World Values Survey and the European Values Study.

4. Consumer surveys on media that ask questions about media usage as well as consumption or usage of products. The surveys used are the Reader's Digest Surveys *A Survey of Europe Today 1970* and *Eurodata 1991,* the European Media and Marketing Surveys (EMS) of 1995, 1997, 1999, and 2007, PAX 2009, and Synovate Media Atlas, Asia.

5. Industry-driven studies, for example, by the tourism trade, car industry, or telecommunications industry. Examples are ITU (International Telecommunications Union), which offers data on telephones, Hotrec on tourism, and the Beverage Marketing Corporation of New York.

6. Various survey data published by market research agencies, media, or companies. Examples are studies by Roper Starch, Nielsen, Synovate or TGI, and the "Trusted Brands" study by Reader's Digest or data on sales or data analysis of various products from commercial sources like Euromonitor.

ECONOMIC STATISTICS

World Bank. *Annual World Development Reports* include economic data and data on infrastructure; separate reports on *World Development Indicators*; data on most countries in the world (World Bank, New York, http://www.worlbank.org). Income data from Table 1. *Key indicators of development*. Data on daily newspapers, Internet, PCs, and from Table 5.11. *The information age*.

United Nations. *UN statistical yearbooks* include economic data and data on product ownership and media, data on most countries in the world. New York: United Nations. http://unstats.un.org/unsd/methods/inter-natlinks/refs3.htm

UN Demographic yearbooks 2008 (data 2006) and 2009 (data 2007) New York: United Nations, Department of Economic and Social Affairs. UN Demographic yearbook 2007. Data available from http://unstats.un.org/unsd/demographic/products/dyb/dyb2007.htm

From the United Nations Statistics Division on the United Nations Website several data can be downloaded, some in Excel format.

For example, statistics and indicators on women and men, http://unstats.un.org/unsd/demographic/products/indwm/tab5b.htm.

The United Nations World Tourism Organization publishes UN Tourism Reports. www.unwto.org/facts/eng/pdf/indicators/ITE.pdf

World Health Organization (WHO). World Health Statistics. World Health Organization, 20 Avenue Appia, 1211 Geneva 27, Switzerland. http://www.who.org. Go to Data and statistics.

Eurostat. (a) *Yearbooks*: Annual Reports include demographic data and data on consumption. Data cover the member states of the European Union. (b) Social Indicators Reports. (c) *Family Budget Surveys*. The report *Consumers in Europe: Facts and figures* (2001) covers data from 1996 to 2000, published by the Office for Official Publications of the European Communities, Luxembourg, http://europ.eu.int/general/en/index_en.htm. Data are on European Union member countries Austria, Belgium, Denmark, Finland, France, Germany, Greece, Ireland, Italy, Luxembourg, the Netherlands, Portugal, Spain, Sweden, the United Kingdom, and some data for candidate member countries Bulgaria, Cyprus, Czech Republic, Estonia, Hungary, Lithuania, Latvia, Malta, Poland, Romania, Slovenia, Slovakia, and Turkey. The report *How Europeans spend their time* (2002) covers data from 1998 to 2002. In 2010, for 25 countries many indicators (in Excel or other formats) could be retrieved from the Eurostat statistics database, for example, from http://epp.eurostat.ec.europa.eu/portal/page/portal/euroindicators/peeis. Examples of databases are *Structure of consumption* (2005); *Euro indicators* (2009) Eurostat statistics database; *Cinema, TV and*

RADIO in the EU (2003) Eurostat Statistics on audiovisual services, data 1980–2002; Community survey on ICT usage in households and by individuals (2006). Eurostat, 21 countries.

OECD. The Organisation for Economic Co-Operation and Development. Member countries are Australia, Austria, Belgium, Canada, Czech Republic, Denmark, Finland, France, Germany, Greece, Hungary, Iceland, Ireland, Italy, Japan, Korea, Luxembourg, Mexico, Netherlands, New Zealand, Norway, Poland, Portugal, Slovak Republic, Spain, Sweden, Switzerland, Turkey, United Kingdom, United States. Several statistical databases can be retrieved from the website: http://www.oecd.org. Examples of databases are *Key ICT Indicators* (2006–2007); *Society at a glance* (2009) OECD Social Indicators.

GOVERNMENTAL OPINION SURVEYS

Eurobarometer. The standard Eurobarometer reports cover the resident populations (ages 15 years and over) of the European Union (EU) member states. The basic sample design applied in all member states is a multistage, random (probability) one. The results of Eurobarometer studies are reported in the form of tables, data files, and analyses and published by the European Commission Directorate, Brussels. Until 2004 separate surveys were conducted for the EU member states and for the EU candidate countries. After the EU enlargements in 2004 and 2007 the candidate countries were included in the standard Eurobarometer. Since 2007 surveys cover 24 or 27 countries. Some go beyond the EU and add countries like Switzerland, Turkey, and Israel.

The results are published on and can be downloaded from the Internet server of the European Commission: http://ec.europa.eu.int/public_opinion/index_en.htm. Next to a few specialized reports, four categories reports are available: Standard EB, Special EB (EBS), CCEB (mostly surveys among Eastern European member states before they joined the EU), and Flash EB.

General reports referred to in this book are *Measuring the information society* 1997 and 2000, *Trend variables 1974–1994* (November 1994), *How Europeans see themselves* (2001).

The Standard Eurobarometer was established in 1973. Each survey consists of approximately 1,000 face-to-face interviews per Member State (except Germany: 2,000, Luxembourg: 600, United Kingdom 1,300, including 300 in Northern Ireland). Reports are published twice yearly. Standard EB reports used for this book are Standard EB 47 (October 1997), EB 47.1 (1999), EB 50.1 (1999), EB 53 (2000) *Measuring information society*; EB 55 (2001), EB 56, *Views on financial services* (2001); EB 58 (March 2003); EB 65 (2007); EB 69, *Globalisation, Values of Europeans, Europeans' state of mind* (November 2008).

Flash Eurobarometer reports used are Flash EB 117, *Consumer survey* (January 2002); Flash EB 151b, *Globalisation* (October 2003); Flash EB 199, Audiovisual communication (2007); Flash EB 202 *Young Europeans* (2007); Flash EB 241, *Information society* (2008); Flash EB 243, *Consumers' view on switching service providers* (2009); Flash EB 247, *Satisfaction with family life* (2008); Flash EB 248, *Towards a safer use of the Internet for children in the EU: A parents' perspective* (December 2008); Flash EB 250, *Confidence in the information society* (May 2009); Flash EB 256, *Europeans' attitudes towards the issue of sustainable consumption and production* (2009); Flash EB 258, *Survey on the attitudes of Europeans towards tourism* (2009).

Special Eurobarometer (EBS). Data from the following special Eurobarometer surveys were used for this book. EBS 114, *Young Europeans* (1997), EBS 120, *Food safety* (September 3, 1998); EBS 151, *Young Europeans* (2001); EBS 197, *European citizens and sports* (2003); EBS 213, *Citizens of the European Union and sport* (November 2004); EBS 225, *Social values, Science and technology* (June 2005); EBS 238 (2005) *Risk issues;* EBS 239, *Attitudes of Europeans towards tobacco.* (2005); EBS 243, *Europeans and their languages* (February 2006); EBS 249 and 293, *E-communications household survey* (July 2006 and June 2008); EBS 273, *European social reality* (February 2007); EBS 278, *European cultural values* (September 2007); EBS 295, *Attitudes of European citizens towards the environment* (March 2008); EBS 298 *Consumer protection in the Internet market* (October 2008).

ACADEMICALLY DRIVEN VALUE STUDIES

World Values Survey. A study of values via public opinion surveys was started in the early 1980s as the European Values Study. In 1981 it was carried out in 10 EU member states. In 1990, a second round was started, and 16 countries were added. It was renamed the World Values Survey (WVS). Four waves have been conducted in 1981–1984, 1990–1993, 1995–1997, and 1999–2004. It eventually covered 53 countries, representing about 70% of the world's population, with a questionnaire including more than 360 forced-choice questions. Examples of areas covered are ecology, economy, education, emotion, family, health, happiness, religion, leisure, and friends.

The 1990 data are published in the following:

Inglehart, R., Basañez, M., & Moreno, A. (1998). *Human values and beliefs: A cross-cultural sourcebook.* Ann Arbor: University of Michigan Press.

Data for Europe of 1999/2000 are published in the following:

European Values Study: A third wave. Source Book of the 1999/2000 European Values Study Surveys. Loek Halman, Tilburg University. PO Box 90153, 5000 LE Tilburg, The Netherlands (evs@uvt.nl).

The complete data files 1981–2005 can be downloaded from http://www.worldvaluessurvey.org

The European Social Survey (R. Jowell and the Central Co-ordinating Team, Centre for Comparative Social Surveys, City University, London). The European Social Survey (the ESS) is a biennial multicountry survey covering over 30 nations. The first round was fielded in

2002/2003, the second in 2004/2005, and the third in 2006/2007. The project is funded jointly by the European Commission, the European Science Foundation, and academic funding bodies in each participating country. The project is directed by a Central Co-ordinating Team led by Roger Jowell at the Centre for Comparative Social Surveys, City University, London. The study covers 23 mostly European countries: Austria, Belgium, Czechia, Denmark, Finland, France, Germany, Greece, Hungary, Ireland, Israel, Italy, Luxembourg, Netherlands, Norway, Poland, Portugal, Slovenia, Spain, Sweden, Switzerland, Turkey, and United Kingdom.

The questionnaire includes two main sections, each consisting of approximately 120 items: a "core" module that will remain relatively constant from round to round, plus two or more "rotating" modules repeated at intervals. The core module aims to monitor change and continuity in a wide range of social variables, including media use, social and public trust; political interest and participation; sociopolitical orientations, governance and efficacy; moral, political and social values; social exclusion, national, ethnic and religious allegiances; well-being, health and security; demographics and socioeconomics. In addition, a supplementary questionnaire is presented to respondents at the end of the main interview. The first part of this questionnaire is a human values scale (part of the core), while the second is devoted to measures to help evaluate the reliability and validity of items in the main questionnaire. The full data file (in SPSS) can be downloaded from http://ess.nsd.uib.no

Interactive Generation in Ibero-America. In 2008 Telefonica, the University of Navarra (Spain) and the Inter-American Organization for Higher Education founded the "Interactive generations Forum," an initiative that is open to public and private corporations, with the aim to foster and promote a responsible and safe use of the new technologies by children and young, the people that constitute the new "interactive generation," Internet address: http://www.generacionesinteractivas.org. The first findings were published in Bringué Sala, X. and Sádaba Chalezquer, C. (2008), *The interactive generation in Ibero-America: Children and adolescents faced with the screens.* Madrid: Collección Fundación Telefónica. Countries: Argentina, Brazil, Chile, Colombia, Mexico, Peru, and Venezuela.

CONSUMER SURVEYS ON MEDIA USAGE

The Reader's Digest Surveys. Studies of the lifestyles, consumer spending habits, and attitudes of people in 17 European countries, published in 1970 and 1991. The data of the 1970 survey were the results of a probability sample representative of the national population ages 18 and over. Comparable sample surveys were conducted in 16 western European countries in early 1969. Approximately 24,000 personal interviews were involved. Eurodata 1991 was based on comparable sample surveys conducted in the early summer (May/June) of 1990. Approximately 22,500 personal interviews were involved. The study was commissioned by the Reader's Digest Association, Inc., in cooperation with its editions and offices in Europe. With the exception of Sweden, it was conducted by the

Gallup-affiliated companies and institutes in Europe and was coordinated by Gallup, London. Probability samples were employed in each of the 17 countries, representative of the population ages 18 and over, living in private households. Reader's Digest Association Limited, London. Countries surveyed were Austria, Belgium, Denmark, Finland, France, Germany, Greece, Ireland, Italy, Luxembourg, the Netherlands, Norway, Portugal, Spain, Sweden, Switzerland, and the United Kingdom.

The European Media and Marketing Survey (EMS) is conducted by Inter/View-NSS (http://www.interview-nss.com), Amsterdam, the Netherlands. Data used from surveys of 1995, 1997, 1999, and 2007. The survey consists of a combination of telephone interviewing and written questionnaire (n = 6.680). Inter/View-NSS now is owned by Synovate, which continues conducting the surveys (http://www.synovate.com). EMS is a European "industry" survey, which measures national and international media usage as well as ownership of some products and services. EMS covers the main income earners living in the top 20% of households in each of 20 survey countries, an estimated population of almost 44 million affluent Europeans. Data are based on interviews and self-completion questionnaires. Reports are available to subscribers only. Countries surveyed were Austria, Belgium, Denmark, Finland, France, Germany, Greece, Ireland, Italy, Luxembourg, the Netherlands, Norway, Portugal, Spain, Sweden, Switzerland, and the United Kingdom. In 2008 Poland, Hungary, and the Czech Republic were added. Data courtesy Reinier Schaper.

Synovate PAX 2009. In Asia a similar survey is conducted called Synovate PAX. The Pan Asia-Pacific Cross Media Survey (PAX) was (in 2010) the only upscale media tracking survey in Asia. It reveals media audiences and consumption trends. It is based on continuous tracking data. Fieldwork is carried out continuously throughout the year to pinpoint shifts in media habits and consumption behavior. PAX covers 11 countries across Asia Pacific (Hong Kong, Singapore, Malaysia, Taiwan, Thailand, Indonesia, Philippines, Korea, India, Australia, and Japan). The sample for a typical market is 1,700 per annum. Annual sample for Asia Pacific is more than 20,000. Data courtesy of Clare Lui.

Synovate PAX Digital Life. Survey of media habits, lifestyle, products, and services among affluent adults across eight cities in Asia: Sydney, Melbourne, Hong Kong, Taipei, Singapore, Seoul, Kuala Lumpur, Bangkok. Measurement of media usage, personal activities, business life, air travel, product usage and ownership. Data courtesy of Clare Lui.

IP-network. IP measures the time spent on TV viewing and offers data on ownership of audio and video electronics. http://www.ip-network.com/tvkeyfacts

Telefónica (Spain) has published data on media usage in Latin America in 2007: Medios de comunicacion Annuario de Medios. El escenario Iberoamericano. (2007). Madrid: Fundacion Telefonica.

INDUSTRY-DRIVEN ORGANIZATIONS

ITU (International Telecommunications Union) offers data on telephony worldwide, http://www.itu.org.ITU measuring the Information Society 2009.

The Beverage Marketing Corporation of New York sells worldwide data on soft drinks, http://www.beveragemarketing.com

Hotrec publishes data for the tourism trade: hotels, restaurants, and cafes in Europe, http://www.hotrec.org

ComScore, Inc. is a Global Internet Information Provider. It maintains proprietary databases that provide a continuous, real-time measurement of the myriad ways in which the Internet is used and the wide variety of activities that are occurring online, http://www.comscore.com

Ofcom. Office of Communication is an independent organization that regulates the United Kingdom's broadcasting, telecommunications, and wireless communications sectors. Publications are communication market reports providing data on television, radio, and telecommunications for several countries, http://www.ofcom.org.uk. Used in this book are Ofcom (2008) *The international communications market*: five telecoms; Ofcom (2006) *International communications market*.

Mediascope Europe is the media consumption study of the European Interactive Advertising Association (EIAA) that provides insight into the evolution of TV, Internet, radio, newspaper, and magazine consumption across Europe, and the role the Internet plays in people's lives. Several studies are published, on the Internet, http://www.eiaa.net/index.asp. Used for this book was the report *Online shoppers* (2008).

VARIOUS SURVEY DATA AND REPORTS PUBLISHED BY MARKET RESEARCH AGENCIES, MEDIA, OR DATA COMPANIES

Global TGI is an international network of harmonized market and media research surveys, present in more than 60 countries around the world. Several free data can be downloaded from http://tgisurveys.com. For this book, several years of data on product ownership and usage were used, for example, *TGI global surveys 2001* and *2003–2004* and from *Product Book 2009*. Specialized surveys are, for example, TGI Europa Internet Report, December 2001; TGI European women report, http://www.bmrb.co.uk. womensreportch2.htm; *Early adopters of technological innovations* (2003) TGI Chile.

Synovate Asia. Young Asians is a syndicated study that covers 8- to 24-year-olds in 12 markets across the region in 2008 (China, Hong Kong China, India, Indonesia, Japan, Korea, Malaysia, Philippines, Singapore, Thailand, and Vietnam). It covers media consumption and digital lifestyles, as well as favorite brands and singers, climate change. and even who's happiest. Data courtesy Clare Lui.

Euromonitor. Euromonitor sells databases on consumption and ownership of products worldwide. Used in this book are *Consumer Europe 1997,* a compendium of pan-European market information on sales, in value and volume, of a large number of products; and *Consumer international 1997,* by Euromonitor PLC, London. Euromonitor publishes databases on consumption and ownership of products worldwide (*Consumer world*) and category-specific data reports, http://www.euromonitor.com. Countries included in *Consumer Europe 1997* were Austria, Belgium, Denmark, Finland, France, Germany, Greece, Ireland, Italy, Luxembourg, the Netherlands, Norway, Portugal, Spain, Sweden, Switzerland, and the United Kingdom.

Nielsen is a worldwide operating marketing and media information company. They measure and analyze how people interact with digital platforms, traditional media and in-store environments—locally as well as globally. The privately held company is active in more than 100 countries, with headquarters in New York. They publish summaries on the Internet. Examples are reports on *Trust in advertising* (2007, October), *Consumers and designer brands* (2006, May), *Health, beauty and personal grooming* (2007, March), and *The power of private label* (2005). http://www.nielsen.com

Future Foundation. A consumer and business trends think tank, the leading consumer insight and strategic futures company, based in the United Kingdom. They publish trends in consumer behavior, based on public domain databases and own surveys. *Trends in clothes-shopping and fashion-following* (2009); *Family life and decision making in the household* (2009).

Reader's Digest annually publishes data on most trusted brands in several parts of the world, together with varying data on consumer attitudes toward brands, http://www.rdtrustedbrands.com

Unilever. The owner of the Dove brand commissioned two studies, in 2004 and 2005, resulting in two reports. Dove 2004 *The real truth about beauty: A global report*, Etcoff, N., Orbach, S., Scott, J., and D'Agostino, H. Quantitative telephone study conducted among 3,200 women ages 18–64 from 10 countries: United States, Canada, Great Britain, Italy, France, Portugal, Netherlands, Brazil, Argentina, and Japan. Dove 2006, by the same authors: *Beyond stereotypes: Rebuilding the foundation of beauty beliefs,* presenting findings of the 2005 Dove Global Study.

Author Index

Subject Index

About the Author

Marieke de Mooij (1943) studied English literature at the University of Amsterdam and after that went to Enschede, the Netherlands, where in 1966 she graduated at the School of Engineering Management with a specialization in textile management. She was public relations and advertising manager for an international textile company; account executive at an advertising agency; a director at the Dutch Institute for Professional Advertising Education; director of education of the International Advertising Association; and managed BBDO College, the educational program for BBDO Europe.

She has worked on the application of the Hofstede model to cross-cultural consumer behavior and international advertising since 1990, doing research, conducting seminars, teaching at various universities worldwide, and advising international companies. As an associate professor, De Mooij has been teaching international advertising on a regular basis at the University of Navarra, Spain. In 2001 she received her PhD at that university at the Department of Communication. The subject of her doctoral research was convergence and divergence in consumer behavior across countries.

De Mooij is a consultant in cross-cultural communications and advises both companies and advertising agencies on international branding and advertising. She is visiting professor to various universities in Europe. She is the author of several publications on the influence of culture on marketing, advertising, and consumer behavior. She is also the author of *Global Marketing and Advertising, Understanding Cultural Paradoxes, Third Edition* (2010), published by SAGE Publications, which is used at universities worldwide. Her website is www.mariekedemooij.com

About the Cover

For the cover of this second edition, I suggested that we feature the same children—now five years older—who appeared on the cover of the first edition to illustrate people's relationships with brands. The children are photographed with national brands from the countries where they live.

Illy Heimeriks from the Netherlands is shown with a package of a typical Dutch brand: Peijnenburg Koek. Illy is a grandchild of my oldest friend Lidi Oepts-Hutter. Illy's father, Hans Heimeriks, made the picture.

Pablo Zambonino Rodríguez from Spain is pictured with his two brothers, Miguel and Nicolas, showing their favorite Spanish brand: Chupa Chups. They are the children of my friend and colleague Natalia Rodríguez Salcedo at the University of Navarra. These children were also photographed by their parents.

Carolus Praet, my friend and professor of International Marketing at Otaru University in Japan, photographed his son Alvin and his daughter Layna with Japanese bottled water brands: Calpis Soda and Pocari Sweat.

Marieke de Mooij

Peter Monadjemi

IN NO TIME

Visual Basic 6

An imprint of Pearson Education

PEARSON EDUCATION LIMITED

Head Office:
Edinburgh Gate
Harlow CM20 2JE
Tel: +44 (0)1279 623623
Fax: +44 (0)1270 431059

London Office:
128 Long Acre
London WC2E 9AN
Tel: +44 (0)20 7447 2000
Fax: +44 (0)20 7240 5771
Website: www.it-minds.com

First published in Germany in 2002
© Pearson Education Limited 2002

First published in 2001 as *Easy Visual Basic 6*
by Markt & Technik Buch-und-Software Verlag GmbH
Martin-Kollar-Straße 10-12
D-81629 Munich
Germany

This edition published 2002 by Pearson Education

British Library Cataloguing in Publication Data
A CIP catalogue record for this book can be obtained from the British Library.

ISBN 0-130-66008-6

Almost all hardware and software names that are used in this book are
registered trademarkes or should be regarded as such.

10   9   8   7   6   5   4   3   2   1

Translated and typeset by Cybertechnics, Sheffield.
Printed and bound in Great Britain by Ashford Colour Press, Gosport, Hampshire.

The Publishers' policy is to use paper manufactured from sustainable forests.

Contents

Chapter 10: More advanced Visual Basic 217

Introduction

We wish you a very warm welcome to a new world – a world that will no doubt require a great amount of time, patience and perseverance over the coming few weeks and months. In return, you will have a lot of fun, find a way to occupy your time, and possibly gain a perspective into a professional future.

Initially, you will probably wonder whether programming is difficult to learn. Unfortunately, this question is difficult to answer. (Even if you think that this is hardly a promising start, please read on.) You will only have an honest answer once you have worked your way through this book. Programming requires a certain empathy with a computer's 'way of thinking' (don't worry – this is astonishingly simple, yet special), staying power, perseverance, and above all a genuine readiness to learn. Learning programming always reminds me of windsurfing. It looks (mostly) easy from the safety of the shore – an assumption that soon changes once you stand on a board for the first time. You (usually) make some headway initially, but there are all sorts of things to bother or worry about. Then, at some point, the wind picks up and the whole thing starts becoming enjoyable, and you suddenly find that what initially just seemed easy actually is.

When you start learning programming, you will have a similar experience. It is therefore important not to give up, and not to be put off by error messages, seemingly inexplicable phenomena, and other strange events. Above all, don't be discouraged by the feeling of 'who on earth actually understands any of this?', which will undoubtedly set in at some point. Millions of people the world over have learned how to program.

With Visual Basic, you will learn a programming language that makes an introduction easy, and which, according to programmers, is fairly liberal. Obviously, nobody will share your way of thinking. As with all other books in the In No Time series, everything will be explained. This means that by the end of the book, you will at least have converted a larger Visual Basic program yourself, and learned the most basic programming rules.

I wish you all the best in learning Visual Basic.

Peter Monadjemi

Düsseldorf, April 2001

Tips for a successful start

The following tips should make your introduction to Visual Basic successful:

- Take time in trying out the examples.

- Pay attention to detail when typing in program listing, such as blank spaces, brackets, commas, ampersands (&) and so on.

- You should intially end every command line with the ⏎ key. The command line will then be closed, and the cursor will be placed on the following line. This is not absolutely necessary, but it makes entries a little easier.

- If you wish to split a command line into several lines, use the following procedure. End the line with a blank space, followed by an underscore (_). This is the line continuation operator. You can then continue the command line into the next line. However, this does not work within a character string, i.e. between two quotation marks. Should a character string become separated, it has to be closed with a quotation mark, expanded with a blank space and an ampersand (&), and continued into the next line with a quotation mark.

- Try not to include irrelevant, apparently inexplicable or meaningless messages. As far as the entry of command lines is concerned, Visual Basic is a little stubborn, and often requires a specific style. This is all a matter of practice.

- And finally: should something not work from the outset, don't give up immediately. A supposed error often has a harmless cause (usually a typing error or an overlooked command). This is a delicate point. Even though great care was taken in writing this book, and even though all examples were tested in detail, small discrepancies may be present. Should you come across such a discrepancy, don't be annoyed but look for the cause calmly. Errors can also be educational, and may actually turn out to be not errors, but small misunderstandings, or a form of wording that was not 100% clear.

Chapter 1

Preparing Visual Basic for the first time

So that your first experience of Visual Basic does not fail due to small misunderstandings, and so that the fun is not unnecessarily removed from the programming, you should first make the preparations required for your expedition into the world of programming. The largely problem-free installation of the Visual Basic 6.0 learning edition will also be described in this chapter.

Before you are let loose into the big wide world of programming, you have to meet a few requirements on your PC. Imagine Visual Basic as the off-road vehicle for your expedition into the world of software. There are several things on your checklist, such as checking tyre pressure, changing the oil, filling up with petrol and water, checking the battery and so on. With Visual Basic, there is a host of things you should do with the same precision. This 'safety check' helps to avoid unnecessary errors, 'deviations' and other mishaps, such as incorrectly written variable names or seemingly untraceable files, which are better avoided from the outset.

Here is your mission, if you are ready to accept it:

- Installing the learning edition of Visual Basic 6.0.
- Creating a directory for your sample program.
- Activating the option Required Variable Declaration.
- Activating the option Prompt To Save Changes.
- Modifying the fonts and colours to your settings.
- Familiarising yourself with the 'fittings'.
- Familiarising yourself with the help functions.
- Creating a new project on a trial basis.

Installing Visual Basic 6.0

Visual Basic 6.0 is a development tool used to develop (and program) Windows applications. It was developed by Microsoft, which also developed Windows. Visual Basic 6.0 (the number 6.0 indicates the version number) is available in several *editions*. All editions offer the same programming language and the same *development environment* (the program that appears after Visual Basic starts and in which the programming takes place), and differ in their *accessories*. This is where the price differs. Whereas the Enterprise Edition aimed at companies is available for around £1000, the Professional Edition (about £200) is aimed at professional software developers, who do not require the extras of the Enterprise Edition. Those who program as a hobby, or who wish to learn Visual Basic, should opt for the Standard Edition, which is relatively affordable at around £70. (All prices are approximate, as there is no recommended retail price.) For schoolchildren, students, teachers, and all those who can produce an education certificate, all editions are available half-price, which makes the Standard Edition even more affordable.

However, if this is too costly, or for those who merely wish to learn the basics of Visual Basic 6.0, Microsoft offers another version: the learning edition of Visual Basic 6.0. The learning edition consists of the complete development environment and all commands of the programming languages. You can also load additional control elements and access large databases. Some things are unavailable, including the creation of *.exe files (program files that run outside of the development environment). However, this is not a disadvantage when learning Visual Basic, so the learning edition is almost ideal for learning purposes.

Creating a directory for your sample program

You are advised to create a separate directory for your Visual Basic sample programs created within the framework of this book and beyond. This guarantees that you will easily be able to find your programs again. The MY DOCUMENTS folder is a suitable place, as this is easily accessible from the desktop. Create a directory called VISUAL BASIC SAMPLES (or something similar) in this directory, or directly on the desktop. You should ensure that when saving a Visual Basic project, the project files, along with the individual form files and any others, are saved in this directory.

Activating the Require Variable Declaration option

Immediately after the installation of Visual Basic, the VARIABLE DECLARATION REQUIRED option is not activated. If activated, it is entered in every newly created module of the OPTION EXPLICIT Visual Basic command. In turn, this ensures that all variables have to be declared in order to be used in a program. Even though it is too early to explain the details of this measure (an explanation is provided in Chapter 3), you should activate this option. By doing so, you will avoid an unnecessary and time-consuming search for errors. If you have entered a variable name or command incorrectly, Visual Basic will consider it to be a non-declared variable, so no error message will be displayed.

5

Procedure: activating the Require Variable Declaration option

1 Start *Visual Basic* and create a STANDARD EXE project.

2 Open the EXTRAS menu and select the OPTIONS entry.

3 Select the EDITOR tab (this is generally not declared, as it is selected by default).

4 Tick the REQUIRE VARIABLE DECLARATION option (Figure 1.9).

5 Close the dialogue field using the OK button.

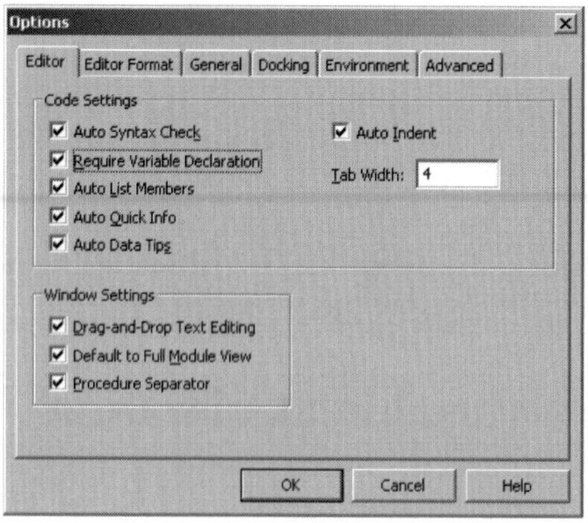

Figure 1.9: The important option REQUIRE VARIABLE DECLARATION *is activated in this dialogue field.*

Activating the Prompt To Save Changes option

In order to ensure that Visual Basic prompts you to save any modifications that may have been made before the program start, you should activate the PROMPT TO SAVE CHANGES option. The advantage is that you have the option of saving the project and associated files. If you fail to save these, and Visual Basic or even Windows happens to crash (however unlikely), the program would be lost as nothing would be saved. Of course, you don't have to wait until the program starts – you can save the project at any time using the PROJECT/SAVE PROJECT menu command.

Procedure: activating the **Prompt To Save Changes** option

1 Start *Visual Basic* (if it is not already open) and create a STANDARD EXE project.

2 Open the EXTRAS menu and select the OPTIONS entry.

3 Select the ENVIRONMENT tab.

4 Select the PROMPT TO SAVE CHANGES option (Figure 1.10).

5 Close the dialogue field using the OK button.

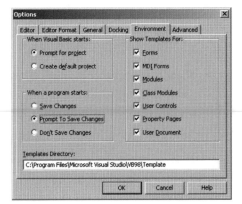

Figure 1.10: The important option PROMPT TO SAVE CHANGES *is activated in this dialogue field.*

Modifying the fonts and colours of your settings

You need to do this only if you are not satisfied with the font used by the program code window. So, where do we find the program code window? This is the window in which all Visual Basic program commands have to be entered. Open it by double-clicking on a form, or by just clicking once (which is recommended, as we do not know yet the consequences of double-clicking) and then press the F7 key. The program code window opens, the contents of which are initially displayed in Times New Roman, size 10. Select a larger font, and, if available, change the font to Arial, as this increases legibility a little (this is, of course, subjective).

You will notice that Visual Basic automatically assigns different colours to different program elements, such as variables or commands. This is quite practical, as you will be able to deduce more easily which name has which function (program errors are always displayed in red). These colours can also be altered, but you should only do so once you are acquainted more fully with Visual Basic.

Procedure: modifying the font and font size

1 Start *Visual Basic* and create a STANDARD EXE project.

2 Open the EXTRAS menu and select the OPTIONS entry.

3 Select the EDITOR FORMAT tab.

4 Select the NORMAL TEXT entry from the list (this is the default entry) (Figure 1.11).

5 Select the font in the FONT selection list, and the size in the SIZE list.

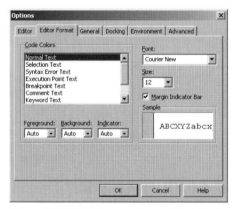

Figure 1.11: The type and size of font for the program code window are set in this dialogue field.

If you wish, you can also set colours in the FOREGROUND and BACKGROUND display lists. However, you should note that you have to set the background colour for all program elements (located in the CODE COLORS selection list). You will see from the preview window how a setting modified for normal text affects the other code elements.

Familiarising yourself with the 'furniture'

The 'furniture' of Visual Basic, or the development environment, refers to the icon bar and icons. All commands are located here – those required for creating new projects, saving projects, and, most importantly, executing the project. The most important button is the one with the small green arrow. The current project is started using this button (you may then be asked whether you wish to save the project files). See Figure 1.12 and Table 1.1.

Figure 1.12: The icon buttons of the main icon bar.

Symbol	Meaning
	Add STANDARD EXE project
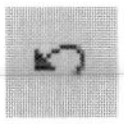	Undo last modification
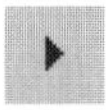	Start program
	Pause program
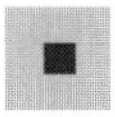	End program
	Make project explorer visible

Table 1.1: The most important icon buttons of the main icon bar.

Familiarising yourself with the help functions

Visual Basic help is the 'handbook' in which all commands, functions, control elements and their properties and methods are explained. It is an indispensable guide when learning Visual Basic, as you will find all information required here at a glance. There is even a search function. Unfortunately, the help function is not available with the Learning Edition of Visual Basic (Figure 1.13). For this, you will require at least the Standard Edition.

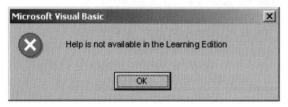

Figure 1.13: Your call cannot be connected – there is no help function in the Learning Edition.

There are three ways of calling the Visual Basic help function:

- Access the internet. A complete documentation of Visual Basic 6.0 can be found at `/msdn.microsoft.com/vbasic/technical/documentation.asp`

- Download the documentation on Visual Basic 5.0 CCE from the internet. The web address is `msdn.microsoft.com/vbasic/downloads/updates.asp` A file called *vb5ccein.exe* is located here. If you execute this file, installation occurs automatically. The help for this version can be found under *Help Files and Documentation* at the following web address: `msdn.microsoft.com/vbasic/downloads/cce/default.asp` The documentation refers to the older Visual Basic Version 5.0, but this is better than nothing at all.

- Buy or borrow a Visual Basic reference book in which all commands are explained (unfortunately, there was no room in this book).

Tip

You may find (e.g. at a computer flea market) a CD entitled 'Microsoft MSDN Library' (there are at least two CDs). This includes the complete documentation. This is the official Visual Basic help, as owners of the Professional or Enterprise Edition also receive these MSDN Library CDs.

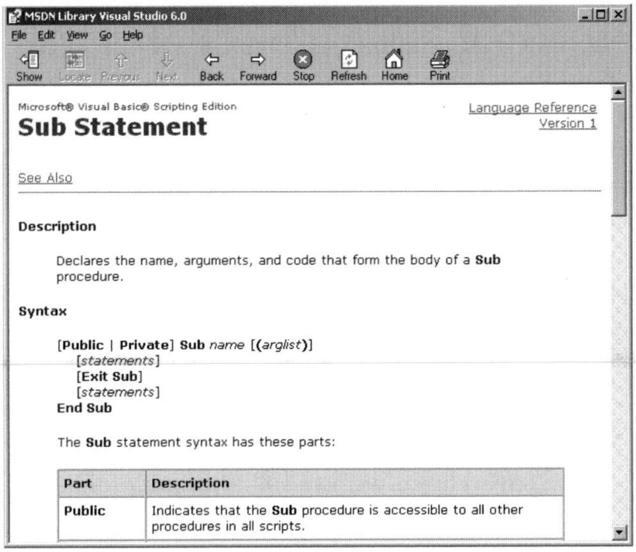

Figure 1.14: The Visual Basic help contains detailed explanations for all commands.

Note

This is not easily done at the outset. Even if you have both MSDN Library CDs, this does not mean that everything functions perfectly. Depending on how much of the MSDN Library you have installed, one help section remains on the CD. When selecting a help topic, you may be prompted to insert a CD called 'MSDN VS 6.0 CD2' (Figure 1.15). Don't worry, this is normal. This is merely an abbreviation for 'MSDN Visual Studio CD No. 2'. Enter the CD, and the help topic should appear.

11

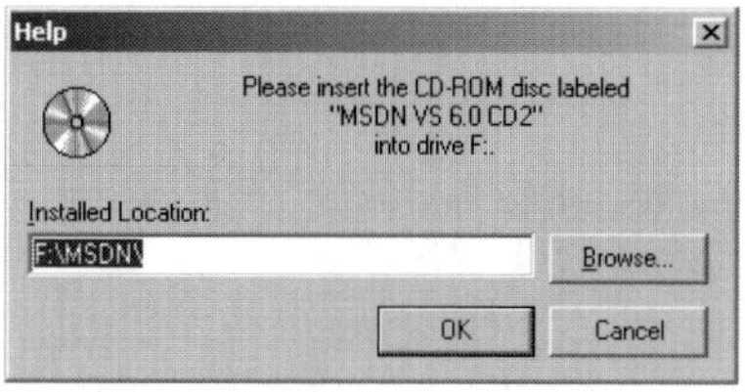

Figure 1.15: This message appears if a requested help topic is not contained on the hard drive.

Creating a new Visual Basic project on a trial basis

In order to try everything that you have learnt in this chapter, you should try to create a project, then execute it using the ⟨F5⟩ key to end it again. You can then check whether you went through your imaginary checklist properly.

Procedure: creating a new Visual Basic project

1 Start *Visual Basic* and create a STANDARD EXE project by selecting the STANDARD EXE entry from the dialogue box, and confirm the selection with OK. A new project is then created consisting of one form.

2 Press the ⟨F5⟩ key to start the project (if you are asked whether you wish to save the files, click on NO).

3 You will now see an empty window, which you can move around the screen.

4 Click on the CLOSE BOX of the window (upper right-hand corner) or on the END icon in the icon bar. The project is then ended.

Is Visual Basic difficult to learn?

Visual Basic is regarded as easy to learn as it does not spit out completed programs at the touch of a button. The word 'visual' refers only to the fact that the input and output elements of a window can easily be arranged with the mouse, rather than by editing the text file brought onto the screen. The rest is just good old programming. Programmers learn best from examples, processed step-by-step on the PC. This is particularly true of Visual Basic, where it is relatively easy to equip small programs with an interface and execute them. Visual Basic is very lenient with errors. Even if blunders are displayed immediately after entry, incorrect data types, unprocessed algorithms or calling unavailable procedures simply leads to the program being stopped. The cause of the error can frequently be corrected in the program code window immediately without having to restart the program. This makes Visual Basic particularly suitable for beginners. It is highly unlikely, almost impossible even, for a Visual Basic program or even Windows to crash completely (you should never say 'never', but Visual Basic is very programmer friendly in this respect).

A further characteristic that makes the introduction far easier is the different forms of entry assistance that Visual Basic offers programmers. Program errors are not corrected automatically, but immediately after the entry of a point, Visual Basic usually offers a selection list with all names concerned, or with functions and methods shows a description of syntax in a small yellow box (the QuickInfo box). This is so that programmers do not have to consult the help function every time, and so they can see what they need from the selection list. Help is available using the F1 key (as mentioned previously – unfortunately not on the learning edition). Simply place the cursor on the command or keyword and press F1. The relevant help section should then appear in which a more detailed explanation of the word in question will be given. Small examples will often be found here, which you can apply to the program directly.

If a personal tutor were embedded in the help function to watch over the programmer constantly, and to make suggestions when you cannot go any further or you wander in the wrong direction, then Visual Basic would be perfect. Unfortunately, this is not so, so there are three suggestions for prospective Visual Basic programmers: practice as much as possible, consult the help function as much as possible, and again practice as much as possible.

What's the next step?

Hopefully, this introduction was not too boring. You may have imagined your debut in the 'exciting' world of programming to be somewhat different. Formalities are an integral part of a programmer's daily life. You should avoid becoming preoccupied with these formalities, yet they are still important, as those described in this chapter will make learning Visual Basic easier in the long run. We will begin programming properly in the next chapter. You will then be able to write your first Visual Basic program step by step and execute it.

Chapter 2

Your very first Visual Basic program

In this chapter, you will have your first taste of success in the world of programming, because this is where you will write your first Visual Basic program step by step.

Things are getting exciting now, as you are about to write and execute your first Visual Basic program. In this chapter, you will get to know two Visual Basic programs. The first example is very easy. This is so you can understand the principles of programming with Visual Basic, and are guaranteed your first taste of success. The second example has more substance. It involves entries being added to the text boxes, actions being resolved by clicking a button, calculations from one unit to another, selection from a menu, and much more. Even bitmaps play a role in creating more pleasant visual impact.

The topics for this chapter are:

- making the computer says hello – the first example;
- converting from feet to metres;
- avoiding errors – checking an entry;
- option fields for selection;
- small images for decoration;
- selecting from a menu.

Say 'hello world'

Programmers love the 'hello world' example. A long time ago, the first computers had to display the phrase 'Hello world' immediately after having begun to operate (often not on a monitor, but on a kind of typewriter connected to the computer). Programmers (or operators, as they were known then) were then able to see that the computer was fully operational. It later became the standard that every decent textbook for beginner programmers used this as a first example. This had several advantages. The example was very simple, so success was practically inevitable; the reader gained a first impression of the general structure of a program; and the author could surreptitiously show that he or she had a certain sense of humour, knew the tradition of the 'hello world' program, and was well versed in the tradition of computer pioneering, able to attain a certain level and able to have his or her work taken seriously. However, let's not dwell too much on the showing-off tricks of authors. You are about to become familiar with a 'hello world' program for Visual Basic.

Follow the instructions below. If anything becomes unclear, or you lose the thread of what you are doing, close down Visual Basic (without saving anything, as there won't be much to save) and start again from the beginning.

1 Start Visual Basic.

As every classic fairytale begins with 'Once upon a time', so every statement in this book begins with this instruction. After the start, you have to decide which type of project is to be created (this question does not always appear). You should select the STANDARD EXE project type for all examples used in this book (Figure 2.1). This creates a new project consisting of a form (or window) (Figure 2.2).

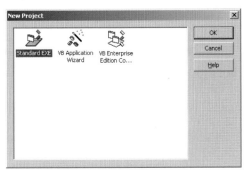

Figure 2.1: At the start you have to select a type of project – opt for STANDARD EXE.

If you no longer wish to see this dialogue field after the start, check the NO LONGER DISPLAY THIS DIALOGUE FIELD option. A new STANDARD EXE project will then always be displayed after starting Visual Basic in future (you make the selection reappear using the IDE options).

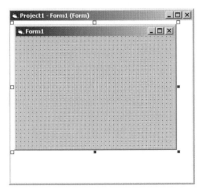

Figure 2.2: Visual Basic programs usually begin with a blank form.

2 The form contains one button.

First, place a button in the form. Click the COMMAND BUTTON icon in the toolbox (underneath the TEXTBOX, the icon with 'ab' as an inscription) once to select it (Figure 2.3). Move the mouse pointer to the form, and the button should be in the upper left-hand corner. Now stretch the frame of the button while holding down the left mouse button. This determines the size of the control element, which can always be modified at any point afterwards. All control elements are created on the form in this way. However, there are some control elements, such as the timer, whose size cannot be altered.

Figure 2.3: The button icon is selected in the toolbox.

The form is the output interface in which the input and output elements are ordered, which the program user can see when the program is executed. These input and output elements are known as *control elements* in Visual Basic. All available control elements are contained in a separate window called the *toolbox*. This is normally located on the left-hand side (if it is not displayed there, it has to be activated using the VIEW menu). Every image (apart from the arrow in the upper left-hand corner, which is only used to highlight a selection) represents a control element. If you wish to see the name of the control element, place the cursor over the icon. A small box is then displayed (Figure 2.4).

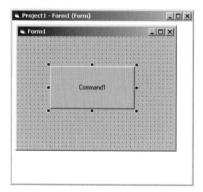

Figure 2.4: A button is created on the form – size and position are not important here.

3 The button is connected with an action.

In this step, the button should be connected with an action. Press the ⌨F7⌨ key to enter into the program code window. You will see a window with a white inner area (as long as the colours have not been modified, as described in

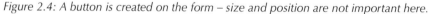

18

Chapter 1) in which words will already be displayed. These words are Visual Basic commands, which you will get to know during the course of this book. You will see the area of the form in which the programming takes place. It is the program code window (Figure 2.5), which can be opened (as long as the program is running) by double-clicking on the form or pressing the ⌨F7 key (⇧+F7 makes the form visible again).

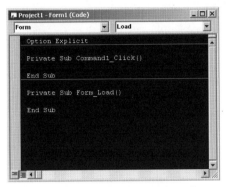

Figure 2.5: The programming takes place in the program code window.

4 The *Click* event is programmed.

Select the COMMAND1 entry from the left-hand selection list (all control elements ordered on the form are listed). This is the name of the button (the name is usually set by default). All events now appear in the right-hand selection list, to which the control elements in the left-hand selection list can react. This also includes the *Click* event, displayed by default. In the program code window, you will see the framework of the event procedure (Figure 2.6):

```
Private Sub Command1_Click ()

End Sub
```

This procedure is always called by Visual Basic whenever the user clicks the button. Here you determine what happens after clicking.

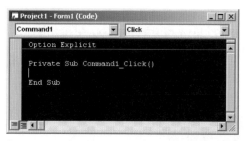

Figure 2.6: The program code window displays the frame of the Click *event procedure of the button.*

5 The *Click* event procedure is given content.

Enter the following commands in the `Command1_Click` procedure (Figure 2.7):

```
Select Case Hour(Time)
  Case 8 To 12
    Msgbox "Good morning!", 64, Time
  Case 13 To 18
    Msgbox "Good afternoon!", 64, Time
  Case Else
    Msgbox "Good evening or goodnight!", 64, Time
End If
```

Note

You will see this at various points throughout the book: upper- and lower-case letters are of no significance when entering commands. Visual Basic automatically modifies the style according to the entry. Remember to press the ⏎ key at the end of every line. Visual Basic then sees that the command line has finished (a command line can be separated into several on-screen lines using the line continuation operator, whereby an underscore is used to denote a blank space).

Not bad for your first program. Visual Basic should now begin to give an indication of what the computer is capable of. You will soon realise that the program is able to make an independent decision, and a welcome message is displayed which is adjusted to the current time of day with scientific precision.

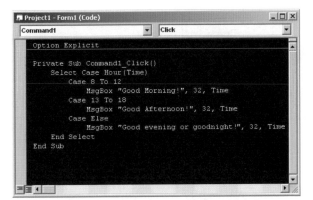

Figure 2.7: The Click *procedure of the* COMMAND1 *button is filled with commands.*

As soon as you type in the name of a function (or a method or object) and Visual Basic recognises this name, the syntax description of the function will be displayed in a small box called the *QuickInfo box* (Figure 2.8). This help function can be cancelled using the Esc key.

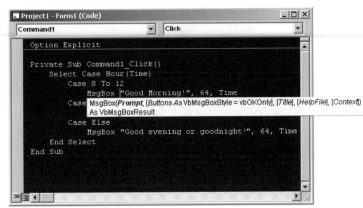

Figure 2.8: When entering functions, Visual Basic displays the syntax description in the help function.

First, you have to start the program. Do so using the F5 key and click on the button. If Visual Basic asks you if you wish to save the project and form file, click on NO (Figure 2.9).

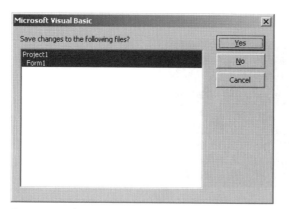

Figure 2.9: This question appears every time the program is started if changes have been made to individual files.

If you have done everything correctly, a welcome message should be displayed, depending on the time of day (Figure 2.10).

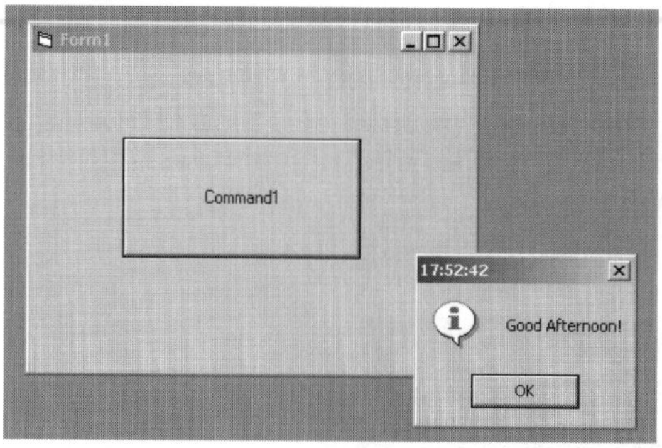

Figure 2.10: The Visual Basic program says 'Good Afternoon' - other messages appear depending on the time of day.

Congratulations! You have brought your first Visual Basic program to life. Though it may be small and its appearance leaves much to be desired, you should have learned two important things:

1. How control elements are arranged on a form.

2. How event procedures are programmed.

Just a small comment to end this first section. The program obviously has no built-in artificial intelligence, and cannot judge the time on the basis of daylight. It involves a simple decision that queries the current time using the Hour function of Visual Basic, and compares it with two (arbitrarily specified) figures: 12 and 18. You will learn how such decisions function on the basis of a SELECT CASE command in Chapter 5.

Converting units

Our next small program will allow us to convert feet to metres. We can than extend the program to other units, such as knots and gallons.

1 Start *Visual Basic*.

You already know this step, so no further explanation is required.

2 Create a STANDARD EXE project

An empty project consisting of an empty form is displayed. The program will now be created.

3 Create a text box in the form.

First, a text box is placed in the form. The number will be entered in feet here later. Click once on the TEXTBOX icon in the toolbox (marked with 'ab') to select it. Now move the mouse pointer to the form, where the text box should be located in the upper left hand corner. Stretch the frame of the text box while holding down the left mouse button.

4 Place a button in the form.

Place a button underneath the textbox. The conversion takes place when you click the button.

5 Place a label in the form.

Create a label underneath the button. The output in metres will appear here later.

The form is now ready (Figure 2.11 shows a rough draft). You can test the program using the F5 key. Clicking the button has no effect as yet. This will soon change when the programming begins.

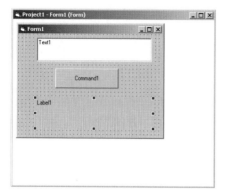

Figure 2.11: A text box, a button and a label are created in the form.

6 Switch to the program code window.

Press the [F7] key to enter the program code window (if you have already started the program, you will have to close it again).

Select the COMMAND1 entry from the left-hand selection list (all control elements placed in the form are listed here). This is the name of the button (the name is usually set by default). All events now appear in the right-hand selection list, to which the control elements set in the left-hand selection list can react. You will see the framework of the event procedure in the program code window:

```
Private Sub Command1_Click ()

End Sub
```

This procedure is always called by Visual Basic whenever the user clicks the button. Here you determine what happens after clicking.

7 The click event procedure is programmed.

In this step, the click procedure is given content, as clicking with the mouse has no effect. Enter the following command in the procedure:

```
Label1.Caption = Text1.Text * 0.305 & " m"
```
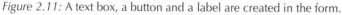

This is a Visual Basic command, which establishes three things at once.

1. The content of the text box is multiplied by 0.305. The asterisk indicates multiplication. So where is the content of the text box? This is made up of two subnames. The name of the text box (Text1) and the name of its properties are displayed in the text box. Both names are separated by a dot. This principle is a fundamental feature of Visual Basic. Most actions

are not processed using commands, but using the properties (and methods) of objects. In this case, `Text1` is the object and `Text` is the property.

2. The letter `m` is added to the result of the calculation. The inconspicuous `&` character (much is inconspicuous in Visual Basic) ensures this. This is known as the **&** operator, which links two character strings together.

3. Finally, the whole process has to be output somewhere. This somewhere is the label, already located in the form. So, which command performs this? Again, no command is used. In order to output in a label, whatever is to be output is assigned to the _Caption property_. The name has to be given in advance so Visual Basic knows which name is being referred to. And how are both names separated? Again, using a dot, which is the most important character in Visual Basic.

8 The program is started.

The program can now be started. Start the program using the F5 key, enter a number in the text box, and click on the button. If you have done everything correctly, the result should appear in the label (Figure 2.12). Congratulations – you have now brought your second Visual Basic program to life!

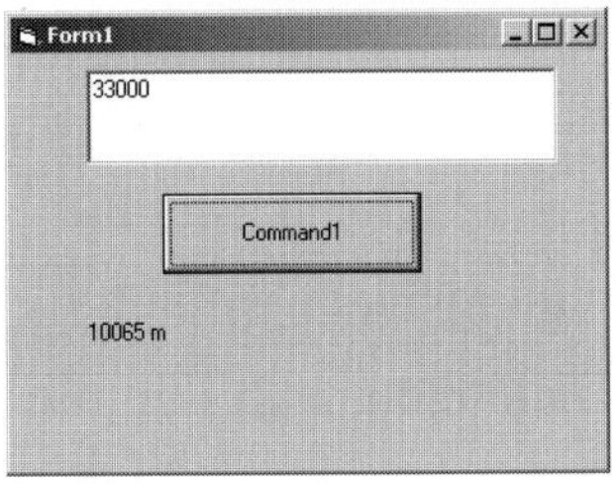

Figure 2.12: The second sample program in action – it converts a value in feet into metres.

Even though this example is small and the visual impact is minimal, you have again learned important things:

1. How control elements are arranged on a form.

2. How event procedures are programmed.

3. How properties of control elements are used in programs.

Before turning to visual refinements, an important topic that plays a central role in every programming language needs to be explained.

The idea of variables

Variables are the short-term memory of a program. Numbers, names and other things are stored here, which should be available during the execution of the program. A variable is a name that represents a number, name or object in a Visual Basic program. In order for a variable to be used, it has to be identified by the program. This is done using the `Dim` command. Identifying a variable is called _declaration_. During declaration, it is usually indicated which sort of data are to be saved. This is called the _data type_. If only integers are to be saved in a variable, select the data type from `Byte`, `Integer` or `Long`, depending on the maximum possible size of the number to be saved. Even though this specification is not absolutely required, Visual Basic helps you convert the program more effectively. In some cases, entering the data type can help the compiler recognise errors earlier, which your PC can execute from the program. Here is an example of a variable declaration:

```
Dim Foot As Integer
```

In this way, a variable is declared with the name `Foot`. It is of no significance to the program that this name has been selected (we could have called it anything). The additional remark `As Integer` indicates that this variable should be an integer. You can only save integers here (from –32,768 to 32,767), which is more than sufficient.

> **Note**
>
> _An overview of all data types can be found in the appendix._

Once the variable has been identified, it can be given a value using the following command:

```
Foot = Text1.Text
```

This is an assignment. The variable `Foot` is assigned the value contained in the _text_ property of the _Text1_ control element. This is the value that was previously entered in the text box. The value of the variables can now be assigned to another variable or property. The following command

```
Label1.Caption = Foot
```

assigns the value of the `Foot` variable to the _Caption_ property of the control element _Label1_. And what effect does this have? The value of the variable is displayed in the control element. Visual Basic, unlike other programming languages, does not recognise direct input and output commands. Instead, inputs and outputs are carried out via the properties of the control element arranged on a form previously.

The response of control elements

Every control element arranged on a form, as well as the form itself, has a name specified in the properties window in the category (name). This name is important, as this is the name to which the control element will respond during program execution. Normally, Visual Basic allocates a name to every control element; however, this should be altered (more on the name selection of control elements in Chapter 3). The name alone is merely an aspect. In most cases, you will want to access a property (or method) of a control element or form. This property (or method) is followed by the name of a control element, separated by a comma. And now for the best part. After entering the dot, Visual Basic (usually) displays a selection list in which all relevant names (i.e. properties and methods) are listed (Figure 2.13). This makes selection very easy, as you need not consult the help function to find out which name is used for a control element. If you want to know what the content of the txtSurname text box is, and assign it to the variable sSurname, the command is as follows:

```
sSurname = txtSurname.Text
```

If you wish to output a word in the text box:

```
txtNachname.Text = "Dr. Hugo"
```

However, if you wish to output the same word in a label, the command is as follows:

```
lblSurname.Caption = "Prof. Dr. Hugo"
```

Figure 2.13: After entering a dot, Visual Basic displays a selection list of all properties and methods.

In this case, the *Caption* property is used, as there is no *text* property with the label. These are the intricacies that separate an experienced Visual Basic programmer from a beginner. It is vital to know the *object principle* of Visual Basic from the outset. Control elements are objects that have properties and methods. The properties and methods of an object always follow the name of an object separated by a dot.

> **Note**
>
> *The term 'method' will be explained in Chapter 3.*

Visual fine tuning

You should (hopefully) have achieved a degree of success fairly quickly with the last Visual Basic program. The onus is on you to add graphic improvements to the form. Visual Basic provides a lot of scope for improving a program visually. The following measures are offered:

- Position the control elements so that they can be recognised.
- Create a label as a description on or after every input or output element (this is the task of the labels).
- Specify a different font and font size in the *Font* property of the properties window.
- Modify the background colour using the *Backcolor* property, and the foreground colour using the *Forecolor* property (you should avoid using too many different colours).
- Set the *TextAlignment* property to centred.
- Set a specific border using the *BorderStyle* property.
- Combine the associated control elements in a frame.
- Assign meaningful names to control elements using the *Name* property. You will find recommendations for name conventions in Chapter 3.

These are only recommendations. Figure 2.14 shows how the improved form may look (its functionality has not changed).

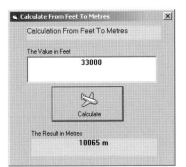

Figure 2.14: The form has been graphically polished up a little.

Setting properties in the Properties window

The recommendations from the last section were well meant, so where do you make the modifications? It is quite simple. All properties of a control element or form are set in the *Properties window*. This is an important window of the development environment, made visible using the F4 key or using the VIEW menu. The program may not already be running. You should always use the same procedure:

1 Select the control element or form by clicking on it once.

2 Switch to the *Properties window* (which has to be visible).

3 Select the left-hand column of the property to be modified, and type the new value in the right-hand column.

4 Confirm the modification by pressing the ⏎ key (this is not compulsory).

This is how new values are assigned to the properties of all control elements. Above all, the *name* property of every control element should be modified according to the suggestions given in Chapter 3. Table 2.1 shows a comparison of the old and new names taken from our sample program.

Old name	New name	Control element
Command1	*cmdConvert*	Button
Text1	*txtFeet*	Text box
Label1	*lblMetres*	Label
Form1	*frmExample01*	Form

Table 2.1: The old and new names of control elements and the form.

29

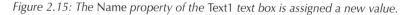

Figure 2.15: The Name property of the Text1 text box is assigned a new value.

The entry check

Optical fine tuning is interesting, but it is much more important that the program functions properly. Have you tried to enter anything other than a number in the text box? If so, Visual Basic will have rejected this with an incomprehensible error message (the program will have been interrupted rather than shut down altogether – look at the status in the title bar of the Visual Basic application). This type of error is no real cause for concern. This is a *runtime error* (as it occurs during program execution, or *runtime*), which Visual Basic reports with the message 'I cannot proceed' (Figure 2.16).

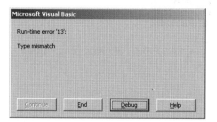

Figure 2.16: An unsuitable entry leads to a runtime error.

Don't worry too much about the exact error message. Type mismatch, in this case, simply means that an error has occurred, in which two data types conflict. If you wish to know what caused the runtime error, click on the DEBUG button. Visual Basic switches to the program code window and displays the program line that caused the runtime error (Figure 2.17). The selection of the error lines in question is not large, as the user currently has only one command line.

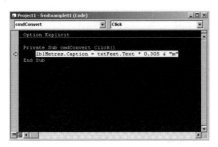

Figure 2.17: This command line has caused a runtime error.

Any idea what the cause of the error is? If you don't, move the mouse pointer to the name txtFeet (the new name of the recently renamed *Text1* text box) and wait a moment. Visual Basic will then show the current value of the *Text* property in a box (Figure 2.18). You may notice that this is not a number. This is hardly surprising, as either text or a combination of numbers and text was entered. This type of 'mix' cannot be multiplied by 0.305. This is the cause of the runtime error and the conflicting data types.

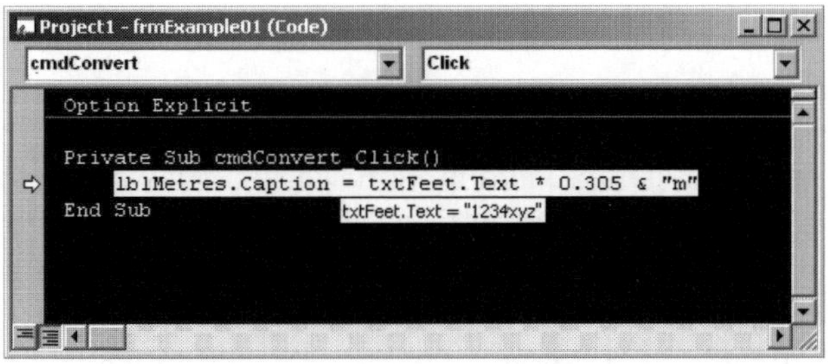

Figure 2.18: By moving the mouse pointer to a variable or property, the current value is displayed during a program's interruption.

The problem has been identified, so what is the solution? First, end the program by clicking on the END button in the icon bar (Figure 2.19). An entry check will now be integrated so that such an error should not occur in future.

Figure 2.19: Program execution is ended by clicking on the END *button.*

Use the following procedure to embed an entry check:

1 Switch to the program code window using F7.

2 Select the CMDCONVERT entry from the left-hand selection list, and the CLICK entry from the right-hand selection list. This is the Click event procedure of the button.

3 Insert new commands in the event procedure. It should contain the following (Figure 2.20):

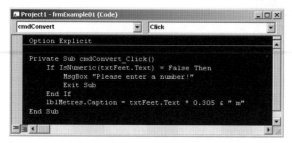

Figure 2.20: The Click event procedure of the button was refined with an entry check.

```
If IsNumeric(txtFeet.Text)= False Then
  Msgbox "Please enter a number!"
  Exit Sub
End If
lblMetres.Caption = txtFeet.Text * 0.305 & " m"
```

The first command line begins with an `If` command. This is followed by an *expression* (i.e. a combination of numbers, variables and arithmetic operators that always produce a result), which can only be true or false. Both terms have nothing to do with conventional meaning – more on this in Chapter 5. True means that the expression is correct, and false means it is incorrect. How the program proceeds now depends on the expression. If the expression is true, the following `If` commands are executed. If it is false, the commands are not executed. There are no further options.

The expression in the above example is

```
IsNumeric(txtFeet.Text) = False
```

This expression can be true or false. The question that has to be answered by the program is: "If `IsNumeric(txtFeet.Text)` false?" If so, then the expression is true (this sounds confusing, but there is a simple logic). The `IsNumeric` function (this a function embedded in Visual Basic) checks whether a number was entered at all:

```
If IsNumeric(txtFeet.Text) = False Then
  Msgbox "Please enter a number!"
  Exit Sub
End If
```

The `Msgbox` function, which displays a small message box on the screen, is only displayed if the condition

```
IsNumeric(txtFeet.Text) = False
```

has been satisfied (i.e. it is true), in other words, if the expression `IsNumeric(txtFeet.Text)` returns the value `False` (i.e. a value of 0)

```
Exit Sub
```

and the event procedure is left. However, if this text box contains a number, the `IsNumeric` function returns the value `True`, and the commands listed between `If` and `End If` are not executed. This means that no conversion is executed and no runtime error is produced.

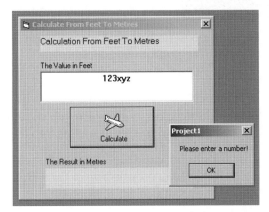

Figure 2.21: If no number is entered, the program reports a message after clicking the button.

If you wish to check whether a number larger than 0 was entered, two `If` commands have to be combined:

```
If IsNumeric(txtFeet.Text) = True Then
    If txtFeet.Text > 0 Then
     Msgbox "You have to enter a number larger than 0"
    End If
Else
     Msgbox "You have to enter a number"
End If
```

33

This is more advanced programming. In this example, the `Else` command is used as an addition to the `If` command. The query has also been switched over. The commands between `Else` and `End If` are now executed if the following condition on the `If` command is false. Integrate this section in the Click event procedure of the button from the sample program. A more comprehensive entry check is then given, which is intercepted with the entry of 0 or a negative number.

From feet to metres and back

Our sample program will be extended in this section so that a conversion from metres to feet is also possible. You will get to know a new control element with the *Options box* provided especially for configurating options. Option boxes appear at least in twos, otherwise there would be no selection. The *Value* property of an option box determines whether the button of an option box is pressed. If another option box is clicked by the user, the *Value* property is automatically given the value *True*. The option box that was pressed until now automatically switches back to the unselected status, and its *Value* property assumes the value 0 once again.

> Note
>
> *If you wish to configure a group of option boxes on a form already containing option boxes, these have to be combined in a frame box.*

The form will now be extended to two option boxes, with which you should be able to set whether a conversion from feet into metres or metres into feet should be processed (Figure 2.22).

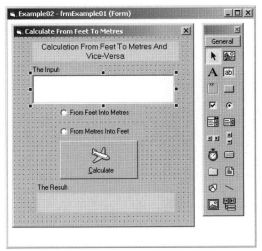

Figure 2.22: The form is extended to two option boxes.

Use the following procedure:

1 Create an option box in the form (The OPTION BUTTON icon is situated at the bottom right of the button).

2 Enter 'From Feet Into Metres' using the *Caption* property.

3 Enter the name *optFeetMetres* for the option field using the *Name* property.

4 Create another option box underneath the existing option box. Enter 'From Metres Into Feet' using the *Caption* property (Figure 2.22).

5 Enter the name *optMetresFeet* for the option box using the *Name* property.

6 Once the button has been clicked, it has to be queried which of the two buttons is pressed. Can you guess which command should be used? Right – the If command. Modify the Click event procedure as shown in Figure 2.23.

7 Finally, both the text box and label box should be assigned new names, as their meanings have changed because of the new conversion variants. The text box can optionally accept metres or feet, and the label box displays these units correspondingly. Rename the text box from *txtFeet* to *txtInput* and the label field from *lblMetres* to *lblOutput*. This makes sense as the meanings of both control elements have changed, and the names should always correspond to the meaning.

8 Start the program using the F5 key. You are now able to select the type of conversion using the option box and obtain another result depending on the setting.

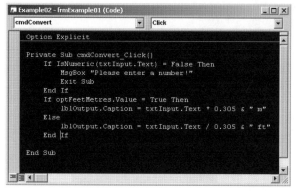

```
Example02 - frmExample01 (Code)                              _ □ ×
cmdConvert                    ▼   Click                          ▼
    Option Explicit

    Private Sub cmdConvert_Click()
        If IsNumeric(txtInput.Text) = False Then
            MsgBox "Please enter a number!"
            Exit Sub
        End If
        If optFeetMetres.Value = True Then
            lblOutput.Caption = txtInput.Text * 0.305 & " m"
        Else
            lblOutput.Caption = txtInput.Text / 0.305 & " ft"
        End If

    End Sub
```

Figure 2.23: The Click procedure of the command button was extended.

Have a look at the new Click procedure of the button in Figure 2.23. It should be easy to see the logic behind this. The `If` command checks the value of the *Value* property of the option box. If it is `True` (i.e. not equal to 0), the following command is executed. However, if it is `False`, the command between `Else` and `End If` is executed.

Figure 2.24: The extended conversion program in action – the graphics are modified a little.

There are still two small details to clear up. If you wish an option box to be set up from the outset, there are two options:

1 Set the *Value* property in the properties window.

2 Insert a command in the *Form_Load* event procedure, which sets the property to true:

```
Option1.Value = True
```

In this example, it becomes clear that you should assign suitable names to control elements from the outset. *optFeetMetres* and *optMetresFeet* are used in place of *Option1* and *Option2* respectively, where *opt* is the prefix used for an option box (more on name conventions in Chapter 3).

The second detail concerns the output of results. Do you think fewer decimal places would be better? Use the `FormatNumber` function to remove unnecessary figures. The output then appears as follows:

```
lblOutput.Caption = FormatNumber(txtInput.Text * 0.305, 2) &
" Metres"
```

and for conversion from metres into feet

```
lblOutput.Caption = FormatNumber(txtInput.Text / 0.305, 2) &
" Metres"
```

The 2 indicates that only two decimal places are to be displayed. Figure 2.25 shows what effect these small changes have.

Figure 2.25: Only two decimal places are displayed now, and rounding off occurs automatically.

And now for something completely different

After so much serious programming, we should do something about the graphics. We will display a flag according to the unit selected. So where do the flags come from? The following exercise can only function if you have selected the graphics when installing the working model. In this case you will find the flags of over 30 different nations in the directory with the name `\Programs\Microsoft Visual Studio\Common\Graphics\Icons\Flags`. If you cannot find this directory, you can find suitable flags (in this case the British and German flags) on the internet. The images are displayed in a *display control element*.

37

Use the following procedure to extend the program (Figure 2.26):

1 Create three display control elements on the form. The images are located in the lower left-hand corner of the toolbox (the one with the mountain and sun, not the one showing the desert).

2 Enter new names for the three displays: call them *imgflag*, *imgUK* and *imgGerman*.

3 Place *imgflag* in the centre, and the other two in the lower right-hand corner. You can easily overlap them, as later they will be invisible during program execution.

4 Set the *Stretch* property of all three displays to the *True* (double-click the *False* value in the right-hand column or select the name from the list). This makes a loaded bitmap fit the size of the frame.

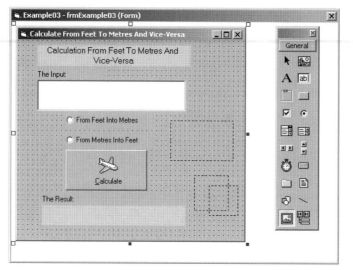

Figure 2.26: Three display control elements are created on the form.

5 Both displays, *imgUK* and *imgGerman*, now receive an image. First click on *imgUK*, switch to the properties window, select the *Picture* property and click on the three small dots. A dialogue box opens, from which you should select the file *Ctruk* (Figure 2.27). Confirm your selection with OK. Shortly afterwards, the flag should be displayed.

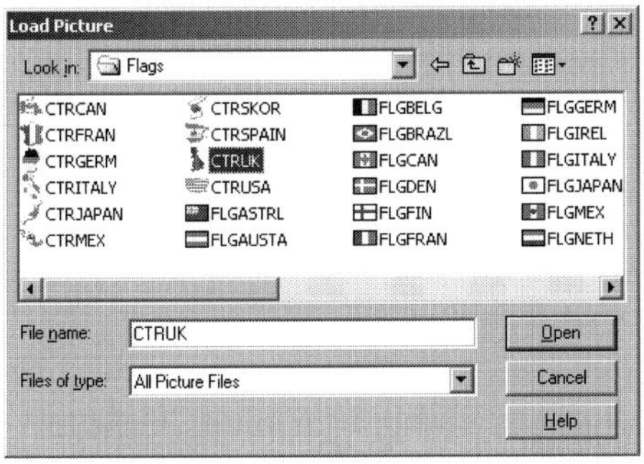

Figure 2.27: The flag icons are selected from the Flags *directory.*

6 Now click on the *imgGerman* display, switch to the properties window, select the *Picture* property, click on the three small dots and select the file *CtrGerm*. Both flag icons should now appear in the lower right-hand corner (Figure 2.28).

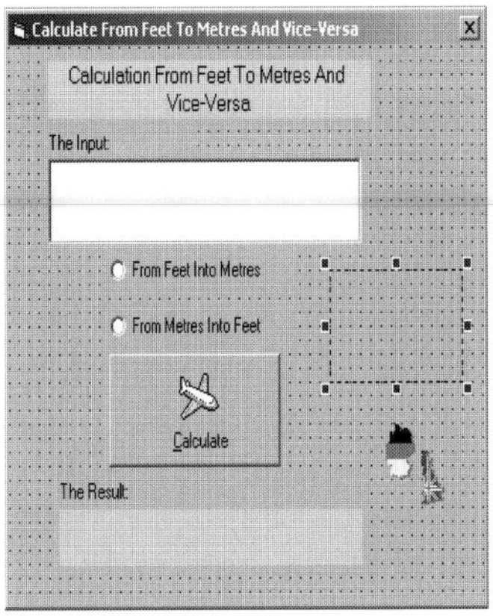

Figure 2.28: Both the imgUK *and* imgGerman *displays have been given an image.*

7 The program should now be configured so that whenever one of the two option boxes is clicked, the suitable flag icon is displayed. Switch to the program code window using ⌈F7⌋ and select *optFeetMetres* from the left-hand selection list. The entry *Click* appears in the right-hand selection list:

```
imgflag.Picture = imgUK.Picture
```

8 Select the *optMetresFeet* entry from the left-hand selection list. The *Click* entry reappears in the right-hand selection list and the procedure margins of the procedure *optMetresFeet_Click*. Insert the following command in this procedure:

```
imgFlag.Picture = imgGerman.Picture
```

9 Finally, both the *imgUK* and *imgGerman* images have to be made invisible during program execution. This can either be done by setting the *Visible* property to *False*, or, more elegantly, by placing the setting on *False* in an event procedure that is always executed when the form is loaded. This is the *Form_Load* event procedure. Select the *Form* entry from the left-hand selection list, and the *Load* entry from the right-hand selection list. Insert the following command in the procedure:

```
imgUK.Visible = False
imgGerman.Visible = False
```

10 That's it. Start the program using ⌨F5. The suitable flag should be displayed whenever either of the option boxes are clicked (Figure 2.29).

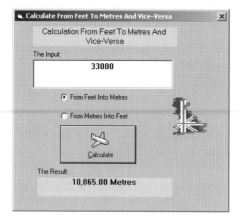

Figure 2.29: Selecting a conversion leads to the suitable flag being displayed.

Selecting using a menu

Option boxes are just one way of offering a selection to the program user. In this section, you will learn a second option using the menu. This time, we will convert from gallons to litres and vice versa. The form does not have to be completely surrounded. The question instead is how the different conversion possibilities should be offered (there are currently four, but there could be more). It would not be a problem to add an extra option box for every conversion variant, but menus are better suited for this.

You will become familiar with the Visual Basic MENU EDITOR used in Chapter 9. Every form can be assigned a menu using the Menu Editor. In turn, a menu is a name displayed in the menu bar, which when clicked opens into a list of names, also known as menu entries. A menu can be assigned to every form using the Menu Editor, which is called with ⌨Ctrl + ⌨E (the form has to be selected).

The Visual Basic program will now be modified a little:

1 End the program (if still running), select the form, and press ⌈Ctrl⌉ + ⌈E⌉. This opens the Menu Editor.

2 Specify the entries for a menu in the Menu Editor. Two details are required for each menu entry: the title, i.e. the text to be displayed, and the name to which the entry responds in the program. First, specify the heading for the menu. You should call it *Conversion*, and the name should be *mnuConversion* accordingly (the *mnu* prefix stands for 'menu') (Figure 2.30).

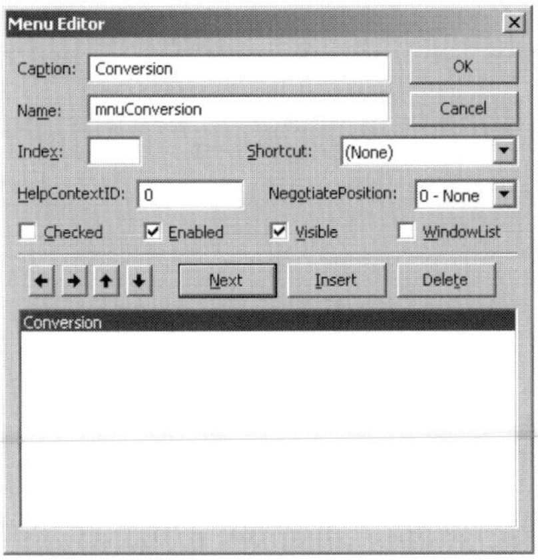

Figure 2.30: The menu is specified in the Menu Editor – *a menu is already available.*

3 Click on NEXT and enter *Feet into Metres* for the caption, and *mnuFeetMetres* for the name. As this is a menu entry rather than a menu, the position is moved to the left. Click on the left arrow (Figure 2.31).

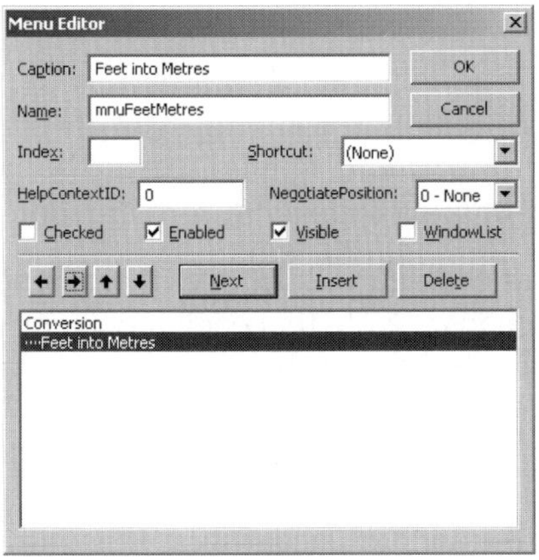

Figure 2.31: The menu is assigned its first entry.

4 The entry for conversion from metres into feet is next. Click on NEXT and enter *Metres into feet* for the caption, and *mnuMetresFeet* for the name. The indent to the left is not required this time as this has already been done.

5 Repeat the last steps for conversion from gallons to litres (the entry should be called *mnuGallonsLitres*) and from litres into gallons (the entry should be called *mnuLitresGallons*). The final menu is shown in Figure 2.32.

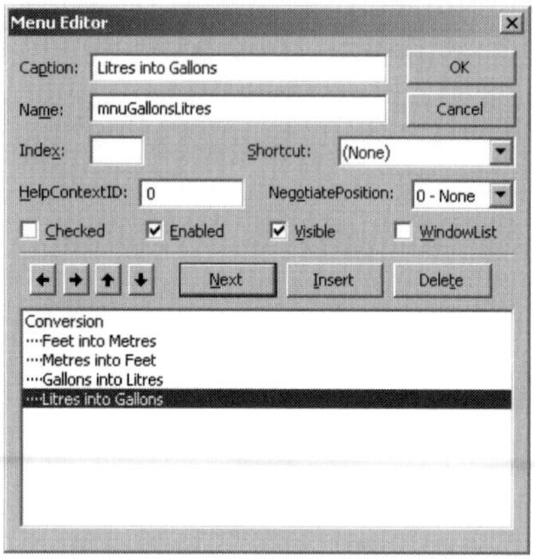

Figure 2.32: The finished menu in the Menu Editor.

Close the Menu Editor using the OK button. The form now has a menu called *Conversion*. The menu entries appear once it has been clicked.

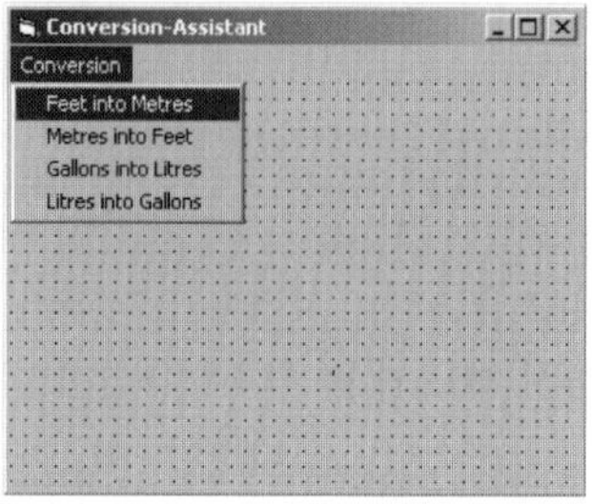

Figure 2.33: The conversion *menu contains four entries.*

The form now has a menu with four entries (Figure 2.33), yet there is no action behind the entries. This will soon change. Note that each menu entry can react to a mouse click, and there is a *Click* event that can react to the conversion. If a conversion is selected, three things should happen:

6 The type of conversion should be saved in a variable with the name *ConversionType* (this is assigned the value 0 for conversion from feet into metres, 1 for conversion from metres into feet, 2 for conversion from gallons into litres, and 3 for conversion from litres into gallons).

7 The units to be converted should be displayed above the text box for the input, and above the label for the output, so that the user can see which conversion is taking place.

8 The selected entry should be marked in the menu with a cross.

Use the following procedure to extend the program:

1 First remove both option boxes (if you have not created a new program), as these are no longer required. Select the first option box and press the Del key. Repeat this with the second option box (both *Click* event procedures remain in the program code window – these are general procedures; as these are also no longer required, they can be deleted or they can remain in the program).

2 Switch to the program code window using F7.

3 Select the GENERAL entry from the left-hand selection list. This is the *General* section of the form. For example, variables are declared here that should be valid in all procedures of the form. Insert the following command:

```
Dim ConversionType As Integer
```

4 Select the MNUFEETMETRES entry from the left-hand selection list. This is the *Click* procedure of the menu entry. Insert the following command:

```
ConversionType = 0
```

5 Select the MNUMETRESFEET entry from the left-hand selection list. This is the *Click* procedure of this menu entry. Insert the following command:

```
ConversionType = 1
```

6 Select the mnuGallonsLitres entry from the left-hand selection list. This is the *Click* procedure of this menu entry. Insert the following command:

```
ConversionType = 2
```

7 Select the MNULITRESGALLONS entry from the left-hand selection list. This is the *Click* procedure of this menu entry. Insert the following command:

```
ConversionType = 3
```

Each time one of the four entries is selected, the variable `ConversionType` is assigned another number. It is later queried via this variant as to which conversion should be used.

8 The conversion now has to be switched. Select the CMDCONVERT entry from the left-hand selection list. This is the *Click* procedure of the button. This already contains a range of commands. As both option boxes no longer exist, the query as to which type of conversion should be used will look different. Figure 2.34 shows the complete event procedure of the button. The query of the conversion type is processed using a SELECT CASE command, as this command is best suited for this. Modify the *Click* procedure in your program so that the procedure corresponds to that in Figure 2.34.

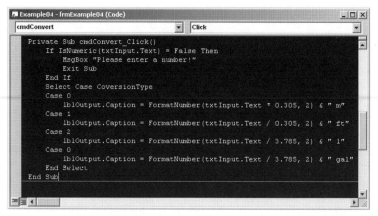

```
Example04 - frmExample04 (Code)                                    _ □ ×
cmdConvert                          ▼    Click                            ▼
    Private Sub cmdConvert_Click()
        If IsNumeric(txtInput.Text) = False Then
            MsgBox "Please enter a number!"
            Exit Sub
        End If
        Select Case ConversionType
        Case 0
            lblOutput.Caption = FormatNumber(txtInput.Text * 0.305, 2) & " m"
        Case 1
            lblOutput.Caption = FormatNumber(txtInput.Text / 0.305, 2) & " ft"
        Case 2
            lblOutput.Caption = FormatNumber(txtInput.Text / 3.785, 2) & " l"
        Case 0
            lblOutput.Caption = FormatNumber(txtInput.Text / 3.785, 2) & " gal"
        End Select
    End Sub
```

Figure 2.34: The new Click *event procedure takes the type of conversion into consideration.*

9 Start the program using the F5 key. What happens? If you have done everything correctly, you must first select a conversion from the menu. Then enter a number in the text box and click on the button. According to the type of conversion selected, a corresponding result should be displayed.

Extensions required

A small modification to a program can lead to a host of other changes, which may not have been foreseen initially. The introduction of further types of conversions into our relatively small and comprehensible program already leads to at least half a dozen necessary alterations in order for the program to be coherent and complete. In turn, these modifications should not be reset. Now it's your turn. Consider how the individual extensions should be carried out. This is an excellent opportunity to test your new knowledge of Visual Basic programming.

Here are the tasks to be processed:

1 If a conversion type was selected from the menu, the entry selected should be marked with a check. The *Checked* property of the menu object should therefore be set to *True*. Here is an example for the *mnuFeetMetres_Click* menu entry:

```
ConversionType = 0
mnuFeetMetres.Checked = True
```

Setting a check means that an existing check has to removed. This does not happen automatically. The simplest way is to set the *Checked* property of all menu entries to *False* before setting a check. So that these commands do not have to be listed in every *Click* procedure of a menu entry, they will be combined in a procedure. Insert the following procedure somewhere in the program code window (preferably at the end):

```
Sub RemoveAllChecks ()
  mnuFeetMetres.Checked = False
  mnuMetresFeet.Checked = False
  mnuGallonsLitres.Checked = False
  mnuLitresGallons.Checked = False
End Sub
```

2 This procedure should be called before making a check in each of the four *Click* procedures of the four menu entries. The *mnuFeetMetres_Click* event procedures looks like this:

```
RemoveAllChecks
ConversionType = 0
mnuFeetMetres.Checked = True
```

3 The selection of a conversion should have an effect on the title of the text box. The heading is represented by a label that should contain another name. Rename this as *lblConversion*. The heading now has to be set in each of the four *Click* procedures of the four menu entries. The event procedure *mnuFeetMetres* should be used as a model:

```
RemoveAllChecks
ConversionType = 0
mnuFeetMetres.Checked = True
lblConversion.Caption = "Enter the value in feet:"
```

If you wish, you can also give a suitable heading to the label that displays the result. This can also occur in the *Click* event of a menu entry.

4 What happened to the flags? A third flag came into play with US gallons, for which another display control element is required. Create this on the form (preferably in the lower left-hand corner), label it *imgUSA*, and allocate to it the file *CtrUsa* using the *Picture* property in the properties window. Remember to set the *Stretch* property to *True* (this is only important for graphics). Furthermore, this display should be invisible during program execution, which happens inside the *Form_Load* event procedure by setting the *Visible* property to *False*.

5 Finally, selecting a conversion from the menu should lead to the corresponding flag being displayed. Again, this occurs in the *Click* event procedure of the respective menu entry. What would it be like if the flag were to appear in the button this time? The *Click* procedure in the *mnuFeetMetres* example has to contain the following command:

```
cmdConversion.Picture = imgUK.Picture
```

The display control element *imgFlag* is no longer required in this case and can be deleted.

6 You are now nearly ready. Just a few details remain, such as the form heading which is set using the *Caption* property, and which should now be called 'Conversion Assistant'.

Have you made all of the alterations? If so, congratulations – you have already learned a lot about Visual Basic programming. However, if something remains to be done, or if you cannot proceed any further: take some time to try out the different options. Look at Figure 2.35, which displays the complete version of the conversion program. You should keep this in mind: practice is more important than theory for beginners in Visual Basic programming.

Figure 2.35: All extensions have been applied to the program. The conversion assistant is ready.

The next step

This chapter addresses one issue in particular: getting to know Visual Basic as a development tool and 'programmer's program' with simple examples. The next chapter systematically explores the basics of programming, and addresses the ABC of Visual Basic programming with which all programmers need to become familiar. You will learn about control elements in more detail in Chapter 4.

Chapter 3

The ABC of programming

In this chapter, the basics of programming will be explained that apply not only to Visual Basic but to most programming languages. The most important passages are explained using short Visual Basic examples so that you don't get bogged down with too much theory. You will learn how to work with Visual Basic projects, which is essential for Visual Basic programming.

Can you remember learning to read? You may have learned a new letter every week, beginning with small words and building up to larger ones over time. When you reached the letter X, you had probably learned some complicated words such as xylophone. Nobody would have given you the complete alphabet on one day and expected you to understand everything the following day. The letters came in sequence and you learned to work with them. The bigger picture unfolded much later. When learning your first programming language, things are very similar. You learn one or two commands and try to work with them. Then comes a new command, with which new possibilities unfold and you can spell more complicated words, meaning that you can combine program commands. There are also some differences. For example, you do not need to learn every single Visual Basic command. Of the (approximately) 90 commands available, only 10 or 20 are important. The rest are so specialised that you may well never use them. The other difference is that 'programming school' lasts for many years. Those who work in software development are immersed in a constant learning process.

In this chapter, we address the ABC of programming. You will learn simple commands of the Visual Basic programming language and construct small programs, which you enter and start using the F5 key. This is a theory chapter first and foremost, and you should read through it several times.

Topics in this chapter include:

- the role of commands;
- error messages – when Visual Basic is unhappy;
- the general structure of a program;
- comments;
- variables;
- using computers to calculate;
- decisions;
- program loops;
- simple output using the `Msgbox` function;
- simple input using the `Inputbox` function;
- useful functions that Visual Basic programmers should know.

The role of commands

A programming language does not contain any vocabulary – it contains commands. A command is a word that has special meaning for a programming language. If the programming language is installed on a PC and the programmer types the word in a file, which is then saved and 'interpreted' by the programming language (all this occurs in the 'development environment' in Visual Basic), the command is executed. If several commands appear in sequence, this results in a program. The commands of a program always belong to a programming language, such as Visual Basic. It is generally not possible to combine the commands of different programming languages in one program (it is possible in Windows script languages, but this is the only exception). A program is only a file (usually a normal text file with a special extension, such as `*.bas` for Basic command files). In order for the program to become active, it has to be executed. This means that the interpreter responsible for the programming language (already embedded in Visual Basic) processes the program one command at a time, analyses the individual commands, and does what is specified by the command.

In order for a program to become active, it has to be executed by another program, which interprets the program commands and converts them into computer commands. This program is known as the *Interpreter*. In Visual Basic, the interpreter is embedded in the development environment and becomes active whenever the [F5] key is pressed.

Here is a simple example for a program that simulates a cash machine:

```
If PinNumber = 1234 Then
   Msgbox "The pin number is correct"
End If
```

These three command lines contain Visual Basic commands. The commands are called `If`, `Then` and `End If`. You have processed a decision (more on decisions in Chapter 5). `Msgbox` is written in the second command line. This is not a command, but a function. Functions are very similar to commands, although there are differences, which you will learn about later on. The function with the name `Msgbox` is there to display something in the message box on the screen. The message to be displayed is in quotation marks. These instruct Visual Basic to ignore anything that appears in quotation marks. This means that you can write anything within the quotation marks. As this has no significance in Visual Basic, it does not matter how you write it. The important thing is that these *character strings* are enclosed in quotation marks, otherwise a syntax error occurs (more about this later).

The task of the `If` command is to check whether that which immediately follows the `If` command produces a value larger than is applicable – programmers call this a comparison. In this case the comparison is

```
PinNumber = 1234
```

So what is `PinNumber`? As this question already indicates, it is not a command. It is a variable, or a name that stands for a value. If Visual Basic comes across this word, it 'thinks' 'This isn't a command, so it must be a variable or function.' It consults its internal memory store and finds the value of this variable (previously entered by someone).

If the value of the variable `PinNumber` is 1234, then (and only then) the condition is satisfied. The term used is a true condition. As far as program execution is concerned, this means that all commands that follow the `If` command are executed. However, if the value of the variable `PinNumber` is *not* 1234, then the condition is not satisfied. This is known as an untrue or false condition (the term 'false' is not a value judgement, but merely describes the status). In this case, the commands between `If` and `End If` are not executed – Visual Basic reacts as if they were not there.

This is an example of the computer's way of thinking. Throughout the course of this book, you will notice that computers are structured far more simply than you may have thought. Computers often think in a very simple manner. They appear so intelligent because they think so incredibly quickly. But they are not intelligent at all.

The role of syntax

The fact that computers use a simple way of thinking means that the programmer has to conform to a certain way of writing. This style of writing is called *syntax*. If this is not adhered to, a *syntax error* occurs. A syntax error means that the computer, Visual Basic in this case, does not understand a program command. Not because it was formulated in too complicated a way, but because somewhere a blank space or comma was overlooked, or a typing error was made. The following example contains two syntax errors:

```
If PinNumber = 1234 Ten
  Msgbox "The PIN number is correct"
Endif
```

The first error is easy to spot – the `Then` command is missing a letter `H`. The second error is more subtle: there should be a blank space between the `End` and the `If`.

Figure 3.1: The incorrect Ten *command leads to a syntax error.*

Figure 3.1 shows how Visual Basic displays such a syntax error. So why was the second error not noticed? The first reason is that an error message can query only one error. The other reason is that Visual Basic has already inserted the blank space between the End and the If, so the syntax error no longer exists. Sometimes Visual Basic realises this type of error on entry.

From theory to practice

So that you can understand the general way of thinking of a computer and Visual Basic better, you should put the small cash machine example from the last section into practice. Use the following procedure to do so:

1 Start *Visual Basic*.

2 Create a STANDARD EXE project. If a selection box does not appear immediately after the start, a STANDARD EXE project has already been created.

3 Double-click on the form window. This switches you to the program code window and the *Form_Load* event procedure. This is the procedure that is called automatically after the program start before the form is displayed. If any commands are to be executed when the program is started, they should be inserted here.

4 Insert the following commands in the *Form_Load* procedure:

```
Dim PinNumber As Integer
PinNumber = Inputbox("Please enter PIN:")
If PinNumber = 1234 Then
  Msgbox "The PIN is correct!"
Else
  Msgbox "The PIN is incorrect", 48, "Try 1234"
End If
```

53

5 Start the program using the [F5] key.

Immediately after the start, a small input box and prompt should appear (Figure 3.2). Visual Basic is now waiting for your input. Enter a number in the input field and click on OK. If the number is 1234, then (and only then) the condition is checked by the `If` command satisfied. The commands between `Then` and `Else` are executed. This is computer logic in action. Chapter 5 addresses this in more detail, as it deals exclusively with decisions.

Figure 3.2: An input box appears after the program starts.

If you wish to repeat the entry, the program has to be shut down (using the END button in the icon bar) and then restarted. In Chapter 4 you will learn how to repeat program functions as often as you wish using a command button.

When Visual Basic complains

At the outset you will often make mistakes in typing a command line, then press the [↵] key only to find that Visual Basic starts to 'complain' (programmers call this a *compiler error*). This is because when entering command lines, you have to adhere to a certain construction, and Visual Basic checks your entry immediately after pressing the [↵] key (this is turned off using the options in the IDE). You should be familiar with this syntax error from the previous section.

Don't worry – this type of error has no negative consequences and is easily remedied. You need only click the OK button (clicking the HELP button does not really achieve much), correct the error and try again. If everything is correct, Visual Basic proceeds.

However, there are errors that occur while the program is running, i.e. after it has been started using the [F5] key. Everything goes well at first, and then something happens. Visual Basic stops the program and complains about a certain command line. This is called a *runtime error*, as it occurred while the program was running. If a runtime error occurs, Visual Basic provides three options (Figure 3.3):

1. End the program.

2. *Debug* the program. This means that the program switches to halt mode.

3. Use the help function.

Ending the program is always the easiest option. You could check the program text, correct the errors if required and then restart the program. However, Visual Basic gives no advice as to where the error(s) may be located. It is experience, a degree of tact, and sometimes a little luck that are decisive in finding errors in large programs.

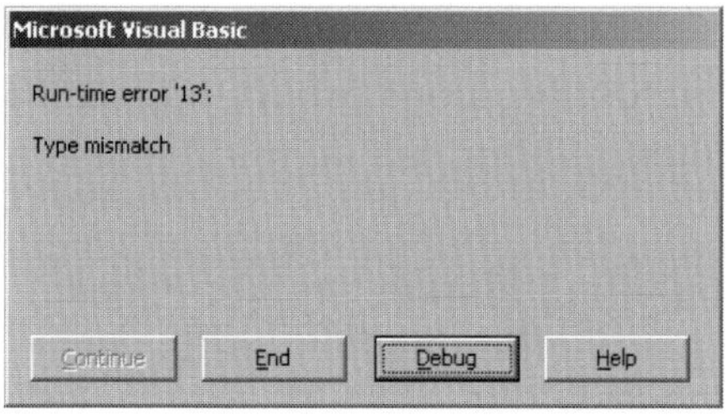

Figure 3.3: END, DEBUG, HELP *or what? If a runtime error occurs, there are generally three ways of proceeding.*

The second option is to debug the program. This term is introduced in more detail in Chapter 10. Noting that the program switches to halt mode by clicking the DEBUG button should be enough for now. This is the best part: Visual Basic shows you the program line where the runtime error occurred (usually underlined in yellow). You can now look at the command line, output the values of variables or other properties involved in the direct window, and much more. You can even modify the program text to a certain extent. If a restart is required after an alteration (not by Visual Basic), a corresponding message appears. If you confirm the dialogue box with OK, the alteration is made, but the project switches to design mode. Cancel the modification by clicking CANCEL (Figure 3.4).

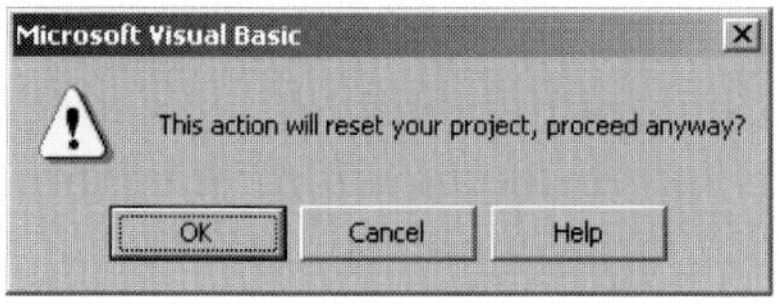

Figure 3.4: This message appears if a modification causes the project to be reset.

The Visual Basic help function is the third option. Don't expect too much of this, as the help texts tend to be very general.

General structure of a Visual Basic program

You already know that a program consists of commands. However, Visual Basic is not quite as simple as this. In Visual Basic, you do not work with programs, but with projects. In Visual Basic, the term 'project' is equivalent to the term 'program'. Every project consists of forms, modules, class modules, and so on. If you select a STANDARD EXE project at the start of Visual Basic, a blank form appears. Even though a Visual Basic project does not have to contain a form, this is the case with all of the programs you will get to know in this book. It therefore depends on knowing the structure of a form. This is very simple, as a form consists of two areas: the form interface where the control elements are created and the program code window. The programming takes place here, i.e. this is where the commands are entered that are executed after the program has started. The program area of a form consists of two further areas:

- the *General* section
- the event procedures.

The *General* section contains declarations that apply to the entire form. For example, if a variable is declared here with the `Dim` command, this variable is recognised in all procedures of the form. The general section can also contain constant definitions (using the `Const` command), the `Option Explicit` command and procedure and function definitions (Figure 3.5). Except for the commands listed, individual commands are not permitted in the *General* section. The *General* section of a form is displayed by selecting the entry (GENERAL) from the left-hand selection list in the program code window. Direct selection is not necessary, so you can scroll upwards from your position in the program code window and enter the *General* selection automatically. There are no fixed subdivisions in the program code window. The dividing line is often displayed immediately after the `Option Explicit` command, which only helps orientation. It has no real function and cannot be moved.

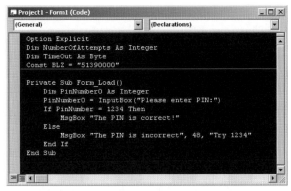

```
Project1 - Form1 (Code)                                    _ □ ×
(General)                  ▼    (Declarations)                ▼
    Option Explicit
    Dim NumberOfAttempts As Integer
    Dim TimeOut As Byte
    Const BLZ = "51390000"

    Private Sub Form_Load()
        Dim PinNumber0 As Integer
        PinNumber0 = InputBox("Please enter PIN:")
        If PinNumber = 1234 Then
            MsgBox "The PIN is correct!"
        Else
            MsgBox "The PIN is incorrect", 48, "Try 1234"
        End If
    End Sub
```

Figure 3.5: Constants and variables are declared in the General section of a form.

You can extend a Visual Basic project at any time with forms, modules and so on by selecting the corresponding command from the PROJECT menu. Every new module is displayed in the Project Explorer with its name allocated by Visual Basic, and can (and should) be modified using the properties window ([F4] key).

Everything happens in procedures

As a programming language, Visual Basic has an important feature. All commands, except those authorised in the *General* section, are always located within a procedure or function. A procedure is a program area initiated by a `Sub` command followed by the name of the procedure, and ended using an `End Sub` command. Here is an example for a procedure:

```
Sub AllNew ()

End Sub
```

The `Sub` command defines a procedure with the name *AllNew*. The `End Sub` command ends the procedure. Both of these commands define the framework of the procedure. It does not matter which commands are within a procedure.

An instance event procedure

In the first examples in this book you will only learn event procedures. These are procedures whose frameworks do not have to be (and should not be) exceeded, and which are always called by Visual Basic if the event concerned occurs, such as by clicking on a button with the mouse. Event procedures differ from normal procedures not only in their structure but also in that they are called automatically by Visual Basic.

Private or public?

This determines whether a procedure should be called only within a form (or module), or also by other project modules. This is already an advanced theme of Visual Basic programming and has only been mentioned at this point as event procedures precede the word `Private`:

```
Private Sub Form_Load ()

End Sub
```

This is a procedure that can only be called within a form. This is known as a private procedure. The opposite is a public procedure. Either the word `Public` precedes the `Sub` command, or it is not executed at all, as Visual Basic assumes a public procedure. So the procedure

```
Sub AllNew ()

End Sub
```

is public, which means it is visible for other project modules. For example, if a procedure is to be called from several forms, it has to be part of the module added to the projected using the PROJECT/ADD MODULE menu command.

Comments

Comments are an important function in programming languages. They help describe the source text of a program. This happens less often in smaller programs. Imagine working as a programmer in a large team, in which other programmers have to read and understand your source code (another name for program commands). Or imagine submitting your source code to a firm or successor. A comment is an annotation in the source text describing a certain point in the program. Every comment line is introduced by an apostrophe. Anything that follows is ignored by Visual Basic, so no error message will be displayed:

```
' I have no idea what this should be
```

The computer's memory — variables

For most programs, it is essential that the program is able to remember numbers, names and other things. Imagine an accounting program where all numbers are forgotten immediately after the entry of a booking. This type of program would be unusable in practice. All programming languages enable the input of values as variables. A *variable* is a name that stands for a value while the program is running, which was previously stored in the variables.

A memory cell stands behind a variable in the huge data store of the PC (the RAM). It is of no significance for Visual Basic programming where this memory cell is stored. It is a type of secret shared by Visual Basic and Windows (and the stubborn Visual Basic programmer can find out using the `VarPtr` function).

Variables have to be declared

Because programmers seem to like expressing themselves in a complicated way, variables do not have to be made known, but have to be declared. On declaring a variable, you are letting Visual Basic know that a name should play the role of a variable from then on. If Visual Basic comes across this name later in the program, it knows it is dealing with a variable. There are five commands for declaring a variable in Visual Basic: `Dim`, `ReDim`, `Public`, `Private` and `Static`, all of which are fully entitled. In this book you will only learn about the `Dim` command, which is suitable for most tasks.

The following command declares a variable with the name `Balance`:

```
Dim Balance As Integer
```

The name of a variable always follows the `Dim` command. You can use any name you wish. However, certain rules apply. Variable names may not contain any blank spaces and may not exceed a certain length (the Visual Basic help function, invisible until now, will advise you of this). In addition, certain characters may not be used (such as &, $, !, # and @) as these have special meaning. There is no distinction between lower- and upper-case letters. You will notice that Visual Basic modifies the style on entry to conform with that of the declaration.

First declare, then assign

A variable is only recognised after being declared. It will receive a value later:

```
Dim Balance As Single

Balance = -6567.89
```

Assigning a value to a variable is known as *allocation*. With Visual Basic 6.0 it is not possible to combine allocation and declaration.

The role of the data type

The *data type* should also be given when a variable is declared. This specifies which sort of data may be placed in the variable later. Not all variables are identical. This is like choosing a cake tin before baking, which determines what shape the cake will be later. The 'cake shapes' in variable terms are `Integer`, `Long`, `Single`, `Currency` or `String`. If a variable is only to take whole numbers, `Integer` is used. If you use numbers with one decimal place, you should use `Single`. If character strings are to be used, then use `String`. There are 12 data types in all, but you need not know all of them at the moment. In order to simplify selection, Visual Basic offers a list of all similar types after the entry of `As`. The most important data types are listed in Table 3.1, and a complete list can be found in the appendix.

Data type	What is it suitable for?
`Currency`	For numbers where accuracy to four decimal places is important, such as in money transfer.
`Integer`	For integers between −32 768 and 32 767.
`Long`	For integers between −2 147 483 648 and 2 147 483 647.
`String`	For character strings (text).

Table 3.1: The most important data types in Visual Basic.

Two remarks to finish on: if no data type is given when declaring a variable, Visual Basic always uses the `Variant` data type. This is the head data type, which comprises all other data types. You should make the effort and indicate data types explicitly. A `Dim` command can also declare several variables:

```
Dim iNumberPoint As Integer, nNumberHit As Long
```

The data type has to be given for each variable individually. A well-known question in interviews for Visual Basic programmers in large software firms is: which data type does Variable `A` have after the following declaration:

```
Dim A, B, C As Integer
```

The answer is `Variant`, as no data type was given for either `A` or `B`. Even though this is a little advanced for Chapter 3 of an introductory book, you should not fall into the trap too easily (this will no longer apply in the next version of Visual Basic, VB.Net).

Constants – when everything should remain the same

As in most programming languages, there are *constants* as well as variables in Visual Basic. These are variables whose values cannot be modified. However, constants offer two important advantages when inputting the value directly:

- If the value changes, only the constants have to be modified. Whenever the constant name appears in the program, the new value is used.

- The constant name is often shorter than the actual value, which is very practical with character strings (think of long directory names).

Constants are therefore very important for programmers, as they can be used without having to think which value they have or whether another part of the program may have changed the value. Constants are rarely required in smaller Visual Basic programs.

A constant is declared with the `Const` command:

```
Const MwstSatz1 = 16
```

A constant is assigned its value differently from a variable on declaration, as allocation at a later stage is not possible.

Constants are very practical when it comes to directory names:

```
Const Path = "C:\My Documents\My Programs\VB\"
```

It is far quicker to give the `Path` constant in a command than a value that stands for the constant.

> **Note**
>
> *Constants are usually written in upper-case letters. This convention is of little significance to Visual Basic.*

Visual Basic knows many constants

With Visual Basic, many constants are already embedded. You should not be surprised if names appear in an example that seem to not have been declared anywhere. Examples of this are `vbCrLf`, which stands for ASCII codes 13 and 10, i.e. a line break, or colour constants such as `vbRed` or `vbBlack`. In total, Visual Basic has well over 100 constants.

61

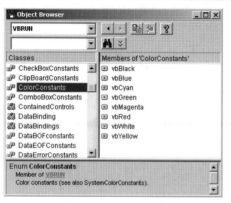

Figure 3.6: The object dialogue shows the built-in constants in Visual Basic.

Calculating your age in days

The following sample program should illustrate the role of variables in a Visual Basic program. After the start, enter your date of birth in the input box. After clicking the command button your age will be shown in days. In the centre of the program is a variable that notes the date entered, so the program can calculate the number of days in the next step.

Use the following procedure for the calculation:

1 Start *Visual Basic.*

2 Create a STANDARD EXE project. If a selection box does not appear immediately after the start, a STANDARD EXE has already been selected.

3 Double-click the form window. This switches to the program code window and the *Form_Load* event procedure. This is the procedure that is called automatically after the program start.

4 Insert the following command in the *Form_Load* procedure:

```
Dim DateofBirth As Date
Dim NumberofDays As Integer
DateofBirth = InputBox("Please enter the date of birth:")
NumberofDays = DateDiff("d", DateofBirth, Now)
MsgBox "You are " & NumberofDays & " old"
```

5 Start the program using the [F5] key (if a query for the program appears, click the No button).

After the start, an input box appears in which you should enter the date (Figure 3.7). After clicking OK, this input is saved in the variable called `DateofBirth` (the name is not important). In the next step, the value of this variable is calculated by the `DateDiff` function in Visual Basic, and the result is saved in another variable called `NumberofDays`. The value of these variables is displayed in a small message box by the following `Msgbox` function. The variables store the values with which the program is to work. If the program is ended, the variables and their values also disappear.

Figure 3.7: The value entered in the input box is saved in a variable, calculated and output.

If the program displays an error message (e.g. 'Types incompatible'), this is probably because the date was not entered in the correct format (the correct format is 25.10.1963). Click on END and restart the program.

A computer can also compute

You may be surprised to learn that a computer can also compute. However, there is no computing command in Visual Basic. Instead, calculations are processed using operators and functions. A list of all operators and functions can be found in the appendix. The following examples should clarify the principle of calculations.

A calculation always consists of numbers, variables and operators, and in which the correct formula of certain rules has to be adhered to. In most cases the result of a calculation is assigned to a variable. The following command processes a simple addition:

```
iSum = 4 + 5
```

The result of this calculation is not displayed, but is assigned to the variable *iSum*, which now has a value of 9. This is a very simple calculation. Visual Basic can do far more:

```
sMwst = GrossAmount / 100 * 16
```

or

```
sFormulaX = Sqr(Force * Mass) ^2 / (SpeedofLight / (1 -
SolarConstant)
```

This calculation clearly involves more operators. In addition, brackets have to be used here, as the rule of arithmetic logic applies in Visual Basic.

Not all calculations can be accommodated in a single line. Calculations in which a temporal variance is used (which is repeated several times according to the length of time) cannot be processed with one command. This is where program loops are used. You will learn one example in Chapter 6, where an amount of money is increased over a number of years, and the interest proceeds for each year are output.

Here is a sample of the kind of calculation in a Visual Basic program: the following small program calculates the circumference according to the rule $c = pi * r^2$. However, Visual Basic does not recognise 'pi', which has to be added using a constant:

```
Const Pi = 3.14
Dim snRadius As Single
Dim snCircumference As Single
snRadius = 2.5
snCircumference = Pi * snRadius ^2
Msgbox "The circumference: " & snUmfang
```

This example clarifies that a single computer cannot process simple calculations in one step, and that several steps in sequence are always required.

The computer makes decisions

Decisions are amongst the most important commands of a programming language. As you are already familiar with the principle of decisions from the If command at the beginning of this chapter (when addressing how a computer 'thinks'), and as all the details can be found in Chapter 5, we give only a brief summary in this section.

Whenever a program has to make a decision, this is based on a simple condition that the value of an expression is greater than null (i.e. true) or is equal to null (i.e. false). All decisions taken while a computer program is running are based on this simple principle.

An example of a very simple decision

It takes a while for newcomers to programming to fathom the basics of binary logic (based on the statuses of true and false), so instead of further explanations, some examples are now given. The first example processes a simple check. Enter your date of birth at the start, and the computer tells you whether you are over 18.

Use the following procedure:

1 Start *Visual Basic*.

2 Create a STANDARD EXE project. If a selection box does not appear immediately after the start, a STANDARD EXE has already been selected.

3 Double-click on the form window. This switches to the program code window and the *Form_Load* event procedure. This is the procedure that is called automatically after the program start.

4 Insert the following command in the *Form_Load* procedure:

```
Dim Alter As Integer
 Alter = InputBox("Please enter your age:")
If Alter > 18 Then
    Msgbox "You are over 18!"
Else
    Msgbox "Unfortunately you are under 18!"
End If
```

5 Start the program using the [F5] key (if a program query appears, click the NO button).

After the start, a small input box appears in which you should enter your age. After clicking OK, the computer tells you whether you are over 18. Of course, you don't need a computer to tell you this. The example is merely there to give you an idea of how a computer thinks. The program knows neither your true age nor any concept of the age of adulthood. It simply processes a comparison between two numbers, which when used in the context of the program can be interpreted as a decision of the computer program.

The last example was really easy. Something a bit more realistic would be a program that accepts a date of birth and then calculates whether you are 18 using the current date. A computer program is only ever as good as the commands that it is made of. If you replace the commands in *Form_Load* with the following commands, you will be asked for your date of birth after the start:

```
Dim DateofBirth As Date
 DateofBirth = InputBox("Please enter your date of birth:")

If DateDiff("yyyy", DateofBirth, Date) > 18 Then

    Msgbox "You are over 18!"
Else
    Msgbox "Unfortunately you are under 18!"
End If
```

The above program is anything but perfect. For example, if you are 18 years old on 31.12.2002, and run the program on 1.1.2002, the computer would consider you to be 18 years old already, as it only calculates the difference in years with the DateDiff function. If the program is to work properly, the decision rule has to be refined somewhat. The day and month also have to be compared, as well as the year. The new content of the *Form_Load* procedure has to look as follows:

```
Dim DateofBirth As Date
DateofBirth = InputBox("Please enter the date of birth:")
If Year(Date) - Year(DateofBirth) >= 18 _
    And Month(Date) >= Month(DateofBirth) _
    And Day(Date) >= Day(DateofBirth) Then
    MsgBox "You are over 18!"
Else
    MsgBox "Unfortunately you are under 18!"
End If
End
```

You now know to the exact day whether you are over 18. Apart from the And operator, three commands are combined. This expression, divided into several lines using the line continuation operator, produces only a single value, which is either true or false. We can draw two important lessons from this small example: a computer program is only ever as good as it has been prepared by the programmer. And seemingly simple tasks can sometimes be tricky to solve.

When computers cheat

The last example in this section should prove that computers will quite readily cheat, insofar as the program allows it.

The following program acts as a cash machine, and dispenses amounts of money up to a maximum of £400 from a balance of £1500. Secretly (which cash machines never really do), it sets aside £50 on every withdrawal, and displays the apparently true, but actually incorrect, balance.

The following example is more extensive and uses several procedures that will be explained in the next few chapters. Try it out – it is not too difficult to use.

1 Start *Visual Basic*.

2 Create a STANDARD EXE project. If a selection box does not appear immediately after the start, a STANDARD EXE has already been selected.

3 Double-click the form window. This switches to the program code window and the *Form_Load* event procedure. This is the procedure that is called automatically after the program start.

4 Enter the following command in the procedure:

```
Balance = 1500
```

5 This command specifies the starting balance.

6 Select the (GENERAL) entry from the left-hand selection list. This selects the *General* section of the form. Enter the following command:

```
Private Balance As Integer
Private SecretAccount As Integer
Private Withdrawal As Integer
```

7 Create a text box on the form. This can be found in the toolbox at the top of the screen (with the inscription 'ab'). The toolbox is the small narrow window with the many small images. Click on the icon once, release the mouse button, move the mouse pointer to a free area on the form, and draw a frame while holding down the left mouse button. You have created a text box on the form.

8 Create a button on the form. You will find this in the toolbox underneath the text box.

Double-click the button. This is the *Click* event procedure. Enter the following commands:

```
Withdrawal = text1.Text
If Withdrawal <= Balance And Withdrawal <= 400 Then
  Balance = Balance - Withdrawal
  If Balance > 50 Then
    Balance = Balance - 50
    SecretAccount = SecretAccount + 50
  End If
  MsgBox "You have " & Withdrawal & " - new balance: " _
& Balance + SecretAccount
  Else
    MsgBox "Withdrawal not possible - Balance: " & Balance
End If
```

9 Start the program using the F5 key.

Enter an amount in the text box, such as £300, and click on the button (first you will have to delete the content of the text box, *Text1*). You will receive a message displaying the new balance. Repeat the withdrawals. At some point you will no longer be able to withdraw any money, even though there appears to be sufficient credit. A corresponding message should appear in which the true balance is displayed.

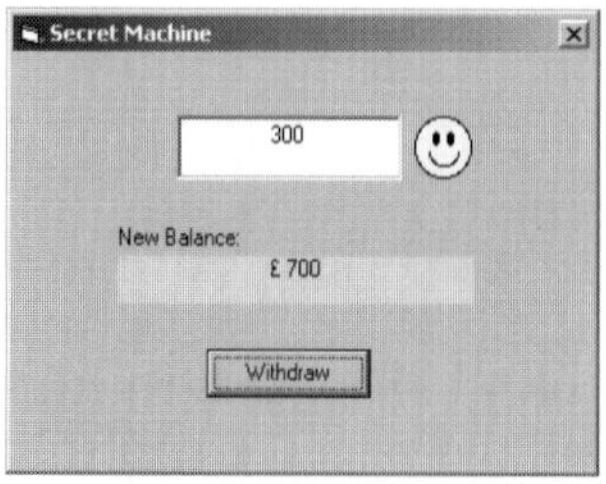

Figure 3.8: Should you trust the program? The balance displayed is not true.

Figure 3.8 shows a version in which the current dummy balance is displayed in a label.

Program loops

In programming language, a *loop* is a repeated command. Repeats are a speciality of every programming language. Loops enable a command or group of commands to be repeated a certain number of times. This is done using either a limiting value which may not be exceeded, and an increment, or by using an abort condition which is checked in every loop sequence at the beginning or the end. You will learn the details of program loops in

Chapter 6. Here is a small example for a `For Next` command, using the value of a variable that is doubled at every loop:

```
Dim cuAmount As Currency
Dim inDays As Integer
For inDays = 1 To 21
   cuAmount = cuAmount * 2
Next inDays
Msgbox "At the end there are: " & cuAmount
```

In this example, the `cuAmount` variable is assigned the `Currency` data type, which is particularly suitable for calculating amounts of money because of its four decimal places.

Here is a question for the more experienced programmer. Why does the variable `cuAmount` still have a value of 0 at the end of the loop, even though the value was doubled on every loop? Quite simple. Each variable with a numerical data type begins with the number 0. And 0 times 2 always gives 0, no matter how many times it is repeated. We forgot to initialise the variable with a value of 0.01 (which stands for an amount in £). The following command has to be executed before the `For Next` command.

```
cuAmount = 0.01
```

Simple outputs using the Msgbox function

Visual Basic does not recognise output commands with which text or numbers can be output on the screen, as control elements such as the label are normally used for this. There is only the *Msgbox* function with which general messages consisting of individual phrases and numbers can be displayed in a small box (Figure 3.9).

```
Msgbox "Hello, this is an important message"
```

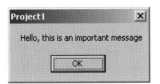

Figure 3.9: The message box is an easy solution for simple messages.

If the message box displays a small icon, this has to be specified using a second number:

```
Msgbox "What's this?", 32
```

Figure 3.10: A question mark appears in the message box.

A question mark now appears in the message box (Figure 3.10). The selection of icons is simple:

- `16` – stop
- `32` – question mark
- `48` – exclamation mark
- `65` – information signal

It is standard practice to use the constants provided for this:

```
Msgbox "What is?", vbQuestion
```

The constant `vbQuestion` stands for the number `32` and is predefined in Visual Basic, so it does not have to be defined using the `Const` command.

A third option is to specify the text that appears in the heading of the message box (Figure 3.11):

```
Msgbox "Everything will be better tomorrow", vbExclamation,
_
 "Motto of the week"
```

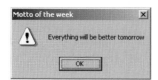

Figure 3.11: A heading appears in the message box.

There are no further ways of modifying the appearance of the message box. Anyone wishing to create more attractive message boxes should refer back to the form, where a project can be added to at any time using the menu command PROJECT/ADD FORM.

Easy entries using the Inputbox function

The opposite of the `Msgbox` function in Visual Basic is the `InputBox` function. Its task is to display a small box in which the user can enter arbitrary text. The text entered is assigned to a variable after the entry is confirmed with OK, and can then be used later in the program. The following command asks for your name (Figure 3.12):

```
Dim sName As String
sName = Inputbox("What is your name?")
Msgbox sName & " is a very nice name!"
```

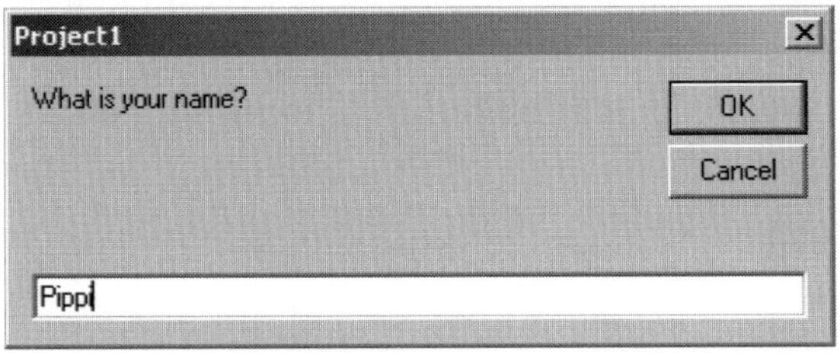

Figure 3.12: The input box asks for a name.

If the heading of the input box is specified, this is used as a second parameter (Figure 3.13):

```
Dim sName As String
sName = Inputbox("What is your name?", "Name check")
```

Figure 3.13: The input box has a heading this time.

To make input a little easier, a value can be provided that need only be confirmed. This *default value* is submitted as a third parameter (Figure 3.14):

```
Dim sName As String
sName = Inputbox("What is your name?", "Name check", "Max")
```

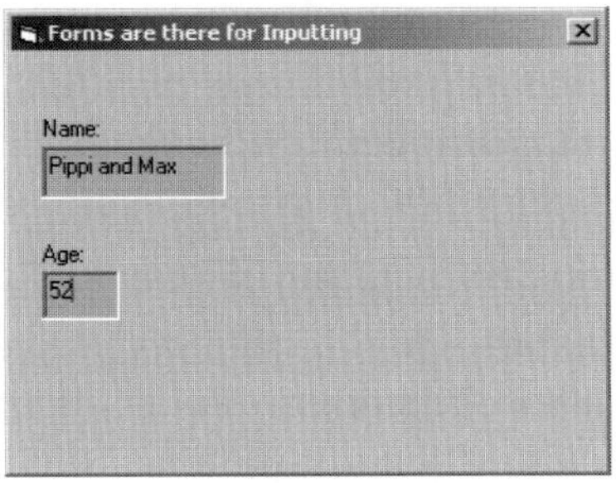

Figure 3.14: The input box displays a default *value.*

There are no other ways to refine the `Inputbox` function (the position where the box is to be displayed on the screen can be specified). This isn't the end of the world, as the forms and their control elements are responsible for making input easier (Figure 3.15).

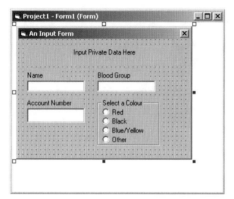

Figure 3.15: A form is the better alternative for easy input.

Useful functions

The difference between commands and functions is emphasised in Visual Basic. Apart from the 90 odd commands, there are also over 150 functions. These have special tasks, such as breaking down a string into component parts, or processing a simple mathematical operation. There are also *service functions*, which advise the program of the current time, specify whether a value submitted is a number (you are already familiar with the `IsNumeric` function from Chapter 2), or assign another data type to a value. There are even financial mathematical functions, with which a term of credit can be calculated, for example. These functions are described in detail in the Visual Basic help function, usually with examples. Table 3.2 summarises the most interesting functions.

Function	What does this do best?
DateAdd	Adds or subtracts a unit of time from a date.
DateDiff	Gives the difference between two dates in the desired units.
Dir	Gives the name of the first file in the specified directory that corresponds to the search string submitted, consisting of the filename and/or the wild cards * and?

Function	What does this do best?
FileLen	Gives the size of a file.
Format Currency	Gives a character string containing an amount of money to two decimal places, using the currency symbol set in the control panel.
Format DateTime	Gives a character string containing a date and/or time in a specified format.
FormatNumber	Gives a character string containing a number with a fixed number of decimal places.
Hex	Gives the hexadecimal value of a number as a character string.
Int	Removes decimal places from numbers and gives only integers.
IsNumeric	Checks to see whether a character string can be converted into a numerical value.
Log	Calculates the logarithm to base 10.
Now	Stands for current system time.
Rnd	Issues a random number between 0 and 1.
Round	Rounds a number to a certain number of decimal places.
Sqr	Calculates the square root of a number.

Table 3.2: Useful Visual Basic functions

Command and functions – what's the difference?

What is the difference between a function and a command – don't they both do the same thing? The answer requires a certain amount of advanced programming. Functions may only be listed on the right-hand side of a statement. Here is an example for the root function `Sqr`:

```
Sqr(10)
```

The function call is correct, but it is not yet complete as something has to happen with the result of the functions (programmers call this the *return value*). It can be assigned to a variable:

73

```
r = Sqr(10)
```

The command is now complete. If executed, the variable `r` contains the result of the function call. It should now be clearer as to what was meant by the ominous assertion that functions always have to stand on the right-hand side of a statement. The following command is not permitted:

```
Sqr(10) = w
```

With commands, there is no return value. These always stand to the left of the equals sign, as long as there is an equals sign. A command that comes after a function is the `Date` command, modified using the system date:

```
Date = "25.10.63"
```

The command is on the left-hand side of the equals sign. There is nothing wrong with combining a command with a function, provided the function assumes its correct position on the right-hand side of the equals sign:

```
Date = DateAdd("d", Date, -1)
```

This command puts the current date back by one day, whereby `Date` is a second function (it is a function as it stands for the current time). It makes no difference to Visual Basic that both a `Date` command and a `Date` function are used, as it can differentiate between the two using a simple rule: the rule that a function may never be placed on the left-hand side of the equals sign.

Working with projects

To finish this chapter, we will end on a more practical note. Working with projects is something a Visual Basic programmer has to master. You already know that Visual Basic programs are always saved in projects. A project comprises all forms, modules, class modules and so on that belong to the program, and that will be loaded into the project over time. The contents of a project are displayed in the project explorer window. Important actions related to projects include:

- creating a new project;
- opening an existing project;
- saving a project.

Creating a new project

This step should be familiar from Chapter 2. A new project may be created at the start of Visual Basic, which you can finish at any time. Open the FILE menu and select the NEW PROJECT entry (Figure 3.16) (or use $\boxed{\text{Ctrl}}$+$\boxed{\text{N}}$). Visual Basic displays the usual selection dialogue from which you can select the project type to be created (this selection dialogue does not always appear – in this case a STANDARD EXE is being created). Individual projects only differ in their details, such as by how many modules are loaded at the beginning, or by specific project properties, all of which can be modified at a later stage. In this sense, the type of project selected is not of paramount importance.

Figure 3.16: A new project is created using the FILE *menu.*

Opening an existing project

If you want to reload a project that has already been saved, you have to open the project file (marked with the *.vbp file extension). Open the FILE menu and select the OPEN PROJECT entry (or use $\boxed{\text{Ctrl}}$+$\boxed{\text{O}}$). If a project is already loaded and you want to make alterations to it, you will be prompted to save it (probably immediately). Visual Basic displays a special selection dialog with two options:

- Selecting a project file from an arbitrary directory (EXISTING tab) (Figure 3.17).

- Selecting the most recently saved project (RECENT tab) (Figure 3.18).

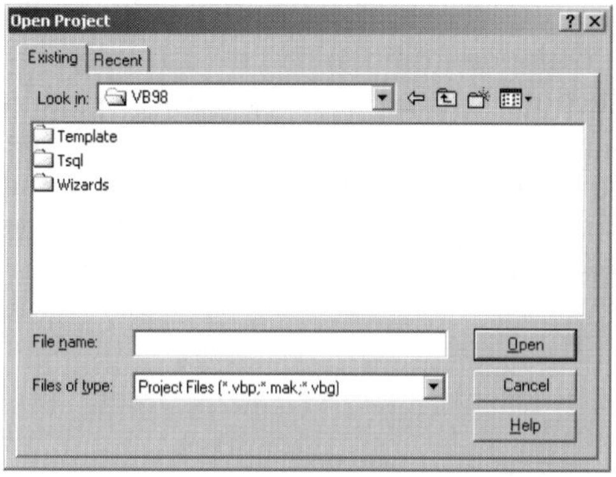

Figure 3.17: A presaved project can be opened from this dialogue box.

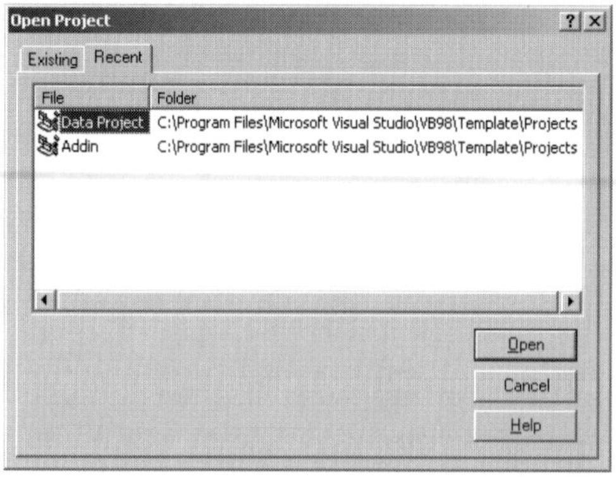

Figure 3.18: The most recently saved projects can be called from the RECENT tab.

It is not desirable for the Visual Basic program directory to be in the EXISTING tab by default. Visual Basic projects should not be saved here.

The last four entries of the FILE menu are a third option. The four most recently accessed projects are listed here. This is often the quickest way of reopening an existing project.

Saving a project

Before you shut down Visual Basic, you have to save the project, otherwise any modifications you have made since you last saved it may be lost. If you made the suggested modifications in OPTIONS as described in Chapter 1, a query should appear whenever you start the program for saving any modifications made since you last saved.

Before you end a project, Visual Basic displays all modules to which modifications have been made since they were saved last (Figure 3.19). You can confirm the selection with *OK*, or unselect individual modules that are not to be saved.

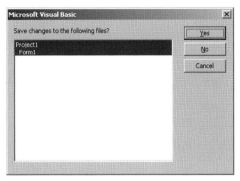

Figure 3.19: A list of modules to be saved is displayed before a project is closed down.

Tip

The entire project, i.e. all modified modules, is saved using the FILE/ SAVE PROJECT menu command (or using the disk icon in the icon bar). This is the quickest way of saving a project. If you use the familiar Word command, Ctrl+S, this saves the current project.

The next step

This is the most important chapter of the book. In this chapter you have become familiar with the ABC of programming with Visual Basic, i.e. the most important commands of the programming language. You have also learned how a computer thinks, by learning the principle of decisions and program loops. These are integral parts of nearly all programming languages. You are not expected to understand everything immediately to be able to progress. However, you will require all the commands introduced in this chapter for almost all of your future programs, so you should browse through this chapter and repeat individual passages now and again.

The next chapter will be very practical. Using the control elements, you will get to know a large number of constituents provided by the toolbox (a window of the Visual Basic development environment) and created on a form, and different options for entering texts and numbers, or for selecting options or names from a list. Working with control elements is very easy. These are some of the reasons why Visual Basic has become so popular in such a short space of time.

Chapter 4

Control elements and forms

Control elements and forms are the basic components of a Visual Basic user interface. In this chapter, you will become familiar with the ever-present toolbox.

In this chapter, you will get to know one of the best aspects of Visual Basic. What programmers in the pioneer years of Windows could only dream of has now become reality for Visual Basic programmers. Instead of typing in reams of descriptions or having to work with temperamental editors, the user interface of a program is easily clicked together using the mouse. Of course, this type of visual programming still requires programming skills and some careful thinking. However, it is clear progress, as programmers are now able to concentrate on actual programming rather than becoming preoccupied with minor details.

In this chapter, you will learn how to construct a user interface for your program by creating control elements on a form. The most important control elements will therefore be introduced. With the text box, label, command button, combination box, control box, frame, picture box, display, line and figure control elements, you will have almost an entire team of control elements. This chapter is not entirely devoid of theory, as in order to be able to use a control element, you have to know what events and their associated event procedures are.

The topics for this chapter are:

- an introduction to the toolbox;
- how a control element appears on the form;
- configuring properties;
- the role of events;
- the form that holds everything together;
- output using the label;
- input using the text box;
- the command button in action;
- using the combination box and control box for selection;
- using the frame for better clarity;
- using the picture box and display to show colour pictures;
- using line and figure control elements for added effect;
- regularity using the timer;
- how control elements respond to mouse clicks;
- how control elements respond to keyboard input;
- naming conventions with control elements.

Not all control elements of the toolbox are introduced in this chapter. The list box and its narrow counterpart, the combination box, will not be described until Chapter 6, as you need to know more about program loops before programming with these control elements.

Introduction to the toolbox

The *toolbox* is the window in which all available control elements are displayed (Figure 4.1). An icon is displayed for every control element. If you place the mouse pointer over the icon, the name of the control element is displayed.

If the toolbox is not visible, make it appear using the VIEW/TOOLBOX menu command. If the option is not available, this is because the program is still running.

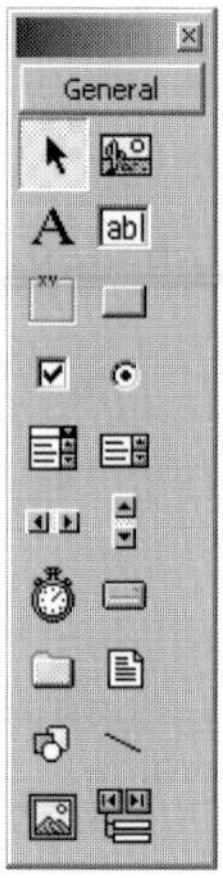

Figure 4.1: The toolbox displays all available control elements for the current project.

The toolbox has an important property – it is expandable. New control elements (already registered on the PC) are added to the toolbox using the PROJECT/COMPONENTS menu command. These control elements are called *additional control elements* or *ActiveX control elements*. Try not to let the wealth of names offered in the selection list confuse you. We will begin working with additional control elements in Chapter 9. Table 4.1 lists the most important control elements of the toolbox.

Control element	Function
Picture box	Displaying bitmaps, the output of text and graphics.
Label	Displaying simple text, usually just one line.
Text Box	Inputting and displaying text, possibly with several lines and using scrollbars. Formatting always applies to the entire text.
Command Button	Triggering actions.
Check Box	Selecting an option where many check boxes can be checked simultaneously.
Option Button	Selecting an option where only one option button can be pressed in a group.
List Box	Displays a list of names from which either one or several (with *MultiSelect=True*) names can be selected.
Combo Box	Combination of text box and list box.
Timer	Triggers an event regularly within a specified interval.

Control element	Function
Shape	Enables the creation of simple shapes.
Image	Displays bitmaps like the picture box. Bitmaps can be modified to the size of the display by setting the *Stretch* property to *True*, which leads to bitmaps being either stretched or compressed.

Table 4.1: The most important control elements of the toolbox.

How does a control element appear on the form?

In order to use a control element, it has to be created on the form. This happens in the following way:

1 Select the control element from the toolbox by selecting the appropriate icon.

2 Release the mouse button and move the mouse pointer to the position of the form where the upper left-hand corner of the control element is to be located.

3 Draw a frame for the control elemnt by holding down the left mouse button. This fixes the size of the control element on the form. Both the size and the position can be modified at any time (also using the *Left, Top, Height* and *Width* properties in the properties window).

You should note the following when creating a control element on a form:

- You can create as many control elements on a form as you wish. If the form is too small, you will have to enlarge it. A form can only be as large as the screen.

- Visual Basic assigns a standard name to each control element (e.g. *Command1*). This name should always be changed to something meaningful using the Properties window, especially if the program is to respond to the control element.

- A few control elements are invisible while the program is running. It does not matter where they are arranged on the form (the size of these control elements cannot be modified). The *Timer* control element is an example.

83

- If a control element is to be deleted, select it and press the Del button.

- If you double-click a control element by mistake, you will switch to the program code window. Pressing Alt + F7 makes the form visible again.

- Observe correct proportions from the outset. This makes small forms visually more attractive.

Configuring properties

Properties determine the appearance of a control element. If a button is to be labelled differently, a text box is to be non-editable or a label is to have a different background colour, this is done using properties. Every control element has a set of properties with which the appearance and characteristics can be configured while a program is running. Properties are configured using the *Properties window*, which is called up by pressing the F4 key or the VIEW menu (Figure 4.2). The properties of a control element or form are always displayed in the Properties window. The control element whose properties are displayed is set using the upper selection list. Configuring properties is always done in the same way. Select the property from the left-hand column and enter the new value in the right-hand column. However, there are different ways of setting values:

- by using direct input in the text box;

- by selecting it from a list;

- by entering it in a dialogue box displayed by clicking the three dots.

The correct method depends on the type of property. For example, a colour is set using a dialogue box, whereas a text is entered directly in the column.

> **Note**
>
> *Not all properties of a control element are configured during the design. Properties that are available only while the program is running are not displayed in the properties window.*

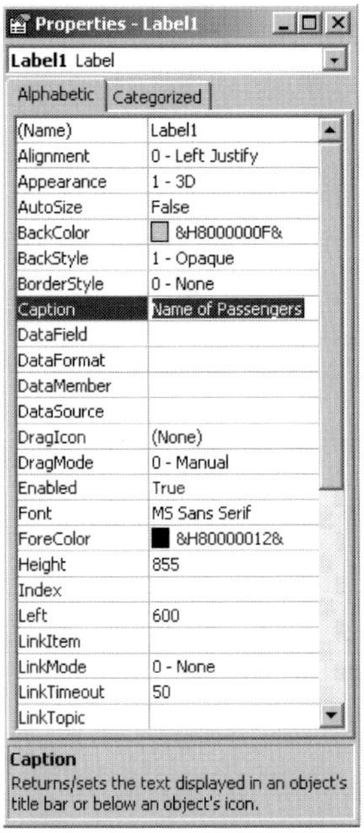

Figure 4.2: The properties of a control element or form are configured in the Properties window.

The role of events

Control elements are dependent on events. This is the only way in which they can inform the program that something is happening, such as a mouse click.

Whenever an action connected with an event is triggered with a control element while the program is running, the associated event procedure is called. The important principle of event-controlled program execution should become clear with the example of the command button. Whenever a button is clicked while the program is running, it results in a *click* event. The *click* event automatically leads to the event procedure being called. Its name consists of the name of the button, an underline and the name of the event procedure, in this case *click*.

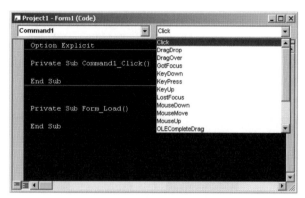

Figure 4.3: The left-hand selection list shows all events to which the control element selected in the right-hand selection list can react.

If you want your program to react to an event, you have to fill the event procedure with the commands to be executed when the event is triggered. The event procedure is selected as follows:

1 Switch to the program code window (e.g. using the [F7] key).

2 Select the name of the control element or form from the left-hand selection list (usually called FORM1).

3 Select the name of the event from the right-hand list. You will see every procedure frame of the event procedure.

4 Enter the commands to be executed by Visual Basic after calling the event procedure between the command lines with SUB and END SUB.

The form holds everything together

Forms are the central component of the user interface in a Visual Basic program. You could also refer to them as windows, but the term 'form' describes their function better. Just like a traditional form, they can contain a range of boxes in which the user can enter something. It makes no difference what you create on a form. The size of a form is also adjustable.

Getting to know the form

Getting to know a form is not too difficult. There is only very little that can initially be configured on a form, and as about 98% of Visual Basic programs contain forms, you can learn as you go along.

In this chapter, we will construct a small input dialogue window step by step, which will be based on a form and will involve all of the important control elements.

Use the following procedure to familiarise yourself with forms:

1 Start *Visual Basic* and create a STANDARD EXE project. A blank form will appear. This form should gradually evolve into an input mask using the following steps.

2 Switch to the Properties window, and enter the phrase *Space Shuttle Ticket Machine* in the *Caption* property. You will notice that this phrase appears in the form header (Figure 4.4).

3 Start the program using the F5 key. You can move the form across the screen using the mouse, as with any other window. Nothing else happens yet.

4 Close down the program by clicking the END button in the icon bar (this is not mentioned every time).

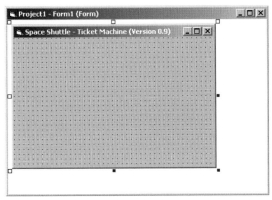

Figure 4.4: An empty form with a specific heading.

- Forms can be any size but no larger than the visible screen area. If the form is to be displayed in full-screen mode, the *WindowsState* property should be set to 2.

- The *BorderStyle* property specifies whether the form has a fixed margin, and whether its size can be modified while the program is running. You can specify where the form should appear on the screen at startup using the *StartUpPosition* property.

- As with the control elements, the form should be given a meaningful name. Call it *MainForm*, or something relating to the content of the form. The name is set using the NAME entry in the properties window.

- The content of the title bar of a form is configured using the *Caption* property.

Output using the label

The *label* is used for simple output. A label cannot be used for input. The label is used whenever a small text should appear on the form. However, the main task of labels is to describe other control elements. For example, if a name indicating the content of the text box is to be placed above the text box itself, a label is placed above the text box.

The content of the label is set using the *Caption* property. There is no way of modifying the appearance of individual letters. The appearance and colour of letters can be modified using the *Font* and *ForeColor* properties.

Getting to know the label

Use the following procedure to familiarise yourself with the label:

1 Create a label in the upper area of the form.

2 Switch to the properties window and enter the value *Name of Passenger* in the *Caption* property.

3 Start the program using the F5 key.

The text entered in the *Caption* property is now displayed on the form after the start (Figure 4.5). A border cannot be seen. Nothing else happens. This is not surprising, as the label is a rather inconspicuous control element. If you want to liven things up, you should set another font (e.g. Arial, size 10) in the properties window, and set the font to *bold*.

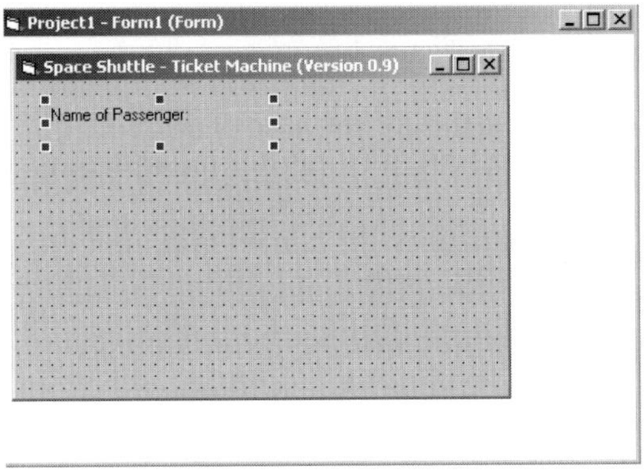

Figure 4.5: The label displays a short heading.

You should note the following about labels:

- The label is not suited for outputs consisting of several lines. If you wish to start a new line, the constant vbCrLf has to be added to the character string assigned in the Caption property. A text box is better suited for outputs of several lines as a scrollbar can be used.

- A simple border can be displayed using the *BorderStyle* property.

- The *Alignment* property specifies whether the text is to be left-aligned, centred or right-aligned.

- If a letter is to be underlined, an ampersand (&) has to precede the letter in the *Caption* property.

Input using the text box

The text box is used for input. After you have created this on the form, you can enter a name or an entire phrase while the program is running. The text you enter is available via the *Text* property of the text box.

Getting to know the text box

Use the following procedure to get to know the text box:

1 Extend the form from the last section to include two text boxes.

2 Create the first text box on the form underneath the upper label.

3 Create another text box underneath the form.

4 Insert a label above the second text box. Switch to the Properties window and enter *Age of Passenger* for the *Caption* property (Figure 4.6).

5 Switch to the Properties window and delete the current value of the *Text* property in both text boxes. This is not essential – it merely gives a more pleasant visual impact.

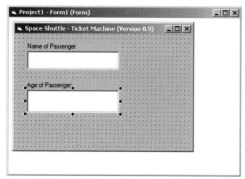

Figure 4.6: Two text fields and a label are created on the form.

- There is no *Caption* property with text boxes. The corresponding property is called *Text*.

- The maximum number of characters per entry can be restricted using the *MaxChar* property.

- If only text is to be displayed in a text box, but no input is permitted, the *Locked* property should be set to *True*.

- If an entry is to be hidden, such as when a password is being entered, the character that hides the actual entered character (such as '*' if it is to be an asterisk) should be set in the *PasswordChar* property.

- Pressing the ⏎ key has no real effect with a text box. If something special is to happen when this button is pressed, a corresponding query should be embedded in the *KeyPress* property. This is explained in more detail later in this chapter.

- If an entry consisting of several lines is to be enabled in a text box, the *MultiLine* property should be set to *True*. In this case, it is recommended that the *Scrollbars* property be set to *1, 2* or *3*. This displays scrollbars so the user can scroll through the text.

The command button in action

The command button enables the user to trigger an action.

Getting to know the command button

The dialogue boxes are slowly taking shape. In order for an input to produce an action, command buttons are required, which will later be assigned a function. Use the following procedure to familiarise yourself with the command button:

1 Create a command button in the lower area of the form used in the last section.

2 Switch to the properties window and enter *Purchase Ticket* in the *Caption* property.

3 Create another command button on the right-hand side of the first one on the form.

4 Enter *Cancel* for the *Caption* property of the second command button (Figure 4.7).

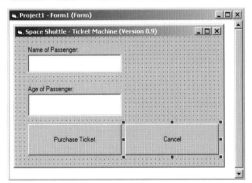

Figure 4.7: Two command buttons are created on the form.

- Command buttons have relatively few properties. The most important one is *Caption*, as this determines the inscription.

- A bitmap can be displayed in the button using the *Picture* property. The *Style* property needs to have a value of *1*.

Using the frame for better clarity

The *frame* is a rather unprepossessing control element that usually plays a passive role. However, it does perform at least two important tasks: it summarises option boxes in a group, in which only one option box can be active, and it also groups control elements into one optical unit.

Getting to know the frame

Use the following procedure to familiarise yourself with the frame:

1 Create a frame on the right of the two text boxes. The size can be modified at a later stage.

2 Switch to the properties window and enter *Additional information* for the *Caption* property (Figure 4.8).

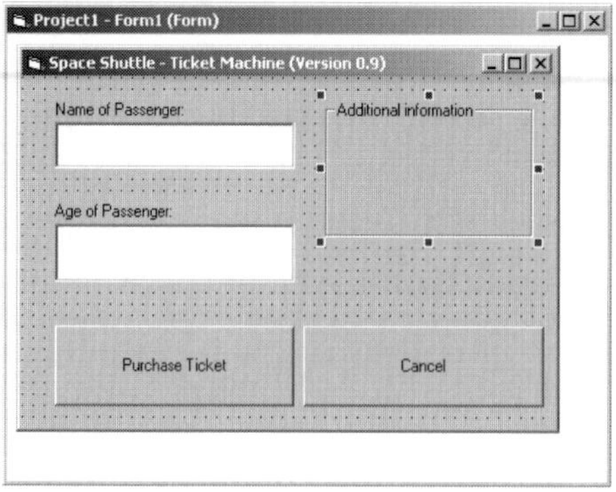

Figure 4.8: A frame is created on the form.

The margin of a frame can be made invisible by setting the BorderStyle property to 0.

Using the option box and check box for selection

Options are offered via the option box and the check box. Both control elements are fairly similar, but with two major differences:

- Only one option box can ever be pressed in a group of option boxes. If an option box is pressed, the previously selected option box assumes its 'unpressed' position. Any number can be checked with check boxes.

- The *Value* property of an option box can only assume the values *True* (pressed) or *False* (unpressed). With check boxes, *Value* can assume the values *0* (not checked), *1* (checked) and *2* (not available).

Getting to know the check box

Use the following procedure to familiarise yourself with the check box:

1 Create a check box in the frame. You may have to enlarge the frame to make room for the check box.

2 Switch to the properties window and enter *Extra Provisions* in the *Caption* property.

3 Create another check box underneath the first one. Enter *XXL Spacesuit* for the *Caption* property.

4 Create a third check box underneath the second one. Enter *Spaceboots* for the *Caption* property (the actual description is not important) (Figure 4.9).

5 Start the program using the F5 key. You will notice that all check boxes can be clicked, which makes a check either appear or disappear.

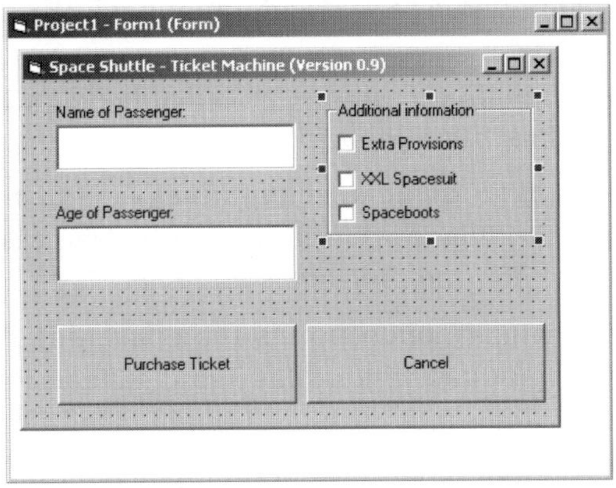

Figure 4.9: Three check boxes are created in the frame.

Getting to know the option box

Use the following procedure to familiarise yourself with the option box:

1 Create an option box underneath the frame. Switch to the Properties window and enter *Single Journey* for the *Caption* property.

2 Create another option box underneath the first one. Switch to the Properties window and enter *Return Journey* for the *Caption* property (Figure 4.10).

3 Start the program using the [F5] key. You will notice that only one of the two option boxes can be clicked. When you select one option, the other is no longer selected.

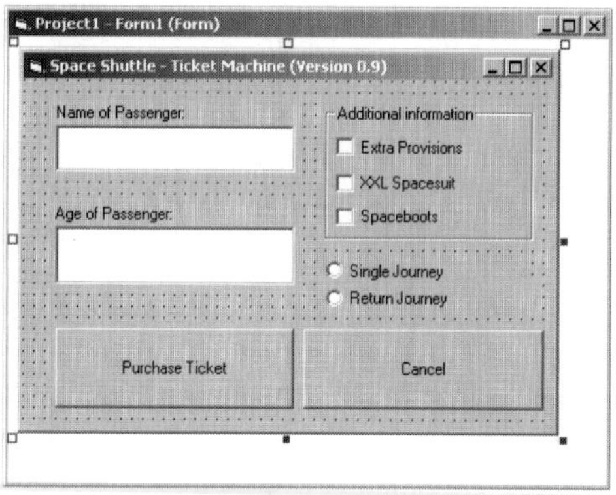

Figure 4.10: Two option boxes are created on the form.

- Option boxes and check boxes are very simple to work with.

- You can specify whether the point or check is aligned to the left or the right using the *Alignment* property.

- The option box or check box can be made into a button that behaves in exactly the same way using the *Style* property.

- If an option box or check box is to be set as soon as the program starts, the *Value* property in the properties window has to be set (this can also be done in the *Form_Load* event while the program is running).

- It is not possible to determine which option box is set in a group of option boxes (there is no property for querying this).

Picture boxes and displaying colour pictures

Picture boxes and displays bring boring forms to life, as they enable bitmaps and graphic files to be displayed in the *Wmf* format. The *Picture* property determines which picture is displayed. Its value is assigned either using the properties window or at a later stage using the LOADPICTURE function while the program is running.

Getting to know the display

Use the following procedure to familiarise yourself with the display:

1 Enlarge the form a little and create a display (the icon in the lower area of the toolbox) to the right of the frame.

2 Switch to the properties window and set the value of the *Stretch* property to *True*. This is done either by double-clicking the entry or selecting the entry *True* from the list.

3 Now switch to the *Picture* property in the Properties window and click on the three dots on the right-hand side. A file selection dialogue box opens. Open the \PROGRAMS\MICROSOFT VISUAL STUDIO\COMMON\GRAPHICS\ICONS\INDUSTRY directory and select the ROCKET file (Figure 4.11).

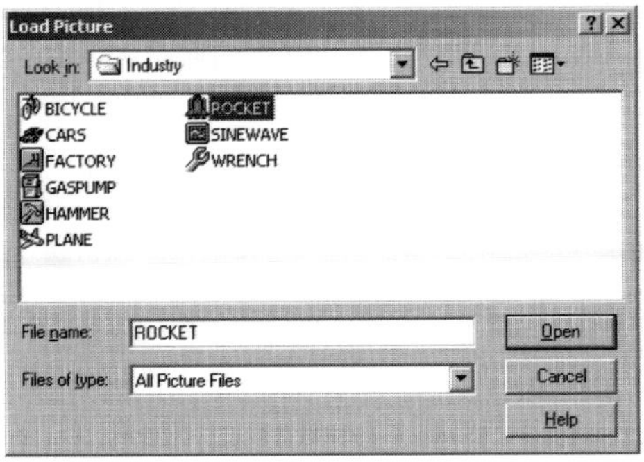

Figure 4.11: The bitmap to be displayed is selected from the list of files.

If you cannot see the \COMMON\GRAPHICS directory, the graphics were installed when Visual Basic 6.0 was installed. Access the directory by inserting the Visual Basic 6.0 CD and starting the SETUP.EXE program and follow the instructions on the screen.

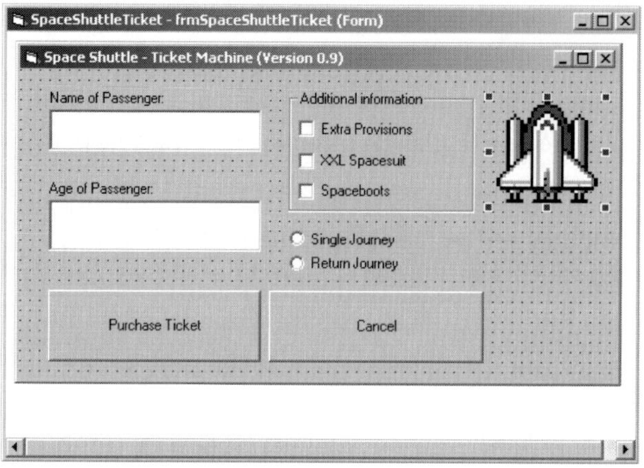

Figure 4.12: A display is created on the form, in which a bitmap is displayed.

- The image to be displayed in a picture box or display is specified using the *Picture* property.

- A picture is selected either in the properties window or while the program is running using the LoadPicture function in the *Picture* property.

- An image from the clipboard can also be inserted into a picture box or display.

- Displays have a *Stretch* property, and picture boxes have an *AutoSize* property. When either of these is set to *True*, the size of the picture box is modified to fit the shape of the picture loaded.

- Both the picture box and display support only a limited selection of graphic formats. The formats supported are *Bmp, Cur, Dib, Gif, Ico, Jpeg* and *Wmf*. Animated *Gif* or *Png* files cannot be displayed.

- Picture boxes are 'proper' windows (according to Windows) that have a number of properties, methods and events, which are usually not required. You are advised to use the display, as too many picture boxes can make a form look overcrowded.

Loading images while the program is running

For an image to be assigned to a picture box or display while the program is running, it has to be loaded using the LoadPicture function:

```
imgPicture.Picture = LoadPicture("C:\Windows\Wood.bmp")
```

This command loads the *bmp* file entered. The complete directory path of the image file always has to be specified (as well as the file extension).

It is also possible to assign the image in a picture box to another display:

`imgPictureNew.Picture = imgPicture.Picture`

This command assigns the content of the IMGPICTURE display to the IMGPICTURENEW display.

> **Note**
>
> *If a display or picture is loaded during runtime, Visual Basic saves the content in a file with a .frx extension. If the Visual Basic project is compiled in an exe or dll file, all pictures that are part of this file, i.e. the frx file will only work when a program is run in the development environment.*

Other control elements also have a picture property

Images can be displayed in control elements other than the picture box and display. The *Picture* property used for displaying images can also be found in the following control elements:

- As well as the *Picture* property, there is also a *DisabledPicture* property (the picture is displayed when the button is disabled using *Enabled=False*) and a *DownPicture* property (displayed when the button is pressed) with command buttons, check boxes and option boxes.

- A form also has a *Picture* property. The image selected using this property is displayed in the inner area of the form.

Line and figure control elements for added effect

Line and figure control elements enable you to draw on a form in which options are limited. The special feature of these control elements is that lines, circles and rectangles can be displayed on the form in design mode.

Getting to know the line control element

Use the following procedure to familiarise yourself with the line control element:

1 Create a line control element immediately above both command buttons, so that the line separates the control buttons from the rest of the form.

2 Switch to the properties window and set the *BorderWidth* to *2 (Figure 4.13)*.

- The width of a line and shape is set using the *BorderWidth* property.

- It specifies which shape (rectangle, square, oval, circle, rounded rectangle or rounded square) is displayed in a shape control element using the *Shape* property.

- The inner section of a shape control element is selected using the *FillStyle* property. For the inner area of a shape to be filled, the *FillStyle* value has to be set to *0*. The colour is selected using the *FillColor* property.

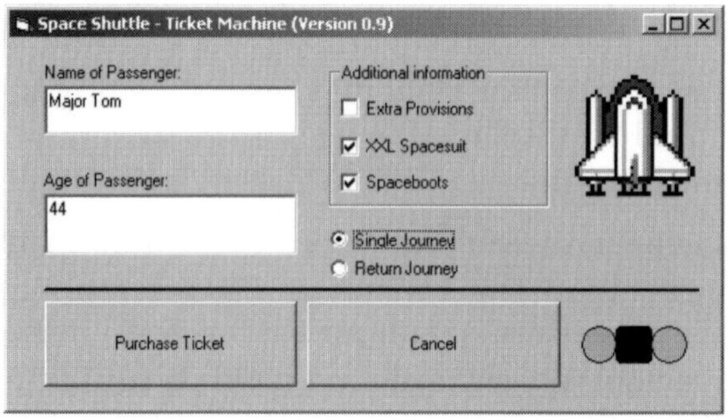

Figure 4.13: The form should look something like this.

Regularity using the timer

The toolbox has a small control element with a stopwatch icon. This is the *Timer*. It has only one task: to call the *Timer* event procedure at regular intervals (set using the *Interval* property). In this way, commands can be repeated automatically at regular intervals. It makes no difference whether a shape is being moved across the screen, keyboard entries are being made or you are checking your e-mail – the timer will not be affected.

Getting to know the timer

Use the following procedure to familiarise yourself with the timer:

1 Create a timing circuit on the form. It does not matter where it is positioned, as the control element is invisible while the program is running.

2 Switch to the properties window and set the *Interval* property to *1000*. This means that the *Timer* event procedure will be called approximately once per second.

3 The timer involves a certain amount of programming, as there is no other way of determining what happens after the specified interval. Double-click on the *Timer* control element. This takes you directly into the *Timer* event procedure.

4 Insert the following command in the event procedure (Figure 4.14):

```
Image1.Visible = Not Image1.Visible
```

This command switches the display from visible to invisible and back again when called. The *Visible* property has to be set to *False* or *True*.

5 Start the program using the F5 key. You will notice that the display begins to flash.

Figure 4.14: A command is inserted in the Timer event procedure.

- The *Interval* property of the timer determines the interval in milliseconds in which the *Timer* event procedure will be called.

- Even if the value of the *Interval* property is set to *1*, the smallest measurable interval is 55 ms because of internal limitations.

- The maximum value permitted for the *Interval* property is 65 535, meaning that the longest interval is just over one minute. If a longer interval is required, a query has to be embedded in the *Timer* event procedure with the effect of making something happen every tenth or fiftieth minute, for example.

- If any value other than *0* is entered for the *Interval* property, the timer starts. If this is not desirable at this stage, the *Enabled* property should be set to *False*.

How do control elements respond to mouse clicks?

Whenever a control element on a form is clicked, a mouse event is triggered. Mouse events include:

- the *Click* event;
- the *DblClick* event;
- the *MouseDown* event;
- the *MouseUp* event;
- the *MouseMove* event.

The Click event

This event is triggered when a control element is clicked with the left mouse button.

The DblClick event

The DblClick event is triggered when a control element is double-clicked with the left mouse button. In Windows, a double click is the result of two single clicks in quick succession. The sensitivity of two single clicks in making a double click can be configured using the mouse program in the control panel.

The MouseDown event

The MouseDown event is triggered whenever the left or right mouse button is pressed. Additional information is given when the event procedure is called, as well as with a *Click* event:

- A number for the mouse button pressed (*Button* parameter).
- A number for the status of the Alt , Ctrl and ⇧ keys.

- The *x* and *y* co-ordinates of the mouse pointer in the inner area of the container, i.e. the surrounding form or picture box in which the mouse pointer is located.

The MouseUp event

The MouseUp event is triggered whenever the depressed mouse button is released again. It always follows a *MouseDown* event. The same information is given as with a *MouseDown* event.

The MouseMove event

The MouseMove event is triggered whenever the mouse pointer is moved in the inner area of the control element. Continual movement results in corresponding continual events. The same information is given as with the *MouseDown* event.

Getting to know the Click event

Use the following procedure to experience the Click procedure in action:

1 End the Visual Basic program if it is still running, and double-click the button entitled *Purchase ticket* to switch to the program code window. You should see the frame of the *Click* event procedure.

2 Enter the following commands in the procedure:

```
Dim sOutput As String
Dim cFlightPrice As Currency
sOutput = "Booking confirmed for " & Text1.Text & vbCrLf
sOutput = sOutput & String(32, "=") & vbCrLf
If Text2.Text < 12 Then
  cFlightPrice = 1245
Else
  cFlightPrice = 32500
End If
If Option2.Value = True Then
  sOutput = sOutput & "Flight price for return flight: "
  cFlightPrice = cFlightPrice * 2
Else
  sOutput = sOutput & "FlightPrice for single ticket: "
End If
MsgBox sOutput & FormatCurrency(cFlightPrice)
```

These commands (you will learn about the IF command in Chapter 5) calculate the price of a flight depending on the age of the passenger and the route selected using the option boxes.

The Click event procedure of the second button should also be connected with an action. Double-click on the button entitled *Abort* to switch to the program code window. You should see the frame of the Click event procedure.

3 Enter the following command in the procedure:

```
Unload Me
```

This command causes the form to be unloaded (the word 'Me' stands for the form) and the program ends.

4 Start the program using the [F5] key. If you click on the BOOK FLIGHT button, your booking should be confirmed. Click on the ABORT button to end the program.

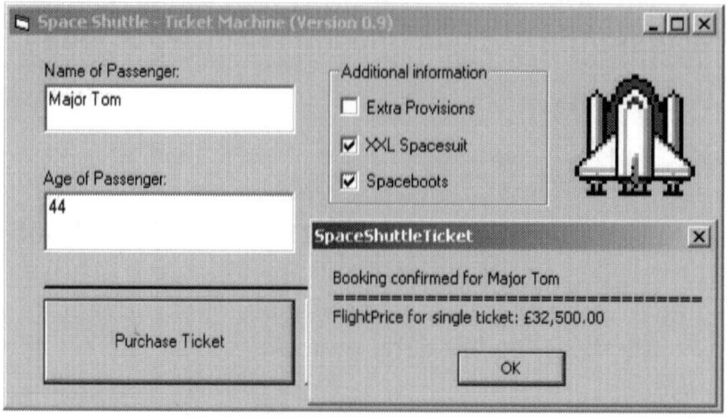

Figure 4.15: Clicking the button calls the Click event procedure

Getting to know the MouseMove event

Use the following procedure to see the MouseMove event in action:

1 End the Visual Basic program if it is still running, and create another label on the lower margin of the form.

2 Switch to the Properties window and name the label *lblStatus* using the *(Name)* property.

3 Double-click the upper text box to switch to the program code window.

4 Select the MOUSEMOVE entry from the right-hand selection list. This displays the frame of the procedure *Text1_MouseMove*.

5 Enter the following command in the event procedure:

```
lblStatus.Caption = "Please enter the name here"
```

6 Select the TEXGT2 entry from the left-hand selection list, and the MOUSEMOVE entry from the right. This displays the frame of the event procedure *Text2_MouseMove*. Enter the following command in the event procedure:

```
lblStatus.Caption = "Please enter age here"
```

7 Start the program using the F5 key. Move the mouse pointer over the upper text box and then the lower text box. Depending on which text box the mouse pointer is placed over, a corresponding note should appear in the label.

How do control elements react to keyboard entries?

Most control elements can react to keyboard entries. However, the control element needs to have a specific *focus*. Only one control element on a form can be given a focus at any one time.

The following keyboard events are used:

- the *KeyPress* event;
- the *KeyDown* event;
- the *KeyUp* event.

The KeyPress event

The KeyPress event is produced whenever a key with a representable character is pressed, i.e. a character with an ASCII code (the ⇆ key is an exception, as this always switches the focus to the next control element – it does not trigger a KeyPress event). Keys that produce a KeyPress event include the ⇧, Ctrl and function keys (F1 to F12). This is not easy to understand for most beginners. If a letter is pressed, the ASCII code for the lower case letter is submitted.

The character ASCII code is also submitted to the KeyPress event as additional information. If the ⇧ key is pressed, the ASCII code for the upper-case letter is submitted (this is why the ⇧ key by itself does not trigger a KeyPress event).

The KeyDown event

The KeyDown event is produced whenever a key is held down. Unlike the KeyPress event, it is produced with every key. Also unlike the KeyPress event, the internal keyboard code is given instead of the ASCII code.

103

The KeyUp event

The KeyUp event is produced whenever a depressed key is released. It always follows a KeyDown event. The internal keyboard code is also given at this event.

Getting to know the KeyPress event

Use the following procedure to see the KeyPress event in action:

1 End the Visual Basic program if it is still running, and double-click on the upper text box to switch to the program code window.

2 Select the KEYPRESS entry from the right-hand selection list. This displays the frame of the event procedure *Text2_KeyPress*.

3 Enter the following command in the event procedure:

```
If KeyAscii = 13 Then
   lblStatus.Caption = "Passenger name: " & Text1.Text
   Text2.SetFocus
End If
```

4 Start the program using the F5 key and set the prompt with the mouse in the upper text box. Enter a name and press the ↵ key. After the name has been displayed in the status box, the prompt jumps automatically to the second text box.

Name conventions with control elements

Assigning names to control elements is standard practice as it also indicates their function. A text box for entering a surname could be called *txtSurname*, and a label for displaying a high score could be called *lblHiScore*. The three letters that precede the name, the *prefix*, are typical for the class of a control element. The name also gives a good indication of what the control element does (remember that a program listing should also be readable for other programmers). Apart from inserting comments, name conventions are an important means of improving the readability and comprehensibility of a program. A list of prefixes for common control elements can be found in Table 4.2. Remember that these are only recommendations.

Control element	Prefix	Example
Command button	cmd or btn	cmdStart
Label	lbl	lblOutput
Text box	txt	txtInput
Form	frm	frmMain
Option box	opt	optGender
List box	lst	lstTeams
Combo box	cbo	cboTeams
Frame	fra	fraExtras
Picture box	pic	picFoto
Image	img	imgFoto
Check box	chk	chkDownload
File selection	fil	filFile
Directory selection	dir	dirDirectory
Drive selection	Drv	drvDrive

Table 4.2: Standard name prefixes for control elements of the toolbox.

Chapter 5

The computer thinks for itself

Don't worry – the computer isn't about to achieve mastery over the human race just yet. Any decisions the computer makes are not of great consequence. In this chapter, the simple yet important principle of the computer thinking for itself will be explained.

In the '70s and '80s, films in which computers went mad and hatched sinister plots to take over the world were very popular. A giant computer responsible for the control of an imaginary town would run amok, triggering destructive intercontinental missiles, and computer-controlled actors would fire blank cartridges aimlessly. Even electronic brains were prone to mental illness.

Only the computer of the good old Starship Enterprise did not develop any sinister plans – it just blinked ahead happily. The computer lost its image as an all-powerful being as it gradually began to appear in offices, studies and children's bedrooms. It soon became evident that computers do not think; nor are they able to make important decisions. Rather, they can only process the details given by the programmer. A PC does not make decisions, but merely makes simple comparisons with numbers, which sometimes give the impression of being important decisions to the outsider.

In this chapter, you will learn how 'decisions' are made in a Visual Basic program, or, to put it more accurately, how comparisons are made. You will learn the `If`, `End If`, `Else` and `ElseIf` commands with which the computer can process simple comparisons independently at various points during the course of the program.

Can computers really think?

In the philosophical sense, this question cannot be answered with a single sentence. However, it can safely be said that computers, and above all PCs as we know them, cannot think, nor are they able to make decisions independently, despite the fact that the spectacular chess match between world champion Gary Kasparov and the IBM supercomputer Deep Blue in 1997, where Kasparov lost by 3.5 points to 2.5, created the misconception that the superiority of artificial intelligence had been firmly established.

A computer program that predicts the future world champion, Prime Minister or Pope is only computing probabilities, and works on the fairly basic principle of formulae with numbers being obtained empirically (either by surveys or votes) and 'fed' into it. This has nothing to do with intelligence (or the future). However, affordable PCs can calculate so ridiculously quickly these days that it is becoming increasingly more difficult to draw the line between the addition and subtraction of simple numbers, and predicting more complex sequences of operations. Even Deep Blue knew nothing about chess, but with the ability to process an unbelievable 250 million calculations per second, and the rules of chess having been programmed in by its programmer, it beat its human opponent hands down.

So, if a computer can predict business statistics or the dynamics of social systems, this is similar to what a human 'computer' can produce. This has nothing to do with independent thinking. The computer on your desk will not develop a mind of its own (even though it may sometimes appear to do so – but this is usually due to a virus or the program Windows).

Comparing instructions

A computer program that does not involve decisions is similar to a train that can only ever travel in a straight line. It is only the strength of the track network that has so many points and allows the train to travel from the northernmost tip of Finland to the southernmost point of Italy. Whenever the train comes to a set of points, a decision has to be made. Should the train go to the left or the right? This decision is obviously not made at random. It has to conform to the timetable. The train reports to a signal box and a rail employee presses a button to set the points correctly.

A computer program functions in much the same way. Decision instructions play the role of points – they decide whether the program should progress to the 'left' or 'right'. However, in a computer program, there is no signal box. The decision as to which direction to take is made by a command. In Visual Basic, this is called the `If` command. It is one of the most important commands in Visual Basic. You will get to know this in detail in this chapter. But before we begin programming and start testing If & Co., we need to do a little brainstorming and try to immerse ourselves in the principle of logical decision making.

Imagine that you are a doorperson in a central bank. You have to make sure that only the correct people pass through the heavily guarded door. Thankfully, your job is very simple as your only instruction is:

```
If ID valid then open door
```

If the ID is invalid, the door remains closed and the person is turned away without further discussion. No further instructions are required, as this results 100% from the original instruction. This is known as an `If Then` instruction. The `Then` instruction is only executed if the `If` criterion is satisfied (programmers refer to this condition with the attribute 'true', even though this has nothing to do with the everyday meaning of the word). If the `If` condition is not fulfilled, nothing happens and the following instruction is ignored. If something in your instruction states that anybody who passes through the door is subject to a body search, or a simple welcome greeting, then these actions are not processed if the person is turned away. As you have a lot of time, you can formulate your instruction in more detail:

```
If ID valid Then
   Open door
   Search person
   Welcome them
Otherwise
   Turn person away
   Explain why
End If
```

This says everything, although there is a glaring error in this instruction. What happens if, after you have opened the door and let the person in, they are wearing baggy trousers or carrying something that poses a security threat to the bank and the vault? In this case, another decision is required, this time more complicated (what makes someone unsafe, and what happens if this person is an employee or the MD?). This makes everything far more complex. So hand in your notice and decide to become a programmer!

Introduction to the If command

In this section, you will get to know the If command. This is the command responsible for decisions in Visual Basic. Even though this command is very important, it is structured very simply. The If command is followed by a variable or a combination of variables, numbers and operators – programmers refer to this as an *expression*. The value of the variable (or the expression) makes no difference, as the If command is concerned with only two things:

- Whether the variable has a value other than 0 (this is the *true condition*);
- Whether the variable has a value of 0 (this is the *false condition*).

In the first case, the *condition* is fulfilled, and in the second case it is not. As with the points on the railway track, there are only two ways for the program to proceed. If the condition is fulfilled, all commands that immediately follow the Then command are executed (if there is an Else command, then all commands following this command will be executed instead). Just as the points do, the If command specifies the way in which the program proceeds.

The If command has the following general construction:

```
If condition Then
   commands
End If
```

Just to reiterate: the commands between `Then` and `End If` are executed only if the condition is 'true', i.e. if the expression has a value other than 0. Otherwise the commands are not executed. There is nothing other than these two options. Figure 5.1 clarifies this important principle.

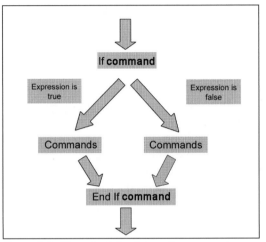

Figure 5.1: The principle of the `If` command.

As the `If` command is very important (you cannot become a Visual Basic programmer if you do not understand this), you should practice using it as much as possible.

Exercise 1: If command with true condition

```
A = 7
If A = 7 Then
  Msgbox "Welcome!"
End If
```

Is the `Msgbox` function used? The answer is yes, as the variable `A` has a value of `7`, and so it fulfils the condition `A = 7`.

Exercise 2: If command with false condition

```
A = 7
If A = 6 Then
  Msgbox "Welcome"
End If
```

111

Is the `Msgbox` function used this time? The answer is no, as the variable `A` has a value of 6. 6 is not equal to 7, so the condition is not fulfilled, and it is false. The commands between `If` and `End If` are thus omitted.

Exercise 3: If command with unequal operator (1)

```
A = 7
If A <> 7 Then
   Msgbox "Welcome!"
End If
```

This is a bit trickier as you have to know what the greater than and less than signs mean when written together. This is known as the *unequal* operator in Visual Basic. It checks whether the numbers or variables (i.e. expressions) on the right- and left-hand sides are different. If so, a true value is produced; if not, a false value is produced. This should make it clear as to what the answer will be. The condition is not satisfied, as `A` is not equal to 7. The commands between `If` and `End If` are not executed.

Exercise 4: If command with unequal operator (2)

```
A = 6
If A <> 7 Then
   Msgbox "Welcome"
End If
```

The solution here is easy, as you now understand the unequal operator. The commands between *If* and *End If* are executed as the condition is fulfilled. Why? Because *A* has a value of 6, and therefore is not equal to 7.

Exercise 5: If command with NOT operator

```
A = 6
If NOT A <> 7 Then
   Msgbox "Welcome"
End If
```

This exercise is deliberately more difficult, as programmers sometimes have to solve more tricky problems. Did the word 'NOT' stand out? This is another operator in Visual Basic, and is fairly tricky. It makes everything opposite. If that which follows NOT is true, it becomes false; and that which is false becomes true. The NOT operator is not there to confuse you; it is simply a logical operator that can be very useful in some cases.

Exercise 6: If command with IsNumeric function

Visual Basic uses a function named `IsNumeric` (you will learn about functions in Chapter 10). It checks whether that which is submitted in brackets when the function is called is a number. If so, the true value is returned, otherwise a false value is returned. So, if a command is only to be executed if a variable contains a number, the `If` command is written as:

```
If IsNumeric(sInput) = True Then
   Commands
End If
```

The word `True` is the official way of writing a true value. It is a constant embedded in Visual Basic (you could also have written 1 or –1). The style for a false value is `False`. This is also constant, with a value of 0.

So how is a condition written when the commands are not to be executed if the variable `sInput` is a number? Easy – the `NOT` operator is used. As this makes everything opposite, the query is written as follows:

```
If NOT IsNumeric(sInput) = True Then
   Commands
End If
```

The commands are only executed if the variable `sInput` is not numerical. This is when the `NOT` operator comes into play.

The Else command

This important command means nothing on its own – it always complements the `If` command. Until now, every situation has involved the `Then` command, where the commands that follow it are only executed if the `If` condition is satisfied. There are also many cases where other commands must be executed if the condition is not true. This is not a problem as the `Else` command will look after this.

Exercise 7: If command with Else section

```
If IsNumeric(sInput) = False Then
   Msgbox "Please enter a number!"
Else
   Msgbox "Thankyou for entering a number!"
End If
```

This exercise is an extension of that in Exercise 6. First, the `If` command checks whether the variable `sInput` contains a number. If not, the function returns a false value and the condition is fulfilled. The variable does not contain a number. So the following `Msgbox` function is called, which produces a corresponding message (this simple output function was introduced briefly in Chapter 3). But there is always a second option, i.e. that the variable *sInput* contains a number. In this case, the `IsNumeric` function returns a true value, so that the condition `IsNumeric(sInput) = False` returns a false value, as it is not fulfilled. The first `Msgbox` function is therefore omitted. The `Else` command is now used. As the `If` condition was not fulfilled, all commands between `Else` and `End If` are executed, meaning that the second `Msgbox` function is called.

Was that complicated? It probably seemed a little strange, but don't worry, you will soon be able to manage it with a little practice. Try to formulate everyday events logically. For example, the barrier in the car park is only raised if your parking ticket is valid, so the condition is:

```
If ParkingTicket = Paid Then
   OpenBarrier
Else
   Output MessageInDisplay
End If
```

You will soon find dozens of examples with logical comparisons. This doesn't always help. If you wish to learn programming, you have to learn how a computer 'thinks'. This is all based on simple logical decisions.

The ElseIf command

This command is similar to the `Else` command. It is a combination of the `If` and `Else` commands. Imagine a program simulating a cash machine. As different things have to be checked (validity of card, validation of PIN number, account balance and permitted limit) before any money actually materialises, several `If` queries have to be combined. A simpler version follows, made up of the familiar `If`, `Else` and `End If` commands:

```
If Card = Invalid Then
   IssueMessage
Else
If Not PINNumber Then
   IssueMessage
Else
If AccountBalanceOK = False Then
   IssueMessage
Else
If Amount > LIMIT Then
   IssueMessage
Else
   DispenseMoney
```

```
End If
End If
End If
End If
```

The `ElseIf` command allows us to shorten the text somewhat:

```
If Card = Invalid Then
   IssueMessage
ElseIf Not PINNumber Then
   IssueMessage
ElseIf AccountBalanceOK = False Then
   IssueMessage
ElseIf Amount > LIMIT Then
   IssueMessage
Else
   DispenseMoney
End If
```

You will notice that the `ElseIf` command makes the query string shorter, as the final `If` command needs only be written once.

Logical combinations

One condition is not always enough to make a decision. Think of an alarm system. This consists of several sensors, where every sensor reports a true value (the sensor is triggered) or a false value (everything OK). So what is the condition that triggers the alarm? A sensor report is already enough to trigger the alarm when `Sensor1 = True` or `Sensor2 = True` or `Sensor3 = True`, and so on. Several true/false values have to be combined. This type of logical combination is called an *OR combination*, as *Condition1* or *Condition2* or *Condition3* has to be true for the combination to return a true value. An OR combination is formulated with the `OR` operator in Visual Basic:

```
If Sensor1=True OR Sensor2=True OR Sensor3=True Then
   Alarm
End If
```

The counterpart of the OR combination is the AND combination. Here, the combination is only true, as all conditions produce a true value. Think of an alarm system again. How is the condition formulated, where the alarm is not triggered after the living room has been entered, the light switched on and the correct code entered?

```
If Light = True AND SecretCodeOk = True Then
   AlarmOff
Else
   AlarmOn
End If
```

The condition is fulfilled if both the first and second subconditions are fulfilled. The above condition can be formulated slightly differently:

```
If Light = False OR SecretCodeOk = False Then
  AlarmOn
Else
  AlarmOff
End If
```

The alarm is triggered this time if either the light is not switched on or the secret number is incorrect.

When If and Else are not enough – the Select Case command

To conclude this chapter, you will learn a command for making decisions. Even though it may not be difficult to understand, it is hard for programmers who have just completed their first steps. Imagine creating a Visual Basic program that assesses the result of an exam. After entering the mark that has been achieved, an appraisal is output. You already know the `If` command, which, in combination with its colleague `ElseIf`, has to be the correct command:

```
Dim Marks As Integer
Points = InputBox("Please enter mark:")
If Points <= 100 AND Marks >= 90 Then
  Msgbox "Top of the class!"
ElseIf Points < 90 AND Points >= 70 Then
  Msgbox "An excellent performance"
ElseIf Points < 70 AND Points >=50 Then
  Msgbox "A good performance"
ElseIf Points < 50 AND Points >=30 Then
  Msgbox "Not bad"
ElseIf Points < 30 AND Points >=10 Then
  Msgbox "Room for improvement"
Else
  Msgbox "I think we need to talk"
End If
```

Every `If` or `ElseIf` command checks whether the variable `Marks` lies within a certain range, whereas the `AND` operator is required to check whether the number is less than or equal to the upper limit (the `<=` operator is the *less than* operator, and the `>=` operator is the *greater than* operator), and at the same time that the number is greater than or equal to the lower limit. Even though this construction is hopefully not totally confusing, it is much simpler to use the `Select Case` command:

```
Dim Marks As Integer
Points = InputBox("Please enter mark:")
Select Case Points
   Case 90 To 100
     MsgBox "Top of the class!"
   Case 70 To 90
     MsgBox "An excellent performance"
   Case 50 To 70
     MsgBox "A good performance"
   Case 30 To 50
     MsgBox "Not badl"
   Case 10 To 30
     MsgBox "Room for improvement"
   Case Else
     MsgBox "I think we need to talk"
End Select
```

Even though both the logical sequence of operations and the result agree in both cases, the second version is shorter and clearer.

The `Select Case` command is always constructed the same way. First, the expression to be checked is specified:

```
Select Case Marks
```

This is followed by an arbitrary number of `Case` branches containing a value (or value range), with which the expression to be checked is compared:

```
Case 90 To 100
```

If the expression to be checked is equal to this value or lies within this range, all commands until `End Select` or the next `Case` command are executed. A `Select Case` command can also contain a `Case Else` branch at the end:

```
Case Else
  MsgBox "I think we need to talk"
```

The command contained in this branch is only executed if none of the previous `Case` branches were fulfilled.

Using the Select Case command

The following command should illustrate the principle of the `Select Case` command. The central point is a form on which a colour is selected using a text box. After clicking the button, a picture box is displayed in the colour selected. The `Select Case` command checks which colour is entered, and assigns the corresponding colour constant (predefined in Visual Basic) to the *Backcolor* property of the picture box.

1 Start *Visual Basic* and create a new STANDARD EXE project. A project appears containing a blank form.

117

2 Create a picture box on the form to fill about two-thirds of the form area.

3 Create a text box underneath the picture box. Switch to the Properties window and delete the current value of the *Text* property (called *Text1*).

4 Create a command button on the right of the text box. Switch to the properties window and enter *&Colour* in the *Caption* property (the ampersand (&) ensures the C is underlined – the command button can also be activated using the [Alt] key and the [B] key). The form should now look like that in Figure 5.2.

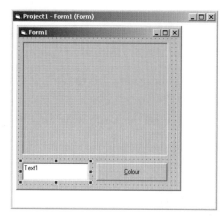

Figure 5.2: A picture box, text box and command button are created on the form.

5 Double-click the command button. This takes you into the *Click* procedure of the command button. Here it is determined what happens after the command button is clicked. Enter the following commands in the *Click* procedure:

```
Select Case Text1.Text
  Case "Red"
    Picture1.BackColor = vbRed
  Case "Blue"
    Picture1.BackColor = vbBlue
  Case "Yellow"
    Picture1.BackColor = vbYellow
  Case "Green"
    Picture1.BackColor = vbGreen
  Case Else
    MsgBox "I don't know that colour!"
End Select
```

6 Start the program using the [F5] key. Enter the name of a colour in the text box, such as Red. After clicking the command button, the picture box should assume this colour. Try the remaining colours. If the program does not recognise the name of a colour, a message will be displayed.

One final exercise

In this section, you will use your knowledge of Visual Basic acquired so far (which is actually quite a lot) to solve a simple task. An online bookstore offers its customers two different options for shipping costs:

Version A: £2 per order and £12 per book.

Version B: £19 per order and £5.95 per book.

Your task is to create a small Visual Basic program in which the number of books is entered in a text box. After clicking the button, both alternatives for shipping costs are displayed, and a suggestion indicating the best value for money is given. Take time to do this; it should not be too difficult considering everything you have learned in this chapter. The following steps should prove successful:

1 Start *Visual Basic* and create a new STANDARD EXE project.

2 Create a text box and a command button on the form. Assign the name *txtAmount* to the text box and *cmdShippingCosts* to the command button.

3 Insert the command for calculating shipping costs in the *Click* event procedure of the command button, depending on the number entered in the text box, and display the result using the MSGBOX function.

Did it work? If so, then congratulations! You have learned something about Visual Basic programming, and you are no longer a beginner. If this program did not work, then you should read the chapter again before progressing any further. You will find a suggested solution for the *Click* event procedure at the end of the chapter.

Summary

In this chapter, you have learned one of the most important commands in Visual Basic in the shape of the If command (and also learned that computers cannot really think for themselves). A program makes decisions using the If command. A decision is therefore based on a simple comparison, which is either true or false. If the comparison is true, all commands between Then and the next End If or Else are executed. If the comparison is false, the commands are not executed. If an Else branch is available, the commands between Else and End If are executed.

An alternative to several `If` commands is the `Select Case` command. This is used if an expression consisting of several different values or ranges of values is to be checked.

In the next chapter, you will learn that computers are not especially clever, but what they can do they do very quickly indeed. You will learn the loops of Visual Basic with the `For Next` and `Do Loop` loop commands. How many additions do you think your PC can process per second? 100? 10 000? Maybe even a million? You will be surprised.

Suggested solution for the Click event procedure

Here is a suggested solution for the exercise on page 130.

```
Private Sub cmdShippingCosts_Click()
  Dim iAmount As Integer
  Dim cPriceA As Currency, cPriceB As Currency
  iAmount = txtAmount.Text
  cPriceA = 2 + 12 * iAmount
  cPriceB = 19 + 5.95 * iAmount
  MsgBox "Price A: " & FormatCurrency(cPreisA) _
  & vbCrLf & "Price B: " & FormatCurrency(cPreisB)
End Sub
```

The `FormatCurrency` function is only there for visual impact. It outputs an arbitrary number in the currency format selected in the control panel. Incidentally, the decision for outputting which of the two costs is better value for money is not yet embedded. So there is still a little left to do ...

Chapter 6

The computer reaches top form using loops

A computer only reveals its full potential when certain commands are repeated in a program loop. A modern 1GHz processor manages to process the almost incredible figure of 1 billion additions per second in the form of machine commands. Visual Basic is not as quick as this, as many machine commands are always involved, but it is still quick enough for most applications.

We trust computers to a certain extent. Some people believe that they can work miracles and solve all of mankind's problems with the right software. Others are more sceptical, and some distrust these electronic players altogether. However, we should all agree on one thing: that computers are unbeatable electronic artists, as they can process operations inconceivably quickly. Even if a (human) computing genius were able to work out the 153rd root of a number with 23 digits in several seconds in his or her head, computers would beat us hands down.

Here is an example from the unofficial records book. One of the quickest (civilian) computers in the world (as of January 2001) is the Hitachi SR8000-F1. The 9 m x 8 m computer, situated in the Leibniz Computer Centre of the Bavarian Academy of Science in Munich, creates 2 teraflops (TFlops) per second. Try not to be put off by the impressive number or the awful sounding units of measurement. One teraflop is equal to 1000 gigaflops (Gflops), which equates to 1 000 000 000 000 (12 zeros) *Floating-Point Operations* (i.e. calculations with floating-point numbers) per second. This inconceivably large number becomes somewhat relative when you look at the number of processors (896 in the first construction stage of the F1) and the construction costs (about £16 million). In comparison, it should be mentioned that the next stage, the petaflop range, is already being envisaged by the manufacturers of this supercomputer. A petaflop is one thousand billion operations per second.

Anybody interested in the development of this ambitious and highly interesting *Blue Generation* IBM project, should look at www.research.ibm.com/news/detail/bluegene.html for more information.

Such computers are obviously not used to run Windows and Visual Basic. Instead, they are used for highly complicated simulations or the analysis of genes and proteins, where huge amounts of data need to be processed in a short amount of time. Our PCs are not capable of such operations, but a basic 800-MHz Pentium from your local shop theoretically processes 800 million additions per second. The technicians and engineers who had to plan the flight to the moon could only dream of such possibilities. In this chapter, you will learn that the basic prerequisite for computers to perform on this level is the loop command. A program loop enables groups of commands to be repeated a certain number of times. It makes no difference whether this is 10 operations or 1 million. The Visual Basic commands For Next and Do Loop are two loop commands that you will get to know in this chapter.

Just how quick is your PC?

Before we start using loops, you should first determine exactly what your PC is capable of, i.e. how quickly it can process operations. This section involves a benchmark program that indicates the performance of a PC in SpecMark or another units. In other words, you can determine how many additions per second a program can process using a small Visual Basic program.

Use the following procedure to activate the example:

1 Start *Visual Basic* and a create a new STANDARD EXE project

2 Create a command button on the form and enter the name *cmdStart*, and enter the heading *Start* for the *Caption* property.

3 Double-click on the command button so the procedure setting of the *Click* event procedure appears.

4 Enter the following commands of the *cmdStart_Click* procedure in the procedure setting:

```
Dim sTimet As Single
Dim n As Long
cmdStart.Enabled = False
sTime = Timer
Do
   n = n + 1
Loop Until Timer > sTime + 1
cmdStart.Enabled = True
MsgBox n & " Addition(s)"
```

Start the program using the F5 key and click on the command button. A few seconds later you should see a number. This is the number of operations that the Visual Basic program can process per second (the number is 290 000 on my 300-MHz laptop with 128 MB RAM – if the program were compiled as an Exe file, the value would increase to 320 000, as Visual Basic programs are run outside the development environment as machine code programs in the processor language). This number is only meaningful to a certain extent. Firstly, Visual Basic is not the quickest of programming languages, so the same program in C or Assembler (the mother tongue of the PC) would have run much quicker (a Pentium 300 processor requires about 1 second to process 10 million additions under ideal circumstances – Visual Basic is relatively slow from this point of view). Secondly, increasing the number by one is not a valid operation. Instead, you should look at the example as providing an insight into the possibilities of a Visual Basic program. More importantly, it is a nice example of the Do Loop command, which you will get to know in detail in this chapter.

Program loops

Similar to the variables and decisions from the last chapter, program loops are commands without which no programming language can function. Think of the train analogy again, representing the course of a program. You should now think of it in terms of whether the train runs at all. Imagine that the train has just one carriage. How should the transport capacity be increased? Quite simply by attaching other carriages, or by the train making several trips.

Program loops function according to a similar principle. Instead of executing a command or a group of commands only once, they are executed several times. The result is a *program loop*. A program loop consists of a start point and an end point. All commands within this range are a part of the program loop. However, if a program loop is not to last forever, an abort condition is required. This specifies when the loop ends. In the following sections, you will learn that the abort condition is determined differently from the For Next and Do Loop loop commands. Whereas with a For Next command the abort condition is specified by the value of a variable, with a Do Loop command it is specified by an expression that is either true or false, and can optionally be checked at the beginning or the end of a loop. So the abort condition is checked in the same way as the If command (you should know this from Chapter 5).

A program loop is a group of commands repeated a certain number of times. Figure 6.1 shows the general principles.

Figure 6.1: The principle of the program loop.

The For Next command

With the `For Next` command, the number of times a variable is repeated is determined, which begins with a default start value and increases every time the loop is repeated, which is known as an increment. The loop is repeated until the start value is greater than the end value. The following command makes Visual Basic count from 1 to 10 (Figure 6.2).

```
Dim nNumber As Long
For nNumber = 1 To 10
  Debug.Print nNumber
Next nNumber
```

The loop variable is `nNumber` (it could be anything). It is assigned a value of `1` on the first loop. Its value increases by one every time the loop is repeated. As no increment is indicated, it is 1. There is only one command within the loop. Calling the *Print* method in Visual Basic's embedded *Debug* object causes the value of `nNumber` to be displayed in the direct window of the development environment. The next command ends the loop. It increases the loop counter by 1 and, by comparing the end value, determines whether the loop should be repeated once more, or whether the command should be executed following the `Next` command.

Figure 6.2: The result of the For Next *loop in the direct window*

Visual Basic learns to count

The following exercise is built around the `For Next` command, used for counting loops in Visual Basic. As the following exercises are very similar, they will be used in the same Visual Basic program, which you will now create.

Use the following procedure to activate the example:

1 Start *Visual Basic* and create a new STANDARD EXE project.

2 Create a text box on the form, name it *txtStartvalue*, and enter *0* in the *Text* property. This will be the default value.

3 Create another text box on the form, name it *txtEndvalue*, and enter *10* in the *Text* property. This will be the default value.

4 Create a third text box on the form, name it *txtIncrement*, and enter *1* in the *Text* property. This will be the default value.

5 Create a list box on the form and name it *lstLoopCounter*.

6 Create a command button on the form, name it *cmdStart*, and enter the heading *Start* in the *Caption* property. Use Figure 6.3 to help you.

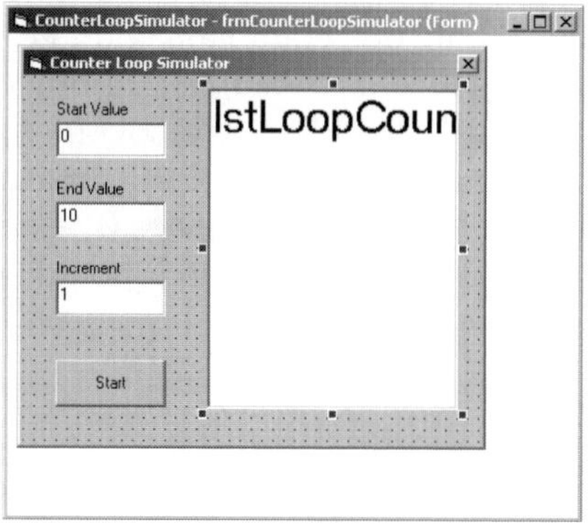

Figure 6.3: The user interface of the loop simulator consists of three text boxes, one list box and one command button.

7 Double-click the command button so the procedure setting of the *Click* event procedure appears.

8 Enter the following command in the procedure setting:

```
Dim snStart As Single
Dim snEnd As Single
Dim snIncrement As Single
Dim snN As Single
snStart = txtStartvalue.Text
snEnd = txtEndvalue.Text
snIncrement = txtIncrement.Text
lstLoopCounter.Clear
For snN = snStart To snEnd Step snIncrement
    lstLoopCounter.AddItem snN
Next snN
```

9 Start the program using the F5 key. In the text boxes, specify where the number variable should start, where it should end, and by how much it should be increased on every loop.

If you click on the command button without altering anything, the loop counts from 0 to 10. This means that 11 loops occur. It should be remembered that a counting loop does not necessarily have to count. Any commands can be executed between For and Next, even further program loops (this is known as an encapsulated loop). It does not matter which commands are in the loop. They are executed until the start value of the loop counter has reached the end value, where the loop counter increases by the increment every time the loop is repeated (if not specified, this is automatically 1).

Counting backwards

If a loop is to run backwards, the start value has to be larger than the end value. Furthermore, the increment has to be a negative number. Enter 10 as the start value, 0 as the end value and –1 as the increment. Visual Basic then counts down from 10 to 0 (figure 6.4).

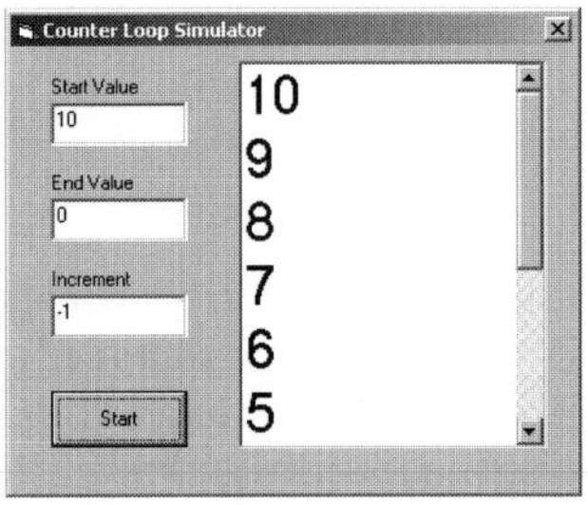

Figure 6.4: Visual Basic can also count backwards; this program loop will run from 10 to 0.

And what happens if the increment is not negative? Try it. In this case, nothing happens, as the abort condition *Loop counter larger than end value* is fulfilled.

Counting 'crookedly'

The loop counter does not always have to be an integer. Set a start value of 1.5, an end value of 2.5, and an increment of 0.25. Visual Basic now counts in decimal values, with five loops completed in total (figure 6.5). One basic rule also applies here: the loop is repeated until the loop counter is larger than the end value.

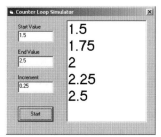

Figure 6.5: The loop counter can also assume decimal values.

When the computer produces nonsense

If you don't think a computer is capable of making mistakes, you'll find that the old box is quite capable of producing false results. But this is usually the programmer's fault, as they will have overlooked some small detail. However, a Visual Basic program can produce rubbish, even if the programmers have done everything correctly. Try out the following program loop by starting Visual Basic, creating a new project, double-clicking the form, and entering the following command in the *Form_Load* event procedure (you can test all the examples in the book this way):

```
Dim n
For n = -10 To 10 Step .1
  Debug.Print n
Next n
```

It seems harmless, but be careful. When you start this program loop, strange numbers appear in the output window (figure 6.6). So instead of 8.6, the number –8.60000000000001 is displayed. Even stranger is that instead of 0, the number –1.87905246917808E-14 appears, a number where 14 zeros follow the decimal point, before the digits 187905 etc. appear. This number is not far off 0, but it is not equal to 0. The program is obviously unable to round it off, and runs into difficulty with small numbers.

```
Immediate                                    ×
 -0.800000000000019
 -0.700000000000019
 -0.600000000000019
 -0.500000000000019
 -0.400000000000019
 -0.300000000000019
 -0.200000000000019
 -0.100000000000019
 -1.87905246917808E-14
  9.99999999999812E-02
```

Figure 6.6: Beware of rounding errors – strange numbers appear, even though the
programmer hasn't done anything wrong.

The reason for this inaccuracy is not a calculation error on the part of Microsoft programmers (the creators of Visual Basic), but has something to do with the way in which numbers are displayed after a decimal point. This process specifies that every number with a decimal point is represented with a negative power of 2. This sounds complicated, but is actually quite simple. For example, the number 1.8 is rounded off as follows:

```
1 + 2 to the power -1 = 1.5
1.5 + 2 to the power -2 = 1.75
1.75 + 2 to the power -3 = 1.78125
1.78125 + 2 to the power -4 = 1.796875
1.796875 + 2 to the power -5 = 1.98828125
and so on.
```

The more additions the computer processes, the closer the result approaches 1.8, yet it never actually reaches it. At some point, the number of decimal places will be exhausted (a maximum of 14 with `Double` type numbers, and a maximum of 28 with `Decimal` type numbers). The number is rounded. But as a rounded number does not correspond exactly to the number it appears to represent, a rounded number can cause inaccuracy with some calculations. The problem lies in the way in which digits following a decimal point are represented (which, incidentally, conforms to the IEEE 754 standard), and so affects all other programming languages.

The Do Loop command

In this section, you will learn the rival of the `For Next` command: the `Do Loop` command. This command produces slightly different program loops from the `For Next` command. `Do Loop` decides whether another loop is required every time. This can be specified either at the start (also with the `Do` command) or at the end (only with the `Loop` command). Visual Basic enables the use of the `Until` and `While` commands, which complement each other as shown by their name, and can mutually replace each other using the NOT Operator.

Here is an easy example for a `Do Loop` loop, where the variable *n* increases from 1 to 10 in steps of one:

```
Dim n As Integer
Do
  n = n + 1
 Debug.Print "The value of n is: " & n
Loop Until n = 10
```

And now the exact same loop using the `While` command:

```
Dim n As Integer
Do
  n = n + 1
 Debug.Print "The value of n is: " & n
Loop While n < 10
```

You will notice that it makes no difference whether `Until` or `While` is used. You only need to reverse the logical condition or place the `NOT` operator before it.

Now let's create a Visual Basic program that takes a virtual 'penny' and doubles it in a certain number of days. The core of the example is a `Do Loop` loop, which repeats the doubling command until the preset amount of days is reached.

Use the following procedure to activate the example:

1 Start *Visual Basic* and create a new STANDARD EXE project.

2 Create a command button on the form, call it *cmdStart*, and enter the value *Start* in the *Caption* property.

3 Double-click the command button to open the program code window.

4 Enter the following commands in the *cmdStart_Click* event procedure:

```
Dim iDays As Integer
Dim dcAmount As Variant
iDays = InputBox("Number of days:", "Moneyspinner game", 21)
dcAmount = 0.01
Do
  dcAmount = CDec(dcAmount) * CDec(2)
  iDays = iDays - 1
 Loop Until iDays = 0
MsgBox "You have " & FormatCurrency(dcAmount)
```

5 Start the program using the F5 key. Click on the command button and enter the number of days. After confirming the entry, the amount is returned.

Isn't it amazing what you can make from a penny? 102 is the maximum number of days you can enter, as resulting amounts of money larger than this cannot be represented in Visual Basic without additional computing miracles.

> **Note**
>
> The CDec *function converts the amount into a* decimal *data type of the highest accuracy in Visual Basic (up to 28 decimal places). The example can also be programmed using a* For Next *loop. However, the* Do Loop *loop is more elegant in this example, as the abort condition has a built-in highest amount, which may not be exceeded.*

Calculating interest

The following example assumes a fixed amount of money (let's say £1000) invested at a fixed rate of interest for a certain number of years. Our program will display the increase in capital for each year. A grid will be used for display purposes. However, as this involves calculation in a program loop, the simple version is introduced using the output in the inner area of the form. The more visually attractive output in a grid is introduced as a small extension.

Use the following procedure to activate the example:

1 Start *Visual Basic* and create a Standard Exe project.

2 Create a text box on the form, name it *txtStartCapital,* and enter a value of *1000* in the *Text* property. This should be the default value.

3 Create a text box on the form, name it *txtInterestRate,* and enter a value of *5.5* in the *Text* property. This should be the default value.

4 Create a text box on the form, name it *txtRuntime,* and enter a value of *10* for the *text* property. This should be the default value.

5 Create a label underneath the text box, name it *lblResult,* and delete the value in the *Caption* property. Set another colour using the *BackColor* property so the label stands out from the background.

6 Create a command button on the form, name it *cmdStart,* and enter the value *Start* in the *Caption* property.

7 Double-click the command button to open the program code window.

8 Enter the following commands in the *cmdStart_Click* event procedure:

```
Dim inRuntime As Integer
Dim inYears As Integer
Dim cuCapital As Currency
Dim cuAmount As Currency
Dim snInterestRate As Single
cuCapital = txtStartCapital.Text
inRuntime = txtRuntime.Text
snInterestRate = txtInterestRate.Text
Do
  inYears = inYears + 1
  cuCapital = cuCapital * (1 + snInterestRate / 100)
Loop Until inYears = inRuntime
lblResult.Caption = FormatCurrency(cuCapital)
```

9 Start the program using the F5 key. Use the default value, or modify it slightly. After clicking the start button, the capital result will be displayed in the label, where the `FormatCurrency` function ensures that the amount of money appears correctly (figure 6.7).

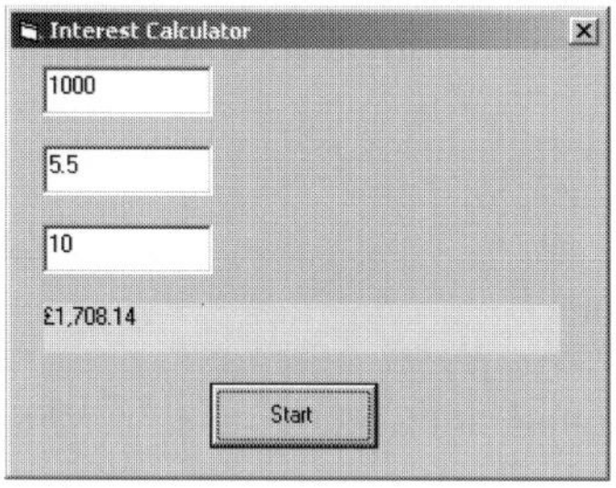

Figure 6.7: The interest calculator.

Drawing lottery numbers

This example 'draws' six numbers betweeen 1 and 49 for a virtual lottery.

Use the following procedure to activate the example:

1 Start *Visual Basic* and create a STANDARD EXE project.

2 Create a command button on the form, name it *cmdStart1,* and enter *Start1* in the *Caption* property.

3 Double-click on the command button to open the program code window.

4 Enter the following commands in the *cmdStart1_Click* in the event procedure:

```
Dim inNumber As Integer
Dim inLotto As Integer
Dim stOutput As String
For inNumber = 1 To 6
   inLotto = Int(Rnd * 49) + 1
   stOutput = stOutput & vbTab & inLotto
Next inNumber
MsgBox stOutput & vbTab, vbOKOnly, "Lottery numbers with
duplicates"
```

In this example, the For Next loop is used again as this is a more compact variant.

5 Start the program using the F5 key and click on the command button. The six lottery numbers should appear in a message box (figure 6.8).

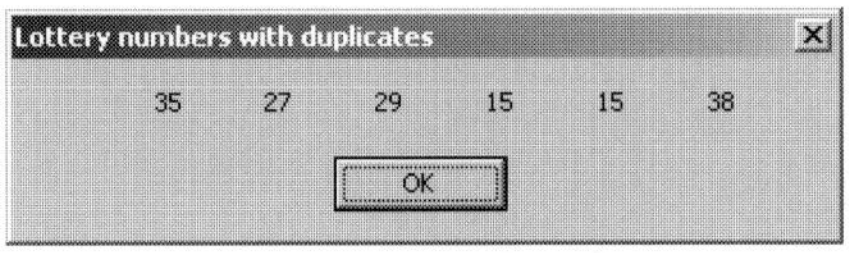

Figure 6.8: Drawing lottery numbers at the weekend.

But in this case, the number '15' appears twice. This is because an appropriate query is missing. So how does the program remember that a number has already been 'drawn'? The easiest way is to use a field variable, which will be explained in Chapter 10. The following example should convert with the aid of the field variable:

1 Create a second command button on the form, name it *cmdStart2*, and enter *Start2* in the *Caption* property.

2 Double-click the command button to open the program code window.

3 Enter the following commands in the *cmdStart2_Click* event procedure:

```
Dim aNumberField(1 To 49) As Boolean
Dim inNumber As Integer
Dim inLotto As Integer
Dim stOutput As String
For inNumber = 1 To 6
   Do
      inLotto = Int(Rnd * 49) + 1
   Loop Until aNumberField(inLotto) = False
   aNumberField(inLotto) = True
   stOutput = stOutput & vbTab & inLotto
```

```
Next inNumber
MsgBox stOutput & vbTab, vbOKOnly, _
  "Lottery numbers without duplicates"
```

4 Start the program using the F5 key and click on the command button.

The six lottery numbers should appear in a message box, but this time without duplicates. This is due to the field variable `aNumberField`, which contains a true value for every number drawn in the position corresponding to the value of the number. The `Do Loop` loop within the `For Next` loop is repeated until it finds a random number, where the field element of the number drawn has a *False* value. This field value is then set to true, and the number is marked as having been drawn (figure 6.9).

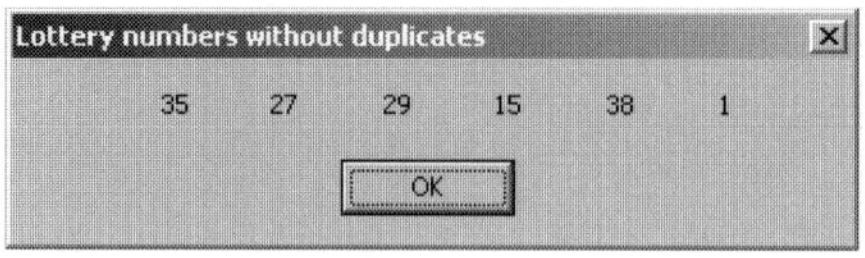

Figure 6.9: Random numbers – this time without duplicates.

Now the program only has one small error. The random numbers do not appear in ascending order. To arrange this, we need only go through the individual settings of the field variables `aNumberField` beginning with 1, and output every field number with a true value.

Use the following procedure to activate the add-on:

1 Create a new command button on the form, name it *cmdStart3*, and enter *Start3* for the caption property.

2 Double-click the command button to open the program code window.

3 Enter the following commands in the *cmdStart3_Click* event procedure:

```
Dim aNumberField(1 To 49) As Boolean
Dim inNumber As Integer
Dim inLotto As Integer
Dim stOutput As String
For inNumber = 1 To 6
  Do
    inLotto = Int(Rnd * 49) + 1
  Loop Until aNumberField(inLotto) = False
  aNumberField(inLotto) = True
Next inNumber
For inNumber = 1 To 49
  If aNumberField(inNumber) = True Then
    stOutput = stOutput & vbTab & inNumber
  End If
```

```
Next inNumber
MsgBox stOutput & vbTab, vbOKOnly, _
 "Lottery numbers in ascending order"
```

4 Start the program using the F5 key and click on the command button.

Again, six numbers appear in a message box, but this time in sequence (Figure 6.10). Another `For Next` loop accounts for this, which goes through all field elements in sequence, and only outputs in the case of those field elements whose number corresponds to the random number drawn, whereby the field element that has a true value is a previously drawn number. Don't worry if this doesn't make much sense yet. Field variables will be explained in more detail in Chapter 10.

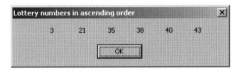

Figure 6.10: Lottery numbers again – in sequence this time.

The Exit command

To conclude this chapter, you should get to know the `Exit` command, one of the program loop commands of Visual Basic. This breaks a loop prematurely. However, as this doesn't happen in every case, it is always dependent on a decision.

The following example uses the `Dir` function to obtain the complete name of a file in a directory, only a part of which is submitted in combination with a dummy:

```
Dim stDir As String
Dim stFilename As String
stDir = "C:\My Documents\"
stFilename = Dir(stDir & "*.doc")
Do
  Debug.Print "Filename: " & stFilename
  Debug.Print "File size: " & FileLen(stDir & stFilename)
  stFilename = Dir()
Loop Until stFilename = ""
```

If you enter this command sequence in the *Form_Load* event procedure and start the program, the names and sizes of all files with the `*.doc` extension are displayed. The `Do Loop` loop is repeated until the `Dir` function returns a filename. Only when there are no more suitable files does the `Dir` function return an empty string (`""`) and the abort condition of the `Do` loop is fulfilled. If there is no file with this extension in the directory, this causes a runtime error, as the `FileLen` function cannot work with an unavailable filename. In order to prevent this runtime error, the query of the `stDFilename` variable is embedded in an empty string at the beginning of the `Do` loop. If the comparison is true, the `Do` loop is ended prematurely using the `Exit` command:

```
Dim stDir As String
Dim stFilename As String
stDir = "C:\My Documents\"
stFilename = Dir(stDir & "*.xls")
Do
  If stFilename = "" Then
    Exit Do
  End If
  Debug.Print "Filename: " & stFilename
  Debug.Print "File size: " & FileLen(stDir & stFilename)
  stFilename = Dir()
Loop
```

The query at the end of the `Do` loop is now no longer required, even if a `Do` loop can have two exit points.

Filling list fields

Now that you have learned about program loops in detail, you should learn how to use this knowledge to fill in a list box with names. Just to remind you: a list box is a control element in the toolbox (explained in Chapter 4), which displays an abitrary amount of names (maximum of 32 768). The names derive from the order of names in a list. It makes no difference which names are displayed. Any character string can appear in a list box. A list box should give the user the selection of one or more names. Usually, only one name can be selected. If several names are to be selected, the *MultiSelect* property should be set to true in the Properties window (figure 6.11).

Figure 6.11: This property decides whether one or several entries in a list box can be selected.

There are two ways of entering names in a list box:

1. In the properties window during programming.

Select the *List* property. A small text box opens in which names can be entered in sequence. A name is entered by pressing the ⏎ key, which also closes the list.

2. During runtime using the *AddItem* method.

The second option is the more interesting, as the names to be added often appear during the runtime, e.g. as they were entered from a file (as shown in Chapter 9) or database. The *AddItem* method is used for adding names (remember that a method is simply a command that always belongs to a class). The following example should answer all your questions. Imagine you have created a list box on a form amd named it *lstTowns*. The list box should return the names of towns in the Greater Manchester area during runtime. The following command ensures that the first name appears in the list box:

```
lstTowns.AddItem "Bolton"
```

The name is displayed when you start the program with F5. The *AddItem* method is used to display more names (figure 6.12):

```
lstTowns.AddItem "Bolton"
lstTowns.AddItem "Bury"
lstTowns.AddItem "Manchester"
lstTowns.AddItem "Oldham"
lstTowns.AddItem "Rochdale"
lstTowns.AddItem "Salford"
lstTowns.AddItem "Stockport"
lstTowns.AddItem "Trafford"
lstTowns.AddItem "Wigan"
```

This still requires more attention. It is not possible to add all entries to a list box at one time. They have to be entered individually.

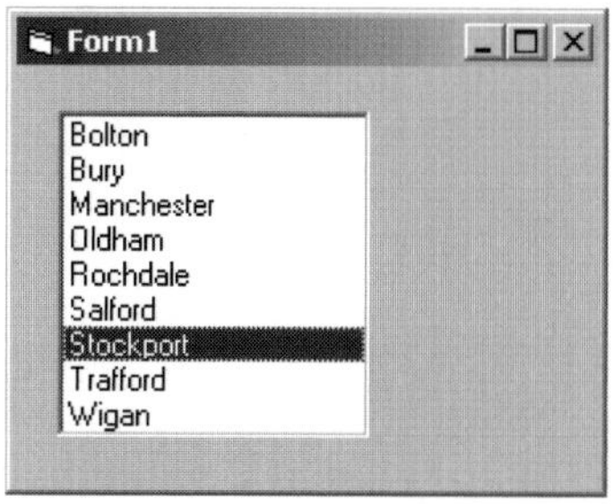

Figure 6.12: The list field displays a number of entries.

The *ListCount* property shows how many entries the list box contains:

```
Msgbox "There are " & lstTowns.ListCount & " entries"
```

Things now get a little more complicated. We want to know how a certain name can be picked out. For this, the number of the entry has to be known. The *ListCount* property always informs you of the number of elements in the list box. The last entry in the list contains the number produced by the value of *ListCount* −1. This is always the case, as the elements are numbered beginning with 0. All entries are summarised in the *List* property. If you wish to query a specific entry, the number of the entry has to be placed in brackets. The following command outputs the first entry in the *lstTowns* list box:

```
Msgbox lstTowns.List(0)
```

The next command outputs the second entry:

```
Msgbox lstTowns.List(1)
```

So what will the command that outputs the last entry look like? As follows:

```
Msgbox lstTowns.List(lstTowns.ListCount)
```

Is that right? Unfortunately not, as the last entry has the number (number of elements -1). The correct command is as follows:

```
Msgbox lstTowns.List(lstTowns.ListCount -1)
```

Don't let it bother you that the name *lstTowns* appears twice. This is because both the *List* and the *ListCount* properties have to precede the name of an object. In both cases, this is the control element *lstTowns*.

So far so good. Things become more interesting if you wish to output all elements in sequence, without having to type in a new command for each element. This is the least optimal solution:

```
Msgbox lstTowns.List(0)
Msgbox lstTowns.List(1)
Msgbox lstTowns.List(2)
Msgbox lstTowns.List(3)
Msgbox lstTowns.List(4)
etc.
```

The disadvantage of this process should be obvious. A new command has to be entered for each element. And what if the list has 5467 entries? There has to be a better way – and there is. So how is a distinction made between the individual commands? Through the number in brackets. This increases by one each time. There also has to be a command that works with a variable instead of a fixed number:

```
Msgbox lstTowns.List(iNr)
```

The variable is called iNr in this case. Its value is initially 0. No problem – we will increase the value by 1.

```
iNr = iNr + 1
Msgbox lstTowns.List(iNr)
INr = iNr + 1
Msgbox lstTowns.List(iNr)
etc.
```

This is hardly progress. On the contrary, the program has become even more extensive. Somehow, the Msgbox function had to be repeated constantly, and the variable iNr increased by one each time. Now comes the decisive step. What is the Visual Basic command called that automatically increases a variable by one? This is the For Next command, introduced earier. This command ensures that all commands between For and Next are executed until a variable is counted from a start value through to an end value by a certain increment (usually 1). There are two advantages of the For Next command:

- The command for displaying a name is repeated automatically.

- The loop variable can be used to select the element.

It now remains only to explain how the start and end values are determined. This is also easy. The start value has to be 0, as this is the number of the first name in the list. The end value has to be the same as the number of entries contained in the list box. This number also informs us of the *ListCount* property, from which we usually have to subtract 1. The *For Next* command looks as follows:

```
For iNr = 0 To lstTowns.ListCount - 1
  Msgbox lstTowns.List(iNr)
Next iNr
```

This is a real step forward, as regardless of whether the list has 5 or 5000 entries, the loop does not have to be repeated.

Removing elements from a list box

If you wish to remove a name from a list box during runtime, use the *Remove* method. The number of the entry should be given. All subsequent entries will move up one position:

```
lstTowns.Remove iNr
```

If all entries are to be removed at once, use the *Clear* method:

```
lstTowns.Clear
```

Which entry is selected?

Either one or several (if the *MultiSelect* property is set to true) entries can be selected in a list box. If only one entry is selected, things are quite simple. So what distinguishes an entry from its neighbour? Not its content, but the position number within the list. It is precisely this position number of the selected entry that is made available using the *ListIndex* property:

```
Msgbox "The number of the selected entry is: " &
lstTowns.ListIndex
```

And how do we find the content of the selected entry? Using the command

```
sContent = lstTowns.List(lstTowns.ListIndex)?
```

However, in principle, this is easier using the *Text* property:

```
sContent = lstTowns.Text
```

Incidentally, you can assign a value to both the *Text* and *ListIndex* properties. The latter causes every entry whose number contains the *ListIndex* property to be selected.

Tip

If you wish the most recently added entry to be selected, execute the following command after calling the AddItem *method:*

```
lstTowns.ListIndex = lstTest.NewIndex
```

The NewIndex *property always contains the number of the most recently added entry.*

What happens if several entries are selected?

Things now become slightly more difficult. You already know that several entries can be selected with *MultiSelect=True*. So how do you know which entries these are? The *ListIndex* property is of no use here, as it can only ever contain one number. Instead, the *Selected* property is used here. You have to submit the number of the entry to check whether it is selected.

The following example processes the *lstTowns* list box and outputs all selected entries in the direct window:

```
Dim n As Long
For n = 0 To lstTowns.ListCount -1
  If lstTowns.Selected(n) = True Then
    Debug.Print lstTowns.List(n)
  End If
Next n
```

The *SelCount* property informs you how many entries are selected in the list box (figure 6.13).

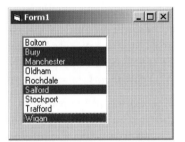

Figure 6.13: Several entries in the list box are selected due to MultiSelect=True.

Tip

To make the list box look different, set the Style *property in the properties window to* 1. *Every entry will now be displayed with a check box (figure 6.14).*

141

Figure 6.14:   *Every entry in the list box is displayed as a check box by setting the Style to 1.*

The combination box

To conclude, the *combination box* will now be introduced. This is a combination of a list box and text box (Figure 6.15). Most properties will already be familiar to you. It has the advantage of the user being able to select a name from the list or a name in the text box.

There is hardly any difference between the properties and methods. Only the *Style* property is worth mentioning, as this controls the list box display, and determines whether an entry can be made in the text box, for example. The combination box does not allow check boxes to be displayed for each entry.

Images cannot be displayed using either the list box or combination field. If you wish to do so, you should either use the image display from the Windows default control elements, or look for an alternative on the Internet (e.g. at www.active-x.com).

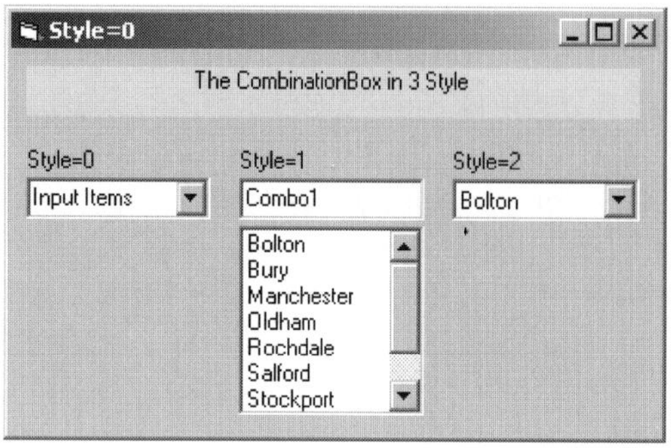

Figure 6.15: The combination box is a combination of the text and list boxes.

Summary

In this chapter, you have learned about the three pillars of program loops, variables and decisions on which nearly all programming languages are based (the fourth pillar, classes, are not introduced in this book as they are not used at the outset). A program loop enables a group of commands to be repeated a certain number of times. Using program loops, computer programs are able to live up to their reputation as electronic artists and make decisions independently.

You now know the most important part of the Visual Basic command set. The more specialised themes of Visual Basic programming will be introduced in the following chapters. In the next chapter, you will also learn how to save data from the end of the program, by placing the data in a file from which they can be read the next time the program is started.

Chapter 7

Files as the computer's long-term memory

In order for data entered during runtime to remain in the memory, they must be saved in files. This chapter uses simple examples to show you how text and numbers are saved in files, and how they can be accessed again.

This chapter addresses a very important topic. You may well wonder how a Visual Basic program 'remembers' entries (i.e. data) on a permanent basis. It used to be the case that whenever numbers or names were entered in a form, they were no longer there after the machine was rebooted. All variables were deleted when the program was ended (provided this had not already happened during runtime). Variables are the short-term memory of a program.

It should therefore be possible for a program to retain its entries in memory. You already know that the contents of the working memory of a computer are deleted when the computer is shut down, but the contents of the hard drive (or of a floppy disk) are retained. Hard drives, floppy disks, CD-ROMs, Zip drives, or anything that can be attached to the PC, are the long-term memory of the computer. Consequently, a Visual Basic program also has to place its data here. This is done in almost the same way as all applications, in that the data are saved in files. When you close down Word, for example, the application always asks whether any changes made to the document should be saved. If you want to see the document again, for example to edit it, you can load the file and everything is there again. Of course, files can also go missing, although this is one of those catastrophes that cannot be attributed to the program.

In this chapter, you will learn how to create files in a Visual Basic program in order to be able to save data, so they will be available the next time you start the program. The whole concept is very simple. You need only follow a few rules.

This chapter addresses the following topics:

- What is a file?
- Files have to be opened.
- The secret of the channel number.
- Saving texts.
- Selecting saved texts.
- Saving and reading numbers.
- Selecting lottery numbers for the entire year.
- Creating a personal horoscope.

What is a file?

The term 'file' is so important that its meaning should not be taken lightly. A file is the 'place' on the hard drive, floppy disk, CD, or any data carrier where data are stored. Where and how these data are placed does not matter, as the file is identified exclusively by its name, which it was given when the data were saved. So if you open Notepad, type in a few words, and save the text in a file called *Justanote.txt*, Notepad creates a file with this name in which the text entered is saved. If you search for the file in Explorer, you will find it in the directory that was selected when the file was saved. It will occupy a certain number of bytes (the smallest data unit in computer terms), whereby the number of bytes depends on the number of characters entered. Depending on which version of Windows you are using, 1 or 2 bytes are saved per character.

A file is therefore a way of saving data on a drive, so that programmers need not concern themselves with the way in which the data are saved. If the file is opened, only its name is indicated.

Files save data

The term 'data' should also be explained. Data simply means everything that a computer program can work with. The most frequently used types of data are numbers and character strings (these are text, also known as *strings* in Visual Basic). A Visual Basic program saves data in variables, where a data type has to be given for every variable. This indicates which type of data (such as integers or numbers with decimal places) are saved in the variables. At the same time, the data type of a variable determines how many bytes of the working memory are occupied. This brings us back to the topic of files, as, if the variable is stored in a file, this occupies a certain number of bytes, as determined by the data type. Table 7.1 gives a brief list of the most important data types in Visual Basic (a complete list can be found in the appendix).

Data type	Number of bytes
Byte	1
Integer	2
Long	4
Single	4
Double	8
String	1 byte per character

Table 7.1: The most important data types in Visual Basic.

147

Opening, accessing, closing — the principles of file access

In order to be able to access the data contained in a file (i.e. used in a Visual Basic program), the file has to be opened. The (physical) status of the file is not altered (in Windows Explorer, you cannot see from a file whether it has been opened by a program). Opening a file merely means that Windows recognises that this file is being used by a program. If another program also wishes to open the same file, Windows can determine whether this is permitted (files are opened exclusively, so that they can only be used by one program at any one time), and displays a note if required. Don't be too concerned with the process of opening files. You should remember that each file has to be opened once. The command used for opening files is the OPEN command.

The following command opens a file called *Horoscope.txt*:

```
Open "C:\My Documents\Horoscope.txt" For Input As 1
```

Note that the full path of the file is given. This is always required, as the file is not located in the same directory as the Visual Basic program. Two other details have to be added to the file path:

- the file access mode, in this case `Input`;
- the channel number, in this case `1`.

When opening, Visual Basic expects you to indicate whether the file should be read (*Input mode*) or described (*Output mode*), or whether something should be attached to an existing file (*Append mode*).

What are reading and writing?

The vterms 'read' and 'write' are specific programming words that won't necessarily mean much to some readers. Reading a file means transferring its content to the program. The reverse process, namely transferring data into a file, is called writing. This has nothing to do with reading and writing in the normal sense of the words. The term 'access' also falls into this category. Accessing a file means either reading its content or writing to the file.

Using the keywords Input, Output and Append, it is determined whether you wish to read or write a file when accessing the text files with the OPEN command. A file can therefore only be written or read. It makes no difference if you wish to save numbers. In this case, the file is opened in *binary* mode, where it makes no difference whether numbers are written or read.

The secret of the channel number

The channel number is also required. This is so that as soon as a file is opened successfully, all further access to this file has to be carried out using a channel number. If you wish to read a line from a file, enter the channel number instead of the filename. The channel number is specified when the OPEN command is executed by the programmer. What was the channel number in the above example? It was 1. Why 1? Well, why not? The channel numbers start with 1 and end with 255, so there is nothing wrong with beginning with 1 (we could also have used 2, 3, 4, etc.). If the file is closed again using the

CLOSE command, the channel number is free for use, so it can be used again when the OPEN command is next used.

Saving texts

When saving texts, the file is first opened using the OPEN command. You have to decide whether to create a new file (or overwrite an existing file) or attach something to an existing file. This is specified using the `Output` or `Append` keywords. The text is then saved using the PRINT command. The notation of this command is rather strange, as the hash character '#' has to follow the compulsory channel number. As long as the file is open, as many PRINT commands as you want can follow. At the end, the file is closed using the CLOSE command.

The following command sequence saves a phrase in a file called *MyManifesto.txt*:

```
iChannel Nr = FreeFile()
Open "MyManifesto.txt" For Output As iChannel Nr
  Print # Channel, "A funny voyage at sea"
Close iChannelNr
```

And what will it look like if the content of a text box is saved? Quite simple: in this case, you don't save the text box as a whole, but the actual content of the *Text* property of the text box. The PRINT command looks as follows:

```
Print # iChannelNr, txtManifesto.txt
```

This command saves the entire content of the *txtManifesto* text box in the file that is opened.

> **Tip**
>
> *If you wish to save only a portion of a text box, you have to work with the* SelText *property of the text box. This contains the text that is currently selected in the text box. The* SelStart *and* SelLength *(number of characters selected) properties enable you to specify the selected area in the program, and save a section of the text box.*

Selecting saved texts

In principle, reading texts from a file corresponds to saving texts, but with two differences:

1. 'Input' is always given as the file mode.

2. The Input or Line Input commands or Input function are used instead of the Print command.

The following example reads the text saved in the last section from the file *MyManifesto.text* again and displays it in a message box:

```
iChannel Nr = FreeFile()
Open "MyManifesto.txt" For Input As iChannelNr
  Input # iChannelNr, sFilecontent
Close iChannelNr
Msgbox "My manifesto is: " & sFilecontent
```

If you execute the example, the text saved in the last section is displayed. The entire text? No, not quite: only those characters up to the comma are displayed. The comma is a type of 'stop sign' for the Input command. If you wish to read a complete line (including the characters following the comma), you will need to use the LINE INPUT command.

The Line Input command

Visual Basic offers two commands for reading texts in the INPUT and LINE INPUT command, which differ from each other only slightly. The INPUT command does not know how many characters are to be read. This is not a problem, as all characters are always read until the next separator. The separator is the comma. If you wish to read an entire line, meaning all characters until the next line break character (ASCII characters 13 and 10), the LINE INPUT command will need to be used. Separators are not involved here.

The following exercise should show you how all lines of a file created in Notepad (the editor for Windows) are read with the LINE INPUT command. You will also learn the EOF function.

Use the following procedure:

1 Start *Notepad* (the program is located in Accessories) and type in a few lines.

2 Save the lines in a file called *MyManifesto2* (the exact name is not important – the *.txt* extension is attached automatically by Notepad). Select *C:\My Documents* as an example.

3 Start *Visual Basic* and create a new STANDARD EXE project.

4 Double-click on the form to switch to the program code window.

5 Enter the following commands in the *Form_Load* event procedure:

```
Dim sFilecontent As String
Dim sLine As String
Dim iChannelNr As Integer
Const Filename = "C:\My Documents\MyManifesto2.txt"
iChannelNr = FreeFile()
Open Filename For Input As iChannelNr
Do While Not EOF(iChannelNr)
  Line Input #iChannelNr, sLine
  sFilecontent = sFilecontent & sLine
Loop
Close iChannelNr
Msgbox "The file content is: " & sFilecontent
```

The Do loop is repeated until the EOF function returns the value true. The channel number of the previously opened file is given so this function knows which file to check.

6 Start the program. The previously saved content of the file should now be displayed (Figure 7.1).

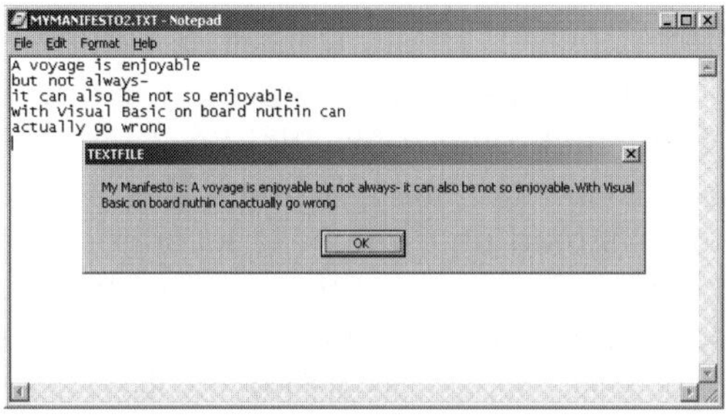

Figure 7.1: The content of a text file previously saved with Notepad is displayed.

The Input function for reading the entire file content

Neither the `Input` nor the `Line Input` command are really optimal, as they assume a line-by-line construction of the text file. If you wish to read the entire content of a file, there are two alternatives:

1. All lines with `Line Input` return the value true until the `EOF` function.

2. Use the `Input` function. Here you can indicate how many characters are to be read. Using the `LOF` function, which determines the number of characters in a file, you obtain a number, which you will need to read the complete file contents.

The following example shows how simply the entire contents of a file can be read using the `Input` function. Use the following procedure:

1 Start *Visual Basic* and create a new STANDARD EXE project.

2 Switch to the program code window using the F7 key.

3 Enter the following commands in the *Form_Load* event procedure:

```
Dim sFilecontent As String
Dim sLine As String
Dim iChannelNr As Integer
Dim Filename As String
Filename = "C:\Config.sys"
iChannelNr = FreeFile()
Open Filename For Input As iChannelNr
  sFilecontent = Input(LOF(iChannelNr), iChannelNr)
Close iChannelNr
MsgBox sFilecontent
```

4 Start the program using the F5 key. Shortly afterwards, the content of the configuration file *Config.sys* (not always available in Windows 2000 – use the file *C:\Msdos.sys* in this case) should be displayed.

In this case, the line break character is also read, as opposed to when the `Line Input` command is used.

Saving and reading numbers

Numbers can also be saved. It doesn't really matter which data are saved in the file. In principle, this also applies to a Visual Basic program. For example, if a string reads '123', this can easily be assigned to a string variable. Visual Basic then determines the suitable data type, such as `Integer` or `Long`. A distinction between numbers and text is therefore not necessary in most cases. This will be explained later in this chapter.

Changing binary code

If numbers are to be saved and read, there is no difference between `Input`, `Output` and `Append` when opening the file. Rather, the files are opened in *Binary* mode. This simply means that you should use the keyword `Binary` with the `Open` command:

```
Open Filename For Binary As iChannelNr
```

As opposed to accessing text files, there is no difference between the filename and channel number.

Saving and reading with Put and Get

The `Put` command controls the saving of data, and the `Get` command controls the reading of data.

The following example enters three numbers in a file called *Measurements.dat*, created using an `Open` command. Use the following procedure:

1 Start *Visual Basic* and create a new a STANDARD EXE project.

2 Switch to the program code window using the F7 key.

3 Enter the following commands in the *Form_Load* event procedure:

```
Dim Filename As String
Dim iChannelNr As Integer
iChannelNr = FreeFile()
Filename = App.Path & "\Measurements.dat"
Open Filename For Binary As iChannelNr
   Put #iChannelNr, , CInt(1234)
   Put #iChannelNr, , CLng(1000000#)
   Put #iChannelNr, , CSng(3.1498754)
Close #iChannelNr
```

4 Start the program using the F5 key. It seems as though nothing happens, but the file *Measurements.dat* is created, and three numbers are saved in it (you can locate the file in Explorer – it should be 18 bytes in size, but note that Explorer always indicates two different sizes: the size on the hard drive and its true size).

Before the file is read again, you need to know something important. The `Put` command always saves as many bytes as are predefined for the data type, be it the variable or number. This is clear with variables, as every variable has a data type – one exception is the `Variant` type of variable (which is always used if you have not indicated a data type when declaring the variable). In this case, Visual Basic adapts the data type to the content of the variable. The data type is therefore very important, as it specifies the number of bytes and their arrangement. A variable saved as `Long` also has to be read as `Long`. If you assigned the Integer type to the variables that the content fed in, you can assume that there would be no error message, as the `Get` command used for reading would read only two bytes rather than four.

It is not quite as simple if numbers are entered. This is because Visual Basic only specifies the data type here, and you have to know which data type is being used and when. The following command clarifies this:

```
Put #iChannelNr, , 1234
```

The number '1234' is always saved as an `Integer`. However, the next command is not quite so clear:

```
Put #iChannelNr, , 1000000#
```

Is the number really saved as `Long`, as the appended # sign would indicate? As specified by the `Typename` function, for example, this number is converted into a `Double` by Visual Basic. This means that a variable used with a corresponding `Get` command also has to be a `Double` type. Or you could tell Visual Basic which data type should be used when saving. This occurs in the above example, for which reason the numbers to be saved are converted into the data types desired with the different type conversion functions (`CInt`, `CDbl` and `CLng`).

You need to know a little more about the `Get` and `Put` commands. A *record number* can be entered with both. This refers to a special Visual Basic file type, called a *random file*. A random file consists of one or more records, where each record has the same field construction. To give an example, one field could be an `Integer` variable, and the next a `String` or `Double` variable. The composition of this field is determined by the `Type` command. A variable is then declared with the data type defined using the `Type` command, which can then be saved in a file using `Put`. In this case, the number of the record is given as a second parameter. If you only wish to save simple numbers, this record number is irrelevant, and the space between the two commas remains empty.

This should clarify everything, and the 'number cocktail' saved in this way should be read and displayed again.

5 Insert the following commands at the end of the *Form_Load* procedure:

```
Dim Number1 As Integer
Dim Number2 As Long
Dim Number3 As Single
iChannelNr = FreeFile()
Filename = App.Path & "\Measurements.dat"
Open Filename For Binary As iChannelNr
  Get #iChannelNr, , Number1
  Get #iChannelNr, , Number2
  Get #iChannelNr, , Number3
Close #iChannelNr
MsgBox "Number1: " & Number1 & vbCrLf _
 & "Number2: " & Number2 & vbCrLf _
 & "Number3: " & Number3 & vbCrLf _
 & "vNumber: " & vNumber
```

6 Start the program using the ⌗F5⌗ key. Three numbers are now saved in *Measurements.dat* and then displayed.

Of course, the whole point of file commands is that you do not have to save data in order to display the data again. These are only brief examples intended to illustrate how to use these important commands. Data are saved so they are permanently available. It will be read either the next time the program is started, or when called at some point in the future. When and how this occurs depends on the programmer.

Overview of file access commands

The principle of file access is not especially complicated, but the Visual Basic help function (if available at all) is not exactly the most comprehensive guide. Table 7.2 contains an overview of all commands and functions, so you can proceed confidently with the different variants of file access.

Command/function	Explanation
`Close` command	Closes an opened file. All opened files without an indicated channel number are also closed.
`FileAttr` function	Indicates the current file mode of a file, where the channel number of the file is given (1=Input, 2=Output, 4=Random, 8=Append, 32=Binary).
`Get` command	Selects a number or record from an opened file, where the channel number is given.

Command/function	Explanation
Input command	Selects all characters until the next separator from an opened file, where the channel number is given.
Input function	Selects the number of characters indicated from an opened file, where the channel number is given.
Line Input command	Selects all characters until the next pair of line break symbols from an opened file, where the channel number is given.
LOC function	Returns the current position of the invisible file pointer of a file, where the channel number is given.
LOF function	Returns the length of an opened file, where the channel number is given.
Open command	Opens a file from the path details, access modes and channel number. Security settings can also be configured.
Print command	Writes the following text into the opened file, where the channel number is given.
Put command	Writes a number or record in an opened file, where the channel number is given.
Seek command	Positions the invisible file pointer to the position indicated, and determines the point in the file that is to be written to or read from, where the channel number of the file is given.
Seek function	As opposed to the LOC function which indicates the current position, the Seek function indicates the position for the next read or write access.
Write command	As opposed to the Print command, character strings are placed in quotation marks.

Table 7.2: Overview of commands and functions for file access.

Selecting lottery numbers for the entire year

No computer program can predict next week's lottery numbers, but we can pretend. The following example simulates the drawing of six random numbers between 1 and 49 over the period of one year. You are already familiar with program loops and the Rnd function from Chapter 6, where random numbers between 0 and 1 were generated in a previous example. This time, the numbers drawn are saved in a file, so you can print them out, for example.

Use the following procedure to activate the example:

1 Start *Visual Basic* and create a new STANDARD EXE project.

2 Create a command button on the form, name it *cmdStart*, and enter *Start* in the *Caption* property.

3 Switch to the program code window using the F7 key.

4 Enter the following commands in the *cmdStart_Click* event procedure:

```
Dim iWeek As Integer
Dim iChannelNr As Integer
Dim iAmount As Integer
Dim iNumber As Integer
Dim aNumberfield(1 To 49) As Boolean
Dim sLottery As String
Dim dDate As Date
Randomize Timer
dDate = DateAdd("d", 7 - Weekday("1.1." & Year(Now)), _
 "1.1." & Year(Now))
iChannelNr = FreeFile
Open "Lotterynumbers.txt" For Output As iChannelNr
  For iWeek = 1 To 52
    For iAmount = 1 To 6
      Do
        iNumber = Int(Rnd * 49) + 1
      Loop Until aNumberfield(iZahl) = False
      aNumberfield(iNumber) = True
    Next iAmount
    For iAmount = 1 To 49
      If aNumberfield(iAmount) = True Then
        sLottery = sLottery & vbTab & Format(iAmount, "##")
      End If
    Next iAmount
    Print #iChannelNr, "The Lottery numbers from " & dDate
Print #iChannelNr, String(64, "=")
    Print #iChannelNr, sLottery
    Print #iChannelNr, ""
    sLottery = ""
    Erase aNumberfield
    dDate = DateAdd("d", 7, dDate)
  Next Week
  Close iChannelNr
  Shell "Explorer Lotterynumbers.txt", vbNormalFocus
```

5 Start the program using the F5 key and click on the command button. Shortly afterwards, the lottery numbers for the whole year, i.e. the content of the text file *Lotterynumbers.txt* created in the program, will be displayed in Internet Explorer (Figure 7.2).

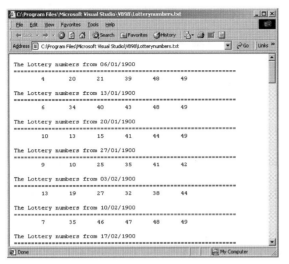

Figure 7.2: Straight from the file to the screen – the content of the file Lotterynumbers.txt.

Explanation of the program

This is probably the most extensive Visual Basic program you have worked with so far. At the beginning of the program, a little date arithmetic occurs, as it searches for the date of the first Saturday in the year. The following command calculates this date:

```
dDate = DateAdd("d", 7 - Weekday("1.1." & Year(Now)), _
  "1.1." & Year(Now))
```

This is the first `DateAdd` function that adds the number of days from 1 January required to reach the next Saturday. Within the function, two further date functions appear: `Weekday`, to determine the number of the weekday of 1 January, and `Year`, to determine the current year. The `DateAdd` function is later used once more to calculate the date of the next respective Saturday.

```
dDate = DateAdd("d", 7, dDate)
```

That was the main difficulty in this program. You should be familiar with the way in which lottery numbers are drawn from the exercise in Chapter 6. Of course, numbers are sorted and saved without duplicates in the file *Lotterynumbers.txt*. However, they will not be displayed by a Visual Basic program. Internet Explorer is instructed to display the file using the `Shell` function, with which programs from the Visual Basic program can be tested (you could also use Notepad or another program):

```
Shell "Explorer Lotterynumbers.txt", vbNormalFocus
```

159

Summary and outlook

Files are where you save data at the end of the program. Saving and reading text and numbers is simple using the file commands and functions. You need note only that when saving text, different file modes (Input, Output and Append) are used, that the Input command only reads all characters up to the next comma, and that the channel number is used for all types of access, which is initially obtained using the Freefile function. If you are saving and reading numbers, it is better to open the file in *Binary* mode. This time, the Put command is used for saving, and the Get command is used for reading. *Binary* mode differs from the text mode in saving characters only in that the number is saved as a binary value, rather than as a sequence of figures. So, the number '1234' is saved as 2 bytes in binary mode, and as 4 bytes in text mode.

If you have worked through the book up to this point, you should now be familiar with the most important functions of Visual Basic programming. In the next chapter, you will not learn any new Visual Basic commands. Instead, a larger sample project will be created step by step. This is a program for displaying images in the form of a screen saver. Chapter 10 explores theory in more detail, and the more advanced topics of Visual Basic programming, such as function calls, working with character strings, and saving numbers and texts in an array.

Chapter 8

A slide show for the PC

In this chapter, a large Visual Basic program will be created step by step with which your scanned holiday photos can be displayed in sequence.

You will not learn any new commands in this chapter. Instead, you will execute a large Visual Basic program step by step. This program will enable you to display image files in a specified order. As this happens in full-screen mode (the program window is not visible), and the images change automatically, it looks like a slide show. The program allows you to achieve an attractive optical effect. Finally, you will also learn how the program produces a proper slide show that can be configured as a Windows screen saver, and started automatically after a certain period of time.

This is about a large Visual Basic program first and foremost, and the program techniques used. In this sense, the program is a repeat of the previous seven chapters.

Topics covered in this chapter are:

- beginning activation;
- creating the start form;
- beginning programming;
- using the second form to show the slides;
- carring out an initial test run;
- suggestions for expansion;
- saving the file path in the registry;
- moving from slide show to screen saver.

Beginning activation

Firstly, gather about half a dozen bitmaps in *JPEG*, *GIF* or *BMP* format, e.g. from the internet. Although resolution matters little, they should be as large as possible so when they are enlarged to screen size, they won't be stretched noticeably. Save the image files in a directory called *Slideshow* so you can find them easily later on.

Step 1: starting Visual Basic and creating a standard exe project

Start Visual Basic and create a new STANDARD EXE project. As usual in Visual Basic, you will see an empty window after selecting a new project. This is the start form window, the window that is displayed automatically after the program is started. During the slide show, this form should be able to specify the files to be selected, and other settings such as the length of the interval. The image display is carried out on a second form, which is added to the project later.

Name the existing form *frmSlideshow* by clicking on the form, activating the properties window using the F4 key, and entering the name in the uppermost entry field *(Name)*. The project should be given a different name. It should be called *Slideshow* (this specifies the predefined filename under which the project file will be saved later). A project name is also set using the properties window, but you should select the project file in the Project Explorer first (Figure 8.1), which is opened using Ctrl+R or using the VIEW menu.

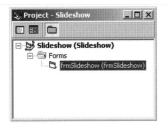

Figure 8.1: Project Explorer shows the new name of the project and the form.

Before we start working on the form, two important questions have to be answered:

1. How do we select files to be displayed?

2. How does the program know which files were selected so it does not need to reselect them every time the program is started?

The answer to the first question is called *Default dialogue box control element*. This *ActiveX* control element is a component part of Visual Basic (more on this important topic in Chapter 9). It makes five general dialogue boxes available, which belong to Windows, and which are also used by other programs (such as the Paint and WordPad accessories). One of the dialogue boxes is used to select a filename. In the slide show, it ensures that a user can easily select an image file (as one would expect from a Windows program). The great advantage of the standard dialogue box is that you don't need to program it – it's already done. One small disadvantage is that the graphics cannot be modified.

There are several answers to the second question. One option is to save the directory path of the selected files in a text file. This text file is read when the program is loaded (in the *Form_Load* event of the start form) and updated again before the program is ended (in the *Form_Unload* event of the start form). You should have learned how such file access works in Chapter 7. The advantage of this version is that the text file can be edited outside the program. One small disadvantage is that when this file is deleted or moved, the memory for the selected images also goes missing. The alternative is to save the filenames in the registry. This is far easier than it sounds, as Visual Basic provides the `SaveSettings` command and the `GetSettings` function. `SaveSettings` does not save arbitrary values anywhere in the registry, but in the *\Software\VB and VBA Program Settings* branch of the respective user, so they cannot be edited externally afterwards.

The first version is used in this project, but it is shown at the end as the directory path is saved in the registry.

Creating the start form

The start form does not show the image (no more than a preview – more about this later) but is used to select images to be displayed. Create the required control elements in sequence on the form by selecting them from the toolbox, drawing on the form, and arranging them in the desired position at the size required. In particular, these are:

- one list box;
- six command buttons;
- one text box;
- one control box;
- two labels;
- one timer.

The standard dialogue box control element is also required, but this is not initially an integral part of the toolbox. This can be added afterwards using the PROJECT/COMPONENTS menu command, and selecting the MICROSOFT COMMON DIALOGUE CONTROL 6.0 entry.

So that creating the different properties (there aren't that many) does not require lengthy explanations, Table 8.1 shows all the properties containing a new value. This is essentially the *Name* property, as all other properties are configured during runtime. Control elements whose properties have to be modified (such as the labels) are not listed. Take a look at Figure 8.2, which shows the finished *frnSlideshow* form.

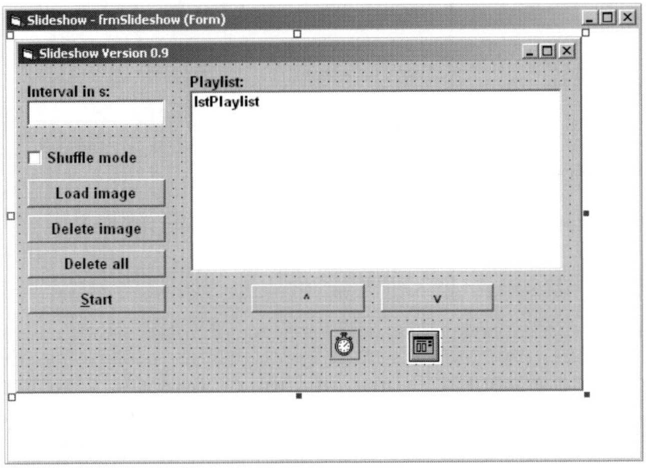

Figure 8.2: The finished frmSlideshow *form should look like this.*

Control element	Property	Old value	New value
Label	Caption	Label1	Interval in seconds:
Textbox	Name	Text1	txtInterval
Label1	Caption	Label2	Playlist:
Listbox	Name	List1	lstPlaylist
Timer	Name	Timer1	tmrTime
Commondialogue	Name	Commondialogue1	cdlFile
Checkbox	Name	Check1	chkShuffle
Checkbox	Caption	Check1	Shuffle mode

Control element	Property	Old value	New value
CommandButton	Name	Command1	cmdLoad
CommandButton	Caption	Command1	&Load image
CommandButton	Name	Command2	cmdDelete
CommandButton	Caption	Command2	&Delete image
CommandButton	Name	Command3	cmdDeleteAll
CommandButton	Caption	Command3	&Delete all
CommandButton	Name	Command4	cmdStart
CommandButton	Caption	Command4	&Start
CommandButton	Name	Command5	cmdUp
CommandButton	Caption	CommandButton	^
CommandButton	Name	Command6	cmdDown
CommandButton	Caption	Command6	V

Table 8.1:   These properties receive new values with the form control elements.

Finally, the form should have a suitable heading. Select the form, switch to the properties window using [F4], and enter *Slideshow Version 0.9* in the *Caption* property (the version number merely indicates that this is a preliminary version).

Beginning programming

The programming starts now. Click on the form and press [F7] to open the program code window. Enter the following two commands in the *General* section of the form (i.e. outside a procedure):

```
Private stPathname As String
Const Slidelist = "C:\My Documents\Slidelist.dat"
```

The first command declares the stPathname variable, which later opens the directory path of an image file. The second command declares the Slidelist constant. Its value is the directory path of the file *Slideshow.dat*, in which the directory paths of the images to be displayed are saved. If this file is going to be placed in another directory, the constant must also be modified accordingly.

The next step determines what happens immediately after the start form is loaded, i.e. directly after the program has started. Select the FORM entry from the left-hand selection list and the LOAD entry from the right -hand selection list (this should be the default entry) and enter the following commands in the procedure frame:

```
Dim stTemp As String
Dim iChannelNr As Integer
On Error Resume Next
iChannelNr = FreeFile()
Open Slidelist For Input As iChannelNr
  If Err.Number > 0 Then
    Exit Sub
  End If
  Do While Not EOF(iKanalNr)
   Input #iChannelNr, stTemp
   lstPlaylist.AddItem stTemp
  Loop
Close iChannelNr
txtInterval.Text = "1"
```

The main section of the procedure consists of reading directory paths saved in the *lstPlaylist* list box. If the *Slidelist.dat* file does not yet contain entries (e.g. because the program has just been started for the first time), the Do loop is not processed. At the end, a value of 1 is entered in the txtInterval text box, as this is the default value for the interval. Closing the form triggers an Unload event. In this case, the content of the list box is saved in the *Slidelist.dat* file. Select the FORM entry from the left-hand selection list in the program code window and the UNLOAD entry from the right-hand selection list, and enter the following commands:

```
Dim iSlideNr As Integer
Dim iChannelNr As Integer
iChannelNr = FreeFile()
Open Slidelist For Output As iChannelNr
 For iSlideNr = 0 To lstPlaylist.ListCount - 1
   Print # iChannelNr, lstPlaylist.List(iSlideNr)
 Next iSlideNr
Close iChannelNr
```

Now for the most important part of the program, the *Timer* event procedure. Whenever a *Timer* event occurs, the next slide is displayed, i.e. the next image is loaded. Only the content of the next list entry need be used as a directory path, and the image file determined in this way is loaded. Select the TMRTIME entry from the left-hand selection list (the name of the timer control element), and the TIMER entry from the right-hand selection list (this is the default entry), and enter the following commands:

```
Static iSlideNr As Integer
If chkShuffle.Value = 0 Then
  iSlideNr = Int(Rnd * lstPlaylist.ListCount) + 1
Else
  iSlideNr = iSlideNr Mod lstPlaylist.ListCount + 1
End If
stPathname = lstPlaylist.List(iSlideNr - 1)
With frmDia
  .Show
  .Caption = stPathname
  .imgDia.Picture = LoadPicture(stPathname)
End With
```

Pay particular attention to the inconspicuous *Show* method. This ensures that the second form *frmSlide* is displayed. However, this form is not available and still has to be added. A Visual Basic program can consist of any number of forms, but only the start form is displayed automatically (specified in the project properties using the PROJECT/PROPERTIES menu command). All other forms have to be displayed using the *Show* method, and later made invisible when no longer required using the *Hide* method, or removed from the working memory using the *Unload* command.

Use the following procedure to add the second form:

1 Open the PROJECT menu and select the ADD FORM entry.

2 If a selection dialogue appears, select the FORM entry (Figure 8.3).

3 Name the new form *frmSlide* in Project Explorer.

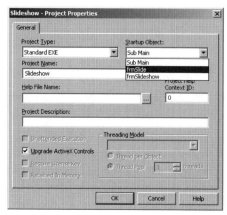

Figure 8.3: The start form of the project is selected in this dialogue of the properties window.

The centre of the program now exists. The procedures that add to the convenience of the program now follow. First comes the loading of further images in the selection list. The command button named *cmdLoad* is used for this task. An image from the standard dialogue box is selected In the *cmdLoad_Click* event procedure and then loaded. Select the procedure settings of the event procedure in the program code window, and insert the following commands:

```
With cdlFile
  .Filter = "GIF|*.GIF|JPEG|*.JPG|BMP|*.BMP|All|*.*"
  .ShowOpen
  stPathname = .FileName
End With
lstPlaylist.AddItem stPathname
```

`cdlFile` is the standard dialogue control element that displays the selection dialogue for the image file. Each file extension is selected using the *Filter* property. The extension should then appear in the corresponding selection list. The *ShowOpen* method displays the dialogue box. The complete directory path is assigned by the file selected by the user (as long as a file was selected) using the *FileName* property of the `stPathname` variable, and then inserted in the list box using the *AddItem* method. Don't let the new `With` command worry you (this is introduced in Chapter 10). Experienced Visual basic programmers use this as an abbreviation so they do not need to list names of an object unnecessarily. However, this can also be omitted. In this case, the name of the list box is placed in front of every point.

The filenames are now not only selected but can also be deleted from the list altogether. The *cmdDelete* (only the selected entry is deleted, not the file) and *cmdDeleteAll* (all entries are deleted from the list) buttons are used for this. Select the *Click* procedure of *cmdDelete* from the program code window and insert the following commands:

```
If lstPlaylist.ListIndex = -1 Then
  MsgBox "Please select an entry", vbExclamation
  Exit Sub
End If
lstPlaylist.RemoveItem lstPlaylist.ListIndex
```

Then select the *Click* procedure of *cmdDeleteAll* from the program code window and insert the following commands:

```
lstPlaylist.Clear
tmrTime.Enabled = False
```

Finally, the form also allows you to modify the sequence of entries in the list box, and therefore the sequence in which the individual images will be displayed using the *cmdDown* (selected entry to move down one place) and *cmdUp* (selected entry to move up one place) buttons. Both buttons call the *MoveEntry* procedure where the direction is given as an argument.

Select the procedure settings of the *cmdDown_Click* in the program code window and insert the following command:

```
MoveEntry 1
```

Select the procedure settings of the *cmdUp_Click* in the program code window and insert the following command:

```
MoveEntry -1
```

The *MoveEntry* procedure does not yet exist. This will now be created. Select the GENERAL entry from the left-hand selection list in the program code window (or simply scroll up), and enter the following commands underneath the `Const` command, which defines the *MoveEntry* procedure:

```
Sub MoveEntry(Direction As Integer)
  Dim stPathOld As String
  Dim iNrNew As Integer, iNrOld As Integer
  With lstPlaylist
    If .ListIndex = -1 Then
      MsgBox "Please select an entry first!", vbExclamation
      Exit Sub
    End If
    If .ListIndex = .ListCount And Direction = 1 Then
     Exit Sub
    End If
    If .ListIndex = 0 And Direction = -1 Then
     Exit Sub
    End If
    iNrOld = .ListIndex
    iNrNew = iNrOld + Direction
    If iNrNew = lstPlaylist.ListCount Then
     Exit Sub
    End If
'Nr., Retrieve name and path of current entry
    iNrOld = .ListIndex
    stPathOld = .Text
' Delete current entry
    .RemoveItem iNrOld
' New Entry
    .AddItem stPfadAlt, iNrNew
    .ListIndex = iNrNew
  End With
End Sub
```

The general *MoveEntry* procedure is not explained in detail here as it is relatively simple. The *lstPlaylist* list box is located in the middle and is explained in Chapter 6.

Finally, the *cmdStart* button that starts the slide show has to be assigned some program code. Select the CMDSTART entry from the left-hand selection list in the program code window and enter the following commands in the *Click* event procedure:

```
With tmrTime
   .Interval = txtIntervall.Text * 1000
   .Enabled = True
End With
' Call Timer event
   tmrTime_Timer
```

The random mode of the program has not yet been mentioned. If the corresponding *chkShuffle* control box is set, the program uses a random sequence instead of the default one so that the next image is determined using a random number (Rnd function). Program commands are not required for this as control boxes play a purely passive role.

Using the second form to display the slides

Everything has been entirely preparatory until now. Our program cannot yet show slides. A second form, already added to the project, is required for this task. Create the *Display* control element on the form. It should be called *imgSlide*. The size and position of the display are not important as they will automatically be modified at a later stage to fit the size of the form. By setting the *Stretch* property to *1*, the size of the image displayed is automatically adapted to the size of the display.

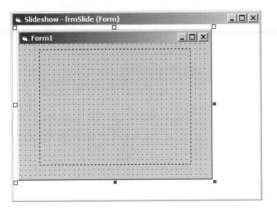

Figure 8.4: The frmSlide *form contains only one display.*

We will now begin programming the second form. Firstly, the *Form_Load* event procedure has to contain something. Select the form, switch to the program code window using ⑦, and select the FORM entry from the left-hand selection list. The procedure settings of the *Form_Load* procedure then appear, and should contain the following:

```
With imgSlide
   .Left = 0
   .Top = 0
   .Stretch = True
End With
Me.WindowState = 2
```

The settings in the *Left* and *Top* properties of the display place the image in the upper left-hand corner. However, the *Stretch* property is set to 1, so the image appears in full-screen mode. The command

```
Me.WindowState = 2
```

causes the window to be maximised. One property of the form that cannot be adjusted during runtime is *BorderStyle*, which specifies the appearance of the border. This property has to be set to 0 in the program code window during the design process. If this happens during runtime, the title bar of the form remains visible.

The size of the display is adapted to that of the surrounding form in the *Resize* property, which is always called after the size of the form has been altered (as well as immediately after the first display). This is actually much easier than it sounds, as the *ScaleHeight* and *ScaleWidth* properties of a form are used specifically for this. These stand for the inner height and width of the form display area. Insert the following commands in the *Form_Resize* event procedure:

```
With imgSlide
  .Width = Me.ScaleWidth
  .Height = Me.ScaleHeight
End With
```

Finally, the slide show ends as soon as the user clicks on the screen. This ends the display *Click* procedure, which unloads the form using the *Unload* command and stops the timer:

```
Private Sub imgSlide_Click()
   frmSlideShow.tmrTime.Enabled _= False
   Unload Me
End Sub
```

The *Click* event normally only refers to the surface of the display element, but as this takes the full area of the form, it doesn't matter where the screen is clicked.

An initial test run

The program is now ready. Start it using the ⌨F5 key (as long as you have set the corresponding option, you will be prompted to save the project file and both form files). Select all images to be displayed in sequence using the LOAD button, and set an other interval length if required. If you now click on the Start button, all images should be displayed in sequence, and also in full-screen mode.

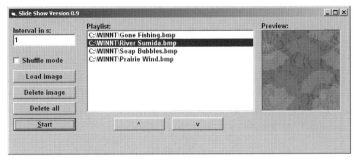

Figure 8.5: The images to be displayed are loaded – clicking the Start button begins the process.

Suggestions for expansion

No program is perfect from the outset, and our slide show is no exception. Two improvements are obvious. Firstly, it would be good if the form had a small preview of the picture selected in the list. To do this, you need only create another display on the form and set the *Stretch* property to 1, so the image is modified to fit the size of the display (Figure 8.6).

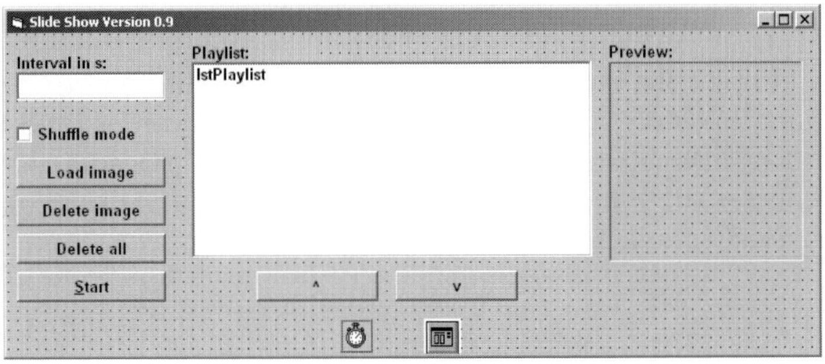

Figure 8.6: Another display is created on the form for a preview.

173

The second improvement is not as easy to achieve. It would be good if the long directory path were removed from the list box (the path can be especially long in Windows 2000). As a normal list box has no scroll function without a few tricks (in the shape of a *SendMessage* API call – more on this in Chapter 10), there has to be a solution. This could be by displaying just a section of the directory path. As the content of the list box is used for loading the file, you would have to save both a full and an abbreviated version of the path, which makes programming rather more extensive. You should always think in terms of the easiest solution being the best in programming. A simple solution would be to select a list entry and assign it to the *TooltipText* property of the list box. This causes the entire directory path (note that there is also a limit here) to be displayed as a tooltip when the mouse pointer is moved over the entry. One command has to be added to the program. This is inserted in the *Click* event of the *lstFiles* list box:

```
lstFiles.ToolTipText = _
  lstFiles.Text
```

This is a typical example of a solution that gives a satisfactory result with a minimum amount of effort. This type of solution is easily prepared and removes the need for a more complicated alternative. This sets an experienced (or talented) programmer apart from the rest.

Saving file paths in the registry

As promised at the beginning of this chapter, an opportunity will be given to save selected filenames in the registry at the end of the program (you will learn more about the registry in Chapter 9). The SaveSetting command is used here, which consists of four main details: the key name (this is usually the name of the application as made available using *App.Title*), the subkey name (an arbitrary category name, called *Imagelist* in this case), the entry name (called *Filename* in this example, supplemented by a number that increases continually), and finally the value to be saved.

```
SaveSetting App.Title, "Imagelist", "Filename" _
  & intSlideNr, lstPlaylist.List(iSlideNr)
```

So, where should this command be inserted? In the program loop of the *Unload* procedure that stores the content of the list box. In order for the entries to be read again when the program is started, the *Load* procedure has to contain the counterpart to the SaveSetting command, the GetSetting function, which is called in a Do loop this time:

```
Dim iSlideNr As Integer
```

```
Do
 stTemp = GetSetting(App.Title, "Imagelist", "Filename" &
iSlideNr)
 If stTemp = "" Then Exit Do
  lstPlaylist.AddItem stTemp
  iSlideNr = iSlideNr + 1
Loop
```

From slide show to screen saver

To finish, we will take a look at the world of Windows programming. We will program a screen saver, which requires some special knowledge. A screen saver is a Windows program selected using the *Display* applet of the control panel, and called by Windows at specified regular intervals. In order for our slide show to become a screen saver, the following additions have to be made:

- Screen savers do not usually begin with a start form, but with a general module containing a procedure called *Main*. A general module therefore has to be added to the project, and the project properties configured accordingly.

- The project must be compiled in an *Exe* file using the FILE/MAKE menu command (this is not possible in the working model of Visual Basic 6.0), which before compilation has the typical *.Scr* extension and has to be placed in the SYSTEM32 directory (all screen savers are placed here).

- The program should be prevented from being called several times by querying App.PrevInstance = True in the *Form_Load* event.

- The command line option /c is evaluated using the Command function, as Windows passes these parameters if the user wishes to configure the screen saver using the control panel. If this parameter is passed, the *frmSlideShow* form is displayed.

- The command line option /s is the test mode of the screen saver. This causes the program to be called by Windows in the interval specified.

- Whenever a screen saver is selected in the tab, the /p option is passed, which can be used for display purposes in the small preview window. This is already more advanced to program, as the *frmSlide* form needs to run in the small rectangular area of the configuration dialogue. This can be achieved by calling half a dozen API functions (more on API functions in Chapter 10), but does require a good knowledge of Visual Basic programming.

- The mouse pointer is made invisible using the *ShowCursor* API function.

- As Windows calls the *frmSlide* form directly, some adjustments are required. Testing the program is also difficult, as it must be compiled in an *Exe* file first. When testing the program, it is recommended that the individual program areas be provided with `Msgbox` functions in order to be able to follow the development of the program and work with runtime error handling using the `On Error Goto` command, so that runtime errors do not immediately cause the program to crash, and so that they can be better localised.

These extensions are not too difficult for an experienced Visual Basic programmer, but one number is still too large at the beginning. You should use this view as an incentive to learn more Visual Basic programming.

Chapter 9

Point, Point, Brush stroke

User interfaces play a very important role in Visual Basic. We now follow on from the control elements explained in Chapter 4. This chapter outlines more advanced topics, such as menus, toolbars and how to insert additional control elements.

A well-thought-out user interface is very important for the utility value of a program. This applies especially when the program is going to be used for more than recreational purposes, and has to stand up to the critical scrutiny of an experienced user. Therefore, we are now going to outline the ABC of user interfaces with this program. Please note that a user interface is far more than just a form on which a few control elements are created. Its success depends on minor details, such as the order in which the entry fields are controlled using the ⬅ key, and the condition that individual fields can controlled on the basis of key combinations.

You will learn that an application can work freely with several forms, and that it is just as easy to make a form the 'chief' (the MDI form) within the inner area of which other forms are created automatically. You will find that the biggest surprise is that the toolbox is extendable, and you can extend it for a project every time in order to create new control elements with special properties. If you require an improved text box for input, a calendar for selecting dates easily, integrated media playback for playing MP3 files, or even a complete Web browser, all these building blocks can easily be called, added to the toolbox and created on a form. This is one of the strongest properties of Visual Basic, with which programmers are able to conjure up unusual interfaces on screen with very little effort.

So that this chapter does not concentrate solely on the theory, you will get to know the ABC of user interfaces using a small Visual Basic application. This is an image viewer, with which you can display, enlarge, reduce and copy images to the clipboard. Other programs can also do the same, but the special feature of this program is that it will be constructed step by step. A list of favourites will be implemented at the end of the chapter as an added extra. Your favourite images can then be displayed directly. Not every image program offers this facility.

Topics for this chapter are:

- an introduction to the image viewer;
- the MDI form;
- the application framework;
- the application contains a menu;
- the secret of ActiveX;
- standard dialogue boxes for file selection;
- implementing the window menu;

- the toolbar;
- the status bar;
- favourites list;
- suggestions for expansion.

Introduction to the image viewer

In this chapter, you will write a small Visual Basic program with which you can (in principle) display your favourite images. Certain similarities to the slide show from Chapter 8 are intended, but this example is an application that works with menus and several windows, rather than being simply an accessories program for the desktop. The special feature of the program is that it consists of a main form, where image files are opened using its menu bar. Every image loaded is displayed in a separate form. The image viewer will also offer a range of additional functions, such as transferring a displayed image to the clipboard or creating a favourite, so a loaded image can easily be displayed directly without having to select it via a file selection dialogue. Figure 9.1 shows the finished article in action.

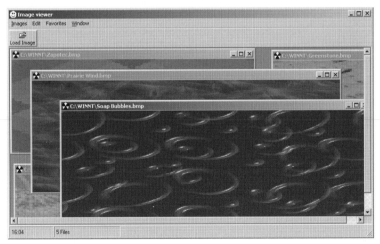

Figure 9.1: The image viewer in action.

The MDI form

As soon as a Visual Basic program contains several forms, an agreement has to be reached regarding the interaction of forms (i.e. the windows displayed). Two models can be selected in Windows. Either all Windows have equal rights, and can be moved and arranged anywhere on the screen, or one window is designated to be the 'chief', and therefore all other windows are subordinate to it. In this case, subordinate means that the other windows can only move within the main window inner area. Since this form of interaction is known as MDI (*Multiple Document Interface*) for historical reasons, the main form is known as the MDI form. You insert in a project using the PROJECT/ADD MDI FORM menu command (Figure 9.2). Please note that there can only be one MDI form per project.

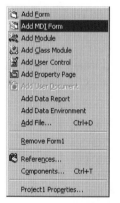

Figure 9.2: An MDI form is added using a separate menu command.

It is important to understand that the use of an MDI form in Visual Basic is not compulsory. The MDI concept always offers a few advantages if there is a main window and several (as many as required, in principle) subordinate windows with equal rights, labelled as 'child windows' in this context.

Compared with a normal form, an MDI form has some small differences. It has fewer properties, and only a few control elements can be created in the inner area of the form. However, this restriction is welcomed, as the MDI form usually exceeds the limits of the application, and, for example, contains no entry fields as child forms are provided for this.

The application framework

You know the idea behind an MDI application. Now we will create one. In this section the framework is created – the programming comes later on.

Use the following procedure to activate the program framework:

1 Start *Visual Basic* and create a new STANDARD EXE project.

2 Name the project *ImageViewer*.

3 Add an MDI form using the PROJECT/ADD MDI FORM command. The project is then extended to include a second form, which appears in Project Explorer.

4 Name the MDI form *mdiMain* in the properties window.

5 Enter *Image viewer* in the *Caption* property of the MDI form.

6 Name the existing form *frmImage* in the properties window.

7 Create an image control element on the *frmImage* form (at the bottom of the toolbox – the icon shows a hilly landscape with a sun). Name this *imgImage*.

8 Open the PROJECT menu, select the PROPERTIES entry and select the MDIMAIN MDI main form in the STARTOBJECT selection list as a start form.

9 Set the *MDIChild* property on the *frmImage* form to *True*. This is an important step, as this ensures that the form becomes an MDI child form.

10 Set the *AutoShowChildren* property to *False* in the properties window of the MDI form. This ensures that the existing child form is not displayed immediately when the program starts.

11 Start the test program using the F5 key. The MDI form is started (Figure 9.3), but the child form is not yet displayed. End the program again.

Figure 9.3: The MDI form is displayed.

The menu bar

There are no command buttons with an MDI form. The program functions are selected using menu and toolbars. A menu bar will now be added. A small program that is part of Visual Basic takes on this task. This is the *Menu Editor*, which is called using either the VIEW menu or Ctrl+E. Note that the form that is to contain the menu bar will need to be selected in advance.

Use the following procedure to add a menu to the MDI form:

1 Select the MDI form.

2 Press Ctrl+E to open the *Menu Editor (Figure 9.4)*. You will see a dialogue box in which the names of all menus and their entries are specified in the menu bar of the form. Use the four arrow buttons to specify where the entry is to appear. A name that is to appear in a menu, rather than as a menu in the menu bar, has to be indented to the right using the arrow keys. As menus can contain submenus, an entry can be indented several times. Two things are required per menu entry: the name to be displayed, and the name that the menu entry in the program is to respond to. The prefix *mnu* is usually added to the name here.

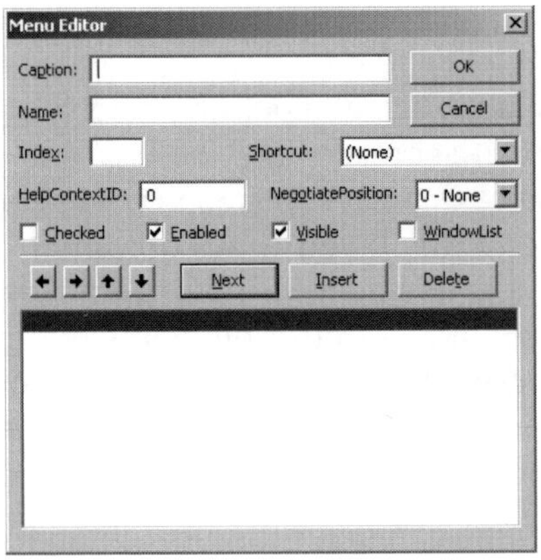

Figure 9.4: The menu is put together using the Menu Editor.

3 Enter *Images* in the *Caption* in the entry field and *mnuImages* in the *Name* entry field.

4 Click on the Next button and on the right arrow. This determines the next entry as a menu entry.

5 Enter *Load image* in the *Caption* property and *mnuLoadImage* in the *Name* entry field. This determines the first menu entry.

6 Click on the NEXT button and enter – (a minus sign) in the *Caption* entry field and *mnuPoint01* in the *Name* entry field. This inserts a horizontal hyphen.

7 Click on the NEXT button, enter *Exit* in the *Caption* entry field and *mnuExit* in the *Name* entry field.

8 The menu is now almost ready. Click on OK to close the Menu Editor.

9 Open the IMAGES menu, which should contain three entries (the hyphen counts as an entry, even though it cannot be selected) in total.

10 Start the program using the [F5] key. The menu bar is displayed.

Clicking a menu entry has no effect. This comes next – first you have to learn the standard dialogue box additional control element. Behind this peculiar name lies a simple but clever idea: the extension of the toolbox to *ActiveX control elements*.

The secret of ActiveX

There is no real secret behind *ActiveX*. In fact, ActiveX control elements are easy to operate. However, there is a small secret for the toolbox – it is extendable. Whenever you select the PROJECT/COMPONENTS menu command (or press Ctrl+T) a selection dialogue is displayed that contains the additional control elements that are available (Figure 9.5). These additional control elements used to be known as *ActiveX* control elements (when Microsoft was looking for an effective commercial measure to try and counteract the success of the Java programming language). These are normal control elements that, in principle, do not differ from the default control elements of the toolbox.

So, how should these additional control elements be approached? Quite simple. Check one of the names in the selection list and an icon is inserted in the toolbox, with which the control element can later be created on the form. Not all of the names displayed are used in Visual Basic (in fact, other applications can also work with ActiveX control elements), and nothing works without a corresponding explanation (this usually comes in the form of a help file).

Figure 9.5: All additional control elements available on the PC are displayed in the selection dialogue.

The toolbox will now be extended to include an additional control element that enables a small but very useful function: the display used for selecting a file in a 'built-in' Windows standard dialogue box for selecting a colour, font attributes or a printer. This additional control element is called the *Standard dialogue box*.

Use the following procedure to create a standard dialogue box control element on the form:

1 Select the MDI form (not the *frmImage* form).

2 Open the PROJECT menu and select the COMPONENTS entry. You will see an extensive dialogue box (Figure 9.6). Check the MICROSOFT COMMON DIALOGUE CONTROL 6.0 entry (SP3 or SP4 may be written at the end) and click on OK (you will find this somewhere in the centre of the list). A new icon appears in the toolbox.

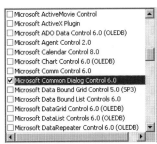

Figure 9.6: The standard dialogue box control element is now selected from the component list.

3 Create the standard dialogue box control element on the form. It is irrelevant where you position it, and the size cannot be modified, as the control element is invisible during runtime.

4 Name the standard dialogue box control element *cdlFile* (its original name was *Commondialogue1*).

Nothing happens yet In order for a dialogue box to be displayed so that you can select a filename, the *ShowOpen* method must be called. This is what happens in the next step.

Displaying the file selection dialogue box

The file selection dialogue should always be displayed if the user clicks the LOAD IMAGE entry in the IMAGES menu. As this occurs whenever the *Click* event is triggered with the menu entry, the dialogue box must be displayed in the *Click* event procedure

Use the following procedure to display the file selection:

1 Select the MDI form and switch to the program code window using F7.

2 Insert the following commands in the *General* section (underneath the explicit option):

```
Private sFilename As String
```

The `sFilename` variable later contains the path of the selected file. This should apply to the whole module, as the *General* section is declared here.

3 Switch to the MDI form using ⇧+F7, open the IMAGES menu, and click on the LOAD IMAGE entry. This takes you back to the program code window, but this time in the framework of the *Click* event procedure, which is always called when the entry is selected.

4 Enter the following commands in the *Click* event procedure:

```
With cdlFile
  .Filter = "Bitmaps (*.bmp, *.gif, *.jpg,
*.wmf)|*.bmp;*.gif;*.jpg;*.wmf)|All Files|*.*"
  .InitDir = "C:\My Documents\My Pictures"
  .dialogueTitle = "Select an image file"
  .FileName = ""
  .ShowOpen
  sFilename = .FileName
End With
If sFilename = "" Then
  Exit Sub
End If
MsgBox "Selected file:" & sFilename
```

Be careful when entering data in the line where the *Filter* property contains a value: there should be no line break in this line. A filter offers different file types for selection in the FILETYPE selection list of the standard dialogue box (Figure 9.7). It specifies which file types are displayed at the beginning, and which are not. The filter consists of two parts: a general description (which could be anything) and one or several file filters (e.g. *.bmp). The sections are both separated by a vertical line, and the individual filters by a semicolon.

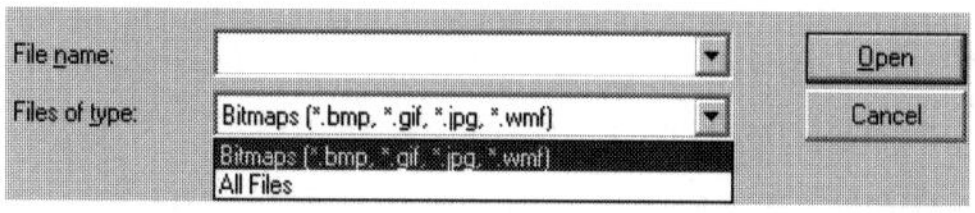

Figure 9.7: The file selection dialogue box offers several file types using a filter.

5 Start the program using the F5 key. Select LOAD IMAGE from the IMAGES menu. The usual file selection dialogue should appear in Windows, from which any image file can be selected. After confirming with OK, the path of the selected file will be displayed. Nothing more happens at this point.

6 End the program and remove the `Msgbox` call in the *Click* procedure, as this is for test purposes only.

Displaying a selected image file

Selecting a file using the file selection dialogue box causes the full directory path to become available using the *FileName* property of the standard dialogue box. The file is not yet loaded. The program will need to do this. An image selected using the file selection should be displayed in an image box on a new form. In other words, for every image selected, a new form should also be displayed.

We now turn to a more complicated topic. It is not possible to insert a form in the project for every image to be loaded. Three or five images are fine, but trying to load 100 or more images would cause chaos. Instead, the form for every new image selected has to be created and displayed during runtime. This produces the following command sequence:

```
Dim oImageFrm As frmImage
Set oImageFrm = New frmImage
oImageFrm.imgImage.Picture = LoadPicture(sFilename)
oBildFrm.Visible = True
```

These commands are fairly tricky. First, a variable is declared. This is called `oImageFrm` (the exact name of the variable doesn't really matter) and has the name of the form *frmImage* as a data type. This means that it can later stand for a *frmImage* type of form. Just like a photocopier, a form can duplicate itself in this way without having to be added to the project several times. However, the variable is currently empty (it has the special value *Nothing*). This will now change. A new *frmImage* form (currently invisible) will now be created using the `Set` command in connection with `New`. The image box on this newly created form will contain its content. In this example, you will learn how control elements on other forms react. Simply place the name of the form in front. Finally, the form will be made visible by setting the *Visible* property to true. The loaded image will then be displayed.

Use the following procedure:

1 Add a module using the PROJECT/ADD MODULE menu command. This module should contain variables that can be used by all program forms (another form will be added later).

2 Name the new module *basGeneral* by selecting the module then changing the name in the properties window (the original name is *Module1*) (Figure 9.8).

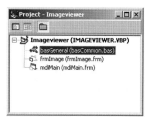

Figure 9.8: The project is extended to include a general module.

3 Select the module in Project Explorer and switch to the program code window using [F7].

4 Enter the following command in the program code window:

```
Public oImageFrm As frmImage
```

This command defines the variable `oImageFrm`, which also responds to the MDI form. This is a public variable.

5 Select the MDI form in Project Explorer, switch to the program code window, change to the *Click* event procedure from *mnuLoadImage,* and insert the following commands at the end of the procedure (the procedure already contains commands):

```
Set oImageFrm = New frmImage
oImageFrm.imgImage.Picture = LoadPicture(sFilename)
oImageFrm.Visible = True
oImageFrm.Caption = sFilename
```

6 Start the program using the [F5] key. Open the IMAGES menu, select the LOAD IMAGE entry, and then select an image. This will now be displayed in a form. If you modify the size of the form, the size of the image will also change. If you load another image, this will be displayed in a new form.

Ending the program

Even though almost every application can be closed using the close box in the right-hand corner of the title bar, the menu on the far left-hand side (which is usually the FILE menu in most applications) should also contain an EXIT command.

Use the following procedure to install the EXIT command:

1 Switch to the program code window of the MDI form using [F7].

2 Select the MNUEXIT command from the left hand selection list.

3 Insert the following command in the *Click* event procedure:

```
Unload Me
```

This command unloads the MDI form (Me always stands for the form in which the command is located), which ends the program.

Small enhancements to the menu

The menu is now fully functional, but it could be improved in two ways to simplify its operation:

1. Selecting the menu using the [Alt] key.

2. Selecting a menu entry using a key combination.

Both modifications are made in the Menu Editor. You must use the following procedure:

1 Select the MDI form and open the *Menu Editor* using [Ctrl]+[E].

2 Place a & character before the I in the IMAGES menu name. The menu can now be called using [Alt]+[B].

3 Select the Load image entry and select the Ctrl+O key combination from the SHORTCUT selection list. This entry can now be called using [Ctrl]+[O].

4 Close the Menu Editor again.

Proceed with all important menus and menu entries in this way. Look at the menus of other applications – you will find similar shortcuts.

Improving the image display

So far, so good. But the image display is not yet particularly attractive. The image appears completely out of place. This can be improved with a little effort. You have to inform the display that you will place the image in the upper left-hand corner immediately after loading the form, and that whenever the size of the form is modified, the image should likewise be modified accordingly. This is done using the *Load* and *Resize* event procedures.

Use the following procedure to modify the display automatically according to the size of the form:

1 Switch to the program code window from *frmImage* and select the *Form_Load* event procedure. Insert the following commands:

```
With imgImage
  .Left = 0
  .Top = 0
  .Stretch = True
End With
```

2 Select the *Form_Resize* event procedure and enter the following commands:

```
With imgImage
  .Width = Me.ScaleWidth
  .Height = Me.ScaleHeight
End With
```

3 Start the program using F5 and load an image. The image will be displayed in full size in the inner area of the form. If you modify the size of the form, the size of the image should also change accordingly.

Implementing the window menu

MDI forms offer the programmer a convenient function. A menu that lists all previously opened (child) windows can be displayed without the need for additional program commands. If the windows need to be displayed on top of or next to each other, the *Arrange* method of the MDI form is required. You will find this WINDOW menu with nearly all MDI applications.

Use the following procedure to implement a WINDOW menu in the menu bar:

1 Select the MDI form and open the *Menu Editor* using Ctrl+E (the program will have to be closed again).

2 Select the bottom entry, and enter *Window* in the *Caption* and *mnuWindow* in the *Name* properties.

3 Select the WINDOWLIST option in the *Menu Editor*.

4 Click on NEXT to add another entry.

5 Enter *Vertical* for the *Caption* and *mnuVertical* for the *Name* properties. Click once on the *Right arrow* button to indent the entry toward the right.

6 Click on NEXT to add another entry.

7 Enter *Horizontal* for *Caption* and *mnuHorizontal* for *Name*.

8 Click on NEXT to add another entry.

9 Enter *Cascade* for *Caption* and *mnuCascade* for *Name*.

10 Click on NEXT to add another entry.

11 Enter *Arrange icons* for *Caption* and *mnu ArrangeIcons* for *Name*.

12 Click on OK to close the Menu Editor.

13 Open the WINDOW menu and select the HORIZONTAL entry. Enter the following command in the *Click* event procedure settings:

```
mdiMain.Arrange vbTileHorizontal
```

14 Select the MNUVERTICAL entry from the left-hand selection list. Enter the following command in the *Click* event procedure settings:

```
mdiMain.Arrange vbTileVertical
```

15 Select the MNUCASCADE entry from the left-hand selection list. Enter the following command in the *Click* event procedure settings:

```
mdiMain.Arrange vbCascade
```

16 Select the MNUARRANGEICONS entry from the left-hand selection list. Enter the following command in the *Click* event procedure settings:

```
mdiMain.Arrange vbArrangeIcons
```

17 Start the program using the [F5] key (don't forget to save the project in the meantime, as this does not happen automatically when the program is started after modifications have been made). Load some images and open the WINDOW menu (Figure 9.9). The name of all image files loaded should be displayed here. Test the different commands when arranging the sequence. The ARRANGE ICONS command can only work if a few windows are reduced to icon size and moved.

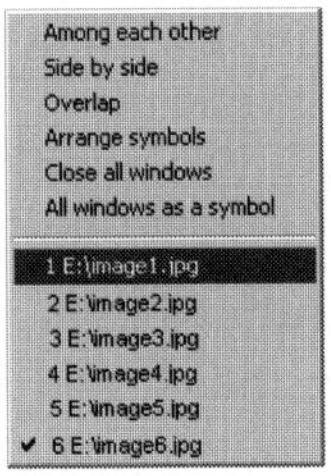

Figure 9.9: The WINDOW *menu lists all opened windows.*

The toolbar

Every modern application has a toolbar as well as a menu bar. There is no editor for the toolbar. Instead, an additional control element is added to the application.

So where do we find this toolbar – is it contained in the toolbox? Yes, but not at the start. The toolbar is one of Windows' standard control elements that has to be added to the toolbox after a project has been created. You should always use the following procedure:

1 Open the PROJECT menu and select COMPONENTS. The current component selection list appears.

Figure 9.10: The MICROSOFT WINDOWS COMMON CONTROLS 6.0 *additional control element is selected from the component selection list.*

2 Check the MICROSOFT WINDOWS COMMON CONTROLS 6.0 entry (Figure 9.10). Please note the exact notation (the name may be followed by SP3 or SP4).

3 Confirm your selection with OK. Eight new images appear in the toolbox (if they don't, you have not selected the right entry). The toolbar is also one of the new control elements.

Adding a control element always occurs in the same way, so nothing more will be mentioned in the following steps.

A word of warning: programming a toolbar is an extensive process. You will see that the images are not added easily. They come from an image list, an additional control element that has to be created on the form.

Use the following procedure to add a toolbar to the MDI form:

1 Execute the PROJECT/COMPONENTS menu command, check the MICROSOFT WINDOWS COMMON CONTROLS 6.0 entry, and confirm the selection with OK.

2 Select the MDI form and add a toolbar and image list from the toolbox. The toolbar is positioned automatically on the upper margin (Figure 9.11). The position of the image list is not important.

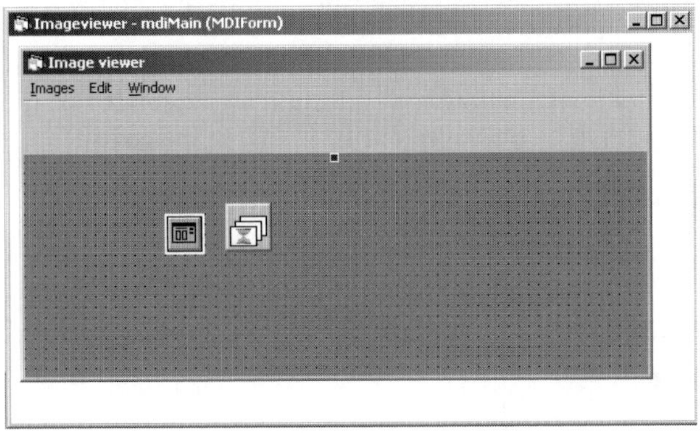

Figure 9.11: The MDI form is extended to include a toolbar.

3 Name the toolbar *tlbMain* and the image list *imlIcons*.

4 Select the image list, switch to the Properties window, and click on the three points in the *Custom* entry. A dialogue box opens in which the most important settings of the image list are summarised.

5 Select the IMAGES tab (Figure 9.12).

6 Click on Insert Image to add images to the image list. It doesn't matter which images you use, *Ico* or *Bmp* files with a size of 32x32 pixels (such icons can be made using Paint or a special icon editor).

7 Insert at least one icon for each planned tool button. For our example, you currently require only one icon for an OPEN button.

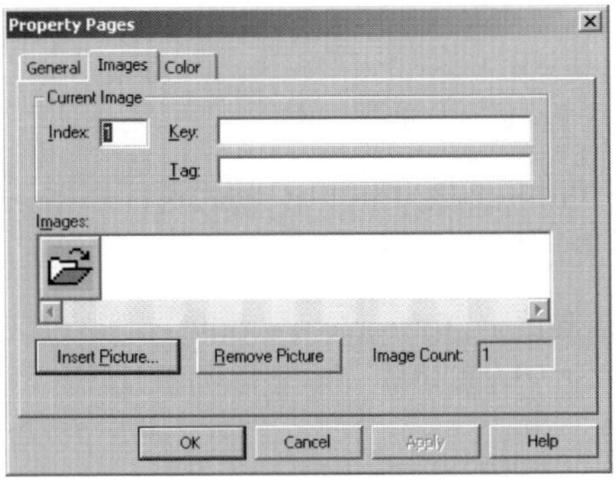

Figure 9.12: The image list is filled with icons in the IMAGES tab.

8 Close the dialogue box using the OK button.

9 Select the tool button, switch to the Properties window, and click on the three points in the *Custom* entry. A dialogue box opens in which the most important settings of the tool button are summarised.

10 Select the IMLIMAGES entry from the IMAGELIST selection list (Figure 9.13). This is our image list. It makes images to be displayed available for the image list.

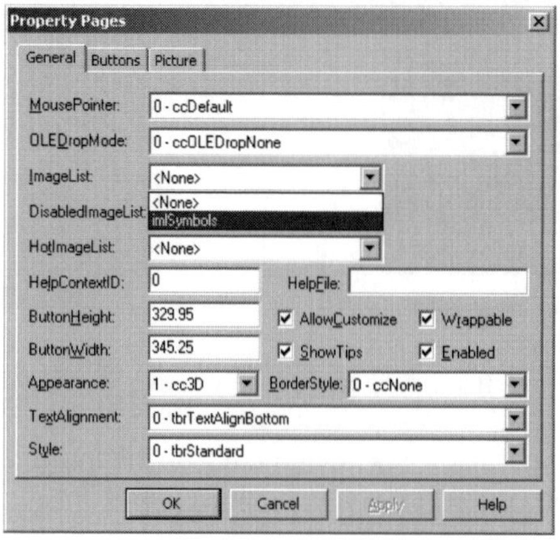

Figure 9.13: The tool button is connected to the image list with this selection list.

11 Switch to the BUTTONS tab.

12 Click on ADD BUTTON.

13 Enter *Load image* in the *Caption* file.

14 Enter the number *1* in the *Image* box. This assigns the image with an index of 1 from the image list to the button.

15 Enter *Load* in the *Key* field. The button can later alternatively respond to its index number using this key, the name of which does not matter.

16 Enter *Loads a new image* in the *ToolTipText* box. This text appears later when the mouse pointer is moved over the tool button.

17 Close the dialogue box using the OK button. The toolbar should contain a tool button in which the OPEN icon can be seen (Figure 9.14).

Figure 9.14: The toolbar contains its first button.

18 The toolbar now has to be subject to a little programming, as it has yet to be specified what happens when a button is clicked. Double-click the toolbar. This takes you into the *ButtonClick* event procedure. This procedure is always called when one of the buttons is clicked. The button is defined with the *Button* argument, which is passed when called.

So what happens when the OPEN button is clicked? Exactly the same should happen as when the LOAD IMAGE menu entry in the IMAGE menu is selected. You now have three options:

1. You can enter the commands again from the *mnuLoadimage_Click* event procedure.

2. You can call the *mnuLoadimage_Click* event procedure from *tlbMain_ButtonClick*.

3. You can create a new procedure called *Loadimage* that contains the commands from *mnuLoadimage_Click*. This procedure is called both by *mnuLoadimage_Click* and *tlbMain_ButtonClick*.

Option 1 should not be used given your relatively advanced knowledge as using identical commands in the same program is never a good solution. Option 3 is the best, but you have already typed enough, so creating a new procedure should be left alone for the time being. Option 2 is therefore the best for this example.

19 Insert the following command in the *tlbMain_ButtonClick* event procedure:

```
If Button.Key = "Load" Then
  mnuLoadimage_Click
End If
```

The query of the *Key* property regarding the *Button* object is required, otherwise it could not be determined which button was clicked. The value of the *Key* property was entered in the properties dialogue of the toolbar. If the value agrees (which is always the case in the current development stage of the program), the *mnuLoadimage_Click* procedure is called. For this, only the name of the procedure needs to be given. Visual Basic recognises the CALL command for this purpose, but this is merely the intricacies of detail, and is surplus to requirements.

20 Start the program using the F5 key. If you click on the new tool button, the same selection field as when the LOAD IMAGE menu entry was selected should appear. This is hardly surprising, as the same commands were executed.

The status bar

As a final visual improvement, the MDI form should contain a status bar. The status bar is an area on the lower margin where text, bitmaps or other control elements can be displayed.

Use the following procedure to add a status bar to the MDI form:

1 Select the MDI form and transfer a status bar from the toolbox on to the form. This will be positioned automatically at the lower edge of the form in full width (Figure 9.15).

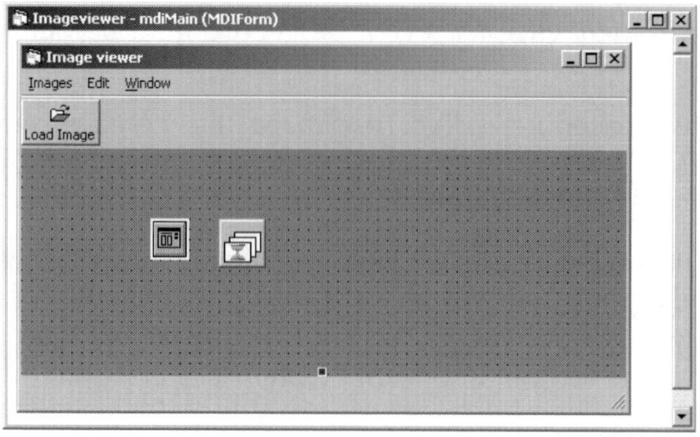

Figure 9.15: A status bar is arranged on the form.

2 Name the status bar *staStatus*.

3 Select the status bar, switch to the properties window and click on the three points in the *Custom* entry. A dialogue box opens that summarises the most important settings of the status bar.

4 Switch to the BASES tab.

5 Click on the ADD BASES button. A second button is then inserted.

6 Set STYLE SBRTIME in the selection list for the first button. This causes the current time to be displayed in this button.

7 Switch to the second button using the small *Right arrow* button on the right-hand side of the *Index* entry field.

8 Enter *Amount* in the *Key* entry field. The button can later respond alternatively to its index number using this key, the name of which does not matter.

9 Enter *Width 2200* in the entry field. This should be the approximate width of the second area. This value may have to be modified at a later stage.

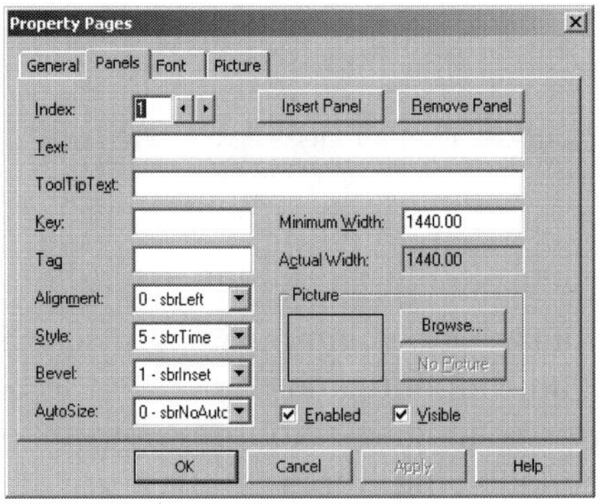

Figure 9.16: The properties of the status bar are also configured in the Properties dialogue box.

10 Close the dialogue box using the OK button.

11 In the second area of the status bar, the number of images currently loaded should be displayed. This number is saved in a variable, which still has to be inserted in the program. Switch to the general module (*basGeneral*) and insert the following declaration:

```
Public iAmountImages As Integer
```

This variable should increase by one every time an image is loaded, and should be decreased by one every time a form with an image is closed. The places in the program responsible for this are the *Form_Load* and *Form_Unload* event procedures of the *frmImage* form. These procedures are always called whenever a new form with an image is loaded or closed. At this point, the `iAmountImages` variable increases or decreases by one. The current value of the variable also has to be output in the status bar.

12 Switch to the program code window of the *frmImage* form.

13 Insert the following commands at the end of the *Form_Load* procedure:

```
iAmountImages = iAmountImages + 1
mdiMain.staStatus.Panels("Amount").Text = _
  iAmountImages & " Files"
```

14 Enter the following commands in the *Form_Unload* procedure:

```
iAmountImages = iAmountImages - 1
mdiMain.staStatus.Panels("Amount").Text = _
  iAmountImages & " Files"
```

197

15 Start the program using the [F5] key. After an image is loaded, the current number of images should be displayed in the status bar. If you close an image, the number decreases by one.

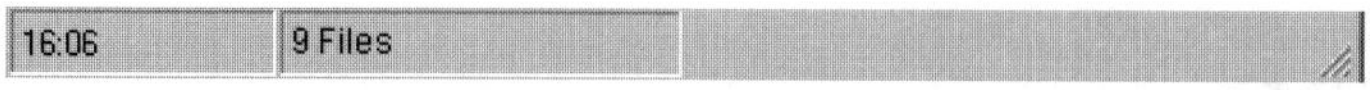

```
16:06        9 Files
```

Figure 9.17: The status bar also shows the number of loaded images next to the time.

A favourites list

It is possible to save the names of previously loaded images in a list so that these images can be called directly next time around, and do not have to be selected using the file selection dialogue. Managing favourites consists of another menu, which should contain the following entries:

- Add favourite
- Organise favourites

When selecting names, one small rule should be applied: menu names should be kept as short and concise as possible. The way in which the program 'remembers' these favourites before being closed is far more important. A favourite is merely the complete directory path of a file containing an image. You have already seen a programming technique in Chapter 7 where individual directory paths were saved. In this section, you will learn a second, more important variant for the long-term storage of data – the registry.

As managing your favourites consists of a form with a list box (for displaying favourites) and two buttons for deleting and displaying favourites, a project will first be extended to include a new form.

Use the following procedure to add an extra form:

1 Switch to the program window of the *basGeneral* general module and enter the following command:

```
Public colFavourites As Collection
```

This defines a *Collection* object (more on this Chapter 10). This should save the directory path of favourite images during runtime. So that it can be used by all other forms, it is declared in the general module.

2 Switch to the program window of the MDI form and enter the following command in the *MDIForm_Load* event procedure:

```
Set colFavourites = New Collection
```

This command creates a new *Collection* object immediately after the actual program is started.

3 Add another form using PROJECT/ADD FORM.

4 Name the form *frmFavourites*.

5 Enter *Organise Favourites* in the *Caption* property.

6 Set the *MDIChild* property of the form to true, as it should also be an MDI child window.

7 Set the *BorderStyle* property to true, as it should not be adjustable in size later.

8 Create a list box on the form and name it *lstFavourites*.

9 Create a command button on the form and name it *cmdImages*. Enter *Display &Image* in the *Caption* property.

10 Create another command button on the form and name it *cmdDelete*. Enter *Delete &Image* in the *Caption* property (Figure 9.18).

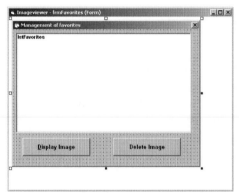

Figure 9.18: The form for organising favourites contains a list box and two command buttons.

11 Insert the following command in the *Form_Load* event procedure of *frmFavourites*:

```
ListFavourites
```

This command simply calls the *ListFavourites* procedure, which has yet to be defined.

12 Scroll to the bottom of the form and enter the following procedure definition:

```
Sub ListFavourites()
  Dim nInx As Long
  lstFavourites.Clear
  For nInx = 1 To colFavourites.Count
     lstFavourites.AddItem colFavourites.Item(nInx)
  Next
  If lstFavourites.ListCount > 1 Then
    lstFavourites.ListIndex = 0
  End If
End Sub
```

This procedure processes all elements of the *Collection* object in sequence and transfers the names (i.e. the directory paths) into the *lstFavourites* list box. Finally, the first entry is selected using the *ListIndex* property, but only if the list box contains an entry.

13 Insert the following commands in the *Click* event procedure of *cmdDisplayImage*:

```
If lstFavourites.ListIndex = -1 Then
  MsgBox "Please select an image first!"
  Exit Sub
End If
Set oImageFrm = New frmImage
oImageFrm.imgImage.Picture = LoadPicture(lstFavour-
ites.Text)
oImageFrm.Caption = lstFavourites.Text
oImageFrm.Visible = True
```

A selected image is displayed in a new *frmImage* type of form after using this command, which should be familiar to you as it is used in the MDI main form after an image is loaded. This time, the file path comes from the list box. The query of the *ListIndex* property is necessary, because an image can only be displayed if an entry is selected in the list box. If this is not the case, you will see that the *ListIndex* entry contains the value *-1*.

14 Enter the following commands in the *Click* event procedure of *cmdDeleteImage*:

```
If lstFavourites.ListIndex = -1 Then
  MsgBox "Please select an image!"
  Exit Sub
End If
colFavourites.Remove lstFavourites.ListIndex + 1
ListFavourites
```

15 The new Favourites form should also be able to be called using the MDI form menu. A new menu is required. It should be named *Favourites*, and should contain the entries ADD FAVOURITE and ORGANISE FAVOURITES. Select the MDI form and press Ctrl+E to call the MENU EDITOR again.

16 Select the WINDOW entry and click on INSERT to insert a new entry.

17 Enter *Favourites* in the *Caption* field and *mnuFavourites* in the *Name* field.

18 Click on INSERT to insert another entry.

19 Enter *Add favourite* in the *Caption* field and *mnuAddFavourite* in the *Name* field.

20 Click on the *Right arrow* button to indent the entry by one position.

21 Click on NEXT and on ADD to add another entry.

22 Enter *Organise favourites* in the *Caption* field and *mnuOrganiseFavourites* in the *Name* field.

23 Click on the *Right arrow* button to indent the entry by one position.

24 Assign the shortcut *Ctrl+L* to the *Organise Favourites* entry, so it can easily be called later.

25 Close the MENU EDITOR using the OK button.

26 Switch to the program code window, select the MNUFAVOURITES entry from the left hand selection list, and then insert the following commands in the *Click* procedure:

```
mnuAddFavourites.Enabled = False
If Not ActiveForm Is Nothing Then
   If TypeOf ActiveForm Is frmImage = True Then
     mnuAddFavourites.Enabled = True
   End If
End If
```

These commands ensure that the *Add Favourite* entry can only be selected if an image form is the active form, otherwise the command would not make sense. Active forms are accessed using `ActiveForm`. Compared with `Nothing`, it is checked whether a form is active at all. If this is the case, the *Enabled* property of the menu entry is set to true, otherwise it remains false.

201

27 Select the ADD TO FAVOURITES entry from the left-hand selection list, and insert the following command in the *Click* procedure:

```
colFavourites.Add ActiveForm.Caption
```

This command inserts the active form heading (remember that this contains the complete path of the loaded image) in the *Collection* object. The *Collection* object is explained in detail in Chapter 10. This is preferable in this case as it is very useful for our image viewer.

28 Select the MNUORGANISEFAVOURITES from the left-hand selection list in the program code window, and then insert the following command in the *Click* event procedure:

```
frmFavourites.Show
frmFavourites.SetFocus
```

This command displays the *frmFavourites* form. The focus is then set using the *SetFocus* method, which is always required if already visible, and should be brought to the foreground be selecting the menu entry.

Figure 9.19: The Favourites *menu is added using the* MENU EDITOR.

The registry

The image viewer can remember favourites and is able to display the image behind a favourite. But what happens when the program is closed and then started again? All the favourites have gone. This is hardly surprising as they weren't saved anywhere. That will change in this section. Even if it is worth saving the name of a directory path behind a favourite in a file, you will learn how to access the registry as an alternative in this section.

The Windows *registry* is not a secret place to which only Windows gurus and specialists have access. It is a general file in which not only Windows but all other programs can save their settings and configuration files. It is very large (and so can be a little disconcerting to many users) and consists of thousands of files. The special feature of the registry is that it has a hierarchical structure. This means that files can have subfiles, subfiles can have subdirectories, and so on. These subfiles are known as *keys*. Here is an example of a key:

`HKEY_CURRENT_USER\Software\VB and VBA Program Settings`

This key path consists of three keys: `HKEY_CURRENT_ USER`, `Software` and `VB and VBA Program Settings`. Don't worry about the names. These are easily determinable and have no profound meaning on the whole. Each key can have a range of entries. These entries subdivide a file (the key) into a number of individual pockets. Each entry has only one value, which could be, for example, a configuration setting. The values are the actual data stored in the registry.

Even though the registry is huge, there is an area reserved for Visual Basic programs. This is the highest listed key. The settings of every Visual Basic program can be stored here. Visual Basic makes the following commands and functions available for accessing this area of the registry:

- the `SaveSetting` command

- the `GetSetting` function

- the `GetAllSettings` function

- the `DeleteSetting` command

The `SaveSetting` command saves a value in a subkey in the `HKEY_CURRENT _USER\Software\VB and VBA Program Settings` area. You have to enter three things to execute the command:

- the name of the subkey

- the name of the entry

- the value to be saved.

The name of the subkey usually corresponds to the name of an application. This is obtained using the *Title* property of the *App* object, i.e. using `App.Title`. The name of the entry can be changed at will. In this case, we will use 'Favourites' to refer to our image viewer. It is important that the same name is used when the `GetSetting` function is used. Finally, enter the value to be saved, which will usually be a character string.

The following command saves the `nColour` command in the registry:

```
Dim nColour As Long
nColour = vbRed
SaveSetting App.Title, "Settings", "Colour", nColour
```

Constructing the `GetSetting` function as follows retrieves this value:

```
nColour = GetSetting(App.Title, "Settings", "Colour")
```

As well as `SaveSetting` and `GetSetting`, Visual Basic also uses the `GetAllSettings` function. This returns all values with their values of a key in the form of a two-dimensional string array (more on arrays in Chapter 10). Even if these are not required for the image viewer, they should be outlined briefly.

The following command sequence returns all entries of the *Settings* subkey:

```
Dim aValues() As String
aValues = GetAllSettings("Project1", "Settings")
Debug.Print aValues(0, 0)
Debug.Print aValues(0, 1)
```

The `DeleteSetting` command is also used. This deletes single or all entries of a key and is required in our example to delete all lists of favourites from the registry before saving again so no card files are left over.

```
DeleteSetting "Project1", "Settings"
```

Both `GetAllSettings` and `DeleteSetting` lead to a runtime error if the value entered does not exist. Because of this, the following extension is used to complement runtime error handling using the `On Error Resume Next` command, which will be introduced in Chapter 10.

That's enough theory – let's concentrate on the add-on to the image viewer. Use the following procedure to implement the extension for saving and re-reading favourite entries:

1 Switch to the program code window of the MDI form and enter the following procedure at the end of the form:

```
Sub SaveFavourites()
  Dim nInx As Long
  Dim sPath As String
  On Error Resume Next
  DeleteSetting App.Title, "Favourites"
  On Error GoTo 0
  For nInx = 1 To colFavouritesCount
    SaveSetting App.Title, "Favourites", "Path" &
CStr(nInx), colFavourites.Item(nInx)
  Next
End Sub
```

The procedure has the purpose of saving the content of the *colFavourites Collection* object, which saves favourites during runtime in the registry.

2 Enter the following procedure in the program code window of the MDI form:

```
Sub ReadFavourites()
  Dim nInx As Long
  Dim sPath As String
  Do
    nInx = nInx + 1
    sPath = GetSetting(App.Title, "Favourites", "Path" &
CStr(nInx), "")
    If sPath = "" Then
      Exit Do
    End If
    colFavourites.Add sPath
  Loop
End Sub
```

The task of this procedure is to select all (possibly) saved entries and insert them in the *colFavourites Collection* object.

3 Insert the following command at the end of the *Form_Load* event procedure:

```
ReadFavourites
```

This is the call of the *ReadFavourites* procedure, which transfers favourites saved in the registry to the *Collection* object.

4 Insert the following command at the end of the *Form_Unload* event procedure:

```
SaveFavourites
```

And this is the call of the *SaveFavourites* procedure, which transfers saved favourites to the registry.

5 Start the program using the F5 key. Load a few images and save these as favourites. End the program, restart it and call the 'Organise Favourites' function. The entries should now be available as before, as they were saved automatically in the registry at the end of the program (Figure 9.20).

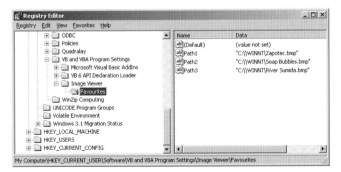

Figure 9.20: The favourite entries are saved in the registry.

205

That's it. Our image viewer is (at least for the time being) ready (Figure 9.21). As a reward, you now have a small program that can do far more than previously. Now, start the program using the [F5] key and try it out. Load an image, add it to the favourites list with FAVOURITES/ADD FAVOURITE and call the 'Organise Favourites' function using FAVOURITES/ORGANISE FAVOURITES.

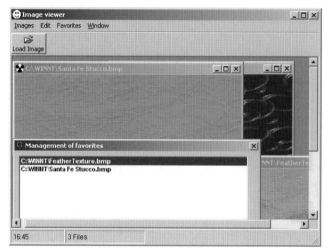

Figure 9.21: It was worth the effort – the extended image viewer in action.

Access to the clipboard

Nearly every application has an EDIT menu, which includes the COPY and PASTE commands. Your image viewer should also be able to do that. Visual Basic offers the *Clipboard* object for access to the clipboard. You will have to know the following methods:

- the *GetFormat* method
- the *GetText* method
- the *GetData* method
- the *SetText* method
- the *SetData* method
- the *Clear* method.

In order to appreciate this wide selection of methods better, you need to become familiar with the principle of the clipboard. It can only ever contain one item of a specified format (bitmap, text, files, and so on) at any one time.

When accessing the clipboard, one generally proceeds by asking the clipboard whether it contains text or a bitmap, and the clipboard duly replies with true or false. Text content is then retrieved using the *GetText* method, and bitmap content is retrieved using the *GetData* method.

The following command sequence first asks whether the clipboard contains text, and if it does places it in a variable:

```
Dim sContent As String
If Clipboard.GetFormat(vbCFText) = True Then
  sContent = Clipboard.GetTex
End If
```

Visual Basic uses constants to determine format, such as vbCFText and vbCFBitmap.

Placing text or bitmaps on the clipboard is easy. Call *SetText* or *SetData*.

Before the EDIT menu is implemented, one last formality should be clarified. The EDIT menu should only contain the PASTE entry if there is a bitmap in the clipboard to paste, and it should only contain the COPY entry if the image form is the active form, so there is something to copy. This is verified in the *Click* event procedure of the EDIT menu.

Use the following procedure to implement the EDIT menu and its two entries.

1 Select the MDI form and press Ctrl+E to open the MENU EDITOR again.

2 Select the FAVOURITES entry and click on INSERT to insert a new entry.

3 Enter *Edit* in the *Caption* field and *mnuEdit* in the *Name* field.

4 Click on NEXT and then INSERT to insert an entry.

5 Enter *Copy* in the *Caption* field and *mnuCopy* in the *Name* field.

6 Assign the shortcut Ctrl+C to the menu entry.

7 Click on the *Right arrow* to indent the entry by one position.

8 Click on NEXT and then on INSERT to insert another entry.

9 Enter *Paste* in the *Caption* field and *mnuPaste* in the *Name* field.

10 Assign the Ctrl+V shortcut to the entry.

11 Click on the *Right arrow* button to indent the entry by one position.

12 Close the Menu Editor using OK.

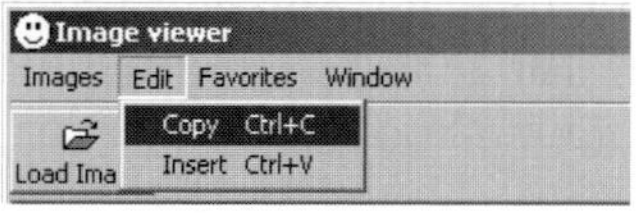

Figure 9.22: The new EDIT *menu contains two entries with which you should be familiar.*

13 Switch to the program code window, select the MNUEDIT entry from the left-hand selection list, and insert the following commands in the *Click* procedure:

```
mnuPaste.Enabled = Clipboard.GetFormat(vbCFBitmap)
mnuCopy.Enabled = False
If Not ActiveForm Is Nothing Then
  If TypeOf ActiveForm Is frmImage Then
    mnuCopy.Enabled = True
  End If
End If
```

Every time the EDIT menu is opened, these commands check whether a bitmap is located in the clipboard, and whether an image form is the active form, so it knows whether it needs to provide the PASTE and COPY commands, respectively.

14 Select the *mnuPaste* entry from the left-hand selection list, and then insert the following commands in the *Click* procedure:

```
Set oImageFrm = New frmImage
oImageFrm.imgImage.Picture = Clipboard.GetData(vbCFBitmap)
oImageFrm.Visible = True
oImageFrm.Caption = "Clipboard " & Time
```

These commands paste the current bitmap content from the clipboard into a newly created image form. The time is appended to the name *Clipboard* as a heading (there is no filename in this case).

15 Select the *mnuCopy* entry from the left-hand selection list, and then enter the following commands in the *Click* procedure:

```
Clipboard.SetData ActiveForm.imgImage.Picture
```

This is a refreshingly short event procedure for a change. The command now copies the content of the display in the active form on to the clipboard.

16 Start the program using the F5 key. Start another graphics program such as Paint, load an image and copy it to the clipboard. Switch to the image viewer. You should be able to insert the image using Ctrl+V.

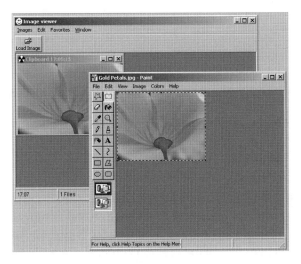

Figure 9.23: Our image viewer is now an integral part of the Windows applications family – at least as far as transferring data via the clipboard is concerned.

Congratulations. You have succeeded in implementing quite a substantial program. If you were to print out the entire program listing using the FILE/ PRINT menu command, it would produce a list several sheets long.

Suggestions for expansion

No program is ever complete. This also applies to our image viewer. A search function would be nice, and a print function very practical, and a few additional tools would look good on the toolbar. This can all be done with relatively little effort. We will now implement an obvious expansion – the option of selecting several files at once. You will realise that an apparently simple extension can lead to a massive alteration of the existing program structure.

Closing all windows at once

The WINDOW menu should contain a command with which all windows can be closed at once. Insert an entry called *mnuCloseAllWindows* at the end of the Window menu using the MENU EDITOR, and enter the *CloseAllWindows* value in the *Caption* property. Insert the following commands in the *Click* event procedure:

```
Dim oF As Form
For Each oF In Forms
```

```
If TypeOf OF Is frmImage Then
  Unload oF
End If
Next oF
```

The `Forms` listing is in the middle of the procedure. This stands for all opened forms. It can be processed using the `For Each` loop (you will learn this version of the `For` loop in Chapter 10). Since the 'Organising Favourites' function can be an open window, it has to be verified whether this is a *frmImage* type of form using the `TypeOf` operator.

Minimising all windows at once

Now that all windows can be closed at once, all windows should be able to be minimised. This command is also made available through the WINDOW menu. With your present knowledge this should be fairly easy, especially as the procedure is almost identical to that of the previous section. Here is a tip for you: a form is minimised by setting the *WindowState* property to *1 (vbMinimized)*.

Selecting several files at once

Wouldn't it be practical if you could select several files in the image viewer? Other programs have this option. No problem, all you need to do is instruct the standard dialogue box to allow multiple selection. This instruction is given by entering a value in the *Flags* property of the standard dialogue box control element, consisting of two constants:

```
cdlOFNAllowMultiselect + cdlOFNExplorer
```

If the user now selects several files, the directory paths of all files selected are transferred to the *FileName* property as before, but according to a certain scheme. As all selected files are located in the same directory, the complete directory path is given first. The names of all the files then follow, separated by a *Chr(0)* character (the `vbNullChar` constant is used for this purpose in Visual Basic). It is not done by assigning the *FileName* property to a variable this time. Instead, its content has to be broken down into component parts. The `Split` function is used for this in Visual Basic, which breaks down a character string with a specified separator. The result is now the component character strings between separators passed in the form of arrays (arrays will be explained in Chapter 10). Since we are already in the realms of advanced Visual Basic programming, only the new *mnuLoadImage_Click* procedure has to be explained. This is always called if the user wishes to load an image.

If you wish to extend the image viewer to include multiple file selection, simply exchange the old procedure for the new one.

The new mnuLoadImage_Click () procedure

```
Sub mnuLoadImage_Click ()
  Dim sPath As String
  Dim aFilenames() As String
  Dim n As Long
  With cdlFile
    .Filter = "Bitmaps (*.bmp, *.gif, *.jpg,
*.wmf)|*.bmp;*.gif;*.jpg;*.wmf|AllFiles|*.*"
    .InitDir = "C:\My Documents\My Pictures"
    .dialogueTitle = "Select an image file"
    .FileName = ""
    .Flags = cdlOFNAllowMultiselect + cdlOFNExplorer
    .ShowOpen
    sFilename = .FileName
  End With
  If sFilename = "" Then
    Exit Sub
  End If
  If InStr(sFilename, vbNullChar) = 0 Then
    Set oImaeFrm = New frmImage
    oImageFrm.imgImage.Picture = LoadPicture(sFilename)
    oImageFrm.Visible = True
    oImageFrm.Caption = sFilename
  Else
    sPath = Left(sFilename, InStr(sFilename, vbNullChar) -
1)
    aFilenames = Split(Mid(sFilename, InStr(sFilename,
vbNullChar) + 1), vbNullChar)
    For n = 0 To UBound(aFilenames)
      Set oImageFrm = New frmImage
      oImageFrm.imgImage.Picture = _
       LoadPicture(aFilenames(n))
      oImageFrm.Visible = True
      oImageFrm.Caption = aFilenames(n)
    Next n
  End If
End Sub
```

Take your time over this – it contains a few advanced commands.

After the program has started, you will notice that several files can now be selected in the file selection dialogue box (Figure 9.24). If you confirm your selection, all images will be loaded in sequence.

211

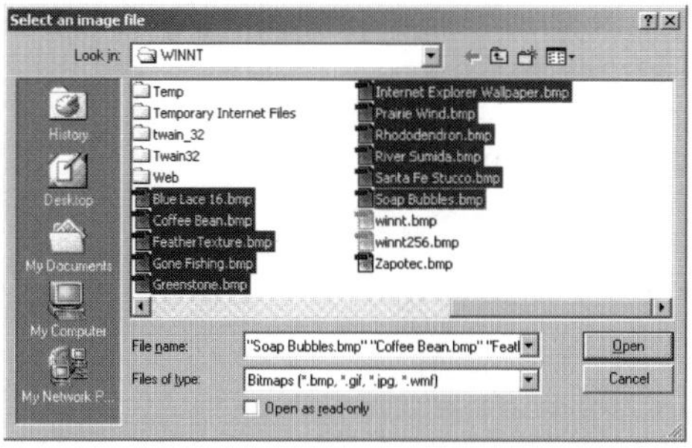

Figure 9.24: Several files can now be selected in the file selection dialogue.

The Windows common controls

We will conclude with a general, yet very difficult, topic, which has nothing to do with the image viewer. These are the Windows common controls. These are about a dozen control elements that are an integral part of Windows, and are made available using three controls. These are a series of operators used by the Windows interface at different points. The most important examples include the tree view (to give an Explorer view), the status bar (which always appears on the lower margin of a window) and the date selection (the calendar used to select dates in several programs). There is not enough room to explain all Windows common controls here (they are described in the Visual Basic help function, and you should already have become familiar with the toolbar and status bar from this chapter). Table 9.1 lists them.

Icon	Control	What can it do?	Where do I find it?
	TabStrip	Display several tabs.	Microsoft Windows Common Controls 6.0
	Toolbar	Extends a form to include a toolbar. The *Buttons* list is the central point.	Microsoft Windows Common Controls 6.0
	StatusBar	Extends a form to include a status bar. The *Panels* list is the central point.	Microsoft Windows Common Controls 6.0
	ProgressBar	Displays a progress bar, which controls the *Value* property.	Microsoft Windows Common Controls 6.0

Icon	Control	What can it do?	Where do I find it?
	TreeView	Displays a tree view with an arbitrary nesting depth. The *Nodes* list is the central point. This is given new nodes using the *Add* method.	Microsoft Windows Common Controls 6.0
	ListView	Displays entries in the same way as a folder window.	Microsoft Windows Common Controls 6.0
	ImageList	Makes icons for other control elements that are available.	Microsoft Windows Common Controls 6.0
	Slider	Enables values to be set using a controller, and is controlled by the *Value* property.	Microsoft Windows Common Controls 6.0
	ImageCombo	Combination box that can also display entries as bitmaps.	Microsoft Windows Common Controls 6.0
	Animation	Enables playback of *Avi* files.	Microsoft Windows Common Controls 6.0-2
	UpDown	Makes a button available for counting up and down through a value in another control element.	Microsoft Windows Common Controls 6.0-2
	MonthView	Displays a calendar for selecting a date, via which the *Value* property can be queried.	Microsoft Windows Common Controls 6.0-2
	DTPicker	Represents a text box for date entry, where it can also display a calendar using an arrow key.	Microsoft Windows Common Controls 6.0-2
	FlatScrollbar	Scrollbar with a flat 3D effect.	Microsoft Windows Common Controls 6.0-2
	Coolbar	Toolbar that can represent compiled toolbars as in Internet Explorer.	Microsoft Windows Common Controls 6.0-3

Table 9.1: An overview of the Windows common controls.

Adding the Windows common controls to the toolbox

Adding a common control to the toolbox was described in the small exercises in Chapters 8 and 9, but we will explain it again here for clarity.

Use the following procedure to add common controls to the toolbox:

1 Open the PROJECT menu and select COMPONENTS. A dialogue box appears with all available components (one entry can stand for several controls).

2 Check the MICROSOFT WINDOWS COMMON CONTROLS 6.0 entry. Pay attention to the notation (SP3 or SP4 may well be added on the end). If you wish to use the additional common controls, check the MICROSOFT WINDOWS COMMON CONTROLS 6.0-2 entry.

3 Confirm your selection with OK. The new controls will now be displayed in the toolbox.

> **Note**
>
> *Programming common controls is explained in the Visual Basic help function (but not with the working model). Select the icon in the toolbox and press the* F1 *key.*

Selecting a date with the date picker

The following little exercise should show how easy a professional-looking date entry can be conjured up on a form using the date picker. You will need to use the following procedure:

1 Create a new Visual basic project (STANDARD EXE as usual).

2 As described in the last section, add MICROSOFT WINDOWS COMMON CONTROLS 6.0-2 (the extended common controls) to the toolbox.

3 Create the month picker on the form. You may be surprised by the visual impact, and should notice that the size of the calendar cannot be modified.

4 Double-click on the calendar control to switch to the program code window. You will see the procedure settings of the *DateClick* event procedure.

5 Enter the following command in the event procedure:

```
MsgBox "The date is: " & DateClicked
```

6 Start the program using the F5 key. If you click the calendar, the selected date is displayed. Both the year and month will change in the head of the sheet (Figure 9.25).

Figure 9.25: The calendar sheet makes a good date picker.

> **Tip**
>
> *The* MonthRows *and* MonthColumns *properties specify how many calendar sheets are displayed horizontally and vertically. A calendar is formed in this way.*

Summary and overview

We are almost at the end of our expedition into the world of Visual Basic programming. Almost all the main topics have been covered. Do you think you can absorb some more info? If so, then you will learn a few more topics in the next chapter that fall into the advanced category of Visual Basic programming. They are all exciting and important topics, such as arrays, the interception of runtime errors, and the definition of separate functions. You should only attempt these once you are sufficiently familiar with basic topics such as variables, decisions and program loops.

215

Chapter 10

More advanced Visual Basic

In this chapter, a few programming topics are introduced, such as working with arrays, intercepting runtime errors, string functions and executing Visual Basic programs with an integrated debugger.

This chapter outlines the more advanced themes of Visual Basic programming. Visual Basic has far more to offer as a programming language than elementary commands such as `Dim`, `If`, `Then`, `For`, `Next`, `Do`, `Loop`, `Sub` and `End Sub`, which exist in almost every programming language. We begin with relatively easy topics, such as the formatted output of numbers, processing character strings and defining separate functions, before tackling more demanding tasks, such as the definition of objects on the basis of class modules. In this chapter, the most important topics of Visual Basic not yet discussed will be introduced using small examples. Finally, you will learn how to make your programs fully operational using a wizard, so they can run on another PC.

This chapter is constructed such that you do not need to work through everything, but can consult the most interesting topics and try out the examples in a form or directly in a window.

Topics for this chapter are:

- the formatted output of numbers;
- rounding numbers;
- using strings;
- defining functions;
- tuning with API functions;
- variables in XXL with arrays;
- the *Collection* object;
- the `For Each` program loop;
- the `With` command;
- the runtime error;
- the Visual Basic debugger;
- from project to *Exe* file.

The formatted output of numbers

The formatted output of numbers or a date means that these are represented in a certain format. Why should this be so important? Quite simple. If a program is calculating with amounts of money, this should not merely displayed as a number (e.g. 1234567.89), but in currency form at (i.e. £1 234 567.89). It would be even better if the currency sign were used automatically, configured using the control panel. So that this does not have to be programmed every time, Visual Basic uses *formatting functions* to carry out these tasks. A number is passed to one of these functions, and a character string in a certain format is returned. Table 10.1 gives an overview of the formatting functions used in Visual Basic (since Version 6.0). Here is an example. The expression

```
?100 / 2.25
44.4444444444444
```

produces an unnecessarily long number. We don't need a number as exact as this. No problem – the FormatNumber function can tame this monster:

```
?FormatNumber(100 / 2.25, "2")
44.44
```

The result is a character string. Rounding takes place at the same time:

```
?100/2.2499
44.4464198408818
```

or

```
?FormatNumber(100/2.2499, 2)
44.45
```

> **Note**
>
> *Very large numbers are output in scientific notation in Visual Basic, where the exponential form is abbreviated with a letter E. So 1E6 means 10 to the power of 6, or one million:*
>
> ```
> ?1E6*1E08
>   100000000000000
> ```
>
> FormatNumber *represents this number in a more familiar way:*
>
> ```
> ?FormatNumber(1E6*1E08,0)
> 100,000,000,000,000
> ```

The scientific notation causes a decimal point to be displayed with integers, as an exponent is usually produced, with a number between 1 and 9 before the decimal point:

```
?120^8
4,29981696E+16
```

If you want a number to be output in scientific format regardless of its size, the global `Format` function has to be used with the `Scientific` format identifier:

```
?Format(100/2.25, "Scientific")
4.44E+01
```

The `Format` function is a function with many options. This is described in detail in the Visual Basic help function.

Function	What does it do?	Example
FormatNumber	Formats a number, e.g. by limiting the number of decimal places.	FormatNumber(22/7.2)
FormatCurrency	Formats a number as a currency, taking into account the settings in the control panel.	FormatCurrency("29.95")
FormatDateTime	Formats a number as a date, taking into account the settings in the control panel.	FormatDatetime(now, vbShortDate)
FormatPercent	Formats a number in a special percentage notation.	FormatPercent("0.125",0)

Table 10.1: The formatting functions of Visual Basic 6.0

Rounding numbers

The `Round` function is used for rounding numbers in Visual Basic 6.0. It isn't perfect, but it is sufficient for most circumstances:

```
?100/-6
-16.6666666666667
?Round(100/-6. 2)
-16.67
```

Magic with strings

A string, or character string, is a sequence of characters. Strings are saved in a Visual Basic program in `String` type variables, or they occur as string constants. The following example assigns a string constant to a string variable:

```
sStatement = "A funny sea voyage"
```

In some program listings, you will find the $ character used in connection with string variables and string functions. This is a fairly old-fashioned way of indicating a variable or function as a string variable or string function.

Visual Basic offers users a huge selection of functions when working with character strings. These *string functions* are very versatile. If, for example, you wish to see the first ten characters of a string, or know where in the above string the word 'sea' appears, you need only call the right string function.

Working with string functions is best learned in small examples. The immediate window of the Visual Basic development environment is best suited for this (Figure 10.1). Just start Visual Basic, create a new project and open the immediate window using Ctrl+G to use the following mini-examples.

First, define a character string in the immediate window. This will be edited later:

```
sStatement = "A fairly funny sea voyage"
```

If you wish to separate the word 'A' from the string, use the *Left* function. This returns a certain number of characters beginning from the left:

```
?Left(sStatement, 1)
A
```

The word 'voyage' is affected by the `Right` function, which returns a certain number of characters beginning from the right:

```
?Right(sStatement, 5)
oyage
```

A letter was forgotten here. Six letters should be removed instead of five. So how do you get to the word 'fair'? Use the `Mid` function. The number of characters has to be given as a second argument next to the position of the first character:

```
?Mid(sStatement, 3, 4)
fair
```

You won't always recognise the composition of a string. If you wish to separate a word from an unknown string, Visual Basic has to search for it.

221

The `Instr` function is used for this, which returns the position of a substring as a string

```
?Instr(sStatement, "fair")
 3
```

We now know that the word 'fair' in the `sStatement` string begins at position no. 3.

And how is the word 'fair' returned, without knowing its exact position in the string? You have to combine the `Mid` and `Instr` functions:

```
?Mid(sStatement, Instr(sStatement, "fair"), 4)
fair
```

Separating a null character

This is an important task, because as soon as a string is accepted from an API function, a second string is received, ending with a null character (vbNullChar). As the appended `vbNullChar` character can sometimes interfere with the further processing of the string, it has to be separated. A string formula is required for this, which separates all characters of the string until the first `vbNullChar` character. The `Instr` function is used again here, in combination with the `Left` function.

```
sNew = Left(sTeststring, Instr(sTestString, vbNullChar) -1)
```

Extracting a filename from a path name

A frequently occurring programming problem is having to separate the filename from a path name. The filename consists of those characters followed by the last \ sign. The `InstrRev` function is used here, which searches for a string from the end backwards.

```
sPath = "C:\Programs\Microsoft Visual Basic\Test\MyProg.vbp"
?Mid(sPath, InstrRev(sPath, "\")+1)
MyProg.vbp
```

This version makes use of the fact that the number of characters to be separated can be omitted using the `Mid` function. All characters up to the end of the string are then returned.

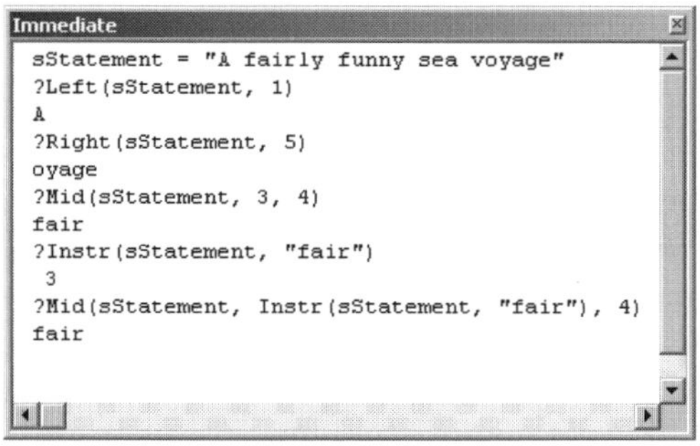

```
Immediate                                    ×
sStatement = "A fairly funny sea voyage"
?Left(sStatement, 1)
A
?Right(sStatement, 5)
oyage
?Mid(sStatement, 3, 4)
fair
?Instr(sStatement, "fair")
 3
?Mid(sStatement, Instr(sStatement, "fair"), 4)
fair
```

Figure 10.1: The immediate window is ideally suited for getting to know string functions.

The role of ANSI codes

A string consists of characters. Each individual character is represented internally by a number between 32 and 255. These characters are not specified arbitrarily, but standardised globally by the *American National Standard Institute* (ANSI). According to this table, A has the code 65, B the code 66, and so on. A lower-case 'a' has the code 97, a lower-case 'b', 98, and so on. Special characters also have codes – the ANSI code for the '!' character is 33, the code for the comma is 44, and 32 is a blank space. The following loop outputs all characters with ANSI codes between 32 and 255 in the immediate window (Figure 10.2):

```
For c = 32 to 255 : ?"ANSI code: ",c,Chr(c) : Next
```

The `Asc` function gives the ANSI code of a character (ASCII code was used previously, hence the name of the function), and the `Chr` function gives the character behind the ANSI code.

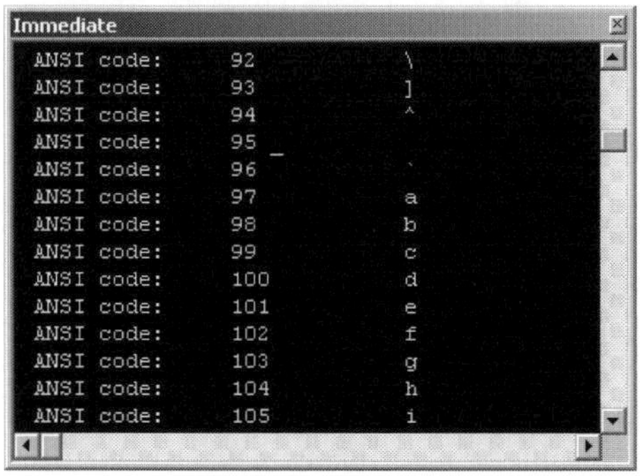

```
Immediate                                    ×
ANSI code:    92          \
ANSI code:    93          ]
ANSI code:    94          ^
ANSI code:    95          _
ANSI code:    96          `
ANSI code:    97          a
ANSI code:    98          b
ANSI code:    99          c
ANSI code:    100         d
ANSI code:    101         e
ANSI code:    102         f
ANSI code:    103         g
ANSI code:    104         h
ANSI code:    105         i
```

Figure 10.2: The ANSI codes appear in the immediate window.

Defining functions

Functions are small subprograms within a Visual Basic program. A function is a name that stands for a group of commands. Even though functions frequently process calculations, they have nothing to do with mathematical functions. The name comes from the fact that they can be used in the same way as mathematical functions, and always return one value. A function is defined with the `Function` command, which follows the name of the function. Then follow those commands that are to be executed when the function is called later. The function definition is ended with the `End Function` command.

The following example shows a function that returns the number of days until the end of the year.

```
Function NewYear() As Integer
  NewYear = DateDiff("d", Date, "31.12")
End Function
```

As a function always returns a value (even though this is not processed further in the program – functions can also be called as well as procedures), a data type has to follow the end of the function header, as with a variable declaration. In this example, the function is an `Integer` type, as it can return numbers in a range from 0 to 365.

> **Note**
>
> *If the data type is omitted, the function is a `Variant` type, which is not optimal.*

A function has to be called whenever the following command outputs the number of days left until the champagne corks can start to pop again, using the `NewYear` function

```
MsgBox "Still " & NewYear() & " days to go"
```

Only the empty brackets (which could also be omitted) indicate that NewYear is a function name. It could also have been the name of a variable. Function names should always be displayed in this way. It can be used wherever a variable name is permitted. The difference between a function and a variable is that a function name stands for one or more commands, and functions can be given values when called.

Entering functions

A function can be entered anywhere in the program code window, but it has to happen outside an existing function or procedure. Visual Basic recognises after the `Function` command has been entered that a function is about be entered, and automatically completes the `End Function` command. All functions (and procedures) of a form are included in the *General* section. If you select the *General* section in the selection list, all the functions (and procedures) of the module are listed in the right-hand selection list (Figure 10.3).

Figure 10.3: Function and procedure definitions are included in the General *section of a form.*

> **Note**
>
> *Visual Basic displays a small dialogue box via the* EXTRAS/ADD MENU *command, with which the settings of a function or procedure can be entered. However, this method is not especially advantageous.*

Calling functions

Functions are called by entering the name of the function. As with a variable, a function name can be part of the expression, and stand on the right-hand side of the statement. But unlike a variable, a function name cannot stand on the left-hand side of a statement, as a value cannot be assigned to a variable.

The following command calls the `NewYear()` function, and assigns the return value of the function to a variable:

```
nNumberofDays = NewYear()
```

225

The question of whether brackets have to be added to a function has already puzzled generations of learning Visual Basic programmers. Visual Basic is very flexible in this sense, *and* allows the brackets to be omitted. However, brackets are compulsory if parameters are passed to the function *and* the return value of the function is processed further.

Determining the return value of the function

Every function returns a value, otherwise it would be a procedure (more on this later). The return value is processed by assigning an arbitrary value to the function name within a function. It doesn't matter where this assignment takes place. It is usually listed at the end of the function. As our sample function consists of only one command, this command is also responsible for the assignment of the return value:

```
NewYear = DateDiff("d", Date, "31.12")
```

This command assigns the difference in the number of days to the function name, thus determining the return value.

Functions with arguments

Working with functions only becomes really interesting when they are assigned values known as *arguments* in this context. The arguments of a function are placed in brackets following the name of the function. Each name plays the role of a variable, which is valid within the function. As with the declaration of a variable, a data type has to be given with the arguments (otherwise the `Variant` data type is returned). It doesn't matter how many arguments a function has. When a function is called, a value, or *parameter* in this context, has to be passed for every argument. The value can be a number, variable or another function or valid expression.

The following function calculates power (HP) in kilowatts (kW) (the example should be fairly familiar).

```
Function HPkW (HPValue As Integer) As Single
   If HPValue > 0 Then
     HPkW = HPValue / 1.341
   Else
     HPkW = -1
   End If
End Function
```

So that something else happens in this simple function, it is verified whether the value contained in the `HPValue` variable is smaller than 0. If so, the function returns the value -1, otherwise the kW is value calculated.

When the function is called, a parameter is passed for the `HPValue` argument:

```
kW = HPkW (340)
```

The parameter could also be a variable:

```
HPNumber = 340
kW = HPkW (HPNumber)
```

The name of the variable passed does not matter, as it depends only on the value. It could also read `HPValue`, even though this name already appears in the function header. This duplication of names is irrelevant in Visual basic, as it is a variable with a different validity range.

Note that when calling a function, Visual Basic displays the function header as a syntax description. This also simplifies working with self-defined functions.

Functions with optional arguments

If an argument has the keyword `Optional` in front of it, a value does not have to be passed for this argument when called. It is even possible to specify a default value, as the optional argument does not contain a value if a parameter was not passed.

The following extension of the `HPkW` function also controls the conversion from kW into HP. It is determined which conversion is processed using an optional argument called `Mode`. If no value is passed for `Mode`, the function uses the default value of 1, and then converts from HP into kW.

```
Function HPkW2 (Value As Single, Optional Modus As Integer = 1)
    If Modus = 1 Then
        HPkW2 = Value / 1.341
    Else
        HPkW2 = Value * 1.341
    End If
End Function
```

Our function could be called like this:

```
HP = HPkW2(75, 0)
```

or like this:

```
kW = HPkW2(150)
```

Calling with named arguments

As every argument of a function has a name, this can be indicated when called. This has the advantage that the parameter sequence can be exchanged when called, making the program more legible.

The following command calls the HPkW2 function, where the names are placed in front of the arguments, so their sequences can be exchanged.

```
HP = HPkW2(Mode:=0, Value:=155)
```

Note that a named argument receives its value through a combination of equals signs and colons.

Procedures are functions without return values

Visual Basic also recognises *procedures* as a variant of functions. A procedure only differs from a function in that it does not return a value, and so does not have a data type. Apart from this, there is no difference. A procedure is introduced with the Sub command, and ended with the End Sub command. You learned about procedures at the beginning of this book, as every event procedure is a normal procedure, the only difference being that it is called automatically by Visual Basic after an event occurs.

The following commands define a procedure called DateInCaption, where the current date is entered in the heading of all project forms. The optional argument bTime determines whether the time is also entered.

```
Sub DateInCaption (Optional bTime As Boolean)
  Dim n As Long
  For n = 0 To Forms.Count - 1
    Forms(n).Caption = = Forms(n).Caption & "  " & Date
    If bTime = True Then
      Forms(n).Caption = Forms(n).Caption & " " & Time
    End If
  Next n
End Sub
```

Determining the date of Easter

To conclude, we will take an example that can generally be used to determine the date of Easter. The date of Easter Sunday is calculated according to a complicated rule, summarised by the famous mathematician Carl Friedrich Gauss (1777–1855). As other religious festivals can be calculated from the date of Easter Sunday, such as Ascension Day (+39days), Whitsun (+49days), Corpus Christi (+60days) and Ash Wednesday (–46days), all important holiday dates within the year can be calculated using this formula. The following Holidays function expects a year as an argument, and gives the date of Easter Sunday of a return value.

If you wish to calculate other holidays instead, these have to be given as optional parameters. In this context, you will learn a practical facility with the *enumeration constant* and the Enum command, using which constants can be combined in a group (the enumeration). This has the advantage that whenever such a constant can be entered, Visual Basic displays a selection list with all relevant names. However, the enumeration constant uses normal Long values.

Use the following procedure to implement the Easter formula:

1 Start *Visual Basic* and create a STANDARD EXE project.

2 Add a general module to the project and name it *basEaster*. A general module is used so that it can be used in any project.

3 Switch to the program code window of the module and enter the following commands:

```
Enum eHolidays
   AshWednesday = -46
   EasterSunday = 0
   AscensionDay = 39
   Whitsun = 49
   CorpusChristi = 60
End Enum
```

This enumeration of constants helps working with constants, simplifying the selection of the desired holiday. They are not compulsory.

4 Enter the following function in the general module. The function is fairly extensive and contains many small variable names. Take time in entering everything.

```
Function HolidayDate(ByVal intYear As Integer, _
 Optional Holiday As eHolidays) As Date
  Dim X As Integer, K As Integer, M As Integer
  Dim S As Integer, A As Integer, D As Integer
  Dim R As Integer, OG As Integer, SZ As Integer
  Dim OE As Integer, OS As Integer
  Dim Month As Integer
  X = intYear
  K = Int(X / 100)
  M = 15 + Int((K * 3 + 3) / 4) - Int((K * 8 + 13) / 25)
  S = 2 - Int((3 * K + 3) / 4)
  A = X Mod 19
  D = (19 * A + M) Mod 30
  R = Int(D / 29) + (Int(D / 28) - Int(D / 29)) _
    * Int(A / 11)
  OG = 21 + D - R
  SZ = 7 - (X + Int(X / 4) + S) Mod 7
  OE = 7 - (OG - SZ) Mod 7
```

```
   OS = OG + OE
    Month = 3
   If OS > 31 Then
     OS = OS - 31
     Month = Month + 1
   End If
   HolidayDate = DateSerial(X, Month, OS)
   Select Case Holiday
     Case eHolidays.AscensionDay
      HolidayDate = DateAdd("d", HolidayDate, _
       eHolidays.AscensionDay)
     Case AshWednesday
      HolidayDate = DateAdd("d", HolidayDate, _
       eHolidays.AshWednesday)


     Case eHolidays.CorpusChristi
      HolidayDate = DateAdd("d", HolidayDate, _
       eHolidays.CorpusChristi)
     Case eHolidays.Whitsun
      HolidayDate = DateAdd("d", HolidayDate, _
       eHolidays.Whitsun)
     Case Else
   End Select
End Function
```

5 Switch to the program code window of the form and enter the following commands in *Form_Load*:

```
Dim intYear As Integer
intYear = InputBox("Please enter year:")
MsgBox Prompt:="Ash Wednesday is on " &
HolidayDate(intYear:=intYear, Holiday:=AshWednesday)
MsgBox Prompt:="Easter Sunday is on " &
HolidayDate(intYear:=intYear)
MsgBox Prompt:="Ascension Day is on " &
HolidayDate(intYear:=intYear, Holiday:=AscensionDay)
MsgBox Prompt:="Whitsun is on " &
HolidayDate(intYear:=intYear, Holiday:=Whitsun)
MsgBox Prompt:="Corpus Christi is on " &
HolidayDate(intYear:=intYear, Holiday:=CorpusChristi)
```

6 Start the program using the F5 key. If you have entered everything correctly, an entry field appears in which you have to enter a year. All holidays will then be displayed. You should check this against a reliable calendar the first time.

Figure 10.4: The computer tells us when Easter is.

Tuning with API functions

Windows offers several thousand functions to programmers, known as API (*Application Programming Interface*) functions. These functions are not located in a particular place, but placed in different files known as DLLs (*Dynamic Link Libraries*). An API function is therefore a function contained in the operating system. If you wish to call them in a Visual Basic program, they have to be declared using the `Declare` command.

For this reason, API functions are much sought after by Visual Basic programmers, as they enable things that Visual Basic commands and functions do not. This includes direct access to windows behind a form, querying system information, and establishing a dial-up connection. The 'tuning' mentioned in the heading of this section refers primarily to construction rather than acceleration.

The following example should demonstrate that calling simple API functions is anything but complicated. The central point is the `GetTickCount` function, which displays the time elapsed in milliseconds since Windows started up. `GetTickCount` is a good first example, as the function does not require a call parameter, so no confusion should arise from this.

Use the following procedure to test the API function:

1 Start *Visual Basic* and create a new STANDARD EXE project.

2 Enter the following command in the *General* section of the form:

```
Private Declare Function GetTickCount Lib "kernel32" () As
Long
```

3 Create a label on the form, set the *Font* property to *Arial,* and set as large a font size as possible (e.g. 24).

4 Create a timer on the form, set the *Interval* property to *1000*, and enter the following command in the *Timer* procedure:

```
Label1.Caption =  GetTickCount()
```

5 Start the program using the F5 key. The time elapsed since the system was started will then be displayed in the label (figure 10.5).

That was easy – due to the API function, your program can process something that a Visual Basic command set alone cannot.

Figure 10.5: The GetTickCount() *API function tells us how many ticks of the clock have gone by.*

The Declare command

Every API function requires a Declare command to be made known to the program. In this way Visual Basic learns the name of the DLL file in which the function is located, as well as the data types of the individual parameters and return value. Haven't we forgotten something? Of course – Visual Basic has to know the name of the function. The Declare command consists of the following elements:

- The keyword Function or Sub, which indicates whether it is a function or procedure. Functions are always used in the case of API functions, but if a return value is not required, they can also be declared as Sub.

- The name of the function. No distinction is made between upper- and lower-case characters.

- The keyword Lib, followed by the name of the file containing the function. If this is not located in the Windows directory, the complete path has to be given. With system DLLs such as Kernel32, the *.dll* extension can be omitted.

- The (optional) keyword Alias, followed by the true name of the function. No distinction is made between upper- and lower-case characters.

- The list of arguments passed when called. The data types are important, whereas names are not. If the data type is not declared, or if it may vary, As Any is used. The ByVal prefix is important, as practically all arguments have to be passed by Visual Basic as values.

- In the case of a function, the declaration ends with the data type of the function (usually written as Long), which usually stands for an error code, which determines whether the function was executed successfully.

The following `Declare` command declares the `SendMessage` API function used in the following examples. Table 10.2 shows the command broken down into component parts.

```
Private Declare Function SendMessage Lib "user32" Alias
"SendMessageA" (ByVal hwnd As Long, ByVal wMsg As Long,
ByVal wParam As Long, lParam As Any) As Long
```

Element	What does it mean?
`Private`	The function is private, so it responds in only one module.
`Declare`	The command itself.
`Function`	Its function is to be declared.
`SendMessage`	The name of the function.
`Lib "user32"`	The function is part of the *User32.dll* file.
`Alias "SendMessageA"`	The true name of the function is `SendMessageA`.
`ByVal hwnd As Long`	The first argument is a `Long` type.
`ByVal wMsg As Long`	The second argument is a `Long` type.
`ByVal wParam As Long`	The third argument is a `Long` type.
`lParam As Any`	The fourth argument can be any data type.
`As Long`	The return value of the function is `Long`.

Table 10.2: The components of a `Declare` *command.*

The API viewer as a friendly adviser

One program easy to befriend is the API viewer, as this makes around 1500 `Declare` commands available, as well as the constants and type declarations for the most important API functions (Figure 10.6). This not only saves you having to type in the long-winded `Declare` command, but it also avoids typing error.

The API viewer is not available in the working model. This does not mean that it is not possible to call API functions with the working model. It merely means that the `Declare` commands may have to be typed sometimes.

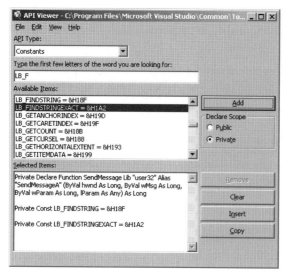

Figure 10.6: The Declare *command is a good friend – the API viewer makes over 1500 declarations available.*

Calling the API viewer

The API viewer can be called in two different ways – either using the program group called MICROSOFT VISUAL BASIC 6.0 TOOLS, or using the ADD-INS menu of the development environment. In this case, select the ADD-IN MANAGER, then VB 6 API VIEWER entries, check LOAD/UNLOAD, and confirm with OK (Figure 10.7). The API viewer will then be available via the ADD-INS menu. After calling the API viewer, you have to load a text file with the Declare commands via the FILE menu. This is usually *Win32api.txt*. The API Viewer is now ready for use.

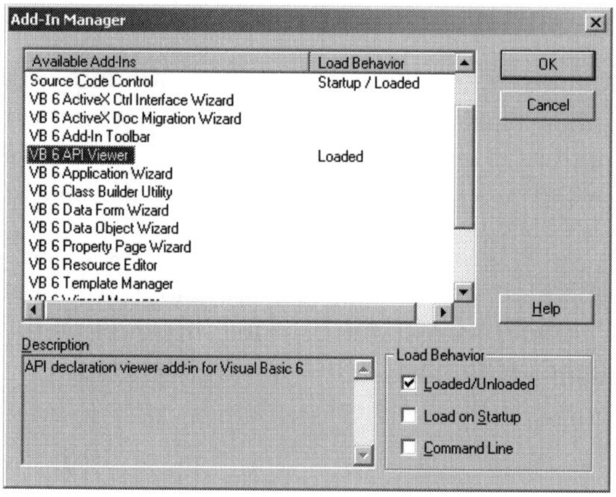

Figure 10.7: The API viewer is called using the ADD-IN-MANAGER.

It is determined whether `Declare` commands, constants or types are to be displayed using the selection list. Then look for the desired function (e.g. `SendMessage`) and add it to the selection area. Once all required function declarations, constants and type declarations have been arranged, experienced programmers copy these into a slide in the program. The PUBLIC and PRIVATE options refer to whether the word `Public` or `Private` is set before the `Declare` command. This is required if the `Declare` command is to be inserted in a form (otherwise an error message appears after the start). However, if the `Declare` command is to be callable by several modules, select the PUBLIC option and insert the declaration in a module.

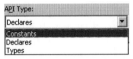

Figure 10.8: The API viewer makes declarations, constants and types available.

Searching through list boxes quickly

List boxes are practical, but they have at least one disadvantage (apart from not being able to display bitmaps). If you wish to determine whether a certain entry is contained, you have to process all entries in a loop, which can bring programs with long lists to an abrupt end. The paradox here is that the list box has a built-in search function. Fortunately, there is a solution using the `SendMessage` function, which is very simple. If you wish to know what lies behind `SendMessage`, then read on. If you wish to see an example in action, then you can skip the following section.

What lies behind SendMessage?

`SendMessage` is a universal function with one particular task: sending a message to a window (windows are also control elements, even though they may not look like windows). This simply means calling the internal window function of this function with a parameter. In the case of `SendMessage`, the function waits until the window has processed and answered the message. In this way, `SendMessage` can ask in which line the character with the position *xy* is located, and the text box returns the line number as a return value of `SendMessage`. Don't worry if this sounds complicated. Everything should be clear once you have tested the following example. So how does `SendMessage` know which window or text box should contain the message? Does the name have to be given? You couldn't have known this, but each window (or text box, list box, etc.) has a unique identification number after being created. This is called the window handle, made available by both forms as well as window-based control elements (not including the label and display) via the *hWnd* property. The `SendMessage` API function requires four parameters:

- the window number (the *hWnd* property of a control element or form);
- the message (in the form of a number determined using a constant);
- the first message content;
- the second message content.

In the following exercise, the `SendMessage` API function is used to pass the message *LB_FINDSTRINGEXACT* (a constant also originating from the API Viewer) to the `lstTowns` list box. A search string is given as variable for the second message content (`lParam`-Parameter). The list box verifies whether the search string is contained in the list, and if so, returns the number of the entry in the list. In order to enable the highest degree of flexibility possible, it can be determined at which list entry the search should begin (this can reduce searching time in long lists) using the first message content (the `wParam` parameter). It should therefore be clear what `SendMessage` is used for. It merely activates an existing function, not made available using a method for whatever reason. If you like experimenting and aren't afraid of large tasks, then program an ActiveX control element with Visual Basic 6.0 containing a list box extended to include a find method (if you only have the Working Model, you will have to avoid Visual Basic 5.0 CCE).

> **Note**
>
> *Additionally,* `SendMessage` *is also suited for sending a message to a window in a Visual Basic application (although these are rarely used). In this case the window has to be able to react to individual messages. How this* subclassing *works is described on many internet help sites.*

Implementing the exercise

Use the following procedure to extend the list box to include a search function:

1 Start *Visual Basic*, create a STANDARD EXE project, create a list box on the form and name it *lstTowns*.

2 Create a text box (it should be called *txtSearchname*) and a command button (called *cmdSearch*) on the form.

3 Start the Add-In Viewer using the Add-Ins Menu and load the file *Win32api.txt* using the menu command FILE/LOAD TEXT FILE.

4 Enter *SendMessage* in the search field, select the PRIVATE option, and click on ADD.

5 Select the Constants entry from the API Type selection list, enter the name *LB_FINDSTRINGEXACT*, and click on ADD.

6 Click on COPY, switch to the *General* section of the form (Figure 10.9) and press [Ctrl]+[V] to insert the content of the clipboard.

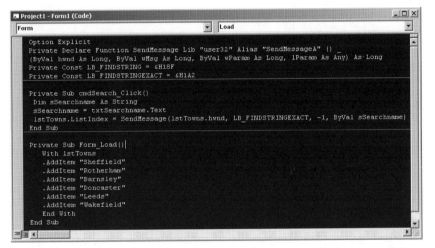

```
Project1 - Form1 (Code)
Form                                          Load
  Option Explicit
  Private Declare Function SendMessage Lib "user32" Alias "SendMessageA" () _
  (ByVal hwnd As Long, ByVal wMsg As Long, ByVal wParam As Long, lParam As Any) As Long
  Private Const LB_FINDSTRING = &H18F
  Private Const LB_FINDSTRINGEXACT = &H1A2

  Private Sub cmdSearch_Click()
   Dim sSearchname As String
   sSearchname = txtSearchname.Text
   lstTowns.ListIndex = SendMessage(lstTowns.hwnd, LB_FINDSTRINGEXACT, -1, ByVal sSearchname)
  End Sub

  Private Sub Form_Load()
   With lstTowns
    .AddItem "Sheffield"
    .AddItem "Rotherham"
    .AddItem "Barnsley"
    .AddItem "Doncaster"
    .AddItem "Leeds"
    .AddItem "Wakefield"
   End With
  End Sub
```

Figure 10.9: The General *section of the form contains an API declaration and the constants required.*

7 Add the following commands in the *Form_Load* event procedure:

```
With lsttowns
   .AddItem "Sheffield"
   .AddItem "Rotherham"
   .AddItem "Barnsley"
   .AddItem "Doncaster"
   .AddItem "Leeds"
   .AddItem "Wakefield"
End With
```

These commands merely fill the list box with content.

8 Add the following commands in the *Click* procedure of the command button:

```
Dim sSearchname As String
sSearchname = txtSearchname.Text
lstTowns.ListIndex = SendMessage(lstTowns.hwnd,
LB_FINDSTRINGEXACT, -1, ByVal sSearchname)
```

237

9 Start the program using the $\boxed{\text{F5}}$ key. Enter the name of an entry in the text box and click on the command button. The list entry should then be highlighted (Figure 10.10).

Figure 10.10: The search function highlights the entry in the list that agrees with the name in the text box.

> **Tip**
>
> *If you wish the first name that agrees partly with the entry to be found in the search, use* LB_FINDSTRING *as a constant (its value is* &H18F, *where* &H *stands for a hexadecimal number, which has 16 characters, the standard numbers 0–9 being followed by the letters A–F).*

Horizontal scrollbars with SendMessage with a list box

The last example clarified that toolbox control elements, such as the text box and list box, can actually do more than it first seems. Some options of these constituents contained in Windows are simply not available via the properties and methods. However, if you wish to use these, you have to tease them out using the SendMessage API function. In this section, you will learn another example for extending a list box. Wouldn't it be practical if a list box also had a horizontal scrollbar? It would then be easy to scroll through long names. As opposed to the text box, this scrollbar is not available from the start – it has to be activated afterwards.

Use the following procedure to extend the list box to include a horizontal scrollbar:

1 Start *Visual Basic*, create a STANDARD EXE project, and create a list box on the form. Name the list box *lstFilenames*.

2 Create a command button on the form, name it *cmdStart,* and enter *&Start* for the *Caption* property.

3 Switch to the program code window and insert the following declaration using the API Viewer in the *General* section of the form:

```
Private Declare Function SendMessage Lib "user32" Alias
"SendMessageA" (ByVal hwnd As Long, ByVal wMsg As Long,
ByVal wParam As Long, lParam As Any) As Long

Private Const LB_SETHORIZONTALEXTENT = &H194
```

4 Insert the following commands in *Form_Load*:

```
Dim sFilename As String
Dim nRet As Long
sFilename = Dir("*.*")
Do While sFilename <> ""
  lstFilenames.AddItem CurDir & "\" & sFilename
  sFilename = Dir()
Loop
nRet = SendMessage(lstFilenames.hwnd,_
  LB_SETHORIZONTALEXTENT, 400, 0)
```

5 Start the program using the F5 key.

The `Dir` function enters the names of all files in the current directory, where the directory path is given, into the list box. As the list box is a little too condensed, calling the `SendMessage` API function with the message `LB_SETHORIZONTALEXTENT` and the dimensional information 400 causes the width to be extended, causing a scrollbar to appear. You can now scroll through the names (Figure 10.11).

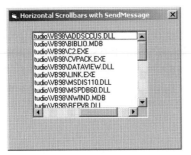

Figure 10.11: The list box now has a horizontal scrollbar.

An API viewer on the internet

The topic of API calls is apparently a taboo subject for Visual Basic help. The `Declare` function may be described, but there is nothing interesting about API functions or how they are built into a Visual Basic program. Fortunately, the internet provides this information, as committed programmers have made the effort to compile examples and descriptions for API functions and offer their know-how free of charge. A particularly laudable example is the API guide (the web address is `http://www.allapi.net/`) by KDP, a group of Visual Basic programmers from Belgium. The API guide not only replaces the API viewer, but also acts as an API reference due to its countless examples (Figure 10.12).

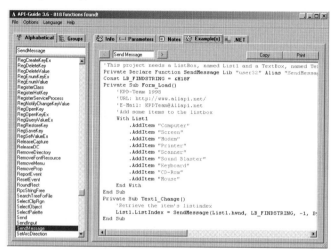

Figure 10.12: The API guide is an extremely useful helper for Visual Basic programmers who wish to use API functions.

Variables in XXL with arrays

As well as simple variables, Visual Basic also offers arrays. An array is a variable consisting of a number of subvariables, all with the same name (and the same data type). Arrays therefore accommodate several values in principle, and so can be very large. So that the individual subvariables can be identified, they always respond to an index, which is a number.

Declaring arrays

When declaring an array, it can be indicated how many elements an array may have. The number of elements is set in brackets. If this number is not known, for example because the array increases or decreases during runtime, it can be left open. In this case, the brackets remain empty.

The following command defines an array called `LotteryNumbers`, containing exactly 49 numbers of the `Byte` type.

```
Dim Lotterynumbers (1 To 49) As Byte
```

Both the upper and lower limits are specified in brackets. If the lower limit is omitted, it is automatically set to 0. This means that the following command defines an array with 11 rather than 10 elements:

```
Dim TrickyField (10)
```

The great advantage of arrays is that all its elements can be used conveniently in one loop. The following `For` loop outputs the numbers of all elements with content not equal to 0:

```
For n = 1 To 49
  If LotteryNumbers(n) <> 0 Then
    Debug.Print n
  End If
Next n
```

The LBound und Ubound functions

The `LBound` and `UBound` functions return the lower and upper limits of an array.

The following loop always runs from the lower to the upper limit of the array, regardless of where these limits are.

```
Dim n As Integer
For n = LBound(MysteryField) To UBound(MysteryField)

Next n
```

The Array function

Several files can be grouped in one field using the `Array` function. However, this is not an actual field but a `Variant` variable (but this doesn't matter for programming purposes).

Which is the most beautiful city in the world? You will soon know the answer. First, several candidates have to be arranged in an array:

```
Dim Towns As Variant
Towns = Array("Rio de Janeiro", "Paris", "New York",
"Rotherham")
```

Now things get exciting. Our infallible random number generator now makes its choice:

```
Randomise Timer
Msgbox "The most beautiful city in the world is: " &
Cities(Int(Rnd * UBound(Towns) + 1))
```

Would you ever have thought that? Don't worry, the next time you try you will get a different result.

241

Dynamic arrays

A *dynamic variable* is an array whose size can change during runtime. This is very practical, as if you only wish to save 20 numeric values, it would be a waste of space to reserve 200 arrays from the outset. On the other hand, if it shows that these 200 fields are not enough, a runtime error (number 9) would be the inevitable consequence.

There is no official restriction of size with dynamic arrays. However, the index cannot be larger than about 2 billion, as this is a *Long* type value. However, this is not the absolute limit, as an array can, in principle, be as large as required. The size of a dynamic array is generally limited by the amount of memory available.

Dynamic arrays are then declared without details of field limits:

```
Dim Field ()
```

The `ReDim` command then specifies the actual amount:

```
ReDim Field(0 To 50)
```

When using the `ReDim` command, note that in the above form the entire array is deleted. All previously saved values are also lost. If this is not desirable, the keyword `Preserve` has to be added to the `ReDim` command.

```
ReDim Preserve Field(0 To 50)
```

Deleting arrays

The `Erase` command is used to delete arrays:

```
Erase LotteryNumbers
```

The Collection object

A *Collection* object is a type of super-array (but it has no real advantages). As in an array, any amount of numbers and names etc. can be saved in a *Collection* object. However, as opposed to an array, values can be mixed, meaning that individual elements could have any data type.

Creating a Collection object

In order to be able to use a Collection object, work through the following two steps:

1 Declare a Collection type variable.

2 Instance the variable with the keyword New.

The following command sequence creates a new Collection object called `colTest`:

```
Dim colTest As Collection
```

An instanced Collection object is then assigned to the `colTest` object variable:

```
Set colTest = New Collection
```

Remember that this allocation is always processed using the `Set` command, as it is an object variable.

Adding elements

If you have a *Collection* object, add values to it using its *Add* method:

```
colTest.Add 1234
colTest.Add txtInput
colTest.Add "Julie and Hannah"
```

This small example should show you that it doesn't matter what you add to a collection.

In order to save the values given, the *Item* method is used (which can be omitted):

```
number = colTest.Item(1)
```

This command fetches the first element in the collection. Note that the numbering starts at 1 (as opposed to an array). You should also note that you have to know which type the element is. The following command produces a runtime error:

```
Dim Number As Long
```

243

```
Number = colTest.Item(2)
```

This will not work, as the number is a `Long` variable, but the element concerned is a text box.

Adding elements with a key

You will probably not require the most important property of a Collection object at the outset. When saving an element, you can create a *key*, which can later be used for access, as an alternative to the sequence. Using a key offers one decisive advantage: speed. In collections with many elements, an element responds much quicker using its key instead of its number. As this works only in large collections, this issue isn't so important at the start. Keys have two conditions:

1. It has to be a character string.

2. It may not happen within the collection.

A Collection object has a few special features, such as that once a key has been allocated, it may not be queried or modified further. Collections also become sluggish if they contain many elements. However, we need not worry about these things just yet.

The following small example adds the names of towns to a collection, where the STD code is used as a key.

```
Dim colTowns As Collection
Set colTowns = New Collection
colTowns.Add "Liverpool", "0151"
colTowns.Add "Manchester", "0161"
colTowns.Add "Leeds", "0113"
colTowns.Add "Sheffield", "0114"
```

A town can now be accessed using either its sequence or its key:

```
sTowns = colTowns.Item(3)
sTowns = colTowns.Item("040")
```

Determining the number of elements

Every collection has a *Count* property, which contains the number of elements:

```
AmountTowns = colTowns.Count
```

Removing elements

Elements are removed from a collection using the *Remove* method. Either the number or the key of the element is given.

```
colTowns.Remove 2
colTowns.Remove "0161"
```

If the requested element is no longer available, runtime error number 5 is produced.

The For Each program loop

If several objects are summarised under one name, this is known as a *listing*. The collections introduced in the previous section are listings. However, Visual Basic also has several built-in listings such as *Controls* and *Forms*. Whereas Controls stands for all control elements of a form, Forms stands for all forms of a project. All listings can be processed using the For Each loop. This type of loop processes a pass for each element of the list, where the loop variable stands for the next element on every loop. In this way, all items of a list can be visited in turn.

The following example processes all loaded forms in the project, loads and displays them, and sets the background colour to a random value.

```
Dim oF As Form
For Each oF In Forms
  oF.Show
  oF.Backcolor = QBColor(Int(Rnd*15)+1)
Next oF
```

The oF loop variable stands for another form every loop.

The For Each loop is more convenient, but it is not compulsory. As all listings have a *Count* property, the above example could also have been formulated as follows:

```
Dim n As Long
For n = 0 To Forms.Count - 1
  Forms(n).Show
  Forms(n).Backcolor = QBColor(Int(Rnd*15)+1)
Next n
```

Organising favourite images in the image viewer in Chapter 9 was a useful example of a Collection object in connection with a For Each loop.

The With command gives a better overview

If you wish to assign a value to several properties of the same object, or call several methods in sequence, the `With` command offers a highly practical shortcut.

```
With txtInput
   .Text = "Start Value"
   .Backcolor = vbRed
   .ForeColor = vbYellow
   .SelStart = 0
   .SelLength = Len(.Text)
   .SetFocus
End With
```

The `With` command assigns a range of properties to the `txtInput` object (a text box), and the *SetFocus* method is called. The advantage of the `With` command is that the object name has to be written only once. Note that the object name can be omitted on both the left- and right-hand sides, as is the case with the previous allocation to the *SelLength* property.

The runtime error

A *runtime error* is an error that occurs during runtime. Runtime errors are generally caused not by the program code directly, but by adverse external circumstances over which the programmer has very little influence. The classic example of a runtime error is a disk drive that has not yet closed, causing the common error message 'Drive not ready'. A good example of an internal runtime error is trying to divide by zero, or using something that lies outside the specified area of a field: errors the compiler cannot determine during compile time. As untreated runtime errors within the Exe file cause the program to abort immediately without the user having the opportunity to save the program and its data, every Visual Basic program has to take measures to prevent runtime errors being passed on to the user. There is some good news: the overwhelming majority of runtime errors can be intercepted, so the program does not abort.

The On Error Goto command

Every (trappable) runtime error can be intercepted using an `On Error` command. This does not lead to a program abort, but calls a specially designed procedure, where the program controls the situation.

> **Note**
>
> *A list of all (documented) trappable runtime errors can be found in the Visual Basic help function. Don't be surprised by the number, as the errors listed here are very specialised and occur rarely.*

The `On Error Goto` command appears in three different versions:

1. On Error Goto <label>

2. On Error Resume Next

3. On Error Goto 0

Even though this error may initially seem fairly strange (why `Goto`?), its application is very simple. Variant 1 is the most commonly occurring version. This command is listed at the beginning of a procedure and activates error handling (more on this later). Variant 2 also activates error handling, but the program itself has to query the error using the *Err* object. Variant 3 is there to deactivate error handling.

Constructing an error handling routine

The `On Error Goto` command activates an error handling routine. This is a part of the procedure marked with a *label*, and is called in the case of a runtime error. An error handling routine is generally ended by a `Resume`, `Resume Next`, `End Sub` or `End Function` command. This specifies the position in the program where runtime is to continue once error handling has finished.

The following example shows a procedure containing an error handling routine, activated using an `On Error Goto` command.

```
Sub Test()
  On Error Goto Test_Err
  ' Any command
  Exit Sub
Test_Err:    ' The error handling routine begins here
  ' Any command
  Resume Next
End Sub
```

You will see that as opposed to a procedure without error handling, there are only two additional commands and one label. If any (trappable) runtime errors occur during execution of the commands between `On Error` and `Exit Sub`, runtime continues not with the next command, but with the label called `Test_Err`, the error handling routine. What happens here depends on the type of procedure. In many cases, the errors are simply pointed out to the user, and as long as it is not a fatal error, the program can resume using the `Resume Next` command. If the cause of the error can be eliminated during the error handling routine, the program continues using the `Resume` command, which executes the command that originally caused the error (if this happens regularly, you will have to switch to a `Resume Next` or `Exit Sub` command at some point). Don't forget the `Exit Sub` command before the beginning of the error handling routine, as this prevents the error handling routine from running when there are no runtime errors.

The following example shows a procedure with an error handling routine. The letters at the beginning of the lines are only there to clarify the example for the purpose of this book. They will usually be omitted:

```
Sub FindeFile()
A       On Error Goto FindeFile
        Dim CheckName As String, Result As String
B       CheckName = Dir("A:*.txt")
        If CheckName <> "" Then
         Result = "The file found is called: " _
         & CheckName
        Else
         Result = "Sorry! No file found"
        End If
C       Exit Sub
D     FindeFile_Err:
E       Select Case Err.Number
F        Case 71
           Msgbox "Please close drive A:"
G          Resume
H        Case Else
             Msgbox Error & "-" & Err, 48, _
             "Runtime error"
I            Stop
         End Select
      End Sub
```

So that you can understand fully the individual steps in this procedure, Table 10.3 contains an explanation of the letters and their respective program lines.

Line	Description
A	The error handling routine is installed. As soon as a runtime error occurs in the procedure, the `FindeFile_Err` label is used.
B	This is the command that causes the error. The `Dir` function accesses drive A. If no disk is inserted, this causes a runtime error.
C	This command is compulsory, so the error handling routine is not processed automatically.
D	The error handling routine begins here.
E	The `Select Case` command verifies the error code, which then returns the *Number* property of the *Err* object.
F	Error code 71 stands for a drive that is not ready.
G	The `Resume` command causes the command that caused the error to be executed again.
H	All other error codes are treated in the same way.
I	The `Stop` command makes sense in the test mode of an application if the program is not yet prepared for all types of error. On the other hand, there is nothing to be found in an Exe file, although it is better than an abrupt end to the program.

Table 10.3: The individual steps of an error handling routine.

What happens if the `FindFile` procedure is executed and the A drive is not closed. In this case, a small message box is displayed. The `Dir` function is executed once again using the `Resume` command. If drive A is still not closed (ready), the error handling routine is called again. So that this process is not repeated endlessly, a counter variable should ensure that the procedure continues after the third or fifth time using a `Resume Next` command, or aborted using an `Exit Sub` command.

The Err object

The *Err* object is the central feature of error handling, as it delivers all information about any runtime errors that have occurred. The most important properties are *Description* and *Number*. The error text or number corresponding to the runtime error is displayed.

Error number	Error text	How can it be fixed?
7	Insufficient memory	Internal program error. Delete the Recycle Bin if possible.
9	Index outside defined range	Verify index. Insert `Debug.Assert` before field access if possible.
11	Division by zero	Verify operand.
28	Stack overflow	Occurs in recursions executed unchecked or nested too deep. You can see which procedure the recursion has overwritten from the call list.
52	Wrong filename or number	Error in filename.
53	File not found	The file does not exist or has been written wrongly. Verify filenames for vaildity and check whether the file exists using the `Dir` function.
71	Disk not ready	
91	Object variable or With-Block variable not specified	Object variable not properly initialised; the `New` keyword may be missing.
94	Illegal use of null	Check that null has not been used using the `Iszero` function.

Table 10.4: The most prominent runtime errors and their causes.

The Resume command

This command specifies at which position the procedure is continued after the error handling routine has been processed:

1. The procedure continues via the `Resume` command with the command following that which originally caused the error.

2. The procedure continues via the `Resume Next` command with the command that originally caused the error. However, this requires the option of eliminating the error within the error handling routine, otherwise a new runtime error is produced immediately.

3. The procedure continues via a `Resume <Label>` with a particular program line within the procedure.

The option you decide on depends primarily on the type of runtime error. An incorrect filename or drive not being ready can be rectified by the user within the error handling routine. In this case, the command that caused the error can be executed again using the *Resume* command. A full hard drive, access denial due to insufficient rights, or stack overflow cannot be eliminated in this way. In this case, the command that caused the error has to be skipped using a `Resume Next` command, or if this is not viable, the procedure should be exited using the `Exit Sub` command.

Querying runtime errors directly

In some cases, the *On Error Resume Next* command enables a more flexible handling of runtime errors. This command activates the interception of runtime errors, but it does not activate an error handling routine. Instead, the programmer has to query the runtime error directly using the *Number* and *Description* properties. The advantage is that you do not need to write an error handling routine or consider the case that the error is passed on to higher levels.

In the following example, error handling is executed in a procedure immediately after a command that caused an error:

```
Sub Test()
  On Error Resume Next
  Open Filename For Random As 1
  If Err.Number = 53 Then
   Msgbox "Error in accessing file", 48, "Runtime error"
   Exit Sub
  End If
```

Immediately after the `Open` command is executed, it is verified whether runtime error no. 53 has occurred ('File not found').

The Visual Basic debugger

Visual Basic offers an integrated debugger for error searches, which is operated using the command button and the commands in the DEBUG menu (Figure 10.13). Even though the term 'debugging' in computer jargon means the removal of errors from programs (one of the first computer errors in the 1940s was caused by a small moth flying into one of the huge tube computers, hence the name), the debugger is unfortunately not an automatic corrector that analyses your program and removes all bugs. Instead, the integrated debugger is a facility that processes a Visual Basic program step by step, contacts the break points in a program, and displays the values of variables, properties and other expressions during a program interruption. The debugger offers the following services to the Visual Basic development environment:

- The gradual execution of a program using the F8 or ⇧+F8 keys.

- Setting break points using the F9 key, so the program can stop at different points during runtime where possible and make certain amendments to the program.

- Setting watches (using the DEBUG/ADD MONITOR menu command). A watch either displays the current value of variables, properties and so on, or stops the program if values change, or if a predefined expression becomes true.

- Tracks the call list of procedures.

You will see from this list that the debugger is not a tool that displays logical errors in the program. It is a tool used for tracking down these errors. However, you should still know how it works.

Figure 10.13: The DEBUG menu lists the debugger commands

The debugger window

The debugger works with four different windows, containing important information about the program during a program interruption:

- the immediate window

- the monitoring window

- the local window

- the call list.

The most important debugging techniques

Even though it may not seem so at the outset, the Visual Basic development environment debugger is really easy to use. You don't have to be a Visual Basic pro to use it. However, if you are new to Visual Basic programming, you can learn a lot from the gradual execution of a program or monitoring individual expressions. All debugger commands are available via the DEBUG menu, usually activated with a key combination. It is far more convenient to press the F8 key than to use the DEBUG/SINGLE STEP menu command. You can also do a lot with the mouse. Clicking the character bar (the left-hand column in the program code window) in break mode in the relevant program line cancels a break point.

> **Tip**
>
> *If you wish to determine the next command during a program interrupt, drag the yellow arrow icon inside the current procedure to the desired line.*

Figure 10.14: All important debug commands are listed in the toolbar.

Interrupting a program using Ctrl + Pause

This is the simplest technique for tracking down program errors. If the program does not behave as you want it to, interrupt it using the Ctrl + Pause key combination. The command line currently being processed is displayed using a yellow background. Interruption is required if the program is stuck in an endless loop or no longer reacts to user entries.

Stopping a program using a Stop command

This is a simple debug method, useful if you want to learn more about the operation of a program. If you wish to stop a program at any point, simply insert a Stop command. This causes the development environment to switch to break mode.

Program execution in single-step mode using F8

The most obvious debugging technique is executing a program in single-step mode using F8 and watching the behaviour of the program carefully. You should note the following points:

- In order to be able to execute a program in a single step, you either have to start it using F8 or place a particular break point and continue with the program using the F5 key.

- Executing the program within an event procedure can continue only as far as the next End Sub command. The next program course depends on which event occurs next. Pay attention to the title bar of the development environment. The heading 'Interrupt' shows that the program is in break mode, and can be executed in single-step mode. The heading 'Run' shows that the program is running and is waiting for further input. The F8 key has no effect in this case.

- If a procedure call or function call is listed in a step, and not processed step by step, the ⇧ + F8 key combination has to be used instead of the F8 key.

254

Ending the current procedure using Ctrl+⇧+F8

This key combination executes all commands until the end of the procedure.

Executing to the cursor position

Executes all commands up to the program line where the cursor is currently located. This is very practical, as certain passages of a procedure can quickly be skipped in this way.

Executing to the end of a loop

In larger loops, you may not wish to repeat every command in single-step mode, but to continue runtime after the Next or Loop command. The debugger has no appropriate tool for this, but the same effect is achieved by placing a break point at the first command after the end of the loop, after pressing the [F5] key and resetting the break point.

Continuing runtime from another position using Ctrl+F9

A very efficient technique is available using the Ctrl+F9 key combination, which enables runtime to continue within a procedure with a command different from that which follows. A command can be repeated in this way. It should be noted that only runtime is affected, and variable values are not reset. Only the command sequence is changed – the program does not retire to a particular state.

Repeating the last command

Even though such a command would be very practical, unfortunately there isn't one. If you wish to see the effect of a certain command, you have to set the cursor on the line as described in the last section, and press Ctrl+F9. Note that Visual Basic only resets the internal program counter, but does not restore the environment, i.e. the values of the individual variables and properties.

Setting break points using F9

A break point can be placed on every executable program line using the F9 key. A break point is a program line where the program halts and switches to break mode. You can now display the values of variables or properties and modify them, either in the immediate window or using the ⟨⇧⟩+⟨F9⟩ key combination.

> **Tip**
>
> *In principle, modifications are also possible in interrupt mode, as long as reconfiguration is not required. So, deleting or adding program lines is usually very easy. However, it is not usually possible (there are exceptions though) to add declarations or modify the data type of variables.*

Setting watches

A watch is an arbitrary expression monitored during runtime. The monitoring causes the program to stop. This is known as a conditional break point, as the point itself depends on a condition. The following can be monitored:

- the value of an expression;
- whether an expression is true;
- whether an expression changes its value.

Watches are inserted using the DEBUG/ADD WATCH menu command. If, for example, the program stops if the variable m contains a negative value, the expression m<0 has to be entered in the EXPRESSION entry field. The expression to be watched does not have to be restricted to simple comparisons of variables or properties. For example, in order to be able to determine when the m variable contains a decimal place, the expression Int(m) – m <>0 has to be watched. All watches are shown with their current values in the watch window during runtime, provided this is not hidden by the program window.

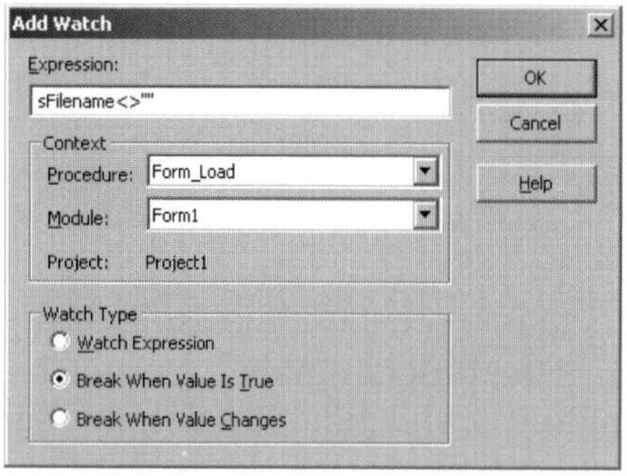

Figure 10.15: Watches are edited in this dialog box.

Displaying the value of an expression

During a program interrupt you can see the values of almost all expressions in the current procedure by moving the mouse pointer over the expression. Should this not work for any reason, the same effect is achieved by using the ⇧ + F9 key combination.

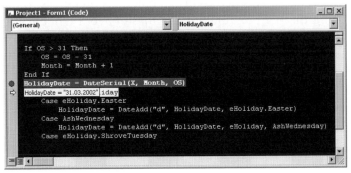

Figure 10.16: The value of a (valid) expression can be displayed in a QuickInfo box during runtime.

Working with the immediate window

The immediate window is one of the most important debugging techniques. Commands can be executed in the immediate window during a program interrupt, to display variable values or modify property values, for example. The immediate window is a type of interactive Visual Basic, in which almost all commands can be tested and API functions called (as long as the declaration is located in the currrent validity range).

The immediate window has a range of features:

- A variable declaration is not possible in the immediate window. However, you can use all variables as long as they are currently valid during the program interrupt.

- It is easier to insert commands in the immediate window using the normal Copy and Paste commands (or using the right mouse button).

- Deleting the immediate window is only possible by selecting the text to be deleted and then deleting it (this cannnot be done in run mode).

- Commands have to be restricted to one line, or spread over several lines using a line separator. In this case, a line is separated using the : operator.

The following commands output the numbers 1 to 10 in the immediate window:

```
For n = 1 To 10 : _
  Print n : _
Next n
```

One important function of the immediate window is to output control messages using the *Print* method of the *Debug* object. The values of expressions can be watched or signalled when the program has reached a certain point in the program. This debugging technique is preferable to the message boxes using the MsgBox function, as these have a tendency to 'swallow' messages and so distort the course of the program.

> **Tip**
>
> *Outputs in the immediate window using the* Debug.Print *command are not transferred into the* Exe *file, and so do not need to be removed.*

Table 10.5 shows all the key combinations for executing a program in single-step mode.

Key combination	Description
F5	Starts the program or continues runtime after an interrupt.
⇧ +F5	Restarts the program.
F8	Executes the next command.
F9	Sets or deletes a break point.
Ctrl +L	Displays the call list that led to the call of the current procedure or function.
Ctrl +W	Opens the dialogue field to edit conditional break points.
Ctrl +F5	Compiles the entire program.
Ctrl +F8	Executes the program up to the program line where the cursor is currently situated.
Ctrl +F9	Specifies the command where the cursor is currently located as the next command to be executed.

Key combination	Description
Ctrl + G	Switches to the immediate window during a program interrupt.
Ctrl + Pause	Interrupts the program and switches to break mode.
Ctrl + ⇧ + F9	Deletes all break points.
⇧ + F1	Displays the definition of the procedure or function whose name the cursor is currently placed over.
⇧ + F8	Executes the next command where procedures and functions are executed in one step.
⇧ + F9	Displays the value of the expression where the cursor is currently located or selected.
Ctrl + ⇧ + F8	Executes all commands up to the end of the current procedure.

Table 10.5: The key combinations for executing a program in single-step mode.

The local window

Along with the immediate window, the local window is one of the most important properties of the integrated debugger. The local window allows you to see all properties as well as variable values during a program interrupt (Figure 10.17). A special feature of the local window is its hierarchical structure. If you wish to see the properties of a control element, you first have to open the form where the control element is situated, and then open the layer of the control element and its properties. Individual properties refer to other objects, as is the case with the *Parent* or *Container* properties, for example, where opening the layer referring to the program takes you one level lower down the hierarchy indicated (this can be confusing at first). There is something else worth mentioning about the local window. If the program contains arrays, you can see the entire field at once, removing the need to output individual values in the immediate window. Anyone who wishes to explore Visual Basic programming further should work more closely with the local window.

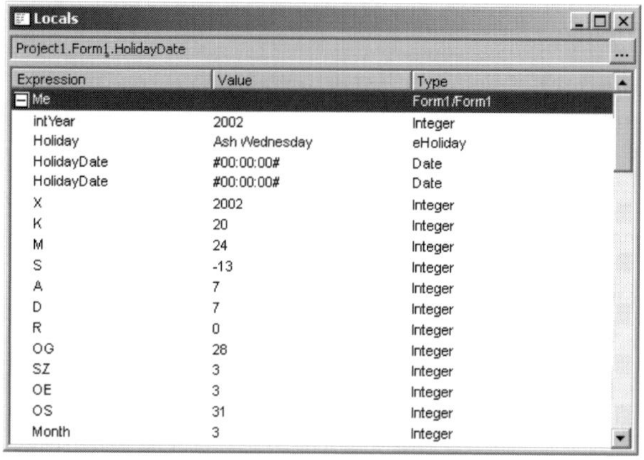

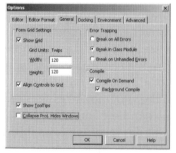

Figure 10.17: The program under the microscope - the local window shows the values of all variables and properties during a program interrupt.

Compiling fully

Visual Basic allows you to compile a program only partly. This makes the programming time much shorter. However, convenience comes at a fee. As the program is compiled only partly, not all errors are displayed. In order to achieve a full compilation, either the COMPILE IF REQUIRED option in the GENERAL dialogue box of the IDE OPTIONS should be disabled (Figure 10.18), or the program should be started using Ctrl+F5.

Figure 10.18: Compile is disabled in IDE Options if required.

Small, compact, independent – from project to Exe file

At some point, you may wish to execute a program not within the development environment but on other PCs. You may wish to post your program on the internet, or sell it to a large software company. Regardless of the grand plans you may have for your program, it has to be compiled in an *Exe* file.

Note

Compilation of Visual Basic programs in an Exe *file is not possible with the working model.*

Converting a Visual Basic project into an *Exe* file is very simple. Open the File menu and select the Make <PROJECT NAME>.EXE, where <PROJECT NAME> stands for the current project name. A dialogue box appears in which you have to confirm the name of the *Exe* file (Figure 10.19). You can also configure different compiler options (such as the version number), but this cannot be discussed at this point. If everything goes according to plan, you should have an *Exe* file which can be executed outside the Visual Basic development environment.

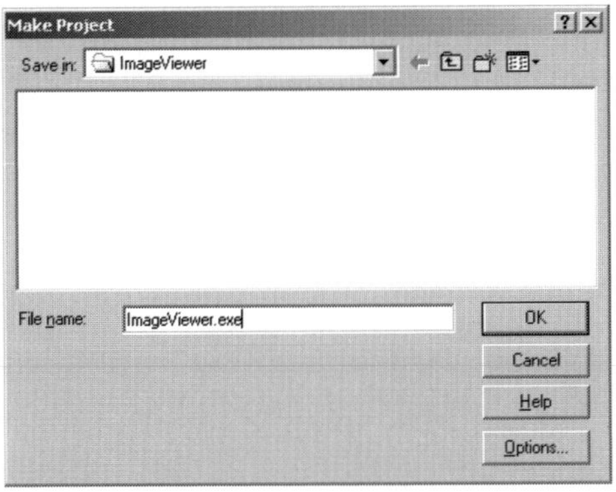

Figure 10.19: The name of the Exe *file to be compiled is determined in this dialogue box.*

Tip

If you prefer not to assign the default icon to your Exe *file, modify it using the* Icon *property of a form. Click on* OPTIONS *before creating the* Exe *file, and select the icon for the file using the* Icon *selection list (Figure 10.20).*

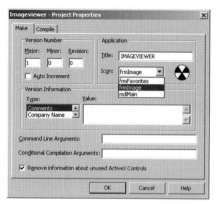

Figure 10.20: The icon is also selected in the Exe files options.

Chapter 11

Playing around with Visual Basic

This chapter is about the fun side of programming, including graphic output, card games, playing sound files, and a small MP3 player.

To conclude this book, we will talk about the fun side of programming. In the last chapter, you leant about all of the important ("serious") topics of Visual Basic programming; now you have earned yourself a change.

We owe a lot to Windows, whose powerful multimedia components have been extended in the last few years. If you want to play a video clip or an MP3 song, your program doesn't have to know anything about the details of the MP2 coding, or how to conjure up a moving image on the screen. Windows takes care of these technical details.

Since Windows 95 there has been a very powerful multimedia extension for Windows with *DirectX*, which can be used by almost all Windows games. As a reward for the efforts, Visual Basic also allows for the programming of great games, which, for example, contain advanced 3D graphics, stereo sound, and the heading of the newest game developments. Anyone interested in this topic should look around for programming introductions in book shops or on the web (the Microsoft Homepage of DirectX for Programmers is found at *http://msdn.microsoft .com/directx*).

The topics covered in this chapter are:

- playing wave files;
- construction of an MP3 music box;
- small card tricks.

Playing wave files

A *wave file* is a file with the extension *.Wav*, in which a short sound or an entire piece of music is contained in digital form. Wave files are the default format in Windows for sounds and short sequences of music. Wave files are also used for the creation of voice files using the Windows audio recorder, particularly since Windows offers effective compression methods through which the spoken text that is saved possibly only occupies very few kilobytes. The wave format is less suitable when saving pieces of music. However, it would not be a problem to save a Verdi opera or a Pink Floyd song completely as a wave file if there were no problems with space. Since the music data are not compressed in the wave format, the wave files swell. The MP3 format became a mega-topic practically overnight because it compresses music in hi-fi quality to a tenth of its size, which is put into wave format and appears on the display area at the right time. For small sequences and system sounds, the wave format is absolutely fine. For some obscure reason, Visual Basic has no play sound command, so you have to fall back on the API function `sndPlaySound`, which is very easy to use.

```
nRet = sndPlaySound ("C:\Windows\Media\Woosh.wav", _
  SND_ASYNC Or SND_NODEFAULT)
```

This call plays the wave file *Woosh.wav*. The prerequisite is that the API function was declared using a `Declare` command in the *public* part of the formula:

```
Private Declare Function sndPlaySound Lib "winmm.dll" Alias
"sndPlaySoundA" (ByVal lpszSoundName As String, ByVal uFlags
As Long) As Long
```

The constants `SND_ASYNC` make sure that the play happens asynchronously (therefore in the background) and the program does not have to wait until the playing has ended. This is typical for Visual Basic. The command sentence does not contain a single command that is in the multimedia category. Nevertheless, almost anything is possible. You only have to know where to find the missing functions and how to call them.

Constants	Meaning	Value
SND_ASYNC	The program doesn't wait until the entire sound has been played.	1
SND_NODEFAULT	If the file cannot be found, the default sound is not played.	2
SND_SYNC	The program continues only if the sound is played.	0

Constants	Meaning	Value
SND_LOOP	The sound will be repeated as until the sndPlay Sound function is replaced; this time, it is called with vbNullString instead of a file name.	8
SND_NOSTOP	The sound is not played if another sound is played.	16

Table 11.1: Constants for the sndPlaySound API function

Playing all wave files in the Windows directory

The following small exercise consists of a Visual Basic program that enables all wave files that are contained in the *Media* subdirectory to be played.

To map the program, carry out the following steps:

1 Create a new STANDARD EXE project and order a list field on the form (*lstWaves*) and a button (*cmdPlay*).

2 In the *public* part of the form, add the following declaration:

```
Private Declare Function sndPlaySound Lib "winmm.dll" _
  Alias _"sndPlaySoundA" (ByVal lpszSoundName As String,
ByVal uFlags As Long) As Long

Private Declare Function GetWindowsDirectoryA _
  Lib "Kernel32" (ByVal lpBuffer As String, _
  ByVal nSize As Long) As Long

Private sWinDir As String
```

The API function *GetWindowsDirectory* gives the directory name of the Windows directory back, as this can be different on every PC.

3 Add the following commands in the *Form_Load* procedure:

```
Dim nRet As Long
Dim sWavFile As String
sWinDir = Space(255)
nRet = GetWindowsDirectoryA(sWinDir, Len(sWinDir))
sWinDir = Left(sWinDir, nRet)
sWavFile = Dir(sWinDir & "\media\*.wav")
Do While sWavFile <> ""
  lstWaves.AddItem sWavFile
  sWavFile = Dir()
Loop
```

4 Add the following commands in the *Click* procedure of the button:

```
Dim nRet As Long
If lstWaves.ListIndex = -1 Then Exit Sub
nRet = sndPlaySound(sWinDir & "\media\" & lstWaves.Text, 0)
```

5 Start the program using the [F5] key. Now the name of a number of wave files should appear in the list, which you can play using the button.

Making an MP3 player

MP3 players are ten a penny, and nobody has the inclination to reprogram the program WinAmp or the very expensive Media Player 7.0 from Windows Me. Nevertheless, the home-made MP3 player is a fine thing. You can put a few ideas into effect, impress friends, and learn something about Visual Basic programming and working with the Windows Media Player control element using this example. The MP3 player introduced in this section is a bog standard model, but it behaves like a top-of-the-range player in much the same way as a Morris Minor gets you from A to B using the same principle as an Aston Martin. Our MP3 player is basically a form with which the Media Player stands in the foreground, and which is supplemented with a few additional functions, such as the compilation of a play list and the reading and editing of MP3 tags.

The conversion begins

The MP3 player that is converted step by step in the following example is deliberately kept very simple. You will be able to select MP3 files, compile in a list field, and play them one after the other. Feel free to extend the program and install your own ideas.

1 Start *Visual Basic*, create a STANDARD EXE Project, call it *Mini music box*, call the form *frmMinimusicbox* and type in *Mini-Musicbox* for the *Caption* property.

2 First of all, you need the Windows Media Player control element. Using the menu command PROJECT/COMPONENTS, open the component selection, cross the entry WINDOWS MEDIA PLAYER, and confirm the selection with OK (Figure 11.1). If this entry is not available as expected, the media reproduction (from Version 6.2) or the new Windows Media Player has not yet been installed.

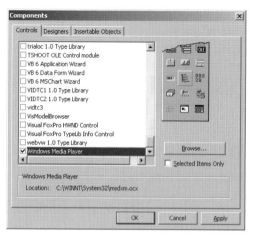

Figure 11.1: The Media Player was selected from the component list...

3 Arrange the Windows Media Player into the bottom area of the form so that only the control buttons are visible. Call the control element *mmplayer*.

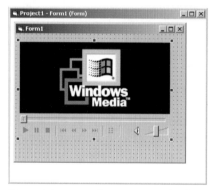

Figure 11.2: ... and arranges on the form

4 In the left corner of the form, arrange a frame area, type in *Playlist* in the *Caption* property, and arrange a list field (*lstplaylist*) and three buttons (*cmdadd, cmddelete* and *cmdplayplaylist*) in the frame area. Look at figure 11.3, which shows the finished form with its control elements.

5 Next to the frame area, arrange another frame area and type in *titleinfo* for *caption*. Arrange four text fields (*txttitle, txtinterpret, txtalbum, txtyear* and *txtcomment* in which *True* and *Scrollbars* are set to 2) together in the frame area as well as the suitable name fields.

6 Arrange a button (*cmdupdate*) in the frame area whose *Caption* property will be *Update*.

7 Arrange a name field (*lblposition*) outside of the frame area, as well as a timer (*tmrtime*) and a default dialogue field control element (*cdlfile*), which you add as usual using PROJECT/COMPONENTS.

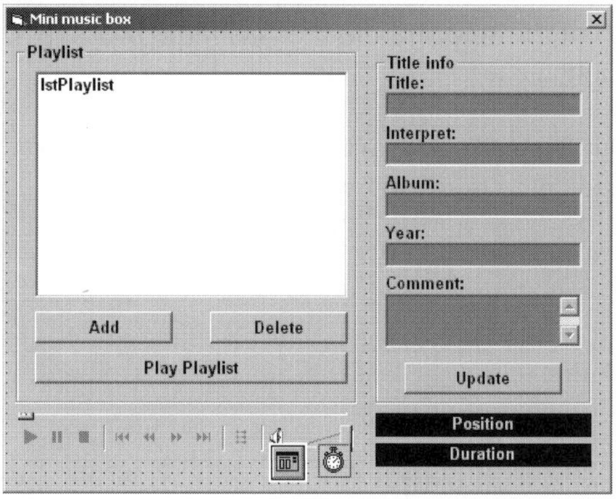

Figure 11.3: The form of the music box will look like this in the end.

The form is now finished. Now let's look at the programming.

8 In the *common* part of the form add the following declaration:

```
Private bPlayMode As Boolean
Private iPlayNr As Integer
Private sFilePfad As String
```

9 Add the following commands in the *click* event procedure of the *cmdsdd* button:

```
With cdlFile
   .Filter = "Mp3-Files (*.mp3)|*.mp3|All files|*.*"
   .InitDir = Environ("userprofile") _
     & "\own files\own music"
   .ShowOpen
   sFilePath = .FileName
End With
   If sFilePath = "" Then
     Exit Sub
   End If
   lstPlaylist.AddItem sFilePath
```

These commands display the file selection and enable the selection of an MP3 file, which is added to the selection list. In Windows 95/98, the *Environ* function, which calls up the value of the environmental variable *UserProfile*, which is only in Windows NT/2000, queries the path of the Windows directory to be changed to.

10 Add the following commands in the event procedure *cmddelete_Click*:

```
If lstPlaylist.ListIndex <> -1 Then
  lstPlaylist.RemoveItem lstPlaylist.ListIndex
End If
```

These commands remove an entry from the playlist.

The playing of the selected media file is easier than you might think. You merely have to assign the path of the selected file the *FileName* property of the Media Player control element.

11 Add the following commands in the event procedure *cmdPlayListPlay_Click*:

```
If bPlayMode = False Then
  bPlayMode = True
  cmdPlaylistPlay.Caption = "interrupt"
  iPlayNr = 0
  lstPlaylist.ListIndex = iPlayNr
  PlaySong lstPlaylist.List(iPlayNr)
  tmrTime.Enabled = True
Else
  mmPlayer.Stop
  tmrTime.Enabled = False
  cmdPlaylistPlay.Caption = "play playlist"
  bPlayMode = False
End If
```

When the button is clicked for the first time, the playlist begins to play. Another click on this button leads to the interruption of the piece that is being played. The playing adopts the procedure *playsong*, which is entered next.

12 Input the following procedure (outside of the event procedure) :

```
Sub PlaySong(MusicFile As String)
  With mmPlayer
    .FileName = MusicFile
    .Play
  End With
  TitleInfodelete
  TitleTagRead MusicFile
  TitleTagOutput
End Sub
```

13 Input the following procedure in the event procedure *cmdUpdate_Click* :

```
With TitleInfo
  .Tag = "TAG"
  .Album = txtAlbum.Text
  .Artist = txtArtist.Text
```

```
    .Year = txtYear.Text
    .Comment = txtCommentr.Text
    .Title = txtTitle.Text
  End With
mmPlayer.FileName = ""
mmPlayer.Stop
TitleTagWrite sFilePath
```

After clicking on the UPDATE button, the content of the text field and the title information in the MP3 file is transferred, which means that title information cam be input in this way. So that the program is not too extensive, the allocation to a music category is not used.

14 Input the following commands in the *Form_Load* event procedure:

```
mmPlayer.AutoStart = False
tmrTime.Interval = 1000
```

So that the file is not played straight away, the *AutoStart* property is set to false. The MP3 Player is now already functional.

15 Input the following command in the event procedure *lstPlaylist_DblClick*:

```
PlaySong lstPlaylist.Text
```

In doing so, it is possible that a double click on the list entry leads to the title being played.

Selecting the title information

The title information of an MP3 file should also be displayed. Under the name of *ID3*, a kind of unofficial standard for the storage of title information has been established. Therefore, at the end of an MP3 file, 128 bytes are appended with the following construction:

```
Private Type TagInfo
  Tag As String * 3
  Title As String * 30
  Artist As String * 30
  Album As String * 30
  Year As String * 4
  Comment As String * 30
  Category As String * 1
End Type
```

271

This block is copied very easily into a program using a variable with a data type defined with the `Type` command from Visual Basic, and which defines a subvariable for every element. The individual names of the subvariables do not play a part; it is only important that the data type is correct. The `TagInfo` type represents the construction of the tag information in the MP3 file. Another advantage is that the entire area in the variable can be read using the `Get` command, and access to the individual subregions about the name of the interpreters using the subvariables of the type is possible. This makes access to the title information very easy. The access itself is carried out using the classic file access commands of Visual Basic. First, the file is opened using the instruction of the file name and a channel number (provided by the `FreeFile` function). Then the data are read using either the `Get` command or the `Put` command. At the end, the file is closed using the `Close` command.

1 Add a new module using the menu command PROJECT/ADD MODULE and give it the name *basMusic*.

2 Add the following variable declaration to the module:

```
Public TitleInfo As TagInfo
Public bFileOpen As Boolean
```

3 Next, add the type declaration that has already been introduced:

```
Private Type TagInfo
   Tag As String * 3
   Title As String * 30
   Artist As String * 30
   Album As String * 30
   Year As String * 4
   Comment As String * 30
   Category As String * 1
End Type
```

4 Add the function `TitleTagRead()`:

```
Function TitleTagRead(sFilename As String) As Boolean
   On Error GoTo errTitleTagRead
   Dim iChannelNr As Integer
   iChannelNr = FreeFile
   Open sFilename For Binary As iChannelNr
    With TitleInfo
      Get #iChannelNr, LOF(iChannelNr) - 127, .Tag
      If .Tag <> "TAG" Then
        TitleTagRead = True
        Exit Function
      End If
```

```
      Get #iChannelNr, , .Title
      Get #iChannelNr, , .Artist
      Get #iChannelNr, , .Album
      Get #iChannelNr, , .Year
      Get #iChannelNr, , .Comment
      Get #iChannelNr, , .Category
    End With
    Close iChannelNr
    Exit Function
errTitleTagRead:
  MsgBox "Error during the reading of tag info (" &
Err.Number & ")", vbExclamation, Err.Description
End Function
```

5 Add the procedure `TitleTagWrite`:

```
Sub TitleTagWrite(sFilename As String)
  On Error GoTo errTitleTagWrite
  Dim iChannelNr As Integer
  iChannelNr = FreeFile
  Open sFilename For Binary As iChannelNr
    Seek #iChannelNr, LOF(iChannelNr) - 127
    Put #iChannelNr, , TitleInfo
  Close iChannelNr
  Exit Sub
errTitleTagWrite:
  MsgBox "Error during update (" & _
  Err.Number & ")", vbExclamation, Err.Description
End Sub
```

While the function loads the title information from an MP3 file, write the proceedure `TitleTagWrite` information using the text field into the file. As already mentioned, the category information is not used.

6 Switch to the program code window of the form and input the following procedure in the *public* part:

```
Sub TitleInfodelete()
  With TitleInfo
    .Title = "---"
    .Album = "---"
    .Artist = "---"
    .Year = "---"
    .Comment = "---"
  End With
End Sub

Sub TitleTagOutput()
  Dim sAlbum As String
  Dim sTitle As String
  Dim sArtist As String
  Dim sComment As String
  Dim sYear As String
```

```
   With TitleInfo
     txtAlbum.Text = RTrim(.Album)
     txtComment.Text = RTrim(.Comment)
     txtTitle.Text = RTrim(.Title)
     txtArtist.Text = RTrim(.Artist)
     txtYear.Text = RTrim(.Year)
   End With
End Sub
```

While the procedure `TitleInfodelete` deletes the subvariables of the variable `TitleInfo`, transfer the procedure `TitleTagOutput` to the content of the variable in the corresponding text field.

Displaying the play duration

Our mini-music box should display the length of a piece as well as the remaining play duration. This information is available on the media player by means of its properties *Duration* and *CurrentPosition*. So that this information is constantly displayed, a *Timer* control element is required. Its task is to call its *Timer* event procedure about once every second in which the update takes place.

Carry out the following steps for the conversion:

1 Organise a *Timer* control element from the tool collection (the clock symbol) (somewhere) on the form and give it the name *tmrTime*.

2 Switch over to the program code window and add the following commands to the *Timer*event procedure:

```
Dim iMin As Integer, iSec As Integer
iMin = mmPlayer.CurrentPosition \ 60
iSek = mmPlayer.CurrentPosition - iMin * 60
If iMin > 0 Or iSec > 0 Then
   lblPosition.Caption = Format(iMin, "0#") & ":" _
     & Format(iSek, "0#")
Else
   lblPosition.Caption = "00:00"
End If
```

3 The total duration of the play will not be updated using the *Timer* event procedure as it stays constant. It will be output in a special event procedure of the media player, which is called *OpenStateChange* and is then always called if the internal status of the player is changed. Input the following commands in the event procedure *mmPlayer_OpenStateChange*:

```
Dim iMin As Integer, iSec As Integer
iMin = mmPlayer.Duration \ 60
iSek = mmPlayer.Duration - iMin * 60
lblPosition.Caption = Format(iMin, "0#") & ":" _
 & Format(iSec, "0#")
lblDuration.Caption = Format(iMin, "0#") & ":" _
 & Format(iSek, "0#")
cmdUpdate.Enabled = CBool(NewState)
If NewState = 0 Then
  tmrTime.Enabled = False
End If
```

4 Lastly, it will also be the case that after one song has been played, the next song in the play list is played, provided it is available. In order to do this, the *EndOfStream* event is available. Add the following commands in the event procedure *mmPlayer_EndOfStream*:

```
If bPlayMode = True Then
  iPlayNr = iPlayNr + 1
  If iPlayNr < lstPlaylist.ListCount Then
    lstPlaylist.ListIndex = iPlayNr
    PlaySong lstPlaylist.List(iPlayNr)
  Else
    cmdPlaylistPlay_Click
  End If
End If
```

For the moment, the music box is complete.

5 Start the program using the [F5] key, select a couple of MP3 pieces of music, click on the PLAY PLAYLIST button and enjoy the digital sounds that hopefully resound from the load speaker shortly afterwards.

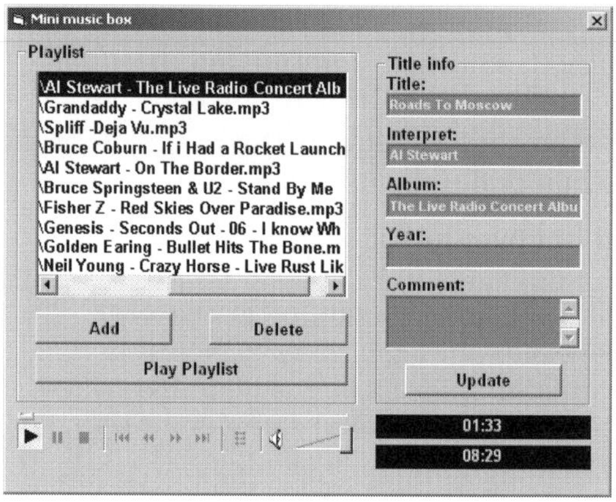

Figure 11.4: The mini-music box in action

275

Suggestions for expansion

The music box is now ready and you can enjoy downloaded titles fresh from the Web. A list of favourites would be a good idea with which you could call your favourite title quicker. Such a list is converted using the *Collection* object, which contains the path of the individual MP3 files (see the example of the image viewer in Chapter 9). It shouldn't be too difficult to use the part of the program from the image viewer in this project, in which the `SaveSetting` command is used to save the content of the *Collection* object in the registration, so that it can read the `GetSetting` function in the *Form_Load* event.

Simple games

One of the classic computer game genres of the last few years was throwing custard pies. The rule of the game was simple. After inputting a throwing angle and a starting speed, a custard pie is thrown at a virtual figure. The aim was to hit the figure. So that the whole thing looks a bit more realistic, the flight path of the custard pies were calculated according to the following formula:

```
x = v₀ * cos (a) * t
y = v₀ * sin (a)* t - g/2 * t²

x = throwing distance
y = throwing height
v₀ = starting speed
a = throwing angle
t = time
```

The game was used by physics teachers to demonstrate the laws of mechanics. In the following example you will learn a somewhat more modern version. The game primarily demonstrates the principle of the output of graphics of Visual Basic using the example of a image field.

Execute the following steps for the conversion of the game:

1 Start *Visual Basic*, create a DEFAULT EXE project, give the project the name *frmCrookedThrow*, and type in *CustardpieThrow* for the *Caption* property.

2 Arrange a frame area on the form and two text fields in the frame area (*txtStartingspeed* and *txtAngle*) with the suitable name fields.

3 Arrange a check box (*chkProtocol*) under the text field and type in *&Protocollisation* for the *Caption* property.

4 Arrange a key (*cmdStart*) below the frame area and type in *&Start* for the *Caption* feature.

5 Arrange a timer (*tmrTime*) on the form.

6 Arrange an image field (*picOutput*) to the right of the frame area. The flight path is drawn here later.

The form is now ready. Figure 11.5 shows how the finished form should look.

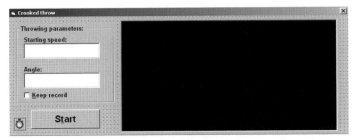

Figure 11.5: The finished form will look like this.

7 Add the following declaration in the *public* part of the form:

```
Private X As Single
Private Y As Single
Private v As Single
Private w As Single
Private x_Platt As Single
Private sFilename As String
Private iChannelNr As Integer
```

8 Add the following function to the *public* part of the form:

```
Private Function Xvalue(ByVal t As Single) As Single
  Xvalue = v * Cos(w) * t
End Function
```

This is the function that calculates the current value for the coordinate of the throwing object from the time value *t*.

9 Add the following function to the *public* part of the form:

```
Private Function Yvalue(ByVal t As Single) As Single
  YValue = v * Sin(w) * t - 4.9 * t ^ 2
End Function
```

This is the function that calculates the current value for the *y* coordinate of the throwing object from the time value *t*.

10 Add the following commands to the *Click* event proceedure of *cmdStart*:

```
w = txtAngle.Text
w = w / 180 * 3.14
v = txtStartingspeed.Text
picOutput.ForeColor = QBColor(Int(Rnd * 15))
If chkProtocol.Value = 1 Then
   sFilename = "Throw_" & Hour(Time) & Minute(Time) & ".dat"
   iChannelNr = FreeFile
   Open sFilename For Output As iChannelNr
End If
tmrTime.Enabled = True
cmdStart.Enabled = False
chkProtocll.Enabled = False
```

After the start of this procedure, a number of things take place that have nothing to do with the throw itself. After the angle and the starting speed have been transferred to the variables w and v (the angle has to be converted from degrees to radian measure, since all trigonometrical functions in Visual basic use radian measures), the character colours for the flight path are determined by the number randomiser. It is also checked whether the flight data will be recorded in a file. Next, the timer is activated and the start button is deactivated so that it cannot be clicked on immediately after the start (there is only one timer).

11 Add the following commands to the *Form_Load* event procedure :

```
Randomize Timer
tmrTime.Interval = 100
tmrTime.Enabled = False
picOutput.DrawWidth = 2
txtStartingspeed.Text = "100"
txtAngle.Text = "45"
picOutput.Scale (0, 400)-(1200, 0)
picOutput.AutoRedraw = True
x_Platt = Rnd * 500 + 600
picOutput.Line (x_Platt, 0)-(x_Platt + 50, 2), , BF
```

Pay attention to the *Scale* method of the image field *picOutput*. It introduces another subdivision in the image field so that the calculated flight coordinates fit better in the image field. Without this subdivision, you would see a small curve in the top left area of the image field. The following command is also important:

```
picOutput.AutoRedraw = True
```

By using this, the internal image memory is activated so that all outputs are copied simultaneously into this image memory using the *Pset* method. This has the advantage that if the image field has to be drawn again, maybe because it has been covered up by a window, Visual Basic copies the content of the image memory into the output area and the programmer does not have to be concerned with this aspect (with `AutoRedraw = False` a *Paint* event will be deleted, where this can happen).

In addition to this, the small platform is drawn in *Form_Load* that has to hit the custard pie. It is a small dash whose *x* position is determined by the number randomiser.

12 Add the following commands to the *Timer* event procedure:

```
Static Time As Single
Time = Time + 0.2
X = XValue(Time)
Y = YValue(time)
If Y <= 0 Then
  Time = 0
  tmrTime.Enabled = False
  cmdStart.Enabled = True
  chkProtocol.Enabled = True
  If X >= x_Platt And X <= x_Platt + 50 Then
    MsgBox "Hit!"
  Else
    MsgBox "miss!"
  End If
  If chkProtocol.Value = 1 Then
    Close iChannelNr
    Shell "Notepad " & sFilename, vbNormalFocus
  End If
    Exit Sub
End If
picOutput.PSet (X, Y)
If chkProtocol.Value = 1 Then
  Print #iChannelNr, X, Y
End If
```

The main work of the program takes place here. In the set time intervals (the more time events that take place, the more points are drawn), the current flight paths are calculated. Next it has to be checked whether the ground was reached (if the *y* coordinate is 0), and whether a hit was made, i.e. whether the *x* coordinate is in the area of the platform. It depends whether a corresponding message is output. In addition, the flight data are saved in the file in the procedure whose name is determined in the *Click* procedure of the start button as follows:

```
sFilename = "throw_" & Hour(Time) & Minute(Time) & ".dat"
```

If the custard pie has reached its destination, and if the check box has been clicked on, the protocol file is output using the command

```
Shell "Notepad " & sFilename, vbNormalFocus
```

It is a simple text file that contains the *x* and *y* coordinates.

13 Add the following commands to the *KeyPress* event procedure of the text field *txtStartingspeed*:

```
If KeyAscii = vbKeyReturn Then
  txtAngle.SetFocus
End If
```

This query makes sure that after pressing the ⏎ key the focus automatically skips from the *SetFocus* method to the text field for the input of the angle.

14 Add the following commands to the *KeyPress* event procedure of the text field *txtAngle*:

```
If KeyAscii = vbKeyReturn Then
  SendKeys "+{TAB}"
End If
```

This query also makes sure that after pressing the ⏎ key, the focus skips automatically to the text field for the input of the starting speed. However, this time the SendKeys command is used, which sends the key combination Alt+⇆ to the current window as if the user had pressed these buttons. The setting of the focus can therefore work only if the text field goes in front in the tab sequence.

15 The conversion/mapping is then complete. Start the program using the F5 key. Set the starting speed and the throwing angle and launch a custard pie. An optimal throwing angle is 45 degrees. Good luck!

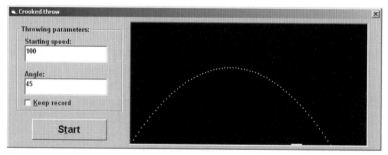

Figure 11.6: The custard pie is about to land.

Suggestions for expansion

- After the impact of the custard pie there should be an appropriate noise. After a hit, you could have applause. The suitable wave file is found on the hard drive or on the internet.

- The custard pie could hit a stick person who collapses theatrically after a hit. This is easily carried out with the *Line* and *Circle* methods.

- The scaling of the *x* axis is established relatively arbitrarily. With the form for the crooked throw, it is, however, also possible to calculate the maximal throwing distance and call the *Scale* method to do so. Look at your physics books or on the internet. You will soon strike lucky.

- You could add a high score list of course, a website, an internet version...

A little bit of maths

We now come to mathematics. Do not worry, it isn't difficult. We will merely show how to display simple mathematical functions in the image field. In addition, you will learn about the scroll bar.

Carry out the following steps:

1 Start *Visual Basic*, create a new DEFAULT EXE project, give the form the name *frmFunPlotter*, and give the project the name *FunPlotter*.

2 Arrange an image field (*picfun*), a horizontal scroll bar (*hsczoom*), a name field (*lblZoom*) and two buttons (*cmddraw* und *cmddelete*) on the form.

3 Switch to the program code window and input the following command in the *public* part:

```
Private sZoom As Single
```

4 Input the following command in the event procedure *cmddelete_Click*:

```
picFun.Cls
```

5 Input the following commands in the event procedure *cmddraw_Click*:

```
Dim sTitle As String
Dim x As Single, y As Single
Dim nColor As Long
picFun.Scale (-15, 120)-(15, -10)
sTitle = "Function of x height 2"
picFun.CurrentY = 120
picFun.CurrentX = -picFun.TextWidth(sTitle) / 2
picFun.Print sTitle
picFun.Line (-10, 0)-(10, 0)
picFun.Line (0, 100)-(0, 0)
For x = -10 To 10
  picFun.Line (x, 2)-(x, -2)
Next x
For y = 5 To 100 Step 5
  picFun.Line (-0.5, y)-(0.5, y)
Next y
sZoom = hscZoom.Value / 10
```

```
nColor = QBColor(Int(Rnd * 15))
For x = -10 To 10 Step 0.01
   y = x ^ 2 * sZoom
   picFun.PSet (x, y), nColor
Next x
```

Pay attention again to the *Scale* method, in which one of function values carries out the suitable subdivision of the *x* and *y* axes. The width of the text is determined using the *TextWidth* method so that this can be placed exactly in the middle.

6 Input the following commands in the *Form_Load* event procedure:

```
With hscZoom
   .Min = 0
   .Max = 10
   .Value = 5
End With
```

7 Input the following command in the event procedure *hscZoom_Change*:

```
lblZoom.Caption = hscZoom.Value / 10
```

8 Start the program using the F5 key and click on draw. Set the expansion of the function curve using the scroll bar. The methods *Line* and *Pset*, which stand in the centre, draw the coordination system and the function curve. The zoom factor is set using the *Value* property of the scroll bar.

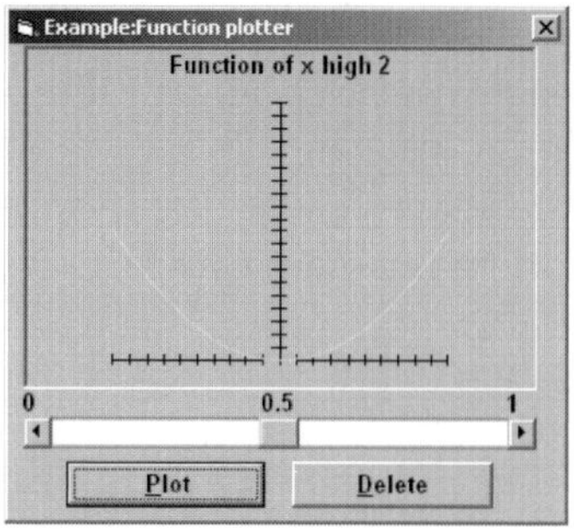

Figure11.7: The function curve.

If you have the time, expand this simple example to a function plotter with extras. A problem is the input of the form, because Visual Basic has no built-in form parser, which evaluates a form available as a string in the runtime, and calculates its value. You have to either program this kind of parser yourself (a bit advanced, but not impossible) or fall back on ready-made Active X control elements that have this functionality (you can get a free parser called *Equator* from Matthew Wells, which also exists as Visual Basic source code on the internet, e.g. at `http://www.active-x.com/download.asp?id=1780`). After installing the download, a file with the name *Equator.ctl.* can be found in the created directory. This is an ActiveX control element that you load in a project and arrange on a form using the tool collection.

Some card tricks

To conclude, Visual Basic will teach you a few card tricks.

The conversion of video poker

In this game, you are given the opportunity to draw five cards and buy new cards. These are things that you should already be able to program yourself. The winning judgement is not difficult, because it consists of a number of `If` commands. For this purpose, you should know that the card bitmaps are in the order: ace of clubs (*card00.bmp*), ace of diamonds (*card01.bmp*), ace of hearts (*card02.bmp*), ace of spades (*card03.bmp*), two of clubs (*card04.bmp*), etc. and are typed in exactly this order in the field variable `ocardfield.` to determine whether, for example, there is a full house.

Carry out the following steps:

1 Start *Visual Basic*, create a new DEFAULT EXE project, give the form the name *frmvideopoker* and give the project the name *videopoker*.

2 Spread out a frame area on the form and type in *gamestable* in the *caption* property.

3 Arrange five display control elements on the form in which the five control elements will be combined in one control element field.

4 Arrange the first display on the form and give it the name *imgcard*.

5 Copy the display onto the clip board with Ctrl+C and add it using Ctrl+V. Confirm whether you want to create a control element field with YES (Figure 11.8).

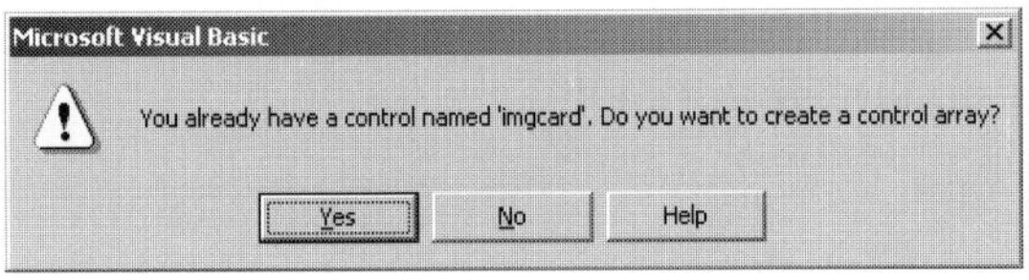

Figure 11.8: Answer this with YES – the result is a control element field.

6 Repeat step 4 three more times so that there are five display control elements on the form.

7 Add a check box underneath every display. Another control element should arise here so that you proceed in the same way as when arranging the display. The first check box contains the name *chkHold*. The other four check boxes have the same name but are different in their *Index* property. Before creating the control element field, set the *Style* property to *1*. By doing so, the check box is displayed as a button.

8 Arrange three buttons underneath the frame field: *cmdnewgame*, *cmdplay* and *cmdfouraces*.

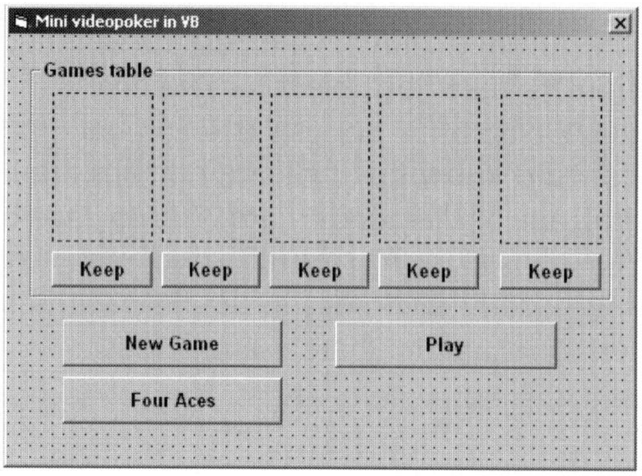

Figure 11.9: The form will look like this – the five displays and the five check boxes are combined in one control element field.

9 Switch to the program code window and input the following commands in the *public* part:

```
Private bcardsfillfield(0 To 51) As Boolean
Private ocardsfield(0 To 51) As StdPicture

Private Declare Sub Sleep Lib "Kernel32" (ByVal ms As Long)
```

Above all, pay attention to the second declaration as a field is defined here that consists of 52 *StdPicture* objects. These are invisible image fields from which each can take on a bitmap. The API function *Sleep* then needs to slow down the drawing of the four aces.

10 Input the following commands in the *Cli*

11

lay:

```
Dim iNr As Integer
Dim iCard As Integer
For iNr = 0 To 4
   If chkHold.Item(iNr).Value = 0 Then
      Do
         iCard = Int(Rnd * 52)
      Loop Until bKcardsfillfield(icard) = False
      bcardsfillfield(icard) = True
      imcard(iNr) = ocardfield(icard)
   End If
Next iNr
cmdplay.Enabled = False
```

12 Input the following commands in the *Form_Loa*

13

```
Sub pullcard()
   Dim iNr As Integer
   Dim icard As Integer
   Erase bcardsfillfield
   For iNr = 0 To 4
      chkhold.Item(iNr).Value = 0
   Next iNr
   For iNr = 0 To 4
      Do
         icard = Int(Rnd * 52)
      Loop Until bcardfillfield(icard) = False
      bcardsfillfield(icard) = True
      imgcard(iNr) = ocardfield(icard)
   Next iNr
End Sub
```

14 Even if the video poker doesn't contain a winning table, it will be possible to determine when four aces appear. The following event procedure of the button *cmdfouraces* runs until four aces have been drawn. Add the following commands to the *Click* event procedure:

```
Dim iCheck As Integer
Dim iNr As Integer
Do
   iCheck = 0
```

```
  draw_cards
  Sleep 500
  DoEvents
  For iNr = 0 To 3
    iCheck = iCheck + bcards_fill_field(iNr)
  Next iNr
Loop Until iCheck = -4
```

15 Start the program using the ⌧ key. Click on NEW GAME and five different playing cards will appear (no multiple cards can appear). Click on HOLD for the cards to be held and then click on PLAY.

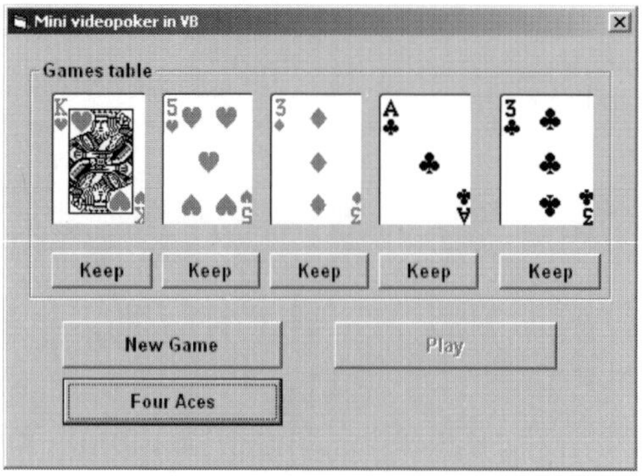

Figure 11.10: Video poker in action.

Outlook

We are now at the end of our expedition into the world of programming with Visual Basic. You have found out about lots of new areas, hopefully learnt something, and had some fun converting small programs and penetrating the secrets of binary logic (do you still think that computers are intelligent?). You have met all of the important areas of Visual Basic programming. Do you now want to learn more about Visual Basic programming? There are many possibilities. The internet offers dozens of websites exclusively dedicated to Visual Basic programming. Simply start your favourite search engine and as a search string enter "Visual Basic, Tips, Know-how" etc. and you will soon find something. It is surprising how many people sacrifice their free time in order to make (free) knowledge available to other programmers. There are also lots of good books on Visual Basic.

No matter how you become familiar with the intricacies of Visual Basic programming, you should always take one principle to heart: practise as much as possible and don't be discouraged by minor setbacks.

Appendix

Visual Basic reference

Here, we list the most important Visual Basic functions. You can also find these functions in the Visual Basic help.

Arithmetic functions

Function	Calculates
Abs	The absolute value of a number, i.e. the number value without a plus of a minus.
Atn	The arcus tangent of a length ratio. The argument has to be given in radian measure. The result is an angle and is in the region of –Pi/2 to Pi/2.
Cos	The cosine. The argument has to be given in radian measure. The radian measure is calculated according to the formula degrees * Pi / 180.
Exp	The exponents to the base e (2.718282). The result can amount to a maximum of 709 782 712 893, otherwise there is an overflow of results.
Fix	The integral share. The function cuts off the fractional share of the number. The difference from the Int function is the treatment of negative numbers. Whilst the Int function returns the integral number value that is the next smallest (from –4.6 it would be –5), with the Fix function it would be the next biggest integral number value (from –4,6 it would be –4).
Int	The integral share of a number.
Log	The natural logarithm of a number applied to the base e.
Rnd	A random number between 0 and 1.
Sgn	The type of the sign. The result is –1 with negative numbers, 1 with positive numbers, and 0 if the argument is also zero.
Sin	The sine. The argument has to be given in radian measure. The radian measure is calculated according to the formula degrees * Pi / 180.
Sqr	The square root. Negative values are not allowed because VBA cannot calculate complex numbers.
Tan	The tangent. The argument has to be given in radian measure. The radian measure is calculated according to the formula degrees * Pi / 180.

Data functions

Function	Meaning
CVDate	Changes an arbitrary (valid) data string into a date type (data type Date).
Date	This function provides the current system data in the form as a date type. The data can be set using the Data command (it has to be between 1 January 1980 and 31 December 2099 in DOS).
DateSerial	Changes a date into a data type. The data are submitted in the form of three values, which set the year, the month and the day.
DateValue	Changes a date into a data type. The date is submitted in the form of a character string, which displays a valid date.
Date	This command sets the system's date. The assigned value has to be a string expression or a date type.
DateAdd	Calculates a date from another date and a time difference.
DateDiff	Calculates the time difference between dates in days.
DatePart	Calculates a particular share from a date type, for example the number of weeks or quarters.
Day	Extracts the day number from a date.
Hour	Extracts the hour number from a date.
Minute	Extracts the minute number from a date.
Month	Extracts the months number from a date.
MonthName	Returns the name of the month due to the number of the month submitted.
Now	Provides the current system date and the current system time in the form of a date type.
Second	Extracts the number of seconds from a date.
Time	Provides the current system time in the form of a date type.
Time	Sets the system time.
Timer	Provides the number of seconds that have passed since midnight.

289

Function	Meaning
Weekday	Extracts a number for the week day from a data type (1 = Sunday, ... 7 = Saturday).
WeekdayName	Returns the name of the week day to a week day number.
Year	Extracts the year number from a date type.

String functions

Function	Syntax	Meaning
Chr	Chr(b)	Changes the character code b (0–255) into a 1–character string.
Instr	Instr([Start], substring, totalstring, [comparison])	Returns the position of a substring in a large string, in which the starting position and the kind of comparison can be determined (0 = binary search, 1= upper–/lower– case).
Left	Left(string, n)	Removes n characters beginning from the left and returns them as a string.
Len	Len(string)	Determines the length of a string.
Ltrim	Ltrim(string)	Cuts off all leading blank spaces from a string.
Mid	Mid(string, n, number)	Removes a number of characters from the n position and returns them as a string.
Right	Right(string, n)	Removes n characters beginning on the right and returns them as a string.
Rtrim	Rtrim(string)	Cuts off all appended blank spaces from a string.

Function	Syntax	Meaning
Str	Str(expression)	Changes the expression into a string. The format function is generally better as you can determine how the string is formed.
StrComp	StrComp(string1, string2 [, comparison])	Compares two strings with each other and returns a true/false value.
StrConv	StrConv(string,conversion type)	Efficient conversion function that changes one string, for example from ANSI into Unicode or from lower to upper case.
String	String(number, character)	Creates a string that consists of a number of characters with the ANSI code characters.
Trim	Trim(string)	Cuts off all leading blank spaces and all appended blank spaces.

Query functions

Function	Meaning
IsArray	Establishes whether an expression has the array subdata type (field).
IsDate	Establishes whether a expression has the date subdata type.
IsVariant	Establishes whether an expression has the variant type.
IsEmpty	Establishes whether a variable was initialised or occupies the empty condition. This requires that the variable has the variant type.
IsObject	Establishes whether it is a reference to an object (object variable) in an expression.

Function	Meaning
IsError	Establishes whether an expression has the error type, i.e. whether it is an error object.
IsMissing	Estalishes whether a value was submited to an optional procedure argument of the variant type.
IsNull	Establishes whether an expression has the special value zero (not 0). This is, for example, returned if a databank field has no content.
IsNumeric	Establishes whether an expression is numeric.
TypeName	Returns the data or object type of an expression as a character string.
VarType	Gives the data type of an expression as a number.

Conversion functions

Function	Meaning
Asc	Determines the ANSI code of a string character. If the string consists of more than one character, only the first character is used.
CBool	Changes a numeric expression into a number of the boolean type. A boolean value can only take on the value of 0 (false) and −1 (true).
CByte	Changes a numeric expression into a number of the byte type.
CCur	Changes a numeric expression into a number of the currency type and reduces the number of fractional digits to 4.
Cdate	Changes a numeric expression into a number of the date type.
Cdec	Changes a numeric expression into a number of the decimal type.
CDbl	Changes a numeric expression into a number of the double type.
CErr	Changes a numeric expression into a number of the error type.
CInt	Changes a numeric expression into a number of the integer type, in which a floating-point value is rounded up to the next even integral number.
CLng	Changes a numeric expression into a number of the long type, in which a floating-point value is rounded up to the next even integral number.

Function	Meaning
CSng	Changes a numeric expression into a number of the single type.
CStr	Changes a numeric expression into a number of the string type.
CVar	Changes a numeric number into a number of the variant type.
Hex	Changes a numeric integral expression into the corresponding hexadecimal number.
Oct	Changes a numeric integral expression into the corresponding octal number (to the base 8).
Val	Calculates the numericnumber of a string. Since the converison is not carried out on numeric characters first, the string does not have to consist only of numbers. You have to make sure that the Val function does not take into account country-specific settings. In principle, you should use the various Cx functions instead of Val.

General functions

Function	Meaning
Environ	Returns the value of an environmental value created in a operating system whose name was submitted. Alternatively, a number can also be submitted that stands for the position of the variables in the pool of the environmental variables.
Dir	Returns the name of a file in the current directory whose name agrees with the submitted pattern (e.g. *.Txt) In order to obtain other file names that agree with the pattern, the dir function has to be called using empty brackets.
FileAttr	Returns the access mode of a file opened in VBA (e.g. binary or random) as a number.
FileDateTime	Returns the date of the last modification as a data type.
FileLen	Returns the length of a file in bytes whose file name was submitted.
FreeFile	Returns the next free file reference number (file handle), which can be used for the open command.
LOC	Returns the current position of the file pointer for an open file, which the writing/reading position determines with the next access.

293

Function	Meaning
LOF	Returns the length in bytes of a file that is already open.
Partition	Returns the number of an area as a string in which a value is submitted, and in which the area is subdivided into fixed intervals.

Index

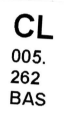